I0038799

ACT
Prep Course

JEFF KOLBY

NOVA
PRESS

ACT is a registered trademark of
ACT, Inc., which was not involved
in the production of, and does not
endorse, this book.

Additional educational titles from Nova Press (available at novapress.net):

➢ **SAT Prep Course** (640 pages, includes software)
  SAT Math Prep Course (480 pages)
  SAT Critical Reading and Writing Prep Course (350 pages)
➢ **GRE Prep Course** (624 pages, includes software)
  GRE Math Prep Course (528 pages)
➢ **GMAT Prep Course** (624 pages, includes software)
  GMAT Math Prep Course (528 pages)
  GMAT Data Sufficiency Prep Course (422 pages)
  Full Potential GMAT Sentence Correction Intensive (372 pages)
➢ **Master The LSAT** (560 pages, includes software, and 2 official LSAT exams)
➢ **The MCAT Physics Book** (444 pages)
  The MCAT Biology Book (416 pages)
  The MCAT Chemistry Book (428 pages)
➢ **Scoring Strategies for the TOEFL® iBT:** (800 pages, includes audio CD)
  Speaking and Writing Strategies for the TOEFL® iBT: (394 pages, includes audio CD)
  500 Words, Phrases, and Idioms for the TOEFL® iBT: (238 pages, includes audio CD)
  Practice Tests for the TOEFL® iBT: (292 pages, includes audio CD)
  Business Idioms in America: (220 pages)
  Americanize Your Language and Emotionalize Your Speech! (210 pages)
➢ **Postal Exam Book** (276 pages)
➢ **Law School Basics:** A Preview of Law School and Legal Reasoning (224 pages)
➢ **Vocabulary 4000:** The 4000 Words Essential for an Educated Vocabulary (160 pages)

ISBN 10: 1-944595-06-6
ISBN 13: 978-1-944595-06-7

ACT is a registered trademark of ACT Inc., which was not involved in the production of, and does not endorse, this book.

NP NOVA PRESS

P. O. Box 692023
West Hollywood, CA 90069

Phone: 1-310-275-3513
E-mail: info@novapress.net
Website: www.novapress.net

ABOUT THIS BOOK

If you don't have a pencil in your hand, get one now! Don't just read this book—write on it, study it, scrutinize it! In short, for the next six weeks, this book should be a part of your life. When you have finished the book, it should be marked-up, dog-eared, tattered and torn.

Although the ACT is a difficult test, it is a *very* learnable test. This is not to say that the ACT is "beatable." There is no bag of tricks that will show you how to master it overnight. You probably have already realized this. Some books, nevertheless, offer "inside stuff" or "tricks" which they claim will enable you to beat the test. These include declaring that answer-choices B or C are more likely to be correct than choices A or D. This tactic, like most of its type, does not work. It is offered to give the student the feeling that he or she is getting the scoop on the test.

The ACT cannot be "beaten." But it can be mastered—through hard work, analytical thought, and by training yourself to think like a test writer. Many of the exercises in this book are designed to prompt you to think like a test writer. For example, you will find "Duals." These are pairs of similar problems in which only one property is different. They illustrate the process of creating ACT questions.

The ACT is not easy—nor is this book. To improve your ACT score, you must be willing to work; if you study hard and master the techniques in this book, your score will improve—significantly.

This book will introduce you to numerous analytic techniques that will help you immensely, not only on the ACT but in college as well. For this reason, studying for the ACT can be a rewarding and satisfying experience.

To insure that you perform at your expected level on the actual ACT, you need to develop a level of skill that is greater than what is tested on the ACT. Hence, about 10% of the problems in this book are harder than actual ACT problems.

Although the quick-fix method is not offered in this book, about 15% of the material is dedicated to studying how the questions are constructed. Knowing how the problems are written and how the test writers think will give you useful insight into the problems and make them less mysterious. Moreover, familiarity with the ACT's structure will help reduce your anxiety. The more you know about this test, the less anxious you will be the day you take it.

CONTENTS

OVERVIEW

Format of the ACT

Math

The math section contains 60 multiple-choice questions and is 60 minutes long. The test measures mathematical skills typically obtained through grade 11 or 12, that is, through Trigonometry.

The questions are listed roughly in ascending order of difficulty. The section typically begins with Pre-Algebra questions, and progresses to Elementary Algebra, then to Intermediate Algebra, and then finally to Trigonometry. But there can be considerable overlap in these categories.

Section	Type	Time
Math	60 Multiple-choice Questions	60 minutes

The math section is always the second section of the test.

Verbal

The Verbal Section[1] contains three parts: English Test, Reading Test, and Writing Test.

English Test

The English Test is 45 minutes long and consists of 75 multiple-choice questions. The test is designed to measure your ability to revise and edit a piece of writing. Two categories of questions appear on the test:

- **Usage/Mechanics**
  Punctuation
  Basic grammar
  Sentence structure

- **Rhetorical Skills**
  General writing style
  Organization

These subsections have their own scores: The Usage/Mechanics score is based on 40 questions, and the Rhetorical Skills score is based on 35 questions.

The English Test is always the first test given.

---

[1] The ACT does use the term Verbal Section. They view and grade each of the three parts of the Verbal Section separately. We are using the term Verbal Section to conveniently distinguish these sections from the Math and Science sections.

Reading Test

The Reading Test is 35 minutes long and consists of 40 multiple-choice questions. It's too late now to pretend that you can't read, so strap on your reading hat and get ready to read about the following subjects:

> **Humanities:** This passage can be about music, dance, theater, art, architecture, language, ethics, literary criticism, and even philosophy.
> **Social Studies:** The social studies passage can include sociology, anthropology, history, geography, psychology, political science, and economics.
> **Natural Sciences:** The natural science passage can cover chemistry, biology, physics, and other physical sciences.
> **Prose Fiction:** The fiction passage can be taken from a novel or a short story; however, don't expect to have read the passage before.

The Reading Test is always the third section of the test.

Writing Test

The Writing Test is 40 minutes long and consists of one prompt from which to write an essay. Although the Writing Test is optional, three-quarters of colleges and universities require this section of the ACT, so it might be in your best interest to take it.

The Writing Test is always the last test given.

Section	Type	Time
English	75 Multiple-choice Questions	45 minutes
Reading	40 Multiple-choice Questions	35 minutes
Writing	1 Prompt	40 minutes

Science

The science section typically includes 40 multiple-choice questions based on 7 passages and is 35 minutes long. The test measures analytical and problem-solving skills associated with the basics of science.

You will not be tested on advanced concepts in science, but you will need to know the basic concepts and nomenclature of science. The test assumes that you are in the process of taking three or more years of science courses and have complete two years of study.

Section	Type	Time
Science	40 Multiple-choice Questions	35 minutes

Advanced mathematical skills are not needed for the science section, but you do need basics computational skills. So, you don't need any knowledge of Calculus, Trigonometry, or even much Algebra.

The science section is always the fourth section of the test.

Pacing

Although time is strictly limited on the ACT, working too quickly can damage your score. Many problems hinge on subtle points, and most require careful reading of the setup. Because high school can put heavy reading loads on students, many will follow their academic conditioning and read questions quickly, looking only for the gist of what each is asking. Once they have found it, they mark their answer and move on, confident they have answered it correctly. Later, many are startled to discover that they missed questions because they either misread the problems or overlooked subtle points.

To do well in your classes, you have to attempt to solve every, or nearly every, problem on a test. Not so with the ACT. In fact, if you try to solve every problem on the test, you will probably hurt your score. For the vast majority of people, the key to performing well on the ACT is not the number of questions they answer, within reason, but the percentage they answer correctly.

Scoring the ACT

Each of the four sections of the ACT, English, Math, Reading, and Science, is assigned a scaled score on a scale from 1 to 36, with 36 being the highest score possible. These section scores are then averaged into a composite score, which is also scored on a scale from 1 to 36.

Here is the conversion chart for converting raw scores into scaled scores:

Scale Score	Raw Scores					Scale Score
	Test 1 English	Test 2 Mathematics	Test 3 Reading	Test 4 Science	Writing	
36	75	60	40	40	47-48	36
35	72-74	58-59	39	39	46	35
34	71	57	38	38	44-45	34
33	70	55-56	37	37	42-43	33
32	68-69	54	35-36	—	41	32
31	67	52-53	34	36	40	31
30	66	50-51	33	35	38-39	30
29	65	48-49	32	34	37	29
28	63-64	45-47	32	33	35-36	28
27	62	43-44	30	32	34	27
26	60-61	40-42	29	30-31	33	26
25	58-59	38-39	28	28-29	32	25
24	56-57	36-37	27	26-27	31	24
23	53-55	34-35	25-26	24-25	29-30	23
22	51-52	32-33	24	22-23	28	22
21	48-50	30-31	22-23	21	26-27	21
20	45-47	29	21	19-20	25	20
19	43-44	27-28	19-20	17-18	24	19
18	41-42	24-26	18	16	23	18
17	39-40	21-23	17	14-15	21-22	17
16	36-38	17-20	15-16	13	20	16
15	32-35	13-46	14	12	—	15
14	29-31	11-12	12-13	11	18-19	14
13	27-28	8-10	11	10	17	13
12	25-26	7	9-10	9	16	12
11	23-24	5-6	8	8	—	11
10	20-22	4	6-7	7	14-15	10
9	18-19	—	—	5-6	13	9
8	15-17	3	5	—	12	8
7	12-14	—	4	4	—	7
6	10-11	2	3	3	10-11	6
5	8-9	—	—	2	9	5
4	6-7	1	2	—	—	4
3	4-5	—	—	1	—	3
2	2-3	—	1	—	—	2
1	0-1	0	0	0	8	1

In addition to the scaled score, you will be assigned a percentile ranking, which gives the percentage of students with scores below yours. For instance, if you score in the 80th percentile, then you will have scored better than 80 out of every 100 test takers.

Skipping and Guessing

Some questions on the ACT are rather hard, and it is a time-pressured test. So, you may not be able to finish the section.

Often students become obsessed with a particular problem and waste valuable time trying to solve it. To get a top score, learn to cut your losses and move on because all questions are worth the same number of points, regardless of difficulty level. So, often it is best to skip the hardest questions and concentrate on the easy and medium ones.

There is no guessing penalty on the ACT. So, if you skip a question or do not finish the section in time, be sure to mark an answer for every question.

The "2 out of 4" Rule

It is significantly harder to create a good but incorrect answer-choice than it is to produce the correct answer. For this reason usually only two attractive answer-choices are offered. One correct; the other either intentionally misleading or only partially correct. The other answer-choices are usually fluff. This makes educated guessing on the ACT immensely effective. If you can dismiss the two fluff choices, your probability of answering the question successfully will increase from 25% to 50%.

Questions and Answers

When is the ACT given?

The test is administered six times a year—usually in September, October, December, February, April, and June—on Saturday mornings. Special arrangements for schedule changes are available.

How important is the ACT and how is it used?

It is crucial! Although colleges may consider other factors, the majority of admission decisions are based on only two criteria: your ACT score and your GPA.

How many times should I take the ACT?

Most people are better off preparing thoroughly for the test, taking it one time and getting their top score. You can take the test up to 12 times, but some schools will average your scores. You should call the schools to which you are applying to find out their policy. Then plan your strategy accordingly.

Can I cancel my score?

No. But if you feel you did poorly on a test, you can ask that your score not be sent to a school. You have at most five days to make the request.

Where can I register for the test?

You can register for the test online at

www.actstudent.org

Or by calling

319-337-1270

Part One

MATH

- **ORIENTATION**
- **SUBSTITUTION**
- **MATH NOTES**
- **NUMBER THEORY**
- **GEOMETRY**
- **COORDINATE GEOMETRY**
- **ELIMINATION STRATEGIES**
- **INEQUALITIES**
- **FRACTIONS & DECIMALS**
- **EQUATIONS**
- **AVERAGES**
- **RATIO & PROPORTION**
- **EXPONENTS & ROOTS**
- **FACTORING**
- **ALGEBRAIC EXPRESSIONS**
- **PERCENTS**
- **GRAPHS**
- **WORD PROBLEMS**
- **SEQUENCES & SERIES**
- **COUNTING**
- **PROBABILITY & STATISTICS**
- **FUNCTIONS**
- **LOGARITHMS**
- **COMPLEX NUMBERS**
- **MATRICES**
- **TRIGONOMETRY**
- **DIAGNOSTIC/REVIEW TEST**

ORIENTATION

Format of the Math Section

The math section contains 60 multiple-choice questions and is 60 minutes long. The test measures mathematical skills typically obtained through grade 11 or 12, that is, through Trigonometry.

The questions are listed roughly in ascending order of difficulty. The section typically begins with Pre-Algebra questions, and progresses to Elementary Algebra, then to Intermediate Algebra, and then finally to Trigonometry. But there can be considerable overlap in these categories.

Section	Type	Time
Math	60 Multiple-choice Questions	60 minutes

Here are the approximate percentages of the content categories on the math section:

1) Pre-Algebra/Elementary Algebra (40%)
2) Intermediate Algebra/Coordinate Geometry (30%)
3) Trigonometry/Plane Geometry (23%)

The math section is always the second section of the test.

Scoring the Math Section

There are four scores recorded:

1) Total score (based on all 60 questions)
2) Elementary Algebra (based on 24 questions)
3) Intermediate Algebra (based on 18 questions)
4) Trigonometry (based on 18 questions)

The total score is reported on a scale from 1 to 36, with 36 being the highest score possible. And the sub-scores are reported on a scale from 1 to 18, with 18 being the highest score possible. The average total score is about 21. Do not become discouraged if you "blow" a few questions. The average ACT student misses more than half of the questions on the math section.

In addition to the scaled score, you will be assigned a percentile ranking, which gives the percentage of students with scores below yours. For instance, if you score in the 80th percentile, then you will have scored better than 80 out of every 100 test takers. Both the total score and the sub-scores are given a percentile ranking.

Calculators

You may use a calculator on the test, but all problems can be solved without a calculator. Be careful not to overuse the calculator; it can slow you down. But if you are accustomed to using a calculator for even simple calculations, you should continue doing so.

You can use any standard scientific or graphing calculator. You cannot use advanced calculators, such as ones with built-in computer algebra systems (for example, TI-89). You also cannot use the calculator in a cell phone or any other electronic communication device.

Skipping and Guessing

Some questions on the ACT are rather hard, and it is a time-pressured test. So, you may not be able to finish the section.

Often students become obsessed with a particular problem and waste valuable time trying to solve it. To get a top score, learn to cut your losses and move on because all questions are worth the same number of points, regardless of difficulty level. So, often it is best to skip the hardest questions and concentrate on the easy and medium ones.

There is no guessing penalty on the ACT. So, if you skip a question or do not finish the section in time, be sure to mark an answer for every question.

The Structure of this Part of the Book

Because it can be rather dull to spend a lot of time reviewing basic math before tackling full-fledged ACT problems, the first few chapters present techniques that don't require much foundational knowledge of mathematics. Then, in latter chapters, review is introduced as needed.

Directions and Reference Material

Be sure you understand the directions below so that you do not need to read or interpret them during the test.

Directions

Solve each problem and decide which one of the choices given is best. Fill in the corresponding oval on your answer sheet.

Do not linger over problems that take too much time. Solve as many as you; then return to the others in the time you have left for this test.

You are permitted to use a calculator on this test. You may use your calculator for any problems you choose, but some problems may best be done without a calculator.

Notes

Unless otherwise stated, all of the following should be assumed.

1. Illustrative figures are NOT necessarily drawn to scale.

2. Geometric figures lie in a plane.

3. The word *line* indicates a straight line.

4. The word *average* indicates arithmetic mean.

Here is some reference material. You will not see this information on the actual test.

Reference Information

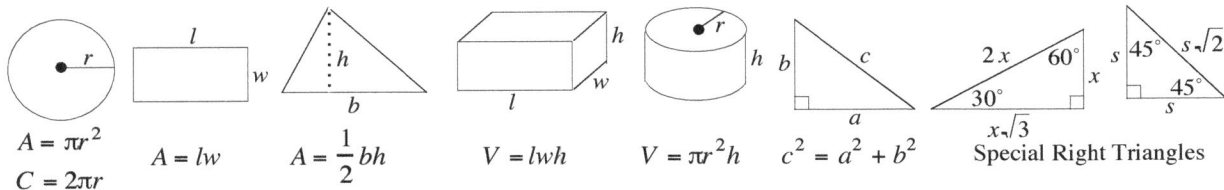

$A = \pi r^2$
$C = 2\pi r$

$A = lw$

$A = \dfrac{1}{2}bh$

$V = lwh$

$V = \pi r^2 h$

$c^2 = a^2 + b^2$

Special Right Triangles

The number of degrees of arc in a circle is 360.
The sum of the measures in degrees of the angles of a triangle is 180.

Substitution

Substitution is a very useful technique for solving ACT math problems. It often reduces hard problems to routine ones. In the substitution method, we choose numbers that have the properties given in the problem and plug them into the answer-choices. A few examples will illustrate.

Example 1: If n is an odd integer, which one of the following is an even integer?

      (A) n^3
      (B) $n/4$
      (C) $2n + 3$
      (D) $n(n + 3)$
      (E) $\sqrt{n}$

We are told that n is an odd integer. So choose an odd integer for n, say, 1 and substitute it into each answer-choice. Now, n^3 becomes $1^3 = 1$, which is not an even integer. So eliminate (A). Next, $n/4 = 1/4$ is not an even integer—eliminate (B). Next, $2n + 3 = 2 \cdot 1 + 3 = 5$ is not an even integer—eliminate (C). Next, $n(n + 3) = 1(1 + 3) = 4$ is even and hence the answer is possibly (D). Finally, $\sqrt{n} = \sqrt{1} = 1$, which is not even—eliminate (E). The answer is (D).

➤ **When using the substitution method, be sure to check every answer-choice because the number you choose may work for more than one answer-choice. If this does occur, then choose another number and plug it in, and so on, until you have eliminated all but the answer. This may sound like a lot of computing, but the calculations can usually be done in a few seconds.**

Example 2: If n is an integer, which of the following CANNOT be an even integer?

      (A) $2n + 2$
      (B) $n - 5$
      (C) $2n$
      (D) $2n + 3$
      (E) $5n + 2$

Choose n to be 1. Then $2n + 2 = 2(1) + 2 = 4$, which is even. So eliminate (A). Next, $n - 5 = 1 - 5 = -4$. Eliminate (B). Next, $2n = 2(1) = 2$. Eliminate (C). Next, $2n + 3 = 2(1) + 3 = 5$ is not even—it *may* be our answer. However, $5n + 2 = 5(1) + 2 = 7$ is not even as well. So we choose another number, say, 2. Then $5n + 2 = 5(2) + 2 = 12$ is even, which eliminates (E). Thus, choice (D), $2n + 3$, is the answer.

Example 3: If x/y is a fraction greater than 1, then which of the following must be less than 1?

(A) $3y/x$
(B) $x/3y$
(C) $\sqrt{\dfrac{x}{y}}$
(D) y/x
(E) y

We must choose x and y so that $x/y > 1$. So choose $x = 3$ and $y = 2$. Now, $\dfrac{3y}{x} = \dfrac{3 \cdot 2}{3} = 2$ is greater than 1,

so eliminate (A). Next, $\dfrac{x}{3y} = \dfrac{3}{3 \cdot 2} = \dfrac{1}{2}$, which is less than 1—it may be our answer. Next, $\sqrt{\dfrac{x}{y}} = \sqrt{\dfrac{3}{2}} > 1$;

eliminate (C). Now, $\dfrac{y}{x} = \dfrac{2}{3} < 1$. So it too may be our answer. Next, $y = 2 > 1$; eliminate (E). Hence, we

must decide between answer-choices (B) and (D). Let $x = 6$ and $y = 2$. Then $\dfrac{x}{3y} = \dfrac{6}{3 \cdot 2} = 1$, which

eliminates (B). Therefore, the answer is (D).

Problem Set A:

Solve the following problems by using substitution.

1. If n is an odd integer, which of the
    following must be an even integer?

    (A) $n/2$
    (B) $4n + 3$
    (C) $2n$
    (D) n^4
    (E) $\sqrt{n}$

2. If x and y are perfect squares, then which of
    the following is <u>not</u> necessarily a perfect
    square?

    (A) x^2
    (B) xy
    (C) $4x$
    (D) $x + y$
    (E) x^5

3. If y is an even integer and x is an odd
    integer, which of the following expressions
    could be an even integer?

    (A) $3x + y/2$
    (B) $(x + y)/2$
    (C) $x + y$
    (D) $x/4 - y/2$
    (E) $x^2 + y^2$

4. If $0 < k < 1$, then which of the following
    must be less than k?

    (A) $3k/2$
    (B) $1/k$
    (C) $|k|$
    (D) $\sqrt{k}$
    (E) k^2

5. Suppose you begin reading a book on page
    h and end on page k. If you read each page
    completely and the pages are numbered and
    read consecutively, then how many pages
    have you read?

    (A) $h + k$
    (B) $h - k$
    (C) $k - h + 2$
    (D) $k - h - 1$
    (E) $k - h + 1$

6. If m is an even integer, then which of the
    following is the sum of the next two even
    integers greater than $4m + 1$?

    (A) $8m + 2$
    (B) $8m + 4$
    (C) $8m + 6$
    (D) $8m + 8$
    (E) $8m + 10$

7. If x^2 is even, which of the following must be true?

   I. x is odd.
   II. x is even.
   III. x^3 is odd.

  (A)   I only
  (B)   II only
  (C)   III only
  (D)   I and II only
  (E)   II and III only

8. Suppose x is divisible by 8 but not by 3. Then which of the following CANNOT be an integer?

  (A) $x/2$
  (B) $x/4$
  (C) $x/6$
  (D) $x/8$
  (E) x

9. If p and q are positive integers, how many integers are larger than pq and smaller than $p(q + 2)$?

  (A)   3
  (B) $p + 2$
  (C) $p - 2$
  (D) $2p - 1$
  (E) $2p + 1$

10. If x and y are prime numbers, then which one of the following cannot equal $x - y$?

  (A)   1
  (B)   2
  (C)   13
  (D)   14
  (E)   20

11. If x is an integer, then which of the following is the product of the next two integers greater than $2(x + 1)$?

  (A) $4x^2 + 14x + 12$
  (B) $4x^2 + 12$
  (C) $x^2 + 14x + 12$
  (D) $x^2 + x + 12$
  (E) $4x^2 + 14x$

12. If the integer x is divisible by 3 but not by 2, then which one of the following expressions is NEVER an integer?

  (A) $(x + 1)/2$
  (B) $x/7$
  (C) $x^2/3$
  (D) $x^3/3$
  (E) $x/24$

13. If both x and y are positive even integers, then which of the following expressions must also be even?

   I. y^{x-1}
   II. $y - 1$
   III. $x/2$

  (A)   I only
  (B)   II only
  (C)   III only
  (D)   I and III only
  (E)   I, II, and III

14. Which one of the following is a solution to the equation $x^4 - 2x^2 = -1$?

  (A)   0
  (B)   1
  (C)   2
  (D)   3
  (E)   4

15. If $x \neq 3/4$, which one of the following will equal -2 when multiplied by $\dfrac{3 - 4x}{5}$?

  (A) $\dfrac{5 - 4x}{4}$
  (B) $\dfrac{10}{3 - 4x}$
  (C) $\dfrac{10}{4x - 3}$
  (D) $\dfrac{3 - 4x}{5}$
  (E) $\dfrac{4x - 3}{10}$

Answers and Solutions to Problem Set A

1. Choose $n = 1$. Then $n/2 = 1/2$, which is not even—eliminate (A). Next, $4n + 3 = 4 \cdot 1 + 3 = 7$, which is not even—eliminate (B). Next, $2n = 2 \cdot 1 = 2$ which is even and may therefore be the answer. Next, both (D) and (E) equal 1, which is not even. Hence, the answer is (C).

2. Choose $x = 4$ and $y = 9$. Then $x^2 = 4^2 = 16$ which is a perfect square. (Note, we cannot eliminate x^2 because it may not be a perfect square for another choice of x.) Next, $xy = 4 \cdot 9 = 36$ which is a perfect square. Next, $4x = 4 \cdot 4 = 16$, which is a perfect square. Next, $x + y = 4 + 9 = 13$, which is not a perfect square. Hence, the answer is (D).

3. Choose $x = 1$ and $y = 2$. Then $3x + y/2 = 3 \cdot 1 + 2/2 = 4$, which is even. The answer is (A). Note: We don't need to check the other answer-choices because the problem asked for the expression that *could be* even. Thus, the first answer-choice that turns out even is the answer.

4. Choose $k = 1/4$ Then $\dfrac{3}{2}k = \dfrac{3}{2} \cdot \dfrac{1}{4} = \dfrac{3}{8} > \dfrac{1}{4}$; eliminate (A). Next, $\dfrac{1}{k} = \dfrac{1}{1/4} = 4 > \dfrac{1}{4}$; eliminate (B). Next, $|k| = \left|\dfrac{1}{4}\right| = \dfrac{1}{4}$; eliminate (C). Next, $\sqrt{k} = \sqrt{\dfrac{1}{4}} = \dfrac{1}{2} > \dfrac{1}{4}$; eliminate (D). Thus, by process of elimination, the answer is (E).

5. Without substitution, this is a hard problem. With substitution, it's quite easy. Suppose you begin reading on page 1 and stop on page 2. Then you will have read 2 pages. Now, merely substitute $h = 1$ and $k = 2$ into the answer-choices to see which one(s) equal 2. Only $k - h + 1 = 2 - 1 + 1 = 2$ does. (Verify this.) The answer is (E).

6. Suppose $m = 2$, an even integer. Then $4m + 1 = 9$, which is odd. Hence, the next even integer greater than 9 is 10. And the next even integer after 10 is 12. Now, $10 + 12 = 22$. So look for an answer-choice which equals 22 when $m = 2$.

Begin with choice (A). Since $m = 2$, $8m + 2 = 18$—eliminate (A). Next, $8m + 4 = 20$—eliminate (B). Next, $8m + 6 = 22$. Hence, the answer is (C).

7. Suppose $x^2 = 4$. Then $x = 2$ or $x = -2$. In either case, x is even. Hence, Statement I need not be true, which eliminates (A) and (D). Further, $x^3 = 8$ or $x^3 = -8$. In either case, x^3 is even. Hence, Statement III need not be true, which eliminates (C) and (E). Therefore, by process of elimination, the answer is (B).

8. Suppose $x = 8$. Then x is divisible by 8 and is not divisible by 3. Now, $x/2 = 4$, $x/4 = 2$, $x/8 = 1$ and $x = 8$, which are all integers—eliminate (A), (B), (D), and (E). Hence, by process of elimination, the answer is (C).

9. Let $p = 1$ and $q = 2$. Then $pq = 2$ and $p(q + 2) = 4$. This scenario has one integer, 3, greater than pq and less than $p(q + 2)$. Now, we plug $p = 1$ and $q = 2$ into the answer-choices until we find one that has the value 1. Look at choice (D): $2p - 1 = 2(1) - 1 = 1$. Thus, the answer is (D).

10. If $x = 3$ and $y = 2$, then $x - y = 3 - 2 = 1$. This eliminates (A). If $x = 5$ and $y = 3$, then $x - y = 5 - 3 = 2$. This eliminates (B). If $x = 17$ and $y = 3$, then $x - y = 17 - 3 = 14$. This eliminates (D). If $x = 23$ and $y = 3$, then $x - y = 23 - 3 = 20$. This eliminates (E). Hence, by process of elimination, the answer is (C).

Method II (without substitution): Suppose $x - y = 13$. Now, let x and y be distinct prime numbers, both greater than 2. Then both x and y are odd numbers since the only even prime is 2. Hence, $x = 2k + 1$, and $y = 2h + 1$, for some positive integers k and h. And $x - y = (2k + 1) - (2h + 1) = 2k - 2h = 2(k - h)$. Hence, $x - y$ is even. This contradicts the assumption that $x - y = 13$, an odd number. Hence, x and y cannot both be greater than 2. Next, suppose $y = 2$, then $x - y = 13$ becomes $x - 2 = 13$. Solving yields $x = 15$. But 15 is not prime. Hence, there does not exist prime numbers x and y such that $x - y = 13$. The answer is (C).

11. Suppose $x = 1$, an integer. Then $2(x + 1) = 2(1 + 1) = 4$. The next two integers greater than 4 are 5 and 6, and their product is 30. Now, check which of the answer-choices equal 30 when $x = 1$. Begin with (A): $4x^2 + 14x + 12 = 4(1)^2 + 14 \cdot 1 + 12 = 30$. No other answer-choice equals 30 when $x = 1$. Hence, the answer is (A).

12. The number 3 itself is divisible by 3 but not by 2. With this value for x, Choice (A) becomes $\frac{3+1}{2} = \frac{4}{2} = 2$, eliminate; Choice (C) becomes $\frac{3^2}{3} = \frac{9}{3} = 3$, eliminate; Choice (D) becomes $\frac{3^3}{3} = \frac{27}{3} = 9$, eliminate. Next, if $x = 21$, then Choice (B) becomes $21/7 = 3$, eliminate. Hence, by process of elimination, the answer is (E).

13. If $x = y = 2$, then $y^{x-1} = 2^{2-1} = 2^1 = 2$, which is even. But $y - 1 = 2 - 1 = 1$ is odd, and $x/2 = 2/2 = 1$ is also odd. This eliminates choices (B), (C), (D), and (E). The answer is (A).

14. We could solve the equation, but it is much faster to just plug in the answer-choices. Begin with 0:

$$x^4 - 2x^2 = 0^4 - 2 \cdot 0^2 = 0 - 0 = 0$$

Hence, eliminate (A). Next, plug in 1:

$$x^4 - 2x^2 = 1^4 - 2 \cdot 1^2 = 1 - 2 = -1$$

Hence, the answer is (B).

15. If $x = 0$, then $\dfrac{3 - 4x}{5}$ becomes 3/5 and the answer-choices become

(A) 5/4
(B) 10/3
(C) −10/3
(D) 3/5
(E) −3/10

Multiplying Choice (C) by 3/5, gives

$$\left(\frac{3}{5}\right)\left(-\frac{10}{3}\right) = -2$$

The answer is (C).

Substitution (Plugging In): Sometimes instead of making up numbers to substitute into the problem, we can use the actual answer-choices. This is called "Plugging In." It is a very effective technique, but not as common as Substitution.

Example 1: The digits of a three-digit number add up to 18. If the ten's digit is twice the hundred's digit and the hundred's digit is 1/3 the unit's digit, what is the number?

(A) 246
(B) 369
(C) 531
(D) 855
(E) 893

First, check to see which of the answer-choices has a sum of digits equal to 18. For choice (A), $2 + 4 + 6 \neq 18$. Eliminate. For choice (B), $3 + 6 + 9 = 18$. This may be the answer. For choice (C), $5 + 3 + 1 \neq 18$. Eliminate. For choice (D), $8 + 5 + 5 = 18$. This too may be the answer. For choice (E), $8 + 9 + 3 \neq 18$. Eliminate. Now, in choice (D), the ten's digit is not twice the hundred's digit, $5 \neq 2 \cdot 8$. Eliminate. Hence, by process of elimination, the answer is (B). Note that we did not need the fact that the hundred's digit is 1/3 the unit's digit.

Problem Set B:
Use the method of Plugging In to solve the following problems.

1. The ten's digit of a two-digit number is twice the unit's digit. Reversing the digits yields a new number that is 27 less than the original number. Which one of the following is the original number?

    (A) 12
    (B) 21
    (C) 43
    (D) 63
    (E) 83

2. If $\dfrac{N + N}{N^2} = 1$, then $N =$

    (A) 1/6
    (B) 1/3
    (C) 1
    (D) 2
    (E) 3

3. Suppose half the people on a bus exit at each stop and no additional passengers board the bus. If on the third stop the next to last person exits the bus, then how many people were on the bus?

    (A) 20
    (B) 16
    (C) 8
    (D) 6
    (E) 4

4. The sum of the digits of a two-digit number is 12, and the ten's digit is one-third the unit's digit. What is the number?

    (A) 93
    (B) 54
    (C) 48
    (D) 39
    (E) 31

5. If $\dfrac{x^6 - 5x^3 - 16}{8} = 1$, then x could be

    (A) 1
    (B) 2
    (C) 3
    (D) 5
    (E) 8

6. Which one of the following is a solution to the equation $x^4 - 2x^2 = -1$?

    (A) 0
    (B) 1
    (C) 2
    (D) 3
    (E) 4

Answers and Solutions to Problem Set B

1. The ten's digit must be twice the unit's digit. This eliminates (A), (C), and (E). Now reversing the digits in choice (B) yields 12. But $21 - 12 \neq 27$. This eliminates (B). Hence, by process of elimination, the answer is (D). $(63 - 36 = 27.)$

2. Here we need only plug in answer-choices until we find the one that yields a result of 1. Start with 1, the easiest number to calculate with. $\frac{1+1}{1^2} = 2 \neq 1$. Eliminate (C). Next, choosing $N = 2$, we get

$\frac{2+2}{2^2} = \frac{4}{4} = 1$. Hence, the answer is (D).

3. Suppose there were 8 people on the bus—choice (C). Then after the first stop, there would be 4 people left on the bus. After the second stop, there would be 2 people left on the bus. After the third stop, there would be only one person left on the bus. Hence, on the third stop the next to last person would have exited the bus. The answer is (C).

4. In choice (D), $3 + 9 = 12$ and $3 = \frac{1}{3} \cdot 9$. Hence, the answer is (D).

5. We could solve the equation, but it is much faster to just plug in the answer-choices.

Begin with 1:

$$\frac{1^6 - 5(1)^3 - 16}{8} = \frac{1 - 5 - 16}{8} = \frac{-20}{8}$$

Hence, eliminate (A).

Next, plug in 2:

$$\frac{2^6 - 5(2)^3 - 16}{8} = \frac{64 - 5(8) - 16}{8} = \frac{64 - 40 - 16}{8} = \frac{8}{8} = 1$$

Hence, the answer is (B).

6. Begin with 0:

$$x^4 - 2x^2 = 0^4 - 2 \cdot 0^2 = 0 - 0 = 0$$

Hence, eliminate (A). Next, plug in 1:

$$x^4 - 2x^2 = 1^4 - 2 \cdot 1^2 = 1 - 2 = -1$$

Hence, the answer is (B).

Math Notes

We'll discuss many of the concepts in this chapter in depth later. But for now, we need a brief review of these concepts for many of the problems that follow.

1. **To compare two fractions, cross-multiply. The larger product will be on the same side as the larger fraction.**

   Example: Given 5/6 vs. 6/7. Cross-multiplying gives $5 \cdot 7$ vs. $6 \cdot 6$, or 35 vs. 36. Now 36 is larger than 35, so 6/7 is larger than 5/6.

2. **Taking the square root of a fraction between 0 and 1 makes it larger.**

   Example: $\sqrt{\frac{1}{4}} = \frac{1}{2}$ and 1/2 is greater than 1/4.

   Caution: This is not true for fractions greater than 1. For example, $\sqrt{\frac{9}{4}} = \frac{3}{2}$. But $\frac{3}{2} < \frac{9}{4}$.

3. **Squaring a fraction between 0 and 1 makes it smaller.**

   Example: $\left(\frac{1}{2}\right)^2 = \frac{1}{4}$ and 1/4 is less than 1/2.

4. $ax^2 \neq (ax)^2$. **In fact,** $a^2 x^2 = (ax)^2$.

   Example: $3 \cdot 2^2 = 3 \cdot 4 = 12$. But $(3 \cdot 2)^2 = 6^2 = 36$. This mistake is often seen in the following form: $-x^2 = (-x)^2$. To see more clearly why this is wrong, write $-x^2 = (-1)x^2$, which is negative. But $(-x)^2 = (-x)(-x) = x^2$, which is positive.

   Example: $-5^2 = (-1)5^2 = (-1)25 = -25$. But $(-5)^2 = (-5)(-5) = 5 \cdot 5 = 25$.

5. $\dfrac{1/a}{b} \neq \dfrac{1}{a/b}$. **In fact,** $\dfrac{1/a}{b} = \dfrac{1}{ab}$ **and** $\dfrac{1}{a/b} = \dfrac{b}{a}$.

   Example: $\dfrac{1/2}{3} = \dfrac{1}{2} \cdot \dfrac{1}{3} = \dfrac{1}{6}$. But $\dfrac{1}{2/3} = 1 \cdot \dfrac{3}{2} = \dfrac{3}{2}$.

6. $-(a + b) \neq -a + b$. **In fact,** $-(a + b) = -a - b$.

   Example: $-(2 + 3) = -5$. But $-2 + 3 = 1$.

   Example: $-(2 + x) = -2 - x$.

7. **Memorize the following factoring formulas—they occur frequently on the test.**

   A. $x^2 - y^2 = (x + y)(x - y)$
   B. $x^2 \pm 2xy + y^2 = (x \pm y)^2$
   C. $a(b + c) = ab + ac$

8. **Know these rules for radicals:**

A. $\sqrt{x}\sqrt{y} = \sqrt{xy}$

B. $\sqrt{\dfrac{x}{y}} = \dfrac{\sqrt{x}}{\sqrt{y}}$

9. **Pythagorean Theorem (For right triangles only):**

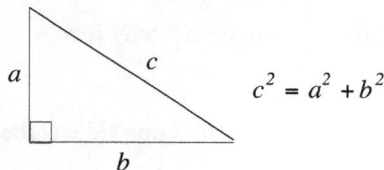

$$c^2 = a^2 + b^2$$

Example: What is the area of the triangle?

(A)   6
(B)   7.5
(C)   8
(D)   11
(E)   15

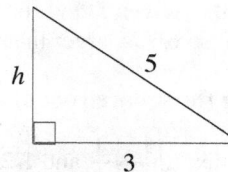

Since the triangle is a right triangle, the Pythagorean Theorem applies: $h^2 + 3^2 = 5^2$, where h is the height of the triangle. Solving for h yields $h = 4$. Hence, the area of the triangle is $\dfrac{1}{2}(base)(height) = \dfrac{1}{2}(3)(4) = 6$. The answer is (A).

10. **When parallel lines are cut by a transversal, three important angle relationships are formed:**

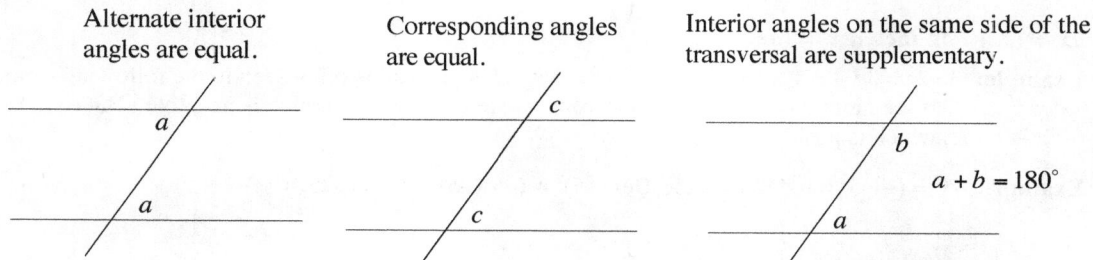

Alternate interior angles are equal.

Corresponding angles are equal.

Interior angles on the same side of the transversal are supplementary.

$$a + b = 180°$$

11. **In a triangle, an exterior angle is equal to the sum of its remote interior angles and therefore greater than either of them.**

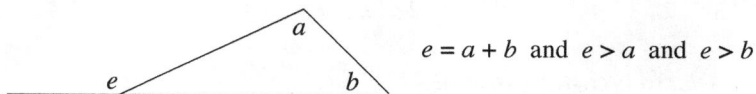

$e = a + b$ and $e > a$ and $e > b$

12. **A central angle has by definition the same measure as its intercepted arc.**

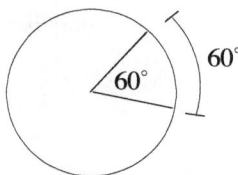

$60°$ $60°$ $60°$

13. An inscribed angle has one-half the measure of its intercepted arc.

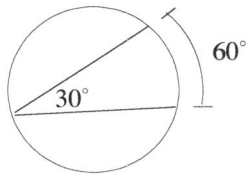

14. There are 180° in a straight angle.

$$x + y = 180°$$

15. The angle sum of a triangle is 180°.

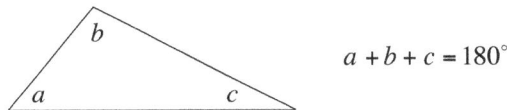

$$a + b + c = 180°$$

Example: In the triangle, what is the degree measure of angle c ?

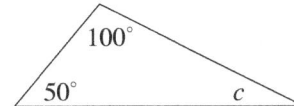

    (A)   17
    (B)   20
    (C)   30
    (D)   40
    (E)   45

Since a triangle has $180°$, we get $100 + 50 + c = 180$. Solving for c yields $c = 30$. Hence, the answer is (C).

16. To find the percentage increase, find the absolute increase and divide by the original amount.

Example: If a shirt selling for $18 is marked up to $20, then the absolute increase is $20 - 18 = 2$. Thus, the percentage increase is

$$\frac{increase}{original\ amount} = \frac{2}{18} = \frac{1}{9} \approx 11\%$$

17. Systems of simultaneous equations can often be solved by merely adding or subtracting the equations.

Example: If $4x + y = 14$ and $3x + 2y = 13$, then $x - y =$

Solution: Merely subtract the second equation from the first:

$$
\begin{array}{r}
4x + y = 14 \\
(-) \quad \underline{3x + 2y = 13} \\
x - y = 1
\end{array}
$$

18. **When counting elements that are in overlapping sets, the total number will equal the number in one group plus the number in the other group minus the number common to both groups. Venn diagrams are very helpful with these problems.**

   Example: If in a certain school 20 students are taking math and 10 are taking history and 7 are taking both, how many students are taking either math or history?

   Solution:

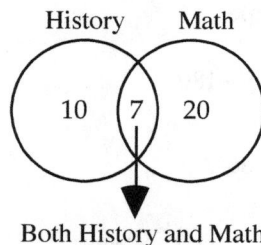

   Both History and Math

   By the principle stated above, we add 10 and 20 and then subtract 7 from the result. Thus, there are (10 + 20) − 7 = 23 students.

19. **The number of integers between two integers <u>inclusive</u> is one more than their difference.**

   For example: The number of integers between 49 and 101 inclusive is (101 − 49) + 1 = 53. To see this more clearly, choose smaller numbers, say, 9 and 11. The difference between 9 and 11 is 2. But there are three numbers between them inclusive—9, 10, and 11—one more than their difference.

20. **Rounding Off:** The convention used for rounding numbers is *"if the following digit is less than five, then the preceding digit is not changed. But if the following digit is greater than or equal to five, then the preceding digit is increased by one."*

   Example: 65,439 —> 65,000 (following digit is 4)
   5.5671 —> 5.5700 (dropping the unnecessary zeros gives 5.57)

21. **Writing a number as a product of a power of 10 and a number $1 \le n < 10$ is called scientific notation. This notation has the following form: $n \times 10^c$, where $1 \le n < 10$ and c is an integer.**

   Example: $326,000,000 = 3.26 \times 10^8$
   Notice that the exponent is the number of significant places that the decimal is moved[*], not the number zeros. Students often use 6 as the exponent in the above example because there are 6 zeros.

   Example: $0.00007 = 7 \times 10^{-5}$
   Notice that for a small number the exponent is negative and for a large number the exponent is positive.

---

[*] Although no decimal is shown in the number 326,000,000, you can place a decimal at the end of the number and add as many trailing zeros as you like without changing the value of the number: 326,000,000 = 326,000,000.00 . . . .

Problem Set C: Use the properties and techniques of this section to solve the following problems.

1. If $x \neq 0$, then which one of the following must be true?

(A) $2x^2 = (2x)^2$

(B) $2x^2 < (2x)^2$

(C) $2x^2 \leq (2x)^2$

(D) $2x^2 > (2x)^2$

(E) $2x^2 \geq (2x)^2$

2. Which one of the following fractions is greatest?

(A) 15/16

(B) 7/9

(C) 13/15

(D) 8/9

(E) 10/11

3. $1 + \dfrac{1}{1 - \dfrac{1}{2}} =$

(A) 3   (B) 5   (C) 7   (D) 9   (E) 11

4. If the ratio of 1/5 to 1/4 is equal to the ratio of 1/4 to x, then what is the value of x ?

(A) 5/16

(B) 4/11

(C) 1

(D) 4

(E) 5

5. Which one of the following numbers is smallest?

(A) $\left(\dfrac{7}{8}\right)^2$

(B) $\sqrt{\dfrac{7}{8}}$

(C) $\sqrt{\dfrac{8}{7}}$

(D) $\left(\dfrac{8}{7}\right)^2$

(E) 8/7

6. Let $a \# b$ be denoted by the expression $a \# b = -b^4$. Then $x \# (-y) =$

(A) $-y^2$

(B) y^4

(C) $-y^4$

(D) y^2

(E) $|y|$

7. $\dfrac{1}{1 - (.2)^2} =$

(A) 25/24

(B) 25/23

(C) 24/15

(D) 23/11

(E) 21/9

8. If $0 < x < 1$, which of the following expressions is greatest?

(A) $\dfrac{1}{\sqrt{x}}$

(B) $\sqrt{x}$

(C) x/π

(D) x^3

(E) x^4

9. Which of the following are true?

I. $\dfrac{\sqrt{\dfrac{5}{6}}}{\left(\dfrac{5}{6}\right)^2} > 1$

II. $\dfrac{\sqrt{\dfrac{5}{6}}}{\left(\dfrac{6}{5}\right)^2} > 1$

III. $\sqrt{\dfrac{\dfrac{5}{6}}{\sqrt{\dfrac{5}{6}}}} > 1$

(A) I only

(B) II only

(C) I and II only

(D) I and III only

(E) I, II, and III

10. If $x > y > 0$, then which of the following are true?

I. $\dfrac{x+2}{y+2} > \dfrac{x}{y}$

II. $\dfrac{x+2}{y+2} = \dfrac{x}{y}$

III. $\dfrac{x+2}{y+2} > 1$

(A) I only

(B) II only

(C) III only

(D) I and III only

(E) II and III only

Answers and Solutions to Problem Set C

1. From the formula $a^2x^2 = (ax)^2$, we see that $(2x)^2 = 2^2 \cdot x^2 = 4x^2$. Now, since $x \neq 0$, $4x^2$ is clearly larger than $2x^2$. Hence, the answer is (B).

2. Begin by comparing 15/16 to each of the other answer-choices. Cross-multiplying 15/16 and 7/9 gives 135 vs. 112. Now, 135 is greater than 112, so 15/16 is greater than 7/9. Using this procedure to compare 15/16 to each of the remaining answer-choices shows that 15/16 is the greatest fraction listed. The answer is (A).

3. $1 + \dfrac{1}{1 - \dfrac{1}{2}} = 1 + \dfrac{1}{\frac{1}{2}} = 1 + 2 = 3$. The answer is (A).

4. "The ratio of 1/5 to 1/4 is equal to the ratio of 1/4 to x" means

$$\frac{\frac{1}{5}}{\frac{1}{4}} = \frac{\frac{1}{4}}{x}, \text{ or } \frac{1}{5} \cdot \frac{4}{1} = \frac{1}{4} \cdot \frac{1}{x}$$

This in turn reduces to $\dfrac{4}{5} = \dfrac{1}{4x}$. Cross-multiplying yields $16x = 5$, or $x = 5/16$. The answer is (A).

5. Squaring a fraction between 0 and 1 makes it smaller, and taking the square root of it makes it larger. Hence, Choice (A) is smaller than Choice (B). Choices (C), (D), (E) are all greater than one since $8/7 > 1$. The answer is (A).

6. $x \# (-y) = -(-y)^4 = -y^4$. Note: The exponent applies only to the negative inside the parentheses. The answer is (C).

7.
$$\frac{1}{1 - (.2)^2} = \frac{1}{1 - .04} = \frac{1}{.96} = \frac{1}{\frac{96}{100}} = 1 \cdot \frac{100}{96} = \frac{100}{96} = \frac{25}{24}$$

The answer is (A).

8. Since x is a fraction between 0 and 1, $\sqrt{x}$ is greater than either x^3 or x^4. It's also greater than x/π since x/π is less than x. To tell which is greater between $\sqrt{x}$ and $\dfrac{1}{\sqrt{x}}$, let $x = 1/4$ and plug it into each expression:

$$\sqrt{x} = \sqrt{\frac{1}{4}} = \frac{1}{2}$$

and

$$\frac{1}{\sqrt{x}} = \frac{1}{\sqrt{\frac{1}{4}}} = \frac{1}{\frac{1}{2}} = 2$$

Hence, $\dfrac{1}{\sqrt{x}}$ is greater than $\sqrt{x}$. The answer is (A).

9. Squaring a fraction between 0 and 1 makes it smaller, and taking the square root of it makes it larger. Therefore, Statement I is true since the top part of the fraction is larger than the bottom. This eliminates (B). Next, Statement II is false. Squaring a fraction makes it smaller only if the fraction is between 0 and 1. This eliminates (C) and (E). Finally, Statement III is false. Since $\dfrac{5}{6} < \sqrt{\dfrac{5}{6}}$, we get

$$\frac{\frac{5}{6}}{\sqrt{\frac{5}{6}}} < 1$$

Although taking the square root of this expression will make it larger, it will still be less than 1. The answer is (A).

10. Statement I is not necessarily true. For example, if $x = 2$ and $y = 1$, then

$$\frac{x + 2}{y + 2} = \frac{2 + 2}{1 + 2} = \frac{4}{3} \neq 2 = \frac{2}{1} = \frac{x}{y}$$

This is also a counterexample to Statement II. Hence, we can eliminate (A), (B), (D), and (E). Thus, by process of elimination, the answer is (C).

However, it is instructive to prove that Statement III is true. From the expression $x > y > 0$, we get

$$x + 2 > y + 2$$

Since $y + 2 > 0$, dividing both sides of the above expression by $y + 2$ will not reverse the inequality:

$$\frac{x + 2}{y + 2} > 1$$

Hence, Statement III is necessarily true.

Number Theory

This broad category is a popular source for ACT questions. At first, students often struggle with these problems since they have forgotten many of the basic properties of arithmetic. So, before we begin solving these problems, let's review some of these basic properties.

➤ *"The remainder is r when p is divided by q"* **means** $p = qz + r$**; the integer** z **is called the quotient. For instance,** *"The remainder is 1 when 7 is divided by 3"* **means** $7 = 3 \cdot 2 + 1$**. Dividing both sides of** $p = kq + r$ **by** k **gives the following alternative form** $p/k = q + r/k$**.**

Example 1:   When the integer n is divided by 2, the quotient is u and the remainder is 1. When the integer n is divided by 5, the quotient is v and the remainder is 3. Which one of the following must be true?

   (A) $2u + 5v = 4$
   (B) $2u - 5v = 2$
   (C) $4u + 5v = 2$
   (D) $4u - 5v = 2$
   (E) $3u - 5v = 2$

Translating *"When the integer n is divided by 2, the quotient is u and the remainder is 1"* into an equation gives

$$n = 2u + 1$$

Translating *"When the integer n is divided by 5, the quotient is v and the remainder is 3"* into an equation gives

$$n = 5v + 3$$

Since both expressions equal n, we can set them equal to each other:

$$2u + 1 = 5v + 3$$

Rearranging and then combining like terms yields

$$2u - 5v = 2$$

The answer is (B).

➤ **A number** n **is even if the remainder is zero when** n **is divided by 2:** $n = 2z + 0$**, or** $n = 2z$**.**

➤ **A number** n **is odd if the remainder is one when** n **is divided by 2:** $n = 2z + 1$**.**

➤ **The following properties for odd and even numbers are very useful—you should memorize them:**

$$even \times even = even$$
$$odd \times odd = odd$$
$$even \times odd = even$$

$$even + even = even$$
$$odd + odd = even$$
$$even + odd = odd$$

Example 2: Suppose p is even and q is odd. Then which of the following CANNOT be an integer?

    I. $(p + q)/p$
    II. $pq/3$
    III. q/p^2

    (A)   I only
    (B)   II only
    (C)   III only
    (D)   I and II only
    (E)   I and III only

For a fractional expression to be an integer, the denominator must divide evenly into the numerator. Now, Statement I cannot be an integer. Since q is odd and p is even, $p + q$ is odd. Further, since $p + q$ is odd, it cannot be divided evenly by the even number p. Hence, $(p + q)/p$ cannot be an integer. Next, Statement II can be an integer. For example, if $p = 2$ and $q = 3$, then $\dfrac{pq}{3} = \dfrac{2 \cdot 3}{3} = 2$. Finally, Statement III cannot be an integer. $p^2 = p \cdot p$ is even since it is the product of two even numbers. Further, since q is odd, it cannot be divided evenly by the even integer p^2. The answer is (E).

➤ **Consecutive integers are written as $x, x + 1, x + 2, \ldots$**

➤ **Consecutive even or odd integers are written as $x, x + 2, x + 4, \ldots$**

➤ **The integer zero is neither positive nor negative, but it is even: $0 = 2 \times 0$.**

➤ **A *prime number* is an integer that is divisible only by itself and 1.**

The prime numbers are $2, 3, 5, 7, 11, 13, 17, 19, 23, 29, 31, 37, 41, \ldots$

➤ **A number is divisible by 3 if the sum of its digits is divisible by 3.**

For example, 135 is divisible by 3 because the sum of its digits $(1 + 3 + 5 = 9)$ is divisible by 3.

➤ **A *common multiple* is a multiple of two or more integers.**

For example, some common multiples of 2 and 5 are 0, 10, 20, 40, and 50.

➤ **The *least common multiple* (LCM) of two integers is the smallest positive integer that is a multiple of both.**

For example, the LCM of 4 and 10 is 20. The standard method of calculating the LCM is to prime factor the numbers and then form a product by selecting each factor the greatest number of times it occurs. For 4 and 10, we get

$$4 = 2^2$$
$$10 = 2 \bullet 5$$

In this case, select 2^2 instead of 2 because it has the greater number of factors of 2, and select 5 by default since there are no other factors of 5. Hence, the LCM is $2^2 \bullet 5 = 4 \bullet 5 = 20$.

For another example, let's find the LCM of 8, 36, and 54. Prime factoring yields

$$8 = 2^3$$
$$36 = 2^2 \bullet 3^2$$
$$54 = 2 \bullet 3^3$$

In this case, select 2^3 because it has more factors of 2 than 2^2 or 2 itself, and select 3^3 because is has more factors of 3 than 3^2 does. Hence, the LCM is $2^3 \bullet 3^3 = 8 \bullet 27 = 216$.

A shortcut for finding the LCM is to just keep adding the largest number to itself until the other numbers divide into it evenly. For 4 and 10, we would add 10 to itself: $10 + 10 = 20$. Since 4 divides evenly in 20, the LCM is 20. For 8, 36, and 54, we would add 54 to itself: $54 + 54 + 54 + 54 = 216$. Since both 8 and 36 divide evenly into 216, the LCM is 216.

➤ **The absolute value of a number, $|\ |$, is always positive. In other words, the absolute value symbol eliminates negative signs.**

For example, $|-7| = 7$ and $|-\pi| = \pi$. Caution, the absolute value symbol acts only on what is inside the symbol, $|\ |$. For example, $-|-(7 - \pi)| = -(7 - \pi)$. Here, only the negative sign inside the absolute value symbol but outside the parentheses is eliminated.

➤ **The product (quotient) of positive numbers is positive.**

➤ **The product (quotient) of a positive number and a negative number is negative.**

For example, $-5(3) = -15$ and $\dfrac{6}{-3} = -2$.

➤ **The product (quotient) of an even number of negative numbers is positive.**

For example, $(-5)(-3)(-2)(-1) = 30$ is positive because there is an even number, 4, of positives.
$\dfrac{-9}{-2} = \dfrac{9}{2}$ is positive because there is an even number, 2, of positives.

➤ **The product (quotient) of an odd number of negative numbers is negative.**

For example, $(-2)(-\pi)(-\sqrt{3}) = -2\pi\sqrt{3}$ is negative because there is an odd number, 3, of negatives.
$\dfrac{(-2)(-9)(-6)}{(-12)\left(-18/2\right)} = -1$ is negative because there is an odd number, 5, of negatives.

➤ **The sum of negative numbers is negative.**

For example, $-3 - 5 = -8$. Some students have trouble recognizing this structure as a sum because there is no plus symbol, $+$. But recall that subtraction is defined as negative addition. So $-3 - 5 = -3 + (-5)$.

➤ **A number raised to an even exponent is greater than or equal to zero.**

For example, $(-\pi)^4 = \pi^4 \geq 0$, and $x^2 \geq 0$, and $0^2 = 0 \cdot 0 = 0 \geq 0$.

Example 3:   If a, b, and c are consecutive integers and $a < b < c$, which of the following must be true?
   I. $b - c = 1$
   II. $abc/3$ is an integer.
   III. $a + b + c$ is even.

   (A)   I only
   (B)   II only
   (C)   III only
   (D)   I and II only
   (E)   II and III only

Let x, $x + 1$, $x + 2$ stand for the consecutive integers a, b, and c, in that order. Plugging this into Statement I yields

$$b - c = (x + 1) - (x + 2) = -1$$

Hence, Statement I is false.

As to Statement II, since a, b, and c are three consecutive integers, one of them must be divisible by 3. Hence, $abc/3$ is an integer, and Statement II is true.

As to Statement III, suppose a is even, b is odd, and c is even. Then $a + b$ is odd since

$$even + odd = odd$$

Hence,

$$a + b + c = (a + b) + c = (odd) + even = odd$$

Thus, Statement III is not necessarily true. The answer is (B).

Example 4:   If both x and y are prime numbers, which of the following CANNOT be the difference of x and y?

   (A) 1   (B) 3   (C) 9   (D) 15   (E) 23

Both 3 and 2 are prime, and $3 - 2 = 1$. This eliminates (A). Next, both 5 and 2 are prime, and $5 - 2 = 3$. This eliminates (B). Next, both 11 and 2 are prime, and $11 - 2 = 9$. This eliminates (C). Next, both 17 and 2 are prime, and $17 - 2 = 15$. This eliminates (D). Hence, by process of elimination, the answer is (E).

Example 5:   If $-x = -|-(-2 + 5)|$, then $x =$

   (A) -7 (B) -3 (C) 3   (D) 7   (E) 9

Working from the innermost parentheses out, we get

$$-x = -|-(-2 + 5)|$$
$$-x = -|-(+3)|$$
$$-x = -|-3|$$
$$-x = -(+3)$$
$$-x = -3$$
$$x = 3$$

The answer is (C).

Problem Set D:

1. If the remainder is 1 when m is divided by 2 and the remainder is 3 when n is divided by 4, which of the following must be true?

    (A) m is even.
    (B) n is even.
    (C) $m + n$ is even.
    (D) mn is even.
    (E) m/n is even.

2. If x and y are both prime and greater than 2, then which of the following CANNOT be a divisor of xy?

    (A) 2
    (B) 3
    (C) 11
    (D) 15
    (E) 17

3. If 2 is the greatest number that will divide evenly into both x and y, what is the greatest number that will divide evenly into both $5x$ and $5y$?

    (A) 2
    (B) 4
    (C) 6
    (D) 8
    (E) 10

4. If the average of the consecutive even integers a, b, and c is less than $a/3$, which of the following best describes the value of a?

    (A) a is prime.
    (B) a is odd.
    (C) a is zero.
    (D) a is positive.
    (E) a is negative.

5. If $\dfrac{x+5}{y}$ is a prime integer, which of the following must be true?

    I. $y = 5x$
    II. y is a prime integer.
    III. $\dfrac{x+5}{y}$ is odd.

    (A) None
    (B) I only
    (C) II only
    (D) I and II only
    (E) II and III only

6. If x is both the cube and the square of an integer and x is between 2 and 200, what is the value of x?

    (A) 8
    (B) 16
    (C) 64
    (D) 125
    (E) 169

7. In the two-digit number x, both the sum and the difference of its digits is 4. What is the value of x?

    (A) 13
    (B) 31
    (C) 40
    (D) 48
    (E) 59

8. If p divided by 9 leaves a remainder of 1, which of the following must be true?

    I. p is even.
    II. p is odd.
    III. $p = 3 \cdot z + 1$ for some integer z.

    (A) I only
    (B) II only
    (C) III only
    (D) I and II only
    (E) I and III only

9. p and q are integers. If p is divided by 2, the remainder is 1; and if q is divided by 6, the remainder is 1. Which of the following must be true.

    I. $pq + 1$ is even.
    II. $pq/2$ is an integer.
    III. pq is a multiple of 12.

    (A) I only
    (B) II only
    (C) III only
    (D) I and II only
    (E) I and III only

10. The smallest prime number greater than 53 is

    (A) 54
    (B) 55
    (C) 57
    (D) 59
    (E) 67

11. Which one of the following numbers is the greatest positive integer x such that 3^x is a factor of 27^5 ?

    (A) 5
    (B) 8
    (C) 10
    (D) 15
    (E) 19

12. If $x, y,$ and z are consecutive integers in that order, which of the following must be true?

    I. xy is even.
    II. $x - z$ is even.
    III. x^z is even.

    (A) I only
    (B) II only
    (C) III only
    (D) I and II only
    (E) I and III only

13. If $-x - 2 = -|-(6 - 2)|$, then $x =$

    (A) −5
    (B) −2
    (C) 0
    (D) 2
    (E) 5

14. If the sum of two prime numbers x and y is odd, then the product of x and y must be divisible by

    (A) 2   (B) 3   (C) 4   (D) 5   (E) 8

15. If $\dfrac{x+y}{x-y} = 3$ and x and y are integers, then

    which one of the following must be true?

    (A) x is divisible by 4
    (B) y is an odd number
    (C) y is an even integer
    (D) x is an even number
    (E) x is an irreducible fraction

16. A two-digit even number is such that reversing its digits creates an odd number greater than the original number. Which one of the following cannot be the first digit of the original number?

    (A) 1
    (B) 3
    (C) 5
    (D) 7
    (E) 9

17. Let $a, b,$ and c be three integers, and let a be a perfect square. If $a/b = b/c$, then which one of the following statements must be true?

    (A) c must be an even number
    (B) c must be an odd number
    (C) c must be a perfect square
    (D) c must not be a perfect square
    (E) c must be a prime number

18. If $n > 2$, then the sum, S, of the integers from 1 through n can be calculated by the following formula: $S = n(n + 1)/2$. Which one of the following statements about S must be true?

    (A) S is always odd.
    (B) S is always even.
    (C) S must be a prime number.
    (D) S must not be a prime number.
    (E) S must be a perfect square.

19. If n is an odd number greater than 5 and a multiple of 5, then what is the remainder when n is divided by 10?

    (A) 1
    (B) 3
    (C) 5
    (D) 7
    (E) 9

20. Which one of the following could be the difference between two numbers both of which are divisible by 2, 3 and 4?

    (A) 71
    (B) 72
    (C) 73
    (D) 74
    (E) 75

21. A number, when divided by 12, gives a remainder of 7. If the same number is divided by 6, then the remainder must be
    (A) 1
    (B) 2
    (C) 3
    (D) 4
    (E) 5

36

Answers and Solutions to Problem Set D

1. The statement *"the remainder is 1 when m is divided by 2"* translates into

$$m = 2u + 1$$

The statement *"the remainder is 3 when n is divided by 4"* translates into

$$n = 4v + 3$$

Forming the sum of m and n gives

$$m + n = 2u + 1 + 4v + 3 =$$
$$2u + 4v + 4 = 2(u + 2v + 2)$$

Since we have written $m + n$ as a multiple of 2, it is even. The answer is (C).

Method II (Substitution)

Let $m = 3$ and $n = 7$. Then

$$3 = 2 \cdot 1 + 1$$

and

$$7 = 4 \cdot 1 + 3$$

Now, both 3 and 7 are odd, which eliminates (A) and (B). Further, $3 \cdot 7 = 21$ is odd, which eliminates (D). Finally, 3/7 is not an integer, which eliminates (E). Hence, by process of elimination, the answer is (C).

2. Since x and y are prime and greater than 2, xy is the product of two odd numbers and is therefore odd. Hence, 2 cannot be a divisor of xy. The answer is (A).

3. Since 2 divides evenly into x, we get $x = 2z$. Hence, $5x = 5(2z) = 10z$. In other words, $5x$ is divisible by 10. A similar analysis shows that $5y$ is also divisible by 10. Since 10 is the greatest number listed, the answer is (E).

4. Let $a, a + 2, a + 4$ stand for the consecutive even integers $a, b,$ and c, in that order. Forming the average of $a, b,$ and c yields

$$\frac{a+b+c}{3} = \frac{a+a+2+a+4}{3} = \frac{3a+6}{3} = a+2$$

Setting this less than $a/3$ gives

$$a + 2 < a/3$$

Multiplying by 3 yields

$$3a + 6 < a$$

Subtracting 6 and a from both sides yields

$$2a < -6$$

Dividing by 2 yields

$$a < -3$$

Hence, a is negative, and the best answer is (E).

5. If $x = 1$ and $y = 3$, then

$$y \neq 5x$$

and

$$\frac{x+5}{y} = \frac{1+5}{3} = \frac{6}{3} = 2,$$

which is prime and not odd. Hence, Statements I and III are not necessarily true. Next, let $x = 3$ and $y = 4$. Then y is not prime and

$$\frac{x+5}{y} = \frac{3+5}{4} = \frac{8}{4} = 2,$$

which is prime. Hence, Statement II is not necessarily true. The answer is (A).

6. Since x is both a cube and between 2 and 200, we are looking at the integers:

$$2^3, 3^3, 4^3, 5^3$$

which reduce to

$$8, 27, 64, 125$$

There is only one perfect square, $64 = 8^2$, in this set. The answer is (C).

7. Since the sum of the digits is 4, x must be $13, 22, 31,$ or 40. Further, since the difference of the digits is 4, x must be $40, 51, 15, 62, 26, 73, 37, 84, 48, 95,$ or 59. We see that 40 and only 40 is common to the two sets of choices for x. Hence, x must be 40. The answer is (C).

8. First, let's briefly review the concept of division. "Seven divided by 3 leaves a remainder of 1" means that $7 = 3 \cdot 2 + 1$. By analogy, "x divided by y leaves a remainder of 1" means that $x = y \cdot q + 1$, where q is an integer.

Hence, *"p divided by 9 leaves a remainder of 1"* translates into $p = 9 \cdot q + 1$. If $q = 1$, then $p = 10$ which is even. But if $q = 2$, then $p = 19$ which is odd. Hence, neither Statement I nor Statement II need be true. This eliminates (A), (B), (D), and (E). Hence, the answer is (C).

Let's verify that Statement III is true.

$p = 9 \cdot q + 1 = 3(3q) + 1 = 3z + 1$, where $z = 3q$.

9.   Statement I is true: From *"If p is divided by 2, the remainder is 1,"* $p = 2u + 1$; and from *"if q is divided by 6, the remainder is 1,"* $q = 6v + 1$. Hence, $pq + 1 =$

$$(2u + 1)(6v + 1) + 1 =$$

$$12uv + 2u + 6v + 1 + 1 =$$

$$12uv + 2u + 6v + 2 =$$

$$2(6uv + u + 3v + 1)$$

Since we have written $pq + 1$ as a multiple of 2, it is even.

Method II

Since p and q each leave a remainder of 1 when divided by an even number, both are odd. Now, the product of two odd numbers is another odd number. Hence, pq is odd, and therefore $pq + 1$ is even.

Now, since $pq + 1$ is even, pq is odd. Hence, $pq/2$ is not an integer, and Statement II is not necessarily true. Next, Statement III is not necessarily true. For example, if $p = 3$ and $q = 7$, then $pq = 21$, which is not a multiple of 12. The answer is (A).

10. Since the question asks for the *smallest* prime greater than 53, we start with the smallest answer-choice. 54 is not prime since $54 = 2(27)$. 55 is not prime since $55 = 5(11)$. 57 is not prime since $57 = 3(19)$. Now, 59 *is* prime. Hence, the answer is (D).

11. $27^5 = \left(3^3\right)^5 = 3^{15}$. Hence, $x = 15$ and the answer is (D).

12. Since x and y are consecutive integers, one of them must be even. Hence, the product xy is even and Statement I is true. As to Statement II, suppose z is odd, then x must be odd as well. Now, the difference of two odd numbers is an even number. Next, suppose z is even, then x must be even as well. Now, the difference of two even numbers is again an even number. Hence, Statement II is true. As to Statement III, let $x = 1$, then $z = 3$ and $x^z = 1^3 = 1$, which is odd. Thus, Statement III is not necessarily true. The answer is (D).

13. Working from the innermost parentheses out, we get

$$-x - 2 = -|-(6 - 2)|$$
$$-x - 2 = -|-4|$$
$$-x - 2 = -(+4)$$
$$-x - 2 = -4$$
$$-x = -2$$
$$x = 2$$

The answer is (D).

14. We are told that the sum of the prime numbers x and y is odd. For a sum of two numbers to be odd, one number must be odd and another even. There is only one even prime number—2; all others are odd. Hence, either x or y must be 2. Thus, the product of x and y is a multiple of 2 and therefore is divisible by 2. The answer is (A).

15. Solution: $\dfrac{x + y}{x - y} = 3$. Multiplying both sides of this equation by $(x - y)$ yields

$$x + y = 3(x - y)$$
$$x + y = 3x - 3y$$
$$-2x = -4y$$
$$x = 2y$$

Since we have expressed x as 2 times an integer, it is even. The answer is (D).

16. Let the original number be represented by *xy*. (Note: here *xy* does not denote multiplication, but merely the position of the digits: *x* first, then *y*.). Reversing the digits of *xy* gives *yx*. We are told that *yx* > *xy*. This implies that *y* > *x*. (For example, 73 > 69 because 7 > 6.) If *x* = 9, then the condition *y* > *x* cannot be satisfied. Hence, *x* cannot equal 9. The answer is (E).

Method II:
Let the original number be represented by *xy*. In expanded form, *xy* can be written as $10x + y$. For example, $53 = 5(10) + 3$. Similarly, $yx = 10y + x$. Since *yx* > *xy*, we get $10y + x > 10x + y$. Subtracting *x* and *y* from both sides of this equation yields $9y > 9x$. Dividing this equation by 9 yields *y* > *x*. Now, if *x* = 9, then the inequality *y* > *x* cannot be satisfied. The answer is (E).

17. Cross multiplying the equation $a/b = b/c$ yields

$$ac = b^2$$

Dividing by *a* yields

$$c = b^2/a$$

We are given that *a* is a perfect square. Hence, $a = k^2$, for some number *k*. Replacing *a* in the bottom equation with k^2, we get

$$c = b^2/k^2 = (b/k)^2$$

Since we have written *c* as the square of a number, it is a perfect square. The answer is (C).

18. Observe that *n* and $(n + 1)$ are consecutive integers. Hence, one of the numbers is even. Therefore, the 2 in the denominator divides evenly into either *n* or $(n + 1)$, eliminating 2 from the denominator. Thus, *S* can be reduced to a product of two integers. Remember, a prime number cannot be written as the product of two integers (other than itself and 1). Hence, *S* is not a prime number, and the answer is (D).

19. The set of numbers greater than 5 and divisible by 5 is

$$\{10, 15, 20, 25, 30, 35, \ldots\}$$

Since *n* is odd, the possible values for *n* are

$$15, 25, 35, \ldots.$$

Any number in this list, when divided by 10, leaves a remainder of 5. The answer is (C).

20. A number divisible by all three numbers 2, 3, and 4 is also divisible by 12. Hence, each number can be written as a multiple of 12. Let the first number be represented as $12a$ and the second number as $12b$. Assuming $a > b$, the difference between the two numbers is $12a - 12b = 12(a - b)$. Observe that this number is also a multiple of 12. Hence, the answer must also be divisible by 12. Since 72 is the only answer-choice divisible by 12, the answer is (B).

21. We are told that the remainder is 7 when the number is divided by 12. Hence, we can represent the number as $12x + 7$. Now, 7 can be written as $6 + 1$. Plugging this into the expression yields

$12x + (6 + 1) =$
$(12x + 6) + 1 =$ by regrouping
$6(2x + 1) + 1$ by factoring 6 out of the first two terms

This shows that the remainder is 1 when the expression $12x + 7$ is divided by 6. The answer is (A).

Method II (Substitution):
Choose the number 19, which gives a remainder of 7 when divided by 12. Now, divide 19 by 6:

$$\frac{19}{6} = 3\frac{1}{6}$$

This shows that 6 divides into 19 with a remainder of 1. The answer is (A).

Geometry

About one-third of the math problems on the ACT involve geometry. (There are no proofs.) Fortunately, the figures on the ACT **are drawn to scale** (even though the official direction say that figures are not necessarily drawn to scale). Hence, you can check your work and in some cases even solve a problem by "eyeballing" the drawing. We'll discuss this technique in detail later.

Following is a discussion of the basic properties of geometry. You probably know many of these properties. Memorize any that you do not know.

Lines & Angles

When two straight lines meet at a point, they form an angle. The point is called the vertex of the angle, and the lines are called the sides of the angle.

The angle in the figure can be identified in three ways:
1. $\angle x$
2. $\angle B$
3. $\angle ABC$ or $\angle CBA$

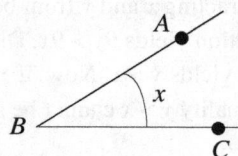

When two straight lines meet at a point, they form four angles. The angles opposite each other are called vertical angles, and they are congruent (equal). In the figure, $a = b$, and $c = d$.

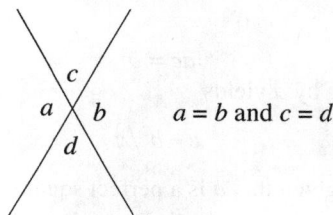

$a = b$ and $c = d$

Angles are measured in degrees, °. By definition, a circle has 360°. So, an angle can be measured by its fractional part of a circle. For example, an angle that is 1/360 of the arc of a circle is 1°. And an angle that is 1/4 of the arc of a circle is $\dfrac{1}{4} \times 360 = 90°$.

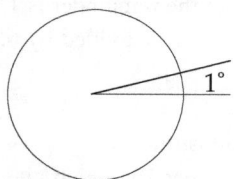

1°	90°	240°
1/360 of an arc of a circle	1/4 of an arc of a circle	2/3 of an arc of a circle

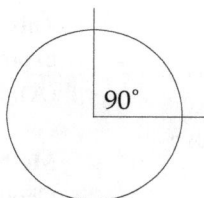

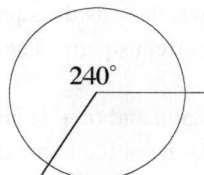

There are four major types of angle measures:

An **acute angle** has measure less than 90°:

A **right angle** has measure 90°:

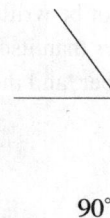

90°

An **obtuse angle** has measure greater than 90°:

A **straight angle** has measure 180°:

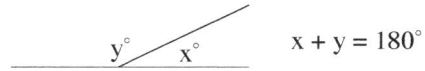

$y°$ $x°$ $x + y = 180°$

Example: In the figure, if the quotient of a and b is 7/2, then $b =$

$a°$ $b°$

    (A)   30
    (B)   35
    (C)   40
    (D)   46
    (E)   50

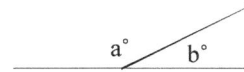

Since a and b form a straight angle, $a + b = 180$. Now, translating "the quotient of a and b is 7/2" into an equation gives $a/b = 7/2$. Solving for a yields $a = 7b/2$. Plugging this into the equation $a + b = 180$ yields

$$7b/2 + b = 180$$
$$7b + 2b = 360$$
$$9b = 360$$
$$b = 40$$

The answer is (C).

Example: In the figure, what is the measure of angle y ?

    (A)   80
    (B)   84
    (C)   85
    (D)   87
    (E)   90

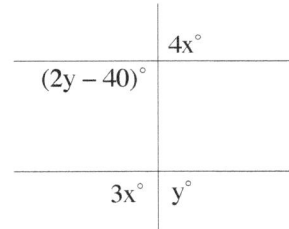

$4x°$
$(2y - 40)°$
$3x°$ $y°$

Since $4x$ and $2y - 40$ represent vertical angles, $4x = 2y - 40$. Since $3x$ and y form a straight angle, $3x + y = 180$. This yields the following system:

$$4x = 2y - 40$$
$$3x + y = 180$$

Solving this system for y yields $y = 84$. Hence, the answer is (B).

Two angles are supplementary if their angle sum is 180°:

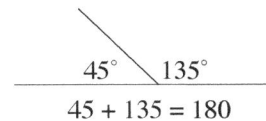

$45°$ $135°$
$45 + 135 = 180$

Two angles are complementary if their angle sum is 90°:

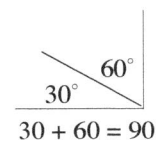

$60°$
$30°$
$30 + 60 = 90$

Perpendicular lines meet at right angles:

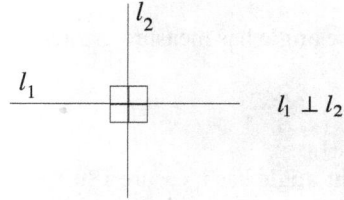

l_2

l_1

$l_1 \perp l_2$

Two lines in the same plane are parallel if they never intersect. Parallel lines have the same slope.

When parallel lines are cut by a transversal, three important angle relationships exist:

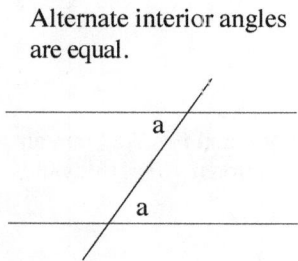

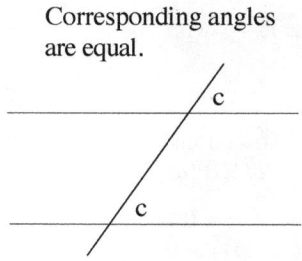

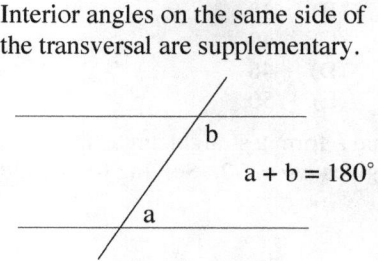

Alternate interior angles are equal.

Corresponding angles are equal.

Interior angles on the same side of the transversal are supplementary.

a

a

c

c

b

a

$a + b = 180°$

The shortest distance from a point to a line is along a new line that passes through the point and is perpendicular to the original line.

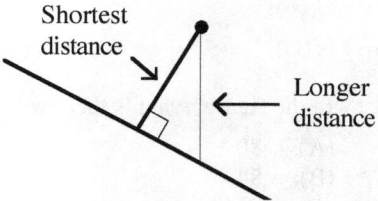

Shortest distance

Longer distance

Triangles

A triangle containing a right angle is called a *right triangle*. The right angle is denoted by a small square:

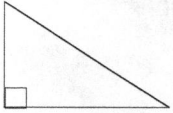

A triangle with two equal sides is called *isosceles*. The angles opposite the equal sides are called the base angles, and they are congruent (equal). A triangle with all three sides equal is called *equilateral*, and each angle is 60°. A triangle with no equal sides (and therefore no equal angles) is called *scalene*:

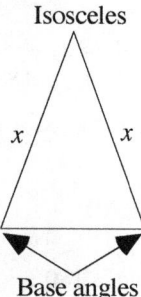

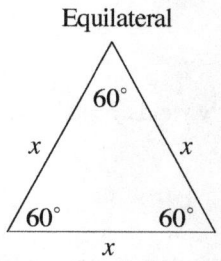

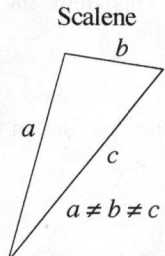

Isosceles

x x

Base angles

Equilateral

60°

x x

60°   60°

x

Scalene

b

a

c

$a \neq b \neq c$

The altitude to the base of an isosceles or equilateral triangle bisects the base and bisects the vertex angle:

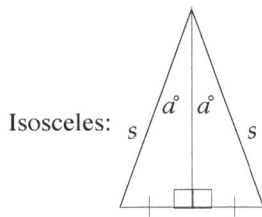

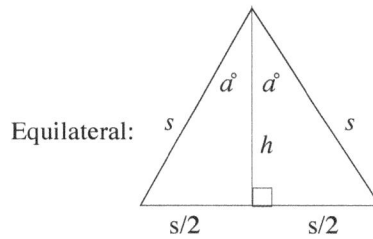

Isosceles:

Equilateral:

$$h = \frac{s\sqrt{3}}{2}$$

The angle sum of a triangle is 180°:

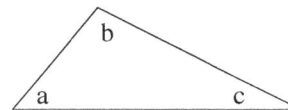

$$a + b + c = 180°$$

Example: In the figure, $w =$
- (A) 30
- (B) 32
- (C) 40
- (D) 52
- (E) 60

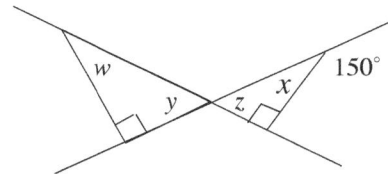

$x + 150 = 180$	since x and 150 form a straight angle
$x = 30$	solving for x
$z + x + 90 = 180$	since the angle sum of a triangle is 180°
$z + 30 + 90 = 180$	replacing x with 30
$z = 60$	solving for z
$z = y = 60$	since y and z are vertical angles
$w + y + 90 = 180$	since the angle sum of a triangle is 180°
$w + 60 + 90 = 180$	replacing y with 60
$w = 30$	solving for w

The answer is (A).

The area of a triangle is $\frac{1}{2}bh$, where b is the base and h is the height. Sometimes the base must be extended in order to draw the altitude, as in the third drawing directly below:

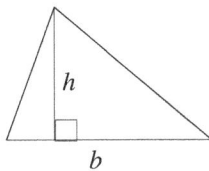

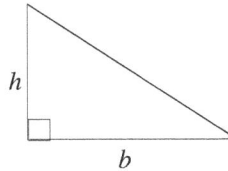

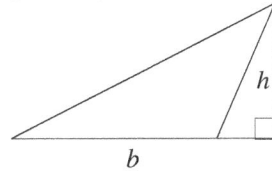

$$A = \frac{1}{2}bh$$

In a triangle, the longer side is opposite the larger angle, and vice versa:

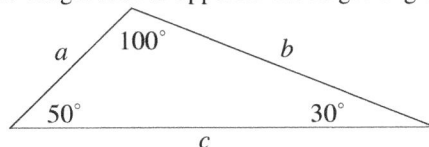

50° is larger than 30°, so side b is longer than side a.

Pythagorean Theorem (right triangles only): The square of the hypotenuse is equal to the sum of the squares of the legs.

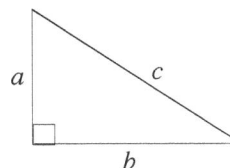

$$c^2 = a^2 + b^2$$

Pythagorean triples: The numbers 3, 4, and 5 can always represent the sides of a right triangle and they appear very often: $5^2 = 3^2 + 4^2$. Another, but less common, Pythagorean Triple is 5, 12, 13: $13^2 = 5^2 + 12^2$.

Two triangles are similar (same shape and usually different sizes) if their corresponding angles are equal. If two triangles are similar, their corresponding sides are proportional:

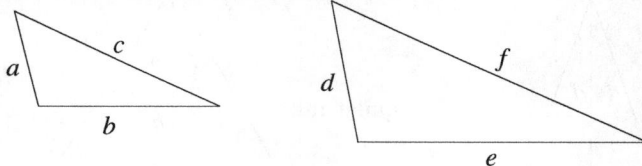

$$\frac{a}{d} = \frac{b}{e} = \frac{c}{f}$$

If two angles of a triangle are congruent to two angles of another triangle, the triangles are similar.

In the figure, the large and small triangles are similar because both contain a right angle and they share $\angle A$..

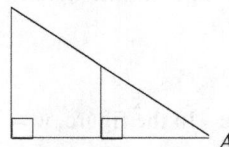

Two triangles are congruent (identical) if they have the same size and shape.

In a triangle, an exterior angle is equal to the sum of its remote interior angles and is therefore greater than either of them:

$e = a + b$ and $e > a$ and $e > b$

In a triangle, the sum of the lengths of any two sides is greater than the length of the remaining side:

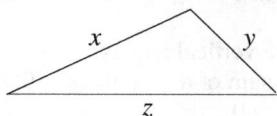

$x + y > z$
$y + z > x$
$x + z > y$

Example: In the figure, what is the value of x ?

   (A)   30
   (B)   32
   (C)   35
   (D)   40
   (E)   47

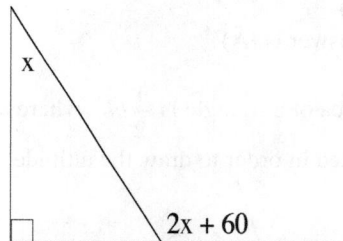

Since $2x + 60$ is an exterior angle, it is equal to the sum of the remote interior angles. That is, $2x + 60 = x + 90$. Solving for x gives $x = 30$. The answer is (A).

In a 30°–60°–90° triangle, the sides have the following relationships:

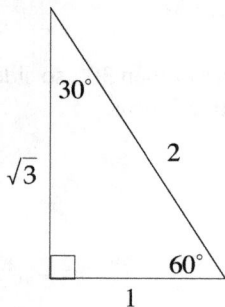

In general —>

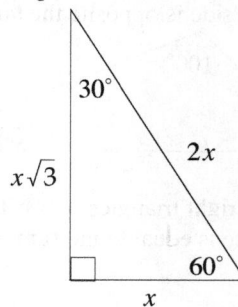

In a 45°–45°–90° triangle, the sides have the following relationships:

Quadrilaterals

A *quadrilateral* is a four-sided closed figure, where each side is a straight line.

The angle sum of a quadrilateral is 360°. You can view a quadrilateral as being composed of two 180-degree triangles:

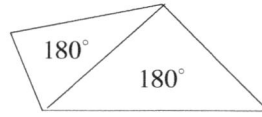

A *parallelogram* is a quadrilateral in which the opposite sides are both parallel and congruent. Its area is *base × height*:

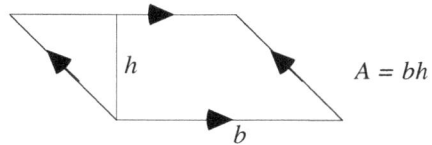

$$A = bh$$

The diagonals of a parallelogram bisect each other:

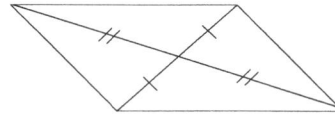

A parallelogram with four right angles is a *rectangle*. If w is the width and l is the length of a rectangle, then its area is $A = l \cdot w$ and its perimeter is $P = 2w + 2l$.

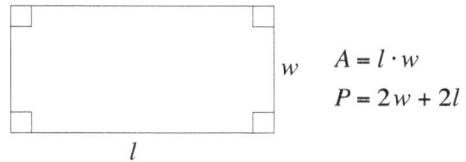

$$A = l \cdot w$$
$$P = 2w + 2l$$

Example: In the figure, what is the perimeter of the pentagon?
- (A) 12
- (B) 13
- (C) 17
- (D) 20
- (E) 25

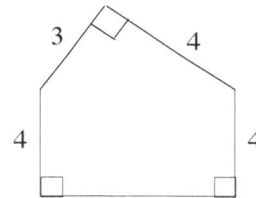

Add the following line to the figure:

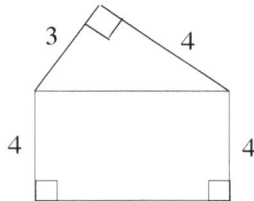

Since the legs of the right triangle formed are of lengths 3 and 4, the triangle must be a 3-4-5 right triangle. Hence, the added line has length 5. Since the bottom figure is a rectangle, the length of the base of the figure is also 5. Hence, the perimeter of the pentagon is $3 + 4 + 4 + 5 + 4 = 20$. The answer is (D).

If the opposite sides of a rectangle are equal, it is a square and its area is $A = s^2$ and its perimeter is $P = 4s$, where s is the length of a side:

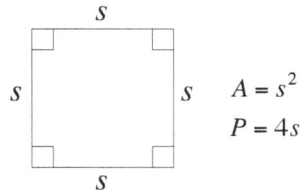

$$A = s^2$$
$$P = 4s$$

The diagonals of a square bisect each other and are perpendicular to each other:

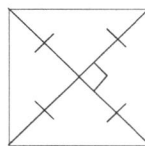

A quadrilateral with only one pair of parallel sides is a *trapezoid*. The parallel sides are called *bases*, and the non-parallel sides are called *legs*:

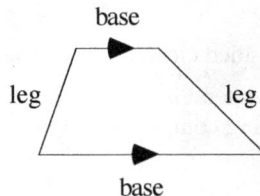

The area of a trapezoid is the average of the two bases times the height:

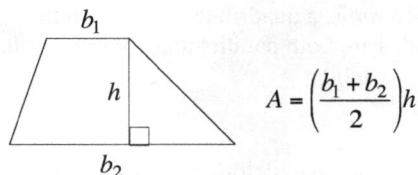

$$A = \left(\frac{b_1 + b_2}{2}\right)h$$

Volume

The volume of a rectangular solid (a box) is the product of the length, width, and height. The surface area is the sum of the area of the six faces:

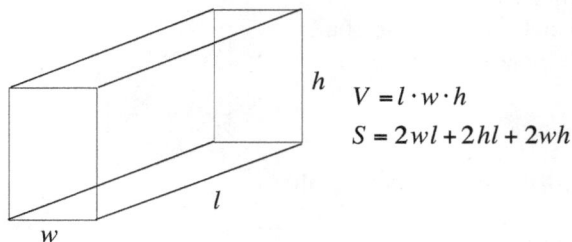

$$V = l \cdot w \cdot h$$
$$S = 2wl + 2hl + 2wh$$

If the length, width, and height of a rectangular solid (a box) are the same, it is a cube. Its volume is the cube of one of its sides, and its surface area is the sum of the areas of the six faces:

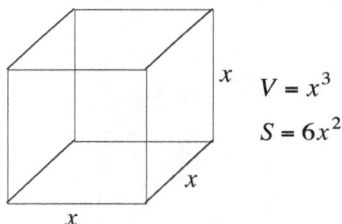

$$V = x^3$$
$$S = 6x^2$$

Example: The volume of the cube is x and its surface area is x.
What is the length of an edge of the cube?

(A)   6
(B)   10
(C)   18
(D)   36
(E)   48

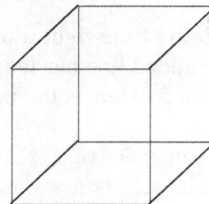

Let e be the length of an edge of the cube. Recall that the volume of a cube is e^3 and its surface area is $6e^2$. Since we are given that both the volume and the surface area are x, these expressions are equal:

$$e^3 = 6e^2$$
$$e^3 - 6e^2 = 0$$
$$e^2(e - 6) = 0$$
$$e^2 = 0 \ \text{ or } \ e - 6 = 0$$
$$e = 0 \ \text{ or } \ e = 6$$

We reject $e = 0$ since in that case no cube would exist. Hence, $e = 6$ and the answer is (A).

The volume of a cylinder is $V = \pi r^2 h$, and the lateral surface (excluding the top and bottom) is $S = 2\pi rh$, where r is the radius and h is the height:

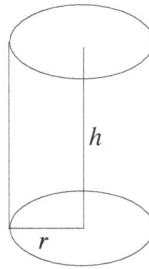

$$V = \pi r^2 h$$
$$S = 2\pi rh + 2\pi r^2$$

Circles

A circle is a set of points in a plane equidistant from a fixed point (the center of the circle). The perimeter of a circle is called the *circumference*.

A line segment from a circle to its center is a *radius*.

A line segment with both end points on a circle is a *chord*.

A chord passing though the center of a circle is a *diameter*.

A diameter can be viewed as two radii, and hence a diameter's length is twice that of a radius.

A line passing through two points on a circle is a *secant*.

A piece of the circumference is an *arc*.

The area bounded by the circumference and an angle with vertex at the center of the circle is a *sector*.

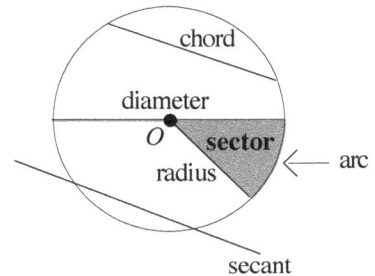

A tangent line to a circle intersects the circle at only one point. The radius of the circle is perpendicular to the tangent line at the point of tangency:

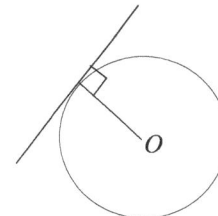

Two tangents to a circle from a common exterior point of the circle are congruent:

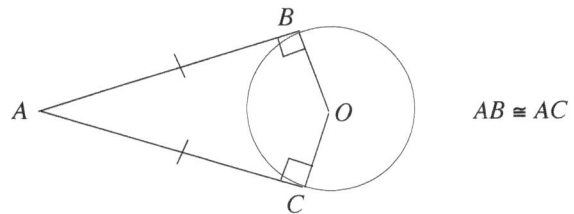

$$AB \cong AC$$

An angle inscribed in a semicircle is a right angle:

A central angle has by definition the same measure as its intercepted arc:

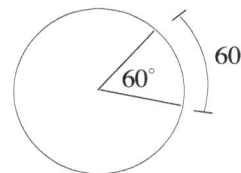

An inscribed angle has one-half the measure of its intercepted arc:

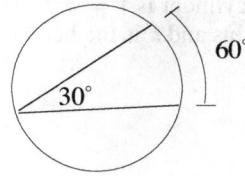

The area of a circle is πr^2, and its circumference (perimeter) is $2\pi r$, where r is the radius:

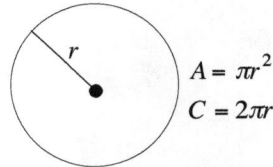

$$A = \pi r^2$$
$$C = 2\pi r$$

On the test, $\pi \approx 3$ is a sufficient approximation for π. You don't need $\pi \approx 3.14$.

Example: In the figure, the circle has center O and its radius is 2. What is the length of arc ACB ?

(A) $\pi/3$
(B) $2\pi/3$
(C) π
(D) $4\pi/3$
(E) $7\pi/3$

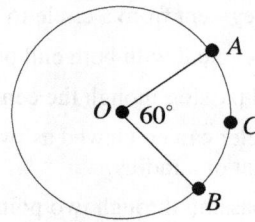

The circumference of the circle is $2\pi r = 2\pi(2) = 4\pi$. A central angle has by definition the same degree measure as its intercepted arc. Hence, arc ACB is also 60°. Now, the circumference of the circle has 360°. So arc ACB is $\frac{1}{6}$ (= 60/360) of the circle's circumference. Hence, arc $ACB = \frac{1}{6}(4\pi) = \frac{2}{3}\pi$. The answer is (B).

Shaded Regions

To find the area of the shaded region of a figure, subtract the area of the unshaded region from the area of the entire figure.

Example: What is the area of the shaded region formed by the circle and the rectangle in the figure?

(A) $15 - 2\pi$
(B) $15 - \pi$
(C) 14
(D) $16 - \pi$
(E) 15π

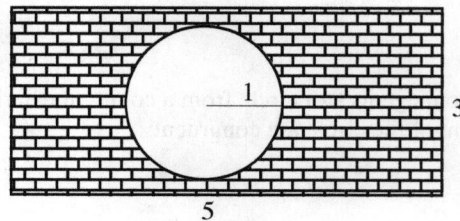

To find the area of the shaded region subtract the area of the circle from the area of the rectangle:

area of rectangle	–	area of circle
$3 \cdot 5$	–	$\pi \cdot 1^2$
15	–	π

The answer is (B).

Example: In the figure, the radius of the larger circle is three times that of the smaller circle. If the circles are concentric, what is the ratio of the shaded region's area to the area of the smaller circle?

(A)   10:1
(B)   9:1
(C)   8:1
(D)   3:1
(E)   5:2

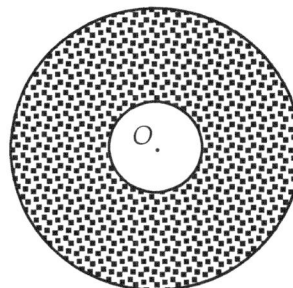

Since we are not given the radii of the circles, we can choose any two positive numbers such that one is three times the other. Let the outer radius be 3 and the inner radius be 1. Then the area of the outer circle is $\pi 3^2 = 9\pi$, and the area of the inner circle is $\pi 1^2 = \pi$. So the area of the shaded region is $9\pi - \pi = 8\pi$.

Hence, the ratio of the area of the shaded region to the area of the smaller circle is $\dfrac{8\pi}{\pi} = \dfrac{8}{1}$. Therefore, the answer is (C).

"Birds-Eye" View

Most geometry problems on the ACT require straightforward calculations. However, some problems measure your insight into the basic rules of geometry. For this type of problem, you should step back and take a "birds-eye" view of the problem. The following example will illustrate.

Example: In the figure, O is both the center of the circle with radius 2 and a vertex of the square $OPRS$. What is the length of diagonal PS ?

(A)   1/2
(B) $\dfrac{\sqrt{2}}{2}$
(C)   4
(D)   2
(E) $2\sqrt{5}$

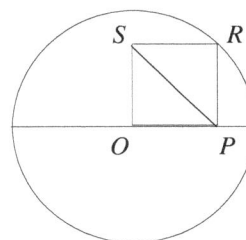

The diagonals of a square are equal. Hence, line segment OR (not shown) is equal to SP. Now, OR is a radius of the circle and therefore $OR = 2$. Hence, $SP = 2$ as well, and the answer is (D).

Problem Set E:

1.   In the figure, what is the value of y ?

(A) $\sqrt{23}$
(B) $\sqrt{27}$
(C) $\sqrt{29}$
(D) $\sqrt{33}$
(E) $\sqrt{35}$

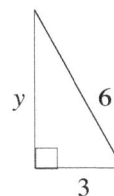

2.   In the figure, circle P has diameter 2 and circle Q has diameter 1. What is the area of the shaded region?

(A) $3\pi/4$
(B) 3π
(C) $7\pi/2$
(D) 5π
(E) 6π

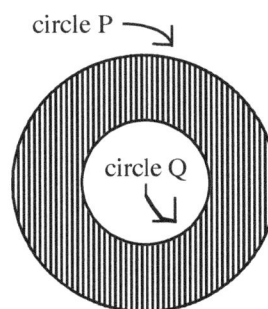

3. In the figure, *QRST* is a square. If the shaded region is bounded by arcs of circles with centers at *Q*, *R*, *S*, and *T*, then the area of the shaded region is

    (A) 9
    (B) 36
    (C) $36 - 9\pi$
    (D) $36 - \pi$
    (E) $9 - 3\pi$

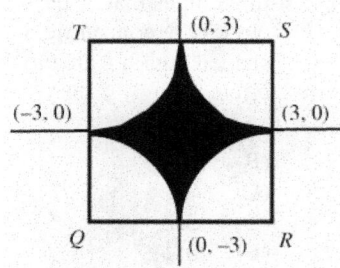

4. In the figure, *QRST* is a square. If the area of each circle is 2π, then the area of square *QRST* is

    (A) $\sqrt{2}$
    (B) 4
    (C) $\sqrt{2}\pi$
    (D) $4\sqrt{2}$
    (E) 32

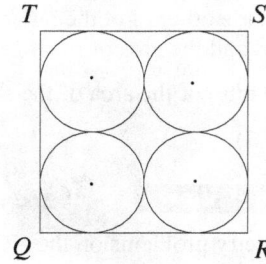

5. In the figure, if *O* is the center of the circle, then *y* =

    (A) 75
    (B) 76
    (C) 77
    (D) 78
    (E) 79

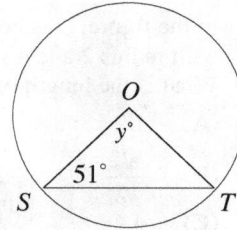

6. In the figure, the value of *a* + *b* is

    (A) 118
    (B) 119
    (C) 120
    (D) 121
    (E) 122

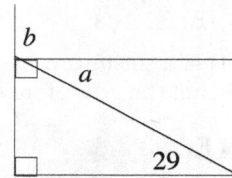

7. If $l_1 \| l_2$ in the figure, what is the value of x?

    (A) 30
    (B) 45
    (C) 60
    (D) 72
    (E) 90

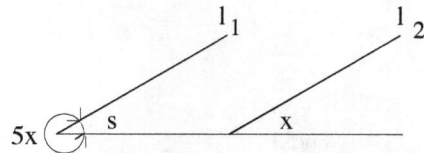

8. In the figure, *O* is the center of the circle. Which one of the following must be true?

    (A) $PQ > OQ$
    (B) $OP \geq OQ$
    (C) $PQ = OQ$
    (D) $OQ < OP$
    (E) $PQ \leq OP$

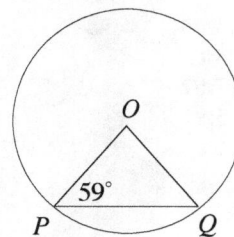

9. In the figure, x is both the radius of the larger circle and the diameter of the smaller circle. The area of the shaded region is

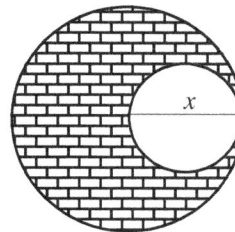

    (A) $3\pi x^2/4$
    (B) $\pi/3$
    (C) $4\pi x^2/3$
    (D) $3\pi x^2/5$
    (E) πx^2

10. In the figure, the circle with center O is inscribed in the square $PQRS$. The combined area of the shaded regions is

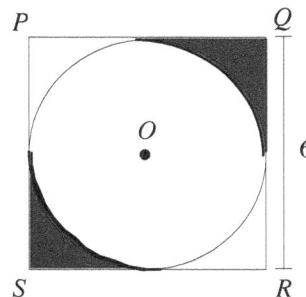

    (A) $36 - 9\pi$
    (B) $36 - 9\pi/2$
    (C) $(36 - 9\pi)/2$
    (D) $18 - 9\pi$
    (E) $9 - 9\pi/4$

11. In the figure, the length of QS is

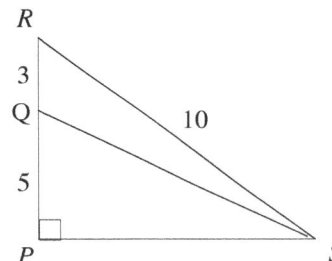

    (A) $\sqrt{51}$
    (B) $\sqrt{61}$
    (C) $\sqrt{69}$
    (D) $\sqrt{77}$
    (E) $\sqrt{89}$

12. In the figure, which one of the following must be true about y ?

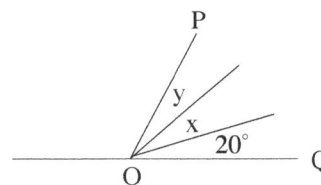

    (A) $y > 37$
    (B) $y < 35$
    (C) $y > 40$
    (D) $y > 42$
    (E) $y > 45$

    $\angle\, POQ = 70°$ and $x > 15$

13. In the figure, if $l \parallel k$, then what is the value of y ?

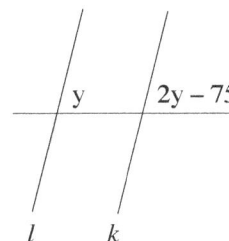

    (A)   20
    (B)   45
    (C)   55
    (D)   75
    (E)   110

14. In the figure, both triangles are right triangles. The area of the shaded region is

    (A) 1/2
    (B) 2/3
    (C) 7/8
    (D) 3/2
    (E) 5/2

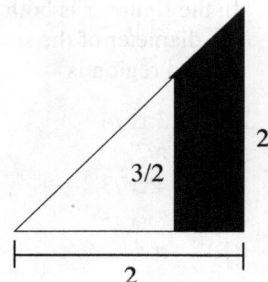

15. In the figure, the radius of the larger circle is twice that of the smaller circle. If the circles are concentric, what is the ratio of the shaded region's area to the area of the smaller circle?

    (A) 10 : 1
    (B) 9 : 1
    (C) 3 : 1
    (D) 2 : 1
    (E) 1 : 1

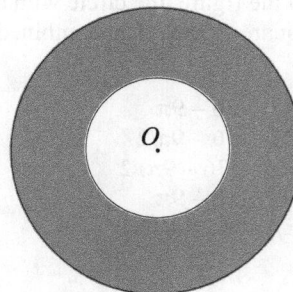

16. In the figure, ΔPST is an isosceles right triangle, and $PS = 2$. What is the area of the shaded region $URST$?

    (A) 4
    (B) 2
    (C) 5/4
    (D) 5/6
    (E) 1/2

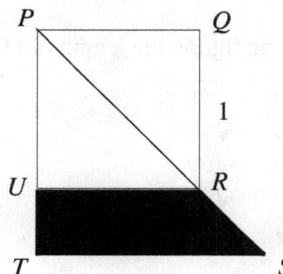

17. In the figure, the area of ΔPQR is 40. What is the area of ΔQRS ?

    (A) 10
    (B) 15
    (C) 20
    (D) 25
    (E) 45

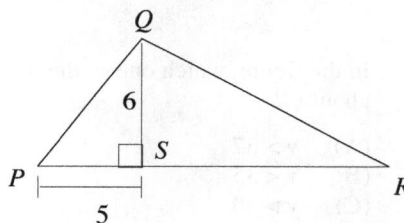

18. In the figure, $PQRS$ is a square and M and N are midpoints of their respective sides. What is the area of quadrilateral $PMRN$?

    (A) 8
    (B) 10
    (C) 12
    (D) 14
    (E) 16

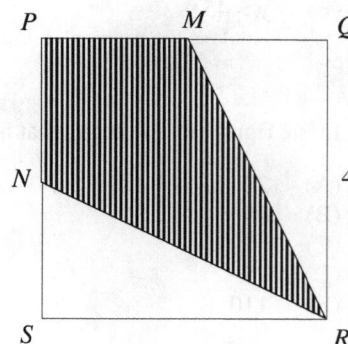

19. In the figure, O is the center of the circle. If the area of the circle is 9π, then the perimeter of the sector *PRQO* is

    (A) $\pi/2 - 6$
    (B) $\pi/2 + 6$
    (C) $3\pi/4 + 6$
    (D) $\pi/2 + 18$
    (E) $3\pi/4 + 18$

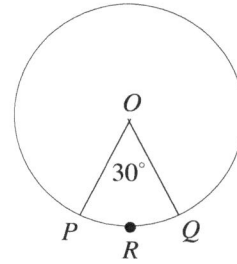

20. Let A denote the area of a circular region. Which of the following denotes the circumference of that circular region?

    (A) $\sqrt{\dfrac{A}{\pi}}$

    (B) $2\dfrac{A}{\sqrt{\pi}}$

    (C) $2\pi\sqrt{A}$

    (D) $2\sqrt{\dfrac{A}{\pi}}$

    (E) $2\pi\sqrt{\dfrac{A}{\pi}}$

21. Ship X and ship Y are 5 miles apart and are on a collision course. Ship X is sailing directly north, and ship Y is sailing directly east. If the point of impact is 1 mile closer to the current position of ship X than to the current position of ship Y, how many miles away from the point of impact is ship Y at this time?

    (A) 1
    (B) 2
    (C) 3
    (D) 4
    (E) 5

22. The figure represents a square with sides of length 4 surmounted by a circle with center O. What is the outer perimeter of the figure?

    (A) $5\pi/6 + 12$
    (B) $\pi + 12$
    (C) $49\pi/9 + 12$
    (D) $20\pi/3 + 12$
    (E) $9\pi + 12$

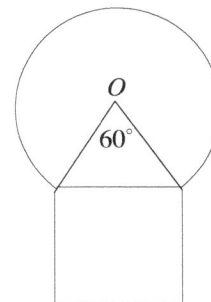

53

23. In $\triangle ABC$, $AB = AC$ and $x = 30$. What is the value of y ?
    - (A) 30
    - (B) 40
    - (C) 50
    - (D) 65
    - (E) 75

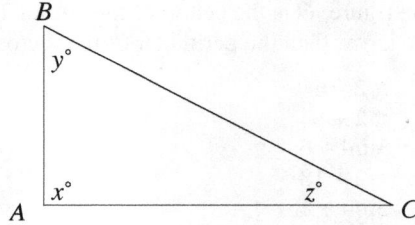

Note, figure not drawn to scale.

24. In the figure, $c^2 = 6^2 + 8^2$. What is the area of the triangle?

    - (A) 12
    - (B) 18
    - (C) 24
    - (D) 30
    - (E) 36

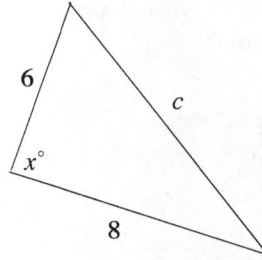

25. If the total surface area of cube S is 22, what is the volume of S ?

    - (A) $\dfrac{1}{3}\sqrt{\dfrac{11}{3}}$
    - (B) $\dfrac{\sqrt{11}}{3}$
    - (C) $11/3$
    - (D) $\dfrac{11}{3}\sqrt{\dfrac{11}{3}}$
    - (E) $121/9$

26. In the figure, what is the area of the triangle?

    - (A) 5
    - (B) 9
    - (C) 10
    - (D) 15
    - (E) It cannot be determined from the information given

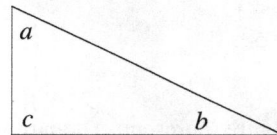

$a = x$, $b = 2x$, and $c = 3x$.

27. In the figure, $\triangle ABC$ is inscribed in the circle and AB is a diameter of the circle. What is the radius of the circle?

    - (A) $3/2$
    - (B) 2
    - (C) $5/2$
    - (D) 5
    - (E) 6

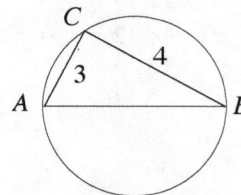

Answers and Solutions to Problem Set E

1. Since we have a right triangle, the Pythagorean Theorem yields

$$y^2 + 3^2 = 6^2$$

Simplifying yields

$$y^2 + 9 = 36$$

Subtracting 9 from both sides yields

$$y^2 = 27$$

Taking the square root of both sides yields

$$y = \sqrt{27}$$

The answer is (B).

2. Since the diameter of circle P is 2, its radius is 1. So the area of circle P is $\pi(1)^2 = \pi$. Since the diameter of circle Q is 1, its radius is 1/2. So the area of circle Q is $\pi\left(\dfrac{1}{2}\right)^2 = \dfrac{1}{4}\pi$. The area of the shaded region is the difference between the area of circle P and the area of circle Q: $\pi - \dfrac{1}{4}\pi = \dfrac{3}{4}\pi$. The answer is (A).

3. Each arc forms a quarter of a circle. Taken together the four arcs constitute one whole circle. From the drawing, we see that the radii of the arcs are each length 3, so the area of the four arcs together is $\pi(3)^2 = 9\pi$. Since the square has sides of length 6, its area is 36. Hence, the area of the shaded region is $36 - 9\pi$. The answer is (C).

4. Setting the area of a circle equal to 2π gives $\qquad\qquad \pi r^2 = 2\pi$
Dividing both sides of this equation by π gives $\qquad r^2 = 2$
Taking the square root of both sides gives $\qquad\quad r = \sqrt{2}$
Hence, the diameter of each circle is $\qquad\qquad\; d = 2r = 2\sqrt{2}$

Adding the diameters to the diagram gives

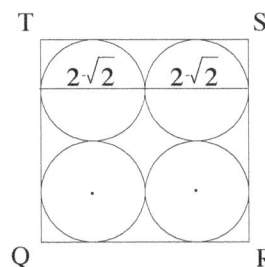

Clearly, in this diagram, the sides of the square are length $2\sqrt{2} + 2\sqrt{2} = 4\sqrt{2}$. Hence, the area of the square is $4\sqrt{2} \cdot 4\sqrt{2} = 16 \cdot 2 = 32$. The answer is (E).

5. *OS* and *OT* are equal since they are radii of the circle. Hence, ΔSOT is isosceles. Therefore, $S = T = 51°$. Recalling that the angle sum of a triangle is $180°$, we get $S + T + y = 51° + 51° + y = 180°$. Solving for y gives $y = 78°$. The answer is (D).

6. Since the two horizontal lines are parallel (Why?), angle a and the angle with measure 29 are alternate interior angles and therefore are equal. Further, from the drawing, angle b is $90°$. Hence, $a + b = 29 + 90 = 119$. The answer is (B).

7. Since $l_1\|l_2$, s and x are corresponding angles and therefore are congruent.

Now, about any point there are 360°. Hence,	$5x + s = 360$
Substituting x for s in this equation gives	$5x + x = 360$
Combining like terms gives	$6x = 360$
Dividing by 6 gives	$x = 60$

The answer is (C).

8. $\triangle OPQ$ is isosceles. (Why?). Hence, $P = Q = 59°$. Now, the angle sum of a triangle is 180. So

$$O + P + Q = 180.$$

Substituting $P = Q = 59°$ into this equation gives 　　　　$O + 59 + 59 = 180.$

Solving for O gives 　　　　$O = 62.$

Now, since O is the largest angle in $\triangle OPQ$, the side opposite it, PQ, is the longest side of the triangle. The answer is (A).

9. Since x is the radius of the larger circle, the area of the larger circle is πx^2. Since x is the diameter of the smaller circle, the radius of the smaller circle is $x/2$. Therefore, the area of the smaller circle is

$\pi\left(\dfrac{x}{2}\right)^2 = \pi\dfrac{x^2}{4}$. Subtracting the area of the smaller circle from the area of the larger circle gives

$$\pi x^2 - \pi\frac{x^2}{4} = \frac{4}{4}\pi x^2 - \pi\frac{x^2}{4} = \frac{4\pi x^2 - \pi x^2}{4} = \frac{3\pi x^2}{4}$$

The answer is (A).

10. The area of square $PQRS$ is $6^2 = 36$. Now, the radius of the circle is 3. (Why?) So the area of the circle is $\pi(3)^2 = 9\pi$. Subtracting the area of the circle from the area of the square yields $36 - 9\pi$. This is the combined area of the regions outside the circle and inside the square. Dividing this quantity by 2 gives $(36 - 9\pi)/2$. The answer is (C).

11. The length of PR is $PR = 3 + 5 = 8$. Applying the Pythagorean Theorem to triangle PRS yields

$$8^2 + (PS)^2 = 10^2$$

Squaring yields

$$64 + (PS)^2 = 100$$

Subtracting 64 from both sides yields

$$(PS)^2 = 36$$

Taking the square root of both sides yields

$$PS = \sqrt{36} = 6$$

Now, applying the Pythagorean Theorem to triangle PQS yields

$$(QS)^2 = 5^2 + 6^2$$

Squaring and adding yields

$$(QS)^2 = 61$$

Taking the square root of both sides yields

$$QS = \sqrt{61}$$

The answer is (B).

12. Since $\angle POQ = 70°$, we get $x + y + 20 = 70$. Solving this equation for y yields $y = 50 - x$. Now, we are given that $x > 15$. Hence, the expression $50 - x$ must be less than 35:

$$x > 15$$
$$-x < -15$$
$$50 - x < 50 - 15$$
$$50 - x < 35$$

The answer is (B).

13. Since lines l and k are parallel, we know that the corresponding angles are equal. Hence, $y = 2y - 75$. Solving this equation for y gives $y = 75$. The answer is (D).

14. Since the height and base of the larger triangle are the same, the slope of the hypotenuse is $45°$. Hence, the base of the smaller triangle is the same as its height, 3/2. Thus,

the area of the shaded region =

(area of the larger triangle) – (area of the smaller triangle) =

$$\left(\frac{1}{2} \cdot 2 \cdot 2\right) - \left(\frac{1}{2} \cdot \frac{3}{2} \cdot \frac{3}{2}\right) = 2 - \frac{9}{8} = \frac{7}{8}$$

The answer is (C).

15. Suppose the radius of the larger circle is 2 and the radius of the smaller circle is 1. Then the area of the larger circle is $\pi r^2 = \pi(2)^2 = 4\pi$, and the area of the smaller circle is $\pi r^2 = \pi(1)^2 = \pi$. Hence, the area of the shaded region is $4\pi - \pi = 3\pi$. Now,

$$\frac{area\ of\ shaded\ region}{area\ of\ smaller\ circle} = \frac{3\pi}{\pi} = \frac{3}{1}$$

The answer is (C).

16. Let x stand for the distances TP and TS. Applying The Pythagorean Theorem to the right triangle PST gives

$$TP^2 + TS^2 = PS^2$$

Substituting x for TP and TS and substituting 2 for PS gives

$$x^2 + x^2 = 2^2$$

Squaring and combining like terms gives

$$2x^2 = 4$$

Dividing by 2 gives

$$x^2 = 2$$

Finally, taking the square root gives

$$x = \sqrt{2}$$

Adding this information to the diagram gives

P   1   Q

1   1

$\sqrt{2}$

U   1   R

T   S

$\sqrt{2}$

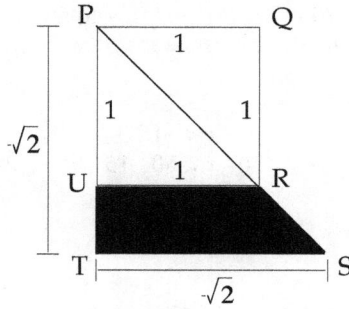

Now, the area of the shaded region equals

(area of triangle PST) – (area of triangle PRU) =

$$\left(\frac{1}{2}\cdot\sqrt{2}\cdot\sqrt{2}\right)-\left(\frac{1}{2}\cdot 1\cdot 1\right)=\left(\frac{1}{2}\cdot 2\right)-\left(\frac{1}{2}\right)=1-\frac{1}{2}=\frac{1}{2}$$

The answer is (E).

17. The area of triangle *PQS* is $\frac{1}{2}\cdot 5\cdot 6 = 15$. Now, (the area of ΔQRS) = (the area of ΔPQR) – (the area of ΔPQS) = $40 - 15 = 25$. The answer is (D).

18. Since M is the midpoint of side *PQ*, the length of *MQ* is 2. Hence, the area of triangle *MQR* is $\frac{1}{2}\cdot 2\cdot 4 = 4$. A similar analysis shows that the area of triangle *NSR* is 4. Thus, the unshaded area of the figure is $4 + 4 = 8$. Subtracting this from the area of the square gives $16 - 8 = 8$. The answer is (A).

19. Since the area of the circle is 9π, we get

$$\pi r^2 = 9\pi$$
$$r^2 = 9$$
$$r = 3$$

Now, the circumference of the circle is

$$C = 2\pi r = 2\pi 3 = 6\pi$$

Since the central angle is $30°$, the length of arc *PRQ* is

$$\frac{30}{360}C = \frac{1}{12}\cdot 6\pi = \frac{1}{2}\pi$$

Hence, the perimeter of the sector is

$$\frac{1}{2}\pi + 3 + 3 = \frac{1}{2}\pi + 6$$

The answer is (B).

20. Since A denotes the area of the circular region, we get

$$A = \pi r^2$$

$$\frac{A}{\pi} = r^2$$

$$\sqrt{\frac{A}{\pi}} = r$$

Hence, the circumference is $C = 2\pi r = 2\pi\sqrt{\frac{A}{\pi}}$

The answer is (E).

21. Let d be the distance ship Y is from the point of collision. Then the distance ship X is from the point of collision is d – 1. The following diagram depicts the situation:

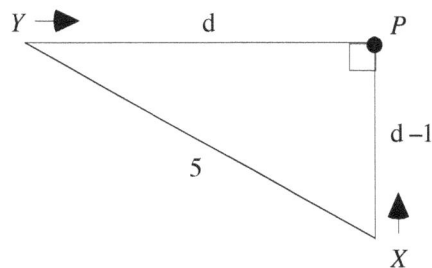

Applying the Pythagorean Theorem to the diagram yields

$$d^2 + (d - 1)^2 = 5^2$$

$$d^2 + d^2 - 2d + 1 = 25$$

$$2d^2 - 2d - 24 = 0$$

$$d^2 - d - 12 = 0$$

$$(d - 4)(d + 3) = 0$$

$$d = 4 \quad \text{or} \quad d = -3$$

Since d denotes distance, we reject $d = -3$. Hence, $d = 4$ and the answer is (D).

22. Since two sides of the triangle are radii of the circle, they are equal. Hence, the triangle is isosceles, and the base angles are equal:

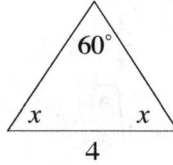

Since the angle sum of a triangle is 180, we get

$$x + x + 60 = 180$$

$$2x = 120$$

$$x = 60$$

Hence, the triangle is equilateral. Therefore, the radius of the circle is 4, and the circumference is $C = 2\pi r = 2\pi 4 = 8\pi$. Now, the portion of the perimeter formed by the circle has length $\frac{360 - 60}{360} \cdot C = \frac{5}{6} \cdot 8\pi = \frac{20}{3}\pi$.

Adding the three sides of the square to this expression gives $\frac{20}{3}\pi + 12$. The answer is (D).

23. Since $AB = AC$, ΔABC is isosceles. Hence, its base angles are equal: $y = z$. Since the angle sum of a triangle is $180°$, we get $x + y + z = 180$. Replacing z with y and x with 30 in this equation and then simplifying yields

$$30 + y + y = 180$$
$$30 + 2y = 180$$
$$2y = 150$$
$$y = 75$$

The answer is (E).

24. Recall that a triangle is a right triangle if and only if the square of the longest side is equal to the sum of the squares of the shorter sides (Pythagorean Theorem). Hence, $c^2 = 6^2 + 8^2$ implies that the triangle is a right triangle. So the area of the triangle is $\frac{1}{2} \cdot 6 \cdot 8 = 24$. The answer is (C).

25. Since the total surface area of the cube is 22 and each of the cube's six faces has the same area, the area of each face is 22/6, or 11/3. Now, each face of the cube is a square with area 11/3, so the length of a side of the cube is $\sqrt{\frac{11}{3}}$. Hence, the volume of the cube is

$$\sqrt{\frac{11}{3}} \cdot \sqrt{\frac{11}{3}} \cdot \sqrt{\frac{11}{3}} = \frac{11}{3} \cdot \sqrt{\frac{11}{3}}$$

The answer is (D).

26. From the information given, we can determine the measures of the angles:

$$a + b + c = x + 2x + 3x = 6x = 180$$

Dividing the last equation by 6 gives

$$x = 30$$

Hence, $a = 30$, $b = 60$, and $c = 90$. However, different size triangles can have these angle measures, as the diagram below illustrates:

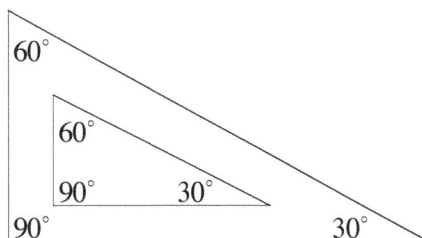

Hence, the information given is not sufficient to determine the area of the triangle. The answer is (E).

27. Recall from geometry that a triangle inscribed in a semicircle is a right triangle. Hence, we can use the Pythagorean Theorem to calculate the length of AB:

$$AC^2 + BC^2 = AB^2$$

or

$$3^2 + 4^2 = AB^2$$

or

$$25 = AB^2$$

or

$$5 = AB$$

Hence, the radius of the circle is

$$\frac{diameter}{2} = \frac{5}{2}$$

The answer is (C).

When Drawing a Geometric Figure or Checking a Given One, Be Sure to Include Drawings of Extreme Cases As Well As Ordinary Ones.

Example 1: In the figure, what is the value of angle x ?

    (A) $x > 45°$
    (B) $x < 45°$
    (C) $x = 45°$
    (D) $x \geq 45°$
    (E)   It cannot be determined from the information given

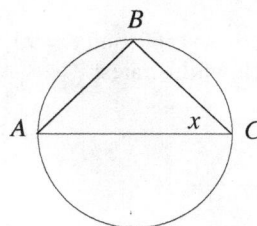

AC is a chord.
B is a point on the circle.

Although in the drawing AC looks to be a diameter, that cannot be assumed. All we know is that AC is a chord. Hence, numerous cases are possible, three of which are illustrated below:

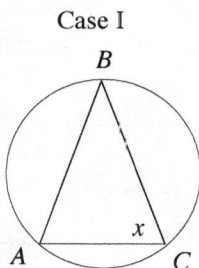

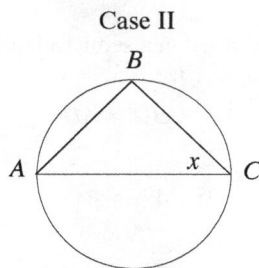

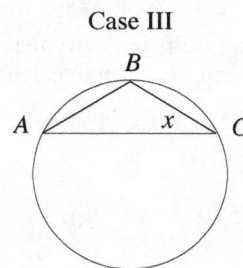

Case I   Case II   Case III

In Case I, x is greater than $45°$; in Case II, x equals $45°$; in Case III, x is less than $45°$. Hence, the answer is (E).

Example 2: Three rays emanate from a common point and form three angles with measures p, q, r. Which one of the following is the measure of angle $q + r$?

    (A) $q + r > 180°$
    (B) $q + r < 180°$
    (C) $q + r = 180°$
    (D) $q + r \leq 180°$
    (E)   It cannot be determined from the information given

It is natural to make the drawing symmetric as follows:

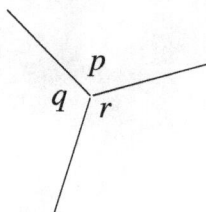

In this case, $p = q = r = 120°$, so $q + r = 240°$. However, there are other drawings possible. For example:

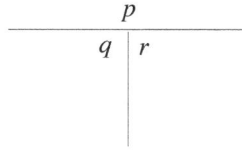

In this case, $q + r = 180°$ and therefore it cannot be determined from the information given. The answer is (E).

Problem Set F:

1. In triangle ABC, $AB = 5$ and $AC = 3$. Which one of the following is the measure of the length of side BC?

    (A) $BC < 7$
    (B) $BC = 7$
    (C) $BC > 7$
    (D) $BC \leq 7$
    (E) It cannot be determined from the information given

2. In the figure, what is the area of $\triangle ABC$?

    (A) 6
    (B) 7
    (C) 8
    (D) 9
    (E) It cannot be determined from the information given

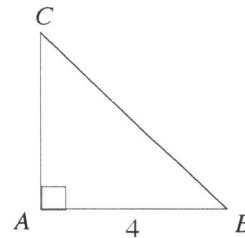

3. In the figure, which one of the following is the measure of angle θ?

    (A) $\theta < 45°$
    (B) $\theta > 45°$
    (C) $\theta = 45°$
    (D) $\theta \leq 45°$
    (E) It cannot be determined from the information given

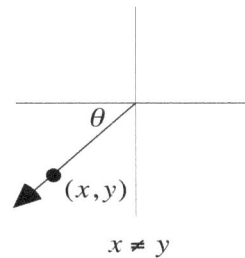

4. In isosceles triangle ABC, $CA = CB = 4$. Which one of the following is the area of triangle ABC?

    (A) 7
    (B) 8
    (C) 9
    (D) 10
    (E) It cannot be determined from the information given

Answers and Solutions to Problem Set F

1. The most natural drawing is the following:

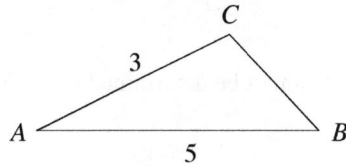

In this case, the length of side *BC* is less than 7. However, there is another drawing possible, as follows:

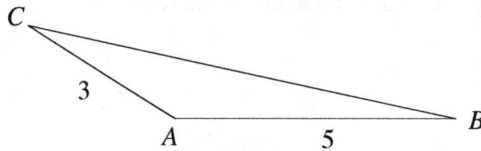

In this case, the length of side *BC* is greater than 7. Hence, there is not enough information to decide, and the answer is (E).

2. Although the drawing looks to be an isosceles triangle, that cannot be assumed. We are not given the length of side *AC*: it could be 4 units long or 100 units long, we don't know. Hence, the answer is (E).

3. There are two possible drawings:

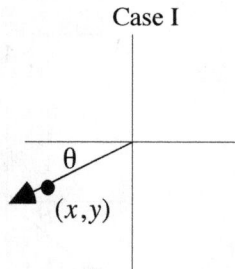

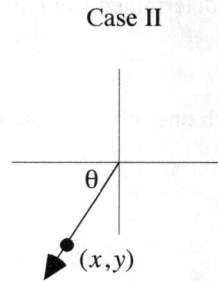

In Case I, $\theta < 45°$. Whereas, in Case II, $\theta > 45°$. This is a double case, and the answer therefore is (E).

4. There are many possible drawings for the triangle, two of which are listed below:

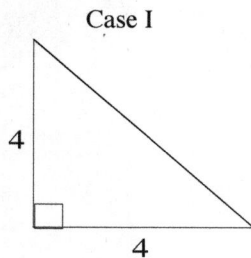

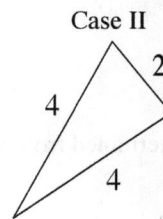

In Case I, the area is 8. In Case II, the area is $\sqrt{15}$. This is a double case and therefore the answer is (E).

Eye-Balling

Surprisingly, on the ACT you can often solve geometry problems by merely "eye-balling" the given drawing. Even on problems whose answers you can't get directly by looking, you often can eliminate a couple of the answer-choices.

- All figures are drawn to scale (even though the official direction say that figures are not necessarily drawn to scale). Hence, if an angle looks like it's about 90°, it is; if one figure looks like it's about twice as large as another figure, it is.

All the problems in this section were solved before. Now, we will solve them by eye-balling the drawings.

Example 1:　In the figure, if $l \| k$, then what is the value of *y* ?

(A)　20
(B)　45
(C)　55
(D)　75
(E)　110

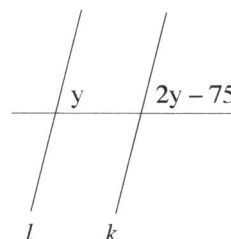

By eye-balling the drawing, we can see that y is less than 90°. It appears to be somewhere between 65° and 85°. But 75° is the only answer-choice in that range. Hence, the answer is (D).

Example 2:　In the figure, the area of the shaded region is

(A)　1/2
(B)　2/3
(C)　7/8
(D)　3/2
(E)　5/2

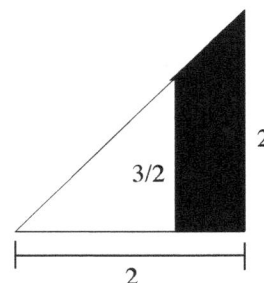

The area of the larger triangle is

$$A = \frac{1}{2}bh = \frac{1}{2} \cdot 2 \cdot 2 = 2$$

Now, by eye-balling the drawing, the area of the shaded region looks to be about half that of the larger triangle. Therefore, the answer should be about $\frac{1}{2} \cdot 2 = 1$. The closest answer-choice to 1 is 7/8. The answer is (C).

Note: On the ACT, answer-choices are listed in order of size: usually from smallest to largest (unless the question asks for the smallest or largest). Hence, in the previous example, 2/3 is smaller than 7/8 because it comes before 7/8.

Problem Set G:

The following problems have been solved before. Now, solve them by eye-balling the figures.

1. In the figure, the radius of the larger circle is twice that of the smaller circle. If the circles are concentric, what is the ratio of the shaded region's area to the area of the smaller circle?

    (A)   10 : 1
    (B)   9 : 1
    (C)   3 : 1
    (D)   2 : 1
    (E)   1 : 1

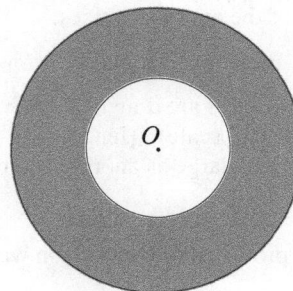

2. In the figure, ΔPST is an isosceles right triangle, and $PS = 2$. What is the area of the shaded region $URST$?

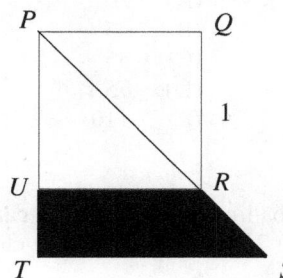

    (A)   4
    (B)   2
    (C)   5/4
    (D)   5/6
    (E)   1/2

3. In the figure, the area of ΔPQR is 40. What is the area of ΔQRS?

    (A)   10
    (B)   15
    (C)   20
    (D)   25
    (E)   45

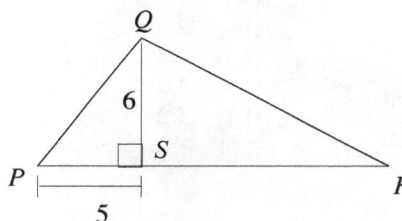

4. and M and N are midpoints of their respective sides. What is the area of quadrilateral $PMRN$?

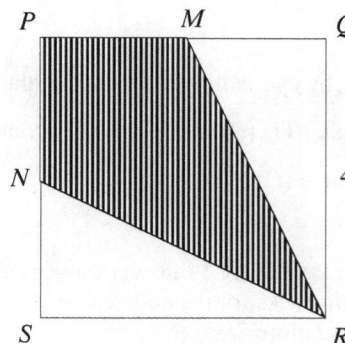

    (A)   8
    (B)   10
    (C)   12
    (D)   14
    (E)   16

Answers and Solutions to Problem Set G

1. In the figure, the radius of the larger circle is twice that of the smaller circle. If the circles are concentric, what is the ratio of the shaded region's area to the area of the smaller circle?

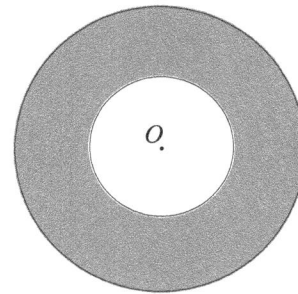

    (A) 10 : 1
    (B) 9 : 1
    (C) 3 : 1
    (D) 2 : 1
    (E) 1 : 1

The area of the shaded region appears to be about three times the area of the smaller circle, so the answer should be (C). Let's verify this. Suppose the radius of the larger circle is 2 and the radius of the smaller circle is 1. Then the area of the larger circle is $\pi r^2 = \pi(2)^2 = 4\pi$, and the area of the smaller circle is $\pi r^2 = \pi(1)^2 = \pi$. Hence, the area of the shaded region is $4\pi - \pi = 3\pi$. Now, $\dfrac{area\ of\ shaded\ region}{area\ of\ smaller\ circle} = \dfrac{3\pi}{\pi} = \dfrac{3}{1}$. The answer is (C).

2. In the figure, ΔPST is an isosceles right triangle, and $PS = 2$. What is the area of the shaded region $URST$?

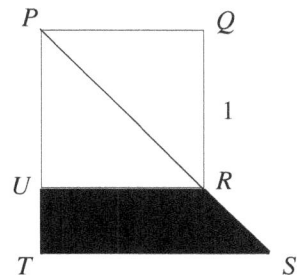

    (A) 4
    (B) 2
    (C) 5/4
    (D) 5/6
    (E) 1/2

The area of the square is $1^2 = 1$. Now, the area of the shaded region appears to be about half that of the square. Hence, the area of the shaded region is about 1/2. The answer is (E).

3. In the figure, the area of ΔPQR is 40. What is the area of ΔQRS?

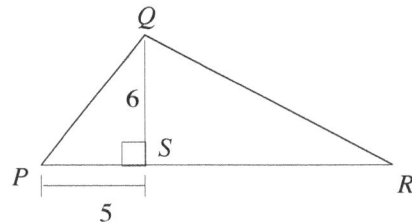

    (A) 10
    (B) 15
    (C) 20
    (D) 25
    (E) 45

Clearly from the drawing, the area of ΔQRS is greater than half the area of ΔPQR. This eliminates (A), (B), and (C). Now, the area of ΔQRS cannot be greater than the area of ΔPQR. This eliminates (E). The answer is (D).

4. In the figure, $PQRS$ is a square and M and N are midpoints of their respective sides. What is the area of quadrilateral $PMRN$?

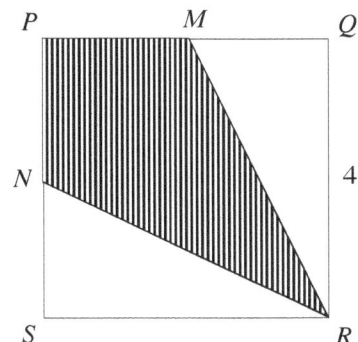

    (A) 8
    (B) 10
    (C) 12
    (D) 14
    (E) 16

Since the square has sides of length 4, its area is 16. Now, the area of the shaded region appears to be half that of the square. Hence, its area is 8. The answer is (A).

Coordinate Geometry

On a number line, the numbers increase in size to the right and decrease to the left:

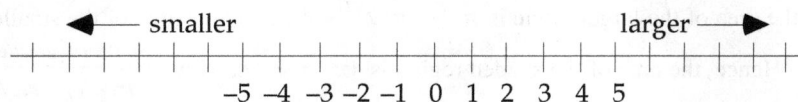

◄—— smaller   larger ——►

-5 -4 -3 -2 -1 0 1 2 3 4 5

If we draw a line through the point 0 perpendicular to the number line, we will form a grid:

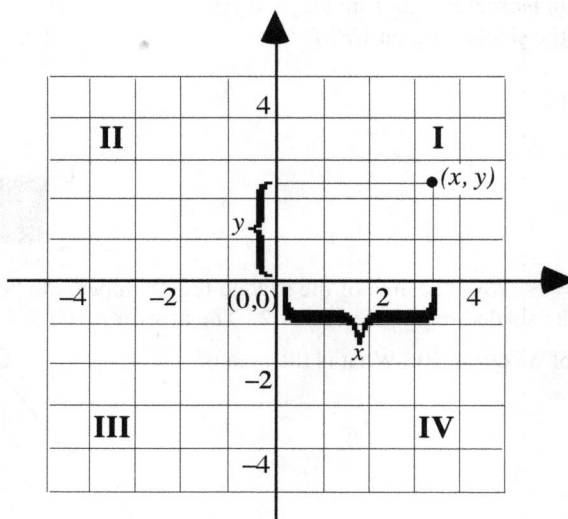

The thick horizontal line in the above diagram is called the x-axis, and the thick vertical line is called the y-axis. The point at which the axes meet, $(0, 0)$, is called the origin. On the x-axis, positive numbers are to the right of the origin and increase in size to the right; further, negative numbers are to the left of the origin and decrease in size to the left. On the y-axis, positive numbers are above the origin and ascend in size; further, negative numbers are below the origin and descend in size. As shown in the diagram, the point represented by the ordered pair (x, y) is reached by moving x units along the x-axis from the origin and then moving y units vertically. In the ordered pair (x, y), x is called the *abscissa* and y is called the *ordinate*; collectively they are called coordinates. The x and y axes divide the plane into four quadrants, numbered I, II, III, and IV counterclockwise. Note, if $x \neq y$, then (x, y) and (y, x) represent different points on the coordinate system. The points $(2, 3)$, $(-3, 1)$, $(-4, -4)$, and $(4, -2)$ are plotted in the following coordinate system:

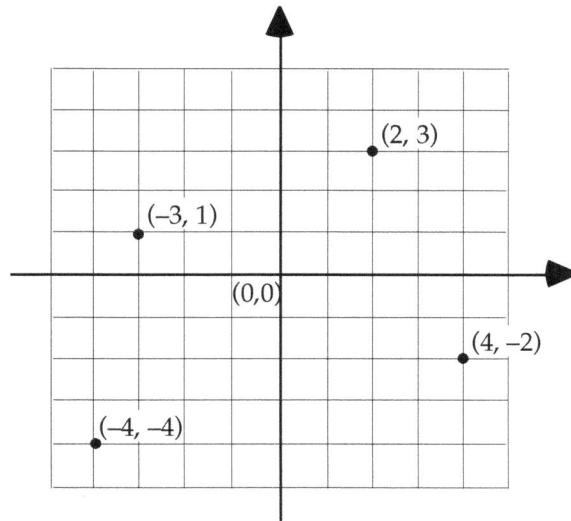

Example: In the figure, polygon *ABCO* is a square. If the coordinates of *B* are $(h, 4)$, what is the value of *h* ?

(A) 4
(B) $4\sqrt{2}$
(C) $-4\sqrt{2}$
(D) -4
(E) not enough information

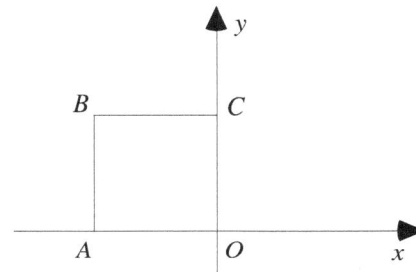

Since the *y*-coordinate of point *B* is 4, line segment *CO* has length 4. Since figure *ABCO* is a square, line segment *AO* also has length 4. Since point *B* is in the second quadrant, the *x*-coordinate of *B* is –4. The answer is (D). Be careful not to choose 4. *h* is the *x*-coordinate of point *B*, not the length of the square's side.

Distance Formula:

The distance formula is derived by using the Pythagorean Theorem. Notice in the figure below that the distance between the points (x, y) and (a, b) is the hypotenuse of a right triangle. The difference $y - b$ is the measure of the height of the triangle, and the difference $x - a$ is the length of base of the triangle. Applying the Pythagorean Theorem yields

$$d^2 = (x - a)^2 + (y - b)^2$$

Taking the square root of both sides this equation yields

$$\boxed{d = \sqrt{(x - a)^2 + (y - b)^2}}$$

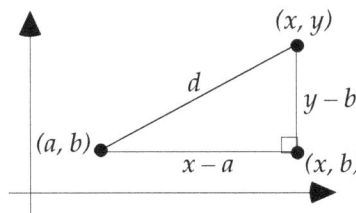

Example: In the figure, the circle is centered at the origin and passes through point P. Which of the following points does it also pass through?

(A) $(3,3)$
(B) $(-2\sqrt{2},-1)$
(C) $(2,6)$
(D) $(-\sqrt{3},\sqrt{3})$
(E) $(-3,4)$

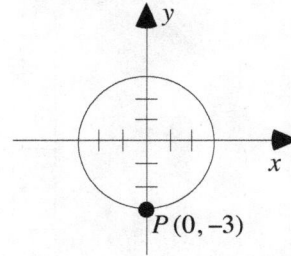

$P(0,-3)$

Since the circle is centered at the origin and passes through the point $(0,-3)$, the radius of the circle is 3. Now, if any other point is on the circle, the distance from that point to the center of the circle (the radius) must also be 3. Look at choice (B). Using the distance formula to calculate the distance between $(-2\sqrt{2},-1)$ and $(0,0)$ (the origin) yields

$$d = \sqrt{\left(-2\sqrt{2}-0\right)^2 + \left(-1-0\right)^2} = \sqrt{\left(-2\sqrt{2}\right)^2 + \left(-1\right)^2} = \sqrt{8+1} = \sqrt{9} = 3$$

Hence, $(-2\sqrt{2},-1)$ is on the circle, and the answer is (B).

Midpoint Formula:

The midpoint M between points (x,y) and (a,b) is given by

$$M = \left(\frac{x+a}{2}, \frac{y+b}{2}\right)$$

In other words, to find the midpoint, simply average the corresponding coordinates of the two points.

Example: In the figure, polygon $PQRO$ is a square and T is the midpoint of side QR. What are the coordinates of T?

(A) $(1,1)$
(B) $(1,2)$
(C) $(1.5,1.5)$
(D) $(2,1)$
(E) $(2,3)$

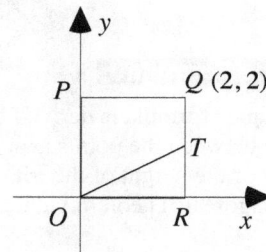

$Q(2,2)$

Since point R is on the x-axis, its y-coordinate is 0. Further, since $PQRO$ is a square and the x-coordinate of Q is 2, the x-coordinate of R is also 2. Since T is the midpoint of side QR, the midpoint formula yields

$$T = \left(\frac{2+2}{2}, \frac{2+0}{2}\right) = \left(\frac{4}{2}, \frac{2}{2}\right) = (2,1)$$

The answer is (D).

Slope Formula:

The slope of a line measures the inclination of the line. By definition, it is the ratio of the vertical change to the horizontal change (see figure below). The vertical change is called the *rise*, and the horizontal change is called the *run*. Thus, the slope is the *rise over the run*.

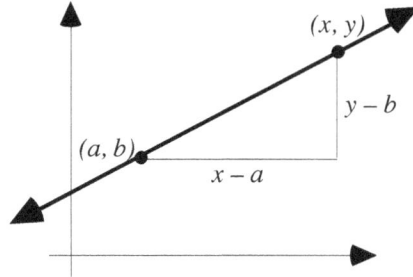

Forming the *rise over the run* in the above figure yields

$$m = \frac{y-b}{x-a}$$

Example: In the figure, what is the slope of line passing through the two points?

(A) 1/4
(B) 1
(C) 1/2
(D) 3/2
(E) 2

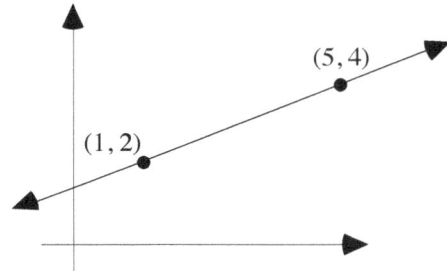

The slope formula yields $m = \dfrac{4-2}{5-1} = \dfrac{2}{4} = \dfrac{1}{2}$. The answer is (C).

Slope-Intercept Form:

Multiplying both sides of the equation $m = \dfrac{y-b}{x-a}$ by $x - a$ yields

$$y - b = m(x - a)$$

Now, if the line passes through the *y*-axis at $(0, b)$, then the equation becomes

$$y - b = m(x - 0)$$

or

$$y - b = mx$$

or

$$y = mx + b$$

This is called the slope-intercept form of the equation of a line, where *m* is the slope and *b* is the *y*-intercept. This form is convenient because it displays the two most important bits of information about a line: its slope and its *y*-intercept.

Example: In the figure, the equation of the line is

$y = \dfrac{9}{10}x + k$. Which one of the following must

be true about line segments *AO* and *BO* ?

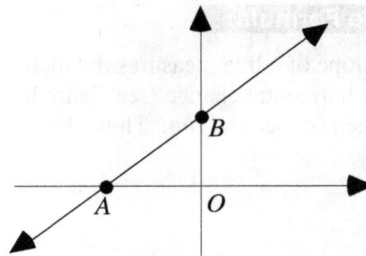

(A) $AO > BO$
(B) $AO < BO$
(C) $AO \le BO$
(D) $AO = BO$
(E) $AO = BO/2$

Since $y = \dfrac{9}{10}x + k$ is in slope-intercept form, we know the slope of the line is 9/10. Now, the ratio of *BO* to

AO is the slope of the line (rise over run). Hence, $\dfrac{BO}{AO} = \dfrac{9}{10}$. Multiplying both sides of this equation by

AO yields $BO = \dfrac{9}{10}AO$. In other words, *BO* is 9/10 the length of *AO*. Hence, *AO* is longer. The answer is

(A).

Intercepts:

The *x*-intercept is the point where the line crosses the *x*-axis. It is found by setting $y = 0$ and solving the resulting equation. The *y*-intercept is the point where the line crosses the *y*-axis. It is found by setting $x = 0$ and solving the resulting equation.

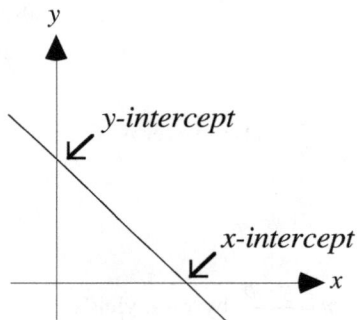

Example: Graph the equation $x - 2y = 4$.

Solution: To find the *x*-intercept, set $y = 0$. This yields $x - 2 \cdot 0 = 4$, or $x = 4$. So the *x*-intercept is $(4, 0)$. To find the *y*-intercept, set $x = 0$. This yields $0 - 2y = 4$, or $y = -2$. So the *y*-intercept is $(0, -2)$. Plotting these two points and connecting them with a straight line yields

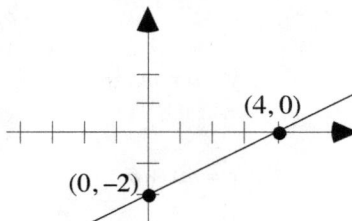

Areas and Perimeters:

Often, you will be given a geometric figure drawn on a coordinate system and will be asked to find its area or perimeter. In these problems, use the properties of the coordinate system to deduce the dimensions of the figure and then calculate the area or perimeter. For complicated figures, you may need to divide the figure into simpler forms, such as squares and triangles. A couple examples will illustrate:

Example: What is the area of the quadrilateral in the coordinate system?

(A) 2
(B) 4
(C) 6
(D) 8
(E) 11

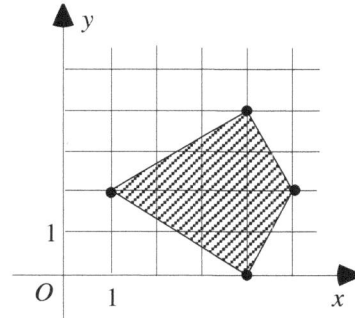

If the quadrilateral is divided horizontally through the line $y = 2$, two congruent triangles are formed. As the figure shows, the top triangle has height 2 and base 4. Hence, its area is

$$A = \frac{1}{2}bh = \frac{1}{2} \cdot 4 \cdot 2 = 4$$

The area of the bottom triangle is the same, so the area of the quadrilateral is $4 + 4 = 8$. The answer is (D).

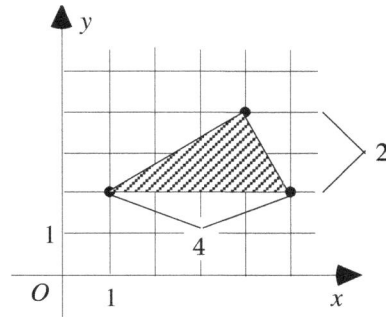

Example: What is the perimeter of Triangle *ABC* in the figure?

(A) $5 + \sqrt{5} + \sqrt{34}$
(B) $10 + \sqrt{34}$
(C) $5 + \sqrt{5} + \sqrt{28}$
(D) $2\sqrt{5} + \sqrt{34}$
(E) $\sqrt{5} + \sqrt{28}$

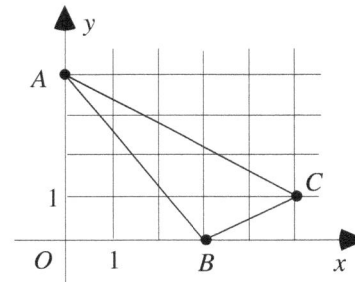

Point *A* has coordinates $(0, 4)$, point *B* has coordinates $(3, 0)$, and point *C* has coordinates $(5, 1)$. Using the distance formula to calculate the distances between points *A* and *B*, *A* and *C*, and *B* and *C* yields

$$\overline{AB} = \sqrt{(0-3)^2 + (4-0)^2} = \sqrt{9+16} = \sqrt{25} = 5$$
$$\overline{AC} = \sqrt{(0-5)^2 + (4-1)^2} = \sqrt{25+9} = \sqrt{34}$$
$$\overline{BC} = \sqrt{(5-3)^2 + (1-0)^2} = \sqrt{4+1} = \sqrt{5}$$

Adding these lengths gives the perimeter of Triangle *ABC*:

$$\overline{AB} + \overline{AC} + \overline{BC} = 5 + \sqrt{34} + \sqrt{5}$$

The answer is (A).

Problem Set H:

1. In the figure, O is the center of the circle. What is the area of the circle?

    (A) 2π
    (B) 3π
    (C) 5.5π
    (D) 7π
    (E) 9π

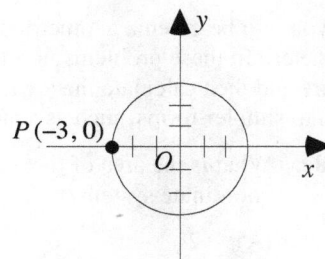

2. In the figure, which one of the following must be true about the value of the y-coordinate of point P ?

    (A) $y < 6$
    (B) $y > 6$
    (C) $y > 5$
    (D) $y = 6$
    (E) $y < 5$

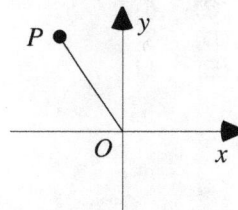

    P is a point in the coordinate system and $OP = 6$.

3. In the figure, the equation of the line is $y = px + a$. Which one of the following is the value of p ?

    (A) $p = -1/2$
    (B) $p = a/b$
    (C) $p = -a/b$
    (D) $p = b/a$
    (E) $p = -b/a$

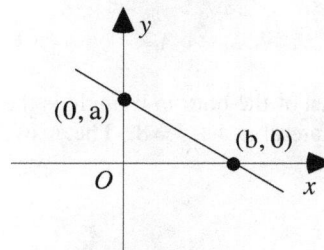

4. In the figure, which one of the following must be true?

    (A) $y < x$
    (B) $y > x$
    (C) $y < 4$
    (D) $y = x$
    (E) $y > 5$

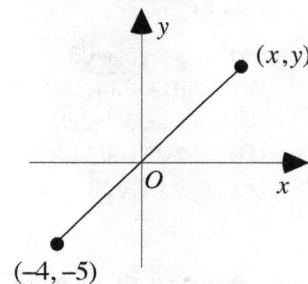

5. In the figure, a is the x-coordinate of point P and b is the y-coordinate of point Q. In which quadrant is the point (a, b) ?

    (A) I
    (B) II
    (C) III
    (D) IV
    (E) cannot be determined from the information given

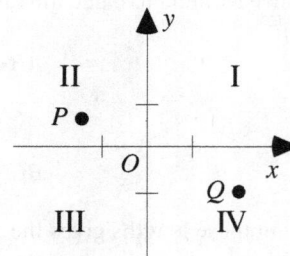

74

6. In the figure, if $x = 4$, then $y =$

    (A) 1
    (B) 2
    (C) 3
    (D) 4
    (E) 5.1

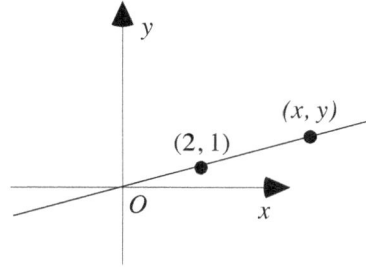

7. In the figure, which of the following could be the coordinates of a point in the shaded region?

    (A) $(1, 2)$
    (B) $(-2, 3)$
    (C) $(3, -5)$
    (D) $(-5, 1)$
    (E) $(-1, -6)$

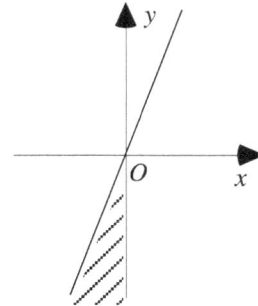

8. In the figure, which of the following points lies within the circle?

    (A) $(3.5, 9.5)$
    (B) $(-7, 7)$
    (C) $(-10, 1)$
    (D) $(0, 11)$
    (E) $(5.5, 8.5)$

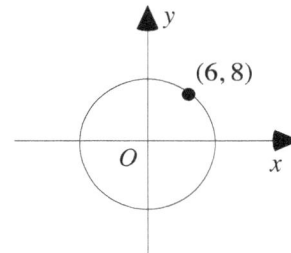

9. In the figure, the grid consists of unit squares. What is the area of the polygon?

    (A) 7
    (B) 9
    (C) 10
    (D) 12
    (E) 15

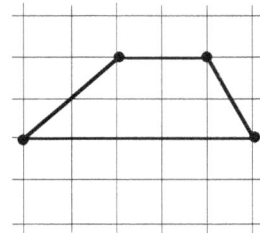

10. In the figure, which of the following points is three times as far from P as from Q ?

    (A) $(0, 3)$
    (B) $(1, 1)$
    (C) $(4, 5)$
    (D) $(2, 3)$
    (E) $(4, 1)$

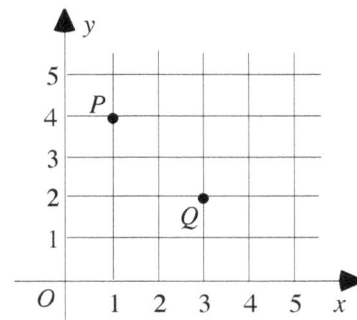

11. In the figure, what is the area of quadrilateral *ABCO* ?

    (A) 3
    (B) 5
    (C) 6.5
    (D) 8
    (E) 13

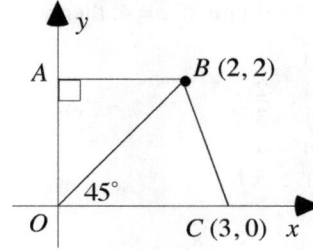

12. In the figure, which quadrants contain points (x, y) such that $xy = -2$?

    (A) I only
    (B) II only
    (C) III and IV only
    (D) II and IV only
    (E) II, III, and IV

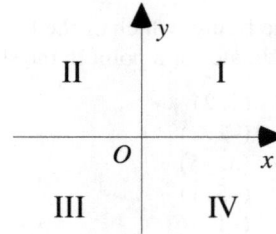

13. If the square in the figure is rotated clockwise about the origin until vertex *V* is on the negative *y*-axis, then the new *y*-coordinate of *V* is

    (A) -2
    (B) $-2\sqrt{2}$
    (C) -4
    (D) $-3\sqrt{2}$
    (E) -8

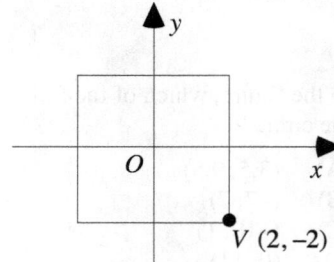

14. In the standard coordinate system, which of the following points is the greatest distance from the origin:

    (A) $(-4, -1)$
    (B) $(-3, 3)$
    (C) $(4, 0)$
    (D) $(2, 3)$
    (E) $(0, 4)$

15. What is the perimeter of Triangle *ABC* in the figure?

    (A) $5 + \sqrt{2} + \sqrt{29}$
    (B) $5 + 2\sqrt{2} + \sqrt{29}$
    (C) $5 + 4\sqrt{2} + \sqrt{29}$
    (D) $3\sqrt{2} + \sqrt{34}$
    (E) $4\sqrt{2} + \sqrt{34}$

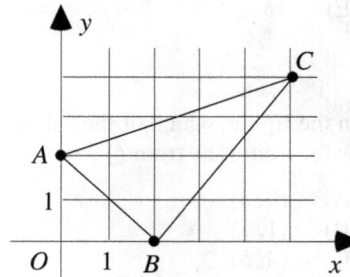

Answers and Solutions to Problem Set H

1. Since the circle is centered at the origin and passes through the point $(-3, 0)$, the radius of the circle is 3. Hence, the area is $A = \pi r^2 = \pi 3^2 = 9\pi$. The answer is (E).

2. Whatever the coordinates of P are, the line OP is the hypotenuse of a right triangle with sides being the absolute value of the x and y coordinates. Hence, OP is greater than the y-coordinate of point P. The answer is (A).

This problem brings up the issue of how much you can assume when viewing a diagram. We are told that P is a point in the coordinate system and that it appears in the second quadrant. Could P be on one of the axes or in another quadrant? No. Although P could be anywhere in Quadrant II (not necessarily where it is displayed), P could not be on the y-axis because the "position of points, angles, regions, etc. can be assumed to be in the order shown." If P were on the y-axis, then it would not be to the left of the y-axis, as it is in the diagram. That is, the order would be different.

3. Since $(b, 0)$ is the x-intercept of the line, it must satisfy the equation:

$$0 = pb + a$$

Subtracting a from both sides yields

$$-a = pb$$

Dividing both sides by b yields

$$-a/b = p$$

The answer is (C).

4. Since the line passes through $(-4, -5)$ and $(0, 0)$, its slope is $m = \dfrac{rise}{run} = \dfrac{-5 - 0}{-4 - 0} = \dfrac{5}{4}$. Notice that the rise, 5, is larger than the run, 4. Hence, the y-coordinate will always be larger than the x-coordinate. The answer is (B).

5. Since P is in Quadrant II, its x-coordinate is negative. That is, a is negative. Since Q is in Quadrant IV, its y-coordinate is negative. That is, b is negative. Hence, (a, b) is in Quadrant III. The answer is (C).

6. Let's write the equation of the line, using the slope-intercept form, $y = mx + b$. Since the line passes through the origin, $b = 0$. This reduces the equation to $y = mx$. Calculating the slope between $(2, 1)$ and $(0, 0)$ yields $m = \dfrac{1 - 0}{2 - 0} = \dfrac{1}{2}$. Plugging this into the equation yields $y = x/2$. Since $x = 4$, we get $y = \dfrac{1}{2} \cdot 4 = 2$. The answer is (B).

7. The shaded region is entirely within the third quadrant. Now, both coordinates of any point in Quadrant III are negative. The only point listed with both coordinates negative is $(-1, -6)$. The answer is (E).

8. For a point to be within a circle, its distance from the center of the circle must be less than the radius of the circle. The distance from $(6, 8)$ to $(0, 0)$ is the radius of the circle: $R = \sqrt{(6 - 0)^2 + (8 - 0)^2} = \sqrt{36 + 64} = \sqrt{100} = 10$. Now, let's calculate the distance between $(-7, 7)$ and $(0, 0)$ $D = \sqrt{(-7 - 0)^2 + (7 - 0)^2} = \sqrt{49 + 49} = \sqrt{98} < 10$. Since the distance D is less than the radius, the point $(-7, 7)$ is within the circle. The answer is (B).

9. Dividing the polygon into triangles and squares yields

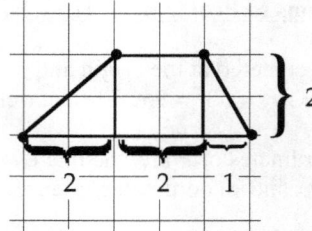

The triangle furthest to the left has area $A = \frac{1}{2}bh = \frac{1}{2} \cdot 2 \cdot 2 = 2$. The square has area $A = s^2 = 2^2 = 4$. The triangle furthest to the right has area $A = \frac{1}{2} \cdot 1 \cdot 2 = 1$. The sum of the areas of these three figures is

$$2 + 4 + 1 = 7$$

The answer is (A).

10. From the distance formula, the distance between $(4,1)$ and Q is $\sqrt{2}$, and the distance between $(4,1)$ and P is $\sqrt{(4-1)^2 + (1-4)^2} = \sqrt{3^2 + (-3)^2} = \sqrt{2 \cdot 3^2} = 3\sqrt{2}$. The answer is (E).

11. Dropping a vertical line from point B perpendicular to the x-axis will form a square and a triangle:

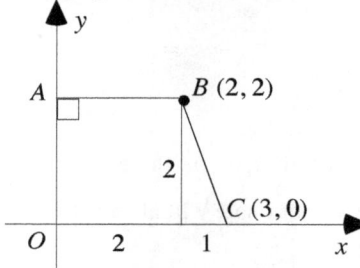

From the figure, we see that the square has area $s^2 = 2^2 = 4$, and the triangle has area

$$\frac{1}{2}bh = \frac{1}{2} \cdot 1 \cdot 2 = 1$$

Hence, the area of the quadrilateral is $4 + 1 = 5$. The answer is (B). Note, with this particular solution, we did not need to use the properties of the diagonal line in the original diagram.

12. If the product of two numbers is negative, the numbers must have opposite signs. Now, only the coordinates of points in quadrants II and IV have opposite signs. The diagram below illustrates the sign pattern of points for all four quadrants. The answer is (D).

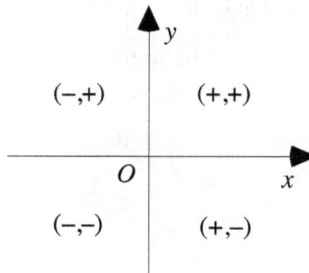

13. Calculating the distance between *V* and the origin yields

$$\sqrt{(2-0)^2 + (-2-0)^2} = \sqrt{4+4} = \sqrt{8} = 2\sqrt{2}$$

Since the square is rotated about the origin, the distance between the origin and *V* is fix. Hence, the new *y*-coordinate of *V* is $-2\sqrt{2}$. The diagram below illustrates the position of *V* after the rotation. The answer is (B).

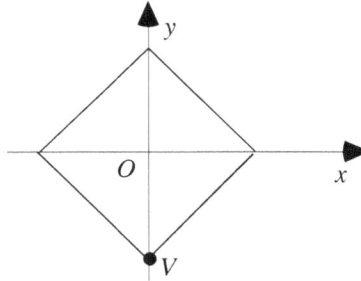

14. Using the distance formula to calculate the distance of each point from the origin yields

$$d = \sqrt{(-4)^2 + (-1)^2} = \sqrt{17}$$
$$d = \sqrt{(-3)^2 + (3)^2} = \sqrt{18}$$
$$d = \sqrt{(4)^2 + (0)^2} = \sqrt{16}$$
$$d = \sqrt{(2)^2 + (3)^2} = \sqrt{13}$$
$$d = \sqrt{(0)^2 + (4)^2} = \sqrt{16}$$

The answer is (B).

15. Point *A* has coordinates $(0, 2)$, point *B* has coordinates $(2, 0)$, and point *C* has coordinates $(5, 4)$. Using the distance formula to calculate the distances between points *A* and *B*, *A* and *C*, and *B* and *C* yields

$$\overline{AB} = \sqrt{(0-2)^2 + (2-0)^2} = \sqrt{4+4} = \sqrt{8} = 2\sqrt{2}$$
$$\overline{AC} = \sqrt{(0-5)^2 + (2-4)^2} = \sqrt{25+4} = \sqrt{29}$$
$$\overline{BC} = \sqrt{(2-5)^2 + (0-4)^2} = \sqrt{9+16} = 5$$

Adding these lengths gives the perimeter of Triangle *ABC*:

$$\overline{AB} + \overline{AC} + \overline{BC} = 2\sqrt{2} + \sqrt{29} + 5$$

The answer is (B).

Elimination Strategies

On hard problems, if you are asked to find the least (or greatest) number, then eliminate the least (or greatest) answer-choice.

Strategy

This rule also applies to easy and medium problems. When people guess on these types of problems, they most often choose either the least or the greatest number. But if the least or the greatest number were the answer, most people would answer the problem correctly, and it therefore would not be a hard problem.

Example: What is the maximum number of points common to the intersection of a square and a triangle if no two sides coincide?

  (A)   4
  (B)   5
  (C)   6
  (D)   8
  (E)   9

By the above rule, we eliminate answer-choice (E).

On hard problems, eliminate the answer-choice "not enough information."

Strategy

When people cannot solve a problem, they most often choose the answer-choice "not enough information." But if this were the answer, then it would not be a "hard" problem.

On hard problems, eliminate answer-choices that <u>merely</u> repeat numbers from the problem.

Strategy

Example: If the sum of x and 20 is 8 more than the difference of 10 and y, what is the value of $x + y$?

  (A)   −2
  (B)   8
  (C)   9
  (D)   28
  (E)   not enough information

By the above rule, we eliminate choice (B) since it merely repeats the number 8 from the problem. By Strategy 2, we would also eliminate choice (E). **Caution:** If choice (B) contained more than the number 8, say, $8 + \sqrt{2}$, then it would not be eliminated by the above rule.

On hard problems, eliminate answer-choices that can be derived from elementary operations.

Strategy

Example: In the figure, what is the perimeter of parallelogram ABCD?

(A)   12
(B)   15
(C) $20 + \sqrt{2}$
(D)   24
(E)   not enough information

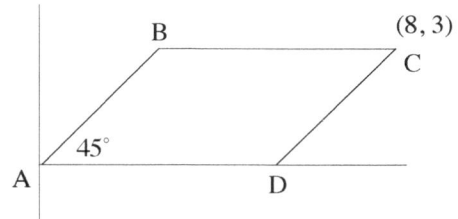

Using the above rule, we eliminate choice (D) since $24 = 8 \cdot 3$. Further, using Strategy 2, eliminate choice (E). Note, 12 was offered as an answer-choice because some people will interpret the drawing as a rectangle tilted halfway on its side and therefore expect it to have one-half its original area.

After you have eliminated as many answer-choices as you can, choose from the more complicated or more unusual answer-choices remaining.

Strategy

Example: Suppose you were offered the following answer-choices:

(A) $4 + \sqrt{3}$
(B) $4 + 2\sqrt{3}$
(C)   8
(D)   10
(E)   12

Then you would choose either (A) or (B).

Problem Set I:

1. What is the maximum number of 3×3 squares that can be formed from the squares in the 6×6 checkerboard?

    (A)   4
    (B)   6
    (C)   12
    (D)   16
    (E)   24

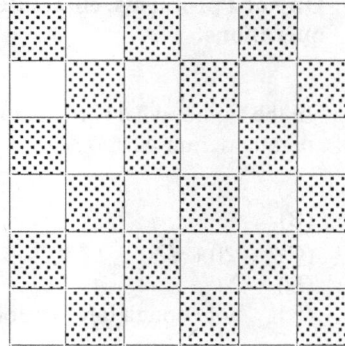

2. Let P stand for the product of the first 5 positive integers. What is the greatest possible value of m if $\frac{P}{10^m}$ is an integer?

    (A)   1
    (B)   2
    (C)   3
    (D)   5
    (E)   10

3. After being marked down 20 percent, a calculator sells for \$10. The original selling price was

    (A)   \$20
    (B)   \$12.5
    (C)   \$12
    (D)   \$9
    (E)   \$7

4. The distance between cities A and B is 120 miles. A car travels from A to B at 60 miles per hour and returns from B to A along the same route at 40 miles per hour. What is the average speed for the round trip?

    (A)   48
    (B)   50
    (C)   52
    (D)   56
    (E)   58

5. If **w** is 10 percent less than **x**, and **y** is 30 percent less than **z**, then **wy** is what percent less than **xz**?

    (A)   10%
    (B)   20%
    (C)   37%
    (D)   40%
    (E)   100%

6. In the game of chess, the Knight can make any of the moves displayed in the diagram. If a Knight is the only piece on the board, what is the greatest number of spaces from which not all 8 moves are possible?

   (A) 8
   (B) 24
   (C) 38
   (D) 48
   (E) 56

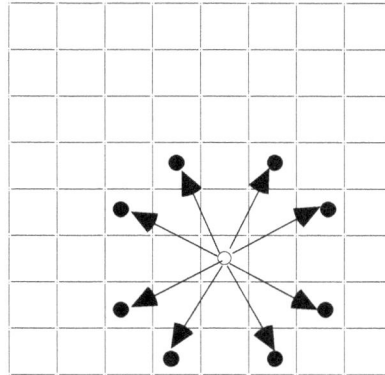

7. How many different ways can 3 cubes be painted if each cube is painted one color and only the 3 colors red, blue, and green are available? (Order is not considered, for example, green, green, blue is considered the same as green, blue, green.)

   (A) 2
   (B) 3
   (C) 9
   (D) 10
   (E) 27

8. What is the greatest prime factor of $\left(2^4\right)^2 - 1$?

   (A) 3
   (B) 5
   (C) 11
   (D) 17
   (E) 19

9. Let C and K be constants. If $x^2 + Kx + 5$ factors into $(x + 1)(x + C)$, the value of K is

   (A) 0
   (B) 5
   (C) 6
   (D) 8
   (E) not enough information

Answers and Solutions to Problem Set I

1. Clearly, there are more than four 3x3 squares in the checker board—eliminate (A). Next, eliminate (B) since it merely repeats a number from the problem. Further, eliminate (E) since it is the greatest. This leaves choices (C) and (D). If you count carefully, you will find sixteen 3x3 squares in the checkerboard. The answer is (D).

2. Since we are to find the greatest value of *m*, we eliminate (E)—the greatest. Also, eliminate 5 because it is repeated from the problem. Now, since we are looking for the largest number, start with the greatest number remaining and work toward the smallest number. The first number that works will be the answer. To this end, let $m = 3$. Then $\dfrac{P}{10^m} = \dfrac{1 \cdot 2 \cdot 3 \cdot 4 \cdot 5}{10^3} = \dfrac{120}{1000} = \dfrac{3}{25}$. This is not an integer, so eliminate (C).

Next, let $m = 2$. Then $\dfrac{P}{10^m} = \dfrac{1 \cdot 2 \cdot 3 \cdot 4 \cdot 5}{10^2} = \dfrac{120}{100} = \dfrac{6}{5}$. This still is not an integer, so eliminate (B). Hence, by process of elimination, the answer is (A).

3. Twenty dollars is too large. The discount was only 20 percent—eliminate (A). Both (D) and (E) are impossible since they are less than the selling price—eliminate. 12 is the eye-catcher: 20% of 10 is 2 and $10 + 2 = 12$. This is too easy for a hard problem—eliminate. Thus, by process of elimination, the answer is (B).

4. We can eliminate 50 (the mere average of 40 and 60) since that would be too elementary. Now, the average must be closer to 40 than to 60 because the car travels for a longer time at 40 mph. But 48 is the only number given that is closer to 40 than to 60. The answer is (A).

It's instructive to also calculate the answer. $Average\ Speed = \dfrac{Total\ Distance}{Total\ Time}$. Now, a car traveling at 40 mph will cover 120 miles in 3 hours. And a car traveling at 60 mph will cover the same 120 miles in 2 hours. So the total traveling time is 5 hours. Hence, for the round trip, the average speed is $\dfrac{120 + 120}{5} = 48$.

5. We eliminate (A) since it repeats the number 10 from the problem. We can also eliminate choices (B), (D), and (E) since they are derivable from elementary operations:

$$20 = 30 - 10$$
$$40 = 30 + 10$$
$$100 = 10 \cdot 10$$

This leaves choice (C) as the answer.

Let's also solve this problem directly. The clause

w is 10 percent less than *x*

translates into

$$w = x - .10x$$

Simplifying yields

1) $\quad w = .9x$

Next, the clause

y is 30 percent less than **z**

translates into

$$y = z - .30z$$

Simplifying yields

2) $\quad y = .7z$

Multiplying 1) and 2) gives

$$wy = (.9x)(.7z) = .63xz = xz - .37xz$$

Hence, **wy** is 37 percent less than **xz**. The answer is (C).

6. Since we are looking for the <u>greatest</u> number of spaces from which not all 8 moves are possible, we can eliminate the greatest number, 56. Now, clearly not all 8 moves are possible from the outer squares, and there are 28 outer squares—not 32. Also, not all 8 moves are possible from the next to outer squares, and there are 20 of them—not 24. All 8 moves are possible from the remaining squares. Hence, the answer is 28 + 20 = 48. The answer is (D). Notice that 56, (32 + 24), is given as an answer-choice to catch those who don't add carefully.

7. Clearly, there are more than 3 color combinations possible. This eliminates (A) and (B). We can also eliminate (C) and (E) because they are both multiples of 3, and that would be too ordinary, too easy, to be the answer. Hence, by process of elimination, the answer is (D).

Let's also solve this problem directly. The following list displays all 27 (= 3 · 3 · 3) color combinations possible (without restriction):

RRR	BBB	GGG
RRB	BBR	GGR
RRG	BBG	GGB
RBR	BRB	GRG
RBB	BRR	GRR
RBG	BRG	GRB
RGR	BGB	GBG
RGB	BGR	GBR
RGG	BGG	GBB

If order is not considered, then there are 10 distinct color combinations in this list. You should count them.

8. $\left(2^4\right)^2 - 1 = (16)^2 - 1 = 256 - 1 = 255$. Since the question asks for the <u>greatest</u> prime factor, we eliminate 19, the greatest number. Now, we start with the next largest number and work our way up the list; the first number that divides into 255 evenly will be the answer. Dividing 17 into 255 gives

$$17\overline{)255} = 15$$

Hence, 17 is the largest prime factor of $\left(2^4\right)^2 - 1$. The answer is (D).

9. Since the number 5 is merely repeated from the problem, we eliminate (B). Further, since this is a hard problem, we eliminate (E), "not enough information."

Now, since 5 is prime, its only factors are 1 and 5. So, the constant C in the expression $(x + 1)(x + C)$ must be 5:

$$(x + 1)(x + 5)$$

Multiplying out this expression yields

$$(x + 1)(x + 5) = x^2 + 5x + x + 5$$

Combining like terms yields

$$(x + 1)(x + 5) = x^2 + 6x + 5$$

Hence, $K = 6$, and the answer is (C).

Inequalities

Inequalities are manipulated algebraically the same way as equations with one exception:

Note! **Multiplying or dividing both sides of an inequality by a negative number reverses the inequality. That is, if $x > y$ and $c < 0$, then $cx < cy$.**

Example: For which values of x is $4x + 3 > 6x - 8$?

Solution: As with equations, our goal is to isolate x on one side:

Subtracting $6x$ from both sides yields

$$-2x + 3 > -8$$

Subtracting 3 from both sides yields

$$-2x > -11$$

Dividing both sides by -2 and reversing the inequality yields

$$x < 11/2$$

Positive & Negative Numbers

A number greater than 0 is positive. On the number line, positive numbers are to the right of 0. A number less than 0 is negative. On the number line, negative numbers are to the left of 0. Zero is the only number that is neither positive nor negative; it divides the two sets of numbers. On the number line, numbers increase to the right and decrease to the left.

The expression $x > y$ means that x is greater than y. In other words, x is to the right of y on the number line:

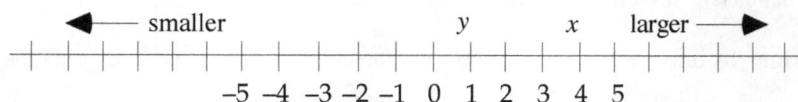

We usually have no trouble determining which of two numbers is larger when both are positive or one is positive and the other negative (e.g., $5 > 2$ and $3.1 > -2$). However, we sometimes hesitate when both numbers are negative (e.g., $-2 > -4.5$). When in doubt, think of the number line: if one number is to the right of the number, then it is larger. As the number line below illustrates, -2 is to the right of -4.5. Hence, -2 is larger than -4.5.

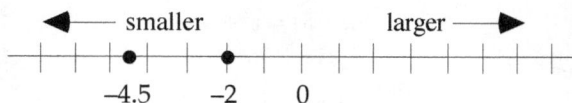

86

Miscellaneous Properties of Positive and Negative Numbers

1. The product (quotient) of positive numbers is positive.

2. The product (quotient) of a positive number and a negative number is negative.

3. The product (quotient) of an even number of negative numbers is positive.

4. The product (quotient) of an odd number of negative numbers is negative.

5. The sum of negative numbers is negative.

6. A number raised to an even exponent is greater than or equal to zero.

Example: If $xy^2z < 0$, then which one of the following statements must also be true?

    I. $xz < 0$
    II. $z < 0$
    III. $xyz < 0$

   (A) None   (B) I only   (C) III only   (D) I and II   (E) II and III

Since a number raised to an even exponent is greater than or equal to zero, we know that y^2 is positive (it cannot be zero because the product xy^2z would then be zero). Hence, we can divide both sides of the inequality $xy^2z < 0$ by y^2:

$$\frac{xy^2z}{y^2} < \frac{0}{y^2}$$

Simplifying yields

$$xz < 0$$

Therefore, I is true, which eliminates (A), (C), and (E). Now, the following illustrates that $z < 0$ is not necessarily true:

$$-1 \cdot 2^2 \cdot 3 = -12 < 0$$

This eliminates (D). Hence, the answer is (B).

Absolute Value

The absolute value of a number is its distance on the number line from 0. Since distance is a positive number, absolute value of a number is positive. Two vertical bars denote the absolute value of a number: $|x|$. For example, $|3| = 3$ and $|-3| = 3$. This can be illustrated on the number line:

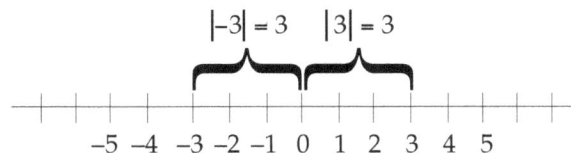

Students rarely struggle with the absolute value of numbers: if the number is negative, simply make it positive; and if it is already positive, leave it as is. For example, since -2.4 is negative, $|-2.4| = 2.4$ and since 5.01 is positive $|5.01| = 5.01$.

Further, students rarely struggle with the absolute value of positive variables: if the variable is positive, simply drop the absolute value symbol. For example, if $x > 0$, then $|x| = x$.

However, negative variables can cause students much consternation. If x is negative, then $|x| = -x$. This often confuses students because the absolute value is positive but the $-x$ appears to be negative. It is actually positive—it is the negative of a negative number, which is positive. To see this more clearly let $x = -k$, where k is a <u>positive</u> number. Then x is a negative number. So $|x| = -x = -(-k) = k$. Since k is positive so is $-x$. Another way to view this is $|x| = -x = (-1) \cdot x = (-1)(\text{a negative number}) = \text{a positive number}$.

Example: If $x = -|x|$, then which one of the following statements could be true?

    I. $x = 0$

    II. $x < 0$

    III. $x > 0$

    (A) None   (B) I only   (C) III only   (D) I and II   (E) II and III

Statement I could be true because $-|0| = -(+0) = -(0) = 0$. Statement II could be true because the right side of the equation is always negative $[-|x| = -(\text{a positive number}) = \text{a negative number}]$. Now, if one side of an equation is always negative, then the other side must always be negative, otherwise the opposite sides of the equation would not be equal. Since Statement III is the opposite of Statement II, it must be false. But let's show this explicitly: Suppose x were positive. Then $|x| = x$, and the equation $|x| = -x$ becomes $x = -x$. Dividing both sides of this equation by x yields $1 = -1$. This is a contradiction. Hence, x cannot be positive. The answer is (D).

Higher Order Inequalities

These inequalities have variables whose exponents are greater than 1. For example, $x^2 + 4 < 2$ and $x^3 - 9 > 0$. The number line is often helpful in solving these types of inequalities.

Example: For which values of x is $x^2 > -6x - 5$?

First, replace the inequality symbol with an equal symbol: $x^2 = -6x - 5$

Adding $6x$ and 5 to both sides yields $x^2 + 6x + 5 = 0$

Factoring yields (see General Trinomials in the chapter Factoring) $(x + 5)(x + 1) = 0$

Setting each factor to 0 yields $x + 5 = 0$ and $x + 1 = 0$

Or $x = -5$ and $x = -1$

Now, the only numbers at which the expression can change sign are -5 and -1. So -5 and -1 divide the number line into three intervals. Let's set up a number line and choose test points in each interval:

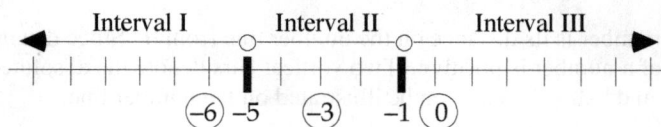

When $x = -6$, $x^2 > -6x - 5$ becomes $36 > 31$. This is true. Hence, all numbers in Interval I satisfy the inequality. That is, $x < -5$. When $x = -3$, $x^2 > -6x - 5$ becomes $9 > 13$. This is false. Hence, no numbers in Interval II satisfy the inequality. When $x = 0$, $x^2 > -6x - 5$ becomes $0 > -5$. This is true. Hence, all numbers in Interval III satisfy the inequality. That is, $x > -1$. The graph of the solution follows:

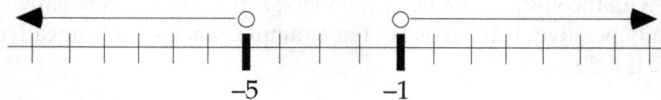

Note, if the original inequality had included the greater-than-or-equal symbol, $\geq$, the solution set would have included both -5 and -1. On the graph, this would have been indicated by filling in the circles above -5 and -1. The open circles indicate that -5 and -1 are not part of the solution.

Summary of steps for solving higher order inequalities:

1. Replace the inequality symbol with an equal symbol.
2. Move all terms to one side of the equation (usually the left side).
3. Factor the equation.
4. Set the factors equal to 0 to find zeros.
5. Choose test points on either side of the zeros.
6. If a test point satisfies the original inequality, then all numbers in that interval satisfy the inequality. Similarly, if a test point does not satisfy the inequality, then no numbers in that interval satisfy the inequality.

Transitive Property

$$\text{If } x < y \text{ and } y < z, \text{ then } x < z$$

Example: If $1/Q > 1$, which of the following must be true?

(A) $1 < Q^2$ (B) $\dfrac{1}{Q^2} > 2$ (C) $1 > Q^2$ (D) $\dfrac{1}{Q^2} < 1$ (E) $Q < Q^2$

Since $1/Q > 1$ and $1 > 0$, we know from the transitive property that $1/Q$ is positive. Hence, Q is positive. Therefore, we can multiply both sides of $1/Q > 1$ by Q without reversing the inequality:

$$Q \cdot \frac{1}{Q} > 1 \cdot Q$$

Reducing yields $1 > Q$

Multiplying both sides again by Q yields $Q > Q^2$

Using the transitive property to combine the last two inequalities yields $1 > Q^2$

The answer is (C).

Like Inequalities Can Be Added

$$\text{If } x < y \text{ and } w < z, \text{ then } x + w < y + z$$

Example: If $2 < x < 5$ and $3 < y < 5$, which of the following best describes $x - y$?

(A) $-3 < x - y < 2$
(B) $-3 < x - y < 5$
(C) $0 < x - y < 2$
(D) $3 < x - y < 5$
(E) $2 < x - y < 5$

Multiplying both sides of $3 < y < 5$ by -1 yields $-3 > -y > -5$. Now, we usually write the smaller number on the left side of the inequality. So $-3 > -y > -5$ becomes $-5 < -y < -3$. Add this inequality to the like inequality $2 < x < 5$:

$$
\begin{array}{r}
2 < x < 5 \\
(+) \quad -5 < -y < -3 \\
\hline
-3 < x - y < 2
\end{array}
$$

The answer is (A).

Problem Set J:

1. If $1 < x < y$, which one of the following must be true?

    (A) $-x^2 < -y^2$ (B) $\dfrac{x}{y} < \dfrac{y}{x}$ (C) $\dfrac{y}{x} < \dfrac{x}{y}$ (D) $\dfrac{-x}{y} < \dfrac{-y}{x}$ (E) $x^2 > y^2$

2. If $-3 < x < -1$ and $3 < y < 7$, which of the following best describes $\dfrac{x-y}{2}$?

    (A) $-5 < \dfrac{x-y}{2} < -2$

    (B) $-3 < \dfrac{x-y}{2} < -1$

    (C) $-2 < \dfrac{x-y}{2} < 0$

    (D) $2 < \dfrac{x-y}{2} < 5$

    (E) $3 < \dfrac{x-y}{2} < 7$

3. If x is an integer and $y = -2x - 8$, what is the least value of x for which y is less than 9?

    (A) -9 (B) -8 (C) -7 (D) -6 (E) -5

4. Which one of the following could be the graph of $3 - 6x \le \dfrac{4x+2}{-2}$?

5. If line segment AD has midpoint M_1 and line segment M_1D has midpoint M_2, what is the value of $\dfrac{M_1D}{AM_2}$?

    (A) 1/2   (B) 2/3   (C) 3/4   (D) 4/5   (E) 5/6

6. If $x < y < -1$, which of the following must be true?

    (A) $\dfrac{x}{y} > xy$ (B) $\dfrac{y}{x} > x+y$ (C) $\dfrac{y}{x} > xy$ (D) $\dfrac{y}{x} < x+y$ (E) $\dfrac{y}{x} > \dfrac{x}{y}$

7. Which of the following represents all solutions of the inequality $x^2 < 2x$?

    (A) $-1 < x < 1$ (B) $0 < x < 2$ (C) $1 < x < 3$ (D) $2 < x < 4$ (E) $4 < x < 6$

$$x \qquad 0 \qquad y$$

8. Given the positions of numbers x and y on the number line above, which of the following must be true?

    I. $xy > 0$

    II. $x/y < 0$

    III. $x - y > 0$

    (A) I only
    (B) II only
    (C) III only
    (D) I and II only
    (E) I, II, and III

9. If $x^4 y < 0$ and $xy^4 > 0$, which of the following must be true?

    (A) $x > y$ (B) $y > x$ (C) $x = y$ (D) $x < 0$ (E) $y > 0$

10. If n is an integer, what is the least value of n such that $\dfrac{1}{3^n} < 0.01$?

    (A) 2
    (B) 3
    (C) 4
    (D) 5
    (E) 6

11. If the average of 10, 14, and n is greater than or equal to 8 and less than or equal to 12, what is the least possible value of n ?

    (A) −12   (B) −6   (C) 0   (D) 6   (E) 12

12. If $3x + y < 4$ and $x > 3$, which of the following must be true?
    (A) $y < -5$ (B) $y < -10$ (C) $x = y$ (D) $x < 3$ (E) $y > 0$

$$2 - 3x \; ? \; 5$$

13. Of the following symbols, which one can be substituted for the question mark in the above expression to make a true statement for all values of x such that $-1 < x \le 2$?

    (A) =   (B) <   (C) ≥   (D) >   (E) ≤

14. Let x, y, z be three different positive integers each less than 20. What is the smallest possible value of expression $\dfrac{x - y}{-z}$?

    (A) −18   (B) −17   (C) −14   (D) −11   (E) −9

Answers and Solutions to Problem Set J

1. From $1 < x < y$, we know that both x and y are positive. So dividing both sides of $x < y$ by x yields $1 < y/x$; and dividing both sides of $x < y$ by y yields $x/y < 1$. Hence, $\dfrac{x}{y} < 1 < \dfrac{y}{x}$. By the transitive property of inequalities, $\dfrac{x}{y} < \dfrac{y}{x}$. The answer is (B).

2. Multiplying both sides of $3 < y < 7$ by -1 yields $-3 > -y > -7$. Now, we usually write the smaller number on the left side of an inequality. So $-3 > -y > -7$ becomes $-7 < -y < -3$. Add this inequality to the like inequality $-3 < x < -1$:

$$
\begin{array}{r}
-3 < x < -1 \\
(+) \quad -7 < -y < -3 \\
\hline
-10 < x - y < -4
\end{array}
$$

Dividing $-10 < x - y < -4$ by 2 yields $\dfrac{-10}{2} < \dfrac{x-y}{2} < \dfrac{-4}{2}$, or $-5 < \dfrac{x-y}{2} < -2$. The answer is (A).

3. Since y is less than 9 and $y = -2x - 8$, we get

$$-2x - 8 < 9$$

Adding 8 to both sides of this inequality yields

$$-2x < 17$$

Dividing by -2 and reversing the inequality yields

$$x > -17/2 = -8.5$$

Since x is an integer and is to be as small as possible,

$$x = -8$$

The answer is (B).

4. Multiplying both sides of the inequality by -2 yields $-2(3 - 6x) \geq 4x + 2$

Distributing the -2 yields $-6 + 12x \geq 4x + 2$

Subtracting $4x$ and adding 6 to both sides yields $8x \geq 8$

Dividing both sides of the inequality by 8 yields $x \geq 1$

The answer is (D).

5. Let 4 be the length of line segment AD. Since M_1 is the midpoint of AD, this yields

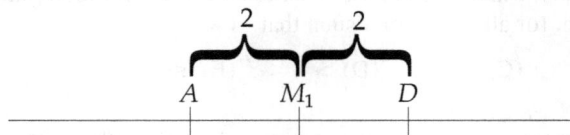

Now, since M_2 is the midpoint of M_1D, this yields

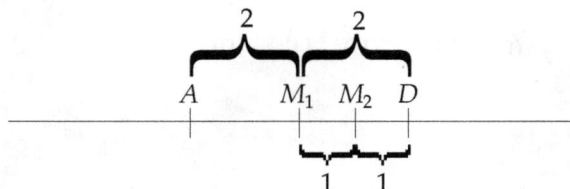

From the diagram, we see that $M_1D = 2$ and $AM_2 = 3$. Hence, $\dfrac{M_1D}{AM_2} = \dfrac{2}{3}$. The answer is (B).

6. Since the sum of negative numbers is negative, $x + y$ is negative. Since the quotient of an even number of negative numbers is positive, y/x is positive. Hence, $\dfrac{y}{x} > x + y$. The answer is (B).

7. Forming an equation from $x^2 < 2x$ yields

$$x^2 = 2x$$

Subtracting $2x$ from both sides yields

$$x^2 - 2x = 0$$

Factoring yields

$$x(x - 2) = 0$$

Setting each factor to zero yields

$$x = 0 \text{ and } x - 2 = 0$$

Solving yields

$$x = 0 \text{ and } x = 2$$

Setting up a number line and choosing test points (the circled numbers on the number line below) yields

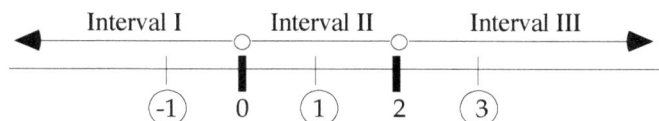

Now, if $x = -1$, the inequality $x^2 < 2x$ becomes $(-1)^2 < 2(-1)$, or $1 < -2$. This is false. Hence, Interval I is not a solution. If $x = 1$, the inequality $x^2 < 2x$ becomes $1^2 < 2(1)$, or $1 < 2$. This is true. Hence, Interval II is a solution. If $x = 3$, the inequality $x^2 < 2x$ becomes $3^2 < 2(3)$, or $9 < 6$. This is false. Hence, Interval III is not a solution. Thus, only Interval II is a solution:

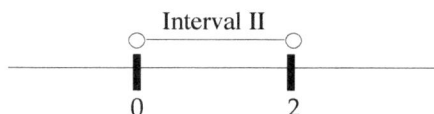

The answer is (B).

8. Since x is to the left of zero on the number line, it's negative. Since y is to the right of zero, it's positive. Now, the product or quotient of a positive number and a negative number is negative. Hence, Statement I is false and Statement II is true. Regarding Statement III, since x is to the left of y on the number line, $x < y$. Subtracting y from both sides of this inequality yields $x - y < 0$. Hence, Statement III is false. Therefore, the answer is (B).

9. Since x is raised to an even exponent, it is greater than or equal to zero. Further, since $x^4 y \neq 0$, we know that neither x nor y is zero (otherwise $x^4 y = 0$). Hence, we may divide $x^4 y < 0$ by x^4 without reversing the inequality:

$$\frac{x^4 y}{x^4} < \frac{0}{x^4}$$

Simplifying yields

$$y < 0$$

A similar analysis of the inequality $xy^4 > 0$ shows that $x > 0$. Hence, $x > y$. The answer is (A).

10. Replacing 0.01 with its fractional equivalent, 1/100, yields

$$\frac{1}{3^n} < \frac{1}{100}$$

Multiplying both sides by 3^n and 100 and then simplifying yields

$$100 < 3^n$$

Beginning with $n = 2$, we plug in larger and larger values of n until we reach one that makes $100 < 3^n$ true. The table below summarizes the results:

n	$100 < 3^n$	
2	$100 < 3^2 = 9$	False
3	$100 < 3^3 = 27$	False
4	$100 < 3^4 = 81$	False
5	$100 < 3^5 = 243$	True

Since 5 is the first integer to work, the answer is (D).

11. Translating the clause "the average of 10, 14, and n is greater than or equal to 8 and less than or equal to 12" into an inequality yields

$$8 \le \frac{10 + 14 + n}{3} \le 12$$

Adding 10 and 14 yields
$$8 \le \frac{24 + n}{3} \le 12$$

Multiplying <u>each</u> term by 3 yields $\quad\quad 24 \le 24 + n \le 36$
Subtracting 24 from each term yields $\quad\quad 0 \le n \le 12$
Hence, the least possible value of n is 0. The answer is (C).

12. Subtracting $3x$ from both sides of $3x + y < 4$ yields $y < 4 - 3x$. Now, multiplying both sides of $x > 3$ by -3 yields $-3x < -9$. Adding 4 to both sides yields $4 - 3x < -5$. Now, using the transitive property to combine $y < 4 - 3x$ and $4 - 3x < -5$ yields $y < 4 - 3x < -5$. Hence, $y < -5$. The answer is (A).

13. Multiply each term of the inequality $-1 < x \le 2$ by -3 (this is done because the original expression involves $-3x$):

$$3 > -3x \ge -6$$

Add 2 to each term of this inequality (this is done because the original expression adds 2 and $-3x$):

$$5 > 2 - 3x \ge -4$$

Rewrite the inequality in standard form (with the smaller number on the left and the larger number on the right):

$$-4 \le 2 - 3x < 5$$

The answer is (B).

14. First, bring the negative symbol in the expression $\dfrac{x-y}{-z}$ to the top: $\dfrac{-(x-y)}{z}$

Then distribute the negative symbol: $\dfrac{y-x}{z}$

To make this expression as small as possible, we need to make both the $y - x$ and z as small as possible. To make $y - x$ as small as possible, let $y = 1$ and $x = 19$. Then $y - x = 1 - 19 = -18$. With these choices for y and x, the smallest remaining value for z is 2. This gives

$$\frac{y-x}{z} = \frac{1-19}{2} = \frac{-18}{2} = -9$$

In this case, we made the numerator as small as possible. Now, let's make the denominator as small as possible. To that end, chose $z = 1$ and $y = 2$ and $x = 19$. This gives

$$\frac{y-x}{z} = \frac{2-19}{1} = \frac{-17}{1} = -17$$

The answer is (B).

Fractions & Decimals

A fraction consists of two parts: a numerator and a denominator.

$$\frac{numerator}{denominator}$$

If the numerator is smaller than the denominator, the fraction is called *proper* and is less than one. For example: $1/2$, $4/5$, and $3/\pi$ are all proper fractions and therefore less than 1.

If the numerator is larger than the denominator, the fraction is called *improper* and is greater than 1. For example: $3/2$, $5/4$, and $\pi/3$ are all improper fractions and therefore greater than 1.

An improper fraction can be converted into a *mixed fraction* by dividing its denominator into its numerator. For example, since 2 divides into 7 three times with a remainder of 1, we get

$$\frac{7}{2} = 3\frac{1}{2}$$

To convert a mixed fraction into an improper fraction, multiply the denominator and the integer and then add the numerator. Then, write the result over the denominator. For example, $5\frac{2}{3} = \frac{3\cdot 5 + 2}{3} = \frac{17}{3}$.

In a negative fraction, the negative symbol can be written on the top, in the middle, or on the bottom; however, when a negative symbol appears on the bottom, it is usually moved to the top or the middle: $\frac{5}{-3} = \frac{-5}{3} = -\frac{5}{3}$. If both terms in the denominator of a fraction are negative, the negative symbol is often factored out and moved to the top or middle of the fraction: $\frac{1}{-x-2} = \frac{1}{-(x+2)} = -\frac{1}{x+2}$ or $\frac{-1}{x+2}$.

To compare two fractions, cross-multiply. The larger number will be on the same side as the larger fraction.

Strategy

Example: Which of the following fractions is larger?

$$9/10 \qquad 10/11$$

Cross-multiplying gives $9 \cdot 11$ versus $10 \cdot 10$, which reduces to 99 versus 100. Now, 100 is greater than 99. Hence, $10/11$ is greater than $9/10$.

Always reduce a fraction to its lowest terms.

Strategy

Example: If $x \neq -1$, then $\dfrac{2x^2 + 4x + 2}{(x+1)^2} =$

   (A) 0   (B) 1   (C) 2   (D) 4   (E) 6

Factor out the 2 in the expression:

$$\frac{2(x^2 + 2x + 1)}{(x+1)^2}$$

Factor the quadratic expressions:

$$\frac{2(x+1)(x+1)}{(x+1)(x+1)}$$

Finally, canceling the $(x + 1)$'s gives 2. The answer is (C).

To solve a fractional equation, multiply both sides by the LCD (lowest common denominator) to clear fractions.

Strategy

Example: If $\dfrac{x+3}{x-3} = y$, what is the value of x in terms of y?

   (A) $3 - y$ (B) $3/y$ (C) $\sqrt{y+12}$ (D) $\dfrac{-3y-3}{1-y}$ (E) $3y^2$

First, multiply both sides of the equation by $x - 3$: $(x-3)\dfrac{x+3}{x-3} = (x-3)y$

Cancel the $(x - 3)$'s on the left side of the equation: $x + 3 = (x - 3)y$
Distribute the y: $x + 3 = xy - 3y$
Subtract xy and 3 from both sides: $x - xy = -3y - 3$
Factor out the x on the left side of the equation: $x(1 - y) = -3y - 3$

Finally, divide both sides of the equation by $1 - y$: $x = \dfrac{-3y-3}{1-y}$

Hence, the answer is (D).

Note!   **Complex Fractions: When dividing a fraction by a whole number (or vice versa), you must keep track of the main division bar:**

$$\frac{\dfrac{a}{b}}{c} = a \cdot \frac{c}{b} = \frac{ac}{b}. \text{ But } \frac{\dfrac{a}{b}}{c} = \frac{a}{b} \cdot \frac{1}{c} = \frac{a}{bc}.$$

Example: $\dfrac{1 - \dfrac{1}{2}}{3} =$

   (A) 6   (B) 3   (C) 1/3   (D) 1/6   (E) 1/8

Solution: $\dfrac{1 - \dfrac{1}{2}}{3} = \dfrac{\dfrac{2}{2} - \dfrac{1}{2}}{3} = \dfrac{\dfrac{2-1}{2}}{3} = \dfrac{\dfrac{1}{2}}{3} = \dfrac{1}{2} \cdot \dfrac{1}{3} = \dfrac{1}{6}$. The answer is (D).

Example: If $z \neq 0$ and $yz \neq 1$, then $\dfrac{1}{y - \dfrac{1}{z}} =$

(A) $\dfrac{yz}{zy - 1}$ (B) $\dfrac{y - z}{z}$ (C) $\dfrac{yz - z}{z - 1}$ (D) $\dfrac{z}{zy - 1}$ (E) $\dfrac{y - z}{zy - 1}$

Solution: $\dfrac{1}{y - \dfrac{1}{z}} = \dfrac{1}{\dfrac{z}{z}y - \dfrac{1}{z}} = \dfrac{1}{\dfrac{zy - 1}{z}} = 1 \cdot \dfrac{z}{zy - 1} = \dfrac{z}{zy - 1}$. The answer is (D).

Note! **Multiplying fractions is routine: merely multiply the numerators and multiply the denominators:** $\dfrac{a}{b} \cdot \dfrac{c}{d} = \dfrac{ac}{bd}$. For example, $\dfrac{1}{2} \cdot \dfrac{3}{4} = \dfrac{1 \cdot 3}{2 \cdot 4} = \dfrac{3}{8}$.

Note! **Two fractions can be added quickly by cross-multiplying:** $\dfrac{a}{b} \pm \dfrac{c}{d} = \dfrac{ad \pm bc}{bd}$

Example: $\dfrac{1}{2} - \dfrac{3}{4} =$

(A) $-5/4$ (B) $-2/3$ (C) $-1/4$ (D) $1/2$ (E) $2/3$

Cross-multiplying the expression $\dfrac{1}{2} - \dfrac{3}{4}$ yields $\dfrac{1 \cdot 4 - 2 \cdot 3}{2 \cdot 4} = \dfrac{4 - 6}{8} = \dfrac{-2}{8} = -\dfrac{1}{4}$. Hence, the answer is (C).

Example: Which of the following equals the average of x and $1/x$?

(A) $\dfrac{x + 2}{x}$ (B) $\dfrac{x^2 + 1}{2x}$ (C) $\dfrac{x + 1}{x^2}$ (D) $\dfrac{2x^2 + 1}{x}$ (E) $\dfrac{x + 1}{x}$

The average of x and $1/x$ is $\dfrac{x + \dfrac{1}{x}}{2} = \dfrac{\dfrac{x^2 + 1}{x}}{2} = \dfrac{x^2 + 1}{x} \cdot \dfrac{1}{2} = \dfrac{x^2 + 1}{2x}$. Thus, the answer is (B).

Note! **To add three or more fractions with different denominators, you need to form a common denominator of all the fractions.**

For example, to add the fractions in the expression $\dfrac{1}{3} + \dfrac{1}{4} + \dfrac{1}{18}$, we have to change the denominator of each fraction into the common denominator 36 (note, 36 is a common denominator because 3, 4, and 18 all divide into it evenly). This is done by multiply the top and bottom of each fraction by an appropriate number (this does not change the value of the expression because any number divided by itself equals 1):

$$\frac{1}{3}\left(\frac{12}{12}\right) + \frac{1}{4}\left(\frac{9}{9}\right) + \frac{1}{18}\left(\frac{2}{2}\right) = \frac{12}{36} + \frac{9}{36} + \frac{2}{36} = \frac{12 + 9 + 2}{36} = \frac{23}{36}$$

You may remember from algebra that to find a common denominator of a set of fractions, you prime factor the denominators and then select each factor the greatest number of times it occurs in any of the factorizations. That is too cumbersome, however. A better way is to simply add the largest denominator to itself until all the other denominators divide into it evenly. In the above example, we just add 18 to itself to get the common denominator 36.

Note! To find a common denominator of a set of fractions, simply add the largest denominator to itself until all the other denominators divide into it evenly.

Note! Fractions often behave in unusual ways: Squaring a fraction makes it smaller, and taking the square root of a fraction makes it larger. (**Caution:** This is true only for proper fractions, that is, fractions between 0 and 1.)

Example: $\left(\frac{1}{3}\right)^2 = \frac{1}{9}$ and 1/9 is less than 1/3. Also $\sqrt{\frac{1}{4}} = \frac{1}{2}$ and 1/2 is greater than 1/4.

Note! You can cancel only over multiplication, not over addition or subtraction.

For example, the c's in the expression $\frac{c+x}{c}$ cannot be canceled. However, the c's in the expression

$\frac{cx+c}{c}$ can be canceled as follows: $\frac{cx+c}{c} = \frac{\cancel{c}(x+1)}{\cancel{c}} = x+1$.

Decimals

If a fraction's denominator is a power of 10, it can be written in a special form called a *decimal fraction*. Some common decimals are $\frac{1}{10} = .1, \frac{2}{100} = .02, \frac{3}{1000} = .003$. Notice that the number of decimal places corresponds to the number of zeros in the denominator of the fraction. Also note that the value of the decimal place decreases to the right of the decimal point:

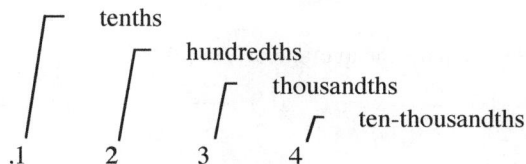

```
       ┌─ tenths
       │   ┌─ hundredths
       │   │   ┌─ thousandths
       │   │   │  ┌─ ten-thousandths
      .1   2   3  4
```

This decimal can be written in expanded form as follows:

$$.1234 = \frac{1}{10} + \frac{2}{100} + \frac{3}{1000} + \frac{4}{10000}$$

Sometimes a zero is placed before the decimal point to prevent misreading the decimal as a whole number. The zero has no affect on the value of the decimal. For example, .2 = 0.2.

Fractions can be converted to decimals by dividing the denominator into the numerator. For example, to convert 5/8 to a decimal, divide 8 into 5 (note, a decimal point and as many zeros as necessary are added after the 5):

```
        .625
    8)5.000
      48
      ──
       20
       16
       ──
        40
        40
        ──
         0
```

The procedures for adding, subtracting, multiplying, and dividing decimals are the same as for whole numbers, except for a few small adjustments.

- **Adding and Subtracting Decimals:** To add or subtract decimals, merely align the decimal points and then add or subtract as you would with whole numbers.

$$\begin{array}{r} 1.369 \\ +\ 9.7 \\ \hline 11.069 \end{array} \qquad \begin{array}{r} 12.45 \\ -\ 6.367 \\ \hline 6.083 \end{array}$$

- **Multiplying Decimals:** Multiply decimals as you would with whole numbers. The answer will have as many decimal places as the sum of the number of decimal places in the numbers being multiplied.

$$\begin{array}{r} 1.23 \\ \times\ 2.4 \\ \hline 492 \\ 246 \\ \hline 2.952 \end{array}$$

1.23 — 2 decimal places
2.4 — 1 decimal place
2.952 — 3 decimal places

- **Dividing Decimals:** Before dividing decimals, move the decimal point of the divisor all the way to the right and move the decimal point of the dividend the same number of spaces to the right (adding zeros if necessary). Then divide as you would with whole numbers.

$$.24\overline{).6} = 24\overline{)60.0} \quad \begin{array}{r} 2.5 \\ \hline 48 \\ \hline 120 \\ 120 \\ \hline 0 \end{array}$$

Example: 1/5 of .1 percent equals:
(A) 2   (B) .2   (C) .02   (D) .002   (E) .0002

Recall that percent means to divide by 100. So .1 percent equals $\frac{.1}{100} = .001$. To convert 1/5 to a decimal, divide 5 into 1:

$$5\overline{)1.0} \quad \begin{array}{r} .2 \\ \hline 10 \\ \hline 0 \end{array}$$

In percent problems, "of" means multiplication. So multiplying .2 and .001 yields

$$\begin{array}{r} .001 \\ \times\ .2 \\ \hline .0002 \end{array}$$

Hence, the answer is (E). Note, you may be surprised to learn that the ACT would consider this to be a hard problem.

Example: The decimal .1 is how many times greater than the decimal $(.001)^3$?

- (A) 10
- (B) 10^2
- (C) 10^5
- (D) 10^8
- (E) 10^{10}

Converting .001 to a fraction gives $\dfrac{1}{1000}$. This fraction, in turn, can be written as $\dfrac{1}{10^3}$, or 10^{-3}. Cubing this expression yields $(.001)^3 = \left(10^{-3}\right)^3 = 10^{-9}$. Now, dividing the larger number, .1, by the smaller number, $(.001)^3$, yields

$$\frac{.1}{(.001)^3} = \frac{10^{-1}}{10^{-9}} = 10^{-1-(-9)} = 10^{-1+9} = 10^8$$

Hence, .1 is 10^8 times as large as $(.001)^3$. The answer is (D).

Example: Let $x = .99$, $y = \sqrt{.99}$, and $z = (.99)^2$. Then which of the following is true?

- (A) $x < z < y$
- (B) $z < y < x$
- (C) $z < x < y$
- (D) $y < x < z$
- (E) $y < z < x$

Converting .99 into a fraction gives 99/100. Since 99/100 is between 0 and 1, squaring it will make it smaller and taking its square root will make it larger. Hence, $(.99)^2 < .99 < \sqrt{.99}$. The answer is (C). Note, this property holds for all proper decimals (decimals between 0 and 1) just as it does for all proper fractions.

Problem Set K:

1. $\dfrac{\frac{2}{4}}{3} =$

- (A) 1/6
- (B) 3/8
- (C) 3/2
- (D) 8/3
- (E) 6

2. Which one of the following fractions is greatest?

- (A) 5/6
- (B) 4/5
- (C) 1/2
- (D) 2/3
- (E) 3/4

3. If $x \neq \pm 3$, then $\dfrac{x^2 + 6x + 9}{x + 3} \cdot \dfrac{x^2 - 9}{x - 3} =$

- (A) $\dfrac{x+3}{x-3}$
- (B) -1
- (C) $(x + 3)2$
- (D) $\left(\dfrac{x+3}{x-3}\right)^2$
- (E) 1

4. $\dfrac{\frac{1}{4}}{\frac{3}{3} - 1} =$

- (A) $-1/3$
- (B) $-1/4$
- (C) 3/4
- (D) 3
- (E) 9/2

5. If $0 < x < 1$, which of the following must be true?

    I. $x^2 < x$

    II. $x < \dfrac{1}{x^2}$

    III. $\sqrt{x} < x$

    (A) I only
    (B) II only
    (C) III only
    (D) I and II only
    (E) I, II, and III

6. In the following pairs of numbers, which are reciprocals of each other?

    I. 1 and 1

    II. 1/11 and −11

    III. $\sqrt{5}$ and $\dfrac{\sqrt{5}}{5}$

    (A) I only
    (B) II only
    (C) I and II only
    (D) I and III only
    (E) II and III only

7. $\dfrac{6^4 - 6^3}{5} =$

    (A) 1/5
    (B) 6^3
    (C) 6/5
    (D) 6^4
    (E) $6^3/5$

8. $\dfrac{1}{1 - \dfrac{1}{1 - \dfrac{1}{2}}} =$

    (A) −2
    (B) −1
    (C) 3/2
    (D) 2
    (E) 4

9. $\dfrac{1}{10^9} - \dfrac{1}{10^{10}} =$

    (A) $-\dfrac{1}{10}$

    (B) $-\dfrac{1}{10^9}$

    (C) $-\dfrac{1}{10^{19}}$

    (D) $\dfrac{9}{10^{10}}$

    (E) $\dfrac{9}{10}$

10. If $x \neq \pm 1$, then $\dfrac{\dfrac{2x^2 - 2}{x - 1}}{2(x + 1)} =$

    (A) $x + 1$
    (B) 1
    (C) $x^2 - 1$
    (D) $x - 1$
    (E) 2

11. If $\left(x^2 - 4\right)\left(\dfrac{4}{x} - 5\right) = 0$, then $x =$

    (A) −4
    (B) −1
    (C) −4/5
    (D) 4/5
    (E) 4

12. If $m = 3^{n-1} = 3^{3n+1}$, what is the value of m/n ?

    (A) 0
    (B) −1/20
    (C) −1/10
    (D) −1/9
    (E) −2

13. For all $p \neq 1/4$ define $p*$ by the equation

    $p* = \dfrac{\dfrac{p}{2}}{4p - 1}$. If $q = 1*$, then $q* =$

    (A) −5/7
    (B) −1/3
    (C) −1/4
    (D) 2/3
    (E) 3/4

Answers and Solutions to Problem Set K

1. $\dfrac{\frac{2}{4}}{3} = 2 \cdot \dfrac{3}{4} = \dfrac{6}{4} = \dfrac{3}{2}$. The answer is (C).

2. Begin with 5/6 and 4/5. Cross-multiplying gives 25 versus 24. Hence, 5/6 > 4/5. Continuing in this manner will show that 5/6 is the greatest fraction listed. The answer is (A).

3. First, factor the expression $\dfrac{x^2 + 6x + 9}{x+3} \cdot \dfrac{x^2 - 9}{x-3}$:

$$\dfrac{(x+3)(x+3)}{x+3} \cdot \dfrac{(x+3)(x-3)}{x-3}$$

Next, canceling the $x + 3$ and the $x - 3$ yields

$$(x+3) \cdot (x-3)$$

or

$$(x+3)^2$$

The answer is (C).

4. $\dfrac{1}{\frac{4}{3} - 1} = \dfrac{1}{\frac{4}{3} - \frac{3}{3}} = \dfrac{1}{\frac{1}{3}} = 3$. The answer is (D).

5. Since squaring a fraction between 0 and 1 makes it smaller, we know Statement I is true. This eliminates both (B) and (C). Also, since taking the square root of a fraction between 0 and 1 makes it larger, we know Statement III is false. This eliminates (E). To analyze Statement II, we'll use substitution. Since $0 < x < 1$, we need only check one fraction, say, $x = 1/2$. Then

$$\dfrac{1}{x^2} = \dfrac{1}{\left(\frac{1}{2}\right)^2} = \dfrac{1}{\left(\frac{1}{4}\right)} = 1 \cdot \dfrac{4}{1} = 4$$

Now, 1/2 < 4. Hence, Statement II is true, and the answer is (D).

6. Let's take the first number in each pair, form its reciprocal, and then try to reduce it to the second number. Now, $1 \Rightarrow \dfrac{1}{1} = 1$. Hence, the pair 1/11 and 1 are reciprocals of each other. Next, $\dfrac{1}{11} \Rightarrow \dfrac{1}{\frac{1}{11}} = 1 \cdot \dfrac{11}{1} = 11 \neq -11$.

Hence, the pair $\dfrac{1}{11}$ and –11 are not reciprocals of each other. Finally, $\sqrt{5} \Rightarrow \dfrac{1}{\sqrt{5}} = \dfrac{1}{\sqrt{5}} \cdot \dfrac{\sqrt{5}}{\sqrt{5}} = \dfrac{\sqrt{5}}{5}$.

Hence, the pair $\sqrt{5}$ and $\dfrac{\sqrt{5}}{5}$ are reciprocals of each other. The answer is (D).

7. $\dfrac{6^4 - 6^3}{5} = \dfrac{6^3(6-1)}{5} = \dfrac{6^3 \cdot 5}{5} = 6^3$. The answer is (B).

8. $\dfrac{1}{1-\dfrac{1}{1-\dfrac{1}{2}}} = \dfrac{1}{1-\dfrac{1}{\dfrac{2}{2}-\dfrac{1}{2}}} = \dfrac{1}{1-\dfrac{1}{\dfrac{1}{2}}} = \dfrac{1}{1-2} = \dfrac{1}{-1} = -1$. The answer is (B).

9. $\dfrac{1}{10^9} - \dfrac{1}{10^{10}} = \dfrac{1}{10^9} - \dfrac{1}{10^9} \cdot \dfrac{1}{10} = \dfrac{1}{10^9}\left(1 - \dfrac{1}{10}\right) = \dfrac{1}{10^9}\left(\dfrac{9}{10}\right) = \dfrac{9}{10^{10}}$. The answer is (D).

10. $\dfrac{\dfrac{2x^2-2}{x-1}}{2(x+1)} = \dfrac{2x^2-2}{x-1} \cdot \dfrac{1}{2(x+1)} = \dfrac{2\left(x^2-1\right)}{x-1} \cdot \dfrac{1}{2(x+1)} = \dfrac{2(x+1)(x-1)}{x-1} \cdot \dfrac{1}{2(x+1)} = \dfrac{2}{2} \cdot \dfrac{x+1}{x+1} \cdot \dfrac{x-1}{x-1} = 1$.
The answer is (B).

11. From the equation $\left(x^2-4\right)\left(\dfrac{4}{x}-5\right) = 0$, we get $x^2 - 4 = 0$ or $\dfrac{4}{x} - 5 = 0$. Consider the equation $x^2 - 4 = 0$ first. Factoring gives

$$(x+2)(x-2) = 0$$

Setting each factor to zero gives

$$x + 2 = 0 \text{ or } x - 2 = 0$$

Hence, $x = 2$ or $x = -2$. But neither number is offered as an answer-choice. So we turn to the equation $\dfrac{4}{x} - 5 = 0$. Adding 5 to both sides yields

$$\dfrac{4}{x} = 5$$

Multiplying both sides by x gives $\qquad\qquad 4 = 5x$

Dividing both sides by 5 gives $\qquad\qquad \dfrac{4}{5} = x$

The answer is (D).

12. $$3^{n-1} = 3^{3n+1}$$
$$n - 1 = 3n + 1$$
$$-2n = 2$$
$$n = -1$$

Since $n = -1$, $m = 3^{n-1} = 3^{-1-1} = 3^{-2} = \dfrac{1}{3^2} = \dfrac{1}{9}$. Hence, $\dfrac{m}{n} = \dfrac{\dfrac{1}{9}}{-1} = -\dfrac{1}{9}$, and the answer is (D).

13. $q = 1* = \dfrac{\dfrac{1}{2}}{4 \cdot 1 - 1} = \dfrac{\dfrac{1}{2}}{3} = \dfrac{1}{2} \cdot \dfrac{1}{3} = \dfrac{1}{6}$.

Hence, $q* = \dfrac{\dfrac{\frac{1}{6}}{2}}{4 \cdot \dfrac{1}{6} - 1} = \dfrac{\dfrac{1}{6} \cdot \dfrac{1}{2}}{\dfrac{2}{3} - 1} = \dfrac{\dfrac{1}{12}}{-\dfrac{1}{3}} = \dfrac{1}{12}\left(-\dfrac{3}{1}\right) = -\dfrac{3}{12} = -\dfrac{1}{4}$.
The answer is (C).

Equations

When simplifying algebraic expressions, we perform operations within parentheses first and then exponents and then multiplication and then division and then addition and lastly subtraction. This can be remembered by the mnemonic:

PEMDAS
Please **E**xcuse **M**y **D**ear **A**unt **S**ally

When solving equations, however, we apply the mnemonic in reverse order: **SADMEP**. This is often expressed as follows: inverse operations in inverse order. The goal in solving an equation is to isolate the variable on one side of the equal sign (usually the left side). This is done by identifying the main operation—addition, multiplication, etc.—and then performing the opposite operation.

Example 1: Solve the following equation for x: $2x + y = 5$

Solution: The main operation is addition (remember addition now comes before multiplication, SADMEP), so subtracting y from both sides yields

$$2x + y - y = 5 - y$$

Simplifying yields

$$2x = 5 - y$$

The only operation remaining on the left side is multiplication. Undoing the multiplication by dividing both sides by 2 yields

$$\frac{2x}{2} = \frac{5-y}{2}$$

Canceling the 2 on the left side yields

$$x = \frac{5-y}{2}$$

Example 2: Solve the following equation for x: $3x - 4 = 2(x - 5)$

Solution: Here x appears on both sides of the equal sign, so let's move the x on the right side to the left side. But the x is trapped inside the parentheses. To release it, distribute the 2:

$$3x - 4 = 2x - 10$$

Now, subtracting $2x$ from both sides yields[*]

$$x - 4 = -10$$

Finally, adding 4 to both sides yields

$$x = -6$$

We often manipulate equations without thinking about what the equations actually say. The ACT likes to test this oversight. Equations are packed with information. Take for example the simple equation $3x + 2 = 5$. Since 5 is positive, the expression $3x + 2$ must be positive as well. An equation means that the terms on

---

[*] Note, students often mistakenly add $2x$ to both sides of this equation because of the minus symbol between $2x$ and 10. But $2x$ is positive, so we subtract it. This can be seen more clearly by rewriting the right side of the equation as $-10 + 2x$.

either side of the equal sign are equal in every way. Hence, any property one side of an equation has the other side will have as well. Following are some immediate deductions that can be made from simple equations.

Equation	Deduction
$y - x = 1$	$y > x$
$y^2 = x^2$	$y = \pm x$, or $|y| = |x|$. That is, x and y can differ only in sign.
$y^3 = x^3$	$y = x$
$y = x^2$	$y \geq 0$
$\dfrac{y}{x^2} = 1$	$y > 0$
$\dfrac{y}{x^3} = 2$	Both x and y are positive or both x and y are negative.
$x^2 + y^2 = 0$	$y = x = 0$
$3y = 4x$ and $x > 0$	$y > x$ and y is positive.
$3y = 4x$ and $x < 0$	$y < x$ and y is negative.
$y = \sqrt{x + 2}$	$y \geq 0$ and $x \geq -2$
$y = 2x$	y is even
$y = 2x + 1$	y is odd
$yx = 0$	$y = 0$ or $x = 0$, or both

Note! **In Algebra, you solve an equation for, say, y by isolating y on one side of the equality symbol. On the ACT, however, you are often asked to solve for an entire term, say, $3 - y$ by isolating it on one side.**

Example 3: If $a + 3a$ is 4 less than $b + 3b$, then $a - b =$

(A) -4 (B) -1 (C) $1/5$ (D) $1/3$ (E) 2

Translating the sentence into an equation gives $a + 3a = b + 3b - 4$

Combining like terms gives $4a = 4b - 4$

Subtracting $4b$ from both sides gives $4a - 4b = -4$

Finally, dividing by 4 gives $a - b = -1$

Hence, the answer is (B).

Note! **Sometimes on the ACT, a system of 3 equations will be written as one long "triple" equation. For example, the three equations $x = y$, $y = z$, $x = z$, can be written more compactly as $x = y = z$.**

Example 4: If $w \neq 0$ and $w = 2x = \sqrt{2}y$, what is the value of $w - x$ in terms of y ?

(A) $2y$ (B) $\dfrac{\sqrt{2}}{2}y$ (C) $\sqrt{2y}$ (D) $\dfrac{4}{\sqrt{2}}y$ (E) y

The equation $w = 2x = \sqrt{2}y$ stands for three equations: $w = 2x$, $2x = \sqrt{2}y$, and $w = \sqrt{2}y$. From the last equation, we get $w = \sqrt{2}y$; and from the second equation, we get $x = \dfrac{\sqrt{2}}{2}y$. Hence, $w - x = \sqrt{2}y - \dfrac{\sqrt{2}}{2}y = \dfrac{2}{2}\sqrt{2}y - \dfrac{\sqrt{2}}{2}y = \dfrac{2\sqrt{2}y - \sqrt{2}y}{2} = \dfrac{\sqrt{2}y}{2}$. Hence, the answer is (B).

Note! **Often on the ACT, you can solve a system of two equations in two unknowns by merely adding or subtracting the equations—instead of solving for one of the variables and then substituting it into the other equation.**

Example 5: If p and q are positive, $p^2 + q^2 = 16$, and $p^2 - q^2 = 8$, then $q =$

    (A)   2

    (B)   4

    (C)   8

    (D) $2\sqrt{2}$

    (E) $2\sqrt{6}$

Subtract the second equation from the first:

$$\begin{array}{r} p^2 + q^2 = 16 \\ (-)\quad p^2 - q^2 = 8 \\ \hline 2q^2 = 8 \end{array}$$

Dividing both sides of the equation by 2 gives

$$q^2 = 4$$

Finally, taking the square root of both sides gives

$$q = \pm 2$$

Hence, the answer is (A).

METHOD OF SUBSTITUTION (Four-Step Method)

Although on the ACT you can often solve a system of two equations in two unknowns by merely adding or subtracting the equations, you still need to know a standard method for solving these types of systems.

The four-step method will be illustrated with the following system:

$$2x + y = 10$$
$$5x - 2y = 7$$

1) *Solve one of the equations for one of the variables*:

    Solving the top equation for y yields $y = 10 - 2x$.

2) *Substitute the result from Step 1 into the other equation*:

    Substituting $y = 10 - 2x$ into the bottom equation yields $5x - 2(10 - 2x) = 7$.

3) *Solve the resulting equation*:

$$5x - 2(10 - 2x) = 7$$
$$5x - 20 + 4x = 7$$
$$9x - 20 = 7$$
$$9x = 27$$
$$x = 3$$

4) *Substitute the result from Step 3 into the equation derived in Step 1*:

    Substituting $x = 3$ into $y = 10 - 2x$ yields $y = 10 - 2(3) = 10 - 6 = 4$.

Hence, the solution of the system of equations is the ordered pair $(3, 4)$.

Problem Set L:

1. If $a > 0$ and $6a = 5b$, which of the following must be true?

   (A) $a = 6b/5$ (B) $ab < 0$ (C) $a > b$ (D) $b = 5a/6$ (E) $b > a$

2. If $p - q + r = 4$ and $p + q + r = 8$, then $p + r =$

   (A) 2 (B) 4 (C) 6 (D) 8 (E) 10

3. Suppose $x = y - 2 = \dfrac{y + 5}{2}$. Then x equals

   (A) 1/3 (B) 1 (C) 7/6 (D) 2 (E) 7

4. Let $p = 3^{q+1}$ and $q = 2r$. Then $\dfrac{p}{3^2} =$

   (A) 3^{2r-1} (B) 3^{2r} (C) 3 (D) r (E) 3^{2r+1}

5. k is a constant in the equation $\dfrac{u - v}{k} = 8$. If $u = 18$ when $v = 2$, then what is the value of u when $v = 4$?

   (A) -3
   (B) 0
   (C) 10
   (D) 23/2
   (E) 20

6. If $x = 3y = 4z$, which of the following must equal $6x$?

   I. $18y$
   II. $3y + 20z$
   III. $\dfrac{4y + 10z}{3}$

   (A) I only
   (B) II only
   (C) III only
   (D) I and II only
   (E) I and III only

7. Let $P = (x + y)k$. If $P = 10$ and $k = 3$, what is the average of x and y?

   (A) 0
   (B) 1/2
   (C) 5/3
   (D) 10/3
   (E) 7/2

8. Let $\dfrac{x}{y} + \dfrac{w}{z} = 2$. Then the value of $\dfrac{y}{x} + \dfrac{z}{w}$ is

   (A) 1/2
   (B) 3/4
   (C) 1
   (D) 5
   (E) It cannot be determined from the information given.

9. If 4 percent of $(p + q)$ is 8 and p is a positive integer, what is the greatest possible value of q?

   (A) 196
   (B) 197
   (C) 198
   (D) 199
   (E) 200

10. If $x^5 = 4$ and $x^4 = 7/y$, then what is the value of x in terms of y?

   (A) $7y/4$
   (B) $4y/7$
   (C) $y/7$
   (D) $7y$
   (E) $7 + 5/y$

11. How many solutions does the above system of equations have?

$$2x + y = 3$$
$$3y = 9 - 6x$$

   (A) None
   (B) One
   (C) Two
   (D) Four
   (E) An infinite number

12. If $p/19$ is 1 less than 3 times $q/19$, then p equals which of the following expressions?

   (A) $3q + 19$
   (B) $3q + 38$
   (C) $19/2$
   (D) $3q - 38$
   (E) $3q - 19$

13. If n is a number such that $(-8)^{2n} = 2^{8 + 2n}$, then $n =$

   (A) $1/2$
   (B) 2
   (C) $3/2$
   (D) 4
   (E) 5

14. If $m = 3^{n-1}$ and $3^{4n-1} = 27$, what is the value of m/n ?

   (A) 0
   (B) 1
   (C) $7/3$
   (D) $9/2$
   (E) 6

15. If $s + S \neq 0$ and $\dfrac{1}{3} = \dfrac{1}{4}\dfrac{s - S}{s + S}$, then what is s in terms of S ?

   (A) $s = S + 3$
   (B) $s = 4S$
   (C) $s = S/12$
   (D) $s = -7S$
   (E) $s = 4S - 6$

Answers and Solutions to Problem Set L

1.   Dividing both sides of the equation $6a = 5b$ by 6 gives $a = \frac{5}{6}b$. Thus, a is a fraction of b. But b is

greater than zero and therefore b is greater than a. (Note, had we been given that a was less than zero, then a would have been greater than b.) The answer is (E).

2.   Adding the two equations $\begin{array}{l} p - q + r = 4 \\ p + q + r = 8 \end{array}$ gives

$$2p + 2r = 12$$

Then dividing by 2 gives

$$p + r = 6$$

Hence, the answer is (C).

3.   Clearing fractions in the equation $y - 2 = (y + 5)/2$ gives $2(y - 2) = y + 5$
Distributing the 2 gives $2y - 4 = y + 5$
Subtracting y and adding 4 to both sides gives $y = 9$
Now, replacing y with 9 in the equation $x = y - 2$ gives $x = y - 2 = 9 - 2 = 7$
Hence, the answer is (E).

4.   Replacing p with 3^{q+1} in the expression $\frac{p}{3^2}$ gives $\frac{p}{3^2} = \frac{3^{q+1}}{3^2} = 3^{q+1-2} = 3^{q-1}$

Now, replacing q with $2r$ in the expression 3^{q-1} gives $3^{q-1} = 3^{2r-1}$
Hence, the answer is (A).

5.   Substituting $u = 18$ and $v = 2$ into the equation $\frac{u-v}{k} = 8$ gives $\frac{18-2}{k} = 8$

Subtracting gives $16/k = 8$

Multiplying both sides of this equation by k gives $16 = 8k$

Dividing by 8 gives $2 = k$

With this value for k, the original equation becomes $\frac{u-v}{2} = 8$

Now, we are asked to find u when $v = 4$.

Replacing v with 4 in the equation $\frac{u-v}{2} = 8$ gives $\frac{u-4}{2} = 8$

Multiplying by 2 gives $u - 4 = 16$

Adding 4 gives $u = 20$

Hence, the answer is (E).

6.   The equation $x = 3y = 4z$ contains three equations:

$$x = 3y$$
$$3y = 4z$$
$$x = 4z$$

Multiplying both sides of the equation $x = 3y$ by 6 gives $6x = 18y$. Hence, Statement I is true. This eliminates (B) and (C). Next, $3y + 20z = 3y + 5(4z)$. Substituting x for $3y$ and for $4z$ in this equation gives $3y + 20z = 3y + 5(4z) = x + 5x = 6x$. Hence, Statement II is true. This eliminates (A) and (E). Hence, by process of elimination, the answer is (D).

7. Plugging $P = 10$ and $k = 3$ into the equation $P = (x + y)k$ gives $10 = (x + y)3$. Dividing by 3 gives $x + y = 10/3$. Finally, to form the average, divide both sides of this equation by 2: $\dfrac{x+y}{2} = \dfrac{10}{6} = \dfrac{5}{3}$. Hence, the answer is (C).

8. There are many different values for $w, x, y,$ and z such that $\dfrac{x}{y} + \dfrac{w}{z} = 2$. Two particular cases are listed below:

If $x = y = w = z = 1$, then $\dfrac{x}{y} + \dfrac{w}{z} = \dfrac{1}{1} + \dfrac{1}{1} = 1 + 1 = 2$ and $\dfrac{y}{x} + \dfrac{z}{w} = \dfrac{1}{1} + \dfrac{1}{1} = 1 + 1 = 2$.

If $x = 3, y = 2, w = 1,$ and $z = 2$, then $\dfrac{x}{y} + \dfrac{w}{z} = \dfrac{3}{2} + \dfrac{1}{2} = \dfrac{3+1}{2} = \dfrac{4}{2} = 2$ and $\dfrac{y}{x} + \dfrac{z}{w} = \dfrac{2}{3} + \dfrac{2}{1} = \dfrac{2}{3} + \dfrac{2}{1} \cdot \dfrac{3}{3} =$

$\dfrac{2}{3} + \dfrac{6}{3} = \dfrac{2+6}{3} = \dfrac{8}{3}$

This is a double case. Hence, the answer is (E).

9. Translating the clause "4 percent of $(p + q)$ is 8" into a mathematical expression yields

$$.04(p + q) = 8$$

Dividing both sides of this equation by .04 yields

$$p + q = 8/.04 = 200$$

Subtracting p from both sides yields

$$q = 200 - p$$

This expression will be greatest when p is as small as possible. This is when $p = 1$:

$$q = 200 - 1 = 199$$

The answer is (D).

10. The expression $x^5 = 4$ can be rewritten as

$$x \cdot x^4 = 4$$

Replacing x^4 in this expression with $7/y$ yields

$$x \cdot \dfrac{7}{y} = 4$$

Multiplying both sides of this equation by y gives

$$x \cdot 7 = 4 \cdot y$$

Dividing both sides of this equation by 7 yields

$$x = \dfrac{4}{7} \cdot y$$

Hence, the answer is (B).

11. Start with the bottom equation $3y = 9 - 6x$:

Dividing by 3 yields $\qquad\qquad y = 3 - 2x$

Adding $2x$ yields $\qquad\qquad 2x + y = 3$

Notice that this is the top equation in the system. Hence, the system is only one equation in two different forms. Thus, there are an infinite number of solutions. For example, the pair $x = 2, y = -1$ is a solution as is the pair $x = 0, y = 3$. The answer is (E).

12. The clause *"p/19 is 1 less than 3 times q/19"* translates into:

$$\frac{p}{19} = 3 \cdot \frac{q}{19} - 1$$

Multiplying both sides of this equation by 19 gives

$$p = 3 \cdot q - 19$$

The answer is (E).

13. Since the right side of the equation is positive, the left side must also be positive. Thus, $(-8)^{2n}$ is equal to

$$8^{2n}$$

This in turn can be written as

$$\left(2^3\right)^{2n}$$

Multiplying the exponents gives

$$2^{6n}$$

Plugging this into the original equation gives

$$2^{6n} = 2^{8+2n}$$

Now, since the bases are the same, the exponents must be equal:

$$6n = 8 + 2n$$

Solving this equation gives

$$n = 2$$

The answer is (B).

14.
$$3^{4n-1} = 27$$
$$3^{4n-1} = 3^3$$
$$4n - 1 = 3$$
$$4n = 4$$
$$n = 1$$

Since $n = 1$, $m = 3^{n-1} = 3^{1-1} = 3^0 = 1$. Hence, $m/n = 1/1 = 1$, and the answer is (B).

15. First, clear fractions by multiplying both sides by $12(s + S)$:

$$4(s + S) = 3(s - S)$$

Next, distribute the 3 and 4:

$$4s + 4S = 3s - 3S$$

Finally, subtract $3s$ and $4S$ from both sides:

$$s = -7S$$

The answer is (D).

Averages

Problems involving averages are very common on the ACT. They can be classified into four major categories as follows.

Note! The average of N numbers is their sum divided by N, that is, $Average = \dfrac{Sum}{N}$.

Example 1: What is the average of $x, 2x$, and 6?
(A) $x/2$
(B) $2x$
(C) $(x + 2)/6$
(D) $x + 2$
(E) $(x + 2)/3$

By the definition of an average, we get $\dfrac{x + 2x + 6}{3} = \dfrac{3x + 6}{3} = \dfrac{3(x + 2)}{3} = x + 2$. Hence, the answer is (D).

Note! *Weighted average:* **The average between two sets of numbers is closer to the set with more numbers.**

Example 2: If on a test three people answered 90% of the questions correctly and two people answered 80% correctly, then the average for the group is not 85% but rather $\dfrac{3 \cdot 90 + 2 \cdot 80}{5} = \dfrac{430}{5} = 86$.
Here, 90 has a weight of 3—it occurs 3 times. Whereas 80 has a weight of 2—it occurs 2 times. So the average is closer to 90 than to 80 as we have just calculated.

Note! Using an average to find a number.

Sometimes you will be asked to find a number by using a given average. An example will illustrate.

Example 3: If the average of five numbers is -10, and the sum of three of the numbers is 16, then what is the average of the other two numbers?

(A) -33
(B) -1
(C) 5
(D) 20
(E) 25

Let the five numbers be a, b, c, d, e. Then their average is $\dfrac{a + b + c + d + e}{5} = -10$. Now three of the numbers have a sum of 16, say, $a + b + c = 16$. So substitute 16 for $a + b + c$ in the average above: $\dfrac{16 + d + e}{5} = -10$. Solving this equation for $d + e$ gives $d + e = -66$. Finally, dividing by 2 (to form the average) gives $\dfrac{d + e}{2} = -33$. Hence, the answer is (A).

Note! $\text{Average Speed} = \dfrac{\text{Total Distance}}{\text{Total Time}}$

Although the formula for average speed is simple, few people solve these problems correctly because most fail to find both the <u>total distance</u> and the <u>total time</u>.

Example 4: In traveling from city A to city B, John drove for 1 hour at 50 mph and for 3 hours at 60 mph. What was his average speed for the whole trip?

(A) 50
(B) 53 ½
(C) 55
(D) 56
(E) 57 ½

The total distance is $1 \cdot 50 + 3 \cdot 60 = 230$. And the total time is 4 hours. Hence,

$$\text{Average Speed} = \frac{\text{Total Distance}}{\text{Total Time}} = \frac{230}{4} = 57\,\tfrac{1}{2}$$

The answer is (E). Note, the answer is not the mere average of 50 and 60. Rather the average is closer to 60 because he traveled longer at 60 mph (3 hrs.) than at 50 mph (1 hr.).

Problem Set M:

1. If the average of p and $4p$ is 10, then $p =$

    (A) 1   (B) 3   (C) 4   (D) 10   (E) 18

2. The average of six consecutive integers in increasing order of size is 9 ½. What is the average of the last three integers?

    (A) 8   (B) 9 ½   (C) 10   (D) 11   (E) 19

3. If S denotes the sum and A the average of the consecutive positive integers 1 through n, then which of the following must be true?

    I. $A = S/n$

    II. $S = A/n$

    III. $A - S = n$

    (A) I only
    (B) II only
    (C) III only
    (D) I and II only
    (E) I, II, and III

4. Cars X and Y leave City A at the same time and travel the same route to City B. Car X takes 30 minutes to complete the trip and car Y takes 20 minutes. Which of the following must be true?

    I.   The average miles per hour at which car X traveled was greater than the average miles per hour at which car Y traveled.

    II.   The distance between the cities is 30 miles.

    III. The average miles per hour at which car Y traveled was greater than the average miles per hour at which car X traveled.

    (A) I only
    (B) II only
    (C) III only
    (D) I and II only
    (E) I and III only

5. If $p + q = r$, what is the average of p, q, and r ?

(A) $r/3$
(B) $(p + q)/3$
(C) $2r/3$
(D) $r/2$
(E) $(p + q)/2$

6. Suppose a train travels x miles in y hours and 15 minutes. Its average speed in miles per hour is

(A) $\dfrac{y + 15}{x}$

(B) $x\left(y - \dfrac{1}{4}\right)$

(C) $\dfrac{x}{y + \dfrac{1}{4}}$

(D) $\dfrac{x}{y + 15}$

(E) $\dfrac{y + \dfrac{1}{4}}{x}$

7. The average of five numbers is 6.9. If one of the numbers is deleted, the average of the remaining numbers is 4.4. What is the value of the number deleted?

   (A) 6.8   (B) 7.4   (C) 12.5   (D) 16.9   (E) 17.2

8. The average of four numbers is 20. If one of the numbers is removed, the average of the remaining numbers is 15. What number was removed?

   (A) 10   (B) 15   (C) 30   (D) 35   (E) 45

9. The average of two numbers is $\pi/2$, and one of the numbers is x. What is the other number in terms of x ?

   (A) $\pi/2 - x$ (B) $\pi/2 + x$ (C) $\pi - x$ (D) $\pi + x$ (E) $2\pi + x$

10. A shopper spends \$25 to purchase CDs at 50¢ each. The next day, the disks go on sale for 30¢ each and the shopper spends \$45 to purchase more disks. What was the average price per disk purchased?

    (A) 25¢   (B) 30¢   (C) 35¢   (D) 40¢   (E) 45¢

11. The average of 8 numbers is A, and one of the numbers is 14. If 14 is replaced with 28, then what is the new average in terms of A ?

    (A) $A + 7/4$ (B) $A + 1/2$ (C) $A + 2$ (D) $2A + 1$ (E) $A + 4$

Answers and Solutions to Problem Set M

1. Since the average of p and $4p$ is 10, we get

$$\frac{p+4p}{2} = 10$$

Combining the p's gives

$$\frac{5p}{2} = 10$$

Multiplying by 2 yields

$$5p = 20$$

Finally, dividing by 5 gives

$$p = 4$$

The answer is (C).

2. We have six consecutive integers whose average is 9 ½, so we have the first three integers less than 9 ½ and the first three integers greater than 9 ½. That is, we are dealing with the numbers 7, 8, 9, 10, 11, 12. Clearly, the average of the last three numbers in this list is 11. Hence, the answer is (D).

3. The average of the consecutive positive integers 1 through n is $A = \dfrac{1+2+...+n}{n}$. Now, we are given that S denotes the sum of the consecutive positive integers 1 through n, that is, $S = 1 + 2 + \cdots + n$. Plugging this into the formula for the average gives $A = S/n$. Hence, Statement I is true, which eliminates (B) and (C). Next, solving the equation $A = S/n$ for S yields $S = A \cdot n$. Thus, Statement II is false, which eliminates (D) and (E). Therefore, the answer is (A).

4. The average speed at which car X traveled is $\dfrac{\text{Total Distance}}{30}$.

    The average speed at which car Y traveled is $\dfrac{\text{Total Distance}}{20}$.

The two fractions have the same numerators, and the denominator for car Y is smaller. Hence, the average miles per hour at which car Y traveled is greater than the average miles per hour at which car X traveled. Thus, Statement I is false and Statement III is true. As to Statement II, we do not have enough information to calculate the distance between the cities. Hence, Statement II need not be true. The answer is (C).

5. The average of p, q, and r is $\dfrac{p+q+r}{3}$. Replacing $p + q$ with r gives $\dfrac{r+r}{3} = \dfrac{2r}{3}$. The answer is (C).

6. Often on the ACT you will be given numbers in different units. When this occurs, you must convert the numbers into the same units. (This is obnoxious but it does occur on the ACT, so be alert to it.) In this problem, we must convert 15 minutes into hours: $15 \cdot \dfrac{1}{60} = \dfrac{1}{4} \, hr$. Hence, the average speed is

$\dfrac{Total\ Distance}{Total\ Time} = \dfrac{x}{y+\dfrac{1}{4}}$. The answer is (C).

7.   Forming the average of the five numbers gives

$$\frac{v + w + x + y + z}{5} = 6.9$$

Let the deleted number be z. Then forming the average of the remaining four numbers gives

$$\frac{v + w + x + y}{4} = 4.4$$

Multiplying both sides of this equation by 4 gives

$$v + w + x + y = 17.6$$

Plugging this value into the original average gives

$$\frac{17.6 + z}{5} = 6.9$$

Solving this equation for z gives

$$z = 16.9$$

The answer is (D).

8.   Let the four numbers be a, b, c, and d. Since their average is 20, we get

$$\frac{a + b + c + d}{4} = 20$$

Let d be the number that is removed. Since the average of the remaining numbers is 15, we get

$$\frac{a + b + c}{3} = 15$$

Solving for $a + b + c$ yields

$$a + b + c = 45$$

Substituting this into the first equation yields

$$\frac{45 + d}{4} = 20$$

Multiplying both sides of this equation by 4 yields

$$45 + d = 80$$

Subtracting 45 from both sides of this equation yields

$$d = 35$$

The answer is (D).

9.   Let the other number be y. Since the average of the two numbers is $\pi/2$, we get

$$\frac{x + y}{2} = \frac{\pi}{2}$$

Multiplying both sides of this equation by 2 yields

$$x + y = \pi$$

Subtracting x from both sides of this equation yields

$$y = \pi - x$$

The answer is (C).

10. This is a weighted-average problem because more disks were purchased on the second day. Let x be the number of disks purchased on the first day. Then $.50x = 25$. Solving for x yields $x = 50$. Let y be the number of disks purchased on the second day. Then $.30y = 45$. Solving for y yields $y = 150$. Forming the weighted average, we get

$$Average\ Cost = \frac{Total\ Cost}{Total\ Number} = \frac{25+45}{50+150} = \frac{70}{200} = .35$$

The answer is (C).

11. Let the seven unknown numbers be represented by $x_1, x_2, ..., x_7$. Forming the average of the eight numbers yields

$$\frac{x_1 + x_2 + \cdots + x_7 + 14}{8} = A$$

Replacing 14 with 28 (= 14 + 14), and forming the average yields

$$\frac{x_1 + x_2 + \cdots + x_7 + (14 + 14)}{8}$$

Breaking up the fraction into the sum of two fractions yields

$$\frac{x_1 + x_2 + \cdots + x_7 + 14}{8} + \frac{14}{8}$$

Since $\dfrac{x_1 + x_2 + \cdots + x_7 + 14}{8} = A$, this becomes

$$A + 14/8$$

Reducing the fraction yields

$$A + 7/4$$

The answer is (A).

Ratio & Proportion

RATIO

A ratio is simply a fraction. The following notations all express the ratio of x to y: $x : y$, $x \div y$, or x/y. Writing two numbers as a ratio provides a convenient way to compare their sizes. For example, since $3/\pi < 1$, we know that 3 is less than π. A ratio compares two numbers. Just as you cannot compare apples and oranges, so to must the numbers you are comparing have the same units. For example, you cannot form the ratio of 2 feet to 4 yards because the two numbers are expressed in different units—feet vs. yards. It is quite common for the ACT to ask for the ratio of two numbers that are expressed in different units. Before you form any ratio, make sure the two numbers are expressed in the same units.

Example 1:   What is the ratio of 2 feet to 4 yards?

       (A)   1 : 9
       (B)   1 : 8
       (C)   1 : 7
       (D)   1 : 6
       (E)   1 : 5

The ratio cannot be formed until the numbers are expressed in the same units. Let's turn the yards into feet. Since there are 3 feet in a yard, 4 yards = 4 × 3 feet = 12 feet. Forming the ratio yields

$$\frac{2 \; feet}{12 \; feet} = \frac{1}{6} \; or \; 1 : 6$$

The answer is (D).

Note, taking the reciprocal of a fraction usually changes its size. For example, $\frac{3}{4} \neq \frac{4}{3}$. So order is important in a ratio: $3 : 4 \neq 4 : 3$.

PROPORTION

A proportion is simply an equality between two ratios (fractions). For example, the ratio of x to y is equal to the ratio of 3 to 2 is translated as

$$\frac{x}{y} = \frac{3}{2}$$

or in ratio notation,

$$x : y :: 3 : 2$$

Two variables are *directly proportional* if one is a constant multiple of the other:

$$y = kx$$

where k is a constant.

The above equation shows that as x increases (or decreases) so does y. This simple concept has numerous applications in mathematics. For example, in constant velocity problems, distance is directly proportional to time: $d = vt$, where v is a constant. Note, sometimes the word *directly* is suppressed.

118

Example 2: If the ratio of y to x is equal to 3 and the sum of y and x is 80, what is the value of y?

(A) –10   (B) –2   (C) 5   (D) 20   (E 60

Translating *"the ratio of y to x is equal to 3"* into an equation yields

$$\frac{y}{x} = 3$$

Translating *"the sum of y and x is 80"* into an equation yields

$$y + x = 80$$

Solving the first equation for y gives $y = 3x$. Substituting this into the second equation yields

$$3x + x = 80$$
$$4x = 80$$
$$x = 20$$

Hence, $y = 3x = 3 \cdot 20 = 60$. The answer is (E).

In many word problems, as one quantity increases (decreases), another quantity also increases (decreases). This type of problem can be solved by setting up a *direct* proportion.

Example 3: If Biff can shape 3 surfboards in 50 minutes, how many surfboards can he shape in 5 hours?

(A) 16   (B) 17   (C) 18   (D) 19   (E) 20

As time increases so does the number of shaped surfboards. Hence, we set up a direct proportion. First, convert 5 hours into minutes: $5 \; hours = 5 \times 60 \; minutes = 300 \; minutes$. Next, let x be the number of surfboards shaped in 5 hours. Finally, forming the proportion yields

$$\frac{3}{50} = \frac{x}{300}$$
$$\frac{3 \cdot 300}{50} = x$$
$$18 = x$$

The answer is (C).

Example 4: On a map, 1 inch represents 150 miles. What is the actual distance between two cities if they are 3½ inches apart on the map?

(A) 225   (B) 300   (C) 450   (D) 525   (E) 600

As the distance on the map increases so does the actual distance. Hence, we set up a direct proportion. Let x be the actual distance between the cities. Forming the proportion yields

$$\frac{1 \, in}{150 \, mi} = \frac{3\frac{1}{2} \, in}{x \, mi}$$

$$x = 3\frac{1}{2} \times 150$$

$$x = 525$$

The answer is (D).

Note, you need not worry about how you form the direct proportion so long as the order is the same on both sides of the equal sign. The proportion in Example 4 could have been written as $\dfrac{1 \, in}{3\frac{1}{2} \, in} = \dfrac{150 \, mi}{x \, mi}$. In this case, the order is inches to inches and miles to miles. However, the following is not a direct proportion because the order is not the same on both sides of the equal sign: $\dfrac{1 \, in}{150 \, mi} = \dfrac{x \, mi}{3\frac{1}{2} \, in}$. In this case, the order is inches to miles on the left side of the equal sign but miles to inches on the right side.

If one quantity increases (or decreases) while another quantity decreases (or increases), the quantities are said to be *inversely* proportional. The statement "*y* is inversely proportional to *x*" is written as

$$y = \frac{k}{x}$$

where *k* is a constant.

Multiplying both sides of $y = \frac{k}{x}$ by *x* yields

$$yx = k$$

Hence, in an inverse proportion, the product of the two quantities is constant. Therefore, instead of setting ratios equal, we set products equal.

In many word problems, as one quantity increases (decreases), another quantity decreases (increases). This type of problem can be solved by setting up a product of terms.

Example 5: If 7 workers can assemble a car in 8 hours, how long would it take 12 workers to assemble the same car?

  (A) 3 hrs.   (B) 3 1/2 hrs.   (C) 4 2/3 hrs.   (D) 5hrs   (E) 6 1/3 hrs.

As the number of workers increases, the amount of time required to assemble the car decreases. Hence, we set the products of the terms equal. Let *x* be the time it takes the 12 workers to assemble the car. Forming the equation yields

$$7 \cdot 8 = 12 \cdot x$$

$$\frac{56}{12} = x$$

$$4\frac{2}{3} = x$$

The answer is (C).

To summarize: if one quantity increases (decreases) as another quantity also increases (decreases), set ratios equal. If one quantity increases (decreases) as another quantity decreases (increases), set products equal.

The concept of proportion can be generalized to three or more ratios. *A*, *B*, and *C* are in the ratio 3 : 4 : 5 means $\frac{A}{B} = \frac{3}{4}$, $\frac{A}{C} = \frac{3}{5}$, and $\frac{B}{C} = \frac{4}{5}$.

Example 6: In the figure, the angles *A*, *B*, *C* of the triangle are in the ratio 5:12:13. What is the measure of angle A?

  (A)   15
  (B)   27
  (C)   30
  (D)   34
  (E)   40

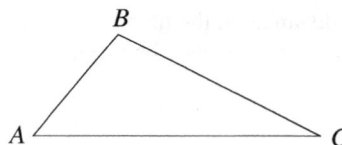

Since the angle sum of a triangle is 180°, $A + B + C = 180$. Forming two of the ratios yields

$$\frac{A}{B} = \frac{5}{12} \qquad \frac{A}{C} = \frac{5}{13}$$

Solving the first equation for *B* yields $B = \frac{12}{5}A$

Solving the second equation for *C* yields $C = \frac{13}{5}A$

Hence, $180 = A + B + C = A + \frac{12}{5}A + \frac{13}{5}A = 6A$. Therefore, $180 = 6A$, or $A = 30$. The answer is choice (C).

Problem Set N:

1. What is the ratio of 2 ft. 3 in. to 2 yds?

    (A) 1/4   (B) 1/3   (C) 3/8   (D) 1/2   (E) 3/4

2. The ratio of two numbers is 10 and their difference is 18. What is the value of the smaller number?

    (A) 2   (B) 5   (C) 10   (D) 21   (E) 27

3. If the degree measures of two angles of an isosceles triangle are in the ratio 1:3, what is the degree measure of the largest angle if it is not a base angle?

    (A) 26°   (B) 36°   (C) 51°   (D) 92°   (E) 108°

4. A jet uses 80 gallons of fuel to fly 320 miles. At this rate, how many gallons of fuel are needed for a 700-mile flight?

    (A) 150   (B) 155   (C) 160   (D) 170   (E) 175

5. Two boys can mow a lawn in 2 hours and 30 minutes. If they are joined by three other boys, how many hours will it take to mow the lawn?

    (A) 1 hr.   (B) 1 ¼ hrs.   (C) 1 ½ hrs.   (D) 1 ¾ hrs.   (E) 2 hrs.

6. A recipe requires 1/2 lb. of shortening and 14 oz. of flour. If the chef accidentally pours in 21 oz. of flour, how many ounces of shortening should be added?

    (A) 9   (B) 10   (C) 11   (D) 12   (E) 13

7. If w widgets cost d dollars, then at this rate how many dollars will 2000 widgets cost?

    (A) $\dfrac{wd}{2000}$ (B) $\dfrac{2000w}{d}$ (C) $\dfrac{2000d}{w}$ (D) $\dfrac{d}{2000w}$ (E) $\dfrac{2000}{wd}$

8. In the system of equations to the right, $z \neq 0$. What is ratio of x to z?

    $$x + 2y - z = 1$$
    $$3x - 2y - 8z = -1$$

    (A) −9/4   (B) −1/3   (C) 1/3   (D) 4/9   (E) 9/4

9. If a sprinter takes 30 steps in 9 seconds, how many steps does he take in 54 seconds?

    (A) 130   (B) 170   (C) 173   (D) 180   (E) 200

10. If $5x = 6y$, then the ratio of x to y is

    (A) 5 : 11   (B) 5 : 6   (C) 1 : 1   (D) 6 : 5   (E) 11 : 6

Answers and Solutions to Problem Set N

1.   First change all the units to inches: 2 ft. 3 in. = 27 in., and 2 yds. = 72 in. Forming the ratio yields

$$\frac{2\,ft.\,3in.}{2\,yds.} = \frac{27\,in.}{72\,in.} = \frac{3}{8}$$

The answer is (C).

2.   Let x and y denote the numbers. Then $x/y = 10$ and $x - y = 18$. Solving the first equation for x and plugging it into the second equation yields

$$10y - y = 18$$

$$9y = 18$$

$$y = 2$$

Plugging this into the equation $x - y = 18$ yields $x = 20$. Hence, y is the smaller number. The answer is (A).

3.   Let x and y denote the angles:

Then $x/y = 1/3$ and since the angle sum of a triangle is $180°$, $x + x + y = 180$. Solving the first equation for y and plugging it into the second equation yields

$$2x + 3x = 180$$

$$5x = 180$$

$$x = 36$$

Plugging this into the equation $x/y = 1/3$ yields $y = 108$. The answer is (E).

4.   This is a direct proportion: as the distance increases, the gallons of fuel consumed also increases. Setting ratios equal yields

$$\frac{80\,gal.}{320\,mi.} = \frac{x\,gal.}{700\,mi.}$$

$$\frac{700 \cdot 80}{320} = x$$

$$175 = x$$

The answer is (E).

5.   This is an inverse proportion: as the number of boys increases the time required to complete the job decreases. Setting products equal yields

$$2 \times 2.5 = 5 \times t$$

$$1 = t$$

The answer is (A).

6. This is a direct proportion: as the amount of flour increases so must the amount of shortening. First change 1/2 lb. into 8 oz., Setting ratios equal yields

$$\frac{8}{14} = \frac{x}{21}$$

$$\frac{21 \cdot 8}{14} = x$$

$$12 = x$$

The answer is (D).

7. Most students struggle with this type of problem, and the ACT considers them to be difficult. However, if you can identify whether a problem is a direct proportion or an inverse proportion, then it is not so challenging. In this problem, as the number of widgets increases so does the absolute cost. This is a direct proportion, and therefore we set ratios equal:

$$\frac{w}{d} = \frac{2000}{x}$$

Cross multiplying yields $\quad w \cdot x = 2000 \cdot d$

Dividing by w yields $\quad x = \dfrac{2000d}{w}$

The answer is (C).

8. This is considered to be a hard problem. Begin by adding the two equations:

$$x + 2y - z = 1$$
$$\underline{3x - 2y - 8z = -1}$$
$$4x - 9z = 0$$
$$4x = 9z$$
$$\frac{x}{z} = \frac{9}{4}$$

The answer is (E).

9. This is a direct proportion: as the time increases so does the number of steps that the sprinter takes. Setting ratios equal yields

$$\frac{30}{9} = \frac{x}{54}$$

$$\frac{30 \cdot 54}{9} = x$$

$$180 = x$$

The answer is (D).

10. Dividing the equation $5x = 6y$ by $5y$ yields

$$\frac{x}{y} = \frac{6}{5} \qquad \text{ratio of } x \text{ to } y$$

or in ratio notation

$$x : y = 6 : 5$$

The answer is (D).

Exponents & Roots

EXPONENTS

Exponents afford a convenient way of expressing long products of the same number. The expression b^n is called a power and it stands for $b \times b \times b \times \cdots \times b$, where there are n factors of b. b is called the base, and n is called the exponent. By definition, $b^0 = 1$.

There are six rules that govern the behavior of exponents:

Rule 1: $x^a \cdot x^b = x^{a+b}$ Example, $2^3 \cdot 2^2 = 2^{3+2} = 2^5 = 32$. Caution, $x^a + x^b \neq x^{a+b}$

Rule 2: $\left(x^a\right)^b = x^{ab}$ Example, $\left(2^3\right)^2 = 2^{3 \cdot 2} = 2^6 = 64$

Rule 3: $(xy)^a = x^a \cdot y^a$ Example, $(2y)^3 = 2^3 \cdot y^3 = 8y^3$

Rule 4: $\left(\dfrac{x}{y}\right)^a = \dfrac{x^a}{y^a}$ Example, $\left(\dfrac{x}{3}\right)^2 = \dfrac{x^2}{3^2} = \dfrac{x^2}{9}$

Rule 5: $\dfrac{x^a}{x^b} = x^{a-b}$, if $a > b$.   Example, $\dfrac{2^6}{2^3} = 2^{6-3} = 2^3 = 8$

          $\dfrac{x^a}{x^b} = \dfrac{1}{x^{b-a}}$, if $b > a$.   Example, $\dfrac{2^3}{2^6} = \dfrac{1}{2^{6-3}} = \dfrac{1}{2^3} = \dfrac{1}{8}$

Rule 6: $x^{-a} = \dfrac{1}{x^a}$ Example, $z^{-3} = \dfrac{1}{z^3}$ Caution, a negative exponent does not make the number negative; it merely indicates that the base should be reciprocated. For example, $3^{-2} \neq -\dfrac{1}{3^2} \text{ or } -\dfrac{1}{9}$.

Problems involving these six rules are common on the test, and they are often listed as hard problems. However, the process of solving these problems is quite mechanical: simply apply the six rules until they can no longer be applied.

Example 1:   If $x \neq 0$, $\dfrac{x\left(x^5\right)^2}{x^4} =$

     (A) x^5 (B) x^6 (C) x^7 (D) x^8 (E) x^9

First, apply the rule $\left(x^a\right)^b = x^{ab}$ to the expression $\dfrac{x\left(x^5\right)^2}{x^4}$:

$$\frac{x \cdot x^{5 \cdot 2}}{x^4} = \frac{x \cdot x^{10}}{x^4}$$

Next, apply the rule $x^a \cdot x^b = x^{a+b}$:

$$\frac{x \cdot x^{10}}{x^4} = \frac{x^{11}}{x^4}$$

Finally, apply the rule $\frac{x^a}{x^b} = x^{a-b}$:

$$\frac{x^{11}}{x^4} = x^{11-4} = x^7$$

The answer is (C).

Note: Typically, there are many ways of solving these types of problems. For this example, we could have begun with Rule 5, $\frac{x^a}{x^b} = \frac{1}{x^{b-a}}$:

$$\frac{x\left(x^5\right)^2}{x^4} = \frac{\left(x^5\right)^2}{x^{4-1}} = \frac{\left(x^5\right)^2}{x^3}$$

Then apply Rule 2, $\left(x^a\right)^b = x^{ab}$:

$$\frac{\left(x^5\right)^2}{x^3} = \frac{x^{10}}{x^3}$$

Finally, apply the other version of Rule 5, $\frac{x^a}{x^b} = x^{a-b}$:

$$\frac{x^{10}}{x^3} = x^7$$

Example 2: $\quad \dfrac{3 \cdot 3 \cdot 3 \cdot 3}{9 \cdot 9 \cdot 9 \cdot 9} =$

(A) $\left(\dfrac{1}{3}\right)^4$ (B) $\left(\dfrac{1}{3}\right)^3$ (C) $1/3$ (D) $4/9$ (E) $4/3$

Canceling the common factor 3 yields $\dfrac{1 \cdot 1 \cdot 1 \cdot 1}{3 \cdot 3 \cdot 3 \cdot 3}$, or $\dfrac{1}{3} \cdot \dfrac{1}{3} \cdot \dfrac{1}{3} \cdot \dfrac{1}{3}$. Now, by the definition of a power,

$\dfrac{1}{3} \cdot \dfrac{1}{3} \cdot \dfrac{1}{3} \cdot \dfrac{1}{3} = \left(\dfrac{1}{3}\right)^4$ Hence, the answer is (A).

Example 3: $\quad \dfrac{6^4}{3^2} =$

(A) 2^4 (B) $2^3 \cdot 3$ (C) 6^2 (D) $2^4 \cdot 3^2$ (E) $2^2 \cdot 3^4$

First, factor the top of the fraction:

$$\frac{(2 \cdot 3)^4}{3^2}$$

Next, apply the rule $(xy)^a = x^a \cdot y^a$: $\qquad\qquad \dfrac{2^4 \cdot 3^4}{3^2}$

Finally, apply the rule $\dfrac{x^a}{x^b} = x^{a-b}$: $\qquad\qquad 2^4 \cdot 3^2$

Hence, the answer is (D).

ROOTS

The symbol $\sqrt[n]{b}$ is read the *n*th root of *b*, where *n* is called the index, *b* is called the base, and $\sqrt{}$ is called the radical. $\sqrt[n]{b}$ denotes that number which raised to the *n*th power yields *b*. In other words, *a* is the *n*th root of *b* if $a^n = b$. For example, $\sqrt{9} = 3$ * because $3^2 = 9$, and $\sqrt[3]{-8} = -2$ because $(-2)^3 = -8$. Even roots occur in pairs: both a positive root and a negative root. For example, $\sqrt[4]{16} = 2$ since $2^4 = 16$, and $\sqrt[4]{16} = -2$ since $(-2)^4 = 16$. Odd roots occur alone and have the same sign as the base: $\sqrt[3]{-27} = -3$ since $(-3)^3 = -27$. If given an even root, you are to assume it is the positive root. However, if you introduce even roots by solving an equation, then you <u>must</u> consider both the positive and negative roots:

$$x^2 = 9$$
$$\sqrt{x^2} = \pm\sqrt{9}$$
$$x = \pm 3$$

Square roots and cube roots can be simplified by removing perfect squares and perfect cubes, respectively. For example,

$$\sqrt{8} = \sqrt{4 \cdot 2} = \sqrt{4}\sqrt{2} = 2\sqrt{2}$$
$$\sqrt[3]{54} = \sqrt[3]{27 \cdot 2} = \sqrt[3]{27}\sqrt[3]{2} = 3\sqrt[3]{2}$$

Radicals are often written with fractional exponents. The expression $\sqrt[n]{b}$ can be written as $b^{1/n}$. This can be generalized as follows:

$$b^{m/n} = \left(\sqrt[n]{b}\right)^m = \sqrt[n]{b^m}$$

Usually, the form $\left(\sqrt[n]{b}\right)^m$ is better when calculating because the part under the radical is smaller in this case. For example, $27^{2/3} = \left(\sqrt[3]{27}\right)^2 = 3^2 = 9$. Using the form $\sqrt[n]{b^m}$ would be much harder in this case: $27^{2/3} = \sqrt[3]{27^2} = \sqrt[3]{729} = 9$. Most students know the value of $\sqrt[3]{27}$, but few know the value of $\sqrt[3]{729}$.

If *n* is even, then

$$\sqrt[n]{x^n} = |x|$$

For example, $\sqrt[4]{(-2)^4} = |-2| = 2$. With odd roots, the absolute value symbol is not needed. For example, $\sqrt[3]{(-2)^3} = \sqrt[3]{-8} = -2$.

To solve radical equations, just apply the rules of exponents to undo the radicals. For example, to solve the radical equation $x^{2/3} = 4$, we cube both sides to eliminate the cube root:

$$\left(x^{2/3}\right)^3 = 4^3$$
$$x^2 = 64$$
$$\sqrt{x^2} = \sqrt{64}$$
$$|x| = 8$$
$$x = \pm 8$$

---

* With square roots, the index is not written, $\sqrt[2]{9} = \sqrt{9}$.

The following rules are useful for manipulating roots:

$$\sqrt[n]{xy} = \sqrt[n]{x}\,\sqrt[n]{y} \qquad\qquad \text{For example, } \sqrt{3x} = \sqrt{3}\,\sqrt{x}\,.$$

$$\sqrt[n]{\frac{x}{y}} = \frac{\sqrt[n]{x}}{\sqrt[n]{y}} \qquad\qquad \text{For example, } \sqrt[3]{\frac{x}{8}} = \frac{\sqrt[3]{x}}{\sqrt[3]{8}} = \frac{\sqrt[3]{x}}{2}\,.$$

Caution: $\sqrt[n]{x+y} \neq \sqrt[n]{x} + \sqrt[n]{y}$. For example, $\sqrt{x+5} \neq \sqrt{x} + \sqrt{5}$. Also, $\sqrt{x^2 + y^2} \neq x + y$. This common mistake occurs because it is similar to the following valid property: $\sqrt{(x+y)^2} = x + y$ (If $x + y$ can be negative, then it must be written with the absolute value symbol: $|x + y|$). Note, in the valid formula, it's the whole term, $x + y$, that is squared, not the individual x and y.

To add two roots, both the index and the base must be the same. For example, $\sqrt[3]{2} + \sqrt[4]{2}$ cannot be added because the indices are different, nor can $\sqrt{2} + \sqrt{3}$ be added because the bases are different. However, $\sqrt[3]{2} + \sqrt[3]{2} = 2\sqrt[3]{2}$. In this case, the roots can be added because both the indices and bases are the same. Sometimes radicals with different bases can actually be added once they have been simplified to look alike. For example, $\sqrt{28} + \sqrt{7} = \sqrt{4 \cdot 7} + \sqrt{7} = \sqrt{4}\sqrt{7} + \sqrt{7} = 2\sqrt{7} + \sqrt{7} = 3\sqrt{7}\,.$

You need to know the approximations of the following roots: $\quad \sqrt{2} \approx 1.4 \qquad \sqrt{3} \approx 1.7 \qquad \sqrt{5} \approx 2.2$

Example 4: Given the system $\begin{array}{c} x^2 = 4 \\ y^3 = -8 \end{array}$, which of the following is NOT necessarily true?

        (A) $y < 0$
        (B) $x < 5$
        (C) y is an integer
        (D) $x > y$
        (E) x/y is an integer

$y^3 = -8$ yields one cube root, $y = -2$. However, $x^2 = 4$ yields two square roots, $x = \pm 2$. Now, if $x = 2$, then $x > y$; but if $x = -2$, then $x = y$. Hence, choice (D) is not necessarily true. The answer is (D).

Example 5: If $x < 0$ and y is 5 more than the square of x, which one of the following expresses x in terms of y?

        (A) $x = \sqrt{y - 5}$
        (B) $x = -\sqrt{y - 5}$
        (C) $x = \sqrt{y + 5}$
        (D) $x = \sqrt{y^2 - 5}$
        (E) $x = -\sqrt{y^2 - 5}$

Translating the expression *"y is 5 more than the square of x"* into an equation yields:

$$y = x^2 + 5$$

$$y - 5 = x^2$$

$$\pm\sqrt{y - 5} = x$$

Since we are given that $x < 0$, we take the negative root, $-\sqrt{y - 5} = x$. The answer is (B).

RATIONALIZING

A fraction is not considered simplified until all the radicals have been removed from the denominator. If a denominator contains a single term with a square root, it can be rationalized by multiplying both the numerator and denominator by that square root. If the denominator contains square roots separated by a plus or minus sign, then multiply both the numerator and denominator by the conjugate, which is formed by merely changing the sign between the roots.

Example: Rationalize the fraction $\dfrac{2}{3\sqrt{5}}$.

Multiply top and bottom of the fraction by $\sqrt{5}$:

$$\frac{2}{3\sqrt{5}}\cdot\frac{\sqrt{5}}{\sqrt{5}}=\frac{2\sqrt{5}}{3\cdot\sqrt{25}}=\frac{2\sqrt{5}}{3\cdot 5}=\frac{2\sqrt{5}}{15}$$

Example: Rationalize the fraction $\dfrac{2}{3-\sqrt{5}}$.

Multiply top and bottom of the fraction by the conjugate $3+\sqrt{5}$:

$$\frac{2}{3-\sqrt{5}}\cdot\frac{3+\sqrt{5}}{3+\sqrt{5}}=\frac{2\left(3+\sqrt{5}\right)}{3^2+3\sqrt{5}-3\sqrt{5}-\left(\sqrt{5}\right)^2}=\frac{2\left(3+\sqrt{5}\right)}{9-5}=\frac{2\left(3+\sqrt{5}\right)}{4}=\frac{3+\sqrt{5}}{2}$$

Problem Set O:

1. If $x\neq 0$, $\left(\dfrac{2y^3}{x^2}\right)^4\cdot x^{10}=$

    (A) $16y^{12}x^2$ 　　(B) $8y^7x^2$ 　　(C) $16\dfrac{y^{12}}{x^8}$ 　　(D) $8\dfrac{y^{12}}{x^8}$ 　　(E) $\dfrac{y^{12}}{16x^8}$

2. $\sqrt{(31-6)(16+9)}=$

    (A) 5 　　(B) 10 　　(C) 25 　　(D) 50 　　(E) 625

3. What is the largest integer n such that 2^n is a factor of 20^8 ?

    (A) 1 　　(B) 2 　　(C) 4 　　(D) 8 　　(E) 16

4. $\dfrac{55^5}{5^{55}}=$

    (A) $\dfrac{11}{5^{50}}$ 　　(B) $\dfrac{11}{5^{55}}$ 　　(C) $\dfrac{11^5}{5^{50}}$ 　　(D) $\dfrac{11^5}{5^5}$ 　　(E) $\dfrac{11^5}{5}$

5. If $x=1/9$, then $\sqrt{x}-x^2=$

    (A) 0 　　(B) 1/9 　　(C) 26/81 　　(D) 1/3 　　(E) 1

6. $\left(9^{x}\right)^{3} =$

    (A) 3^{3x} (B) 3^{2+3x} (C) 3^{6x} (D) $729x^{3}$ (E) $9^{x^{3}}$

7. If $x = 4$, then $-2^{2\sqrt{x}} + 2 =$

    (A) -14 (B) -8 (C) -2 (D) 0 (E) 18

8. $\sqrt{\dfrac{25 + 10x + x^{2}}{2}} =$

    (A) $\dfrac{\sqrt{2}(5 - x)}{2}$ (B) $\dfrac{\sqrt{5 + x}}{\sqrt{2}}$ (C) $\dfrac{\sqrt{2}(5 + x)}{2}$ (D) $\dfrac{5 + x}{2}$ (E) $\dfrac{5 - x}{2}$

9. $\dfrac{2 + \sqrt{5}}{2 - \sqrt{5}} =$

    (A) $-9 - 4\sqrt{5}$ (B) $-1 - \dfrac{4}{9}\sqrt{5}$ (C) $1 + \dfrac{4}{9}\sqrt{5}$ (D) $9 + 4\sqrt{5}$ (E) 20

10. $2^{12} + 2^{12} + 2^{12} + 2^{12} =$

    (A) 4^{12} (B) 2^{14} (C) 2^{16} (D) 4^{16} (E) 2^{48}

11. $\left(\dfrac{\left(x^{2}y\right)^{3} z}{xyz}\right)^{3} =$

    (A) $x^{8}y^{5}$ (B) xy^{6} (C) $x^{15}y^{6}z$ (D) $x^{3}y^{6}$ (E) $x^{15}y^{6}$

12. If $2^{2x} = 16^{x+2}$, what is the value of x ?

    (A) -4 (B) -2 (C) 0 (D) 2 (E) 4

13. If $(x - y)^{\frac{1}{3}} = (x + y)^{-\frac{1}{3}}$, then which one of the following must be true?

    (A) $x = 1$ (B) $y = 1$ (C) $x^{2} - y^{2} = 1$ (D) $x + y^{2} = 1$ (E) $x^{2} - 2xy + y^{2} = 1$

Answers and Solutions to Problem Set O

1.

$$\left(\frac{2y^3}{x^2}\right)^4 \cdot x^{10} = \frac{\left(2y^3\right)^4}{\left(x^2\right)^4} \cdot x^{10} = \qquad \text{by the rule } \left(\frac{x}{y}\right)^a = \frac{x^a}{y^a}$$

$$\frac{2^4 \cdot \left(y^3\right)^4}{\left(x^2\right)^4} \cdot x^{10} = \qquad \text{by the rule } \left(xy\right)^a = x^a \cdot y^a$$

$$\frac{2^4 \cdot y^{12}}{x^8} \cdot x^{10} = \qquad \text{by the rule } \left(x^a\right)^b = x^{ab}$$

$$2^4 \cdot y^{12} \cdot x^2 = \qquad \text{by the rule } \frac{x^a}{x^b} = x^{a-b}$$

$$16 \cdot y^{12} \cdot x^2$$

The answer is (A).

2.

$$\sqrt{(31-6)(16+9)} =$$

$$\sqrt{25 \cdot 25} =$$

$$\sqrt{25}\sqrt{25} =$$

$$5 \cdot 5 =$$

$$25$$

The answer is (C).

3. Begin by completely factoring 20:

$$20^8 = \left(2 \cdot 2 \cdot 5\right)^8 =$$

$$2^8 \cdot 2^8 \cdot 5^8 = \qquad \text{by Rule 3, } \left(xy\right)^a = x^a \cdot y^a *$$

$$2^{16} \cdot 5^8 \qquad \text{by Rule 1, } x^a \cdot x^b = x^{a+b}$$

The expression 2^{16} represents all the factors of 20^8 of the form 2^n. Hence, 16 is the largest such number, and the answer is (D).

4. Begin by factoring 55 in the top of the fraction:

$$\frac{55^5}{5^{55}} = \frac{\left(5 \cdot 11\right)^5}{5^{55}} =$$

$$\frac{5^5 \cdot 11^5}{5^{55}} = \qquad \text{by Rule 3, } \left(xy\right)^a = x^a \cdot y^a$$

$$\frac{11^5}{5^{50}} \qquad \text{by Rule 5, } \frac{x^a}{x^b} = \frac{1}{x^{b-a}}$$

The answer is (C).

5. $\sqrt{x} - x^2 = \sqrt{\frac{1}{9}} - \left(\frac{1}{9}\right)^2 = \frac{1}{3} - \frac{1}{81} = \frac{27}{27} \cdot \frac{1}{3} - \frac{1}{81} = \frac{27-1}{81} = \frac{26}{81}$. The answer is (C).

---

* Note, Rule 3 can be extended to any number of terms by repeatedly applying the rule. For example,
$\left(xyz\right)^a = \left(\left[xy\right]z\right)^a = \left[xy\right]^a \cdot z^a = x^a y^a z^a$.

6.

$$\left(9^x\right)^3 = 9^{3x} = \qquad \text{by the rule } \left(x^a\right)^b = x^{ab}$$

$$\left(3^2\right)^{3x} = \qquad \text{since } 9 = 3^2$$

$$3^{6x} \qquad \text{again by the rule } \left(x^a\right)^b = x^{ab}$$

The answer is (C). Note, this is considered to be a hard problem.

7.   Plugging $x = 4$ into the expression $-2^{2\sqrt{x}} + 2$ yields

$$-2^{2\sqrt{4}} + 2 = -2^{2 \cdot 2} + 2 = -2^4 + 2 = -16 + 2 = -14$$

The answer is (A).

8.

$$\sqrt{\frac{25 + 10x + x^2}{2}} = \sqrt{\frac{(5+x)^2}{2}} = \qquad \text{since } 25 + 10x + x^2 \text{ factors into } (5+x)^2$$

$$\frac{\sqrt{(5+x)^2}}{\sqrt{2}} = \qquad \text{by the rule } \sqrt[n]{\frac{x}{y}} = \frac{\sqrt[n]{x}}{\sqrt[n]{y}}$$

$$\frac{5+x}{\sqrt{2}} = \qquad \text{since } \sqrt{x^2} = x$$

$$\frac{5+x}{\sqrt{2}} \cdot \frac{\sqrt{2}}{\sqrt{2}} = \qquad \text{rationalizing the denominator}$$

$$\frac{\sqrt{2}(5+x)}{2}$$

Hence, the answer is (C).

9. $\dfrac{2+\sqrt{5}}{2-\sqrt{5}} = \dfrac{2+\sqrt{5}}{2-\sqrt{5}} \cdot \dfrac{2+\sqrt{5}}{2+\sqrt{5}} = \dfrac{4+4\sqrt{5}+5}{4-5} = \dfrac{9+4\sqrt{5}}{-1} = -9 - 4\sqrt{5}$. Hence, the answer is (A).

10. $2^{12} + 2^{12} + 2^{12} + 2^{12} = 4 \cdot 2^{12} = 2^2 \cdot 2^{12} = 2^{2+12} = 2^{14}$. The answer is (B).

11. $\left(\dfrac{\left(x^2 y\right)^3 z}{xyz}\right)^3 = \left(\dfrac{\left(x^2 y\right)^3}{xy}\right)^3 = \left(\dfrac{\left(x^2\right)^3 y^3}{xy}\right)^3 = \left(\dfrac{x^6 y^3}{xy}\right)^3 = \left(x^5 y^2\right)^3 = \left(x^5\right)^3 \left(y^2\right)^3 = x^{15} y^6$

Hence, the answer is (E).

12. Our goal here is to write both sides of the equation in terms of the base 2 and then equate the exponents. To that end, write 16 as 2^4:

$$2^{2x} = \left(2^4\right)^{x+2}$$
$$2^{2x} = 2^{4(x+2)}$$

Since we have written both sides of the equation in terms of the base 2, we now equate the exponents:

$$2x = 4(x + 2)$$
$$2x = 4x + 8$$
$$-2x = 8$$
$$x = -4$$

The answer is (A).

13. First, let's reciprocate the expression $(x+y)^{-\frac{1}{3}}$ to eliminate the negative exponent:

$$(x-y)^{-\frac{1}{3}} = \frac{1}{(x+y)^{\frac{1}{3}}}$$

Cubing both sides of this equation to eliminate the cube roots yields

$$x - y = \frac{1}{x+y}$$

Multiplying both sides of this equation by $x + y$ yields

$$(x - y)(x + y) = 1$$

Multiplying out the left side of this equation yields

$$x^2 + xy - xy - y^2 = 1$$

Reducing yields

$$x^2 - y^2 = 1$$

The answer is (C).

Factoring

To factor an algebraic expression is to rewrite it as a product of two or more expressions, called factors. In general, any expression on the test that can be factored should be factored, and any expression that can be unfactored (multiplied out) should be unfactored.

DISTRIBUTIVE RULE

The most basic type of factoring involves the distributive rule:

$$ax + ay = a(x + y)$$

When this rule is applied from left to right, it is called factoring. When the rule is applied from right to left, it is called distributing.

For example, $3h + 3k = 3(h + k)$, and $5xy + 45x = 5xy + 9 \cdot 5x = 5x(y + 9)$. The distributive rule can be generalized to any number of terms. For three terms, it looks like $ax + ay + az = a(x + y + z)$. For example, $2x + 4y + 8 = 2x + 2 \cdot 2y + 2 \cdot 4 = 2(x + 2y + 4)$. For another example, $x^2 y^2 + xy^3 + y^5 = y^2\left(x^2 + xy + y^3\right)$.

Example 1: If $x - y = 9$, then $\left(x - \dfrac{y}{3}\right) - \left(y - \dfrac{x}{3}\right) =$

(A) −4   (B) −3   (C) 0   (D) 12   (E) 27

$$\left(x - \frac{y}{3}\right) - \left(y - \frac{x}{3}\right) =$$

$x - \dfrac{y}{3} - y + \dfrac{x}{3} =$ by distributing the negative sign

$\dfrac{4}{3}x - \dfrac{4}{3}y =$ by combining the fractions

$\dfrac{4}{3}(x - y) =$ by factoring out the common factor 4/3

$\dfrac{4}{3}(9) =$ since $x - y = 9$

12

The answer is (D).

Example 2: $\dfrac{2^{20}-2^{19}}{2^{11}} =$

(A) $2^9 - 2^{19}$ (B) $\dfrac{1}{2^{11}}$ (C) 2^8 (D) 2^{10} (E) 2^{28}

$$\dfrac{2^{20}-2^{19}}{2^{11}} = \dfrac{2^{19+1}-2^{19}}{2^{11}} =$$

$$\dfrac{2^{19}\cdot 2^1 - 2^{19}}{2^{11}} = \qquad \text{by the rule } x^a \cdot x^b = x^{a+b}$$

$$\dfrac{2^{19}(2-1)}{2^{11}} = \qquad \text{by the distributive property } ax + ay = a(x+y)$$

$$\dfrac{2^{19}}{2^{11}} =$$

$$2^8 \qquad \text{by the rule } \dfrac{x^a}{x^b} = x^{a-b}$$

The answer is (C).

DIFFERENCE OF SQUARES

One of the most important formulas on the ACT is the difference of squares:

$$\boxed{x^2 - y^2 = \left(x+y\right)\left(x-y\right)}$$

Caution: a sum of squares, $x^2 + y^2$, does not factor.

Example 3: If $x \neq -2$, then $\dfrac{8x^2 - 32}{4x+8} =$

(A) $2(x-2)$ (B) $2(x-4)$ (C) $8(x+2)$ (D) $x-2$ (E) $x+4$

In most algebraic expressions involving multiplication or division, you won't actually multiply or divide, rather you will factor and cancel, as in this problem.

$$\dfrac{8x^2 - 32}{4x+8} =$$

$$\dfrac{8\left(x^2-4\right)}{4\left(x+2\right)} = \qquad \text{by the distributive property } ax + ay = a(x+y)$$

$$\dfrac{8(x+2)(x-2)}{4(x+2)} = \qquad \text{by the difference of squares } x^2 - y^2 = (x+y)(x-y)$$

$$2(x-2) \qquad \text{by canceling common factors}$$

The answer is (A).

PERFECT SQUARE TRINOMIALS

Like the difference of squares formula, perfect square trinomial formulas are very common on the ACT.

$$x^2 + 2xy + y^2 = (x + y)^2$$
$$x^2 - 2xy + y^2 = (x - y)^2$$

For example, $x^2 + 6x + 9 = x^2 + 2(3x) + 3^2 = (x + 3)^2$. Note, in a perfect square trinomial, the middle term is twice the product of the square roots of the outer terms.

Example 4:   If $r^2 - 2rs + s^2 = 4$, then $(r - s)^6 =$

    (A) -4 (B) 4   (C) 8   (D) 16   (E) 64

$$r^2 - 2rs + s^2 = 4$$

$$(r - s)^2 = 4 \qquad \text{by the formula } x^2 - 2xy + y^2 = (x - y)^2$$

$$\left[(r - s)^2\right]^3 = 4^3 \qquad \text{by cubing both sides of the equation}$$

$$(r - s)^6 = 64 \qquad \text{by the rule } \left(x^a\right)^b = x^{ab}$$

The answer is (E).

GENERAL TRINOMIALS

$$x^2 + (a + b)x + ab = (x + a)(x + b)$$

The expression $x^2 + (a + b)x + ab$ tells us that we need two numbers whose product is the last term and whose sum is the coefficient of the middle term. Consider the trinomial $(x + 2)(x + 3)$. Now, two factors of 6 are 1 and 6, but $1 + 6 \neq 5$. However, 2 and 3 are also factors of 6, and $2 + 3 = 5$. Hence,

$$x^2 + 5x + 6 = (x + 2)(x + 3)$$

Example 5:   Which of the following could be a solution of the equation $x^2 - 7x - 18 = 0$?

    (A) -1 (B) 0   (C) 2   (D) 7   (E) 9

Now, both 2 and -9 are factors of 18, and $2 + (-9) = -7$. Hence, $x^2 - 7x - 18 = (x + 2)(x - 9) = 0$. Setting each factor equal to zero yields $x + 2 = 0$ and $x - 9 = 0$. Solving these equations yields $x = -2$ and 9. The answer is (E).

COMPLETE FACTORING

When factoring an expression, first check for a common factor, then check for a difference of squares, then for a perfect square trinomial, and then for a general trinomial.

Example 6:   Factor the expression $2x^3 - 2x^2 - 12x$ completely.

Solution: First check for a common factor: $2x$ is common to each term. Factoring $2x$ out of each term yields $2x(x^2 - x - 6)$. Next, there is no difference of squares, and $x^2 - x - 6$ is not a perfect square trinomial since x does not equal twice the product of the square roots of x^2 and 6. Now, -3 and 2 are factors of -6 whose sum is -1. Hence, $2x(x^2 - x - 6)$ factors into $2x(x - 3)(x + 2)$.

Problem Set P:

1. If $3y + 5 = 7x$, then $21y - 49x =$

    (A) -40
    (B) -35
    (C) -10
    (D) 0
    (E) 15

2. If $x - y = p$, then $2x^2 - 4xy + 2y^2 =$

    (A) p
    (B) $2p$
    (C) $4p$
    (D) p^2
    (E) $2p^2$

3. If $p \neq 0$ and $p = \sqrt{2pq - q^2}$, then in terms of q, $p =$

    (A) q
    (B) q^2
    (C) $2q$
    (D) $-2q$
    (E) $q/4$

4. If $\dfrac{x^2 + 2x - 10}{5} = 1$, then x could equal

    (A) -5
    (B) -3
    (C) 0
    (D) 10
    (E) 15

5. What is the absolute value of twice the difference of the roots of the equation $5y^2 - 20y + 15 = 0$?

    (A) 0
    (B) 1
    (C) 2
    (D) 3
    (E) 4

6. If $x \neq -2$, then $\dfrac{7x^2 + 28x + 28}{(x+2)^2} =$

    (A) 7
    (B) 8
    (C) 9
    (D) 10
    (E) 11

7. $\dfrac{7^9 + 7^8}{8} =$

(A) 1/8

(B) 7/8

(C) $\dfrac{7^7}{8}$

(D) 7^8

(E) 7^9

8. If $x + y = 10$ and $x - y = 5$, then $x^2 - y^2 =$
(A) 50
(B) 60
(C) 75
(D) 80
(E) 100

9. $x(x - y) - z(x - y) =$
(A) $x - y$
(B) $x - z$
(C) $(x - y)(x - z)$
(D) $(x - y)(x + z)$
(E) $(x - y)(z - x)$

10. If $(x - y)^2 = x^2 + y^2$, then which one of the following statements must also be true?
I. $x = 0$
II. $y = 0$
III. $xy = 0$

(A) None
(B) I only
(C) II only
(D) III only
(E) II and III only

11. If x and y are prime numbers such that $x > y > 2$, then $x^2 - y^2$ must be divisible by which one of the following numbers?
(A) 3
(B) 4
(C) 5
(D) 9
(E) 12

12. If $\dfrac{x + y}{x - y} = \dfrac{1}{2}$, then $\dfrac{xy + x^2}{xy - x^2} =$
(A) −4.2
(B) −1/2
(C) 1.1
(D) 3
(E) 5.3

Answers and Solutions to Problem Set P

1. First, interchanging 5 and $7x$ in the expression $3y + 5 = 7x$ yields $3y - 7x = -5$. Next, factoring $21y - 49x$ yields

$$21y - 49x =$$
$$7 \cdot 3y - 7 \cdot 7x =$$
$$7(3y - 7x) =$$
$$7(-5) = \qquad \text{since } 3y - 7x = -5$$
$$-35$$

The answer is (B).

2. $$2x^2 - 4xy + 2y^2 =$$
$$2(x^2 - 2xy + y^2) = \qquad \text{by factoring out the common factor 2}$$
$$2(x - y)^2 = \qquad \text{by the formula } x^2 - 2xy + y^2 = (x - y)^2$$
$$2p^2 \qquad \text{since } x - y = p$$

The answer is (E).

3. $$p = \sqrt{2pq - q^2}$$
$$p^2 = 2pq - q^2 \qquad \text{by squaring both sides}$$
$$p^2 - 2pq + q^2 = 0 \qquad \text{by subtracting } 2pq \text{ and adding } q^2 \text{ to both sides}$$
$$(p - q)^2 = 0 \qquad \text{by the formula } x^2 - 2xy + y^2 = (x - y)^2$$
$$p - q = 0 \qquad \text{by taking the square root of both sides}$$
$$p = q \qquad \text{by adding } q \text{ to both sides}$$

The answer is (A).

4. $$\frac{x^2 + 2x - 10}{5} = 1$$
$$x^2 + 2x - 10 = 5 \qquad \text{by multiplying both sides by 5}$$
$$x^2 + 2x - 15 = 0 \qquad \text{by subtracting 5 from both sides}$$
$$(x + 5)(x - 3) = 0 \qquad \text{since } 5 \cdot 3 = 15 \text{ and } 5 - 3 = 2$$
$$x + 5 = 0 \text{ and } x - 3 = 0 \qquad \text{by setting each factor equal to zero}$$
$$x = -5 \text{ and } x = 3$$

The answer is (A).

5. Begin by factoring out the common factor in the equation $5y^2 - 20y + 15 = 0$:

$$5(y^2 - 4y + 3) = 0$$

Dividing both sides of this equation by 5 yields $\qquad\qquad y^2 - 4y + 3 = 0$
Since $3 + 1 = 4$, the trinomial factors into $\qquad\qquad (y - 3)(y - 1) = 0$
Setting each factor equal to zero yields $\qquad\qquad y - 3 = 0 \text{ and } y - 1 = 0$

Solving these equations yields $y = 3$ and $y = 1$. Now, the difference of 3 and 1 is 2 and twice 2 is 4. Further, the difference of 1 and 3 is -2 and twice -2 is -4. Now, the absolute value of both 4 and -4 is 4. The answer is (E).

6.
$$\frac{7x^2 + 28x + 28}{(x+2)^2} =$$

$$\frac{7(x^2 + 4x + 4)}{(x+2)^2} = \qquad \text{by factoring out 7}$$

$$\frac{7(x+2)^2}{(x+2)^2} = \qquad \text{by the formula } x^2 + 2xy + y^2 = (x+y)^2$$

$$7 \qquad \text{by canceling the common factor } (x+2)^2$$

The answer is (A).

7.
$$\frac{7^9 + 7^8}{8} =$$

$$\frac{7^8 \cdot 7 + 7^8}{8} = \qquad \text{since } 7^9 = 7^8 \cdot 7$$

$$\frac{7^8(7+1)}{8} = \qquad \text{by factoring out the common factor } 7^8$$

$$\frac{7^8(8)}{8} =$$

$$7^8$$

Hence, the answer is (D). Note, this is considered to be a very hard problem.

8.
$$x^2 - y^2 =$$

$$(x+y)(x-y) = \qquad \text{since } x^2 - y^2 \text{ is a difference of squares}$$

$$(10)(5) = \qquad \text{since } x + y = 10 \text{ and } x - y = 5$$

$$50$$

The answer is (A). This problem can also be solved by adding the two equations. However, that approach will lead to long, messy fractions. Writers of the ACT put questions like this one on the ACT to see whether you will discover the short cut. The premise being that those students who do not see the short cut will take longer to solve the problem and therefore will have less time to finish the test.

9. Noticing that $x - y$ is a common factor, we factor it out:

$$x(x - y) - z(x - y) = (x - y)(x - z)$$

The answer is (C).

Method II
Sometimes a complicated expression can be simplified by making a substitution. In the expression $x(x - y) - z(x - y)$ replace $x - y$ with w:

$$xw - zw$$

Now, the structure appears much simpler. Factoring out the common factor w yields

$$w(x - z)$$

Finally, re-substitute $x - y$ for w:

$$(x - y)(x - z)$$

10. $(x - y)^2 = x^2 + y^2$

   $x^2 - 2xy + y^2 = x^2 + y^2$ by the formula $x^2 - 2xy + y^2 = (x - y)^2$

   $-2xy = 0$ by subtracting x^2 and y^2 from both sides of the equation

   $xy = 0$ by dividing both sides of the equation by -2

Hence, Statement III is true, which eliminates choices (A), (B), and (C). However, Statement II is false. For example, if $y = 5$ and $x = 0$, then $xy = 0 \cdot 5 = 0$. A similar analysis shows that Statement I is false. The answer is (D).

11. The Difference of Squares formula yields $x^2 - y^2 = (x + y)(x - y)$. Now, both x and y must be odd because 2 is the only even prime and $x > y > 2$. Remember that the sum (or difference) of two odd numbers is even. Hence, $(x + y)(x - y)$ is the product of two even numbers and therefore is divisible by 4. To show this explicitly, let $x + y = 2p$ and let $x - y = 2q$. Then $(x + y)(x - y) = 2p \cdot 2q = 4pq$. Since we have written $(x + y)(x - y)$ as a multiple of 4, it is divisible by 4. The answer is (B).

Method II (substitution):
Let $x = 5$ and $y = 3$, then $x > y > 2$ and $x^2 - y^2 = 5^2 - 3^2 = 25 - 9 = 16$. Since 4 is the only number listed that divides evenly into 16, the answer is (B).

12. Solution:

$$\frac{xy + x^2}{xy - x^2} =$$

$$\frac{x(y + x)}{x(y - x)} =$$ by factoring out x from both the top and bottom expressions

$$\frac{y + x}{y - x} =$$ by canceling the common factor x

$$\frac{x + y}{-(x - y)} =$$ by factoring out the negative sign in the bottom and then rearranging

$$-\frac{x + y}{x - y} =$$ by recalling that a negative fraction can be written three ways: $\frac{a}{-b} = -\frac{a}{b} = \frac{-a}{b}$

$$-\frac{1}{2}$$ by replacing $\frac{x + y}{x - y}$ with 1/2

The answer is (B).

Algebraic Expressions

A mathematical expression that contains a variable is called an algebraic expression. Some examples of algebraic expressions are x^2, $3x - 2y$, $2z\left(y^3 - \dfrac{1}{z^2}\right)$. Two algebraic expressions are called like terms if both the variable parts and the exponents are identical. That is, the only parts of the expressions that can differ are the coefficients. For example, $5y^3$ and $\dfrac{3}{2}y^3$ are like terms, as are $x + y^2$ and $-7(x + y^2)$. However, x^3 and y^3 are not like terms, nor are $x - y$ and $2 - y$.

ADDING & SUBTRACTING ALGEBRAIC EXPRESSIONS

Only like terms may be added or subtracted. To add or subtract like terms, merely add or subtract their coefficients:

$$x^2 + 3x^2 = (1 + 3)x^2 = 4x^2$$

$$2\sqrt{x} - 5\sqrt{x} = (2 - 5)\sqrt{x} = -3\sqrt{x}$$

$$.5\left(x + \frac{1}{y}\right)^2 + .2\left(x + \frac{1}{y}\right)^2 = (.5 + .2)\left(x + \frac{1}{y}\right)^2 = .7\left(x + \frac{1}{y}\right)^2$$

$$\left(3x^3 + 7x^2 + 2x + 4\right) + \left(2x^2 - 2x - 6\right) = 3x^3 + (7 + 2)x^2 + (2 - 2)x + (4 - 6) = 3x^3 + 9x^2 - 2$$

You may add or multiply algebraic expressions in any order. This is called the commutative property:

$$\boxed{x + y = y + x}$$

$$\boxed{xy = yx}$$

For example, $-2x + 5x = 5x + (-2x) = (5 - 2)x = 3x$ and $(x - y)(-3) = (-3)(x - y) = (-3)x - (-3)y = -3x + 3y$.

Caution: the commutative property does not apply to division or subtraction:

$$2 = 6 \div 3 \neq 3 \div 6 = 1/2$$

and

$$-1 = 2 - 3 \neq 3 - 2 = 1$$

When adding or multiplying algebraic expressions, you may regroup the terms. This is called the associative property:

$$\boxed{x + (y + z) = (x + y) + z}$$

$$\boxed{x(yz) = (xy)z}$$

Notice in these formulas that the variables have not been moved, only the way they are grouped has changed: on the left side of the formulas the last two variables are grouped together, and on the right side of the formulas the first two variables are grouped together.

For example, $(x - 2x) + 5x = (x + [-2x]) + 5x = x + (-2x + 5x) = x + 3x = 4x$

and

$2(12x) = (2 \cdot 12)x = 24x$

The associative property doesn't apply to division or subtraction: $4 = 8 \div 2 = 8 \div (4 \div 2) \neq (8 \div 4) \div 2 = 2 \div 2 = 1$

and

$-6 = -3 - 3 = (-1 - 2) - 3 \neq -1 - (2 - 3) = -1 - (-1) = -1 + 1 = 0.$

Notice in the first example that we changed the subtraction into negative addition: $(x - 2x) = (x + [-2x])$. This allowed us to apply the associative property over addition.

PARENTHESES

When simplifying expressions with nested parentheses, work from the inner most parentheses out:

$$5x + (y - (2x - 3x)) = 5x + (y - (-x)) = 5x + (y + x) = 6x + y$$

Sometimes when an expression involves several pairs of parentheses, one or more pairs are written as brackets. This makes the expression easier to read:

$$2x(x - [y + 2(x - y)]) =$$
$$2x(x - [y + 2x - 2y]) =$$
$$2x(x - [2x - y]) =$$
$$2x(x - 2x + y) =$$
$$2x(-x + y) =$$
$$-2x^2 + 2xy$$

ORDER OF OPERATIONS: (PEMDAS)

When simplifying algebraic expressions, perform operations within parentheses first and then exponents and then multiplication and then division and then addition and lastly subtraction. This can be remembered by the mnemonic:

PEMDAS
Please **E**xcuse **M**y **D**ear **A**unt **S**ally

This mnemonic isn't quite precise enough. Multiplication and division are actually tied in order of operation, as is the pair addition and subtraction. When multiplication and division, or addition and subtraction, appear at the same level in an expression, perform the operations from left to right. For example, $6 \div 2 \times 4 = (6 \div 2) \times 4 = 3 \times 4 = 12$. To emphasize this left-to-right order, we can use parentheses in the mnemonic: **PE(MD)(AS)**.

Example 1: $2 - \left(5 - 3^3[4 \div 2 + 1]\right) =$

(A) –21   (B) 32   (C) 45   (D) 60   (E) 78

$2 - \left(5 - 3^3[4 \div 2 + 1]\right) =$

$\quad 2 - \left(5 - 3^3[2 + 1]\right) =$ By performing the division within the innermost parentheses

$\quad\quad 2 - \left(5 - 3^3[3]\right) =$ By performing the addition within the innermost parentheses

$\quad\quad\quad 2 - (5 - 27[3]) =$ By performing the exponentiation

$\quad\quad\quad\quad 2 - (5 - 81) =$ By performing the multiplication within the parentheses

$\quad\quad\quad\quad\quad 2 - (-76) =$ By performing the subtraction within the parentheses

$\quad\quad\quad\quad\quad\quad 2 + 76 =$ By multiplying the two negatives

$\quad\quad\quad\quad\quad\quad\quad 78$

The answer is (E).

FOIL MULTIPLICATION

You may recall from algebra that when multiplying two expressions you use the FOIL method: **F**irst, **O**uter, **I**nner, **L**ast:

$$(x + y)(x + y) = xx + xy + xy + yy$$

Simplifying the right side yields $(x + y)(x + y) = x^2 + 2xy + y^2$. For the product $(x - y)(x - y)$ we get $(x - y)(x - y) = x^2 - 2xy + y^2$. These types of products occur often, so it is worthwhile to memorize the formulas. Nevertheless, you should still learn the FOIL method of multiplying because the formulas do not apply in all cases.

Examples (FOIL):

$$(2 - y)(x - y^2) = 2x - 2y^2 - xy + yy^2 = 2x - 2y^2 - xy + y^3$$

$$\left(\frac{1}{x} - y\right)\left(x - \frac{1}{y}\right) = \frac{1}{x}x - \frac{1}{x}\frac{1}{y} - xy + y\frac{1}{y} = 1 - \frac{1}{xy} - xy + 1 = 2 - \frac{1}{xy} - xy$$

$$\left(\frac{1}{2} - y\right)^2 = \left(\frac{1}{2} - y\right)\left(\frac{1}{2} - y\right) = \left(\frac{1}{2}\right)^2 - 2\left(\frac{1}{2}\right)y + y^2 = \frac{1}{4} - y + y^2$$

DIVISION OF ALGEBRAIC EXPRESSIONS

When dividing algebraic expressions, the following formula is useful:

$$\frac{x + y}{z} = \frac{x}{z} + \frac{y}{z}$$

This formula generalizes to any number of terms.

Examples:

$$\frac{x^2 + y}{x} = \frac{x^2}{x} + \frac{y}{x} = x^{2-1} + \frac{y}{x} = x + \frac{y}{x}$$

$$\frac{x^2 + 2y - x^3}{x^2} = \frac{x^2}{x^2} + \frac{2y}{x^2} - \frac{x^3}{x^2} = x^{2-2} + \frac{2y}{x^2} - x^{3-2} = x^0 + \frac{2y}{x^2} - x = 1 + \frac{2y}{x^2} - x$$

When there is more than a single variable in the denomination, we usually factor the expression and then cancel, instead of using the above formula.

Example 2: $\dfrac{x^2 - 2x + 1}{x - 1} =$

        (A) $x + 1$ (B) $-x - 1$ (C) $-x + 1$ (D) $x - 1$ (E) $x - 2$

$\dfrac{x^2 - 2x + 1}{x - 1} = \dfrac{(x-1)(x-1)}{x-1} = x - 1$. The answer is (D).

Problem Set Q:

1. $(x^2 + 2)(x - x^3) =$

    (A) $x^4 - x^2 + 2$ (B) $-x^5 - x^3 + 2x$ (C) $x^5 - 2x$ (D) $3x^3 + 2x$ (E) $x^5 + x^3 + 2x$

2. $-2\left(3 - x\left[\dfrac{5 + y - 2}{x}\right] - 7 + 2 \cdot 3^2\right) =$

    (A) $2y - 11$ (B) $2y + 1$ (C) $x - 2$ (D) $x + 22$ (E) $2y - 22$

3. For all real numbers a and b, where $a \cdot b \neq 0$, let $a \lozenge b = ab - 1$, which of the following must be true?

    I. $a \lozenge b = b \lozenge a$

    II. $\dfrac{a \lozenge a}{a} = 1 \lozenge 1$

    III. $(a \lozenge b) \lozenge c = a \lozenge (b \lozenge c)$

    (A) I only   (B) II only   (C) III only   (D) I and II only   (E) I and III only

4. $\left(x + \dfrac{1}{2}\right)^2 - (2x - 4)^2 =$

    (A) $-3x^2 - 15x + 65/4$ (B) $3x^2 + 16x$ (C) $-3x^2 + 17x - 63/4$ (D) $5x^2 + 65/4$ (E) $3x^2$

5. If $x = 2$ and $y = -3$, then $y^2 - \left(x - \left[y + \dfrac{1}{2}\right]\right) - 2 \cdot 3 =$

    (A) $-39/2$ (B) $-3/2$ (C) 0 (D) 31 (E) 43

6. $4(xy)^3 + (x^3 - y^3)^2 =$

    (A) $x^3 - y^3$ (B) $(x^2 + y^2)^3$ (C) $(x^3 + y^3)^3$ (D) $(x^3 - y^3)^2$ (E) $(x^3 + y^3)^2$

7. If $\dfrac{a}{b} = -\dfrac{2}{3}$, then $\dfrac{b - a}{a} =$

    (A) $-5/2$ (B) $-5/3$ (C) $-1/3$ (D) 0 (E) 7

8. The operation $*$ is defined for all non-zero x and y by the equation $x * y = x/y$. Then the expression $(x - 2)^2 * x$ is equal to

    (A) $x - 4 + 4/x$ (B) $x + 4/x$ (C) $4/x$ (D) $1 + 4/x$ (E) $1 - 4x + 4/x$

9. $\left(2 + \sqrt{7}\right)\left(4 - \sqrt{7}\right)(-2x) =$

    (A) $78x - 4x\sqrt{7}$ (B) $\sqrt{7}x$ (C) $-2x - 4x\sqrt{7}$ (D) $-2x$ (E) $4x\sqrt{7}$

10. If the operation $*$ is defined for all non-zero x and y by the equation $x * y = (xy)^2$, then $(x * y) * z =$

    (A) $x^2 y^2 z^2$ (B) $x^4 y^4 z^2$ (C) $x^2 y^4 z^2$ (D) $x^4 y^2 z^2$ (E) $x^4 y^4 z^4$

11. If $p = z + 1/z$ and $q = z - 1/z$, where z is a real number not equal to zero, then $(p + q)(p - q) =$

    (A) 2 (B) 4 (C) z^2 (D) $1/z^2$ (E) $z^2 - \dfrac{1}{z^2}$

Answers and Solutions to Problem Set Q

1. $\left(x^2 + 2\right)\left(x - x^3\right) = x^2 x - x^2 x^3 + 2x - 2x^3 = x^3 - x^5 + 2x - 2x^3 = -x^5 - x^3 + 2x$. Thus, the answer is (B).

2.
$$-2\left(3 - x\left[\frac{5 + y - 2}{x}\right] - 7 + 2 \cdot 3^2\right) =$$
$$-2\left(3 - x\left[\frac{3 + y}{x}\right] - 7 + 2 \cdot 3^2\right) =$$
$$-2\left(3 - [3 + y] - 7 + 2 \cdot 3^2\right) =$$
$$-2\left(3 - 3 - y - 7 + 2 \cdot 3^2\right) =$$
$$-2(3 - 3 - y - 7 + 2 \cdot 9) =$$
$$-2(3 - 3 - y - 7 + 18) =$$
$$-2(-y + 11) =$$
$$2y - 22$$

The answer is (E).

3. $a \lozenge b = ab - 1 = ba - 1 = b \lozenge a$. Thus, I is true, which eliminates (B) and (C).

$\dfrac{a \lozenge a}{a} = \dfrac{aa - 1}{a} \neq 1 \cdot 1 - 1 = 1 - 1 = 0 = 1 \lozenge 1$. Thus, II is false, which eliminates (D).

$(a \lozenge b) \lozenge c = (ab - 1) \lozenge c = (ab - 1)c - 1 = abc - c - 1 \neq a \lozenge (bc - 1) = a(bc - 1) - 1 = abc - a - 1 = a \lozenge (b \lozenge c)$. Thus, III is false, which eliminates (E). Hence, the answer is (A).

4.
$$\left(x + \frac{1}{2}\right)^2 - (2x - 4)^2 =$$
$$x^2 + 2x\frac{1}{2} + \left(\frac{1}{2}\right)^2 - \left[(2x)^2 - 2(2x)4 + 4^2\right] =$$
$$x^2 + x + \frac{1}{4} - 4x^2 + 16x - 16 =$$
$$-3x^2 + 17x - \frac{63}{4}$$

Hence, the answer is (C).

5.
$$y^2 - \left(x - \left[y + \frac{1}{2}\right]\right) - 2 \cdot 3 =$$
$$(-3)^2 - \left(2 - \left[-3 + \frac{1}{2}\right]\right) - 2 \cdot 3 =$$
$$(-3)^2 - \left(2 - \left[-\frac{5}{2}\right]\right) - 2 \cdot 3 =$$
$$(-3)^2 - \left(2 + \frac{5}{2}\right) - 2 \cdot 3 =$$
$$(-3)^2 - \frac{9}{2} - 2 \cdot 3 =$$

$$9 - \frac{9}{2} - 2 \cdot 3 =$$
$$9 - \frac{9}{2} - 6 =$$
$$3 - \frac{9}{2} =$$
$$-\frac{3}{2}$$

The answer is (B).

6.
$$4(xy)^3 + \left(x^3 - y^3\right)^2 =$$
$$4x^3y^3 + \left(x^3\right)^2 - 2x^3y^3 + \left(y^3\right)^2 =$$
$$\left(x^3\right)^2 + 2x^3y^3 + \left(y^3\right)^2 =$$
$$\left(x^3 + y^3\right)^2$$

The answer is (E).

7.
$$\frac{b-a}{a} = \frac{b}{a} - \frac{a}{a} = \frac{b}{a} - 1 = \frac{-3}{2} - 1 = \frac{-3}{2} - \frac{2}{2} = \frac{-3-2}{2} = \frac{-5}{2}.$$ The answer is (A).

8. $(x-2)^2 * x = \frac{(x-2)^2}{x} = \frac{x^2 - 4x + 4}{x} = \frac{x^2}{x} - \frac{4x}{x} + \frac{4}{x} = x - 4 + \frac{4}{x}$. The answer is (A).

9.
$$\left(2 + \sqrt{7}\right)\left(4 - \sqrt{7}\right)(-2x) =$$
$$\left(2 \cdot 4 - 2\sqrt{7} + 4\sqrt{7} - \sqrt{7}\sqrt{7}\right)(-2x) =$$
$$\left(8 + 2\sqrt{7} - 7\right)(-2x) =$$
$$\left(1 + 2\sqrt{7}\right)(-2x) =$$
$$1(-2x) + 2\sqrt{7}(-2x) =$$
$$-2x - 4x\sqrt{7}$$

The answer is (C).

10. $(x * y) * z = (xy)^2 * z = \left((xy)^2 z\right)^2 = \left((xy)^2\right)^2 z^2 = (xy)^4 z^2 = x^4 y^4 z^2$. The answer is (B).

11. Since we are given that $p = z + 1/z$ and $q = z - 1/z$,

$$p + q = (z + 1/z) + (z - 1/z) = z + 1/z + z - 1/z = 2z.$$
$$p - q = (z + 1/z) - (z - 1/z) = z + 1/z - z + 1/z = 2/z.$$

Therefore, $(p + q)(p - q) = (2z)(2/z) = 4$. The answer is (B).

Percents

Problems involving percent are common on the ACT. The word *percent* means "divided by one hundred." When you see the word "percent," or the symbol %, remember it means 1/100. For example,

$$25 \text{ percent}$$
$$\downarrow \qquad \downarrow$$
$$25 \times \frac{1}{100} = \frac{1}{4}$$

To convert a decimal into a percent, move the decimal point two places to the right. For example,

$$0.25 = 25\%$$
$$0.023 = 2.3\%$$
$$1.3 = 130\%$$

Conversely, to convert a percent into a decimal, move the decimal point two places to the left. For example,

$$47\% = .47$$
$$3.4\% = .034$$
$$175\% = 1.75$$

To convert a fraction into a percent, first change it into a decimal (by dividing the denominator [bottom] into the numerator [top]) and then move the decimal point two places to the right. For example,

$$\frac{7}{8} = 0.875 = 87.5\%$$

Conversely, to convert a percent into a fraction, first change it into a decimal and then change the decimal into a fraction. For example,

$$80\% = .80 = \frac{80}{100} = \frac{4}{5}$$

Following are the most common fractional equivalents of percents:

$$33\frac{1}{3}\% = \frac{1}{3} \qquad\qquad 20\% = \frac{1}{5}$$

$$66\frac{2}{3}\% = \frac{2}{3} \qquad\qquad 40\% = \frac{2}{5}$$

$$25\% = \frac{1}{4} \qquad\qquad 60\% = \frac{3}{5}$$

$$50\% = \frac{1}{2} \qquad\qquad 80\% = \frac{4}{5}$$

Note! **Percent problems often require you to translate a sentence into a mathematical equation.**

Example 1: What percent of 25 is 5?

(A) 10%   (B) 20%   (C) 30%   (D) 35%   (E) 40%

Translate the sentence into a mathematical equation as follows:

What	percent	of	25	is	5
↓	↓	↓	↓	↓	↓
x	$\dfrac{1}{100}$	$\cdot$	25	=	5

$$\frac{25}{100}x = 5$$

$$\frac{1}{4}x = 5$$

$$x = 20$$

The answer is (B).

Example 2: 2 is 10% of what number

(A) 10   (B) 12   (C) 20   (D) 24   (E) 32

Translate the sentence into a mathematical equation as follows:

2	is	10	%	of	what number
↓	↓	↓	↓	↓	↓
2	=	10	$\dfrac{1}{100}$	$\cdot$	x

$$2 = \frac{10}{100}x$$

$$2 = \frac{1}{10}x$$

$$20 = x$$

The answer is (C).

Example 3: What percent of a is $3a$?

(A) 100%   (B) 150%   (C) 200%   (D) 300%   (E) 350%

Translate the sentence into a mathematical equation as follows:

What	percent	of	a	is	$3a$
↓	↓	↓	↓	↓	↓
x	$\dfrac{1}{100}$	$\cdot$	a	=	$3a$

$$\frac{x}{100} \cdot a = 3a$$

$$\frac{x}{100} = 3 \quad \text{(by canceling the } a\text{'s)}$$

$$x = 300$$

The answer is (D).

Example 4:   If there are 15 boys and 25 girls in a class, what percent of the class is boys?

(A)   10%
(B)   15%
(C)   18%
(D)   25%
(E)   37.5%

The total number of students in the class is $15 + 25 = 40$. Now, translate the main part of the sentence into a mathematical equation:

what	percent	of	the class	is	boys
↓	↓	↓	↓	↓	↓
x	$\frac{1}{100}$	$\cdot$	40	$=$	15

$$\frac{40}{100}x = 15$$

$$\frac{2}{5}x = 15$$

$$2x = 75$$

$$x = 37.5$$

The answer is (E).

Note! **Often you will need to find the percent of increase (or decrease). To find it, calculate the increase (or decrease) and divide it by the original amount:**

Percent of change: $\dfrac{Amount\ of\ change}{Original\ amount} \times 100\%$

Example 5:   The population of a town was 12,000, and ten years later it was 16,000. What was the percent increase in the population of the town during this period?

(A) $33\frac{1}{3}\%$

(B)   50%
(C)   75%
(D)   80%
(E)   120%

The population increased from 12,000 to 16,000. Hence, the change in population was 4,000. Now, translate the main part of the sentence into a mathematical equation:

Percent of change: $\dfrac{Amount\ of\ change}{Original\ amount} \times 100\% =$

$$\frac{4000}{12000} \times 100\% =$$

$$\frac{1}{3} \times 100\% = \qquad \text{(by canceling 4000)}$$

$$33\frac{1}{3}\%$$

The answer is (A).

Problem Set R:

1. John spent $25, which is 15 percent of his monthly wage. What is his monthly wage?

    (A) $80   (B) $166 2/3   (C) $225   (D) $312.5   (E) $375

2. If a = 4b, what percent of 2a is 2b?

    (A) 10%   (B) 20%   (C) 25%   (D) 26%   (E) 40%

3. If $p = 5q > 0$, then 40 percent of $3p$ equals

    (A) $6q$ (B) $5.52q$ (C) $13.3q$ (D) $9q$ (E) $20.1q$

4. A jar contains 24 blue balls and 40 red balls. Which one of the following is 50% of the blue balls?

    (A) 10   (B) 11   (C) 12   (D) 13   (E) 14

5. In a company with 180 employees, 108 of the employees are female. What percent of the employees are male?

    (A) 5%   (B) 25%   (C) 35%   (D) 40%   (E) 60%

6. John bought a shirt, a pair of pants, and a pair of shoes, which cost $10, $20, and $30, respectively. What percent of the total expense was spent for the pants?

    (A) $16\frac{2}{3}\%$ (B) 20%   (C) 30%   (D) $33\frac{1}{3}\%$ (E) 60%

7. Last year Jenny was 5 feet tall, and this year she is 5 feet 6 inches. What is the percent increase of her height?

    (A) 5%   (B) 10%   (C) 15%   (D) 20%   (E) 40%

8. Last month the price of a particular pen was $1.20. This month the price of the same pen is $1.50. What is the percent increase in the price of the pen?

    (A) 5%   (B) 10%   (C) 25%   (D) 30%   (E) $33\frac{1}{3}\%$

9. Stella paid $1,500 for a computer after receiving a 20 percent discount. What was the price of the computer before the discount?

    (A) $300   (B) $1,500   (C) $1,875   (D) $2,000   (E) $3,000

10. A town has a population growth rate of 10% per year. The population in 1990 was 2000. What was the population in 1992?

    (A) 1600   (B) 2200   (C) 2400   (D) 2420   (E) 4000

Answers and Solutions to Problem Set R

1.   Consider the first sentence: John spent $25, which is 15 percent of his monthly wage. Now, translate the main part of the sentence into a mathematical equation as follows:

25	is	15	%	of	his monthly wage
↓	↓	↓	↓	↓	↓
25	=	15	$\frac{1}{100}$	·	x

$$25 = \frac{15}{100}x$$
$$2500 = 15x$$
$$x = \frac{2500}{15} = \frac{500}{3} = 166\frac{2}{3}$$

The answer is (B).

2.   Translate the main part of the sentence into a mathematical equation as follows:

What	percent	of	2a	is	2b
↓	↓	↓	↓	↓	↓
x	$\frac{1}{100}$	·	$2a$	=	$2b$

$$\frac{x}{100} \cdot 2a = 2b$$

$$\frac{x}{100} \cdot 2(4b) = 2b \qquad \text{(substituting } a = 4b\text{)}$$

$$\frac{x}{100} \cdot 8 = 2 \qquad \text{(canceling } b \text{ from both sides)}$$

$$\frac{8x}{100} = 2$$
$$8x = 200$$
$$x = 25$$

The answer is (C).

Remark: You can substitute $b = a/4$ instead of $a = 4b$. Whichever letter you substitute, you will get the same answer. However, depending on the question, one substitution may be easier than another.

3.   Since more than one letter is used in this question, we need to substitute one of the letters for the other to minimize the number of unknown quantities (letters).

40	percent	of	3p
↓	↓	↓	↓
40	$\frac{1}{100}$	×	$3p$

$$= \frac{40}{100} \times 3p$$

$$= \frac{40}{100} \times 3(5q) \qquad \text{(substituting } p = 5q\text{)}$$

$$= \frac{600q}{100}$$

$$= 6q$$

The answer is (A).

4.

50	%	of	the blue balls
↓	↓	↓	↓
50	$\dfrac{1}{100}$	×	24

$= \dfrac{50 \times 24}{100}$

$= \dfrac{1200}{100}$

$= 12$

The answer is (C).

5. Since female employees are 108 out of 180, there are $180 - 108 = 72$ male employees. Now, translate the main part of the sentence into a mathematical equation as follows:

What	percent	of	the employees	are	male
↓	↓	↓	↓	↓	↓
x	$\dfrac{1}{100}$	·	180	=	72

$\dfrac{180}{100}x = 72$

$\dfrac{100}{180} \cdot \dfrac{180}{100}x = \dfrac{100}{180} \cdot 72$

$x = 40$

The answer is (D).

6. The total expense is the sum of expenses for the shirt, pants, and shoes, which is $\$10 + \$20 + \$30 = \$60$. Now, translate the main part of the sentence into a mathematical equation:

What	percent	of	the total expense	was spent for	the pants
↓	↓	↓	↓	↓	↓
x	$\dfrac{1}{100}$	·	60	=	20

$\dfrac{60}{100}x = 20$

$60x = 2000$ (by multiplying both sides of the equation by 100)

$x = \dfrac{2000}{60}$ (by dividing both sides of the equation by 60)

$x = \dfrac{100}{3} = 33\dfrac{1}{3}$

The answer is (D).

7. First, express all the numbers in the same units (inches):

The original height is $5 \ feet = 5 \ feet \times \dfrac{12 \ inches}{1 \ feet} = 60 \ inches$

The change in height is $(5 \ feet \ 6 \ inches) - (5 \ feet) = 6 \ inches$. Now, use the formula for percent of change.

Percent of change:

$\dfrac{Amount \ of \ change}{Original \ amount} \times 100\% =$

$\dfrac{6}{60} \times 100\% =$

$\dfrac{1}{10} \times 100\% =$ (by canceling 6)

10%

The answer is (B).

8. The change in price is $\$1.50 - \$1.20 = \$.30$. Now, use the formula for percent of change.

$$\dfrac{Amount \ of \ change}{Original \ amount} \times 100\% =$$

$$\dfrac{.30}{1.20} \times 100\% =$$

$$\dfrac{1}{4} \times 100\% =$$

$$25\%$$

The answer is (C).

9. Let x be the price before the discount. Since Stella received a 20 percent discount, she paid 80 percent of the original price. Thus, 80 percent of the original price is $\$1,500$. Now, translate this sentence into a mathematical equation:

80	percent	of	the original price	is	$\$1,500$
↓	↓	↓	↓	↓	↓
80	$\dfrac{1}{100}$	.	x	=	1500

$\dfrac{80}{100} x = 1500$

$\dfrac{100}{80} \dfrac{80}{100} x = \dfrac{100}{80} 1500$ (by multiplying both sides by the reciprocal of 80/100)

$x = 1875$

The answer is (C).

10. Since the population increased at a rate of 10% per year, the population of any year is the population of the previous year + 10% of that same year. Hence, the population in 1991 is the population of 1990 + 10% of the population of 1990:

$2000 + 10\%$ of $2000 =$
$2000 + 200 =$
2200

Similarly, the population in 1992 is the population of 1991 + 10% of the population of 1991:

$2200 + 10\%$ of $2200 =$
$2200 + 220 =$
2420

Hence, the answer is (D).

Graphs

Questions involving graphs are common on the ACT. Rarely do these questions involve any significant calculating. Usually, the solution is merely a matter of interpreting the graph.

Questions 1-4 refer to the following graphs.

SALES AND EARNINGS OF CONSOLIDATED CONGLOMERATE

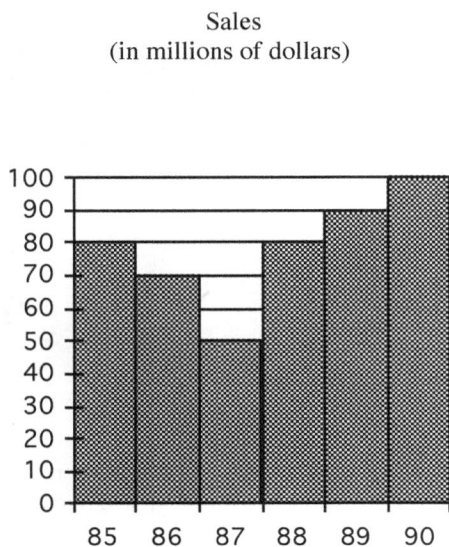

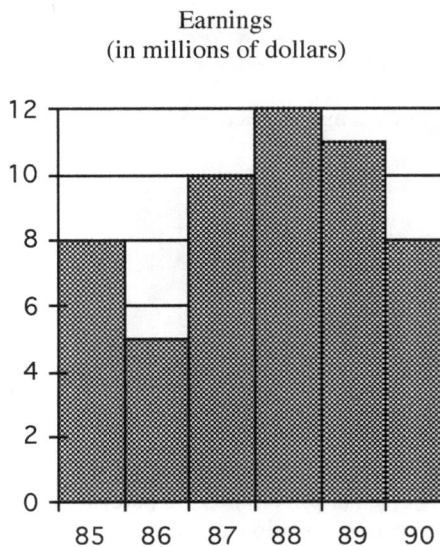

Sales
(in millions of dollars)

Earnings
(in millions of dollars)

Note: Figure drawn to scale.

1. During which year was the company's earnings 10 percent of its sales?

    (A) 85   (B) 86   (C) 87   (D) 88   (E) 90

Reading from the graph, we see that in 1985 the company's earnings were $8 million and its sales were $80 million. This gives

$$\frac{8}{10} = \frac{1}{10} = \frac{10}{100} = 10\%$$

The answer is (A).

2. During the years 1986 through 1988, what were the average earnings per year?

    (A) 6 million   (B) 7.5 million   (C) 9 million   (D) 10 million   (E) 27 million

The graph yields the following information:

Year	Earnings
1986	$5 million
1987	$10 million
1988	$12 million

Forming the average yields $\frac{5+10+12}{3} = \frac{27}{3} = 9$. The answer is (C).

3. In which year did sales increase by the greatest percentage over the previous year?

    (A) 86
    (B) 87
    (C) 88
    (D) 89
    (E) 90

To find the percentage increase (or decrease), divide the numerical change by the original amount. This yields

Year	Percentage increase
86	$\dfrac{70-80}{80} = \dfrac{-10}{80} = \dfrac{-1}{8} = -12.5\%$
87	$\dfrac{50-70}{70} = \dfrac{-20}{70} = \dfrac{-2}{7} \approx -29\%$
88	$\dfrac{80-50}{50} = \dfrac{30}{50} = \dfrac{3}{5} = 60\%$
89	$\dfrac{90-80}{80} = \dfrac{10}{80} = \dfrac{1}{8} = 12.5\%$
90	$\dfrac{100-90}{90} = \dfrac{10}{90} = \dfrac{1}{9} \approx 11\%$

The largest number in the right-hand column, 60%, corresponds to the year 1988. The answer is (C).

4. If Consolidated Conglomerate's earnings are less than or equal to 10 percent of sales during a year, then the stockholders must take a dividend cut at the end of the year. In how many years did the stockholders of Consolidated Conglomerate suffer a dividend cut?

    (A) None
    (B) One
    (C) Two
    (D) Three
    (E) Four

Calculating 10 percent of the sales for each year yields

Year	10% of Sales (millions)	Earnings (millions)
85	$.10 \times 80 = 8$	8
86	$.10 \times 70 = 7$	5
87	$.10 \times 50 = 5$	10
88	$.10 \times 80 = 8$	12
89	$.10 \times 90 = 9$	11
90	$.10 \times 100 = 10$	8

Comparing the right columns shows that earnings were 10 percent or less of sales in 1985, 1986, and 1990. The answer is (D).

Problem Set S:

Questions 1–5 refer to the following graphs.

Profit And Revenue Distribution For Zippy Printing, 1990–1993, Copying And Printing.

Total Profit
(in thousands of dollars)

Total Revenue
(in millions of dollars)

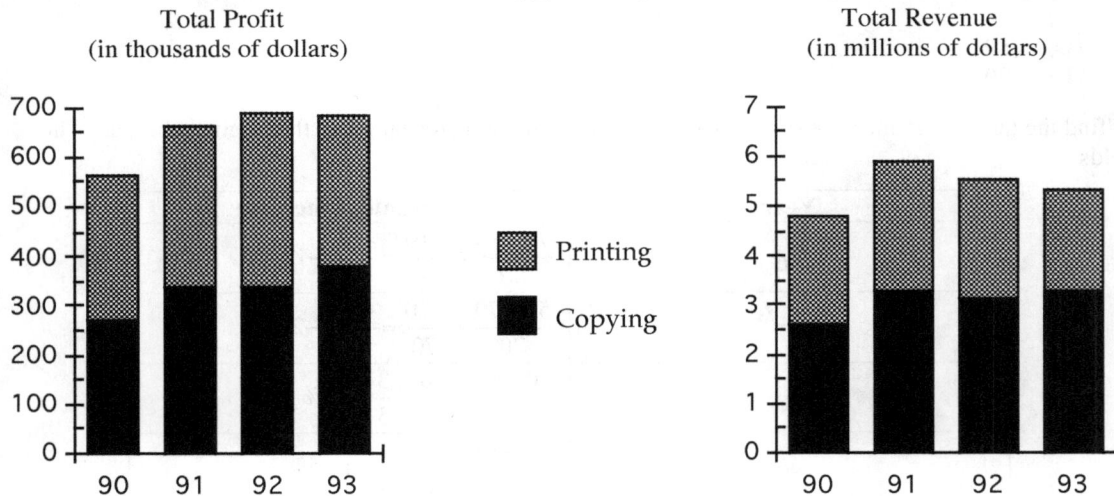

Distribution of Profit from Copying, 1992
(in thousands of dollars)

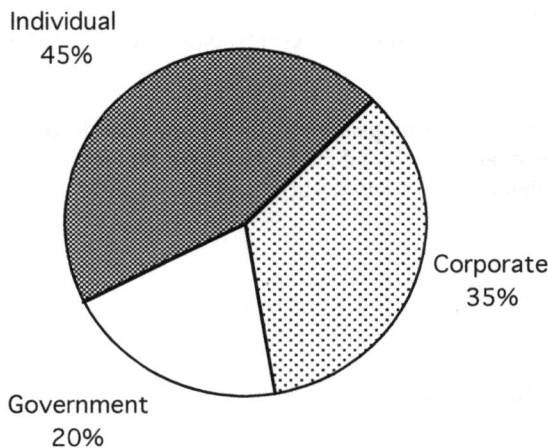

1. In 1993, the total profit was approximately how much greater than the total profit in 1990?

    (A) 50 thousand   (B) 75 thousand   (C) 120 thousand   (D) 200 thousand   (E) 350 thousand

2. In 1990, the profit from copying was approximately what percent of the revenue from copying?

    (A) 2%   (B) 10%   (C) 20%   (D) 35%   (E) 50%

3. In 1992, the profit from copying for corporate customers was approximately how much greater than the profit from copying for government customers?

    (A) 50 thousand   (B) 80 thousand   (C) 105 thousand   (D) 190 thousand   (E) 260 thousand

4. During the two years in which total profit was most nearly equal, the combined revenue from printing was closest to

    (A) 1 million   (B) 2 million   (C) 4.5 million   (D) 6 million   (E) 6.5 million

5. The amount of profit made from government copy sales in 1992 was

    (A) 70 thousand   (B) 100 thousand   (C) 150 thousand   (D) 200 thousand   (E) 350 thousand

Questions 6–10 refer to the following graphs.

**DISTRIBUTION OF CRIMINAL ACTIVITY BY CATEGORY OF CRIME FOR COUNTRY X IN 1990
AND PROJECTED FOR 2000.**

Criminal Population: 10 million   Criminal Population: 20 million

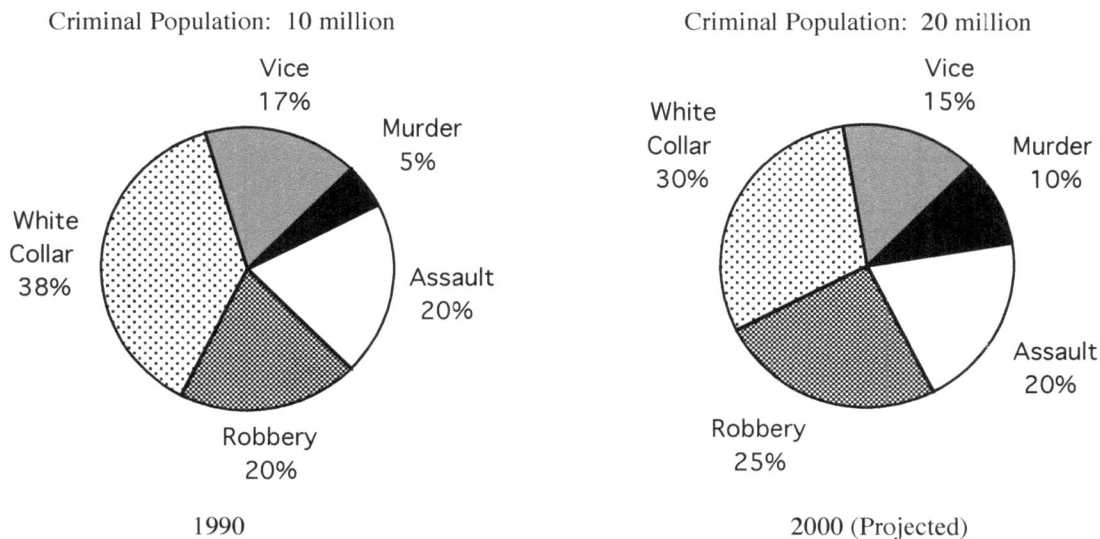

1990   2000 (Projected)

6. What is the projected number of white-collar criminals in 2000?

   (A)   1 million
   (B)   3.8 million
   (C)   6 million
   (D)   8 million
   (E)   10 million

7. The ratio of the number of robbers in 1990 to the number of projected robbers in 2000 is

   (A) 2/5   (B) 3/5   (C) 1   (D) 3/2   (E) 5/2

8. From 1990 to 2000, there is a projected decrease in the number of criminals for which of the
   following categories?
   I.   Vice
   II. Assault
   III. White Collar

   (A) None   (B) I only   (C) II only   (D) II and III only   (E) I, II, and III

9. What is the approximate projected percent increase between 1990 and 2000 in the number of
   criminals involved in vice?

   (A) 25%   (B) 40%   (C) 60%   (D) 75%   (E) 85%

10. The projected number of Robbers in 2000 will exceed the number of white-collar criminals in 1990
    by

   (A) 1.2 million   (B) 2.3 million   (C) 3.4 million   (D) 5.8 million   (E) 7.2 million

Questions 11–15 refer to the following graph.

SALES BY CATEGORY FOR GRAMMERCY PRESS, 1980–1989
(in thousands of books)

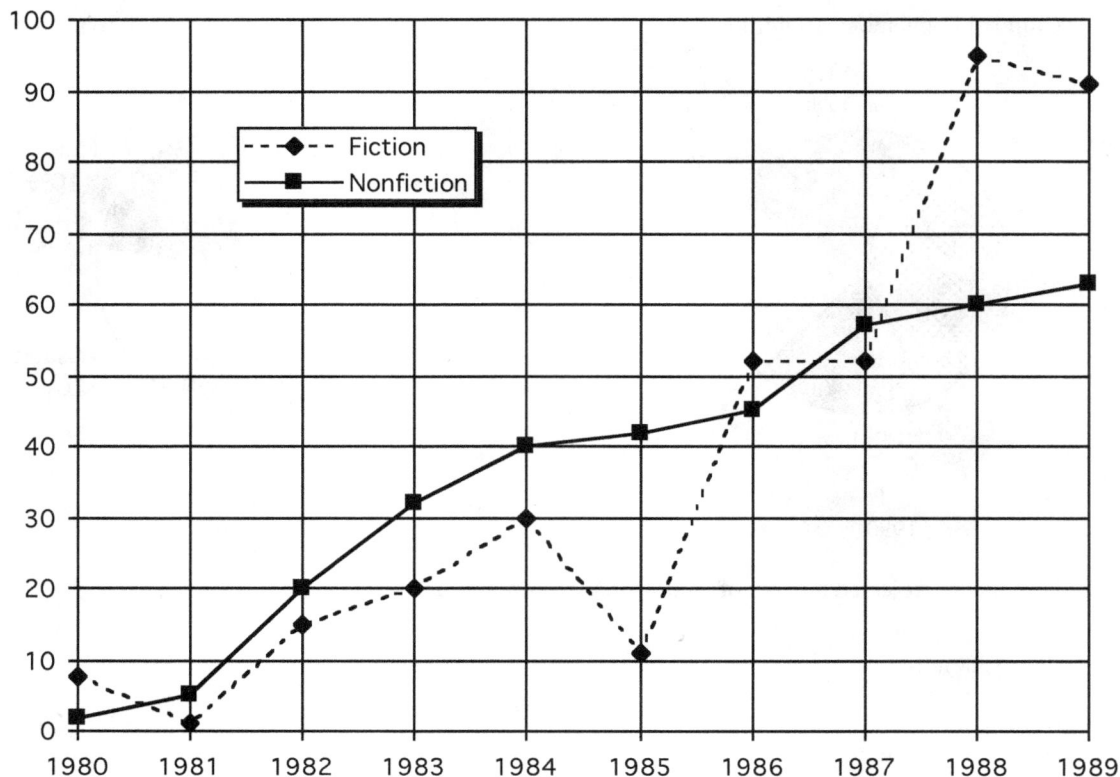

11. In how many years did the sales of nonfiction titles exceed the sales of fiction titles ?

    (A) 2   (B) 3   (C) 4   (D) 5   (E) 6

12. Which of the following best approximates the amount by which the increase in sales of fiction titles from 1985 to 1986 exceeded the increase in sales of fiction titles from 1983 to 1984?

    (A)   31.5   thousand
    (B)   40   thousand
    (C)   49.3   thousand
    (D)   50.9   thousand
    (E)   68   thousand

13. Which of the following periods showed a continual increase in the sales of fiction titles?

    (A) 1980–1982   (B) 1982–1984   (C) 1984–1986   (D) 1986–1988   (E) 1987–1989

14. What was the approximate average number of sales of fiction titles from 1984 to 1988?

    (A) 15 thousand   (B) 30 thousand   (C) 40 thousand   (D) 48 thousand   (E) 60 thousand

15. By approximately what percent did the sale of nonfiction titles increase from 1984 to 1987?

    (A) 42%   (B) 50%   (C) 70%   (D) 90%   (E) 110%

Answers and Solutions to Problem Set S

1. Remember, rarely does a graph question involve significant computation. For this question, we need merely to read the bar graph. The Total Profit graph shows that in 1993 approximately 680 thousand was earned, and in 1990 approximately 560 thousand was earned. Subtracting these numbers yields 680 – 560 = 120. The answer is (C).

2. The Total Revenue graph indicates that in 1990 the revenue from copying was about $2,600,000. The Total Profit graph shows the profit from copying in that same year was about $270,000. The profit margin is

$$\frac{\text{Profit}}{\text{Revenue}} = \frac{270,000}{2,600,000} \approx 10\%$$

The answer is (B).

3. From the chart, the profit in 1992 was approximately $700,000 of which 35% x $700,000 = $245,000 was from corporate customers and 20% x $700,000 = $140,000 was from government customers. Subtracting these amounts yields $245,000 – $140,000 = $105,000. The answer is (C).

4. The Total Profit graph shows that 1992 and 1993 are clearly the two years in which total profit was most nearly equal. Turning to the Total Revenue graph, we see that in 1992 the revenue from printing sales was approximately 2.5 million, and that in 1993 the revenue from printing sales was approximately 2 million. This gives a total of 4.5 million in total printing sales revenue for the period. The answer is (C).

5. The Total Profit graph shows that Zippy Printing earned about $340,000 from copying in 1992. The Pie Chart indicates that 20% of this was earned from government sales. Multiplying these numbers gives $340,000 × 20% ≈ $70,000. The answer is (A).

6. From the projected-crime graph, we see that the criminal population will be 20 million and of these 30 percent are projected to be involved in white-collar crime. Hence, the number of white-collar criminals is (30%)(20 *million*) = (.30)(20 *million*) = 6 *million*. The answer is (C).

7. In 1990, there were 10 million criminals and 20% were robbers. Thus, the number of robbers in 1990 was

$$(20\%)(10 \text{ million}) = (.20)(10 \text{ million}) = 2 \text{ million}$$

In 2000, there are projected to be 20 million criminals of which 25% are projected to be robbers. Thus, the number of robbers in 2000 is projected to be

$$(25\%)(20 \text{ million}) = (.25)(20 \text{ million}) = 5 \text{ million}$$

Forming the ratio of the above numbers yields

$$\frac{number\ of\ robbers\ in\ 1990}{number\ of\ robbers\ in\ 2000} = \frac{2}{5}$$

The answer is (A).

8. The following table lists the number of criminals by category for 1990 and 2000 and the projected increase or decrease:

Category	Number in 1990 (millions)	Number in 2000 (millions)	Projected increase (millions)	Projected decrease (millions)
Vice	1.7	3	1.3	None
Assault	2	4	2	None
White Collar	3.8	6	2.2	None

As the table displays, there is a projected increase (not decrease) in all three categories. Hence, the answer is (A).

9. Remember, to calculate the percentage increase, find the absolute increase and divide it by the original number. Now, in 1990, the number of criminals in vice was 1.7 million, and in 2000 it is projected to be 3 million. The absolute increase is thus:

$$3 - 1.7 = 1.3$$

Hence the projected percent increase in the number of criminals in vice is

$$\frac{absolute\ increase}{original\ number} = \frac{1.3}{1.7} \approx 75\%$$

The answer is (D).

10. In 1990, the number of white-collar criminals was (38%)(10 million) = 3.8 million. From the projected-crime graph, we see that the criminal population in the year 2000 will be 20 million and of these (25%)(20 million) = 5 million will be robbers. Hence, the projected number of Robbers in 2000 will exceed the number of white-collar criminals in 1990 by 5 – 3.8 = 1.2 million. The answer is (A).

11. The graph shows that nonfiction sales exceeded fiction sales in '81, '82, '83, '84, '85, and '87. The answer is (E).

12. The graph shows that the increase in sales of fiction titles from 1985 to 1986 was approximately 40 thousand and the increase in sales of fiction titles from 1983 to 1984 was approximately 10 thousand. Hence, the difference is 40 – 10 = 30. Choice (A) is the only answer-choice close to 30 thousand.

13. According to the chart, sales of fiction increased from 15,000 to 20,000 to 30,000 between 1982 and 1984. The answer is (B).

14. The following chart summarizes the sales for the years 1984 to 1988:

Year	Sales
1984	30 thousand
1985	11 thousand
1986	52 thousand
1987	52 thousand
1988	95 thousand

Forming the average yields:

$$\frac{30 + 11 + 52 + 52 + 95}{5} = 48$$

The answer is (D).

Note, it is important to develop a feel for how the writers of the ACT approximate when calculating. We used 52 thousand to calculate the sales of fiction in 1986, which is the actual number. But from the chart, it is difficult to tell whether the actual number is 51, 52, or 53 thousand. However, using any of the these numbers, the average would still be nearer to 40 than to any other answer-choice.

15. Recall that the percentage increase (decrease) is formed by dividing the absolute increase (decrease) by the original amount:

$$\frac{57 - 40}{40} = .425$$

The answer is (A).

Word Problems

TRANSLATING WORDS INTO MATHEMATICAL SYMBOLS

Before we begin solving word problems, we need to be very comfortable with translating words into mathematical symbols. Following is a partial list of words and their mathematical equivalents.

Concept	Symbol	Words	Example	Translation
equality	=	is	2 plus 2 is 4	$2 + 2 = 4$
		equals	x minus 5 equals 2	$x - 5 = 2$
		is the same as	multiplying x by 2 is the same as dividing x by 7	$2x = x/7$
addition	+	sum	the sum of y and π is 20	$y + \pi = 20$
		plus	x plus y equals 5	$x + y = 5$
		add	how many marbles must John add to collection P so that he has 13 marbles	$x + P = 13$
		increase	a number is increased by 10%	$x + 10\%x$
		more	the perimeter of the square is 3 more than the area	$P = 3 + A$
subtraction	–	minus	x minus y	$x - y$
		difference	the difference of x and y is 8	$\|x - y\| = 8$
		subtracted	x subtracted from y	$y - x$ *
		less than	the circumference is 5 less than the area	$C = A - 5$
multiplication	$\times$ or $\cdot$	times	the acceleration is 5 times the velocity	$a = 5v$
		product	the product of two consecutive integers	$x(x + 1)$
		of	x is 125% of y	$x = 125\%y$
division	$\div$	quotient	the quotient of x and y is 9	$x \div y = 9$
		divided	if x is divided by y, the result is 4	$x \div y = 4$

Although exact steps for solving word problems cannot be given, the following guidelines will help:

(1)   First, choose a variable to stand for the least unknown quantity, and then try to write the other unknown quantities in terms of that variable.

> For example, suppose we are given that Sue's age is 5 years less than twice Jane's and the sum of their ages is 16. Then Jane's age would be the least unknown, and we let $x = Jane's\ age$. Expressing Sue's age in terms of x gives $Sue's\ age = 2x - 5$.

(2)   Second, write an equation that involves the expressions in Step 1. Most (though not all) word problems pivot on the fact that two quantities in the problem are equal. Deciding which two quantities should be set equal is usually the hardest part in solving a word problem since it can require considerable ingenuity to discover which expressions are equal.

> For the example above, we would get $(2x - 5) + x = 16$.

(3)   Third, solve the equation in Step 2 and interpret the result.

> For the example above, we would get by adding the x's: $3x - 5 = 16$
>
> Then adding 5 to both sides gives $3x = 21$
>
> Finally, dividing by 3 gives $x = 7$
>
> Hence, Jane is 7 years old and Sue is $2x - 5 = 2 \cdot 7 - 5 = 9$ years old.

---

* Notice that with "minus" and "difference" the terms are subtracted in the same order as they are written, from left to right (x minus $y \longrightarrow x - y$). However, with "subtracted" and "less than," the order of subtraction is reversed (x subtracted from $y \longrightarrow y - x$). Many students translate "subtracted from" in the wrong order.

MOTION PROBLEMS

Virtually, all motion problems involve the formula *Distance = Rate × Time*, or

$$D = R \times T$$

Overtake: In this type of problem, one person catches up with or overtakes another person. The key to these problems is that at the moment one person overtakes the other they have traveled the same distance.

Example: Scott starts jogging from point X to point Y. A half-hour later his friend Garrett who jogs 1 mile per hour slower than twice Scott's rate starts from the same point and follows the same path. If Garrett overtakes Scott in 2 hours, how many miles will Garrett have covered?

(A) 2 1/5   (B) 3 1/3   (C) 4   (D) 6   (E) 6 2/3

Following Guideline 1, we let *r = Scott's rate*. Then *2r – 1 = Garrett's rate*. Turning to Guideline 2, we look for two quantities that are equal to each other. When Garrett overtakes Scott, they will have traveled the same distance. Now, from the formula $D = R \times T$, Scott's distance is $D = r \times 2\frac{1}{2}$

and Garrett's distance is $D = (2r - 1)2 = 4r - 2$

Setting these expressions equal to each other gives $4r - 2 = r \times 2\frac{1}{2}$

Solving this equation for *r* gives $r = 4/3$

Hence, Garrett will have traveled $D = 4r - 2 = 4\left(\frac{4}{3}\right) - 2 = 3\frac{1}{3}$ miles. The answer is (B).

Opposite Directions: In this type of problem, two people start at the same point and travel in opposite directions. The key to these problems is that the total distance traveled is the sum of the individual distances traveled.

Example: Two people start jogging at the same point and time but in opposite directions. If the rate of one jogger is 2 mph faster than the other and after 3 hours they are 30 miles apart, what is the rate of the faster jogger?

(A) 3   (B) 4   (C) 5   (D) 6   (E) 7

Let *r* be the rate of the slower jogger. Then the rate of the faster jogger is *r + 2*. Since they are jogging for 3 hours, the distance traveled by the slower jogger is $D = rt = 3r$, and the distance traveled by the faster jogger is $3(r + 2)$. Since they are 30 miles apart, adding the distances traveled gives

$$3r + 3(r + 2) = 30$$
$$3r + 3r + 6 = 30$$
$$6r + 6 = 30$$
$$6r = 24$$
$$r = 4$$

Hence, the rate of the faster jogger is *r + 2 = 4 + 2 = 6*. The answer is (D).

<u>**Round Trip:**</u> The key to these problems is that the distance going is the same as the distance returning.

Example: A cyclist travels 20 miles at a speed of 15 miles per hour. If he returns along the same path and the entire trip takes 2 hours, at what speed did he return?

(A) 15 mph
(B) 20 mph
(C) 22 mph
(D) 30 mph
(E) 34 mph

Solving the formula $D = R \times T$ for T yields $T = D/R$. For the first half of the trip, this yields $T = 20/15 = 4/3$ hours. Since the entire trip takes 2 hours, the return trip takes $2 - 4/3$ hours, or 2/3 hours. Now, the return trip is also 20 miles, so solving the formula $D = R \times T$ for R yields

$$R = \frac{D}{T} = \frac{20}{2/3} = 20 \cdot \frac{3}{2} = 30$$

The answer is (D).

<u>**Compass Headings:**</u> In this type of problem, typically two people are traveling in perpendicular directions. The key to these problems is often the Pythagorean Theorem.

Example: At 1 PM, Ship A leaves port heading due west at x miles per hour. Two hours later, Ship B is 100 miles due south of the same port and heading due north at y miles per hour. At 5 PM, how far apart are the ships?

(A) $\sqrt{(4x)^2 + (100 + 2y)^2}$
(B) $x + y$
(C) $\sqrt{x^2 + y^2}$
(D) $\sqrt{(4x)^2 + (2y)^2}$
(E) $\sqrt{(4x)^2 + (100 - 2y)^2}$

Since Ship A is traveling at x miles per hour, its distance traveled at 5 PM is $D = rt = 4x$. The distance traveled by Ship B is $D = rt = 2y$. This can be represented by the following diagram:

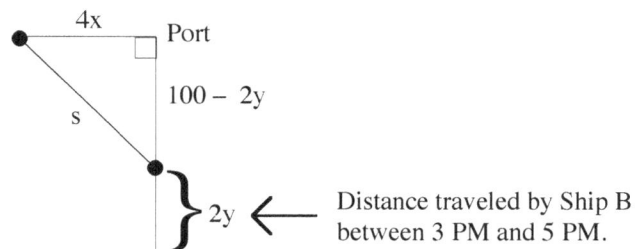

Applying the Pythagorean Theorem yields $s^2 = (4x)^2 + (100 - 2y)^2$. Taking the square root of this equation gives $s = \sqrt{(4x)^2 + (100 - 2y)^2}$. The answer is (E).

Circular Motion: In this type of problem, the key is often the arc length formula $S = R\theta$, where S is the arc length (or distance traveled), R is the radius of the circle, and θ is the angle.

Example: The figure shows the path of a car moving around a circular racetrack. How many miles does the car travel in going from point A to point B ?

(A) $\pi/6$ (B) $\pi/3$ (C) π (D) 30   (E) 60

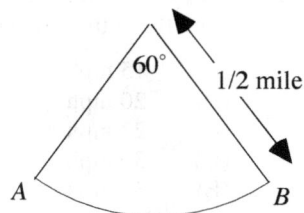

When calculating distance, degree measure must be converted to radian measure. To convert degree measure to radian measure, multiply by the conversion factor $\pi/180$. Multiplying $60°$ by $\pi/180$ yields $60 \cdot \dfrac{\pi}{180} = \dfrac{\pi}{3}$. Now, the length of arc traveled by the car in moving from point A to point B is S. Plugging this information into the formula $S = R\theta$ yields $S = \dfrac{1}{2} \cdot \dfrac{\pi}{3} = \dfrac{\pi}{6}$. The answer is (A).

Example: If a wheel is spinning at 1200 revolutions per minute, how many revolutions will it make in t seconds?

(A) $2t$ (B) $10t$ (C) $20t$ (D) $48t$ (E) $72t$

Since the question asks for the number of revolutions in t seconds, we need to find the number of revolutions per second and multiply that number by t. Since the wheel is spinning at 1200 revolutions per minute and there are 60 seconds in a minute, we get $\dfrac{1200 \text{ revolutions}}{60 \text{ seconds}} = 20\,\text{rev/sec}$. Hence, in t seconds, the wheel will make $20t$ revolutions. The answer is (C).

WORK PROBLEMS

The formula for work problems is *Work = Rate × Time*, or $W = R \times T$. The amount of work done is usually 1 unit. Hence, the formula becomes $1 = R \times T$. Solving this for R gives $R = 1/T$.

Example: If Johnny can mow the lawn in 30 minutes and with the help of his brother, Bobby, they can mow the lawn 20 minutes, how long would it take Bobby working alone to mow the lawn?

(A) 1/2 hour   (B) 3/4 hour   (C) 1 hour   (D) 3/2 hours   (E) 2 hours

Let $r = 1/t$ be Bobby's rate. Now, the rate at which they work together is merely the sum of their rates:

Total Rate = Johnny's Rate + Bobby's Rate

$$\frac{1}{20} = \frac{1}{30} + \frac{1}{t}$$

$$\frac{1}{20} - \frac{1}{30} = \frac{1}{t}$$

$$\frac{30 - 20}{30 \cdot 20} = \frac{1}{t}$$

$$\frac{1}{60} = \frac{1}{t}$$

$$t = 60$$

Hence, working alone, Bobby can do the job in 1 hour. The answer is (C).

Example: A tank is being drained at a constant rate. If it takes 3 hours to drain 6/7 of its capacity, how much longer will it take to drain the tank completely?

(A) 1/2 hour   (B) 3/4 hour   (C) 1 hour   (D) 3/2 hours   (E) 2 hours

Since 6/7 of the tank's capacity was drained in 3 hours, the formula $W = R \times T$ becomes $6/7 = R \times 3$. Solving for R gives $R = 2/7$. Now, since 6/7 of the work has been completed, 1/7 of the work remains. Plugging this information into the formula $W = R \times T$ gives $\frac{1}{7} = \frac{2}{7} \times T$. Solving for T gives $T = 1/2$. The answer is (A).

MIXTURE PROBLEMS

The key to these problems is that the combined total of the concentrations in the two parts must be the same as the whole mixture.

Example: How many ounces of a solution that is 30 percent salt must be added to a 50-ounce solution that is 10 percent salt so that the resulting solution is 20 percent salt?

(A) 20   (B) 30   (C) 40   (D) 50   (E) 60

Let x be the ounces of the 30 percent solution. Then $30\%x$ is the amount of salt in that solution. The final solution will be $50 + x$ ounces, and its concentration of salt will be $20\%(50 + x)$. The original amount of salt in the solution is $10\% \cdot 50$. Now, the concentration of salt in the original solution plus the concentration of salt in the added solution must equal the concentration of salt in the resulting solution:

$$10\% \cdot 50 + 30\%x = 20\%(50 + x)$$

Multiply this equation by 100 to clear the percent symbol and then solving for x yields $x = 50$. The answer is (D).

COIN PROBLEMS

The key to these problems is to keep the quantity of coins distinct from the value of the coins. An example will illustrate.

Example: Laura has 20 coins consisting of quarters and dimes. If she has a total of $3.05, how many dimes does she have?

(A) 3   (B) 7   (C) 10   (D) 13   (E) 16

Let D stand for the number of dimes, and let Q stand for the number of quarters. Since the total number of coins in 20, we get $D + Q = 20$, or $Q = 20 - D$. Now, each dime is worth 10¢, so the value of the dimes is $10D$. Similarly, the value of the quarters is $25Q = 25(20 - D)$. Summarizing this information in a table yields

	Dimes	Quarters	Total
Number	D	$20 - D$	20
Value	$10D$	$25(20 - D)$	305

Notice that the total value entry in the table was converted from $3.05 to 305¢. Adding up the value of the dimes and the quarters yields the following equation:

$$10D + 25(20 - D) = 305$$
$$10D + 500 - 25D = 305$$
$$-15D = -195$$
$$D = 13$$

Hence, there are 13 dimes, and the answer is (D).

AGE PROBLEMS

Typically, in these problems, we start by letting x be a person's current age and then the person's age a years ago will be $x - a$ and the person's age a years in future will be $x + a$. An example will illustrate.

Example: John is 20 years older than Steve. In 10 years, Steve's age will be half that of John's. What is Steve's age?

      (A)   2
      (B)   8
      (C)   10
      (D)   20
      (E)   25

Steve's age is the most unknown quantity. So we let x = Steve's age and then $x + 20$ is John's age. Ten years from now, Steve and John's ages will be $x + 10$ and $x + 30$, respectively. Summarizing this information in a table yields

	Age now	Age in 10 years
Steve	x	$x + 10$
John	$x + 20$	$x + 30$

Since "in 10 years, Steve's age will be half that of John's," we get

$$\frac{1}{2}(x + 30) = x + 10$$
$$x + 30 = 2(x + 10)$$
$$x + 30 = 2x + 20$$
$$x = 10$$

Hence, Steve is 10 years old, and the answer is (C).

INTEREST PROBLEMS

These problems are based on the formula

$$\text{INTEREST} = \text{AMOUNT} \times \text{TIME} \times \text{RATE}$$

Often, the key to these problems is that the interest earned from one account plus the interest earned from another account equals the total interest earned:

Total Interest = (Interest from first account) + (Interest from second account)

An example will illustrate.

Example: A total of $1200 is deposited in two savings accounts for one year, part at 5% and the remainder at 7%. If $72 was earned in interest, how much was deposited at 5%?

      (A)   410
      (B)   520
      (C)   600
      (D)   650
      (E)   760

Let x be the amount deposited at 5%. Then $1200 - x$ is the amount deposited at 7%. The interest on these investments is $.05x$ and $.07(1200 - x)$. Since the total interest is $72, we get

$$.05x + .07(1200 - x) = 72$$
$$.05x + 84 - .07x = 72$$
$$-.02x + 84 = 72$$
$$-.02x = -12$$
$$x = 600$$

The answer is (C).

Problem Set T:

1. Seven years ago, Scott was 3 times as old as Kathy was at that time. If Scott is now 5 years older than Kathy, how old is Scott?

    (A) 12½   (B) 13   (C) 13½   (D) 14   (E) 14½

Duals

2. A dress was initially listed at a price that would have given the store a profit of 20 percent of the wholesale cost. After reducing the asking price by 10 percent, the dress sold for a net profit of 10 dollars. What was the wholesale cost of the dress?

    (A) 200   (B) 125   (C) 100   (D) 20   (E) 10

3. A dress was initially listed at a price that would have given the store a profit of 20 percent of the wholesale cost. The dress sold for 50 dollars. What was the wholesale cost of the dress?

    (A) 100   (B) 90   (C) 75   (D) 60   (E) Not enough information to decide

Duals

4. The capacity of glass X is 80 percent of the capacity of glass Y. Further, glass X contains 6 ounces of punch and is half-full, while glass Y is full. Glass Y contains how many more ounces of punch than glass X?

    (A) 1   (B) 3   (C) 6   (D) 9   (E) Not enough information to decide

5. The capacity of glass X is 80 percent of the capacity of glass Y. Further, Glass X is 70 percent full, and glass Y is 30 percent full. Glass X contains how many more ounces of punch than glass Y?

    (A) 1   (B) 3   (C) 6   (D) 8   (E) Not enough information to decide

6. Car X traveled from city A to city B in 30 minutes. The first half of the distance was covered at 50 miles per hour, and the second half of the distance was covered at 60 miles per hour. What was the average speed of car X?

    (A) 200/11   (B) 400/11   (C) 500/11   (D) 600/11   (E) 700/11

7. Steve bought some apples at a cost of $.60 each and some oranges at a cost of $.50 each. If he paid a total of $4.10 for a total of 8 apples and oranges, how many apples did Steve buy?

    (A) 1   (B) 2   (C) 3   (D) 5   (E) 6

8. Cyclist M leaves point P at 12 noon and travels in a straight path at a constant velocity of 20 miles per hour. Cyclist N leaves point P at 2 PM, travels the same path at a constant velocity, and overtakes M at 4 PM. What was the average speed of N?

    (A) 15   (B) 24   (C) 30   (D) 35   (E) 40

9. A pair of pants and matching shirt cost $52.50. The pants cost two and a half times as much as the shirt. What is the cost of the shirt alone?

    (A) 10   (B) 15   (C) 20   (D) 27   (E) 30

10. Jennifer and Alice are 4 miles apart. If Jennifer starts walking toward Alice at 3 miles per hour and at the same time Alice starts walking toward Jennifer at 2 miles per hour, how much time will pass before they meet?

    (A) 20 minutes   (B) 28 minutes   (C) 43 minutes   (D) 48 minutes   (E) 60 minutes

11. If Robert can assemble a model car in 30 minutes and Craig can assemble the same model car in 20 minutes, how long would it take them, working together, to assemble the model car?

    (A) 12 minutes   (B) 13 minutes   (C) 14 minutes   (D) 15 minutes   (E) 16 minutes

12. How many ounces of nuts costing 80 cents a pound must be mixed with nuts costing 60 cents a pound to make a 10-ounce mixture costing 70 cents a pound?

    (A) 3   (B) 4   (C) 5   (D) 7   (E) 8

13. Tom is 10 years older than Carrie. However, 5 years ago Tom was twice as old as Carrie. How old is Carrie?

    (A) 5   (B) 10   (C) 12   (D) 15   (E) 25

14. Two cars start at the same point and travel in opposite directions. If one car travels at 45 miles per hour and the other at 60 miles per hour, how much time will pass before they are 210 miles apart?

    (A) .5 hours   (B) 1 hour   (C) 1.5 hours   (D) 2 hours   (E) 2.5 hours

15. If the value of x quarters is equal to the value of $x + 32$ nickels, $x =$

    (A) 8   (B) 11   (C) 14   (D) 17   (E) 20

16. Steve has $5.25 in nickels and dimes. If he has 15 more dimes than nickels, how many nickels does he have?

    (A) 20   (B) 25   (C) 27   (D) 30   (E) 33

17. Cathy has equal numbers of nickels and quarters worth a total of $7.50. How many coins does she have?

    (A) 20   (B) 25   (C) 50   (D) 62   (E) 70

Answers and Solutions to Problem Set T

1.   Let S be Scott's age and K be Kathy's age. Then translating the sentence *"If Scott is now 5 years older than Kathy, how old is Scott"* into an equation yields

$$S = K + 5$$

Now, Scott's age 7 years ago can be represented as $S = -7$, and Kathy's age can be represented as $K = -7$. Then translating the sentence *"Seven years ago, Scott was 3 times as old as Kathy was at that time"* into an equation yields $S - 7 = 3(K - 7)$.

Combining this equation with $S = K + 5$ yields the system:

$$S - 7 = 3(K - 7)$$
$$S = K + 5$$

Solving this system gives $S = 14\frac{1}{2}$. The answer is (E).

2.   Since the store would have made a profit of 20 percent on the wholesale cost, the original price P of the dress was 120 percent of the cost: $P = 1.2C$. Now, translating *"After reducing the asking price by 10 percent, the dress sold for a net profit of 10 dollars"* into an equation yields:
$$P - .1P = C + 10$$

Simplifying gives $.9P = C + 10$

Solving for P yields $P = \dfrac{C + 10}{.9}$

Plugging this expression for P into $P = 1.2C$ gives

$$\frac{C + 10}{.9} = 1.2C$$

Solving this equation for C yields $C = 125$. The answer is (B).

3.   There is not sufficient information since the selling price is not related to any other information. Note, the phrase "initially listed" implies that there was more than one asking price. If it wasn't for that phrase, the information would be sufficient. The answer is (E).

4.   Since *"the capacity of glass X is 80 percent of the capacity of glass Y,"* we get

$$X = .8Y$$

Since *"glass X contains 6 ounces of punch and is half-full,"* the capacity of glass X is 12 ounces. Plugging this into the equation yields

$$12 = .8Y$$

$$12/.8 = Y$$

$$15 = Y$$

Hence, glass Y contains $15 - 6 = 9$ more ounces of punch than glass X. The answer is (D).

5. Now, there is not sufficient information to solve the problem since it does not provide any absolute numbers. The following diagram shows two situations: one in which Glass X contains 5.2 more ounces of punch than glass Y, and one in which Glass X contains 2.6 more ounces than glass Y.

Scenario I (Glass X contains 5.2 more ounces than glass Y.)

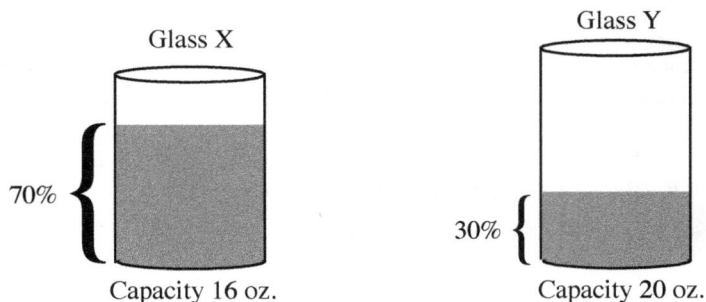

Glass X

Glass Y

70%

30%

Capacity 16 oz.

Capacity 20 oz.

Scenario II (Glass X contains 2.6 more ounces than glass Y.)

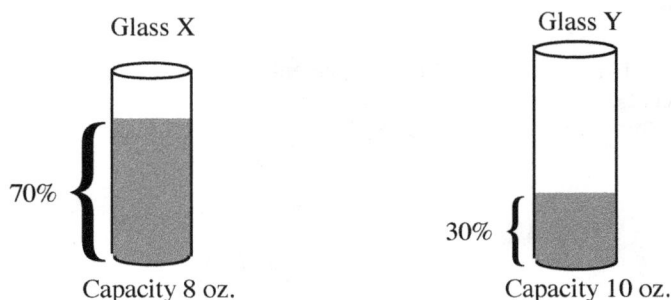

Glass X

Glass Y

70%

30%

Capacity 8 oz.

Capacity 10 oz.

The answer is (E).

6. Recall that $Average\ Speed = \dfrac{Total\ Distance}{Total\ Time}$. Now, the setup to the question gives the total time for the trip—30 minutes. Hence, to answer the question, we need to find the distance of the trip.

Let *t* equal the time for the first half of the trip. Then since the whole trip took 30 minutes (or 1/2 hour), the second half of the trip took $1/2 - t$ hours. Now, from the formula *Distance = Rate × Time*, we get for the first half of the trip:

$$\frac{d}{2} = 50 \cdot t$$

And for the second half of the trip, we get

$$\frac{d}{2} = 60\left(\frac{1}{2} - t\right)$$

Solving this system yields

$$d = 300/11$$

Hence, the $Average\ Speed = \dfrac{Total\ Distance}{Total\ Time} = \dfrac{300/11}{1/2} = \dfrac{600}{11}$. The answer is (D).

7. Let x denote the number of apples bought, and let y denote the number of oranges bought. Then, translating the sentence *"Steve bought some apples at a cost of $.60 each and some oranges at a cost of $.50 each"* into an equation yields

$$.60x + .50y = 4.10$$

Since there are two variables and only one equation, the key to this problem is finding a second equation that relates x and y. Since he bought a total of 8 apples and oranges, we get

$$x + y = 8$$

Solving this system yields $x = 1$. Hence, he bought one apple, and the answer is (A).

8. Recall the formula *Distance = Rate × Time*, or $D = R \cdot T$. From the second sentence, we get for Cyclist N:

$$D = R \cdot 2$$

Now, Cyclist M traveled at 20 miles per hour and took 4 hours. Hence, Cyclist M traveled a total distance of

$$D = R \cdot T = 20 \cdot 4 = 80 \text{ miles}$$

Since the cyclists covered the same distance at the moment they met, we can plug this value for D into the equation $D = R \cdot 2$:

$$80 = R \cdot 2$$
$$40 = R$$

The answer is (E).

9. Let p denote the cost of the pants, and let s denote the cost of the shirt. Then from the question setup, $p + s = 52.50$.

Translating *"The pants cost two and a half times as much as the shirt"* into an equation gives $p = 2.5s$. Plugging this into the above equation gives

$$2.5s + s = 52.50$$
$$3.5s = 52.50$$
$$s = 15$$

The answer is (B).

10. Let the distance Jennifer walks be x. Then since they are 4 miles apart, Alice will walk $4 - x$ miles. The key to this problem is that when they meet each person will have walked for an equal amount of time. Solving the equation $D = R \times T$ for T yields $T = D/R$. Hence,

$$\frac{x}{3} = \frac{4 - x}{2}$$
$$2x = 3(4 - x)$$
$$2x = 12 - 3x$$
$$5x = 12$$
$$x = 12/5$$

Therefore, the time that Jennifer walks is $T = \dfrac{D}{R} = \dfrac{12/5}{3} = \dfrac{12}{5} \times \dfrac{1}{3} = \dfrac{4}{5}$ of an hour. Converting this into minutes gives $\dfrac{4}{5} \times 60 = 48$ minutes. The answer is (D).

11. Let t be the time it takes the boys, working together, to assemble the model car. Then their combined rate is $1/t$, and their individual rates are $1/30$ and $1/20$. Now, their combined rate is merely the sum of their individual rates:

$$\frac{1}{t} = \frac{1}{30} + \frac{1}{20}$$

Solving this equation for t yields $t = 12$. The answer is (A).

12. Let x be the amount of nuts at 80 cents a pound. Then $10 - x$ is the amount of nuts at 60 cents a pound. The cost of the 80-cent nuts is $80x$, the cost of the 60-cent nuts is $60(10 - x)$, and the cost of the mixture is $70(10)$ cents. Since the cost of the mixture is the sum of the costs of the 70- and 80-cent nuts, we get

$$80x + 60(10 - x) = 70(10)$$

Solving this equation for x yields $x = 5$. The answer is (C).

13. Let C be Carrie's age. Then Tom's age is $C + 10$. Now, 5 years ago, Carrie's age was $C - 5$ and Tom's age was $(C + 10) - 5 = C + 5$. Since at that time, Tom was twice as old as Carrie, we get $5 + C = 2(C - 5)$. Solving this equation for C yields $C = 15$. The answer is (D).

14. Since the cars start at the same time, the time each has traveled is the same. Let t be the time when the cars are 210 miles apart. The equation $D = R \times T$, yields

$$210 = 45 \cdot t + 60 \cdot t$$
$$210 = 105 \cdot t$$
$$2 = t$$

The answer is (D).

15. The value of the x quarters is $25x$, and the value of the $x + 32$ nickels is $5(x + 32)$. Since these two quantities are equal, we get

$$25x = 5(x + 32)$$
$$25x = 5x + 160$$
$$20x = 160$$
$$x = 8$$

The answer is (A).

16. Let N stand for the number of nickels. Then the number of dimes is $N + 15$. The value of the nickels is $5N$, and the value of the dimes is $10(N + 15)$. Since the total value of the nickels and dimes is 525¢, we get

$$5N + 10(N + 15) = 525$$
$$15N + 150 = 525$$
$$15N = 375$$
$$N = 25$$

Hence, there are 25 nickels, and the answer is (B).

17. Let x stand for both the number of nickels and the number of quarters. Then the value of the nickels is $5x$ and the value of the quarters is $25x$. Since the total value of the coins is $7.50, we get

$$5x + 25x = 750$$
$$30x = 750$$
$$x = 25$$

Hence, she has $x + x = 25 + 25 = 50$ coins. The answer is (C).

Sequences & Series

A sequence is an ordered list of numbers. The following is a sequence of odd numbers:

$$1, 3, 5, 7, \ldots$$

A term of a sequence is identified by its position in the sequence. In the above sequence, 1 is the first term, 3 is the second term, etc. The ellipsis symbol (. . .) indicates that the sequence continues forever.

Example 1: In sequence S, the 3rd term is 4, the 2nd term is three times the 1st, and the 3rd term is four times the 2nd. What is the 1st term in sequence S?

  (A) 0   (B) 1/3   (C) 1   (D) 3/2   (E) 4

We know *"the 3rd term of S is 4,"* and that *"the 3rd term is four times the 2nd."* This is equivalent to saying the 2nd term is 1/4 the 3rd term: $\frac{1}{4} \cdot 4 = 1$. Further, we know *"the 2nd term is three times the 1st."* This is equivalent to saying the 1st term is 1/3 the 2nd term: $\frac{1}{3} \cdot 1 = \frac{1}{3}$. Hence, the first term of the sequence is fully determined:

$$1/3, 1, 4$$

The answer is (B).

Example 2: Except for the first two numbers, every number in the sequence $-1, 3, -3, \ldots$ is the product of the two immediately preceding numbers. How many numbers of this sequence are odd?

  (A) one   (B) two   (C) three   (D) four   (E) more than four

Since *"every number in the sequence $-1, 3, -3, \ldots$ is the product of the two immediately preceding numbers,"* the forth term of the sequence is $-9 = 3(-3)$. The first 6 terms of this sequence are

$$-1, 3, -3, -9, 27, -243, \ldots$$

At least six numbers in this sequence are odd: $-1, 3, -3, -9, 27, -243$. The answer is (E).

Arithmetic Progressions

An arithmetic progression is a sequence in which the difference between any two consecutive terms is the same. This is the same as saying: each term exceeds the previous term by a fixed amount. For example, $0, 6, 12, 18, \ldots$ is an arithmetic progression in which the common difference is 6. The sequence $8, 4, 0, -4, \ldots$ is arithmetic with a common difference of -4.

Example 3: The seventh number in a sequence of numbers is 31 and each number after the first number in the sequence is 4 less than the number immediately preceding it. What is the fourth number in the sequence?

(A) 15   (B) 19   (C) 35   (D) 43   (E) 51

Since each number *"in the sequence is 4 less than the number immediately preceding it,"* the sixth term is $31 + 4 = 35$; the fifth number in the sequence is $35 + 4 = 39$; and the fourth number in the sequence is $39 + 4 = 43$. The answer is (D). Following is the sequence written out:

$$55, 51, 47, 43, 39, 35, 31, 27, 23, 19, 15, 11, \ldots$$

Sequence Formulas

Students with strong backgrounds in mathematics may prefer to solve sequence problems by using formulas.

Since each term of an arithmetic progression *"exceeds the previous term by a fixed amount,"* we get the following:

first term	$a + 0d$	where a is the first term and d is the common difference
second term	$a + 1d$	
third term	$a + 2d$	
fourth term	$a + 3d$	
	$\ldots$	
nth term	$a + (n - 1)d$	This formula generates the nth term

The sum of the first n terms of an arithmetic sequence is

$$\frac{n}{2}\left[2a + (n - 1)d\right]$$

Geometric Progressions

A geometric progression is a sequence in which the ratio of any two consecutive terms is the same. Thus, each term is generated by multiplying the preceding term by a fixed number. For example, $-3, 6, -12, 24, \ldots$ is a geometric progression in which the common ratio is -2. The sequence $32, 16, 8, 4, \ldots$ is geometric with common ratio $1/2$.

Example 4: What is the sixth term of the sequence $90, -30, 10, -10/3, \ldots$?

(A) 1/3
(B) 0
(C) −10/27
(D) −3
(E) −100/3

Since the common ratio between any two consecutive terms is $-1/3$, the fifth term is $\dfrac{10}{9} = \left(-\dfrac{1}{3}\right) \cdot \left(-\dfrac{10}{3}\right)$.

Hence, the sixth number in the sequence is $-\dfrac{10}{27} = \left(-\dfrac{1}{3}\right) \cdot \left(\dfrac{10}{9}\right)$. The answer is (C).

Sequence Formulas

Since each term of a geometric progression *"is generated by multiplying the preceding term by a fixed number,"* we get the following:

first term	a
second term	ar^1
third term	ar^2
fourth term	ar^3

where r is the common ratio

$$\ldots$$

nth term	$a_n = ar^{n-1}$	This formula generates the nth term

The sum of the first n terms of an geometric sequence is

$$\frac{a\left(1 - r^n\right)}{1 - r}$$

SERIES

A series is simply the sum of the terms of a sequence. The following is a series of even numbers formed from the sequence $2, 4, 6, 8, \ldots$:

$$2 + 4 + 6 + 8 + \cdots$$

A term of a series is identified by its position in the series. In the above series, 2 is the first term, 4 is the second term, etc. The ellipsis symbol ($\ldots$) indicates that the series continues forever.

Example 5: The sum of the squares of the first n positive integers $1^2 + 2^2 + 3^2 + \ldots + n^2$ is $\frac{n(n+1)(2n+1)}{6}$. What is the sum of the squares of the first 9 positive integers?

(A) 90   (B) 125   (C) 200   (D) 285   (E) 682

We are given a formula for the sum of the squares of the first n positive integers. Plugging $n = 9$ into this formula yields

$$\frac{n(n+1)(2n+1)}{6} = \frac{9(9+1)(2 \cdot 9 + 1)}{6} = \frac{9(10)(19)}{6} = 285$$

The answer is (D).

Example 6: For all integers $x > 1$, $<x> = 2x + (2x - 1) + (2x - 2) + \ldots + 2 + 1$. What is the value of $<3> \cdot <2>$?

(A) 60   (B) 116   (C) 210   (D) 263   (E) 478

$<3> = 2(3) + (2 \cdot 3 - 1) + (2 \cdot 3 - 2) + (2 \cdot 3 - 3) + (2 \cdot 3 - 4) + (2 \cdot 3 - 5) = 6 + 5 + 4 + 3 + 2 + 1 = 21$

$<2> = 2(2) + (2 \cdot 2 - 1) + (2 \cdot 2 - 2) + (2 \cdot 2 - 3) = 4 + 3 + 2 + 1 = 10$

Hence, $<3> \cdot <2> = 21 \cdot 10 = 210$, and the answer is (C).

Problem Set U:

1. By dividing 21 into 1, the fraction 1/21 can be written as a repeating decimal: 0.476190476190 . . . where the block of digits 476190 repeats. What is the 54th digit following the decimal point?

    (A) 0   (B) 4   (C) 6   (D) 7   (E) 9

2. The positive integers $P, Q, R, S,$ and T increase in order of size such that the value of each successive integer is one more than the preceding integer and the value of T is 6. What is the value of R?

    (A) 0   (B) 1   (C) 2   (D) 3   (E) 4

3. Let u represent the sum of the integers from 1 through 20, and let v represent the sum of the integers from 21 through 40. What is the value of $v - u$?

    (A) 21   (B) 39   (C) 200   (D) 320   (E) 400

4. In the pattern of dots, each row after the first row has two more dots than the row immediately above it. Row 6 contains how many dots?

    (A) 6   (B) 8   (C) 10   (D) 11   (E) 12

5. In sequence S, all odd numbered terms are equal and all even numbered terms are equal. The first term in the sequence is $\sqrt{2}$ and the second term is -2. What is approximately the sum of two consecutive terms of the sequence?

    (A) -2 (B) -0.6 (C) 0   (D) 2   (E) 0.8

6. The sum of the first n even, positive integers is $2 + 4 + 6 + \cdots + 2n$ is $n(n + 1)$. What is the sum of the first 20 even, positive integers?

    (A) 120   (B) 188   (C) 362   (D) 406   (E) 420

7. In the array of numbers to the right, each number above the bottom row is equal to three times the number immediately below it. What is value of $x + y$?

27	x	81	-108
9	-18	27	-36
3	-6	y	-12
1	-2	3	-4

    (A) -45 (B) -15 (C) -2 (D) 20   (E) 77

8. The first term of a sequence is 2. All subsequent terms are found by adding 3 to the immediately preceding term and then multiplying the sum by 2. Which of the following describes the terms of the sequence?

    (A) Each term is odd   (B) Each term is even   (C) The terms are: even, odd, even, odd, etc.
    (D) The terms are: even, odd, odd, odd, etc.   (E) The terms are: even, odd, odd, even, odd, odd, etc.

9. Except for the first two numbers, every number in the sequence $-1, 3, 2, . . .$ is the sum of the two immediately preceding numbers. How many numbers of this sequence are even?

    (A) none   (B) one   (C) two   (D) three   (E) more than three

10. In the sequence $w, x, y, 30$, adding any one of the first three terms to the term immediately following it yields $w/2$. What is the value of w ?

    (A) -60 (B) -30 (C) 0   (D) 5   (E) 25

Answers and Solutions to Problem Set U

1.   The sixth digit following the decimal point is the number zero: 0.476190476190 . . . Since the digits repeat in blocks of six numbers, 0 will appear in the space for all multiples of six. Since 54 is a multiple of six, the 54th digit following the decimal point is 0. The answer is (A).

2.   We know that T is 6; and therefore from the fact that *"each successive integer is one more than the preceding integer"* we see that S is 5. Continuing in this manner yields the following unique sequence:

$$
\begin{array}{ccccc}
P & Q & R & S & T \\
2 & 3 & 4 & 5 & 6
\end{array}
$$

Hence, the value of R is 4. The answer is (E).

3.   Forming the series for u and v yields

$$u = 1 + 2 + \cdots + 19 + 20$$
$$v = 21 + 22 + \cdots + 39 + 40$$

Subtracting the series for u from the series for v yields

$$v - u = \underbrace{20 + 20 + \cdots + 20 + 20}_{20 \text{ times}} = 20 \cdot 20 = 400$$

The answer is (E).

4.   Extending the dots to six rows yields

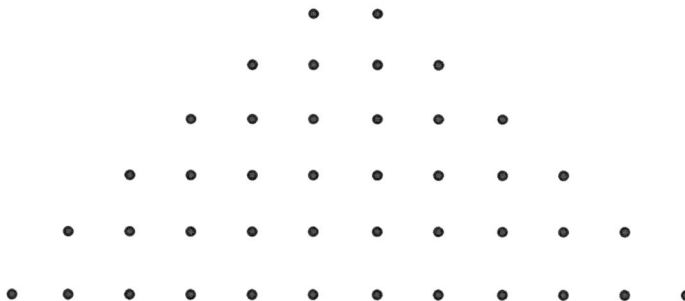

Row 6 has twelve dots. Hence, the answer is (E).

5.   Since the *"the first term in the sequence is $\sqrt{2}$ "* and *"all odd numbered terms are equal,"* all odd numbered terms equal $\sqrt{2}$. Since the *"the second term is –2"* and *"all even numbered terms are equal,"* all even numbered terms equal –2. Hence, the sum of any two consecutive terms of the sequence is $\sqrt{2} + (-2) \approx -0.6$ (remember, $\sqrt{2} \approx 1.4$). The answer is (B).

6.   We are given a formula for the sum of the first n even, positive integers. Plugging $n = 20$ into this formula yields

$$n(n + 1) = 20(20 + 1) = 20(21) = 420$$

The answer is (E).

7.   Since *"each number above the bottom row is equal to three times the number immediately below it,"* $x = 3(-18) = -54$ and $y = 3(3) = 9$. Hence, $x + y = -54 + 9 = -45$. The answer is (A).

8.   The first term is even, and all subsequent terms are found by multiplying a number by 2. Hence, all terms of the sequence are even. The answer is (B). Following is the sequence:

$$2, 10, 26, 58, \ldots$$

9.   Since *"every number in the sequence* $-1, 3, 2, \ldots$ *is the sum of the two immediately preceding numbers,"* the forth term of the sequence is $5 = 3 + 2$. The first 12 terms of this sequence are

$$-1, 3, 2, 5, 7, 12, 19, 31, 50, 81, 131, 212, \ldots$$

At least four numbers in this sequence are even: 2, 12, 50, and 212. The answer is (E).

10. Since *"adding any one of the first three terms to the term immediately following it yields w/2,"* we get

$$w + x = \frac{w}{2}$$
$$x + y = \frac{w}{2}$$
$$y + 30 = \frac{w}{2}$$

Subtracting the last equation from the second equation yields $x - 30 = 0$. That is $x = 30$. Plugging $x = 30$ into the first equation yields

$$w + 30 = w/2$$

Multiplying both sides by 2 yields

$$2w + 60 = w$$

Subtracting w from both sides yields

$$w + 60 = 0$$

Finally, subtracting 60 from both sides yields

$$w = -60$$

The answer is (A).

Counting

Counting may have been one of humankind's first thought processes; nevertheless, counting can be deceptively hard. In part, because we often forget some of the principles of counting, but also because counting can be inherently difficult.

Note! **When counting elements that are in overlapping sets, the total number will equal the number in one group plus the number in the other group minus the number common to both groups. Venn diagrams are very helpful with these problems.**

Example 1: If in a certain school 20 students are taking math and 10 are taking history and 7 are taking both, how many students are taking either math or history?

(A) 20   (B) 22   (C) 23   (D) 25   (E) 29

Solution:

History   Math

10   7   20

Both History and Math

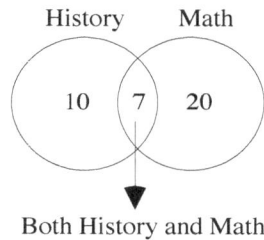

By the principle stated above, we add 10 and 20 and then subtract 7 from the result. Thus, there are $(10 + 20) - 7 = 23$ students. The answer is (C).

Note! **The number of integers between two integers <u>inclusive</u> is one more than their difference.**

Example 2: How many integers are there between 49 and 101, inclusive?

(A) 50   (B) 51   (C) 52   (D) 53   (E) 54

By the principle stated above, the number of integers between 49 and 101 inclusive is $(101 - 49) + 1 = 53$. The answer is (D). To see this more clearly, choose smaller numbers, say, 9 and 11. The difference between 9 and 11 is 2. But there are three numbers between them inclusive—9, 10, and 11—one more than their difference.

Note! *Fundamental Principle of Counting*: **If an event occurs *m* times, and each of the *m* events is followed by a second event which occurs *k* times, then the second event follows the first event *m* · *k* times.**

The following diagram illustrates the fundamental principle of counting for an event that occurs 3 times with each occurrence being followed by a second event that occurs 2 times for a total of $3 \cdot 2 = 6$ events:

Event One: 3 times

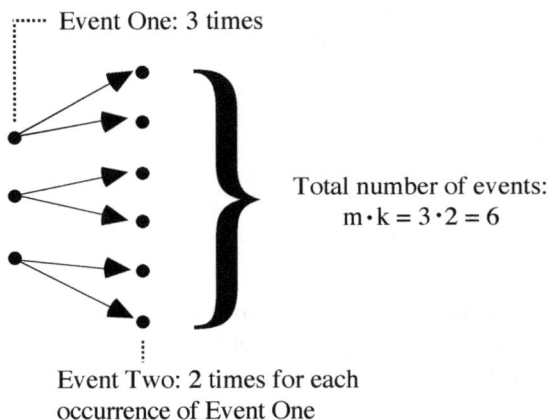

Total number of events:
$m \cdot k = 3 \cdot 2 = 6$

Event Two: 2 times for each
occurrence of Event One

Example 3: A drum contains 3 to 5 jars each of which contains 30 to 40 marbles. If 10 percent of the marbles are flawed, what is the greatest possible number of flawed marbles in the drum?

(A) 51   (B) 40   (C) 30   (D) 20   (E) 12

There is at most 5 jars each of which contains at most 40 marbles; so by the fundamental counting principle, there is at most $5 \cdot 40 = 200$ marbles in the drum. Since 10 percent of the marbles are flawed, there is at most $20 = 10\% \cdot 200$ flawed marbles. The answer is (D).

MISCELLANEOUS COUNTING PROBLEMS

Example 4: In a legislative body of 200 people, the number of Democrats is 50 less than 4 times the number of Republicans. If one fifth of the legislators are neither Republican nor Democrat, how many of the legislators are Republicans?

(A) 42   (B) 50   (C) 71   (D) 95   (E) 124

Let D be the number of Democrats and let R be the number of Republicans. "One fifth of the legislators are neither Republican nor Democrat," so there are $200/5 = 40$ legislators who are neither Republican nor Democrat. Hence, there are $200 - 40 = 160$ Democrats and Republicans, or $D + R = 160$. Translating the clause "the number of Democrats is 50 less than 4 times the number of Republicans" into an equation yields $D = 4R - 50$. Plugging this into the equation $D + R = 160$ yields

$$4R - 50 + R = 160$$
$$5R - 50 = 160$$
$$5R = 210$$
$$R = 42$$

The answer is (A).

Example 5: Speed bumps are being placed at 20-foot intervals along a road 1015 feet long. If the first speed bump is placed at one end of the road, how many speed bumps are needed?

(A) 49   (B) 50   (C) 51   (D) 52   (E) 53

Since the road is 1015 feet long and the speed bumps are 20 feet apart, there are $1015/20 = 50.75$, or 50 full sections in the road. If we ignore the first speed bump and associate the speed bump at the end of each section with that section, then there are 50 speed bumps (one for each of the fifty full sections). Counting the first speed bump gives a total of 51 speed bumps. The answer is (C).

SETS

A *set* is a collection of objects, and the objects are called *elements* of the set. You may be asked to form the *union* of two sets, which contains all the objects from either set. You may also be asked to form the *intersection* of two sets, which contains only the objects that are in both sets. For example, if Set $A = \{1, 2, 5\}$ and Set $B = \{5, 10, 21\}$, then the union of sets A and B would be $\{1, 2, 5, 10, 21\}$ and the intersection would be $\{5\}$.

Problem Set V:

1. The number of integers between 29 and 69, inclusive is
    (A) 39   (B) 40   (C) 41   (D) 42   (E) 43

2. A school has a total enrollment of 150 students. There are 63 students taking French, 48 taking chemistry, and 21 taking both. How many students are taking <u>neither</u> French nor chemistry?
    (A) 60   (B) 65   (C) 71   (D) 75   (E) 97

3. The number of minutes in 1 1/3 hours is
    (A) 60   (B) 65   (C) 71   (D) 80   (E) 97

4. A web press prints 5 pages every 2 seconds. At this rate, how many pages will the press print in 7 minutes?
    (A) 350   (B) 540   (C) 700   (D) 950   (E) 1050

5. A school has a total enrollment of 90 students. There are 30 students taking physics, 25 taking English, and 13 taking both. What percentage of the students are taking either physics or English?
    (A) 30%   (B) 36%   (C) 47%   (D) 51%   (E) 58%

6. Callers 49 through 91 to a radio show won a prize. How many callers won a prize?
    (A) 42   (B) 43   (C) 44   (D) 45   (E) 46

7. A rancher is constructing a fence by stringing wire between posts 20 feet apart. If the fence is 400 feet long, how many posts must the rancher use?
    (A) 18   (B) 19   (C) 20   (D) 21   (E) 22

8. The number of marbles in x jars , each containing 15 marbles, plus the number of marbles in $3x$ jars , each containing 20 marbles is
    (A) $65x$ (B) $70x$ (C) $75x$ (D) $80x$ (E) $85x$

9. The number of integers from 2 to 10^3, inclusive is
    (A) 997   (B) 998   (C) 999   (D) 1000   (E) 1001

10. In a small town, 16 people own Fords and 11 people own Toyotas. If exactly 15 people own only one of the two types of cars, how many people own both types of cars.
    (A) 2   (B) 6   (C) 7   (D) 12   (E) 14

Answers and Solutions to Problem Set V

1. Since the number of integers between two integers inclusive is one more than their difference, we get $69 - 29 + 1 = 41$ integers. The answer is (C).

2. First display the information in a Venn diagram:

French   Chemistry

63 ⟨21⟩ 48

Both French and Chemistry

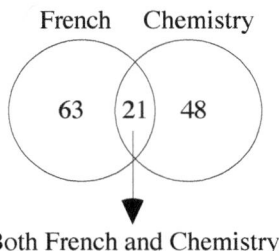

Adding the number of students taking French and the number of students taking chemistry and then subtracting the number of students taking both yields $(63 + 48) - 21 = 90$. This is the number of students enrolled in *either* French or chemistry or both. Since the total school enrollment is 150, there are $150 - 90 = 60$ students enrolled in *neither* French nor chemistry. The answer is (A).

3. There are 60 minutes in an hour. Hence, there are $1\frac{1}{3} \cdot 60 = 80$ minutes in 1 1/3 hours. The answer is (D).

4. Since there are 60 seconds in a minute and the press prints 5 pages every 2 seconds, the press prints $5 \cdot 30 = 150$ pages in one minute. Hence, in 7 minutes, the press will print $7 \cdot 150 = 1050$ pages. The answer is (E).

5. First display the information in a Venn diagram:

Physics   English

30 ⟨13⟩ 25

Both Physics and English

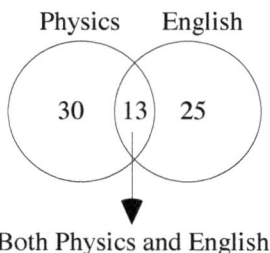

Adding the number of students taking physics and the number of students taking English and then subtracting the number of students taking both yields $(30 + 25) = -13 = 42$. This is the number of students enrolled in *either* physics or English or both. The total school enrollment is 90, so forming the ratio yields

$$\frac{physics\ or\ math\ enrollment}{total\ enrollment} = \frac{42}{90} \approx .47 = 47\%$$

The answer is (C).

6. Since the number of integers between two integers inclusive is one more than their difference, $(91 - 49) + 1 = 43$ callers won a prize. The answer is (B).

7. Since the fence is 400 feet long and the posts are 20 feet apart, there are 400/20 = 20 sections in the fence. Now, if we ignore the first post and associate the post at the end of each section with that section, then there are 20 posts (one for each of the twenty sections). Counting the first post gives a total of 21 posts. The answer is (D).

8. The x jars have $15x$ marbles, and the $3x$ jars have $20 \cdot 3x = 60x$ marbles. Hence, there is a total of

$$15x + 60x = 75x \text{ marbles}$$

The answer is (C).

9. Since the number of integers between two integers inclusive is one more than their difference, we have $(10^3 - 2) + 1 = (1000 - 2) + 1 = 999$ integers. The answer is (C).

10. This is a hard problem. Let x be the number of people who own both types of cars. Then the number of people who own only Fords is $16 - x$, and the number of people who own only Toyotas is $11 - x$. Adding these two expressions gives the number of people who own only one of the two types of cars, which we are told is 15:

$$(16 - x) + (11 - x) = 15$$

Add like terms:

$$27 - 2x = 15$$

Subtract 27 from both sides of the equation:

$$-2x = -12$$

Finally, divide both sides of the equation by –2:

$$x = 6$$

The answer is (B).

Method II (Plugging-In):

We can also solve the problem working backward from the solutions.

Start with Choice (A). If only 2 people own both types of cars, then 14 (= 16 – 2) own only a Ford and 9 (= 11 – 2) own only a Toyota. Hence, exactly 23 (= 14 + 9) own only one type of car, but we are told that exactly 15 (not 23) own only one type of car. This eliminates choice (A).

Now, turn to Choice (B). If only 6 people own both types of cars, then 10 (= 16 – 6) own only a Ford and 5 (= 11 – 6) own only a Toyota. Hence, exactly 15 (= 10 + 5) own only one type of car, *and* we are told that exactly 15 own only one type of car. So, the answer is (B).

Probability & Statistics

PROBABILITY

We know what probability means, but what is its formal definition? Let's use our intuition to define it. If there is no chance that an event will occur, then its probability of occurring should be 0. On the other extreme, if an event is certain to occur, then its probability of occurring should be 100%, or 1. Hence, our *probability* should be a number between 0 and 1, inclusive. But what kind of number? Suppose your favorite actor has a 1 in 3 chance of winning the Oscar for best actor. This can be measured by forming the fraction 1/3. Hence, a *probability* is a fraction where the top is the number of ways an event can occur and the bottom is the total number of possible events:

$$P = \frac{Number\ of\ ways\ an\ event\ can\ occur}{Number\ of\ total\ possible\ events}$$

Example: *Flipping a coin*

What's the probability of getting heads when flipping a coin?

There is only one way to get heads in a coin toss. Hence, the top of the probability fraction is 1. There are two possible results: heads or tails. Forming the probability fraction gives 1/2.

Example: *Tossing a die*

What's the probability of getting a 3 when tossing a die?

A die (a cube) has six faces, numbered 1 through 6. There is only one way to get a 3. Hence, the top of the fraction is 1. There are 6 possible results: 1, 2, 3, 4, 5, and 6. Forming the probability fraction gives 1/6.

Example: *Drawing a card from a deck*

What's the probability of getting a king when drawing a card from a deck of cards?

A deck of cards has four kings, so there are 4 ways to get a king. Hence, the top of the fraction is 4. There are 52 total cards in a deck. Forming the probability fraction gives 4/52, which reduces to 1/13. Hence, there is 1 chance in 13 of getting a king.

Example: *Drawing marbles from a bowl*

What's the probability of drawing a blue marble from a bowl containing 4 red marbles, 5 blue marbles, and 5 green marbles?

There are five ways of drawing a blue marble. Hence, the top of the fraction is 5. There are 14 (= 4 + 5 + 5) possible results. Forming the probability fraction gives 5/14.

Example: *Drawing marbles from a bowl (second drawing)*

What's the probability of drawing a red marble from the same bowl, given that the first marble drawn was blue and was not placed back in the bowl?

There are four ways of drawing a red marble. Hence, the top of the fraction is 4. Since the blue marble from the first drawing was not replaced, there are only 4 blue marbles remaining. Hence, there are 13 (= 4 + 4 + 5) possible results. Forming the probability fraction gives 4/13.

Consecutive Probabilities

What's the probability of getting heads twice in a row when flipping a coin twice? Previously we calculated the probability for the first flip to be 1/2. Since the second flip is not affected by the first (these are called *independent* events), its probability is also 1/2. Forming the product yields the probability of two heads in a row: $\frac{1}{2} \times \frac{1}{2} = \frac{1}{4}$.

What's the probability of drawing a blue marble and then a red marble from a bowl containing 4 red marbles, 5 blue marbles, and 5 green marbles? (Assume that the marbles are not replaced after being selected.) As calculated before, there is a 5/14 likelihood of selecting a blue marble first and a 4/13 likelihood of selecting a red marble second. Forming the product yields the probability of a red marble immediately followed by a blue marble: $\frac{5}{14} \times \frac{4}{13} = \frac{20}{182} = \frac{10}{91}$.

These two examples can be generalized into the following rule for calculating consecutive probabilities:

> **To calculate consecutive probabilities, multiply the individual probabilities.**

This rule applies to two, three, or any number of consecutive probabilities.

Either-Or **Probabilities**

What's the probability of getting either heads or tails when flipping a coin once? Since the only possible outcomes are heads or tails, we expect the probability to be 100%, or 1: $\frac{1}{2} + \frac{1}{2} = 1$. Note that the events heads and tails are independent. That is, if heads occurs, then tails cannot (and vice versa).

What's the probability of drawing a red marble or a green marble from a bowl containing 4 red marbles, 5 blue marbles, and 5 green marbles? There are 4 red marbles out of 14 total marbles. So the probability of selecting a red marble is 4/14 = 2/7. Similarly, the probability of selecting a green marble is 5/14. So the probability of selecting a red or green marble is $\frac{2}{7} + \frac{5}{14} = \frac{9}{14}$. Note again that the events are independent. For instance, if a red marble is selected, then neither a blue marble nor a green marble is selected.

These two examples can be generalized into the following rule for calculating *either-or* probabilities:

> **To calculate *either-or* probabilities, add the individual probabilities (only if the events are independent).**

The probabilities in the two immediately preceding examples can be calculated more naturally by adding up the events that occur and then dividing by the total number of possible events. For the coin example, we get 2 events (heads or tails) divided by the total number of possible events, 2 (heads and tails): 2/2 = 1. For the marble example, we get 9 (= 4 + 5) ways the event can occur divided by 14 (= 4 + 5 + 5) possible events: 9/14.

If it's more natural to calculate the *either-or* probabilities above by adding up the events that occur and then dividing by the total number of possible events, why did we introduce a second way of calculating the probabilities? Because in some cases, you may have to add the individual probabilities. For example, you may be given the individual probabilities of two independent events and be asked for the probability that either could occur. You now know to merely add their individual probabilities.

Geometric Probability

In this type of problem, you will be given two figures, with one inside the other. You'll then be asked what is the probability that a randomly selected point will be in the smaller figure. These problems are solved with the same principle we have been using: $Probability = \dfrac{desired\ outcome}{possible\ outcomes}$.

Example: In the figure, the smaller square has sides of length 2 and the larger square has sides of length 4. If a point is chosen at random from the large square, what is the probability that it will be from the small square?

Applying the probability principle, we get $Probability = \dfrac{area\ of\ the\ small\ square}{area\ of\ the\ large\ square} = \dfrac{2^2}{4^2} = \dfrac{4}{16} = \dfrac{1}{4}$.

STATISTICS

Statistics is the study of the patterns and relationships of numbers and data. There are four main concepts that may appear on the test:

Median

When a set of numbers is arranged in order of size, the *median* is the middle number. For example, the median of the set $\{8, 9, 10, 11, 12\}$ is 10 because it is the middle number. In this case, the median is also the mean (average). But this is usually not the case. For example, the median of the set $\{8, 9, 10, 11, 17\}$ is 10 because it is the middle number, but the mean is $11 = \dfrac{8+9+10+11+17}{5}$. If a set contains an even number of elements, then the median is the average of the two middle elements. For example, the median of the set $\{1, 5, 8, 20\}$ is $6.5 \left(= \dfrac{5+8}{2} \right)$.

Example: What is the median of $0, -2, 256, 18, \sqrt{2}$?

Arranging the numbers from smallest to largest (we could also arrange the numbers from the largest to smallest; the answer would be the same), we get $-2, 0, \sqrt{2}, 18, 256$. The median is the middle number, $\sqrt{2}$.

Mode

The *mode* is the number or numbers that appear most frequently in a set. Note that this definition allows a set of numbers to have more than one mode.

Example: What is the mode of $3, -4, 3, 7, 9, 7.5$?

The number 3 is the mode because it is the only number that is listed more than once.

Example: What is the mode of $2, \pi, 2, -9, \pi, 5$?

Both 2 and π are modes because each occurs twice, which is the greatest number of occurrences for any number in the list.

Range

The *range* is the distance between the smallest and largest numbers in a set. To calculate the range, merely subtract the smallest number from the largest number.

Example: What is the range of $2, 8, 1, -6, \pi, 1/2$?

The largest number in this set is 8, and the smallest number is -6. Hence, the range is $8 - (-6) = 8 + 6 = 14$.

Standard Deviation

On the test, you are not expected to know the definition of standard deviation. However, you may be presented with the definition of standard deviation and then be asked a question based on the definition. To make sure we cover all possible bases, we'll briefly discuss this concept.

Standard deviation measures how far the numbers in a set vary from the set's mean. If the numbers are scattered far from the set's mean, then the standard deviation is large. If the numbers are bunched up near the set's mean, then the standard deviation is small.

Example: Which of the following sets has the larger standard deviation?

$$A = \{1, 2, 3, 4, 5\}$$
$$B = \{1, 4, 15, 21, 34\}$$

All the numbers in Set A are within 2 units of the mean, 3. All the numbers in Set B are greater than 5 units from the mean, 15 (except, or course, the mean itself). Hence, the standard deviation of Set B is greater.

Problem Set W:

1. The median is larger than the average for which one of the following sets of integers?
   (A) $\{8, 9, 10, 11, 12\}$
   (B) $\{8, 9, 10, 11, 13\}$
   (C) $\{8, 10, 10, 10, 12\}$
   (D) $\{10, 10, 10, 10, 10\}$
   (E) $\{7, 9, 10, 11, 12\}$

2. A hat contains 15 marbles, and each marble is numbered with one and only one of the numbers 1, 2, 3. From a group of 15 people, each person selects exactly 1 marble from the hat.

Numbered Marble	Number of People Who Selected The Marble
1	4
2	5
3	6

   What is the probability that a person selected at random picked a marble numbered 2 or greater?
   (A) 5/15   (B) 9/15   (C) 10/15   (D) 11/15   (E) 1

3. If $x < y < z$, $z = ky$, $x = 0$, and the average of the numbers x, y, and z is 3 times the median, what is the value of k?

   (A) –2   (B) 3   (C) 5.5   (D) 6   (E) 8

4. Three positive numbers x, y, and z have the following relationships $y = x + 2$ and $z = y + 2$. When the median of x, y, and z is subtracted from the product of the smallest number and the median, the result is 0. What is the value of the largest number?

   (A) –2   (B) π (C) 5   (D) 8   (E) 21/2

5. A jar contains only three types of objects: red, blue, and silver paper clips. The probability of selecting a red paper clip is 1/4, and the probability of selecting a blue paper clip is 1/6. What is the probability of selecting a silver paper clip?

   (A) 5/12   (B) 1/2   (C) 7/12   (D) 3/4   (E) 11/12

6. A bowl contains one marble labeled 0, one marble labeled 1, one marble labeled 2, and one marble labeled 3. The bowl contains no other objects. If two marbles are drawn randomly without replacement, what is the probability that they will add up to 3?
   (A) 1/12   (B) 1/8   (C) 1/6   (D) 1/4   (E) 1/3

7. A housing subdivision contains only two types of homes: ranch-style homes and townhomes. There are twice as many townhomes as ranch-style homes. There are 3 times as many townhomes with pools than without pools. What is the probability that a home selected at random from the subdivision will be a townhome with a pool?
   (A) 1/6   (B) 1/5   (C) 1/4   (D) 1/3   (E) 1/2

8. The figure shows a small equilateral triangle inscribed in the large equilateral triangle. If a point is chosen at random from the large triangle, what is the probability that it will be from the small triangle?

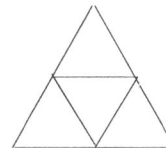

   (A) 1/8   (B) 1/5   (C) 1/4   (D) 1/3   (E) 1/2

Answers and Solutions to Problem Set W

1.   The median in all five answer-choices is 10. By symmetry, the average in answer-choices (A), (C), and (D) is 10 as well. The average in choice (B) is larger than 10 because 13 is further away from 10 than 8 is. Similarly, the average in choice (E) is smaller than 10 because 7 is further away from 10 than 12 is. The exact average is

$$\frac{7+9+10+11+12}{5} = \frac{49}{5} < 10$$

The answer is (E).

2.   There are 11 (= 5 + 6) people who selected a number 2 or number 3 marble, and there are 15 total people. Hence, the probability of selecting a number 2 or number 3 marble is 11/15, and the answer is (D).

3.   Since y is the middle number, it is the median. Forming the average of x, y, and z and setting it equal to 3 times the median yields

$$\frac{x+y+z}{3} = 3y$$

Replacing x with 0 and z with ky yields

$$\frac{0+y+ky}{3} = 3y$$

Multiplying both sides of this equation by 3 yields

$$y + ky = 9y$$

Subtracting $9y$ from both sides yields

$$-8y + ky = 0$$

Factoring out y yields

$$y(-8 + k) = 0$$

Since $y \neq 0$ (why?), $-8 + k = 0$. Hence, $k = 8$ and the answer is (E).

4.   Plugging $y = x + 2$ into the equation $z = y + 2$ gives $z = (x + 2) + 2 = x + 4$. Hence, in terms of x, the three numbers x, y, and z are

$$x, x + 2, x + 4$$

Clearly, x is the smallest number. Further, since $x + 2$ is smaller than $x + 4$, $x + 2$ is the median. Subtracting the median from the product of the smallest number and the median and setting the result equal to 0 yields

$$x(x + 2) - (x + 2) = 0$$

Factoring out the common factor $x + 2$ yields

$$(x + 2)(x - 1) = 0$$

Setting each factor equal to 0 yields

$$x + 2 = 0 \text{ or } x - 1 = 0$$

Hence, $x = -2$ or $x = 1$. Since the three numbers are positive, x must be 1. Hence, the largest number is

$$x + 4 = 1 + 4 = 5$$

The answer is (C).

5. First, let's calculate the probability of selecting a red or a blue paper clip. This is an either-or probability and is therefore the sum of the individual probabilities:

$$1/4 + 1/6 = 5/12$$

Now, since there are only three types of objects, the sum of their probabilities must be 1 (Remember that the sum of the probabilities of all possible outcomes is always 1):

$$P(r) + P(b) + P(s) = 1,$$

where r stands for red, b stands for blue, and s stands for silver.

Replacing $P(r) + P(b)$ with 5/12 yields

$$5/12 + P(s) = 1$$

Subtracting 5/12 from both sides of this equation yields

$$P(s) = 1 - 5/12$$

Performing the subtraction yields

$$P(s) = 7/12$$

The answer is (C).

6. The following list shows all 12 ways of selecting the two marbles:

$(0, 1)$	$(1, 0)$	$(2, 0)$	$\mathbf{(3, 0)}$
$(0, 2)$	$\mathbf{(1, 2)}$	$\mathbf{(2, 1)}$	$(3, 1)$
$\mathbf{(0, 3)}$	$(1, 3)$	$(2, 3)$	$(3, 2)$

The four pairs in bold are the only ones whose sum is 3. Hence, the probability that two randomly drawn marbles will have a sum of 3 is

$$4/12 = 1/3$$

The answer is (E).

7. Since there are twice as many townhomes as ranch-style homes, the probability of selecting a townhome is 2/3.[*] Now, "there are 3 times as many townhomes with pools than without pools." So the probability that a townhome will have a pool is 3/4. Hence, the probability of selecting a townhome with a pool is

$$\frac{2}{3} \cdot \frac{3}{4} = \frac{1}{2}$$

The answer is (E).

8. In the figure, it appears that the small inscribed triangle divides the large triangle into four congruent triangles. Hence, the probability that a point chosen at random from the large triangle will also be from the small triangle is 1/4. (As an exercise, prove that small inscribed triangle divides the large triangle into four congruent triangles.) The answer is (C).

---

[*] Caution: Were you tempted to choose 1/2 for the probability because there are "twice" as many townhomes? One-half (= 50%) would be the probability if there were an equal number of townhomes and ranch-style homes. Remember the probability of selecting a townhome is not the ratio of townhomes to ranch-style homes, but the ratio of townhomes to the total number of homes. To see this more clearly, suppose there are 3 homes in the subdivision. Then 2 would be townhomes and 1 would be a ranch-style home. So the ratio of townhomes to total homes would be 2/3.

Functions

DEFINITION

A function is a special relationship (correspondence) between two sets such that for each element x in its domain there is assigned one and <u>only one</u> element y in its range.

Notice that the correspondence has two parts:

    1) For each x there is assigned *one* y. (This is the ordinary part of the definition.)

    2) For each x there is assigned *only one* y. (This is the special part of the definition.)

The second part of the definition of a function creates the uniqueness of the assignment: There cannot be assigned two values of y to one x. In mathematics, uniqueness is very important. We know that $2 + 2 = 4$, but it would be confusing if $2 + 2$ could also equal something else, say 5. In this case, we could never be sure that the answer to a question was the *right* answer.

The correspondence between x and y is usually expressed with the function notation: $y = f(x)$, where y is called the *dependent variable* and x is called the *independent variable*. In other words, the value of y depends on the value of x plugged into the function. For example, the square root function can be written as $y = f(x) = \sqrt{x}$. To calculate the correspondence for $x = 4$, we get $y = f(4) = \sqrt{4} = 2$. That is, the square root function assigns the unique y value of 2 to the x value of 4. Most expressions can be turned into functions. For example, the expression $2^x - \dfrac{1}{x}$ becomes the function

$$f(x) = 2^x - \frac{1}{x}$$

DOMAIN AND RANGE

We usually identify a function with its correspondence, as in the example above. However, a function consists of three parts: a domain, a range, and correspondence between them.

➢   **The *domain* of a function is the set of x values for which the function is defined.**

For example, the function $f(x) = \dfrac{1}{x-1}$ is defined for all values of $x \neq 1$, which causes division by zero.

There is an infinite variety of functions with restricted domains, but only two types of restricted domains appear on the ACT: division by zero and even roots of negative numbers. For example, the function $f(x) = \sqrt{x-2}$ is defined only if $x - 2 \geq 0$, or $x \geq 2$. The two types of restrictions can be combined. For example, $f(x) = \dfrac{1}{\sqrt{x-2}}$. Here, $x - 2 \geq 0$ since it's under the square root symbol. Further $x - 2 \neq 0$, or $x \neq 2$, because that would cause division by zero. Hence, the domain is all $x > 2$.

> The *range* of a function is the set of *y* values that are assigned to the *x* values in the domain.

For example, the range of the function $y = f(x) = x^2$ is $y \geq 0$ since a square is never negative. The range of the function $y = f(x) = x^2 + 1$ is $y \geq 1$ since $x^2 + 1 \geq 1$. You can always calculate the range of a function algebraically, but it is usually better to graph the function and read off its range from the *y* values of the graph.

GRAPHS

The graph of a function is the set of ordered pairs $(x, f(x))$, where *x* is in the domain of *f* and $y = f(x)$.

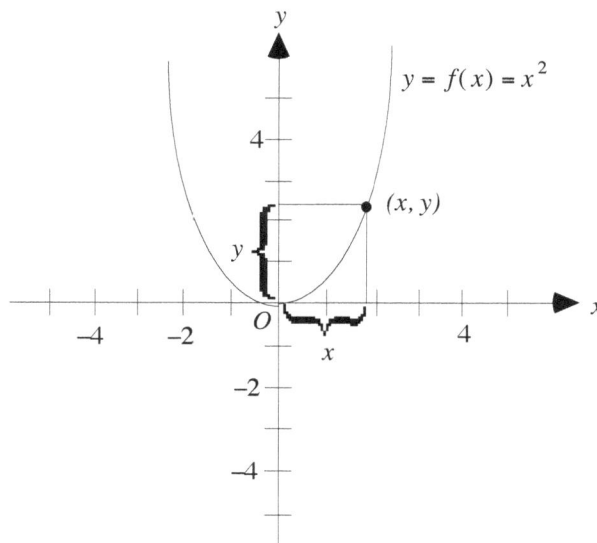

For this function, the domain is all *x* and the range is all $y \geq 0$ (since the graph touches the *x*-axis at the origin and is above the *x*-axis elsewhere).

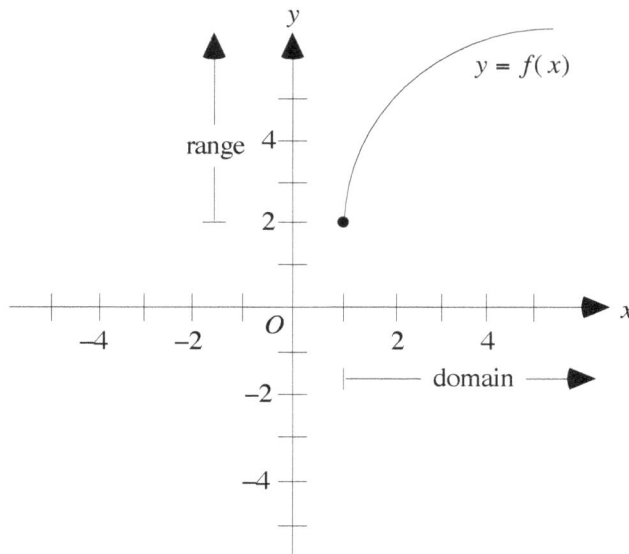

For this function, the domain is all $x \geq 1$ and the range is all $y \geq 2$.

191

TRANSLATIONS OF GRAPHS

Many graphs can be obtained by shifting a base graph around by adding positive or negative numbers to various places in the function. Take for example, the absolute value function $y = |x|$. Its graph is

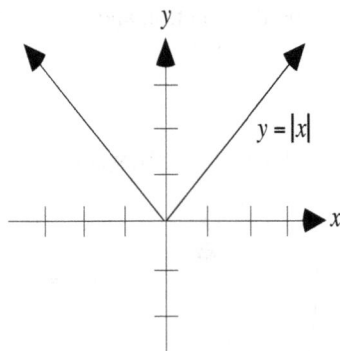

(Notice that sometimes an arrow is added to a graph to indicate the graph continues indefinitely and sometimes nothing is used. To indicate that a graph stops, a dot is added to the terminal point of the graph. Also, notice that the domain of the absolute value function is all x because you can take the absolute value of any number. The range is $y \geq 0$ because the graph touches the x-axis at the origin, is above the x-axis elsewhere, and increases indefinitely.)

To shift this base graph up one unit, we add 1 outside the absolute value symbol, $y = |x| + 1$:

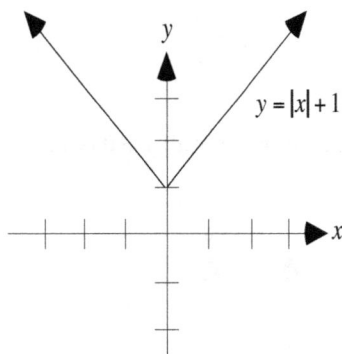

(Notice that the range is now $y \geq 1$.)

To shift the base graph down one unit, we subtract 1 outside the absolute value symbol, $y = |x| - 1$:

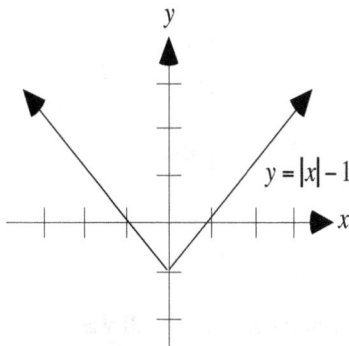

(Notice that the range is now $y \geq -1$.)

192

To shift the base graph to the right one unit, we subtract 1 inside the absolute value symbol, $y = |x - 1|$:

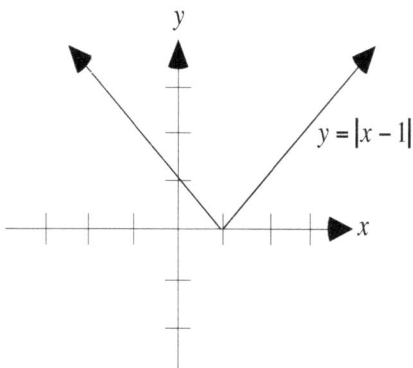

$$y = |x - 1|$$

(Notice that the range did not change; it's still $y \geq 0$. Notice also that subtracting 1 moved the graph to right. Many students will mistakenly move the graph to the left because that's where the negative numbers are.)

To shift the base graph to the left one unit, we add 1 inside the absolute value symbol, $y = |x + 1|$:

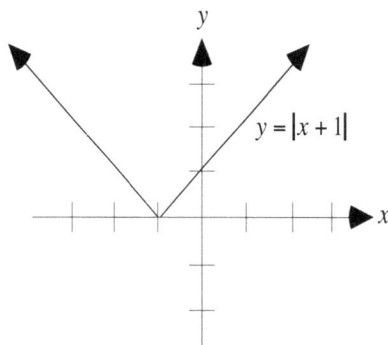

$$y = |x + 1|$$

(Notice that the range did not change; it's still $y \geq 0$. Notice also that adding 1 moved the graph to left. Many students will mistakenly move the graph to the right because that's where the positive numbers are.)

The pattern of the translations above holds for all functions. So to move a function $y = f(x)$ up c units, add the positive constant c to the exterior of the function: $y = f(x) + c$. To move a function $y = f(x)$ to the right c units, subtract the constant c in interior of the function: $y = f(x - c)$. To summarize, we have

To shift up c units:	$y = f(x) + c$
To shift down c units:	$y = f(x) - c$
To shift to the right c units:	$y = f(x - c)$
To shift to the left c units:	$y = f(x + c)$

REFLECTIONS OF GRAPHS

Many graphs can be obtained by reflecting a base graph by multiplying various places in the function by negative numbers. Take for example, the square root function $y = \sqrt{x}$. Its graph is

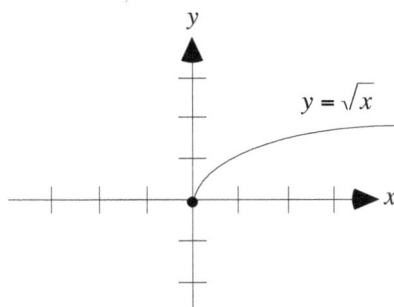

(Notice that the domain of the square root function is all $x \geq 0$ because you cannot take the square root of a negative number. The range is $y \geq 0$ because the graph touches the x-axis at the origin, is above the x-axis elsewhere, and increases indefinitely.)

To reflect this base graph about the x-axis, multiply the exterior of the square root symbol by negative one, $y = -\sqrt{x}$:

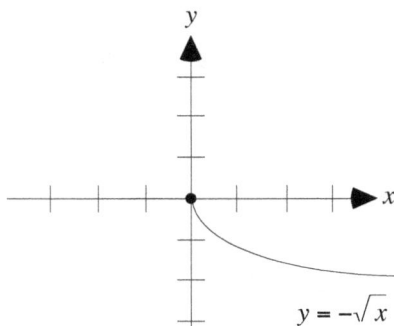

(Notice that the range is now $y \leq 0$ and the domain has not changed.)

To reflect the base graph about the y-axis, multiply the interior of the square root symbol by negative one, $y = \sqrt{-x}$:

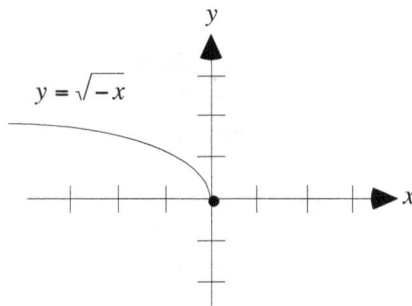

(Notice that the domain is now $x \leq 0$ and the range has not changed.)

The pattern of the reflections above holds for all functions. So to reflect a function $y = f(x)$ about the x-axis, multiply the exterior of the function by negative one: $y = -f(x)$. To reflect a function $y = f(x)$ about the y-axis, multiply the interior of the function by negative one: $y = f(-x)$. To summarize, we have

To reflect about the x-axis:	$y = -f(x)$
To reflect about the y-axis:	$y = f(-x)$

Reflections and translations can be combined. Let's reflect the base graph of the square root function $y = \sqrt{x}$ about the x-axis, the y-axis and then shift it to the right 2 units and finally up 1 unit:

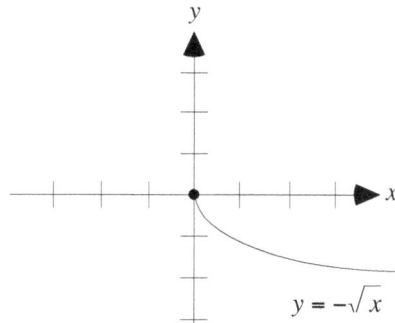

$$y = -\sqrt{x}$$

(Notice that the domain is still $x \geq 0$ and the range is now $y \leq 0$.)

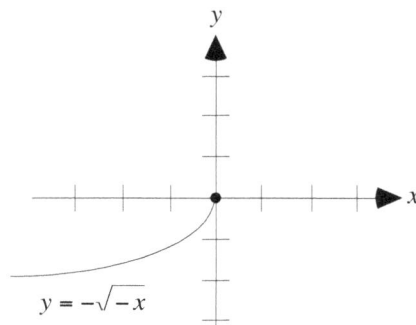

$$y = -\sqrt{-x}$$

(Notice that the domain is now $x \leq 0$ and the range is still $y \leq 0$.)

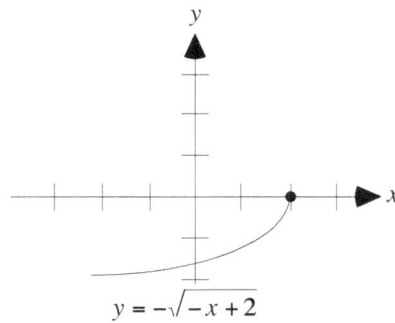

$$y = -\sqrt{-x+2}$$

(Notice that the domain is now $x \leq 2$ and the range is still $y \leq 0$.)

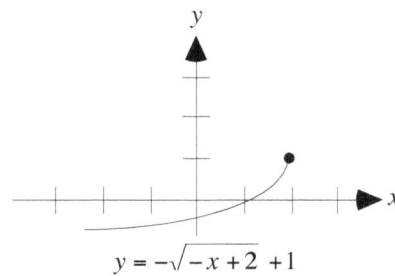

$$y = -\sqrt{-x+2} + 1$$

(Notice that the domain is still $x \leq 2$ and the range is now $y \leq 1$.)

EVALUATION AND COMPOSITION OF FUNCTIONS

EVALUATION

We have been using the function notation $f(x)$ intuitively; we also need to study what it actually means. You can think of the letter f in the function notation $f(x)$ as the name of the function. Instead of using the equation $y = x^3 - 1$ to describe the function, we can write $f(x) = x^3 - 1$. Here, f is the name of the function and $f(x)$ is the value of the function at x. So $f(2) = 2^3 - 1 = 8 - 1 = 7$ is the value of the function at 2. As you can see, this notation affords a convenient way of prompting the evaluation of a function for a particular value of x.

Any letter can be used as the independent variable in a function. So the above function could be written $f(p) = p^3 - 1$. This indicates that the independent variable in a function is just a "placeholder." The function could be written without a variable as follows:

$$f(\ ) = (\ )^3 - 1$$

In this form, the function can be viewed as an input/output operation. If 2 is put into the function $f(2)$, then $2^3 - 1$ is returned.

In addition to plugging numbers into functions, we can plug expressions into functions. Plugging $y + 1$ into the function $f(x) = x^2 - x$ yields

$$f(y+1) = (y+1)^2 - (y+1)$$

You can also plug other expressions in terms of x into a function. Plugging $2x$ into the function $f(x) = x^2 - x$ yields

$$f(2x) = (2x)^2 - 2x$$

This evaluation can be troubling to students because the variable x in the function is being replaced by the same variable. But the x in function is just a placeholder. If the placeholder were removed from the function, the substitution would appear more natural. In $f(\ ) = (\ )^2 - (\ )$, we plug $2x$ into the left side $f(2x)$ and it returns the right side $(2x)^2 - 2x$.

COMPOSITION

We have plugged numbers into functions and expressions into functions; now let's plug in other functions. Since a function is identified with its expression, we have actually already done this. In the example above with $f(x) = x^2 - x$ and $2x$, let's call $2x$ by the name $g(x)$. In other words, $g(x) = 2x$. Then the composition of f with g (that is plugging g into f) is

$$f(g(x)) = f(2x) = (2x)^2 - 2x$$

For another example, let $f(x) = \dfrac{1}{x+1}$ and let $g(x) = x^2$. Then $f(g(x)) = \dfrac{1}{x^2+1}$ and $g(f(x)) = \left(\dfrac{1}{x+1}\right)^2$.

Once you see that the composition of functions merely substitutes one function into another, these problems can become routine. Notice that the composition operation $f(g(x))$ is performed from the inner parentheses out, not from left to right. In the operation $f(g(2))$, the number 2 is first plugged into the function g and then that result is plugged in the function f.

A function can also be composed with itself. That is, substituted into itself. Let $f(x) = \sqrt{x} - 2$. Then

$$f(f(x)) = \sqrt{\sqrt{x} - 2} - 2.$$

Example: The graph of $y = f(x)$ is shown. If $f(-1) = v$, then which one of the following could be the value of $f(v)$?

(A)   0
(B)   1
(C)   2
(D)   2.5
(E)   3

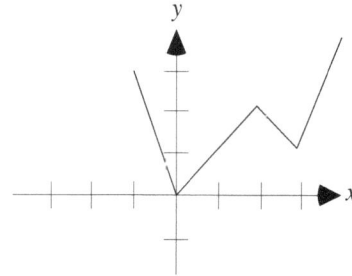

Since we are being asked to evaluate $f(v)$ and we are told that $v = f(-1)$, we are just being asked to compose f(x) with itself. That is, we need to calculate $f(f(-1))$. From the graph, $f(-1) = 3$. So $f(f(-1)) = f(3)$. Again, from the graph, $f(3) = 1$. So $f(f(-1)) = f(3) = 1$. The answer is (B).

QUADRATIC FUNCTIONS

Quadratic functions (parabolas) have the following form:

$$y = f(x) = ax^2 + bx + c$$

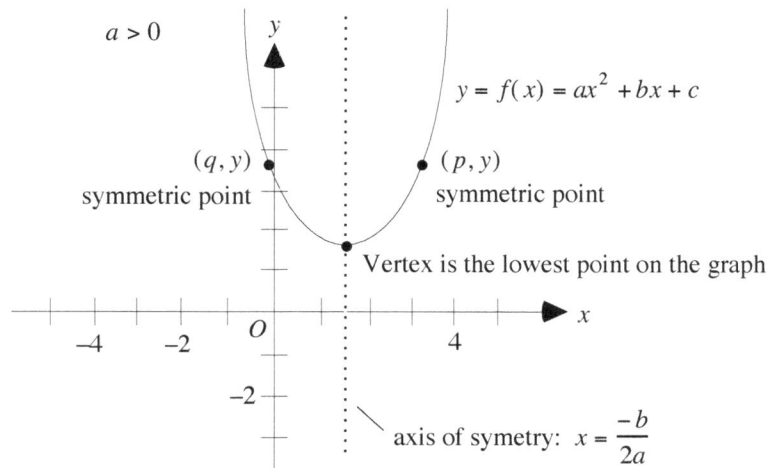

The lowest or highest point on a quadratic graph is called the vertex. The x–coordinate of the vertex occurs at $x = -b/2a$. This vertical line also forms the axis of symmetry of the graph, which means that if the graph were folded along its axis, the left and right sides of the graph would coincide.

In graphs of the form $y = f(x) = ax^2 + bx + c$ if $a > 0$, then the graph opens up.

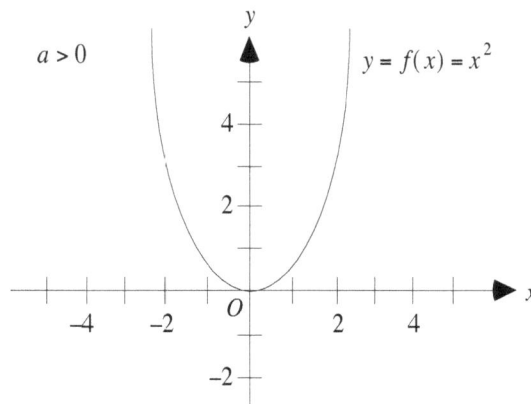

If $a < 0$, then the graph opens down.

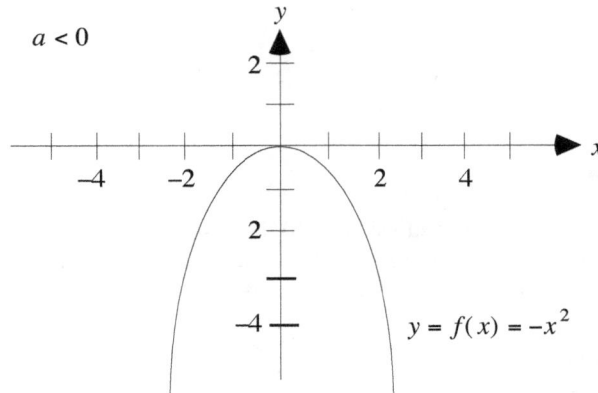

$a < 0$

$y = f(x) = -x^2$

By completing the square, the from $y = ax^2 + bx + c$ can be written as $y = a(x - h)^2 + k$. You are not expected to know this form on the test. But it is a convenient form since the vertex occurs at the point (h, k) and the axis of symmetry is the line $x = h$.

We have been analyzing quadratic functions that are vertically symmetric. Though not as common, quadratic functions can also be horizontally symmetric. They have the following form:

$$x = g(y) = ay^2 + by + c$$

$a > 0$

symmetric point
(x, p)

axis of symetry: $y = \dfrac{-b}{2a}$

$x = g(y) = ay^2 + by + c$

Vertex is the furthest point to the left on the graph

(x, q)
symmetric point

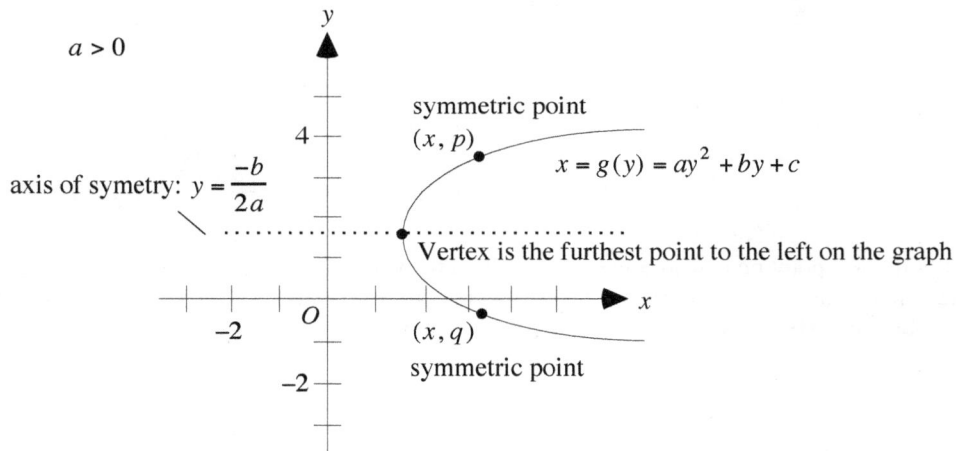

The furthest point to the left on this graph is called the vertex. The y-coordinate of the vertex occurs at $y = -b/2a$. This horizontal line also forms the axis of symmetry of the graph, which means that if the graph were folded along its axis, the top and bottom parts of the graph would coincide.

In graphs of the form $x = ay^2 + by + c$ if $a > 0$, then the graph opens to the right and if $a < 0$ then the graph opens to the left.

Example: The graph of $x = -y^2 + 2$ and the graph of the line k intersect at $(0, p)$ and $(1, q)$. Which one of the following is the smallest possible slope of line k ?

(A) $-\sqrt{2} - 1$
(B) $-\sqrt{2} + 1$
(C) $\sqrt{2} - 1$
(D) $\sqrt{2} + 1$
(E) $\sqrt{2} + 2$

Let's make a rough sketch of the graphs. Expressing $x = -y^2 + 2$ in standard form yields $x = -1y^2 + 0 \cdot y + 2$. Since $a = -1$, $b = 0$, and $c = 2$, the graph opens to the left and its vertex is at $(2, 0)$.

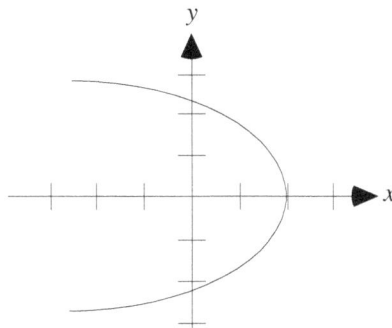

Since p and q can be positive or negative, there are four possible positions for line k (the y-coordinates in the graphs below can be calculated by plugging $x = 0$ and $x = 1$ into the function $x = -y^2 + 2$):

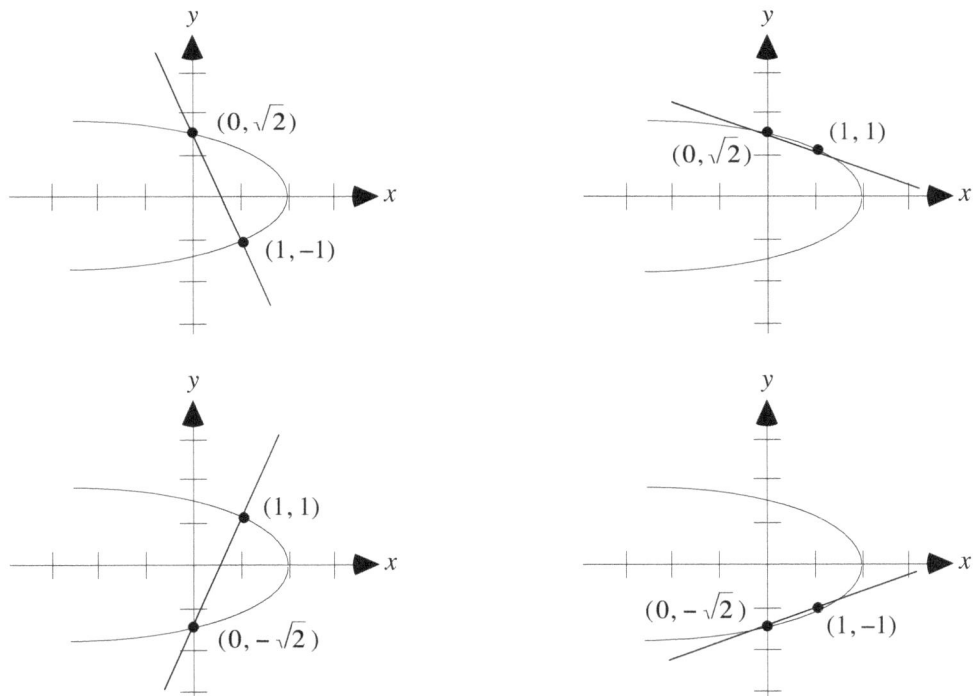

Since the line in the first graph has the steepest negative slope, it is the smallest possible slope. Calculating the slope yields

$$m = \frac{\sqrt{2} - (-1)}{0 - 1} = \frac{\sqrt{2} + 1}{-1} = -\left(\sqrt{2} + 1\right) = -\sqrt{2} - 1$$

The answer is (A).

CIRCLES

The standard form for a circle of radius r centered at (h, k) is

$$(x - h)^2 + (y - k)^2 = r^2$$

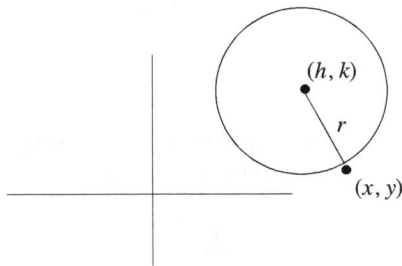

For instance, the equation of a circle of radius 4 centered at $(-1, 3)$ is

$$(x - (-1))^2 + (y - 3)^2 = 2^2$$
$$(x + 1)^2 + (y - 3)^2 = 2^2$$

Note that a circle is not function because for some values of x, there is more than one value of y. For example, with the unit circle, $x^2 + y^2 = 1$, if $x = 0$, then $0^2 + y^2 = 1$, or $y^2 = 1$, or $y = \pm 1$. Since there are two values for y (-1 and $+1$), this is not a function.

Example: A circle of radius 3 in the (x, y) coordinate plane is tangent to x-axis at -2. If the y-coordinate of the center of the circle is negative, which one of the following is an equation of the circle?

(A) $x^2 + y^2 = 9$
(B) $x^2 + y^2 = 3$
(C) $(x - 2)^2 + (y - 3)^2 = 9$
(D) $(x - 2)^2 + (y + 3)^2 = 3$
(E) $(x + 2)^2 + (y + 3)^2 = 9$

Since the circle is tangent to x-axis at -2 and the y-coordinate of the center is negative, the center of the circle is in Quadrant III:

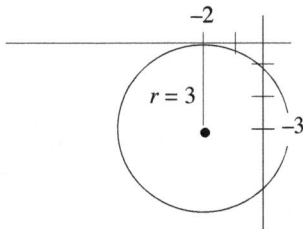

From the figure, it is clear that the center of the circle (h, k) is $(-2, -3)$. Plugging this information along with $r = 3$ into the formula for a circle yields

$$(x - (-2))^2 + (y - (-3))^2 = 3^2$$
$$(x + 2)^2 + (y + 3)^2 = 9$$

The answer is (E).

QUALITATIVE BEHAVIOR OF GRAPHS AND FUNCTIONS

In this rather vague category, you will be asked how a function and its graph are related. You may be asked to identify the zeros of a function based on its graph. The zeros, or roots, of a function are the x-coordinates of where it crosses the x-axis. Or you may be given two graphs and asked for what x values are their functions equal. The functions will be equal where they intersect.

Example: The graphs of $y = f(x)$ and $y = 1$ are shown. For how many x values does $f(x)$ equal 1?

   (A) 0
   (B) 1
   (C) 2
   (D) 3
   (E) 4

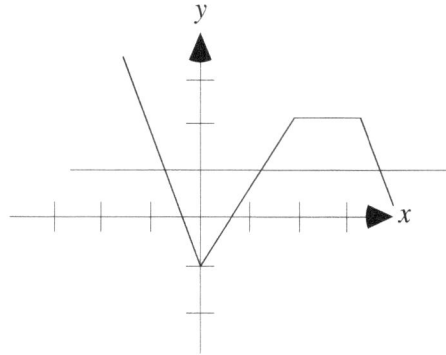

The figure shows that the graphs intersect at three points. At each of these points, both graphs have a height, or y-coordinate, of 1. The points are approximately $(-.8, 1)$, $(1.2, 1)$, and $(4, 1)$. Hence, $f(x) = 1$ for three x values. The answer is (D).

FUNCTIONS AS MODELS OF REAL-LIFE SITUATIONS

Functions can be used to predict the outcomes of certain physical events or real-life situations. For example, a function can predict the maximum height a projectile will reach when fired with an initial velocity, or the number of movie tickets that will be sold at a given price.

Example: The graph shows the number of music CDs sold at various prices. At what price should the CDs be marked to sell the maximum number of CDs?

   (A) 0
   (B) 5
   (C) 10
   (D) 15
   (E) 20

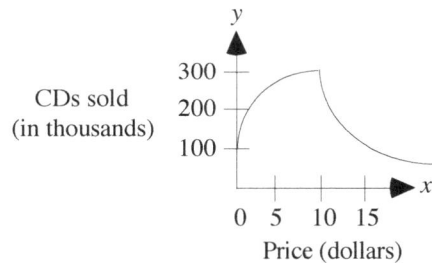

As you read the graph from left to right, it shows that sales initially increase rapidly and then slow to a maximum of about 300,000. From there, sales drop precipitously and then slowly approach zero as the price continues to increase. From the graph, sales of 300,000 units on the y-axis correspond to a price of about \$10 on the x-axis. The answer is (C).

Problem Set X:

$$g(x) = (2x - 3)^{1/4} + 1$$

1. In the function shown, for what values of x is $g(x)$ a real number?

   (A) $x \geq 0$
   (B) $x \geq 1/2$
   (C) $x \geq 3/2$
   (D) $x \geq 2$
   (E) $x \geq 3$

2. The table shows the values of the quadratic function f for several values of x. Which one of the following best represents f?

x	-1	0	1	2
$f(x)$	1	3	1	-5

   (A) $f(x) = -2x^2$
   (B) $f(x) = x^2 + 3$
   (C) $f(x) = -x^2 + 3$
   (D) $f(x) = -2x^2 - 3$
   (E) $f(x) = -2x^2 + 3$

201

3. In the function shown, if $f(k) = 2$, then which one of the following could be a value of k ?

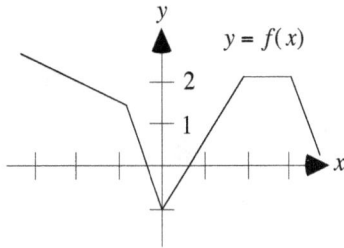

(A) -1
(B) 0
(C) 0.5
(D) 2.5
(E) 4

4. Let the function h be defined by $h(x) = \sqrt{x} + 2$. If $3h(v) = 18$, then which one of the following is the value of $h\left(\dfrac{v}{4}\right)$?

(A) -4
(B) -1
(C) 0
(D) 2
(E) 4

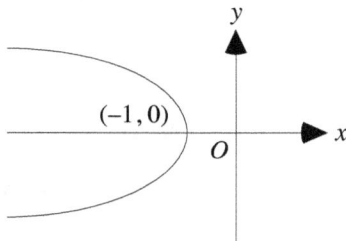

5. The graph shows a parabola that is symmetric about the x-axis. Which one of the following could be the equation of the graph?

(A) $x = -y^2 - 1$
(B) $x = -y^2$
(C) $x = -y^2 + 1$
(D) $x = y^2 - 1$
(E) $x = (y + 1)^2$

6. A pottery store owner determines that the revenue for sales of a particular item can be modeled by the function $r(x) = 50\sqrt{x} - 40$, where x is the number of the items sold. How many of the items must be sold to generate \$110 in revenue?

(A) 5
(B) 6
(C) 7
(D) 8
(E) 9

7. At time $t = 0$, a projectile was fired upward from an initial height of 10 feet. Its height after t seconds is given by the function $h(t) = p - 10(q - t)^2$, where p and q are positive constants. If the projectile reached a maximum height of 100 feet when $t = 3$, then what was the height, in feet, of the projectile when $t = 4$?

(A) 62 (B) 70 (C) 85 (D) 89 (E) 90

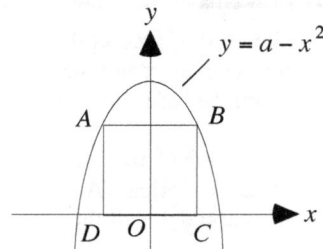

8. The figure shows the graph of $y = a - x^2$ for some constant a. If the square $ABCD$ intersects the graph at points A and B and the area of the square is 16, what is the value of a ?

(A) 2 (B) 4 (C) 6 (D) 8 (E) 10

9. If $f(x) = x^2 + x$, then $f(x - a) =$

(A) $x^2 - (2a - 1)x + a^2 - a$
(B) $x^2 - (2a + 1)x + a^2$
(C) $x^2 + x - a^2 - a$
(D) $x^2 + a^2$
(E) $x^2 a^2$

Answers and Solutions to Problem Set X

1. Let's change the fractional notation to radical notation: $g(x) = \sqrt[4]{2x - 3} + 1$. Since we have an even root, the expression under the radical must be greater than or equal to zero. Hence, $2x - 3 \geq 0$. Adding 3 to both sides of this inequality yields $2x \geq 3$. Dividing both sides by 2 yields $x \geq 3/2$. The answer is (C).

2. We need to plug the x table values into each given function to find the one that returns the function values in the bottom row of the table. Let's start with $x = 0$ since zero is the easiest number to calculate with. According to the table $f(0) = 3$. This eliminates Choice (A) since $f(0) = -2(0)^2 = -2(0) = 0$; and it eliminates Choice (D) since $f(0) = -2(0)^2 - 3 = -2 \cdot 0 - 3 = 0 - 3 = -3$. Now, choose $x = 1$. The next easiest number to calculate with. According to the table $f(1) = 1$. This eliminates Choice (B) since $f(1) = 1^2 + 3 = 1 + 3 = 4$; and it eliminates Choice (C) since $f(1) = -(1)^2 + 3 = -1 + 3 = 2$. Hence, by process of elimination, the answer is (E).

3. The graph has a height of 2 for every value of x between 2 and 3; it also has a height of 2 at about $x = -2$. The only number offered in this interval is 2.5. This is illustrated by the dot and the thick line in the following graph:

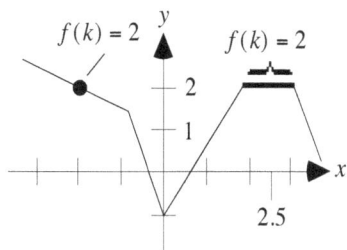

The answer is (D).

4. Evaluating the function $h(x) = \sqrt{x} + 2$ at v yields $h(v) = \sqrt{v} + 2$. Plugging this into the equation $3h(v) = 18$ yields

$3\left(\sqrt{v} + 2\right) = 18$

$\sqrt{v} + 2 = 6$ by dividing both sides by 3

$\sqrt{v} = 4$ by subtracting 2 from both sides

$\left(\sqrt{v}\right)^2 = 4^2$ by squaring both sides

$v = 16$ since $\left(\sqrt{v}\right)^2 = v$

Plugging $v = 16$ into $h\left(\dfrac{v}{4}\right)$ yields

$$h\left(\frac{v}{4}\right) = h\left(\frac{16}{4}\right) = h(4) = \sqrt{4} + 2 = 2 + 2 = 4$$

The answer is (E).

5. Since the graph is symmetric about the x-axis, its base graph is $x = y^2$. Since the graph opens to the left, we know that the exterior of the base function is multiplied by negative one: $-y^2$. Since the graph is shifted one unit to the left, we know that one is subtracted from the exterior of the function: $x = -y^2 - 1$. The answer is (A).

6. We are asked to find the value of x for which revenue is \$110. In mathematical terms, we need to solve the equation $r(x) = 110$. Since $r(x) = 50\sqrt{x} - 40$, we get

$$50\sqrt{x} - 40 = 110$$
$$50\sqrt{x} = 150$$
$$\sqrt{x} = 3$$
$$\left(\sqrt{x}\right)^2 = 3^2$$
$$|x| = 9$$
$$x = 9 \quad \text{or} \quad x = -9$$

Since $x = -9$ has no physical interpretation for this problem, we know that $x = 9$. The answer is (E).

7. Recall that when a quadratic function is written in the form $y = a(x - h)^2 + k$, its vertex (in this case, the maximum height of the projectile) occurs at the point (h, k). So let's rewrite the function $h(t) = p - 10(q - t)^2$ in the form $h(t) = a(t - h)^2 + k$. Notice that we changed y to $h(t)$ and x to t.

$$\begin{aligned}
h(t) &= p - 10(q - t)^2 \\
&= -10(q - t)^2 + p \\
&= -10(-[-q + t])^2 + p \\
&= -10(-[t - q])^2 + p \\
&= -10([-1]^2[t - q])^2 + p \\
&= -10([+1][t - q])^2 + p \\
&= -10(t - q)^2 + p
\end{aligned}$$

In this form, we can see that the vertex (maximum) occurs at the point (q, p). We are given that the maximum height of 100 occurs when t is 3. Hence, $q = 3$ and $p = 100$. Plugging this into our function yields

$$h(t) = -10(t - q)^2 + p = -10(t - 3)^2 + 100$$

We are asked to find the height of the projectile when $t = 4$. Evaluating our function at 4 yields

$$h(4) = -10(4 - 3)^2 + 100$$
$$= -10(1)^2 + 100$$
$$= -10 \cdot 1 + 100$$
$$= -10 + 100$$
$$= 90$$

The answer is (E).

Method II:
In this method, we are going to solve a system of two equations in two unknowns in order to determine the values of p and q in the function $h(t) = p - 10(q - t)^2$. At time $t = 0$, the projectile had a height of 10 feet. In other words, $h(0) = 10$. At time $t = 3$, the projectile had a height of 100 feet. In other words, $h(3) = 100$. Plugging this information into the function $h(t) = p - 10(q - t)^2$ yields

$$h(0) = 10 \implies 10 = p - 10(q - 0)^2$$
$$h(3) = 100 \implies 100 = p - 10(q - 3)^2$$

Now, we solve this system of equations by subtracting the bottom equation from the top equation:

$$10 = p - 10q^2$$
$$(-)\quad 100 = p - 10(q - 3)^2$$
$$\overline{-90 = -10q^2 + 10(q - 3)^2}$$

Solving this equation for q yields

$$-90 = -10q^2 + 10(q - 3)^2$$
$$-90 = -10q^2 + 10(q^2 - 6q + 9)$$
$$-90 = -10q^2 + 10q^2 - 60q + 90$$
$$-90 = -60q + 90$$
$$-180 = -60q$$
$$3 = q$$

Plugging $q = 3$ into the equation $10 = p - 10q^2$ yields

$$10 = p - 10 \cdot 3^2$$
$$10 = p - 10 \cdot 9$$
$$10 = p - 90$$
$$100 = p$$

Hence, the function $h(t) = p - 10(q - t)^2$ becomes $h(t) = 100 - 10(3 - t)^2$. We are asked to find the height of the projectile when $t = 4$. Evaluating this function at 4 yields

$$h(4) = 100 - 10(3 - 4)^2$$
$$= 100 - 10(-1)^2$$
$$= 100 - 10 \cdot 1$$
$$= 100 - 10$$
$$= 90$$

The answer is (E).

8. Let s denote the length of a side of square $ABCD$. Since the area of the square is 16, we get $s^2 = 16$. Taking the square root of both sides of this equation yields $s = 4$. Hence, line segment AB has length 4. Since the parabola is symmetric about the y-axis, Point B is 2 units from the y-axis (as is Point A). That is, the x-coordinate of Point B is 2. Since line segment BC has length 4, the coordinates of Point B are $(2, 4)$. Since the square and the parabola intersect at Point B, the point $(2, 4)$ must satisfy the equation $y = a - x^2$:

$$4 = a - 2^2$$
$$4 = a - 4$$
$$8 = a$$

The answer is (D).

9.

$$f(x - a) = (x - a)^2 + (x - a)$$
$$= x^2 - 2ax + a^2 + x - a$$
$$= x^2 - 2ax + x + a^2 - a$$
$$= x^2 - (2a - 1)x + a^2 - a$$

The answer is (A).

Logarithms

$$\log_b x = y \quad \text{if and only if} \quad b^y = x$$

Note that b is called the base, x is the number whose log is being calculated, and the result y is the log. Both x and b must be positive.

Students often find logs mysterious. Even after studying logs for a while, students may still ask, "what is a log?" It is nothing more than the definition above! Notice that on the right side of the definition that y (the log) is an exponent: it is the power to which you raise the base to get the number you are taking the log of. If this seems contrived, you're right. A log is a pure contrivance. Many subjects in mathematics are created this way. For instance, Trigonometry, which is just the naming of various ratios of the sides of a triangle with respect to an angle of the triangle.

Let's use this definition (rule) to calculate some logs:

1) $\log_2 8 = y$

   Here, the base b is 2, x is 8, and y is itself. Plugging this information into the right side of the definition yields

   $$2^y = 8$$

   Clearly, the solution to this equation is 3: $2^3 = 2 \cdot 2 \cdot 2 = 8$.

2) $\log_3 27$

   Here, we are being asked to find to what power do you raise 3 to get 27. Though y was not written in the problem, we will use it in the solution. Here, the base b is 3, and x is 27. Plugging this information into the right side of the definition yields

   $$3^y = 27$$

   Clearly, the solution to this equation is 3: $3^3 = 3 \cdot 3 \cdot 3 = 27$.

3) $\log_b 4 = 2$

   Here, we are not asked to calculate the log, which is 2. Instead, by the right-hand side of the definition, we are asked what number squared is 4 ($b^2 = 4$). Of course, the answer is 2, so $b = 2$. Note: the base is always positive, so -2 is not a possible answer.

205

Since logs are exponents, they should share the properties of exponents. When multiply two exponential expressions, you add their exponents: $x^m \cdot x^n = x^{m+n}$. The analogous rule for logs is

$$\log_b mn = \log_b m + \log_b n$$

Logs have many exotic properties, which is why students often find logs mysterious. However, these properties are easy to manipulate, which makes logs fundamentally easy—as long as you are not intimidated by the strange properties.

One of the more unusual properties is the "leap frog" rule (with this silly name, you are unlikely to forget the rule):

$$\log_b x^a = a \log_b x$$

Here, the exponent "leaps" in front of the log. For example, $\log_2 (x+1)^5 = 5\log_2(x+1)$. Caution: to apply the "leap frog" rule, the exponent must be on just the argument, not the entire log: $(\log_3 x)^5 \neq 5\log_3 x$.

We have seen logs of base 2 and base 3; the most common base is base 10: $\log_{10} x$. It is called the *common log*, and often the base is not written:

$$\log_{10} x = \log x$$

Pop Quiz: $\log_b b^a =$

If you are struggling to solve this problem (and most students do the first time they see it), don't overlook the obvious. Go back to the definition of a log: the question is asking us to what power do we raise b to get b^a. Of course, the answer is a—it's staring us in the face. Or using the formal definition $b^y = b^a$, so equating exponents yields $y = a$. Whenever you are struggling with a logarithmic problem, stop and look for the simple concept or property that you are probably overlooking—again, logs are fundamentally easy.

Let's summarize the properties we have derived and add a few more.

Properties of Logs:

1) $\log_b xy = \log_b x + \log_b y$ Caution: $\log_b (x + y) \neq \log_b x + \log_b y$

2) $\log_b \dfrac{x}{y} = \log_b x - \log_b y$ Caution: $\log_b (x - y) \neq \log_b x - \log_b y$

3) $\log_b x^a = a \log_b x$ The "leap frog" rule

4) $\log_b b^a = a$

5) $\log_b 1 = 0$ This follows from the fact that $b^0 = 1$.

6) $\log_b b = 1$ This follows from the fact that $b^1 = b$.

Before doing any of the exercises at the end of this chapter, know these log properties cold.

Examples:

1) Solve the following equation: $\log_4(z+2) - \log_4 3 = 1$

$$\log_4 \frac{z+2}{3} = 1$$ by Rule 2

$$4^1 = \frac{z+2}{3}$$ by the definition of a log: $\log_b x = y$ if and only if $b^y = x$

$$12 = z+2$$

$$z = 10$$

2) Solve the following equation: $\log x + \log(x-6) = \log 9$

$\log x(x-6) = \log 9$ by Rule 1

$x(x-6) = 9$ If two logs are equal, then their arguments are equal: If $\log_b x = \log_b y$, then $x = y$. This fact is used often with logs.

$x^2 - 6x = 9$

$x^2 - 6x - 9 = 0$

$(x-3)^2 = 0$

$x - 3 = 0$ by taking the square root of both sides

$x = 3$ Note: We have not yet determined that 3 is the solution. We have merely narrowed the infinite number of possible solutions to just one, 3. With simple equations, the potential solution is usually the solution. But, with more complex equations, such as logarithmic equations, the potential solution often is not a solution. We must plug potential solutions into the original equation to see whether they make the two sides of the equation equal. This is not a check; it is the final step in finding the solution. Plugging 3 into the original equation yields:

$\log 3 + \log(3-6) = \log 3 + \log(-3)$ However, the log of a negative number does not exit, so the equation has no solutions.

3) Write $\log x + \dfrac{1}{3}\log(z+4) - 3\log y^2$ as a single logarithm.

First, apply the "leap frog" rule ($\log_b x^a = a\log_b x$):

$$\log x + \log(z+4)^{1/3} - \log\left(y^2\right)^3$$

Next, apply Rule 1 ($\log_b xy = \log_b x + \log_b y$):

$$\log x(z+4)^{1/3} - \log y^6$$

Finally, apply Rule 2 ($\log_b \dfrac{x}{y} = \log_b x - \log_b y$):

$$\log \frac{x(z+4)^{1/3}}{y^6}$$

4) Write $\log \sqrt[4]{x^2 - 1}$ as a sum of two logs.

First, change to fractional exponents:

$$\log\left(x^2 - 1\right)^{1/4}$$

Next, apply the "leap frog" rule ($\log_b x^a = a \log_b x$):

$$\frac{1}{4} \log\left(x^2 - 1\right)$$

Factoring the difference of squares $x^2 - 1$ yields

$$\frac{1}{4} \log(x + 1)(x - 1)$$

Applying Rule 1 ($\log_b xy = \log_b x + \log_b y$) yields

$$\frac{1}{4}\left[\log(x + 1) + \log(x - 1)\right]$$

Finally, distribute the 1/4:

$$\frac{1}{4} \log(x + 1) + \frac{1}{4} \log(x - 1)$$

Though the manipulations in this problem are a little odd, aren't they actually easy? This would be considered a hard problem on the ACT, not because it is inherently hard, but because most students would get it wrong.

SOLVING EXPONENTIAL EQUATIONS BY USING LOGS

Often, we solve exponential equations by equating exponents:

$$2^{-1/x} = 8$$
$$2^{-1/x} = 2^3$$
$$-1/x = 3 \qquad \text{if the bases are equal (2), the exponents must be equal}$$
$$-1/3 = x$$

But, what if the bases are not equal? In this case, we can use logs to solve the equation.

Example: Solve the equation $3^y = 5$.

In the previous example, we were able to write 8 in terms of the 2: $8 = 2^3$. However, we cannot write 5 in terms of 3, or vice versa. Taking the log of both sides of the equation[1] yields

$$\log 3^y = \log 5$$

Applying the "leap frog" rule yields

$$y \log 3 = \log 5$$

Finally, dividing both sides by $\log 3$ (which is just a number) yields

$$y = \frac{\log 5}{\log 3}$$

---

[1] Just as you can square both sides of an equation or multiply both sides of an equation, you can log both sides of an equation.

We used the common log (base 10) to solve this problem, but we can use any base for the log. Using $\log_3$ would be a more efficient way to solve the equation:

$$\log_3 3^y = \log_3 5$$
$$y = \log_3 5$$

Instead of solving this equation by taking the log of both sides, we can just use the definition of a log: $\log_b x = y$ if and only if $b^y = x$. Note that all definitions read both from left to right and from right to left.

That's what the "if and only if" part of a definition means. Reading the definition from right to left, $3^y = 5$ indicates that the base is 3, the exponent is y, and 5 is the number that we are taking the log of. This yields

$$\log_3 5 = y$$

GRAPHS OF LOGARITHMIC FUNCTIONS

We will graph a typical logarithmic function by plotting points, but the ACT does not expect you to graph functions this way: they assume that you are familiar with the shapes of graphs of common functions, such as the log.

Graph of $y = \log_2 x$

x	1/8	1/4	1/2	1	2	4	8
$f(x) = \log_2 x$	-3	-2	-1	0	1	2	3

Plotting these points in the coordinate system and connecting them with a smooth curve yields the following graph:

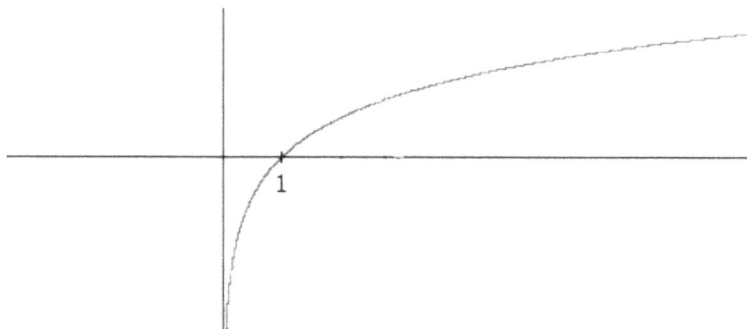

From the graph, notice that the domain (x values) consists of positive numbers only, and the range (y values) is all real numbers (negative, zero, and positive). This is the basic shape of all logarithmic functions with a base greater than 1. They all intersect the x-axis at $(1, 0)$. Notice that the y-values of the graph (the range) increase* slowly when x is greater than 1. In fact, they increase extremely slowly. To get the y-value of the graph of the common log ($y = \log_{10} x$) to 10, you have to go out to 10 billion on the x-axis: $\log_{10} x = 10 \implies x = 10^{10}$, which is 10 billion. On the other hand, the y-values increase rapidly for values of x smaller than 1 (notice that the y-axis is a vertical asymptote). Understanding of these types of graph properties is what the ACT tests.

---

* Note that we "read" graphs just as we read English—from left to right. So, as you view the graph from left to right, it is increasing (going up hill): at first rapidly and then very slowly.

Example: Sketch the graph of $y = 1 + 2\log(x - 3)$.

The number 1 shifts the graph of the common log ($\log_{10} x$) up 1 unit, the number 2 increases the height of the graph by a factor of 2, and the number 3 shifts the graph to the right 3 units:

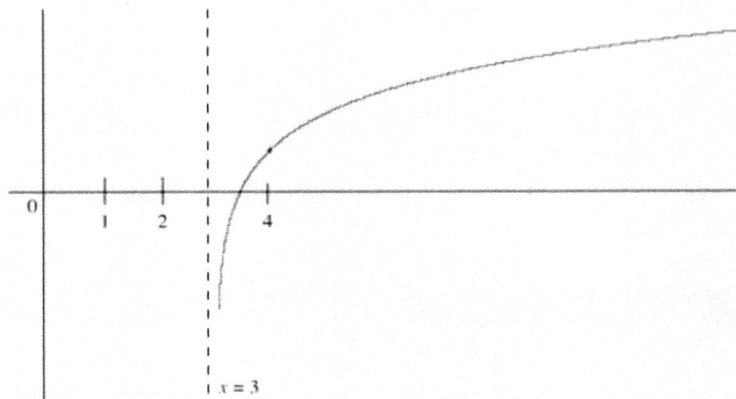

Example: Sketch the graph of $y = \log|x|$.

Usually, we cannot plug negative numbers into a log function. But here, the absolute value turns all negative numbers into positive numbers. So, for negative values of x, the graph looks the same as for positive values of x. This has the affect of reflecting the graph about the y-axis (Note: the y-axis is still the vertical asymptote since $|0| = 0$):

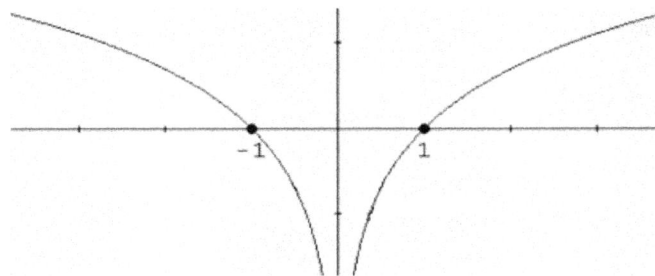

Example: The graphs of the functions $y = \log_3 x$ and $y = \dfrac{1}{2}(x - 1)$ are shown in the standard coordinate system below. For what real values of x is $\log_3 x > \dfrac{1}{2}(x - 1)$?

    (A) $x < 1$ and $x > 3$ (B) $x < 0$ and $x > 3$ (C) $1 < x < 3$ (D) $1 < x < 2$ (E) $x < 3$

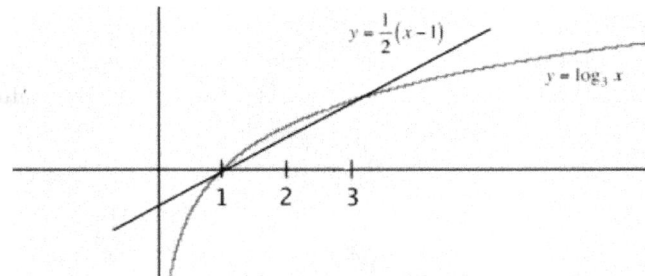

From the graph, we see that the graph of $y = \log_3 x$ is above the graph of $y = \dfrac{1}{2}(x - 1)$ for all values of x between 1 and 3. Hence, the answer is (C).

GRAPHS OF EXPONENTIAL FUNCTIONS

The exponential function can be viewed as the inverse of the logarithm function.

Interchanging x and y (which creates the inverse) in the left-hand side of the definition of the common log ($\log_{10} x = y$) yields

$$\log_{10} y = x$$

Now, use the definition of the logarithm ($\log_b x = y$ if and only if $b^y = x$) to convert this form to the exponential form:

$$y = 10^x$$

As with all inverse functions, we can obtain the graph of $y = 10^x$ by reflecting the graph of $y = \log_{10} x$ about the line $y = x$:

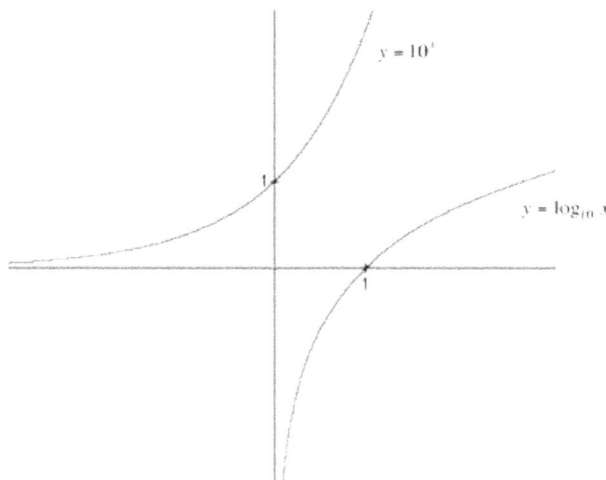

From the graph, notice that the domain (x values) includes all real numbers (negative, zero, and positive), and the range (y values) is only positive numbers. This is the basic shape of all exponential functions with a base greater than 1. They all intersect the y-axis at (0, 1). Notice that the y-values of the graph (the range) increase* slowly when x is less than 0 (notice that the x-axis is a horizontal asymptote), and the y-values increase rapidly for values of x greater than 1. In fact, they increase extremely fast. To get the y-value of the graph of the exponential function ($y = 10^x$) to 10 billion, you have to go out to only 10 on the x-axis: $y = 10^{10}$, which is 10 billion. Notice that our analysis of the exponential function is the same as the logarithm function, just the roles of x and y have been interchanged. This is to be expected since they are inverses of each other.

---

* Note that we "read" graphs just as we read English—from left to right. So, as you view the graph from left to right, it is increasing (going up hill): at first rapidly and then very slowly.

Problem Set Y:

1. $\log_{10} \dfrac{1}{100} =$

         (A) -2
         (B) -1
         (C)   0
         (D)   1
         (E)   2

2.   Which one of the following values of x satisfies the equation $\log_x 16 = 2$?

         (A)   2
         (B)   4
         (C)   8
         (D)   10
         (E)   16

3.   Which one of the following real numbers satisfies the equation $\left(3^x\right)(9) = 27^2$?

         (A)   1
         (B)   2
         (C)   3
         (D)   4
         (E)   5

4.   If $\log_b x = u$ and $\log_b y = v$, then $\log_b \left(\dfrac{x}{y}\right)^3 =$

         (A) $uv/3$
         (B) $3uv$
         (C) $u - v$
         (D) $(u - v)/3$
         (E) $3(u - v)$

5.   Which one of the following functions could represent the graph?

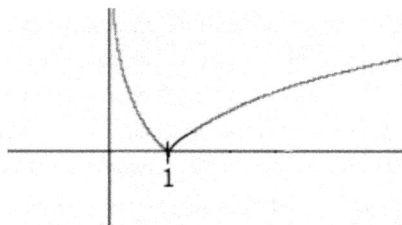

         (A) $y = \dfrac{1}{2}\log(x - 1)$
         (B) $y = \log(x - 1)$
         (C) $y = \log x^2$
         (D) $y = \left(\log x\right)^4 + 2$
         (E) $y = \left(\log x\right)^2$

6. Which one of the following sets of real numbers represents all the solutions of the equation $\log \sqrt{x} = \sqrt{\log x}$?

   (A) $\{0, 10\}$
   (B) $\{1, 100\}$
   (C) $\{1, 10{,}000\}$
   (D) $\{1, 2\}$
   (E) $\{0, 4\}$

7. Which one of the following expressions is equivalent to $\log \dfrac{x^2}{y^2} - 2 \log y + \log \sqrt{xy}$?

   (A) $\dfrac{1}{2} \log \dfrac{x^5}{y^7}$

   (B) $\log \dfrac{x^{5/2}}{y^7}$

   (C) $\log \dfrac{x^5}{y^{7/2}}$

   (D) $\dfrac{5}{2} \log \dfrac{x}{y}$

   (E) $\log \dfrac{x}{y}$

8. The base of a logarithm can be changed by using the following Change of Base Formula: $\log_b x = \dfrac{\log_a x}{\log_a b}$. With the aid of this formula what is the real number solution of the equation $\log_2 x + \log_4 x = 3$?

   (A) 1
   (B) 2
   (C) 3
   (D) 4
   (E) 5

9. Which one of the following real numbers is a solution of the equation $x \log 3 + \log 4^x = 1$?

   (A) $\log 3$
   (B) $\dfrac{1}{\log 12}$
   (C) $\log 12$
   (D) 3
   (E) 4

10. The loudness of sound can be measured by the formula $\alpha = 10 \log \left(\dfrac{I}{I_0} \right)$, where I is the intensity level of the sound and I_0 is a constant. What is the loudness of a sound with an intensity level 100 times greater than I_0 ?

    (A) 1
    (B) 20
    (C) 100
    (D) 2,000
    (E) 10,000

213

Answers and Solutions to Problem Set Y

1. By the definition of a logarithm, $\log_{10} \dfrac{1}{100} = y$ if and only if

$$10^y = \frac{1}{100}$$
$$10^y = 100^{-1}$$
$$10^y = \left(10^2\right)^{-1}$$
$$10^y = 10^{2(-1)}$$
$$10^y = 10^{-2}$$
$$y = -2 \qquad \text{by equating exponents}$$

Hence, the answer is (A).

2. By the definition of a logarithm, $\log_x 16 = 2$ if and only if

$$x^2 = 16$$
$$x = \pm 4 \qquad \text{by taking the square root of both sides}$$

Since the base of a log must be positive, $x = 4$ and the answer is (B).

3. We don't need to use a log to solve this problem because all the numbers are powers of 3, so we will work to equate exponents:

$$\left(3^x\right)(9) = 27^2$$
$$\left(3^x\right)\left(3^2\right) = \left(3^3\right)^2$$
$$\left(3^x\right)\left(3^2\right) = 3^{3 \cdot 2} \qquad \text{by the rule } \left(x^a\right)^b = x^{ab}$$
$$3^{x+2} = 3^6 \qquad \text{by the rule } x^a x^b = x^{a+b}$$
$$x + 2 = 6 \qquad \text{by equating exponents}$$
$$x = 4$$

The answer is (D).

If you chose answer (B), you may have made the mistake of writing $\left(3^x\right)(9) = 27^x$.

If you chose answer (C), you may have made the mistake of writing $\left(3^3\right)^2 = 3^5$.

4.

$$\log_b \left(\frac{x}{y}\right)^3 =$$

$$3\log_b \left(\frac{x}{y}\right) = \qquad \text{by the rule } \log_b x^a = a \log_b x$$

$$3\left(\log_b x - \log_b y\right) = \qquad \text{by the rule } \log_b \frac{x}{y} = \log_b x - \log_b y$$

$$3(u - v) \qquad \text{by substituting } u \text{ for } \log_b x \text{ and } v \text{ for } \log_b y$$

Hence, the answer is (E).

5. The standard log ($y = \log x$) is negative between 0 and 1 (it is below the *x*-axis). But our graph is positive there (it is above the *x*-axis). One way to make it positive is to raise the standard function to an even exponent (even exponents turn negative expressions into positive ones). So, the answer is either (D) or (E). The expression in Choice (D), however, is always greater than or equal to 2 (why?), and, from the graph, the function is 0 when *x* is 1. Hence, by process of elimination, the answer is (E).

Don't make the mistake of choosing (C). $\log x^2$ is still negative between 0 and 1. The even exponent here is affecting just the *x*, not the entire function. For example,

$$\log\left(\frac{1}{10}\right)^2 = \log\left(10^{-1}\right)^2 = \log 10^{-2} = -2$$

6. First, change to fractional exponents:

$$\log x^{1/2} = \left(\log x\right)^{1/2}$$

Using the "leap frog" rule ($\log_b x^a = a\log_b x$) on the left side of the equation yields

$$\frac{1}{2}\log x = \left(\log x\right)^{1/2}$$

Squaring both sides to eliminate the remaining exponent yields

$$\frac{1}{4}\left(\log x\right)^2 = \log x$$

Subtracting $\log x$ from both sides yields

$$\frac{1}{4}\left(\log x\right)^2 - \log x = 0$$

Factoring out $\log x$ yields

$$\log x\left(\frac{1}{4}\log x - 1\right) = 0$$

Setting each factor to zero yields

$$\log x = 0 \quad \text{or} \quad \frac{1}{4}\log x - 1 = 0$$

Or

$$\log x = 0 \quad \text{or} \quad \log x = 4$$

From the first equation, we get $x = 10^0 = 1$; and from the second equation, we get $x = 10^4 = 10,000$. Hence, the answer is (C).

7.

$$\log \frac{x^2}{y^2} - 2\log y + \log \sqrt{xy} =$$

$$\log \frac{x^2}{y^2} - 2\log y + \log(xy)^{1/2} =$$

$$\log \frac{x^2}{y^2} - \log y^2 + \log(xy)^{1/2} =$$

$$\log \frac{x^2/y^2}{y^2} + \log(xy)^{1/2} =$$

$$\log \frac{x^2/y^2}{y^2/1} + \log(xy)^{1/2} =$$

$$\log \left(\frac{x^2}{y^2} \cdot \frac{1}{y^2} \right) + \log(xy)^{1/2} =$$

$$\log \frac{x^2}{y^4} + \log(xy)^{1/2} =$$

$$\log \left(\frac{x^2}{y^4} \cdot (xy)^{1/2} \right) =$$

$$\log \left(\frac{x^2}{y^4} \cdot x^{1/2} \cdot y^{1/2} \right) =$$

$$\log \frac{x^{2+1/2}}{y^{4-1/2}} =$$

$$\log \frac{x^{5/2}}{y^{7/2}} =$$

$$\log \left(\frac{x^5}{y^7} \right)^{1/2} =$$

$$\frac{1}{2}\log \frac{x^5}{y^7}$$

The answer is (A).

8. We cannot apply the rule $\log_b xy = \log_b x + \log_b y$ to the equation $\log_2 x + \log_4 x = 3$ because the bases are different, $2 \neq 4$. Let's use the change of base formula to write the base 4 log in terms of the base 2 log:

$$\log_4 x = \frac{\log_2 x}{\log_2 4} = \frac{\log_2 x}{2}$$

Plugging this result into the equation yields

$$\log_2 x + \frac{\log_2 x}{2} = 3$$

Multiplying the equation by 2 yields

$$2\log_2 x + \log_2 x = 6$$

Adding like terms yields

$$3\log_2 x = 6$$

Dividing by 3 yields

$$\log_2 x = 2$$

Applying the definition of a log yields

$$x = 2^2 = 4$$

The answer is (D). Note: This problem can also be solved efficiently by plugging the answer-choices into the equation.

9. First, apply the "leap frog" rule ($\log_b x^a = a\log_b x$):

$$x\log 3 + x\log 4 = 1$$

Many students are intimidated by equations like this one because of the odd looking logs in it. But the logs here are just numbers. If you were to replace the logs with the numbers 3 and 4, you would get the following simple linear equation:

$$x \cdot 3 + x \cdot 4 = 1$$

Since $\log 3$ and $\log 4$ are just numbers, our equation is also linear. Factoring out the common factor x yields

$$x(\log 3 + \log 4) = 1$$

Dividing both sides of this equation by $\log 3 + \log 4$ yields

$$x = \frac{1}{\log 3 + \log 4}$$

Finally, using the rule $\log_b xy = \log_b x + \log_b y$ to simplify the expression yields

$$x = \frac{1}{\log 3 \cdot 4} = \frac{1}{\log 12}$$

The answer is (B).

10. Since the intensity is 100 times greater than I_0, $I = 100I_0$. Substituting this into the formula for loudness yields

$$\alpha = 10\log\left(\frac{I}{I_0}\right)$$
$$= 10\log\left(\frac{100I_0}{I_0}\right)$$
$$= 10\log 100$$
$$= 10(2)$$
$$= 20$$

The answer is (B).

Complex Numbers

In the previous chapter, we said that logs are fundamentally easy. Well, complex numbers are even easier, mainly, because they do not have the exotic properties of logs, and because, with a few exceptions, the rules for manipulating real numbers apply to complex numbers.

Complex numbers evolved from the need to solve equations like $x^2 + 1 = 0$, or $x^2 = -1$. Equations like this one occur frequently in Algebra, and they have no *real* number solutions. The only possible candidates for solutions of the equation $x^2 = -1$ are 1 and -1, but both equal $+1$ when squared. This prompts the following definition of a new number, i, called an *imaginary number*.

DEFINITION

$$i^2 = -1 \quad \text{or} \quad i = \sqrt{-1}$$

A number written in the form $a + bi$ is called a *complex number*. In this complex number, a is called the real part, and b is called the imaginary part, but both a and b are always real numbers.

Example: Solve the equation $x^2 - 4x + 4 = -1$.

$$x^2 - 4x + 4 = -1$$
$$(x - 2)(x - 2) = -1$$
$$(x - 2)^2 = -1$$
$$\sqrt{(x - 2)^2} = \pm\sqrt{-1}$$
$$x - 2 = \pm i$$
$$x = 2 \pm i$$

There are formulas for adding, multiplying, etc. complex numbers, but they are unnecessary — just use the rules for real numbers, and each time $\sqrt{-1}$ appears, replace it with i and replace i^2 with -1.

Examples:

$$(3 - i) + (-4 + 5i) = (3 - 4) + (-1i + 5i) = (3 - 4) + (-1 + 5)i = -1 + 4i$$

$$\begin{aligned}
(1+i)\sqrt{-4} &= (1+i)\sqrt{4}i \\
&= (1+i)2i \\
&= 1(2i) + i(2i) \\
&= 2i + 2i^2 \\
&= 2i + 2(-1) \\
&= -2 + 2i
\end{aligned}$$

Probably the only algebraic formula for real numbers that you will see that is false for complex numbers is $\sqrt{x}\sqrt{y} = \sqrt{xy}$.

$$\boxed{\textbf{For complex numbers, } \sqrt{x}\sqrt{y} \neq \sqrt{xy}}$$

For example,

$$\sqrt{-2}\sqrt{-2} = \sqrt{2}i \cdot \sqrt{2}i = \left(\sqrt{2} \cdot \sqrt{2}\right)i^2 = 2(-1) = -2$$
$$\sqrt{(-2)(-2)} = \sqrt{4} = 2$$

To avoid this error, and others like it, always replace $\sqrt{-1}$ with i before performing any algebraic operations. For example,

$$\sqrt{-x}\sqrt{-y} = \sqrt{x}i \cdot \sqrt{y}i = \sqrt{x}\sqrt{y}\left(i^2\right) = \sqrt{xy}(-1) = -\sqrt{xy}$$

CONJUGATE

Because complex numbers are based on a radical, we often rationalize fractions involving complex numbers. This makes the conjugate important for complex numbers.

$$\boxed{\textbf{The conjugate of the complex number } a + bi \textbf{ is } a - bi.}$$

Example: Rationalize the expression $\dfrac{1}{1-i}$ by multiplying top and bottom by $1 + i$:

$$\frac{1}{1-i} = \frac{1}{1-i} \cdot \frac{1+i}{1+i} = \frac{1(1+i)}{(1-i)(1+i)} = \frac{1+i}{1+i-i-i^2} = \frac{1+i}{1+i-i-(-1)} = \frac{1+i}{1+i-i+1} = \frac{1+i}{2} = \frac{1}{2} + \frac{1}{2}i$$

Because complex numbers have two parts (real and imaginary), they can be represented in the coordinate plane:

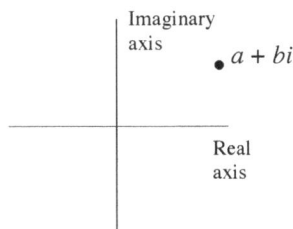

Example: $-1 - 4i$

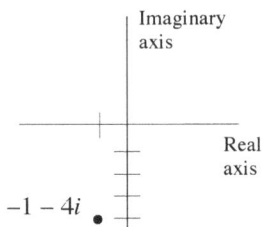

ABSOLUTE VALUE

With real numbers, the absolute value is the distance a number is from the origin. Likewise for complex numbers:

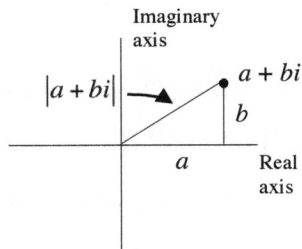

Applying The Pythagorean Theorem to the triangle in the figure gives

> **The absolute value of the complex number $a + bi$ is**
> $$|a + bi| = \sqrt{a^2 + b^2}$$

Notice that the absolute value of a complex number is a real number (the i does not appear in $\sqrt{a^2 + b^2}$).

Examples:

$$|-2 + 3i| = \sqrt{(-2)^2 + (3)^2} = \sqrt{4 + 9} = \sqrt{13}$$

$$|-5i| = |0 + (-5)i| = \sqrt{0^2 + (-5)^2} = \sqrt{0 + 25} = \sqrt{25} = 5$$

$$|0| = |0 + (0)i| = \sqrt{0^2 + 0^2} = \sqrt{0 + 0} = \sqrt{0} = 0$$

Problem Set Z:

1. $\dfrac{-1-2i}{3+2i}\cdot\dfrac{3-2i}{3-2i}=$

   (A) $-\dfrac{7}{10}-\dfrac{4}{10}i$

   (B) $\dfrac{7}{13}+\dfrac{4}{13}i$

   (C) $-\dfrac{7}{13}-\dfrac{4}{13}i$

   (D) $-\dfrac{7}{10}-\dfrac{4}{13}i$

   (E) $\dfrac{7}{13}-\dfrac{6}{13}i$

2. $\left(3-\sqrt{-9}\right)\left(4-\sqrt{-4}\right)=$

   (A) $6-18i$
   (B) $6+18i$
   (C) $-6-18i$
   (D) $6-6i$
   (E) $18-18i$

3. What are the complex solutions of the equation $x^2-6x+9=-4$?

   (A) $3+2i$ and $3-2i$
   (B) $-3+2i$ and $3+2i$
   (C) $-3+2i$ and $-3+2i$
   (D) $2+2i$ and $2+2i$
   (E) $3+2i$ and $3+2i$

4. $-\sqrt{-\dfrac{16}{49}}=$

   (A) $\dfrac{4}{7}i$

   (B) $-\dfrac{4}{7}i$

   (C) $\dfrac{4}{7}$

   (D) $\dfrac{4}{7}i^2$

   (E) $4i$

5. If $p=1+i$ and $q=0.5+1.5i$, then which one of the following must be true?

   (A) $|p|=|q|$
   (B) $|p|>|q|$
   (C) $|p|\geq|q|$
   (D) $|p|<|q|$
   (E) $|p|\leq|q|$

6. $\dfrac{1-i}{i}-\dfrac{2}{2+i}=$

   (A) $-\dfrac{3}{5}i$

   (B) $\dfrac{9}{2}+\dfrac{3}{2}i$

   (C) $\dfrac{9}{5}-\dfrac{3}{5}i$

   (D) $-\dfrac{9}{2}-\dfrac{3}{2}i$

   (E) $-\dfrac{9}{5}-\dfrac{3}{5}i$

7. The conjugate of a complex number $z=a+bi$ is often denoted by $\bar{z}$. That is, $\bar{z}=a-bi$. With this notation $\bar{z}=z$ if and only if

   (A) a is zero
   (B) z is a real number
   (C) $b=1$
   (D) z is an irrational number
   (E) $a=b=0$

8. If $z=a+bi$, then $\overline{z^2}=$

   (A) z
   (B) $\bar{z}$
   (C) z^2
   (D) $\left(\bar{z}\right)^2$
   (E) $z/2$

9. Which one of the complex numbers in the figure has the greatest absolute value?

   (A) z_1
   (B) z_2
   (C) z_3
   (D) z_4
   (E) z_5

10. Two complex numbers are equal if and only if their real parts are equal and their imaginary parts are equal. That is, if $a+bi=c+di$, then $a=c$ and $b=d$. From this definition, what are the values of x and y in the equation $x^3-(x-y)i=8-2i$?

    (A) $x=-8,y=1$
    (B) $x=8,y=2$
    (C) $x=-2,y=2$
    (D) $x=2,y=3$
    (E) $x=2,y=0$

Answers and Solutions to Problem Set Z

1.

$$\frac{-1-2i}{3+2i} \cdot \frac{3-2i}{3-2i} = \frac{-3+2i-6i+4i^2}{9-6i+6i-4i^2}$$

$$= \frac{-3-4i+4(-1)}{9-4(-1)}$$

$$= \frac{-7-4i}{13}$$

$$-\frac{7}{13} - \frac{4}{13}i$$

The answer is (C).

2.

$$\left(3-\sqrt{-9}\right)\left(4-\sqrt{-4}\right) = \left(3-\sqrt{9}i\right)\left(4-\sqrt{4}i\right)$$

$$= \left(3-3i\right)\left(4-2i\right)$$

$$= 12-6i-12i+6i^2$$

$$= 12-18i+6(-1)$$

$$= 6-18i$$

The answer is (A).

3.

$$x^2 - 6x + 9 = -4$$

$$(x-3)(x-3) = -4$$

$$(x-3)^2 = -4$$

$$\sqrt{(x-3)^2} = \pm\sqrt{-4}$$

$$x-3 = \pm 2i$$

$$x = 3 \pm 2i$$

The answer is (E).

4.

$$-\sqrt{-\frac{16}{49}} = -\sqrt{\frac{16}{49}}i$$

$$= -\frac{\sqrt{16}}{\sqrt{49}}i$$

$$= -\frac{4}{7}i$$

The answer is (B).

5.

$$|p| = |1+i| = |1+1i| = \sqrt{1^2+1^2} = \sqrt{1+1} = \sqrt{2}$$

$$|q| = |0.5+1.5i| = \sqrt{(0.5)^2+(1.5)^2} = \sqrt{0.25+2.25} = \sqrt{2.5}$$

Since $\sqrt{2.5} > \sqrt{2}$, $|q| > |p|$ and the answer is (D).

6.

$$\frac{1-i}{i} - \frac{2}{2+i} = \frac{1-i}{i}\cdot\frac{i}{i} - \frac{2}{2+i}\cdot\frac{2-i}{2-i}$$

$$= \frac{(1-i)i}{i\cdot i} - \frac{2(2-i)}{(2+i)(2-i)}$$

$$= \frac{1i-i\cdot i}{i\cdot i} - \frac{2\cdot 2 - 2i}{2\cdot 2 - 2i + 2i - i\cdot i}$$

$$= \frac{i-i^2}{i^2} - \frac{4-2i}{4-i^2}$$

$$= \frac{i-(-1)}{-1} - \frac{4-2i}{4-(-1)}$$

$$= \frac{i+1}{-1} - \frac{4-2i}{4+1}$$

$$= -\frac{i+1}{1} - \frac{4-2i}{5}$$

$$= -\frac{i+1}{1}\cdot\frac{5}{5} - \frac{4-2i}{5}$$

$$= -\frac{5i+5}{5} - \frac{4-2i}{5}$$

$$= \frac{-5i-5}{5} + \frac{-4+2i}{5}$$

$$= \frac{-5i-5-4+2i}{5}$$

$$= \frac{-9-3i}{5}$$

$$= -\frac{9}{5} - \frac{3}{5}i$$

The answer is (E).

7. The equation $\bar{z} = z$ yields

$$\overline{a + bi} = a + bi$$

Applying the conjugate yields

$$a - bi = a + bi$$

Subtracting a from both sides of the equation yields

$$-bi = bi$$

Since a has been removed from the equation, its value is not constrained by the equation. Hence, a can have any value, which eliminates choices (A) and (E). Now, subtracting bi from both sides of the equation yields

$$-2bi = 0$$

Finally, dividing both sides of the equation by $-2i$ yields

$$b = 0$$

Hence, $z = a + bi = a + 0i = a + 0 = a$. Since a is always a real number, z is a real number. The answer is (B).

8.

$$
\begin{aligned}
\overline{z^2} &= \overline{\left(a + bi\right)^2} \\
&= \overline{(a + bi)(a + bi)} \\
&= \overline{a^2 + abi + abi + b^2 i^2} \\
&= \overline{a^2 + 2abi + b^2(-1)} \\
&= \overline{a^2 - b^2 + 2abi} \\
&= a^2 - b^2 - 2abi \\
&= a^2 - 2abi - b^2 \\
&= (a - bi)(a - bi) \\
&= (a - bi)^2 \\
&= \left(\overline{a + bi}\right)^2 \\
&= \left(\bar{z}\right)^2
\end{aligned}
$$

The answer is (D).

9. Remember: The absolute value of a complex number is its distance from the origin. Clearly, from the figure, point z_1 is the farthest from the origin. The answer is (A).

10. Since the real parts must be equal and the imaginary parts must be equal, we get the following system of two equations:

$$x^3 = 8$$
$$-(x - y) = -2$$

Taking the cube root of both sides of the equation $x^3 = 8$ yields $x = 2$. Plugging this result into the equation $-(x - y) = -2$ yields

$$
\begin{aligned}
-(2 - y) &= -2 \\
2 - y &= 2 \\
-y &= 0 \\
y &= 0
\end{aligned}
$$

Hence, $x = 2$ and $y = 0$. The answer is (E).

Matrices

Matrices afford an efficient way of solving systems of equations. We won't study this method, however, because it is very unlikely on the test that you will be asked to solve a system of equations by using matrices. Instead, you will be given problems that require an understanding of the properties of matrices.

A *matrix* is just an array of numbers. Some examples are

$$\begin{bmatrix} 1 & 2 & 3 \end{bmatrix} \qquad \begin{bmatrix} 1 & 2 \\ 3 & 4 \end{bmatrix} \qquad \begin{bmatrix} a & b & c \\ d & e & f \\ g & h & i \end{bmatrix}$$

In general, an $m \times n$ matrix (m rows and n columns) is

$$\begin{bmatrix} a_{11} & a_{12} & a_{13} & \cdots & a_{1n} \\ a_{21} & a_{22} & a_{23} & \cdots & a_{2n} \\ a_{31} & a_{32} & a_{33} & \cdots & a_{3n} \\ \vdots & \vdots & \vdots & \ddots & \vdots \\ a_{m1} & a_{m2} & a_{m3} & \cdots & a_{mn} \end{bmatrix}$$

ADDING MATRICES

To add two matrices, just add their corresponding elements:

$$\begin{bmatrix} a & b \\ c & d \end{bmatrix} + \begin{bmatrix} e & f \\ g & h \end{bmatrix} = \begin{bmatrix} a+e & b+f \\ c+g & d+h \end{bmatrix}$$

Examples:

$$\begin{bmatrix} 1 & 2 \\ 3 & 4 \end{bmatrix} + \begin{bmatrix} 5 & 6 \\ 7 & 8 \end{bmatrix} = \begin{bmatrix} 1+5 & 2+6 \\ 3+7 & 4+8 \end{bmatrix} = \begin{bmatrix} 6 & 8 \\ 10 & 12 \end{bmatrix}$$

$$\begin{bmatrix} a & 0 & 2a \\ 0 & 0 & a \\ 1 & 3a & 0 \end{bmatrix} + \begin{bmatrix} a & 0 & 0 \\ 1 & 0 & 1 \\ 1 & 2a & 0 \end{bmatrix} = \begin{bmatrix} 2a & 0 & 2a \\ 1 & 0 & a+1 \\ 2 & 5a & 0 \end{bmatrix}$$

Note: To add matrices, they must be the same size—same number of rows and columns. You cannot add a 2×2 matrix and a 3×2 matrix.

SUBTRACTING MATRICES

To subtract two matrices, just subtract their corresponding elements:

$$\begin{bmatrix} a & b \\ c & d \end{bmatrix} - \begin{bmatrix} e & f \\ g & h \end{bmatrix} = \begin{bmatrix} a-e & b-f \\ c-g & d-h \end{bmatrix}$$

Examples:

$$\begin{bmatrix} 1 & 2 \\ 3 & 4 \end{bmatrix} - \begin{bmatrix} 5 & 6 \\ 7 & 8 \end{bmatrix} = \begin{bmatrix} 1-5 & 2-6 \\ 3-7 & 4-8 \end{bmatrix} = \begin{bmatrix} -4 & -4 \\ -4 & -4 \end{bmatrix}$$

$$\begin{bmatrix} a & 0 & 2a \\ 0 & 0 & a \\ 1 & 3a & 0 \end{bmatrix} - \begin{bmatrix} a & 0 & 0 \\ 1 & 0 & 1 \\ 1 & 2a & 0 \end{bmatrix} = \begin{bmatrix} 0 & 0 & 2a \\ -1 & 0 & a-1 \\ 0 & a & 0 \end{bmatrix}$$

Note: To subtract matrices, they must be the same size—same number of rows and columns. You cannot subtract a 2×2 matrix and a 3×2 matrix.

THE ZERO MATRIX

The *zero matrix*, appropriately enough, has zeros for all its entries:

$$\begin{bmatrix} 0 & 0 & 0 \end{bmatrix} \qquad \begin{bmatrix} 0 & 0 \\ 0 & 0 \end{bmatrix} \qquad \begin{bmatrix} 0 & 0 & 0 \\ 0 & 0 & 0 \\ 0 & 0 & 0 \end{bmatrix}$$

The zero matrix is the additive identity. That is, adding the zero matrix to any matrix leaves the matrix unchanged:

$$\begin{bmatrix} a & b \\ c & d \end{bmatrix} + \begin{bmatrix} 0 & 0 \\ 0 & 0 \end{bmatrix} = \begin{bmatrix} a+0 & b+0 \\ c+0 & d+0 \end{bmatrix} = \begin{bmatrix} a & b \\ c & d \end{bmatrix}$$

SCALAR MULTIPLICATION

To multiply a matrix by a number, just multiply each element of the matrix by the number:

$$2 \begin{bmatrix} 1 & 0 \\ 3 & \pi \end{bmatrix} = \begin{bmatrix} 2 \cdot 1 & 2 \cdot 0 \\ 2 \cdot 3 & 2 \cdot \pi \end{bmatrix} = \begin{bmatrix} 2 & 0 \\ 6 & 2\pi \end{bmatrix}$$

MULTIPLYING MATRICES

To multiply two matrices, multiply the elements in each row of the first matrix by the corresponding elements in each column of the second matrix.

$$\begin{bmatrix} a & b \\ c & d \end{bmatrix} \begin{bmatrix} e & f \\ g & h \end{bmatrix} = \begin{bmatrix} ae+bg & af+bh \\ ce+dg & cf+dh \end{bmatrix}$$

Examples:

$$\begin{bmatrix} 1 & 2 \end{bmatrix} \begin{bmatrix} 3 \\ 4 \end{bmatrix} = \begin{bmatrix} 1 \cdot 3 + 2 \cdot 4 \end{bmatrix} = \begin{bmatrix} 11 \end{bmatrix}$$

$$\begin{bmatrix} 1 & 0 \\ 0 & 3 \end{bmatrix} \begin{bmatrix} 2 & 4 \\ 4 & 5 \end{bmatrix} = \begin{bmatrix} 1 \cdot 2 + 0 \cdot 4 & 1 \cdot 4 + 0 \cdot 5 \\ 0 \cdot 2 + 3 \cdot 4 & 0 \cdot 4 + 3 \cdot 5 \end{bmatrix} = \begin{bmatrix} 2 & 4 \\ 12 & 15 \end{bmatrix}$$

$$\begin{bmatrix} a & 0 & 2a \\ 0 & 0 & a \\ 1 & 3a & 0 \end{bmatrix} \begin{bmatrix} a & 0 & 0 \\ 1 & 0 & 1 \\ 1 & 2a & 0 \end{bmatrix} = \begin{bmatrix} a \cdot a + 0 \cdot 1 + 2a \cdot 1 & a \cdot 0 + 0 \cdot 0 + 2a \cdot 2a & a \cdot 0 + 0 \cdot 1 + 2a \cdot 0 \\ 0 \cdot a + 0 \cdot 1 + a \cdot 1 & 0 \cdot 0 + 0 \cdot 0 + a \cdot 2a & 0 \cdot 0 + 0 \cdot 1 + a \cdot 0 \\ 1 \cdot a + 3a \cdot 1 + 0 \cdot 1 & 1 \cdot 0 + 3a \cdot 0 + 0 \cdot 2a & 1 \cdot 0 + 3a \cdot 0 + 0 \cdot 0 \end{bmatrix} = \begin{bmatrix} a^2 + 2a & 4a^2 & 0 \\ a & 2a^2 & 0 \\ 4a & 0 & 0 \end{bmatrix}$$

Note: To multiply two matrices, the first matrix must have the same number of columns as the rows in the second matrix: $m \times n$ and $n \times p$. The result of the product will be a matrix of size $m \times p$. Also, matrix multiplication is not commutative. If A and B are matrices, then, in general, $AB \neq BA$.

APPLICATIONS OF MATRICES

Example: The number of people running for political office in a particular state is given by the following matrix:

$$\begin{array}{ccc} \text{Governor} & \text{Legislator} & \text{Controller} \\ \begin{bmatrix} 10 & 90 & 6 \end{bmatrix} \end{array}$$

The percentage of candidates who will qualify to be on the ballot is given by the following matrix:

$$\begin{array}{c} \text{Governor} \\ \text{Legislator} \\ \text{Controller} \end{array} \begin{bmatrix} 40\% \\ 30\% \\ 50\% \end{bmatrix}$$

From these matrices, how many total candidates will qualify to be on the ballot?

(A) 34
(B) 35
(C) 37
(D) 40
(E) 52

This is a fairly complex and abstract problem. Yet, the ACT would not consider it hard, probably because there is only one natural way to solve it—multiply the matrices:

$$\begin{bmatrix} 10 & 90 & 6 \end{bmatrix} \begin{bmatrix} 40\% \\ 30\% \\ 50\% \end{bmatrix} = \begin{bmatrix} 10 \cdot 40\% + 90 \cdot 30\% + 6 \cdot 50\% \end{bmatrix} = \begin{bmatrix} 4 + 27 + 3 \end{bmatrix} = 34$$

The answer is (A).

Problem Set AA:

1. $\begin{bmatrix} 1 & 0 \\ 2 & 3 \end{bmatrix} + \begin{bmatrix} 5 & \sqrt{2} \\ -2 & 0 \end{bmatrix} =$

   (A) $\begin{bmatrix} 6 & \sqrt{2} \\ 0 & 0 \end{bmatrix}$

   (B) $\begin{bmatrix} 6 & \sqrt{2} \\ 0 & 3 \end{bmatrix}$

   (C) $\begin{bmatrix} -4 & -\sqrt{2} \\ 4 & 3 \end{bmatrix}$

   (D) $\begin{bmatrix} 6 & 2 \\ 0 & 3 \end{bmatrix}$

   (E) $\begin{bmatrix} 6 & \sqrt{2} \\ 0 & 0 \end{bmatrix}$

2. If $A = \begin{bmatrix} 1 & 2 \\ 2 & 0 \end{bmatrix}$ and $B = \begin{bmatrix} 0 & 3 \\ 1 & -1 \end{bmatrix}$ then $3A - B =$

   (A) $\begin{bmatrix} 3 & 3 \\ 5 & -1 \end{bmatrix}$

   (B) $\begin{bmatrix} 1 & 3 \\ 5 & 1 \end{bmatrix}$

   (C) $\begin{bmatrix} 3 & 3 \\ 5 & 1 \end{bmatrix}$

   (D) $\begin{bmatrix} 3 & 3 \\ -5 & 1 \end{bmatrix}$

   (E) $\begin{bmatrix} 3 & 3 \\ 5 & 0 \end{bmatrix}$

3. $\begin{bmatrix} 2 & 1 \\ 0 & -2 \end{bmatrix} \begin{bmatrix} 0 & 4 \\ -2 & 3 \end{bmatrix} =$

   (A) $\begin{bmatrix} -2 & 1 \\ 4 & -6 \end{bmatrix}$

   (B) $\begin{bmatrix} -2 & 0 \\ 0 & -6 \end{bmatrix}$

   (C) $\begin{bmatrix} -2 & 11 \\ 4 & 6 \end{bmatrix}$

   (D) $\begin{bmatrix} -2 & 11 \\ 4 & -6 \end{bmatrix}$

   (E) $\begin{bmatrix} 2 & 11 \\ 4 & 6 \end{bmatrix}$

4. What is the product of the matrices $\begin{bmatrix} x \\ 2x \\ 0 \end{bmatrix} \begin{bmatrix} 1 & 0 & 2 \end{bmatrix}$?

(A) $\begin{bmatrix} x & 0 & 0 \end{bmatrix}$

(B) $\begin{bmatrix} x \\ 0 \\ 0 \end{bmatrix}$

(C) $\begin{bmatrix} x \end{bmatrix}$

(D) $\begin{bmatrix} x & 0 & 0 \\ 2 & x & 0 \\ 0 & 4x & x \end{bmatrix}$

(E) $\begin{bmatrix} x & 0 & 2x \\ 2x & 0 & 4x \\ 0 & 0 & 0 \end{bmatrix}$

5. What is the product of the matrices $\begin{bmatrix} x & 1 & 3x \end{bmatrix} \begin{bmatrix} x \\ 0 \\ 4 \end{bmatrix}$?

(A) $\begin{bmatrix} x^2 \\ 1 \\ 12x \end{bmatrix}$

(B) $\begin{bmatrix} x^2 \\ 0 \\ 12x \end{bmatrix}$

(C) $\begin{bmatrix} x^2 + 12 \end{bmatrix}$

(D) $\begin{bmatrix} x^2 + 12x \end{bmatrix}$

(E) Does not exist

6. The number of each type of sandwich on the menu at the Mom & Pop Sandwich shop is given by the following matrix:

$$\begin{matrix} \text{Tuna} & \text{Pastrami} & \text{Chicken} \\ \begin{bmatrix} 5 & 2 & 4 \end{bmatrix} \end{matrix}$$

The number of sides available for each sandwich is given by the following matrix:

$$\begin{matrix} \text{Tuna} \\ \text{Pastrami} \\ \text{Chicken} \end{matrix} \begin{bmatrix} 5 \\ 3 \\ 2 \end{bmatrix}$$

From these matrices, how many total combinations of orders of one sandwich with one side are possible?

(A) 30
(B) 36
(C) 39
(D) 43
(E) 59

Answers and Solutions to Problem Set AA

1.

$$\begin{bmatrix} 1 & 0 \\ 2 & 3 \end{bmatrix} + \begin{bmatrix} 5 & \sqrt{2} \\ -2 & 0 \end{bmatrix} = \begin{bmatrix} 1+5 & 0+\sqrt{2} \\ 2+(-2) & 3+0 \end{bmatrix} = \begin{bmatrix} 6 & \sqrt{2} \\ 0 & 3 \end{bmatrix}$$

The answer is (B).

2.

$$3A - B = 3\begin{bmatrix} 1 & 2 \\ 2 & 0 \end{bmatrix} - \begin{bmatrix} 0 & 3 \\ 1 & -1 \end{bmatrix}$$

$$= \begin{bmatrix} 3\cdot 1 & 3\cdot 2 \\ 3\cdot 2 & 3\cdot 0 \end{bmatrix} - \begin{bmatrix} 0 & 3 \\ 1 & -1 \end{bmatrix}$$

$$= \begin{bmatrix} 3 & 6 \\ 6 & 0 \end{bmatrix} - \begin{bmatrix} 0 & 3 \\ 1 & -1 \end{bmatrix}$$

$$= \begin{bmatrix} 3-0 & 6-3 \\ 6-1 & 0-(-1) \end{bmatrix}$$

$$= \begin{bmatrix} 3 & 3 \\ 5 & 1 \end{bmatrix}$$

The answer is (C).

3.

$$\begin{bmatrix} 2 & 1 \\ 0 & -2 \end{bmatrix}\begin{bmatrix} 0 & 4 \\ -2 & 3 \end{bmatrix} = \begin{bmatrix} 2\cdot 0 + 1(-2) & 2\cdot 4 + 1\cdot 3 \\ 0\cdot 0 + (-2)(-2) & 0\cdot 4 + (-2)\cdot 3 \end{bmatrix}$$

$$= \begin{bmatrix} -2 & 11 \\ 4 & -6 \end{bmatrix}$$

The answer is (D).

4. This problem is harder than it may appear at first glance. Many students mistakenly chose the answer to be (C). For the product to be defined, the number of columns of the first matrix must equal the number of rows of the second matrix. The first matrix in the problem has 1 column, and the second matrix has 1 row. So, the product is defined, and the result is a 3 × 3 matrix.

To form the product, we multiply the first row of $\begin{bmatrix} x \\ 2x \\ 0 \end{bmatrix}$ by the *first* column of $\begin{bmatrix} 1 & 0 & 2 \end{bmatrix}$. This yields

$x \cdot 1 = x$. Adding this calculation to our 3 × 3 matrix yields

$$\begin{bmatrix} x & - & - \\ - & - & - \\ - & - & - \end{bmatrix}$$

Now, multiply the first row of $\begin{bmatrix} x \\ 2x \\ 0 \end{bmatrix}$ by the *second* column of $\begin{bmatrix} 1 & 0 & 2 \end{bmatrix}$. This yields $x \cdot 0 = 0$. Adding this

calculation to our matrix yields

$$\begin{bmatrix} x & 0 & \_ \\ \_ & \_ & \_ \\ \_ & \_ & \_ \end{bmatrix}$$

Now, multiply the first row of $\begin{bmatrix} x \\ 2x \\ 0 \end{bmatrix}$ by the *third* column of $\begin{bmatrix} 1 & 0 & 2 \end{bmatrix}$. This yields $x \cdot 2 = 2x$. Adding this

calculation to our matrix yields

$$\begin{bmatrix} x & 0 & 2x \\ \_ & \_ & \_ \\ \_ & \_ & \_ \end{bmatrix}$$

Performing the same series of calculations for the second and third rows yields

$$\begin{bmatrix} x & 0 & 2x \\ 2x & 0 & 4x \\ 0 & 0 & 0 \end{bmatrix}$$

The answer is (E).

5. For the product to be defined, the number of columns of the first matrix must equal the number of rows of the second matrix. The first matrix in the problem has 3 columns, and the second matrix has 3 rows. So, the product is defined, and the result is a 1 × 1 matrix.

To form the product, we multiply the first and only row of $\begin{bmatrix} x & 1 & 3x \end{bmatrix}$ by the first and only column of

$\begin{bmatrix} x \\ 0 \\ 4 \end{bmatrix}$. This yields

$$\begin{bmatrix} x & 1 & 3x \end{bmatrix}\begin{bmatrix} x \\ 0 \\ 4 \end{bmatrix} = \begin{bmatrix} x \cdot x + 1 \cdot 0 + 3x \cdot 4 \end{bmatrix}$$
$$= \begin{bmatrix} x^2 + 0 + 12x \end{bmatrix}$$
$$= \begin{bmatrix} x^2 + 12x \end{bmatrix}$$

The answer is (D).

6. The only option we have in this problem is to multiply the matrices:

$$\begin{bmatrix} 5 & 2 & 4 \end{bmatrix}\begin{bmatrix} 5 \\ 3 \\ 2 \end{bmatrix} = \begin{bmatrix} 5 \cdot 5 + 2 \cdot 3 + 4 \cdot 2 \end{bmatrix} = \begin{bmatrix} 25 + 6 + 8 \end{bmatrix} = 39$$

Hence, there are 39 combinations of one sandwich with one side. The answer is (C).

Trigonometry

Trigonometry is one of the least elegant math topics. It is just the naming of various ratios of the sides of a triangle with respect to an angle of the triangle. These simple ratios lead to an enormous number of properties, formulas, and applications, most of which you do not need to know for the ACT. Though the basic definitions, you must know cold.

The ACT pretty consistently asks only three or four trig questions. Two of which are just straightforward applications of the basic definitions of sin, cos, etc. This is probably because many students take the test at the end of their junior year or at the beginning of their senior year, so many are just starting their studies of trig.

TRIGONOMETRIC FUNCTIONS AND FORMULAS YOU MUST KNOW

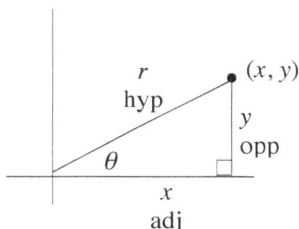

$$\sin\theta = \frac{opp}{hyp} = \frac{y}{r} \qquad \csc\theta = \frac{hyp}{opp} = \frac{r}{y} = \frac{1}{\sin\theta}$$

$$\cos\theta = \frac{adj}{hyp} = \frac{x}{r} \qquad \sec\theta = \frac{hyp}{adj} = \frac{r}{x} = \frac{1}{\cos\theta}$$

$$\tan\theta = \frac{opp}{adj} = \frac{y}{x} = \frac{\sin\theta}{\cos\theta} \qquad \cot\theta = \frac{adj}{hyp} = \frac{x}{y} = \frac{1}{\tan\theta}$$

Example 1: Given right triangle $\triangle ABC$, what is the value of $\cos B$?

(A) c/a
(B) a/c
(C) b/c
(D) b/a
(E) c/b

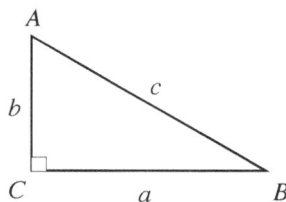

On the test, you will probably get a trig problem as simple as this one. By definition,

$$\cos B = \frac{adj}{hyp} = \frac{a}{c}$$

The answer is (B).

Example 2: Given right triangle $\triangle ABC$, what is the value of $\tan A$?

(A) $\dfrac{\sqrt{1-x^2}}{x}$

(B) $\sqrt{1-x^2}$

(C) $\dfrac{1}{x}$

(D) $\dfrac{1}{\sqrt{1-x^2}}$

(E) $\dfrac{x}{\sqrt{1-x^2}}$

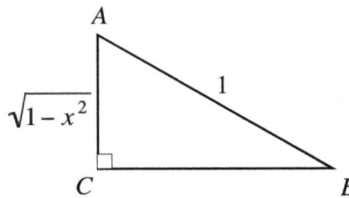

In order to calculate $\tan A$, we need the length of segment CB. Applying The Pythagorean Theorem to $\triangle ABC$ yields

$$1^2 = \left(\sqrt{1-x^2}\right)^2 + \left(\overline{CB}\right)^2$$

$$1 = 1 - x^2 + \left(\overline{CB}\right)^2$$

$$x^2 = \left(\overline{CB}\right)^2$$

$$x = \overline{CB}$$

Now, applying the definition of the tangent yields

$$\tan A = \frac{opp}{adj} = \frac{CB}{AC} = \frac{x}{\sqrt{1-x^2}}$$

The answer is (E).

TRIGONOMETRIC IDENTITIES YOU SHOULD BE FAMILIAR WITH, BUT PROBABLY DO NOT NEED TO MEMORIZE

Sum or Difference formulas:

$$\sin(x \pm y) = \sin x \cos y \pm \cos x \sin y$$

$$\cos(x \pm y) = \cos x \cos y \mp \sin x \sin y$$

$$\tan(x \pm y) = \frac{\tan x \pm \tan y}{1 \mp \tan x \tan y}$$

Double Angle formulas:

$$\sin 2\theta = 2\sin\theta\cos\theta$$

$$\cos 2\theta = 1 - 2\sin^2\theta$$

$$= 2\cos^2\theta - 1$$

$$= \cos^2\theta - \sin^2\theta$$

$$\tan 2\theta = \frac{2\tan\theta}{1 - \tan^2\theta}$$

Pythagorean formulas:

$$\sin^2\theta + \cos^2\theta = 1$$

$$\tan^2\theta + 1 = \sec^2\theta$$

$$\cot^2\theta + 1 = \csc^2\theta$$

Example 3: If $x = a\sin\theta$ for $-\pi/2 < \theta < \pi/2$ and $a > 0$, then $\dfrac{\sqrt{a^2 - x^2}}{x} =$

    (A) $\tan\theta$

    (B) $\cot\theta$

    (C) $a\tan\theta$

    (D) $a\cot\theta$

    (E) $\dfrac{\tan\theta}{a}$

Replacing x with $a\sin\theta$ in the expression $\dfrac{\sqrt{a^2 - x^2}}{x}$ yields

$$
\begin{aligned}
\frac{\sqrt{a^2 - x^2}}{x} &= \frac{\sqrt{a^2 - (a\sin\theta)^2}}{a\sin\theta} \\
&= \frac{\sqrt{a^2 - a^2\sin^2\theta}}{a\sin\theta} \\
&= \frac{\sqrt{a^2(1 - \sin^2\theta)}}{a\sin\theta} \\
&= \frac{\sqrt{a^2\cos^2\theta}}{a\sin\theta} \\
&= \frac{a\cos\theta}{a\sin\theta} \\
&= \frac{\cos\theta}{\sin\theta} \\
&= \cot\theta
\end{aligned}
$$

The answer is (B).

Half Angle formulas:

$$\sin^2\theta = \frac{1}{2}(1 - \cos 2\theta)$$

$$\cos^2\theta = \frac{1}{2}(1 + \cos 2\theta)$$

$$\sin\frac{\theta}{2} = \pm\sqrt{\frac{1 - \cos\theta}{2}}$$

$$\cos\frac{\theta}{2} = \pm\sqrt{\frac{1 + \cos\theta}{2}}$$

$$\tan\frac{\theta}{2} = \frac{\sin\theta}{1 + \cos\theta} = \frac{1 - \cos\theta}{\sin\theta}$$

Sum and Product formulas:

$$\sin x \cos y = \frac{1}{2}[\sin(x+y)+\sin(x-y)]$$

$$\cos x \sin y = \frac{1}{2}[\sin(x+y)-\sin(x-y)]$$

$$\cos x \cos y = \frac{1}{2}[\cos(x+y)+\cos(x-y)]$$

$$\sin x \sin y = \frac{1}{2}[\cos(x-y)-\cos(x+y)]$$

$$\sin x + \sin y = 2\sin\left(\frac{x+y}{2}\right)\cos\left(\frac{x-y}{2}\right)$$

$$\sin x - \sin y = 2\cos\left(\frac{x+y}{2}\right)\sin\left(\frac{x-y}{2}\right)$$

$$\cos x + \cos y = 2\cos\left(\frac{x+y}{2}\right)\cos\left(\frac{x-y}{2}\right)$$

$$\cos x - \cos y = -2\sin\left(\frac{x+y}{2}\right)\sin\left(\frac{x-y}{2}\right)$$

Reduction formulas:

$$\sin(-\theta) = -\sin\theta$$
$$\cos(-\theta) = \cos\theta$$
$$\sin\theta = -\sin(\theta-\pi)$$
$$\cos\theta = -\cos(\theta-\pi)$$

Conversion factors:

$$1° = \frac{\pi}{180} \text{ radians}$$

$$1 \text{ radian } = \frac{180°}{\pi}$$

FORMULAS FOR SOLVING NONRIGHT TRIANGLES

Law of Cosines:

$$c^2 = a^2 + b^2 - 2ab\cos C$$
where a, b, and c are the sides of the triangle and C is the angle opposite side c

The Law of Cosines is one of the favorite formulas of the ACT writers. There is a good chance you will see it on your test. You don't need to memorize the formula. If you do get a problem that requires the Law of Cosines, the formula will be given to you. The ACT is more concerned about measuring the mathematical skills you have developed than how many formulas you have memorized. So, you need to understand how the formula can be used.

Example 4: Given triangle $\triangle ABC$, what is the length of side AB ?

(A) $\sqrt{1^2 + (1.1)^2}$

(B) $\sqrt{1^2 - (1.1)^2}$

(C) $\sqrt{1^2 + (1.1)^2 - 2(1)(1.1)\cos 9°}$

(D) $\sqrt{1^2 + (1.1)^2 + 2(1)(1.1)\cos 9°}$

(E) $\sqrt{1^2 + (1.1)^2 - 2(1)(1.1)\cos(90-9)°}$

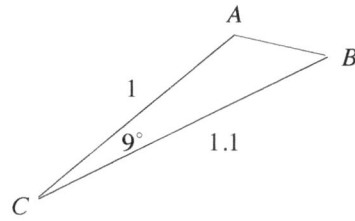

Since side AB is opposite angle C, the Law of Cosines yields

$$AB^2 = a^2 + b^2 - 2ab\cos C$$

Letting $a = 1$, $b = 1.1$ (or you can let $a = 1.1$ and $b = 1$), and $C = 9°$ yields

$$AB^2 = 1^2 + (1.1)^2 - 2(1)(1.1)\cos 9°$$

Finally, taking the square root of both sides of this equation yields

$$AB = \sqrt{1^2 + (1.1)^2 - 2(1)(1.1)\cos 9°}$$

The answer is (C).

Law of Sines:

$$\frac{\sin A}{a} = \frac{\sin B}{b} = \frac{\sin C}{c}$$

where angle A is oppsite side a, etc.

TRIGONOMETRIC VALUES FOR SPECIAL ANGLES

Angle	$\sin \theta$	$\cos \theta$	$\tan \theta$	$\cot \theta$	$\sec \theta$	$\csc \theta$
0 or 0°	0	1	0	Undefined	1	Undefined
$\pi/6$ or 30°	1/2	$\sqrt{3}/2$	$\sqrt{3}/3$	$\sqrt{3}$	$2\sqrt{3}/3$	2
$\pi/4$ or 45°	$\sqrt{2}/2$	$\sqrt{2}/2$	1	1	$\sqrt{2}$	$\sqrt{2}$
$\pi/3$ or 60°	$\sqrt{3}/2$	1/2	$\sqrt{3}$	$\sqrt{3}/3$	2	$2\sqrt{3}/3$

Example 5: What is the value of $\sin \dfrac{\pi}{8}$ given that $\sin \dfrac{\theta}{2} = \sqrt{\dfrac{1-\cos\theta}{2}}$?

(Note: You can use any of the values in the above table.)

(A) $\quad 2 - \sqrt{2}$

(B) $\quad \sqrt{2}$

(C) $\quad \dfrac{\sqrt{2-\sqrt{2}}}{4}$

(D) $\quad \sqrt{2-\sqrt{2}}$

(E) $\quad \dfrac{\sqrt{2-\sqrt{2}}}{2}$

Our goal here is to write $\pi/8$ as half of one of the special angles in the table so that we can use the given

Half Angle Formula: $\sin \dfrac{\theta}{2} = \sqrt{\dfrac{1-\cos\theta}{2}}$. Now, $\dfrac{\pi}{8} = \dfrac{\pi}{2 \cdot 4} = \dfrac{1}{2}\left(\dfrac{\pi}{4}\right) = \dfrac{\pi/4}{2}$, so replacing θ in the formula

with $\pi/4$ yields

$$\sin\frac{\pi}{8} = \sin\frac{\pi/4}{2}$$

$$= \sqrt{\frac{1-\cos\pi/4}{2}}$$

$$= \sqrt{\frac{1-\dfrac{\sqrt{2}}{2}}{2}} \qquad \text{from the table } \cos\pi/4 = \frac{\sqrt{2}}{2}$$

$$= \sqrt{\frac{\dfrac{2}{2}-\dfrac{\sqrt{2}}{2}}{2}}$$

$$= \sqrt{\frac{\dfrac{2-\sqrt{2}}{2}}{2}}$$

$$= \sqrt{\frac{2-\sqrt{2}}{4}}$$

$$= \frac{\sqrt{2-\sqrt{2}}}{2}$$

The answer is (E).

Problem Set BB:

1. In the right triangle $\triangle ABC$, the length of side AC is 2. If the cosine of angle A is 1/2, then what is the length of the hypotenuse AB ?

    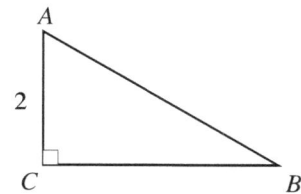

    (A)   4

    (B) $\dfrac{4}{\sqrt{3}}$

    (C) $\sqrt{3}$

    (D)   2

    (E)   1

2. In the right triangle $\triangle ABC$ shown, $\dfrac{\sec B}{\sin a} =$

    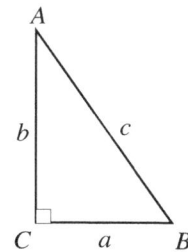

    (A)   1

    (B) a/c

    (C) $\left(\dfrac{c}{a}\right)^2$

    (D) c^2

    (E) a^2

3. If $\cos A = \dfrac{b}{c}$, $b > 0$, and $0 < A < \pi/2$, then $\sin A =$

    (A) $\dfrac{c}{\sqrt{c^2 - b^2}}$

    (B) c/b

    (C) $\dfrac{\sqrt{c^2 + b^2}}{c}$

    (D) $\dfrac{\sqrt{c^2 - b^2}}{c}$

    (E) $\sqrt{c^2 - b^2}$

4. In the right triangle shown, the secant of one of the angles is c/a. What is the tangent of this angle?

    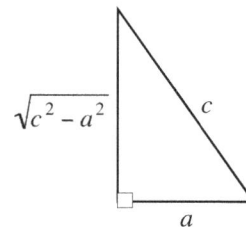

    (A) $\dfrac{a}{\sqrt{c^2 - a^2}}$

    (B) $\dfrac{\sqrt{c^2 - a^2}}{a}$

    (C) $\dfrac{\sqrt{c^2 - a^2}}{c}$

    (D) $\sqrt{c^2 - a^2}$

    (E) c/a

5. Given right triangle $\triangle ABC$, what is the value of csc A ?

    (A) $\dfrac{2}{\sqrt{5}}$

    (B) $\dfrac{\sqrt{5}}{2}$

    (C) 3/2

    (D) $\sqrt{5}$

    (E) 1/2

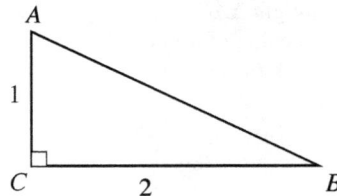

6. What is $\tan\dfrac{\pi}{12}$ given that $\tan(x-y)=\dfrac{\tan x - \tan y}{1+\tan x \tan y}$ and $\dfrac{\pi}{12}=\dfrac{\pi}{3}-\dfrac{\pi}{4}$?

    (Note: You can use the values in the table below.)

θ	$\tan\theta$
$\pi/4$	1
$\pi/3$	$\sqrt{3}$

    (A) $\dfrac{\sqrt{3}-1}{1+\sqrt{3}}$

    (B) $\dfrac{\sqrt{3}+1}{1+\sqrt{3}}$

    (C) $\dfrac{\sqrt{3}+1}{1-\sqrt{3}}$

    (D) $\dfrac{\sqrt{3}-1}{\sqrt{3}}$

    (E) $\dfrac{\sqrt{3}}{1+\sqrt{3}}$

Answers and Solutions to Problem Set BB

1. From the definition of cosine, we get

$$\cos A = \frac{adj}{hyp} = \frac{2}{AB}$$

Since we are given that $\cos A = \frac{1}{2}$, this becomes

$$\frac{2}{AB} = \frac{1}{2}$$

Solving this equation yields $AB = 4$, and the answer is (A).

2. From the definitions of secant and sine, we get

$$\frac{\sec B}{\sin A} = \frac{hyp/adj}{opp/hyp} = \frac{c/a}{a/c} = \frac{c}{a} \cdot \frac{c}{a} = \left(\frac{c}{a}\right)^2$$

The answer is (C).

3. In a triangle, the cosine is the ratio of the adjacent side to the hypotenuse, so we get

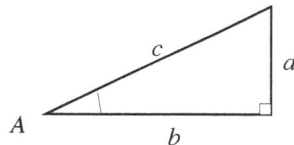

In order to determine $\sin A$, we must find the length of side a. Applying The Pythagorean Theorem to the triangle yields $c^2 = a^2 + b^2$. Solving this equation for a yields $a = \sqrt{c^2 - b^2}$, so the figure becomes

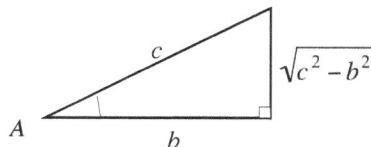

Hence, $\sin A = \frac{opp}{hyp} = \frac{\sqrt{c^2 - b^2}}{c}$. The answer is (D).

4. Since the secant is the hypotenuse divided by the adjacent side, we are dealing with the angle at the lower right-hand corner of the triangle. Let's label it B:

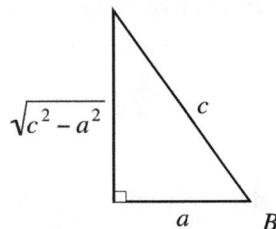

From the definition of tangent, we get

$$\tan B = \frac{opp}{adj} = \frac{\sqrt{c^2 - a^2}}{a}$$

The answer is (B).

5. In order to calculate csc A, we need the length of the hypotenuse AB. Applying The Pythagorean Theorem to $\triangle ABC$ yields

$$AB^2 = 1^2 + 2^2$$
$$AB^2 = 5$$
$$AB = \sqrt{5}$$

Now, applying the definition of the cosecant to angle A yields

$$\csc A = \frac{hyp}{opp} = \frac{AB}{CB} = \frac{\sqrt{5}}{2}$$

The answer is (B).

6. Replacing $\frac{\pi}{12}$ with $\frac{\pi}{3} - \frac{\pi}{4}$ in the expression $\tan\frac{\pi}{12}$ yields

$$\tan\frac{\pi}{12} = \tan\left(\frac{\pi}{3} - \frac{\pi}{4}\right)$$

$$= \frac{\tan\frac{\pi}{3} - \tan\frac{\pi}{4}}{1 + \tan\frac{\pi}{3}\tan\frac{\pi}{4}} \qquad \text{since } \tan(x - y) = \frac{\tan x - \tan y}{1 + \tan x \tan y}$$

$$= \frac{\sqrt{3} - 1}{1 + \sqrt{3} \cdot 1} \qquad \text{from the table}$$

$$= \frac{\sqrt{3} - 1}{1 + \sqrt{3}}$$

The answer is (A).

Diagnostic/Review Test

This diagnostic test appears at the end of the math section because it is probably best for you to use it as a review test. Unless your math skills are very strong, you should thoroughly study every chapter of the math section. Afterwards, you can use this diagnostic/review test to determine which chapters you need to work on more. If you do not have much time to study, this test can also be used to concentrate your studies on your weakest areas.

1. If $3x + 9 = 15$, then $x + 2 =$
    (A) 2
    (B) 3
    (C) 4
    (D) 5
    (E) 6

2. If $a = 3b, b^2 = 2c, 9c = d$, then $a^2/d =$
    (A) 1/2
    (B) 2
    (C) 10/3
    (D) 5
    (E) 6

$$a + b + c/2 = 60$$
$$-a - b + c/2 = -10$$

3. In the system of equations above, what is the value of b ?
    (A) 8
    (B) 20
    (C) 35
    (D) 50
    (E) Not enough information to decide.

4. $3 - (2^3 - 2[3 - 16 \div 2]) =$
    (A) -15
    (B) -5
    (C) 1
    (D) 2
    (E) 30

5. If $(x - 2)(x + 4) - (x - 3)(x - 1) = 0$, then $x =$
    (A) -5
    (B) -1
    (C) 0
    (D) 1/2
    (E) 11/6

6. $-2^4 - (x^2 - 1)^2 =$
    (A) $-x^4 + 2x^2 + 15$
    (B) $-x^4 - 2x^2 + 17$
    (C) $-x^4 + 2x^2 - 17$
    (D) $-x^4 + 2x^2 - 15$
    (E) $-x^4 + 2x^2 + 17$

7. The smallest prime number greater than 48 is
    (A) 49
    (B) 50
    (C) 51
    (D) 52
    (E) 53

8. If a, b, and c are consecutive integers and $a < b < c$, which of the following must be true?
    (A) b^2 is a prime number
    (B) $(a + c)/2 = b$
    (C) $a + b$ is even
    (D) ab/c is an integer
    (E) $c - a = b$

9. $\sqrt{(42 - 6)(20 + 16)} =$
    (A) 2
    (B) 20
    (C) 28
    (D) 30
    (E) 36

10. $\left(4^x\right)^2 =$
    (A) 2^{4x}
    (B) 4^{x+2}
    (C) 2^{2x+2}
    (D) 4^{x^2}
    (E) 2^{2x^2}

11. If $8^{13} = 2^z$, then $z =$
    (A) 10
    (B) 13
    (C) 19
    (D) 26
    (E) 39

12. 1/2 of 0.2 percent equals
    (A) 1
    (B) 0.1
    (C) 0.01
    (D) 0.001
    (E) 0.0001

13. $\dfrac{4}{\frac{1}{3} + 1} =$
    (A) 1
    (B) 1/2
    (C) 2
    (D) 3
    (E) 4

14. If $x + y = k$, then $3x^2 + 6xy + 3y^2 =$

    (A) k
    (B) $3k$
    (C) $6k$
    (D) k^2
    (E) $3k^2$

15. $8x^2 - 18 =$

    (A) $8(x^2 - 2)$
    (B) $2(2x + 3)(2x - 3)$
    (C) $2(4x + 3)(4x - 3)$
    (D) $2(2x + 9)(2x - 9)$
    (E) $2(4x + 3)(x - 3)$

16. For which values of x is the following inequality true: $x^2 < 2x$.

    (A) $x < 0$
    (B) $0 < x < 2$
    (C) $-2 < x < 2$
    (D) $x < 2$
    (E) $x > 2$

17. If x is an integer and $y = -3x + 7$, what is the least value of x for which y is less than 1?

    (A) 1
    (B) 2
    (C) 3
    (D) 4
    (E) 5

18. In the figure shown, triangle ABC is isosceles with base AC. If $x = 60°$, then $AC =$

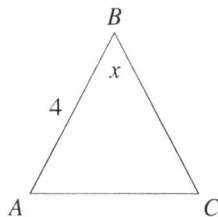

Note, figure not drawn to scale

    (A) 2
    (B) 3
    (C) 4
    (D) 14/3
    (E) $\sqrt{30}$

19. A unit square is circumscribed about a circle. If the circumference of the circle is $q\pi$, what is the value of q?

    (A) 1
    (B) 2
    (C) π
    (D) 2π
    (E) 5π

20. What is the area of the triangle shown?

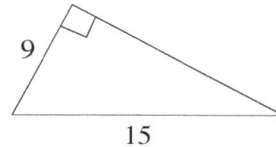

    (A) 20
    (B) 24
    (C) 30
    (D) 54
    (E) 64

21. If the average of $2x$ and $4x$ is 12, then $x =$

    (A) 1
    (B) 2
    (C) 3
    (D) 4
    (E) 24

22. The average of x, y, and z is 8 and the average of y and z is 4. What is the value of x?

    (A) 4
    (B) 9
    (C) 16
    (D) 20
    (E) 24

23. If the ratio of two numbers is 6 and their sum is 21, what is the value of the larger number?

    (A) 1
    (B) 5
    (C) 12
    (D) 17
    (E) 18

24. What percent of $3x$ is $6y$ if $x = 4y$?

    (A) 50%
    (B) 40%
    (C) 30%
    (D) 20%
    (E) 18%

25. If $y = 3x$, then the value of 10% of y is

    (A) $.003x$
    (B) $.3x$
    (C) $3x$
    (D) $30x$
    (E) $300x$

26. How many ounces of water must be added to a 30-ounce solution that is 40 percent alcohol to dilute the solution to 25 percent alcohol?

    (A) 9
    (B) 10
    (C) 15
    (D) 16
    (E) 18

27. What is the value of the 201st term of a sequence if the first term of the sequence is 2 and each successive term is 4 more than the term immediately preceding it?

    (A) 798
    (B) 800
    (C) 802
    (D) 804
    (E) 806

28. A particular carmaker sells four models of cars, and each model comes with 5 options. How many different types of cars does the carmaker sell?

    (A) 15
    (B) 16
    (C) 17
    (D) 18
    (E) 20

29. If $f(x) = x^3 - 1$ and $g(x) = \sqrt[3]{x}$, then $\dfrac{f(2)}{g(1)} =$

    (A) 0
    (B) 2
    (C) 7/3
    (D) 7
    (E) 9

30. Let $f(x) = 1 - x$, for all non-negative x. If $f(f(1-x)) = f(1-x)$, then $x =$

    (A) 1/2
    (B) 3/4
    (C) 1
    (D) 2
    (E) 3

1. Dividing both sides of the equation by 3 yields

$$x + 3 = 5$$

Subtracting 1 from both sides of this equation (because we are looking for $x + 2$) yields

$$x + 2 = 4$$

The answer is (C).

2.

$$\frac{a^2}{d} =$$

$$\frac{(3b)^2}{9c} = \qquad \text{since } a = 3b \text{ and } 9c = d$$

$$\frac{9b^2}{9c} =$$

$$\frac{b^2}{c} =$$

$$\frac{2c}{c} = \qquad \text{since } b^2 = 2c$$

$$2$$

The answer is (B).

3. Merely adding the two equations yields

$$c = 50$$

Next, multiplying the bottom equation by -1 and then adding the equations yields

$$\begin{aligned} a + b + c/2 &= 60 \\ (+) \quad a + b - c/2 &= 10 \\ \hline 2a + 2b &= 70 \end{aligned}$$

Dividing this equation by 2 yields

$$a + b = 35$$

This equation does not allow us to determine the value of b. For example, if $a = 0$, then $b = 35$. Now suppose $a = -15$, then $b = 50$. This is a double case and therefore the answer is (E), not enough information to decide.

4.
$$3 - (2^3 - 2[3 - 16 \div 2]) = \qquad \text{Within the innermost parentheses, division is performed before subtraction:}$$
$$3 - (2^3 - 2[3 - 8]) =$$
$$3 - (2^3 - 2[-5]) =$$
$$3 - (8 - 2[-5]) =$$
$$3 - (8 + 10) =$$
$$3 - 18 =$$
$$-15$$

The answer is (A).

5. Multiplying (using foil multiplication) both terms in the expression yields

$$x^2 + 4x - 2x - 8 - (x^2 - x - 3x + 3) = 0$$

(Notice that parentheses are used in the second expansion but not in the first. Parentheses must be used in the second expansion because the negative sign must be distributed to *every* term within the parentheses.)

Combining like terms yields

$$x^2 + 2x - 8 - (x^2 - 4x + 3) = 0$$

Distributing the negative sign to every term within the parentheses yields

$$x^2 + 2x - 8 - x^2 + 4x - 3 = 0$$

(Note, although distributing the negative sign over the parentheses is an elementary operation, many, if not most, students will apply the negative sign to only the first term:

$$-x^2 - 4x + 3$$

The writers of the test are aware of this common mistake and structure the test so that there are many opportunities to make this mistake.)

Grouping like terms together yields

$$(x^2 - x^2) + (2x + 4x) + (-8 - 3) = 0$$

Combining the like terms yields

$$6x - 11 = 0$$
$$6x = 11$$
$$x = 11/6$$

The answer is (E).

6.
$$-2^4 - (x^2 - 1)^2 =$$
$$-16 - [(x^2)^2 - 2x^2 + 1] =$$
$$-16 - [x^4 - 2x^2 + 1] =$$
$$-16 - x^4 + 2x^2 - 1 =$$
$$-x^4 + 2x^2 - 17$$

The answer is (C).

Notice that $-2^4 = -16$, not 16. This is one of the most common mistakes on the test. To see why $-2^4 = -16$ more clearly, rewrite -2^4 as follows:

$$-2^4 = (-1)2^4$$

In this form, it is clearer that the exponent, 4, applies only to the number 2, not to the number -1. So, $-2^4 = (-1)2^4 = (-1)16 = -16$.

To make the answer positive 16, the -2 could be placed in parentheses:

$$(-2)^4 = [(-1)2]^4 = (-1)^4\, 2^4 = (+1)16 = 16$$

7. Since the question asks for the *smallest* prime greater than 48, we start with the smallest answer-choice. Now, 49 is not prime since $49 = 7 \cdot 7$. Next, 50 is not prime since $50 = 5 \cdot 10$. Next, 51 is not prime since $51 = 3 \cdot 17$. Next, 52 is not prime since $52 = 2 \cdot 26$. Finally, 53 *is* prime since it is divisible by only itself and 1. The answer is (E).

Note, an integer is prime if it greater than 1 and divisible by only itself and 1. The number 2 is the smallest prime (and the only even prime) because the only integers that divide into it evenly are 1 and 2. The number 3 is the next larger prime. The number 4 is not prime because $4 = 2 \cdot 2$. Following is a partial list of the prime numbers. You should memorize it.

$$2, 3, 5, 7, 11, 13, 17, 19, 23, 29, 31, \ldots$$

8. Recall that an integer is prime if it is divisible by only itself and 1. In other words, an integer is prime if it cannot be written as a product of two other integers, other than itself and 1. Now, $b^2 = bb$. Since b^2 can be written as a product of b and b, it is not prime. Statement (A) is false.

   Turning to Choice (B), since a, b, and c are consecutive integers, in that order, b is one unit larger than a: $b = a + 1$, and c is one unit larger than b: $c = b + 1 = (a + 1) + 1 = a + 2$. Now, plugging this information into the expression $\dfrac{a+c}{2}$ yields

$$\frac{a+c}{2} =$$
$$\frac{a+(a+2)}{2} =$$
$$\frac{2a+2}{2} =$$
$$\frac{2a}{2} + \frac{2}{2} =$$
$$a + 1 =$$
$$b$$

The answer is (B).

   Regarding the other answer-choices, Choice (C) is true in some cases and false in others. To show that it can be false, let's plug in some numbers satisfying the given conditions. How about $a = 1$ and $b = 2$. In this case, $a + b = 1 + 2 = 3$, which is odd, not even. This eliminates Choice (C). Notice that to show a statement is false, we need only find one exception. However, to show a statement is true by plugging in numbers, you usually have to plug in more than one set of numbers because the statement may be true for one set of numbers but not for another set. We'll discuss in detail later the conditions under which you can say that a statement is true by plugging in numbers.

   Choice (D) is not necessarily true. For instance, let $a = 1$ and $b = 2$. Then $\dfrac{ab}{3} = \dfrac{1 \cdot 2}{3} = \dfrac{2}{3}$, which is not an integer. This eliminates Choice (D).

   Finally, $c - a = b$ is not necessarily true. For instance, let $a = 2$, $b = 3$, and $c = 4$. Then $c - a = 4 - 2 = 2 \neq 3$. This eliminates Choice (E).

9.
$$\sqrt{(42-6)(20+16)} =$$
$$\sqrt{(36)(36)} =$$
$$\sqrt{36}\sqrt{36} = \qquad \text{from the rule } \sqrt{xy} = \sqrt{x}\sqrt{y}$$
$$6 \cdot 6 =$$
$$36$$

The answer is (E).

10.
$$\left(4^x\right)^2 =$$
$$4^{2x} = \qquad \text{by the rule } \left(x^a\right)^b = x^{ab}$$
$$\left(2^2\right)^{2x} = \qquad \text{by replacing 4 with } 2^2$$
$$(2)^{4x} \qquad \text{by the rule } \left(x^a\right)^b = x^{ab}$$

The answer is (A). Note: This is considered a hard problem.

   As to the other answer-choices, Choice (B) wrongly adds the exponents x and 2. The exponents are added when the same bases are multiplied:

$$a^x a^y = a^{x+y}$$

For example: $2^3 2^2 = 2^{3+2} = 2^5 = 32$. Be careful not to multiply unlike bases. For example, do not add exponents in the following expression: $2^3 4^2$. The exponents cannot be added here because the bases, 2 and 4, are not the same.

Choice (C), first changes 4 into 2^2, and then correctly multiplies 2 and x: $\left(2^2\right)^x = 2^{2x}$. However, it then errs in adding $2x$ and 2: $\left(2^{2x}\right)^2 \neq 2^{2x+2}$.

Choice (D) wrongly squares the x. When a power is raised to another power, the powers are multiplied:

$$\left(x^a\right)^b = x^{ab}$$

So, $\left(4^x\right)^2 = 4^{2x}$.

Choice (E) makes the same mistake as in Choice (D).

11. The number 8 can be written as 2^3. Plugging this into the equation $8^{13} = 2^z$ yields

$$\left(2^3\right)^{13} = 2^z$$

Applying the rule $\left(x^a\right)^b = x^{ab}$ yields

$$2^{39} = 2^z$$

Since the bases are the same, the exponents must be the same. Hence, $z = 39$, and the answer is (E).

12. Recall that percent means to divide by 100. So .2 percent equals $.2/100 = .002$. (Recall that the decimal point is moved to the left one space for each zero in the denominator.) Now, as a decimal $1/2 = .5$.
In percent problems, "of" means multiplication, so multiplying .5 and .002 yields

$$\begin{array}{r} .002 \\ \times\quad .5 \\ \hline .001 \end{array}$$

Hence, the answer is (D).

13.
$$\frac{4}{\frac{1}{3}+1} =$$

$$\frac{4}{\frac{1}{3}+\frac{3}{3}} = \qquad \text{by creating a common denominator of 3}$$

$$\frac{4}{\frac{1+3}{3}} =$$

$$\frac{4}{\frac{4}{3}} =$$

$$4\cdot\frac{3}{4} = \qquad \text{Recall: "to divide" means to invert and multiply}$$

$$3 \qquad\qquad \text{by canceling the 4's}$$

Hence, the answer is (D).

14.
$$3x^2 + 6xy + 3y^2 =$$
$$3(x^2 + 2xy + y^2) = \qquad \text{by factoring out the common factor 3}$$
$$3(x + y)^2 = \qquad \text{by the perfect square trinomial formula } x^2 + 2xy + y^2 = (x + y)^2$$
$$3k^2$$

Hence, the answer is (E).

15. $8x^2 - 18 =$

$2(4x^2 - 9) =$ by the distributive property $ax + ay = a(x + y)$

$2(2^2x^2 - 3^2) =$

$2([2x]^2 - 3^2) =$

$2(2x + 3)(2x - 3)$ by the difference of squares formula $x^2 - y^2 = (x + y)(x - y)$

The answer is (B).

It is common for students to wrongly apply the Difference of Squares formula to a perfect square:

$$(x - y)^2 \neq (x + y)(x - y)$$

The correct formulas follow. Notice that the first formula is the square of a difference, and the second formula is the difference of two squares.

Perfect square trinomial: $(x - y)^2 = x^2 - 2xy + y^2$

Difference of squares: $x^2 - y^2 = (x + y)(x - y)$

It is also common for students to wrongly distribute the 2 in a perfect square:

$$(x - y)^2 \neq x^2 - y^2$$

Note, there is no factoring formula for a sum of squares: $x^2 + y^2$. It cannot be factored.

16. First, replace the inequality symbol with an equal symbol: $x^2 = 2x$

Subtracting $2x$ from both sides yields $x^2 - 2x = 0$

Factoring by the distributive rule yields $x(x - 2) = 0$

Setting each factor to 0 yields $x = 0$ and $x - 2 = 0$

Or $x = 0$ and $x = 2$

Now, the only numbers at which the expression can change sign are 0 and 2. So, 0 and 2 divide the number line into three intervals. Let's set up a number line and choose test points in each interval:

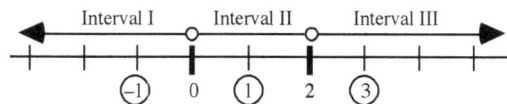

When $x = -1$, $x^2 < 2x$ becomes $1 < -2$. This is false. Hence, no numbers in Interval I satisfy the inequality. When $x = 1$, $x^2 < 2x$ becomes $1 < 2$. This is true. Hence, all numbers in Interval II satisfy the inequality. That is, $0 < x < 2$. When $x = 3$, $x^2 < 2x$ becomes $9 < 6$. This is false. Hence, no numbers in Interval III satisfy the inequality. The answer is (B). The graph of the solution follows:

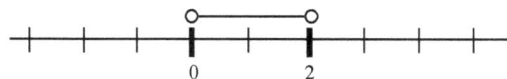

17. Since y is to be less than 1 and $y = -3x + 7$, we get

$-3x + 7 < 1$

$-3x < -6$ by subtracting 7 from both sides of the inequality

$x > 2$ by dividing both sides of the inequality by -3

(Note that the inequality changes direction when we divide both sides by a negative number. This is also the case if you multiply both sides of an inequality by a negative number.)

Since x is an integer and is to be as small as possible, $x = 3$. The answer is (C).

18. Since the triangle is isosceles, with base AC, the base angles are congruent (equal). That is, $A = C$. Since the angle sum of a triangle is 180, we get

$$A + C + x = 180$$

Replacing C with A and x with 60 gives

$$A + A + 60 = 180$$
$$2A + 60 = 180$$
$$2A = 120$$
$$A = 60$$

Hence, the triangle is equilateral (all three sides are congruent). Since we are given that side AB has length 4, side AC also has length 4. The answer is (C).

19. Since the unit square is circumscribed about the circle, the diameter of the circle is 1 and the radius of the circle is $r = d/2 = 1/2$. This is illustrated in the following figure:

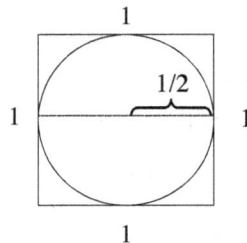

Now, the circumference of a circle is given by the formula $2\pi r$. For this circle the formula becomes $2\pi r = 2\pi(1/2) = \pi$. We are told that the circumference of the circle is $q\pi$. Setting these two expressions equal yields

$$\pi = q\pi$$

Dividing both sides of this equation by π yields

$$1 = q$$

The answer is (A).

20. Let x be the unknown side of the triangle. Applying The Pythagorean Theorem yields

$$9^2 + x^2 = 15^2$$
$$81 + x^2 = 225 \qquad \text{by squaring the terms}$$
$$x^2 = 144 \qquad \text{by subtracting 81 from both sides of the equation}$$
$$x = \pm\sqrt{144} \qquad \text{by taking the square root of both sides of the equation}$$
$$x = 12 \qquad \text{since we are looking for a length, we take the positive root}$$

In a right triangle, the legs are the base and the height of the triangle. Hence, $A = \dfrac{1}{2}bh = \dfrac{1}{2} \cdot 9 \cdot 12 = 54$.

The answer is (D).

21. Since the average of $2x$ and $4x$ is 12, we get

$$\frac{2x + 4x}{2} = 12$$
$$\frac{6x}{2} = 12$$
$$3x = 12$$
$$x = 4$$

The answer is (D).

22. Recall that the average of N numbers is their sum divided by N. That is, average = sum/N. Since the average of x, y, and z is 8 and the average of y and z is 4, this formula yields

$$\frac{x + y + z}{3} = 8$$

$$\frac{y + z}{2} = 4$$

Solving the bottom equation for $y + z$ yields $y + z = 8$. Plugging this into the top equation gives

$$\frac{x + 8}{3} = 8$$

$$x + 8 = 24$$

$$x = 16$$

The answer is (C).

23. Let the two numbers be x and y. Now, a ratio is simply a fraction. Forming the fraction yields $x/y = 6$, and forming the sum yields $x + y = 21$. Solving the first equation for x yields $x = 6y$. Plugging this into the second equation yields

$$6y + y = 21$$
$$7y = 21$$
$$y = 3$$

Plugging this into the equation $x = 6y$ yields

$$x = 6(3) = 18$$

The answer is (E).

24. Let $z\%$ represent the unknown percent. Now, when solving percent problems, "of" means times. Translating the statement "What percent of $3x$ is $6y$" into an equation yields

$$z\%(3x) = 6y$$

Substituting $x = 4y$ into this equation yields

$$z\%(3 \cdot 4y) = 6y$$

$$z\%(12y) = 6y$$

$$z\% = \frac{6y}{12y}$$

$$z\% = 1/2 = .50 = 50\%$$

The answer is (A).

25. The percent symbol, %, means to divide by 100. So $10\% = 10/100 = .10$. Hence, the expression 10% of y translates into $.10y$. Since $y = 3x$, this becomes $.10y = .10(3x) = .30x$. The answer is (B).

26. Let x be the amount of water added. Since there is no alcohol in the water, the percent of alcohol in the water is $0\%x$. The amount of alcohol in the original solution is $40\%(30)$, and the amount of alcohol in the final solution will be $25\%(30 + x)$. Now, the concentration of alcohol in the original solution plus the concentration of alcohol in the added solution (water) must equal the concentration of alcohol in the resulting solution:

$$40\%(30) + 0\%x = 25\%(30 + x)$$

Multiplying this equation by 100 to clear the percent symbol yields

$$40(30) + 0 = 25(30 + x)$$
$$1200 = 750 + 25x$$
$$450 = 25x$$
$$18 = x$$

The answer is (E).

27. Except for the first term, each term of the sequence is found by adding 4 to the term immediately preceding it. In other words, we are simply adding 4 to the sequence 200 times. This yields

$$4 \cdot 200 = 800$$

Adding the 2 in the first term gives $800 + 2 = 802$. The answer is (C).

We can also solve this problem formally. The first term of the sequence is 2, and since each successive term is 4 more than the term immediately preceding it, the second term is $2 + 4$, and the third term is $(2 + 4) + 4$, and the fourth term is $[(2 + 4) + 4] + 4$, etc. Regrouping yields (note that we rewrite the first term as $2 + 4(0)$. You'll see why in a moment.)

$$2 + 4(0), 2 + 4(1), 2 + 4(2), 2 + 4(3), \ldots$$

Notice that the number within each pair of parentheses is 1 less than the numerical order of the term. For instance, the *first* term has a 0 within the parentheses, the *second* term has a 1 within the parentheses, etc. Hence, the nth term of the sequence is

$$2 + 4(n - 1)$$

Using this formula, the 201st term is $2 + 4(201 - 1) = 2 + 4(200) = 2 + 800 = 802$.

28. For the first model, there are 5 options. So there are 5 different types of cars in this model. For the second model, there are the same number of different types of cars. Likewise, for the other two types of models. Hence, there are $5 + 5 + 5 + 5 = 20$ different types of cars. The answer is (E).

This problem illustrates the *Fundamental Principle of Counting*:

> If an event occurs m times, and each of the m events is followed by a second event which occurs k times, then the first event follows the second event $m \cdot k$ times.

29. $\dfrac{f(2)}{g(1)} = \dfrac{2^3 - 1}{\sqrt[3]{1}} = \dfrac{8 - 1}{1} = 7$. The answer is (D).

30.
$$f(f(1 - x)) = f(1 - x)$$
$$f(1 - (1 - x)) = f(1 - x)$$
$$f(1 - 1 + x) = f(1 - x)$$
$$f(0 + x) = f(1 - x)$$
$$f(x) = f(1 - x)$$
$$1 - x = 1 - (1 - x)$$
$$1 - x = 1 - 1 + x$$
$$1 - x = x$$
$$1 = 2x$$
$$\frac{1}{2} = x$$

The answer is (A).

Study Plan

Use the list below to review the appropriate chapters for any questions you missed.

Equations:	**Factoring:**	**Percents:**
Questions: 1, 2, 3	Questions: 14, 15	Questions: 24, 25
Algebraic Expressions:	**Inequalities:**	**Word Problems:**
Questions: 4, 5, 6	Questions: 16, 17	Question: 26
Number Theory:	**Geometry:**	**Sequences & Series:**
Questions: 7, 8	Questions: 18, 19, 20	Question: 27
Exponents & Roots:	**Averages:**	**Counting:**
Questions: 9, 10, 11	Questions: 21, 22	Question: 28
Fractions & Decimals:	**Ratio & Proportion:**	**Functions:**
Questions: 12, 13	Question: 23	Questions: 29, 30

Part Two
VERBAL

ORIENTATION

ENGLISH TEST

- Punctuation
- Grammar
- Rhetoric

READING TEST

- Reading Methods
- The Six Questions
- Pivotal Words
- The Three-Step Method
- Practice Reading Test

WRITING TEST

- The Essay
- Re-Cap
- Presenting a Perspective on an Issue
- Sample Essays
- Practice Test

ORIENTATION

The Verbal Section* contains three parts: English Test, Reading Test, and Writing Test.

English Test

The English Test is 45 minutes long and consists of 75 multiple-choice questions. The test is designed to measure your ability to revise and edit a piece of writing. Two categories of questions appear on the test:

> **Usage/Mechanics**
>> Punctuation
>> Basic grammar
>> Sentence structure

> **Rhetorical Skills**
>> General writing style
>> Organization

These subsections have their own scores: The Usage/Mechanics score is based on 40 questions, and the Rhetorical Skills score is based on 35 questions.

The English Test is always the first test given.

Reading Test

The Reading Test is 35 minutes long and consists of 40 multiple-choice questions. It's too late now to pretend that you can't read, so strap on your reading hat and get ready to read about the following subjects:

> **Humanities:** This passage can be about music, dance, theater, art, architecture, language, ethics, literary criticism, and even philosophy.
> **Social Studies**: The social studies passage can include sociology, anthropology, history, geography, psychology, political science, and economics.
> **Natural Sciences:** The natural science passage can cover chemistry, biology, physics, and other physical sciences.
> **Prose Fiction:** The fiction passage can be taken from a novel or a short story; however, don't expect to have read the passage before.

Writing Test

The Writing Test is 30 minutes long and consists of one prompt from which to write an essay. Although the Writing Test is optional, three-quarters of colleges and universities require this section of the ACT, so it might be in your best interest to take it.

The Writing Test is always the last test given.

---

* The ACT does use the term Verbal Section. They view and grade each of the three parts of the Verbal Section separately. We are using the term Verbal Section to conveniently distinguish these sections from the Math and Science sections.

Skipping and Guessing

Some questions on the ACT are rather hard. And since it is a time-pressured test, you may not be able to answer every question.

Often students become obsessed with a particular problem and waste valuable time trying to solve it. To get a top score, learn to cut your losses and move on. All questions are worth the same number of points, regardless of their difficulty.

There is no penalty for guessing on the ACT. So, if you skip a question or do not finish a section in time, be sure to at least mark an answer for good measure.

Check Your Work

Throughout this chapter, you will come across sections titled "Check Your Work." These sections are designed to shed light on tips that can help you master the ACT, so pay special attention when you see them.

ENGLISH TEST

- **INTRODUCTION**

- **PUNCTUATION**
  Commas
  Semicolons
  Colons
  Dashes
  Apostrophes
  Sentence Fragments
  Run-On Sentences

- **GRAMMAR**
  Pronouns
  Subject-Verb Agreement
  Modifiers
  Parallelism
  Verb Tense
  Diction

- **RHETORIC**
  Style
  Structure

Introduction

The English Test portion of the ACT consists of 75 multiple-choice questions and tests standard written English. The test is designed to measure your ability to revise and edit a piece of writing. Remember those composition classes you took freshmen year? When you knew how to use the subjunctive and actually cared about the differences between adjectives and adverbs? If not, the following chapter will give you an in depth refresh.

Two categories of questions appear on the English Test:

- **Usage/Mechanics**
  Punctuation
  Basic grammar
  Sentence structure

- **Rhetorical Skills**
  General writing style
  Organization

Don't worry if your grammar and punctuation is a little rusty. Just read the following section carefully, and you'll master the English Test in no time.

Punctuation

In this section, we will discuss the most commonly used punctuation marks: commas, semicolons, colons, dashes, apostrophes, and quotation marks. We will also discuss using punctuation to correct run-on sentences and sentence fragments.

Commas

When talking, we separate our ideas by pausing between them. In writing, these pauses are represented by punctuation marks. The shortest of these pauses is indicated by the comma – the most frequently used mark of punctuation in the English language.

Even though commas float around in just about every sentence, it is possible to obtain order in the midst of all this comma chaos. If you can remember a few standard rules, you'll be placing commas in their proper place in no time.

➤ **Rule 1** – Use a comma to separate words, phrases, or clauses in a series.

   Example:
   Will you pick up some <u>hotdogs, chips, and drinks</u> for the party tonight?

When you have three or more items in a series, the final comma before the conjunction (*and, or, nor*) is optional.

   I made the bed, swept the floor, and vacuumed the carpet.

However, you should never use a comma after the conjunction in the series.

   Incorrect:
   I made the bed, swept the floor, vacuumed the carpet, and, cleaned the bathroom.

➤ **Rule 2** – Use a comma to separate two or more adjectives that precede and modify the same noun.

   Example:
   It seemed like a crime to disturb the <u>beautiful, serene lake.</u>

However, when the final adjective is so closely related to the noun that the words form a single expression, no comma is necessary before the final adjective.

   Before you watch TV, I want you to clean the <u>dirty, grimy kitchen sink.</u>

Don't use a comma between the final adjective and its noun.

   When are we going to surf that <u>secret, beautiful</u> beach you used to talk about?

✔ <u>Check your work</u>
Look through your work for any series of words, phrases or clauses. If there are two or more of these elements, place a comma after all but the last one.

Example (without punctuation):
He thought taking a road trip would <u>help him feel rejuvenated</u> <u>allow him to work through his feelings</u> and <u>provide him with some much needed solitude.</u>

In the sentence above, there are three modifying clauses. Each clause modifies the verbal phrase *taking a road trip,* which is acting as the object of the sentence. Once these clauses are identified, a comma should be placed after each except for the last:

He thought taking a road trip would <u>help him feel rejuvenated, allow him to work through his feelings, and provide him some much needed solitude.</u>

Lets try some adjectives:

She looked longingly through the window at the <u>lovely elegant pearl necklace.</u>

First, identify the list of words: *lovely, elegant,* and *pearl* modify *necklace.* Now confirm that each adjective equally modifies the noun *necklace.* To do this, insert the word *and* in between each adjective:

She looked longingly through the window at the <u>lovely *and* elegant *and* pearl necklace.</u>

Clearly, the sentence does not make sense with *and* between *elegant* and *pearl.* Therefore, you should place the commas appropriately:

She looked longingly through the window at the <u>lovely, elegant pearl necklace.</u>

➤ **Rule 3** – Use a comma to separate various introductory elements from the rest of the sentence. Introductory elements include prepositional phrases, subordinating clauses, transitional words or phrases, and verbal phrases.

A *prepositional phrase* begins with a preposition and includes any modifiers or objects. Prepositional phrases usually signal a relationship, particularly a relationship of time or location.

Examples:
Spoiler Alert: <u>In the movie *Titanic*</u>, Leonardo di Caprio's character dies.
<u>Since the accident last year</u>, she has been afraid to drive on the highway.

Both introductory clauses in these examples begin with prepositions. The clauses indicate a relationship of location (*In the movie*...) and time (*Since the accident*...) between the introductory phrases and the independent clause that follows. Therefore, commas must separate them.

A *subordinating clause* begins with a *subordinator,* which is a word that indicates a relationship—usually a relationship of time or location—between the clause and the independent clause that follows. This relationship makes a subordinating clause similar to a prepositional phrase. However, unlike a prepositional phrase, a subordinating clause can also be referred to as a dependent clause because it has both a subject and a verb.

Example:
<u>When I first entered the workforce</u>, we didn't have all the modern technological conveniences that make today's business world move at such a rapid pace.

Here the phrase *When I first entered the workforce* begins with the subordinator *When,* which signals a time relationship between the subordinating clause and the independent clause that follows. Although this clause has a subject (*I*) and a verb (*entered*), it cannot stand alone as a sentence and requires the independent clause to complete the thought.

Transitional words and phrases add coherence to your writing. They help connect one sentence to the next, but beware; transitional words and phrases are often un-needed outside of formal writing, so they should be used with caution.

Here are some of the most commonly used transitional words: *finally*, *furthermore*, *moreover*, and *next* indicate sequence; *again*, *likewise*, and *similarly* indicate comparison; *although*, *but*, *however*, *by contrast*, and *on the other hand* indicate contrast; *for example*, *in fact*, and *specifically* indicate examples; *accordingly*, *as a result*, *consequently*, and *therefore* indicate cause and effect.

> **Example:**
> Dear Employees,
>
> I am writing to tell you about a new incentive program we are beginning here at ABC Company. Specifically, this incentive program will focus on rewarding sales. Our customer base has dropped drastically this year. Consequently, we must look for new ways to increase sales. Although we have offered incentives in the past, this program will be different because it will reward you for improvement in sales rather than for your sales numbers. Furthermore, you will not only be able to earn monetary rewards, but you may also be awarded with extra vacation days.
>
> Happy selling,
> Mr. Smith

In the above text, transitional words and phrases are used to make the text flow more smoothly. A comma is required after each transitional word or phrase.

Verbal phrases contain verb elements but function as nouns, adjectives or adverbs rather than verbs. There are two kinds of verbal phrases that can act as introductory phrases and therefore must be set off by commas: participial phrases and infinitive phrases.

Participial phrases are made up of a present participle (the *–ing* form of a verb) or a past participle (the *–ed* form of a verb) as well as any modifiers or objects. Participial phrases act as adjectives because they describe, or modify, the subject in the independent clause.

> **Examples:**
> Standing alone by the door, Ricky watched the rest of the boys dance with their dates.
> Angered by the kids' cutting remarks, Naomi stormed out of the room and then burst into tears.

The first example contains a participial phrase that contains the present participle *Standing*. The introductory phrase *Standing alone by the door* describes Ricky. In the second example, the past participle *Angered* makes up the participial phrase, and the full introductory phrase describes Naomi.

Infinitive phrases are made up of an infinitive (a verb taking its root form, e.g., *to drink*, *to live*, *to be*) as well as any modifiers or objects.

> **Examples:**
> To win a gold medal, you must work very hard.
> To earn a high score on the ACT, you must study this guide thoroughly.

To win is the infinitive in the first sentence, and *To earn* is the infinitive in the second sentence. Both infinitives serve as part of the introductory phrase, which must be set off by commas.

✔ Check your work

To find introductory phrases that should be set off with a comma, first look for the subject and verb of the independent clause — the core sentence. Then note any words that precede the subject and verb. Other than articles (*a, an, the*) and adjectives, any words or phrases that precede the subject and verb make up the introductory phrase.

Example:

Knowing that the strongest qualities of a teacher are patience and understanding, Beth highlighted these qualities on her résumé.

Beth is the subject and *highlighted* is the verb. The phrase *Knowing that the strongest qualities of a teacher are patience and understanding* is a participial phrase and therefore should be set off with a comma.

Note that introductory preposition phrases of four words or less don't require a comma.

Example:

This morning I stopped at the bagel shop for coffee.

A comma is acceptable after *This morning*, but it's not required. When in doubt, however, use a comma.

➤ **Rule 4** – Use a comma to set off nonrestrictive clauses and phrases — clauses and phrases that are not essential modifiers. Adjectival clauses and appositives (words that rename a noun) are most often nonrestrictive.

Adjectival clauses are phrases that begin with *who, whom, whose, which, that, when, where*, or *why*. In many cases, an adjectival clause is nonrestrictive such as in the following example:

The heart, <u>which pumps the body's blood</u>, is necessary to sustain life.

In this sentence, the adjectival clause *which pumps the body's blood* is set off by commas because it is not essential to the sentence. It's separated because the sentence would have the same meaning without the clause. By contrast, the adjectival clause in the next sentence is restrictive because it is necessary to convey the meaning of the sentence:

The police <u>who are investigating the murders in Maryland</u> are using geographic profiling to aid in their search for the perpetrator.

The adjectival clause *who are investigating the murders in Maryland* is necessary to provide the reader with full details about the police and the murderer for whom they are searching. Without this phrase, the reader would not know that the police are in Maryland and that they are investigating a murderer. *Appositives* act as nouns or noun substitutes by modifying the noun that precedes the appositive. Just as with adjectival clauses, nonrestrictive appositives are set off by commas, whereas restrictive appositives are not.

Nonrestrictive examples:

My high school English teacher, <u>Mr. Roper</u>, taught me how to use commas properly.
She drove her new car, <u>a Honda Accord</u>, to the senior center to pick up her grandmother.
The book club will be meeting this Wednesday to discuss the latest book, <u>Grisham's *Rainmaker*</u>.

In these examples, the underlined phrases are nonrestrictive appositives, which rename the noun preceding them. These phrases add interesting details to the sentences, but are not necessary to make the sentences complete and understandable. On the other hand, some appositives are essential to capture the full meaning of the sentence. Such restrictive appositives should not be set off with commas.

My son <u>Michael</u> is two years old, and my other son <u>Jacob</u> is five months old.
Meet me at 6:00 at the new restaurant <u>*Vinny's Vittles*</u> that just opened on Main Street.
My friend <u>Tammy</u> met me at the beach yesterday.

The appositives in these examples are necessary in specifying the subjects. This information is necessary so the reader has a clear understanding of the subject involved in the text.

✓ Check your work
Review each sentence in your writing. Identify the adjectival phrases and appositives and the nouns they modify. For each adjectival phrase or appositive, ask yourself if the phrase provides important identifying information about the noun, or if it just provides "extra" information. If you are still unsure, read the sentence without the adjectival phrase or appositive. Does the sentence still have its full meaning? If so, set the phrase off with commas. If not, omit the commas.

➢ **Rule 5** – Use a comma to set off interjections and transitional phrases. Use a comma only if the transition or interjection could be removed without changing the basic meaning of the sentence.

An *interjection* is usually one or two words that interrupt the flow of a sentence and give extra information about the content of the sentence. Although an interjection provides added detail that enhances the reader's knowledge, generally the information provided by an interjection could be omitted with little or no effect on the meaning of the sentence.

> I could probably take, <u>say</u>, five people in my van for the carpool.
> She was, <u>oddly enough</u>, the only one who entered the contest.

A *transitional phrase* directs the flow of an essay. Often, transitional phrases are helpful in leading to a conclusion and therefore should not be set off with commas such as in these two examples:

> His strategy was to impress the boss and <u>thus</u> receive the promotion.
> I was tired and <u>therefore</u> did not want to go to the party.

There are instances, however, where a transitional word could be omitted without affecting the meaning of the sentence.

Examples:
I was not confident, <u>however</u>, that he knew the answer.
The message went on to say, <u>furthermore</u>, that he would not be coming home for dinner.

The transitional words in these examples enhance the text by emphasizing the direction in which the meaning of the sentence is moving. However, the meaning of the sentences would be the same without the transitional words.

✓ Check your work
To double-check your use of commas with interjections, identify any word or words that interrupt your sentence and have little or no effect to the meaning of the sentence. Set these words off with commas. Next, check for transitional words, keeping in mind the list of common transitional phrases we discussed earlier. Once you have identified the transitional words, ask yourself if the words are necessary to convey the meaning of the sentence. If they are, don't set them off with commas; if they aren't, use commas.

➢ **Rule 6** – Use a comma before a coordination conjunction (*and, but, or, nor, for, so, yet*) that joins two independent clauses.

An *independent clause* is a group of words that contain both a subject and a verb and can stand alone as a sentence.

Example:
I drove my car to work. (*I* is the subject, and *drove* is the verb.)

A *coordinating conjunction* is a word that serves as a link between a word or group of words. These conjunctions are easy to remember by using the acronym BOYFANS:

But
Or
Yet
For
And
Nor
So

Short, choppy sentences can make your writing tedious to read. To provide some interest and variety, join some of the sentences in your essays. To do so, you will need to use a comma and a coordinating conjunction. Let's look at some examples:

Too choppy:
I took a long lunch. I went back to work. I got behind on my work. I had to stay late.

Better:
I took a long lunch, and I went back to work. I got behind on my work, so I had to stay late.

Too choppy:
My guests were arriving in an hour. I wanted to throw a memorable New Year's Eve party. I made the punch and hors d'oeuvres ahead of time. I found that I still had a lot to get done to get ready. I didn't have enough time. I decided to put the ice in the punch early. Then, I discovered that my icemaker was broken. I didn't have time to go to the store. I wasn't prepared to serve anything else. The punch would just have to be room temperature.

Better:
My guests were arriving in an hour, and I wanted to throw a memorable New Year's Eve party, so I made the punch and hors d'oeuvres ahead of time. I found, however, that I still had a lot to get ready and not enough to do it all, so I decided to put the ice in the punch early. Then, I discovered that my icemaker was broken, but I still didn't have time to go to the store, nor was I prepared to serve anything else, so the punch would just have to be room temperature.

In both examples, combining sentences with commas and conjunctions make them more interesting and conversational. We will learn more ways to create interest in your writing when we discuss writing style later on.

✓ Check your work
To properly combine two independent clauses with a comma and a conjunction, you must check to make sure that the clauses joined by the comma and conjunction are indeed independent clauses. To do this, first find all the conjunctions. Then look at the clauses on either side of each conjunction. Does each clause have a subject and a verb? Can each clause stand alone as sentences? If so, the conjunction is properly placed and a comma should precede the conjunction.

Incorrect:
We went to the mall last night, and bought some new dresses for work.

Correct:
We went to the mall last night and bought some new dresses for work.

Correct:
We went to the mall last night, and Terri bought some new dresses for work.

In the first example, *and* is the conjunction. *We went to the mall last night* is an independent clause (*we* is the subject, *went* is the verb). However, *bought some new dresses for work* is not an independent clause because there is no subject. Therefore, the sentence can be corrected by simply omitting the comma as seen in the second example. Or, if there is a possible subject for the sentence, it can be added and the comma can stay as seen in the third example. Here is another example where the same guidelines apply:

Incorrect:
He committed the crime, but didn't think the judge's ruling was fair.

Correct:
He committed the crime but didn't think the judge's ruling was fair.

Correct:
He committed the crime, but he didn't think the judge's ruling was fair.

Semicolons

What's stronger than a comma yet weaker than a period? A semicolon.

A *semicolon* indicates a major pause or break between thoughts, yet it also shows that the thoughts are logically related. If you want to master the mysterious semicolon, there are, again, only a few simple rules to remember.

➢ **Rule 1** – Use a semicolon to join two independent clauses if they aren't joined by a coordinating conjunction (*and, but, or, nor for, yet*) and are closely related to each other.

Sometimes a period seems like too strong of a pause when separating two closely related sentences. Equally, a comma doesn't always emphasize both sentences adequately. In cases like this, you should use a semicolon to join both independent clauses, giving you, as the writer, a subtle way of showing a close relationship between complete thoughts, especially if the second sentence restates the first or more clearly defines it by giving an example or presenting a contrast.

Example:
Loyalty is the foundation upon which relationships are built; without loyalty, friendships and marriages crumble.

The puppy scooted blindly across the floor; his eyes hadn't opened yet, leaving him totally dependent on his mother.

Using a semicolon with a transitional word is also a good way to join contrasting clauses.

These days there is a cure for every ailment; however, the side effects of many medications are worse than the condition for which the medication is prescribed.

A transitional word may also serve to emphasize a cause-effect relationship.

The drought has greatly affected many farmers; therefore, the price of produce is expected to rise.

The choice to join two clauses with a semicolon and a transitional word may be a stylistic choice rather than a grammatical one. Likewise, adding variety to your writing may be the purpose when it comes to replacing a comma and conjunction with a semicolon.

Correct:
The slippery rock presented the climbers with a challenge, <u>so</u> they watched their footing very closely.

Correct:
The slippery rock presented the climbers with a challenge; they watched their footing very closely.

Sometimes, however, it is necessary to replace the comma with a semicolon in order to provide clarity. In these cases, you may or may not omit the conjunction.

Confusing:
From such a great distance, the man could not make out the faces of the evil, crafty conspirators, but, if he moved any closer, he would be taking an unnecessary, careless risk.

Better:
From such a great distance, the man could not make out the faces of the evil, crafty conspirators; but, if he moved any closer, he would be taking an unnecessary, careless risk.

✔ Check your work
To use a semicolon to join two independent clauses, analyze the two clauses carefully to make sure there is a close relationship between the two before placing the semicolon. Be careful not to misuse semicolons, especially when you use them with a transitional word or in place of a comma and conjunction.

Incorrect:
I was forced; therefore, to take the detour around the construction site.

Correct:
I was forced, therefore, to take the detour around the construction site.

In this example, *therefore* is a transitional word and should be set off with commas. Furthermore, the clause *I was forced* is an independent clause and *to take the detour around the construction site* is not, so the clauses cannot be set apart by a semicolon.

Take the same caution when replacing a comma and conjunction with a semicolon. Remember that, to join two clauses with a comma and a conjunction, both clauses must be independent. Each clause must be able to stand alone as a separate sentence.

Incorrect:
He completed the yard work, and then enjoyed a lemonade break with his mom.

Incorrect:
He completed the yard work; and then enjoyed a lemonade break with his mom.

Correct:
He completed the yard work and then enjoyed a lemonade break with his mom.

The subject in this sentence is *He* and the compound verb is *completed* and *enjoyed*. There is no subject in the second part of the sentence, so it is incorrect to use a comma and conjunction in the sentence. Likewise, a semicolon cannot be used.

➤ **Rule 2** – Use semicolons to join more than two independent clauses.

In Rule 1, we discussed using a semicolon to join two independent clauses. Semicolons can also be used to join multiple independent clauses in more complex sentences:

Example:
Over the past few years, violence has adopted a new calling card; it is more random, gruesome and sinister than ever. In this country of freedom, violence has made its presence known in all areas of life. In schools, students take the lives of other students before taking their own; a close-knit community is gripped by fear because of random shootings; a father kills another father over their sons' hockey game.

This example could be written as a few separate sentences; however, since the independent clauses are all closely related, it is acceptable to link them with semicolons. Joining multiple independent clauses is often a stylistic choice and an effective one because it makes an impact by more closely connecting the sentences.

✔ Check your work
To join multiple independent clauses with a semicolon, make sure the clauses you are joining are closely related. When used conservatively, semicolons can add a great deal of impact while also adding clarity to comma riddled sentences. To avoid overusing semicolons, reread your text and make sure your use of semicolons is sporadic; semicolons should never appear as often as commas or periods.

Too many semicolons:
My next interviewee came in and sat across from me; she tried to put on a confident face; but I could tell she was nervous; she played anxiously with her ring; she shifted positions every few seconds.

Better:
My next interviewee came in and sat across from me. She tried to put on a confident face, but I could tell she was nervous; she played anxiously with her ring and shifted positions every few seconds.

➤ **Rule 3** – Use semicolons to separate a series of items that contain commas.

Use of the semicolon in this manner prevents confusion.

Confusing:
I boarded a flight in Los Angeles, California, had a two-hour layover in Detroit, Michigan, and finally landed in London, England.

Better:
I boarded a flight in Los Angeles, California; had a two-hour layover in Detroit, Michigan; and finally landed in London, England.

Too many commas cause confusion, so in order to simplify the sentence and make it clearer, semicolons must be used to separate the clauses.

All employees must bring a pen, paper, and a notebook to the first day of training; a laptop, highlighter and paperclips to day two; and a sample report, pie chart and three markers to the last day.

✔ Check your work
Check each of the independent clauses you have joined with commas. Do any of the independent clauses contain commas? If so, joining the independent clauses with a semicolon instead of a comma might make the sentence clearer.

Confusing:
My pottery class is on Mondays, Wednesdays, and Fridays, and I babysit my nephew, niece, and neighbor's son on Tuesdays and Thursdays.

Better:
My pottery class is on Mondays, Wednesdays and Fridays; and I babysit my nephew, niece and neighbor's son on Tuesdays and Thursdays.

If, after reviewing your writing, you feel you have used semicolons too often, consider using other methods to join phrases. For example, you might use a period to divide clauses into separate sentences. Semicolons can make a big impact but only when used conservatively and correctly.

Colons

A colon means, in effect, "Note what follows," and is generally considered a very formal mark of punctuation.

➤ **Rule 1** – Use a colon to join two independent clauses when introducing an explanation or example.

When a comma does not place adequate emphasis on the relationship between two independent clauses, use a semicolon. When a semicolon does not provide adequate emphasis, use a colon.

> **Example:**
> When I picture my dream house, I can almost envision all the beautiful scenery: the beach or mountains, for example, would be perfect.

A colon can also introduce an explanation such as in the following:

> Dave and Stephanie's presentation lacked the usual enthusiasm: probably because they were up all night working on the ad campaign again.

✓ Check your work

Just as with semicolons, the choice to use colons can be a stylistic one. If you do choose to use a colon to introduce an explanation or example, make sure that both the preceding clause and the clause that follows are independent clauses.

Capitalize the clause that follows a colon if it is a formal statement or if the content that is introduced contains more than one sentence.

> **Example (formal statement):**
> Our club bylaws shall set forth the following: Rules for meetings, code of conduct, and membership procedures.

> **Example (more than one clause):**
> When thinking of a future career, there are many choices: Becoming a lawyer would be a good financial decision. On the other hand, teaching may provide more personal satisfaction.

➤ **Rule 2** – Use a colon to introduce a series, list, or formal quotation.

Use a colon to introduce a series or list.

> **Examples:**
> We need to get several things done before our trip: pay the bills, water the plants, and take the dog to the kennel.
>
> Before we can take off, you must do the following: fasten your seat belt, turn off your cell phone, and return your tray table to its upright position.
>
> The names of the people who made the volleyball team are as follows: Ruth, Mary Lynn, Amy, Sarah, Alicia, and Elizabeth.

Note that when the word *following* or *follows* is used to introduce a list or series you must use a colon. You should also use a colon to introduce a quotation.

Example:
As people seek to build relationships and, in so doing, break down the walls of racism, they should remember Martin Luther King, Jr.'s famous words: "I have a dream that [we] will one day live in a nation where [we] will not be judged by the color of [our] skin but by the content of [our] character."

✓ Check your work
When introducing a series or list, always use a colon if the clause that introduces the list or series contains the term *follows* or *following*.

Example:
The following improvements need to be made to your house before you try to sell it: new carpet should be installed, the outside trim should be painted, and the fixtures in the downstairs bathroom should be replaced.

Do not use a colon if the list or series is introduced by phrases such as *especially*, *such as*, *namely*, *for instance*, *for example*, or *that is* unless the series is made up of one or more independent clauses.

Incorrect (colon introducing a series of phrases):
Some of my life goals, for example: to ski in the Alps, bungee jump from Victoria Falls, and visit the Great Wall of China.

Correct (colon introducing a series of independent clauses):
I have set some goals that I wish to achieve before I get too old to do so. For example: I want to ski in the Alps, bungee jump from Victoria Falls, and visit the Great Wall of China.

Note that a comma would work in this sentence as well, but the colon following *For example* places more emphasis on the text that follows.

Do not use a colon after a form of the verb *to be*.

Incorrect:
My favorite marks of punctuation are: the dash, the semicolon, and the exclamation point.

Correct:
My favorite marks of punctuation are the dash, the semicolon, and the exclamation point.

You may use a colon to introduce a quotation and, in this instance, you must capitalize the first word of the quotation.

Example:
The principles of this country are founded on the *Declaration of Independence* and its famous words: "We hold these truths to be self-evident, that all men are created equal, that they are endowed by their Creator with certain unalienable Rights, that among these are Life, Liberty and the pursuit of Happiness."

Dashes

Many writers misunderstand dashes. They sprinkle their writing with dashes to indicate pauses where commas, periods, or semicolons should be, but the dash is not a super-powered mark of punctuation that saves the writer from the trouble of determining what other mark is appropriate. A dash merely indicates a break in thought or structure of the sentence.

➤ **Rule 1** – Use dashes for emphasis, to set off a repetition, or indicate an abrupt shift in the sentence structure or thought.

> **Examples:**
> If you are interested in martial arts — and who wouldn't be interested in such a disciplined art? — there are many centers for instruction.
>
> I was unable — unwilling, really — to head up the new committee at the office.

✔ Check your work

Although commas may be used to set off phrases that interrupt a sentence, dashes add emphasis to the set off clause. In addition, dashes set an informal tone in your writing. Because of their informality, dashes should be used sparingly, if ever, in graduate writing. When you do choose to use dashes, you may include question marks and exclamation points in the clauses that are set off by dashes (as in the first example above).

➤ **Rule 2** – Use dashes to set off parenthetical or explanatory information.

> **Example:**
> The editor of the *Banner Herald* often employs hyperbole — deliberate exaggeration or overstatement to show special emphasis or create humor — to express his political views.

Here dashes set apart the definition of *hyperbole*. Though not necessary to the meaning of the sentence, the definition adds useful information. Again, dashes are an informal way of setting off information; a comma could serve the same purpose here.

✔ Check your work

Review each sentence in your writing and identify any information that is parenthetical or that explains a topic in the sentence. You may set this information off with dashes. Remember, though, that dashes should seldom be used in formal writing. In formal writing, you should use commas to set off these elements from the rest of the sentence.

Apostrophes

While some would say that the use of an apostrophe is a mystery, it may, in fact, be the simplest mark of punctuation to truly master.

➤ **Rule 1** – Use an apostrophe to form a contraction, a word that is a shortened combination of two words.

Contractions are used in informal writing and serve to shorten two words by leaving out some letters and joining the two words.

Common Contractions:

Words that combine to form a contraction	Contractions
it is	it's
I am	I'm
he will	he'll
they are	they're
you are	you're
we will	we'll
could not	couldn't
would not	wouldn't
cannot	can't
does not	doesn't
do not	don't
will not	won't
let us	let's
I would	I'd
they would	they'd
was not	wasn't
I will	I'll
should not	shouldn't
we had	we'd
they will	they'll

✔ Check your work

The use of contractions is quite simple: if you wish to shorten two words into one, you must simply replace the words with the correct contraction. There are, however, some common mistakes people make when using contractions. A few contractions sound like possessive words, and these are often confused.

Example (they're):
I don't know where they think *they're* going, but *they're* going to end up at a dead end.

Example (their):
When I saw them heading toward the dead end, I assumed they did not know *their* way.

Example (they're and their):
They're going to run into a dead end because they don't know *their* way.

Remember that *they're* is short for *they are*. *Their* is the third person plural possessive. The next pair of words to watch out for is the contraction *you're* and the possessive *your*.

Example (you're):
You're not going to succeed in school if you don't study hard.

Example (your):
Your success in school is dependent upon hard work.

Example (you're and your):
You're not going to succeed in school if you don't try *your* best.

You're is short for *you are*, and *your* is the second person singular possessive. The final pair of words that can be confusing are *it's* and *its*.

> **Example (it's):**
> *It's* seemingly impossible for a cat to travel that far to get home.

> **Example (its):**
> A cat will travel a long way to find *its* home.

> **Example (it's and its):**
> *It's* amazing the distance a cat will travel to find *its* way back home.

Be careful when you use *it's* or *its*; remember that *it's* is the contraction for *it is* and *its* is the third person singular possessive.

✓ Check your work

To check for proper use of a contraction, especially those that can be tricky, substitute the words that have been replaced by the contraction. If the full-length word makes sense, the contraction is correct. If not, you need to check your spelling. Once again, though, keep in mind that contractions are more appropriate for use in informal writing.

➤ **Rule 2** – Use an apostrophe to show possession.

To show the possessive form of singular nouns, add an apostrophe and an *–s*.

> **Examples:**
> Teddy cleaned the *dog's* house before he and his family went on vacation.
> The teacher used *Julia's* homework as an example because it was exceptional.
> She didn't feel comfortable borrowing *Harris's* car.

To show the possessive form of plural nouns, add an *–s* and an apostrophe.

> **Examples:**
> Coach Hannigan distributed the *girls'* uniforms at soccer practice.

Some plural nouns, however, do not end in *–s*. In these instances, add an apostrophe and an *–s*.

> **Examples:**
> The *women's* meeting will be held in the gymnasium on Thursday night.
> All of the *children's* bikes were parked in the driveway.
> Competition between *men's* sports teams is fierce.

✓ Check your work

Check for the correct use of apostrophes with possessives by first identifying the nouns that show possession. Then identify whether the noun is singular or plural. If the noun is singular, add an apostrophe and an *–s*. If the noun is plural, add an *–s* and an apostrophe. Finally, take note of any irregular plural nouns that do not end in *–s*. Add an apostrophe and an *–s* to irregular nouns.

Quotation Marks

Use quotation marks to set off direct quotations and dialogue.

Example (quotation):
In his famous inaugural address, President John F. Kennedy implored, "My fellow Americans, ask not what your country can do for you: Ask what you can do for your country."

Example (dialog):
"Where are you going tonight?" asked Greg.
"Beth and I are going to the library to get some research done," Susan replied. "Then we're heading to the mall to do some shopping."

➢ **Rule 1** – Commas and periods should be placed inside quotation marks.

Example:
"I don't understand what you're trying to say," Glen said. "You need to speak up."

Don't use a comma and quotation marks for indirect quotes.

Example (direct quote):
He said, "I don't have time to take the car for an oil change today."

Example (indirect quote):
He said that he didn't have time to take the car for an oil change today.

✓ Check your work
To determine if a quote is a direct or indirect quote, ask yourself if the quote comes directly from the speaker and if the quote contains the exact words of the speaker. If so, place quotation marks around the quote. If not, there should be no comma or quotation marks.

➢ **Rule 2** – Place semicolons and colons outside quotation marks.

Example (semicolon):
My mom always used to say, "A stitch in time saves nine"; I always remember that quote when I am tempted to procrastinate.

Example (colon):
Patrick Henry made a strong statement when he said, "Give me liberty or give me death":
he felt that it would be better to die than to live in a country without freedom.

✓ Check your work
When you use quotation marks with a semicolon or colon, first determine whether you are using the semicolon or colon correctly. Then make sure you place the semicolon or colon outside the quotation marks.

➢ **Rule 3** – Place question marks and exclamation points outside quotation marks unless they are a part of the quotation.

Examples (question mark):
Did you hear Professor Johnston say, "You must read the first 500 pages for a quiz on Monday"?

Stunned, she implored, "Why didn't you tell me you were leaving for good?"

In the first example, the quotation is a statement that does not require a question mark; however, the overall sentence that contains the quotation is a question. Therefore, the question mark goes outside the quotation marks. In the second example, though, the quotation is a question, so the question mark goes inside the quotation marks.

Examples (exclamation point):
I can't believe she finally said, "I love you"!

The woman ran after the thief yelling, "Hey, come back with my purse!"

Overall, the first sentence is an exclamatory sentence, but the phrase *I love you* is not; therefore, the exclamation point goes outside the quotation marks. *Hey, come back with my purse* in the second sentence, however, is an exclamation, so the exclamation point goes inside the quotation marks.

✓ Check your work
Examine all quotations in your writing. If the quotation itself is a question or exclamation, place the appropriate punctuation mark inside the quotation marks. If, however, the overall sentence is a question or exclamation but the actual quote is not, the punctuation should be placed outside the quotation marks.

Sentence Fragments

A *sentence fragment* is an incomplete sentence. Sentence fragments are ungrammatical because they lack one or more of the three elements of a complete sentence: a subject, predicate (a fancy name for a verb or group of words that act as a verb), or a complete thought.

Example (independent clause):
I ran down the road.

Examples (sentence fragments):
Ran down the road.

Running down the road.

Fragments generally occur when modifying phrases or dependent clauses aren't attached to an independent clause. To correct sentence fragments in your writing, you must first identify them and then add the right punctuation.

➤ **Step 1** – Identifying sentence fragments.

To find sentence fragments in your writing, first analyze each sentence. If a sentence doesn't have a subject or a verb, or if the sentence is actually a dependent clause that doesn't make sense on it's own, it's probably a fragment.

Fragment:
On our way to the store tomorrow. We need to stop at the bank

Complete sentence:
On our way to the store tomorrow, we need to stop at the bank.

Fragments:
Providing equal opportunity to all citizens. Is of utmost importance.

Complete sentence:
Providing equal opportunity to all citizens is of utmost importance.

In the first example, *On our way to the store tomorrow* is a prepositional phrase that can't stand on its own. In the second example, both sentences are fragments. *Providing equal opportunity to all citizens* is a gerund that acts as the noun of the sentence; therefore, it must be combined with the second sentence to be reunited with its long-lost verb *is*.

➢ **Step 2** – Revising sentence fragments: there are two ways to do this.

    •   Combine sentences to make them complete.

Example:
(Fragments) Because I was at the office working. I didn't make it to dinner.

(Revised) Because I was at the office working, I didn't make it to dinner.

    •   Add the necessary elements to the fragment to make it complete.

Example:
(Fragments) From the beginning. Wanted to practice law in a small town.

(Revised) From the beginning, he wanted to practice law in a small town.

Once you have made your revisions, make sure you reread your writing. Identify that there is a subject and verb in each sentence, but beware of subordinating clauses! They have both a subject and a verb, yet they do not complete a thought.

Example:
When we ran through the hallway.

Sentences that don't complete a thought but that have a subject and a verb are still sentence fragments.

Run-On Sentences

It's a common misconception that run-on sentences are just wordy sentences that "run-on" too long; however, that's not the case. In fact, it's not uncommon to see sentences that have the length of entire paragraphs without being run-on sentences.

A *run-on sentence* refers to two or more sentences written as one.

Example:
David went on a field trip to an aquarium with his classmates and they saw a large variety of fish.

In this example, two independent clauses are joined with a coordinating conjunction, but there is no comma. This type of run-on sentence is called a *fused* sentence. A fused sentence can also lack both a comma and a conjunction.

The debate over alien existence will probably continue for years some are sure they have seen aliens.

This next sentence contains a comma but no coordinating conjunction.

Many people believe in the powers of a psychic, sometimes even detectives depend on psychics to help solve crimes.

Because this sentence contains a comma but no coordinating conjunction, it is called a *comma splice*.

To correct run-on sentences in your writing, you must — you guessed it! — identify them and revise them.

> **Step 1** – Identify run-on sentences in your writing.

To find run-on sentences in your writing, first analyze each sentence. In your analysis, mark the subject and verb by underlining the subject once and the verb twice.

> **Examples:**
> <u>Osteoporosis</u> <u>is</u> very common among women but <u>drinking</u> milk and <u>taking</u> calcium supplements <u>can</u> help <u>prevent</u> it.
>
> <u>History</u> <u>provides</u> us with interesting stories, <u>it</u> also <u>helps</u> us in the future because we can learn from mistakes made in history.

These examples contain two independent clauses that are not combined correctly. Many writers also link multiple clauses incorrectly. If you are prone to this error, it is important that you take the time to go through each sentence and identify the subjects and verbs.

> **Step 2** – Revise your run-on sentences by using one of five methods:

- Separate the clauses into complete sentences.

  Example:
  (Run-on) Working together as a team is more productive than working individually, a team can get more accomplished than one person.

  (Revised) Working together as a team is more productive than working individually. A team can get more accomplished than one person.

- Link the clauses with a semicolon.

  Example:
  (Run-on) Writing is great therapy letting off steam through the written word is a good way to work through frustration.

  (Revised) Writing is great therapy; letting off steam through the written word is a good way to work through frustration.

- Link the clauses with a comma and a coordinating conjunction.

  Example:
  (Run-on) I went to Florida last week to go to Disney World with a friend but it rained the whole time.

  (Revised) I went to Florida last week to go to Disney World with a friend, but it rained the whole time.

- Rewrite the clauses to form just one independent clause.

  Example:
  (Run-on) This summer has been a very hot one, it has been humid also.

  (Revised) This summer has been a very hot and humid.

- Rewrite the clauses to form one independent clause with an introductory dependent clause.

  Example:
  (Run-on) We re-painted our house, the old paint was peeling and fading.

  (Revised) Because the old paint was peeling and fading, we re-painted our house.

✓ Check your work
Make sure you review your work after making revisions to ensure that all run-on sentences have indeed been corrected. In addition, try to use all five methods of revision in your writing; don't correct each run-on with the same method. Using different forms of revision will result in varying sentence patterns, which will enhance your writing style. We will talk more about writing style shortly; but first, let's make sure you can properly apply the rules of punctuation we just covered.

Punctuation Drills

> <u>Directions:</u> Grab a blank sheet of paper, read each sentence, and then make necessary punctuation and spelling corrections. Pay special attention to sentence fragments and run-on sentences and re-write them so that they are grammatically correct.

1. Dana is a foster mother. Takes care of newborns. When babies are put up for adoption a social worker places the baby in Dana's house where the baby stays until the adoption is completed usually the baby stays no longer than six weeks unless there is no adoptee lined up yet.

2. Buying a new car is a big decision their are many factors to consider dependability for example is a key factor in choosing the car to suit your needs.

3. The energetic boisterous boy climbed the jungle gym hung from the monkey bars jumped down and then ran to the merry-go-round.

4. What do you think he meant when he said, "Your going to have to figure that one out on you're own"

5. A cool sparkling stream meandered through the peaceful forest and some deer stopped to take a drink and glanced up for a moment to look at me they disappeared into the trees.

6. Some people claim even boast that they've never read an entire book. This is there loss because reading leads to knowledge knowledge leads to power power enables people to influence those around them.

7. The mens' group did charity work this weekend they completed the following projects they helped rebuild a church that had been damaged in a tornado they completed some of the landscaping on the church grounds and they began repairs to the pastors home nearby the church.

8. Many people suffer from "diet fatigue" they try diet after diet only to meet failure with each one. What they should be focusing on instead is nutritional eating and fitness nutritional eating consists of eating well-balanced servings of meats vegetables fruits and grains drinking lots of water and indulging in junk food sparingly. Proper fitness can come in the form of aerobic exercise walking sports or weight training making just a few adjustments in daily eating and exercise habits can make all the difference in a persons physical and emotional well-being.

9. The beautiful grand stain-glassed windows added a majestic feeling to the old cathedral.

Solutions to Punctuation Drills

1. Dana is a foster <u>mother who takes</u> care of newborns. When babies are put up for <u>adoption,</u> a social worker places the baby in Dana's house where the baby stays until the adoption is <u>completed. Usually</u> the baby stays no longer than six weeks unless there is no adoptee lined up yet.

    Takes care of newborns is a fragment; it was corrected by joining it to the first clause *Dana is a foster mother*. *When babies are put up for adoption* is an introductory dependent clause and should be followed by a comma. The last clause is a run-on sentence, and it was corrected by placing a period after *completed*.

2. Buying a new car is a big <u>decision. There</u> are many factors to <u>consider: dependability, for example,</u> is a key factor in choosing the car to suit your needs.

    The first clause is a run-on sentence and should be divided into two sentences; thus, a period was placed between *decision* and *There*. Moreover, *their* was replaced with the correct word *there*. Once you have divided the sentence into two separate clauses, notice that *dependability* is an example. Therefore, a colon should follow *consider*. In addition, *for example* should be set off by commas because it is an interjection.

3. The <u>energetic, boisterous</u> boy climbed the jungle <u>gym, hung</u> from the monkey <u>bars, jumped</u> <u>down, and</u> then ran to the merry-go-round.

    Energetic and *boisterous* are adjectives that modify *boy*. Because there are two adjectives modifying the same noun, they should be separated by a comma. In addition, a set of four phrases follows — *climbed the jungle gym*, *hung from the monkey bars*, *jumped down*, and *then ran to the merry-go-round* — and should also be separated by commas.

4. What do you think he meant when he said, "<u>Y</u>ou're going to have to figure that one out on <u>your</u> <u>own</u>"?

    Your and *you're* are misspelled. The contraction *you're* should be the first word in the quotation, and the possessive *your* should precede *own*. The question mark in the sentence should be placed outside the quotation marks because the quotation itself is not a question; however, the complete sentence is a question.

5. A <u>cool, sparkling</u> stream meandered through the peaceful <u>forest. Some</u> deer stopped to take a drink. <u>Before they disappeared into the trees, they glanced up for a moment to look at me.</u>

    First, a comma should separate the series of adjectives *cool* and *sparkling*. Second, this clause is a run-on sentence and was corrected by dividing it into two independent clauses by placing a period between *forest* and *Some*. Finally, a third clause was created by converting the sentence fragment into an introductory clause.

6. Some people <u>claim, even boast, that</u> <u>they have</u> never read an entire book. This is <u>their</u> loss because reading leads to <u>knowledge; knowledge</u> leads to <u>power; power</u> enables people to influence those around them.

    Even boast is an interjection and should be set apart by commas. You should use commas instead of dashes because the topic of the sentences is formal. The contraction *they've* should be changed to *they have* to maintain the formality. The next sentence should contain the possessive *their*. Finally, the last clause is a run-on sentence. Because the clauses are closely related, they should be separated by semicolons.

7. The <u>men's</u> group did charity work this <u>weekend. They</u> completed the following <u>projects: they</u> helped rebuild a church that had been damaged in a <u>tornado, they</u> completed some of the landscaping on the church <u>grounds, and</u> they began repairs to the <u>pastor's</u> home nearby the church.

    Because the word *men* is a plural noun that does not end in –*s*, its possessive should be spelled with an apostrophe and then an –*s*. Also, the first clause is a run-on, so there should be a period between *weekend* and *They*. Next, there should be a colon after *projects* in order to introduce the series of clauses that follow. The word *following* is your clue to use a colon in this instance. A comma should separate each clause in the series that follows. Finally, *pastor's* is possessive and should contain an apostrophe.

8. Many people suffer from "diet <u>fatigue";</u> they try diet after diet only to meet failure with each one. What they should be focusing on instead is nutritional eating and <u>fitness. Nutritional</u> eating consists of eating well-balanced servings of <u>meats, vegetables, fruits, and</u> <u>grains; drinking</u> lots of <u>water; and</u> indulging in junk food sparingly. Proper fitness can come in the form of aerobic <u>exercise, walking,</u> <u>sports, or</u> weight <u>training. Making</u> just a few adjustments in daily eating and exercise habits can make all the difference in a <u>person's</u> physical and emotional well-being.

    The first clause is a run-on and should be divided into two separate sentences; since they're so closely related, you may use a semicolon. The semicolon should be placed outside the quotation marks around *diet fatigue*. A period should follow *fitness* in order to separate the next run-on sentence into separate sentences. In the third sentence, you are presented with a series of clauses; one of the clauses contains a list of words that require commas to separate them. Because so many commas can be confusing, semicolons should separate the series of clauses. Commas should separate the series of words in the sentence that follows as well. A final sentence should be set off starting at *Making*. Finally, the possessive of *person's* must contain an apostrophe.

9. The <u>beautiful, grand</u> stain-glassed windows added a majestic feeling to the old cathedral.

    A comma should separate *beautiful* and *grand*. Notice that there is no comma after *grand*. You can double-check this by placing *and* between each adjective: *The beautiful <u>and</u> grand <u>and</u> stain-glassed window*. The *and* between *grand* and *stain-glassed* does not make sense; therefore, there should be no comma preceding *stain-glass*.

Grammar

The field of grammar is a huge and complex world — entire books have been written about it, all with slightly differing opinions. This complexity should be no surprise since grammar deals with the process of English communication.

Grammar can be divided into two parts: Mechanics and Usage.

Mechanics concerns punctuation and capitalization, which we discussed earlier in this chapter, and it is not tested on the ACT to the same extent as usage. So don't spend too much time worrying whether a comma is in the right place or whether a particular word should be capitalized.

Usage deals with how we choose our words and how we express our thoughts. In other words, are the connections between the words in a sentence logically sound? Are they expressed in a way that conforms to standard diction? This is the part of grammar that is most important on the ACT. Six major categories of usage are tested:

- **Pronouns**
- **Subject-Verb Agreement**
- **Misplaced and Redundant Modifiers**
- **Parallelism**
- **Verb Tense**
- **Diction**

The more familiar you are with the parts of speech (*nouns, verbs, pronouns, adjectives, adverbs*, and so forth) and how they function in a sentence, the easier the test will be for you. Let's take a look at some of the rules that dictate proper usage in the English language.

Pronouns

A *pronoun* is a word that takes the place of a noun. In fancy grammatical terms, the noun is the antecedent of the pronoun. There are a few things to keep in mind when it comes to pronouns:

> **Rule 1** – A pronoun must have the same number (singular or plural) as the noun or noun phrase it is replacing.

> > **Examples:**
> > Steve has yet to receive *his* degree.
> > Everybody is on *his* (not their) best behavior during the ACT.

Because the word *everybody* is referring to a singular group of people and not multiple groups, it is almost always a singular noun. Even though the pronoun *their* sounds right, it's not. Whenever you see the word *everybody*, triple-check the pronoun to make sure that it is singular.

> **Rule 2** – A pronoun must have the same gender (feminine, masculine, or neuter) as the noun it is replacing.

> > **Example:**
> > Even though Pat knew *her* wedding was in less than an hour, *she* still didn't feel nervous.

Because *Pat* is a female, the pronouns *she* and *her* were used.

Following is a list of the most commonly used pronouns:

PRONOUNS

Singular	Plural	Both Singular and Plural
I, me	we, us	any
she, her	they	none
he, him	them	all
it	these	most
anyone	those	more
either	some	who
each	that	which
many	both	what
nothing	ourselves	you
one	any	
another	many	
everything	few	
mine	several	
his, hers	others	
this		
that		

> **Rule 3** – A pronoun should refer to one, and only one, noun or compound noun.

This is probably the most common error on the ACT. If a pronoun follows two nouns, it is often unclear which of the nouns the pronoun refers to.

Incorrect:
The breakup of the Soviet Union has left <u>nuclear weapons</u> in the hands of unstable, nascent <u>countries</u>. It is imperative to world security that *they* be destroyed.

<u>George</u> asked <u>Phil</u> to pick up *his* laundry.

An unclear pronoun often requires major sentence surgery to repair.

<u>George,</u> tired of seeing Phil's laundry on the floor, asked <u>Phil</u> to pick *it* up.

Sometimes, however, the pronoun should just be replaced with a clarifying noun.

The breakup of the Soviet Union has left <u>nuclear weapons</u> in the hands of unstable, nascent <u>countries</u>. It is imperative to world security that ***these weapons*** be destroyed.

➤ **Rule 4** – A pronoun must be in the proper case: subjective (*I, you, he, she, it, we, they*), objective (*me, you, him, her, it, us, them*), or possessive (*my, mine, your, yours, his, her, hers, its, our, ours, their, theirs*).

A pronoun following any form of the verb *to be*, is going to be in the subjective form. This form often sounds weird and pretentious, but it is correct. To do well on the ACT, you should store the following phrases in your mental bank:

Phrases:
It is I.
It was he.
It could be they.
It was she who...
This is he.
It was they.

Example:
After much interrogation, I finally confessed to my roommate that <u>it was I</u> who drank the last cup of coffee.

Subject-Verb Agreement

➤ **Rule 1** – A singular subject requires a singular verb.

Example:
Jack Johnson's <u>music</u> *is* (not are) relaxing.

Some words are singular, but they try to pose as plural words, with their plural-sounding, tricky ways. Don't be fooled, however. The following words are always singular and therefore always require a singular verb: *each, every, collection, group, public, club, government, organization*, and *union*.

➤ **Rule 2** – A plural subject requires a plural verb.

Example:
The <u>works</u> of Stephen King and Ted Dekker *are* (not is) terrifying and suspenseful.

The following words are always plural and require a plural verb: *few, both, several, many*.

➤ **Rule 3** – A compound subject, two or more subjects connected by the word *and*, requires a plural verb.

Example:
The *Iliad* and *The Odyssey* are two of the known epics written by Homer.

➤ **Rule 4** – Intervening clauses and phrases, the most common of these prepositional phrases, do not affect subject-verb agreement.

Example:
Only <u>one</u> ~~of the President's nominees~~ *was* confirmed.

Here, the singular verb *was* agrees with its singular subject *one*. The intervening prepositional phrase *of the President's nominees* has no effect on the number or person of the verb.

Collective nouns followed by intervening phrases are particularly easy to miss.

Example:
The <u>content</u> ~~of the boxes~~ *is* what she wants.
The <u>meaning</u> ~~of her sentences~~ *is* not clear.

Be careful when a phrase beginning with *as well as, along with, together with, in addition to*, or a similar expression follows a simple subject. Be sure the verb agrees with the simple subject, not with a noun in the intervening phrase.

Example:
Our <u>Senator</u>, ~~along with most congressmen~~, *opposes* the bill.

Here, the singular verb *opposes* agrees with its singular subject *Senator*. The intervening phrase *along with most congressmen* has no effect on the number or person of the verb.

√ <u>Check your work</u>
In most writing, and on the ACT, sentences will not always follow the same pattern. That is to say, the subject will not always be closely followed by the verb and vise versa. In order to ease some of this confusion, mark a line through any prepositional phrases, like in the above examples, and simply read the noun (subject) next to the verb.

➤ **Rule 5** – When subject and verb are reversed, they still must agree in number and person.

Example:
Attached are <u>copies</u> ~~of the contract~~.

Here, the plural verb *are attached* agrees with its plural subject *copies*. The sentence could be rewritten as

Copies of the contract are attached.

Although it may seem obvious that when reversing the normal order of the subject and the verb their agreement must be preserved, this obvious error is easy to miss.

Incorrect:
Attached ~~to the email~~ *is* <u>the graphic file and the agreement</u>.

This ungrammatical sentence sounds natural perhaps because its error is committed so often. The compound subject of the sentence is *the graphic file and the agreement*, which must take a plural verb:

Correct
Attached ~~to the email~~ *are* (not is) <u>the graphic file and the agreement</u>.

Be careful when an inverted subject-verb order is introduced by a construction such as *there is, there are, here is, here are*.

> There is much disagreement between the parties.

The word *there* introduces the singular verb *is*, which agrees with the singular subject of the sentence *disagreement*.

It's tempting to mistakenly use a singular verb before the plural subject.

> *There is* <u>a wallet and a key</u> on the dresser.

The compound (plural) subject of this sentence is *a wallet and a key*, so it requires a plural verb.

> <u>There are</u> a wallet and a key on the dresser.

Because the verb has to be chosen before we fully form the subject in our minds, this error occurs daily in speech, which makes the mistake all the more easy to commit in writing

Modifiers

A *modifier* is a phrase or a clause that describes something. A misplaced modifier, therefore, is one that describes the wrong item in a sentence, often creating an illogical statement.

> ➤ **Rule 1** – A modifier should be placed as close as possible to what it is modifying.

> **Example:**
> Following are some useful tips for protecting your person and property from the FBI.

This sentence implies that the FBI is a threat to your person and property. To correct the sentence put the modifier *from the FBI* next to the word it modifies, *tips*.

> Following are some useful <u>tips from the FBI</u> for protecting your person and property.

> **Example:**
> I saw the senators debating while watching television.

Here again, this sentence implies that senators were debating and watching TV at the same time. To improve the sentence, simply put the modifier *while watching television* next to the word it modifies, *I*.

> <u>While watching television, I saw</u> the senators debating.

The sentence can be made even clearer and more direct without the modifier:

> I saw the senators debating on television.

> ➤ **Rule 2** – When a phrase begins a sentence, make sure that it modifies the subject of the sentence.

> **Example:**
> Coming around the corner, a few moments passed before I could recognize my old home.

Is it possible for moments to come around the corner? Maybe, but that's probably not what the author is trying to say.

> <u>Coming around the corner, I paused</u> a few moments before I could recognize my old home.

Here's another example:

> While at summer camp, my family moved.

Does the family live at summer camp? If not, then the above sentence doesn't make much sense. It can, however, be corrected.

> While I was at summer camp, my family moved.

> ➤ **Rule 3** – When a prepositional phrase begins a sentence, make sure it modifies the *true* subject of phrase. Beware though: this error is easy to miss.

>> **Example:**
>> As the top programmer, I feel that only Steve can handle this project.

Who is the top programmer in this sentence, *Steve* or *I*? Since only *Steve* can handle the project, it's likely that he is the top programmer.

> As the top programmer, only Steve can handle this project.

> **Or**

> I feel that <u>as the top programmer only Steve can handle</u> this project.

> ➤ **Rule 4** – When a verbal phrase ends a sentence, make sure that it cannot modify more than one idea in the main clause.

>> **Example:**
>> Oddly, the senator known for his ability to close well performed poorly in the final two debates, causing a drop in his poll numbers.

There are two conflicting ideas expressed in the main clause of this sentence: the senator is a strong closer and he did poorly in the final debates. It's not clear which one caused the drop in his poll numbers (though logically the drop was caused by his poor performance). The sentence should be made clearer, often by removing the interfering verbal phrase.

> Though known to be a strong closer, the senator's poor performance in the final two debates caused his poll numbers to drop.

> **Or**

> The senator's poor performance in the final two debates caused his poll numbers to drop, even though he is known to be a strong closer.

> ➤ **Rule 5** – Do not modify a word with a word that means the same thing.

>> **Example:**
>> The old heirlooms are priceless.

By definition, heirlooms (valuables handed down from generation to generation) are old. The sentence can be corrected by dropping the word *old*.

Parallelism

Writers often try to summarize a thought or describe a situation by listing items in a series that are similar in content or function. When all of these parts share the same grammatical form, we say that they are parallel; hence, parallelism. Faulty parallelism occurs when units with similar functions in a sentence are not written with the same structure. Lucky for you, this error is easily fixed and fairly easy to spot. After all, faulty parallelism just doesn't sound right.

> **Rule 1** – When two adjectives modify the same noun, they must share a similar form.

>> **Awkward:**
>> The topology course was both rigorous and a challenge.

>> **Parallel:**
>> The topology course was both rigorous and *challenging*.

> **Rule 2** – When a series of adjective modify the same noun, they must share a similar form.

>> **Awkward:**
>> The interim Prime Minister is strong, compassionate, and wants to defeat the insurgency with a minimum of civilian casualties.

>> **Parallel:**
>> The interim Prime Minister is strong, compassionate, and *determined* to defeat the insurgency with a minimum of civilian casualties.

Often, this imbalance in complexity can make a sentence stilted, and the lesser adjectives will need to be subordinated.

>> The interim Prime Minister, *who is strong and compassionate*, wants to defeat the insurgency with a minimum of civilian casualties.

However, the first rewrite is more natural, active and powerful.

> **Rule 3** – When a series of clauses is listed, the verbs in each clause must have the same form.

>> **Awkward:**
>> During his trip to Europe, the President will discuss ways to stimulate trade, offer economic aid, and trying to forge a new coalition with moderate forces in Russia.

>> **Parallel:**
>> During his trip to Europe, the President will discuss ways to stimulate trade, offer economic aid, and *try* to forge a new coalition with moderate forces in Russia.

> **Rule 4** – When the first half of a sentence has a certain structure, the second half should preserve that structure.

>> **Awkward:**
>> To acknowledge that one is an alcoholic is taking the first and hardest step to recovery.

>> **Parallel:**
>> To acknowledge that one is an alcoholic is *to take* the first and hardest step to recovery.

✓ <u>Check your work</u>

To correct an unparalleled structure, fist try giving the similar parts the same structure. For instance, change an adjective and a noun to two adjectives. However, this can sometimes also make the sentence more awkward. In these cases, you may need to subordinate one part to another.

> **Example:**
> He ranks as one of the top volleyball players in the country and is often solicited by clothing companies for his endorsement.

The first clause in this sentence uses the active verb *ranks*, and the second clause uses the passive verb *solicited*. Making the first clause passive can make the sentence parallel.

> He *is ranked* as one of the top volleyball players in the country and is often solicited by clothing companies for his endorsement.

Be careful though; in writing, the active is preferred over the passive.

> He *ranks* as one of the top volleyball players in the country, and clothing companies often *solicit* him for his endorsement.

But now the sentence sounds awkward. So instead of forcing a parallel structure here, let's just subordinate the first clause to the second clause:

> As one of the top volleyball players in the country, he is often solicited for his endorsement.

➢ **Rule 5** – Correlative conjunctions should be preceded and followed by parallel constructions.

Following are some common correlative conjunctions:

> both . . . and . . .
> either . . . or . . .
> neither . . . nor . . .
> not only . . . but also . . .
> whether . . . or . . .
>
> **Awkward:**
> It was a long vacation *and* very boring.
>
> **Parallel:**
> It was a long *and* very boring vacation.
>
> **Awkward:**
> The game was *not only* a financial success, *but* it *also* succeeded as art.
>
> **Parallel:**
> The game was *not only* a financial success *but also* an artistic success.

Verb Tense

A verb is usually defined as a word that expresses action or state of being. Oddly, this definition is simultaneously nebulous and too precise: "state of being" is vague, and words other than verbs can also carry the weight of action within a sentence. However, any attempt to better define the concept of a verb will lead us into far more detail than we have room to discuss. Let's just use the above definition to reinforce our understanding of the meaning and function of a verb in a sentence.

A verb has four principal forms:

1. **Present Tense**
    a. Used to express present tense: *He studies hard*
    b. Used to express general truths: *During a recession, people are cautious about their money.*
    c. Used with *will* or *shall* to express future time: *He will take the ACT next year.*

2. Past Tense
a. Used to express past tense: *He took the ACT last year.*

3. Past Participle
a. Used to form the *present perfect tense*, which indicates that an action was started in the past and its effects are continuing in the present. It is formed using *have* or *has* and the past participle of the verb: *He has prepared thoroughly for the ACT.*

b. Used to form the *past perfect tense*, which indicates that an action was completed before another past action. It is formed using *had* and the past participle of the verb: *He had prepared thoroughly before taking the ACT.*

c. Used to form the *future perfect tense*, which indicates that an action will be completed before another future action. It is formed using *will have* or *shall have* and the past participle of the verb: *He will have completed the ACT by now.*

4. Present Participle
a. Used to form the *present progressive tense*, which indicates that an action is ongoing. It is formed using *is, am,* or *are* and the present participle of the verb: *He is preparing for the ACT.*

b. Use to form the *past progressive tense*, which indicates that an action was in progress in the past. It is formed using *was* or *were* and the present participle of the verb: *He was preparing for the ACT.*

c. Used to form the *future progressive tense*, which indicates that an action will be in progress in the future. It is formed using *will be* or *shall be* and the present participle of the verb: *He will be preparing for the ACT tonight.*

Much like a talented voice actor, verbs can also change their voice to suit a situation. But unlike a talented voice actor, verbs really only have two flavors to choose from.

The *passive voice* weakens a sentence by removing the subject of the sentence. Instead, the object of the sentence becomes the subject, and the subject becomes encased in a prepositional phrase.

The *active voice* is simply that. The verb shows the action that the subject is performing.

Passive Voice:
The bill *was resubmitted by* the Senator.

Active Voice:
The Senator resubmitted the bill.

Unless you want to de-emphasize the doer of an action, you should favor the active voice. Passive sentences are usually considered weak and timid. Notice in the above example that the sentence with the active verb is more powerful.

✓ Check your work
When passive construction is used in a sentence, the prepositional phrase often points to the wrong doer of action. Not only does this mistake make the writer seem unprofessional, but it will also lead to confusion for the reader.

Example:
The head of the insurgency of *was reported killed* in the first day of action by the press.

This sentence seems to imply that the press killed the head of the insurgency. The sentence is better expressed in the active voice:

The press *reported* that the head of the insurgency *was killed* in the first day of action

Diction

By definition, *diction* is the choice and use of words and phrases in speech or writing. Often, these choices sound alike or even mean similar things. Because of this, diction errors occur daily in speech and writing. Fortunately for the writer, the most common diction errors can be pinpointed and fixed.

Accept/Except

Accept means to receive something that is offered or agree to something.

> The European powers would have *accepted* Iran's offer if it had included on-site and unrestricted inspections.

Except means to leave out or exclude something.

> All the world's industrial powers signed the treaty to reduce global warming *except* the United States.

Affect/Effect

Affect, usually a verb, means to influence or concern. *Effect*, usually a noun, means the cause or result.

> The anti-venom had the desired *effect*, and the boy fully recovered.

Here, *effect* is a noun meaning result.

> The negotiators were not *affected* by the large, violent street protests.

Here, *affected* is a verb meaning influence.

Among/Between

Between compares exactly two things. A*mong* compares more than two things.

> The young lady must choose *between* two suitors.

A*mong* compares more than two things.

> The fault is spread evenly *among* the three defendants.

As/Like

A frequent mistake is to use *like* when *as* is needed. If you are connecting a clause to its subject, use *as*. If you merely need a preposition to introduce a noun, use *like*.

> It appears *as* though the peace plan has failed.

As is introducing the clause *the peace plan has failed*.

> It looks *like* rain.

Like is introducing the noun *rain*

As to

This phrase is usually imprecise. In almost all cases, it should replace with a more precise preposition or deleted.

> **Poor:**
> The prosecuting attorney left little doubt *as to* the defendant's motive for the murder.

> **Better:**
> The prosecuting attorney left little doubt *about* defendant's motive for the murder.

> **Poor:**
> The question *as to* whether it's better to let the bill die in committee or be voted down on the floor of the house is purely political.

> **Better:**
> The question *whether* it's better to let the bill die in committee or be voted down on the floor of the house is purely political.

Being that vs. Since

Being that is nonstandard and should be replaced by *since*.

Beside/Besides

Adding an *s* to *beside* completely changes its meaning: *Beside* means next to.

> We sat *beside* (next to) the host.

Besides means in addition.

> *Besides* (in addition), money was not even an issue in the contract negotiations.

Center on vs. Center around

Center around is colloquial. It should not be used in formal writing.

> **Incorrect:**
> The dispute *centers around* the effects of undocumented workers.

> **Correct:**
> The dispute *centers on* the effects of undocumented workers.

Conform to (not with)

> Stewart's writing does not *conform to* standard literary conventions.

Consensus of opinion

Consensus of opinion is redundant: consensus means general agreement, so *of opinion* is not necessary in the phase.

Correspond to/with

Correspond to means in agreement with.

> The penalty does not the severity of the crime.

Correspond with means to exchange letters.

> He *corresponded with* many of the top European leaders of his time.

Farther/Further

Farther refers to a measurable distance, and *further* refers to a figurative degree or quantity that can't be measured.

> **Examples:**
> They went no *further* (degree) than necking.
> He threw the discs *farther* (distance) than the top seated competitor.

Fewer/Less

Use *fewer* when referring to a number of items. Use *less* when referring to a continuous quantity.

> **Examples:**
> In the past, we had *fewer* options.
> The impact was *less* than what was expected.

Identical with (not to)

> This bid is *identical with* (not to) the one submitted by you.

In contrast to (not of)

> In *contrast to* (not of) the conservative attitudes of her time, Mae West was quite provocative.

Independent of (not from)

> The judiciary is *independent of* (not from) the other branches of government.

On account of vs. Because
Because is always better than *on account of*.

Poor:
On account of his poor behavior, he was expelled.

Better:
Because he behaved poorly, he was expelled.

One another/Each other
Use *each other* when referring to two things and *one another* when referring to more than two things.

Examples:
The members of the basketball team (more than two) congratulated *one another* on their victory.
The business partners (two) congratulated *each other* on their successful first year.

Plus vs. And
Do not use *plus* as a conjunction meaning *and*.

Incorrect:
His contributions to this community are considerable, *plus* his character is beyond reproach.

Correct:
His contributions to this community are considerable, *and* his character is beyond reproach.

Plus can be used to mean *and* as long as it is not being used as a conjunction.
His generous financial contribution *plus* his donated time has made this project a success.

Regard vs. Regards
Unless you are giving best wishes to someone, you should use *regard*.

Regardless vs. Irregardless
Regardless means "not withstanding." Hence, the "ir" in *irregardless* is redundant. *Irregardless* is not a real word and, therefore, should not be used under any circumstances.

Speak to/with
To *speak to* someone is to tell them something.

We *spoke to* Jennings about the alleged embezzlement.

To *speak with* someone is to discuss something with him or her.

Steve *spoke with* his friend Dave for hours yesterday.

Whether vs. As to whether
As to whether is wordy and should be replaced with *whether*.

Whether vs. If
Whether introduces a choice; *if* introduces a condition. A common mistake is to use *if* to present a choice.

Incorrect:
He inquired *if* we had decided to keep the gift.

Correct:
He inquired *whether* we had decided to keep the gift.

✓ Check your work
At times, grammar can seem impossible to conquer, especially when regularly accepted, spoken terms are often incorrect when written down on paper. But if you can remember a few key phrases and rules, you'll be mastering the written word in no time.

Points to Remember

1. A pronoun should be plural when it refers to two nouns joined by *and*.
2. A pronoun should be singular when it refers to two nouns joined by *or* or *nor*.
3. A pronoun should refer to one, and only one, noun or compound noun.
4. A pronoun must agree with its antecedent in both number and person.
5. The subject and verb must agree both in number and person.
6. Intervening phrases and clauses have no effect on subject-verb agreement.
7. When the subject and verb are reversed, they still must agree in both number and person.
8. As a general rule, a modifier should be placed as close as possible to what it modifies.
9. When a phrase begins a sentence, make sure that it modifies the subject of the sentence.
10. For a sentence to be parallel, similar elements must be expressed in similar form.
11. When two adjectives modify the same noun, they should have similar forms.
12. When a series of clauses is listed, the verbs must be in the same forms.
13. When the first half of a sentence has a certain structure, the second half should preserve that structure.
14. An adverb modifies a verb, an adjective, or another adverb.
15. A verb has four principal forms:
    I. Present Tense
        a. Used to express something that is occurring now.
        b. Used to express general truths.
        c. Used with *will* or *shall* to express future time.

    II. Past Tense
        a. Used to express something that occurred in the past.

    III. Past Participle
        a. Used to form the *present perfect tense*, which indicates that an action was started in the past and its effects are continuing in the present. It is formed using *have* or *has* and the past participle of the verb.
        b. Used to form the *past perfect tense*, which indicates that an action was completed before another past action. It is formed using *had* and the past participle of the verb.
        c. Used to form the *future perfect tense*, which indicates that an action is ongoing. It is formed using *is, am,* or *are* and the present participle of the verb.

    IV. Present Participle (*-ing* form of the verb)
        a. Used to form the *present progressive tense*, which indicates that an action is ongoing. It is formed using *is, am,* or *are* and the present participle of the verb.
        b. Used to form the *past progressive tense*, which indicates that an action was in progress in the past. It is formed using *was* or *were* and the present participle of the verb.
        c. Used to form the *future progressive tense*, which indicates that an action will be in progress in the future. It is formed using *will be* or *shall be* and the present participle of the verb.

16. Unless you intend to de-emphasize the doer of an action in a sentence, you should favor the active voice.

17. Attack strategy for identifying misplaced modifiers:
    I. Find the subject and the verb.
    II. Isolate the subject and the verb by deleting intervening phrases.
    III. Follow the rule of proximity: Modifiers should describe what they are next to in a sentence.
    IV. Check the punctuation. Punctuation should create coherence and not confusion.

Grammar Practice Drills

In each of the following sentences, part or all of the sentence is underlined. The answer-choices offer five ways of phrasing the underlined part. If you think the sentence as written is better than the alternatives, choose A, which merely repeats the underlined part; otherwise choose one of the alternatives.

1. Had the President's Administration not lost the vote on the budget reduction package, his first year in office would have been rated an A.
   (A) NO CHANGE
   (B) If the Administration had not lost the vote on the budget reduction package, his first year in office would have been rated an A.
   (C) Had the President's Administration not lost the vote on the budget reduction package, it would have been rated an A.
   (D) Had the President's Administration not lost the vote on its budget reduction package, his first year in office would have been rated an A.
   (E) If the President had not lost the vote on the budget reduction package, the Administration's first year in office would have been rated an A.

2. The new law requires a manufacturer to immediately notify their customers whenever the government is contemplating a forced recall of any of the manufacturer's products.
   (A) NO CHANGE
   (B) to immediately notify customers whenever the government is contemplating a forced recall of their products.
   (C) to immediately, and without delay, notify its customers whenever the government is contemplating a forced recall of any of the manufacture's products.
   (D) to immediately notify whenever the government is contemplating a forced recall of any of the manufacturer's products that the customers may have bought.
   (E) to immediately notify its customers whenever the government is contemplating a forced recall of any of the manufacturer's products.

3. World War II taught the United States the folly of punishing a vanquished aggressor; so after the war, they enacted the Marshall Plan to rebuild Germany.
   (A) NO CHANGE
   (B) after the war, the Marshall Plan was enacted to rebuild Germany.
   (C) after the war, the Marshall Plan was enacted by the United States to rebuild Germany.
   (D) after the war, the United States enacted the Marshall Plan to rebuild Germany.
   (E) after the war, the United States enacted the Marshall Plan in order to rebuild Germany.

4. In the 1950's, integration was an anathema to most Americans; now, however, most Americans accept it as desirable.
   (A) NO CHANGE
   (B) to most Americans, now, however, most Americans accept it.
   (C) to most Americans; now, however, most Americans are desirable of it.
   (D) to most Americans; now, however, most Americans accepted it as desirable.
   (E) to most Americans. Now, however, most Americans will accept it as desirable.

5. Geologists in California have discovered a fault near the famous San Andreas Fault, one that they believe to be a trigger for major quakes on the San Andreas.
   (A) NO CHANGE
   (B) one they believe to be a trigger for
   (C) one that they believe triggers
   (D) that they believe to be a trigger for
   (E) one they believe acts as a trigger for

6. The rising cost of government bureaucracy have made it all but impossible to reign in the budget deficit.
   (A) NO CHANGE
   (B) Since the rising costs
   (C) Because of the rising costs
   (D) The rising costs
   (E) Rising cost

7. In a co-publication agreement, ownership of both the material and its means of distribution are equally shared by the parties.
   (A) NO CHANGE
   (B) its means of distribution are shared equally by each of the parties.
   (C) its means of distribution is equally shared by the parties.
   (D) their means of distribution is equally shared by the parties.
   (E) the means of distribution are equally shared by the parties.

8. The rise in negative attitudes toward foreigners indicate that the country is becoming less tolerant, and therefore that the opportunities are ripe for extremist groups to exploit the illegal immigration problem.
   (A) NO CHANGE
   (B) indicates that the country is becoming less tolerant, and therefore
   (C) indicates that the country is becoming less tolerant, and therefore that
   (D) indicates that the country is being less tolerant, and therefore
   (E) indicates that the country is becoming less tolerant of and therefore that

9. The harvest of grapes in the local valleys decreased in 1990 for the third straight year but were still at a robust level.
   (A) NO CHANGE
   (B) The harvest of grapes in the local valleys began to decrease in 1990 for the third straight year but were
   (C) In 1990, the harvest of grapes in the local valleys decreased for the third straight year but were
   (D) The harvest of grapes in the local valleys decreased for the third straight year in 1990 but was
   (E) The harvest of grapes in the local valleys began decreasing in 1990 for the third straight year but was

10. More important than winning is developing the ability to work with others and developing leadership skills.
    (A) NO CHANGE
    (B) More important than winning are the ability to work with others and leadership skills.
    (C) Developing the ability to work with others and developing leadership skills is more important than winning.
    (D) More important than winning are developing the ability to work with others and developing leadership skills.
    (E) More important than winning has been the development of the ability to work with others and the development leadership skills.

11. There is a number of solutions to the problem of global warming that have not been considered by this committee.
    (A) NO CHANGE
    (B) There are a number of solutions
    (C) There was a number of solutions
    (D) There were a number of solutions
    (E) There have been a number of solutions

12. By focusing on poverty, the other causes of crime—such as the breakup of the nuclear family, changing morals, the loss of community, etc.—have been overlooked by sociologists.
    (A) NO CHANGE
    (B) the other causes of crime have been overlooked by sociologists—such as the breakup of the nuclear family, changing morals, the loss of community, etc.
    (C) there are other causes of crime that have been overlooked by sociologists—such as the breakup of the nuclear family, changing morals, the loss of community, etc.
    (D) crimes—such as the breakup of the nuclear family, changing morals, the loss of community, etc.—have been overlooked by sociologists.
    (E) sociologists have overlooked the other causes of crime—such as the breakup of the nuclear family, changing morals, the loss of community, etc.

13. Using the Hubble telescope, previously unknown galaxies are now being charted.
    (A) NO CHANGE
    (B) Previously unknown galaxies are now being charted, using the Hubble telescope.
    (C) Using the Hubble telescope, previously unknown galaxies are now being charted by astronomers.
    (D) Using the Hubble telescope, astronomers are now charting previously unknown galaxies.
    (E) With the aid of the Hubble telescope, previously unknown galaxies are now being charted.

14. The bitter cold the Midwest is experiencing is potentially life threatening to stranded motorists unless well-insulated with protective clothing.
    (A) NO CHANGE
    (B) stranded motorists unless being insulated
    (C) stranded motorists unless they are well-insulated
    (D) stranded motorists unless there is insulation
    (E) the stranded motorist unless insulated

15. Traveling across and shooting the vast expanse of the Southwest, in 1945 Ansel Adams began his photographic career.
    (A) NO CHANGE
    (B) In 1945, Ansel Adams began his photographic career, traveling across and shooting the vast expanse of the Southwest.
    (C) Having traveled across and shooting the vast expanse of the Southwest, in 1945 Ansel Adams began his photographic career.
    (D) Ansel Adams, in 1945 began his photographic career, traveling across and shooting the vast expanse of the Southwest.
    (E) Traveling across and shooting the vast expanse of the Southwest, Ansel Adams began his photographic career in 1945.

16. The Harmony virus will destroy a computer system unless inoculated by an anti-harmony program.
    (A) NO CHANGE
    (B) a computer system unless the system is inoculated
    (C) a computer system unless it is inoculated
    (D) a computer system unless inoculation occurred
    (E) a system unless it's being inoculated

17. As head of the division, we believe you should make the decision whether to retake the rebel stronghold.
    (A) NO CHANGE
    (B) Seeing as you are the head of the division, we believe
    (C) Being the head of the division, we believe
    (D) As head of the division, we are inclined to believe
    (E) We believe that as head of the division

18. <u>It is well established that the death of a parent during childhood can cause insecurity in adults.</u>
    (A) NO CHANGE
    (B) It is well established that the death of a parent when a child can cause insecurity in adults.
    (C) It is well established that the death of a parent occurring when a child can cause insecurity in adults.
    (D) It is well established that people who during childhood experience the death of a parent can be insecure as adults.
    (E) That people who during childhood experience the death of a parent can be insecure as adults is well established.

19. <u>Based on the yarns of storytellers, linguistic archeologists are compiling a written history of Valhalla and are realizing</u> that much of what was considered myth is in fact true.
    (A) NO CHANGE
    (B) Basing on the yarns of storytellers, linguistic archeologists are compiling a written history of Valhalla and are realizing
    (C) Using the yarns of storytellers, linguistic archeologists are compiling a written history of Valhalla and are realizing
    (D) Based on the yarns of storytellers, linguistic archeologists are compiling a written history of Valhalla and are coming to the realization
    (E) Deriving it from the yarns of storytellers, linguistic archeologists are compiling a written history of Valhalla and are realizing

20. Common knowledge tells us that sensible exercise and <u>eating properly will result</u> in better health.
    (A) NO CHANGE
    (B) proper diet resulted
    (C) dieting will result
    (D) proper diet results
    (E) eating properly results

21. This century began with <u>war brewing in Europe, the industrial revolution well-established, and a nascent communication age.</u>
    (A) NO CHANGE
    (B) war brewing in Europe, the industrial revolution surging, and a nascent communication age.
    (C) war in Europe, the industrial revolution well-established, and a nascent communication age.
    (D) war brewing in Europe, the industrial revolution well-established, and the communication age beginning.
    (E) war brewing in Europe, the industrial revolution well-established, and saw the birth of the communication age.

22. It is often better <u>to try repairing an old car than to junk it.</u>
    (A) NO CHANGE
    (B) to repair an old car than to have it junked.
    (C) to try repairing an old car than to junking it.
    (D) to try and repair an old car than to junk it.
    (E) to try to repair an old car than to junk it.

23. <u>Jurassic Park, written by Michael Crichton, and which was first printed in 1988,</u> is a novel about a theme park of the future in which dinosaurs roam free.
    (A) NO CHANGE
    (B) Jurassic Park, written by Michael Crichton and first printed in 1988,
    (C) Jurassic Park, which was written by Michael Crichton, and which was first printed in 1988,
    (D) Written by Michael Crichton and first printed in 1988, Jurassic Park
    (E) Jurassic Park, which was written by Michael Crichton and first printed in 1988,

The following passage is a first draft of an essay. Some parts of the passage need to be rewritten.

(1) Nestled in the foothills of the Smoky Mountains, *Getaway Lodge* offers its guests hospitality, comfort, and living in luxury. (2) Guests are greeted at the door and ushered to their rooms where they are welcomed with a large gift basket filled with scrumptious snacks and bath oils. (3) Every room has magnificent, breathtaking views of the surrounding mountains. (4) The mountains offer a myriad of activities for travelers including hiking and rock climbing. (5) If outdoor recreation is not appealing, guests can lounge by the free-form pool or soak in the hot tub.

(6) After a full day's activities, dinner is served in a romantic dining room adjacent to a waterfall. (7) By the glow of candlelight, diners will enjoy savory entrees and decadent desserts. (8) After dinner, guests may enjoy a stroll through the garden or sitting by the fireplace. (9) With so many pleasurable activities, guests can easily pass a memorable week at the *Getaway Lodge*.

24. What is the best way to deal with sentence 1 (reproduced below)?

    Nestled in the foothills of the Smoky Mountains, Getaway Lodge offers its guests hospitality, comfort, and living in luxury.

    (A) NO CHANGE
    (B) Change *its* to *their*.
    (C) Change *hospitably* to *hospitable living*.
    (D) Change *comfort* to *comfortable living*.
    (E) Change *living in luxury* to *luxurious living*.

25. Which of the following is the best revision of sentence 4 to better link it to sentence 3?
    (A) Every room also has magnificent, breathtaking views of the surrounding mountains.
    (B) Moreover, every room has magnificent, breathtaking views of the surrounding mountains.
    (C) Guests are also treated to magnificent, breathtaking views of the surrounding mountains.
    (D) In addition, guests are also shown magnificent, breathtaking views of the surrounding mountains.
    (E) Also, guests may view magnificent, breathtaking views of the surrounding mountains.

26. What is the best way to deal with sentence 8 (reproduced below)?

    After dinner, guests may enjoy a stroll through the garden or sitting by the fireplace.

    (A) NO CHANGE
    (B) Change *enjoy* to *take*.
    (C) Change *a stroll* to *strolling*.
    (D) Change *sitting* to *taking a seat*.
    (E) Place *after dinner* at the end of the sentence.

27. In the past few years and to this day, many teachers of math and science had chosen to return to the private sector.
    (A) NO CHANGE
    (B) having chosen to return to the private sector.
    (C) chose to return to the private sector.
    (D) have chosen to return to the private sector.
    (E) have chosen returning to the private sector.

28. Most of the homes that were destroyed in last summer's brush fires were built with wood-shake roofs.
    (A) NO CHANGE
    (B) Last summer, brush fires destroyed most of the homes that were
    (C) Most of the homes that were destroyed in last summer's brush fires had been
    (D) Most of the homes that the brush fires destroyed last summer's have been
    (E) Most of the homes destroyed in last summer's brush fires were being

29. Although World War II ended nearly a half century ago, Russia and Japan still have not signed a formal peace treaty; and both countries have been reticent to develop closer relations.
    (A) NO CHANGE
    (B) did not signed a formal peace treaty; and both countries have been
    (C) have not signed a formal peace treaty; and both countries being
    (D) have not signed a formal peace treaty; and both countries are
    (E) are not signing a formal peace treaty; and both countries have been

30. The Democrats have accused the Republicans of resorting to dirty tricks by planting a mole on the Democrat's planning committee and then used the information obtained to sabotage the Democrat's campaign.
    (A) NO CHANGE
    (B) used the information they had obtained to sabotage
    (C) of using the information they had obtained to sabotage
    (D) using the information obtained to sabotage
    (E) to have used the information obtained to sabotage

31. Unless you maintain at least a 2.0 GPA, you will not graduate medical school.
    (A) NO CHANGE
    (B) you will not be graduated from medical school.
    (C) you will not be graduating medical school.
    (D) you will not graduate from medical school.
    (E) you will graduate medical school.

32. The studio's retrospective art exhibit refers back to a simpler time in American history.
    (A) NO CHANGE
    (B) The studio's retrospective art exhibit harkens back to
    (C) The studio's retrospective art exhibit refers to
    (D) The studio's retrospective art exhibit refers from
    (E) The studio's retrospective art exhibit looks back to

33. Due to the chemical spill, the commute into the city will be delayed by as much as 2 hours.
    (A) NO CHANGE
    (B) The reason that the commute into the city will be delayed by as much as 2 hours is because of the chemical spill.
    (C) Due to the chemical spill, the commute into the city had been delayed by as much as 2 hours.
    (D) Because of the chemical spill, the commute into the city will be delayed by as much as 2 hours.
    (E) The chemical spill will be delaying the commute into the city by as much as 2 hours.

The following passage is a first draft of an essay. Some parts of the passage need to be rewritten.

(1) A best-selling book offers "Seven Ways to Become a Better Person." (2) A radio ad promises you will feel great in 30 days or less just by taking some pills. (3) "If you buy our exercise equipment," a TV ad guarantees, "you'll have the body you've always wanted." (4) In today's society, we are continually bombarded with the latest techniques of how to better ourselves, a focus which some feel is unhealthy. (5) Additionally, a focus on self-improvement is very important in helping people grow in character.

(6) Self-improvement helps build character. (7) Building character involves taking a person's strengths and building on them. (8) Such strengths as unselfishness can be developed into a lifelong habit of generosity, a positive spirit into an unfailing compassion for others. (9) Everyone has strength in character and the ability to build on these strengths through self-improvement.

(10) Weaknesses are not flaws, but rather negative traits that, through self-improvement, can be developed into more positive traits. (11) For example, impatience can be turned into determination to accomplish goals. (12) Strong will turns into perseverance. (13) If a person can just find a way to capitalize on a weakness, it can be turned into a strength. (14) Self-improvement is the best way to do this.

34. What is the best word or phrase to use in place of the word *additionally* in sentence 5 (reproduced below)?

    Additionally, a focus on self-improvement is very important in helping people grow in character.

    (A) Moreover
    (B) On the contrary
    (C) Along those lines
    (D) Consequently
    (E) Accordingly

35. What is the best way to deal with sentence 12 (reproduced below)?

    Strong will turns into perseverance.

    (A) NO CHANGE
    (B) Add *is* before *turns* and change *turns* to *turned*.
    (C) Add *shall* before *turns* and change *turns* to *turn*.
    (D) Change *turns into* to *becomes*.
    (E) Add *can be* before *turns* and change *turns* to *turned*.

Solutions to Grammar Practice Drills

1. The answer is (E).

Choice (A) is incorrect because *his* appears to refer to *the President*, but the subject of the subordinate clause is *the President's Administration*, not *the President*.

Choice (B) changes the structure of the sentence, but retains the same flawed reference.

In choice (C), *it* can refer to either *the President's Administration* or *the budget reduction package*. Thus, the reference is ambiguous.

Choice (D) adds another pronoun, *its*, but still retains the same flawed reference.

Choice (E) corrects the flawed reference by removing all pronouns.

2. The answer is (E).

Choice (A) is incorrect because the plural pronoun *their* cannot have the singular noun *a manufacturer* as its antecedent.

Although choice (B) corrects the given false reference, it introduces another one. *Their* can now refer to either *customers* or *government*, neither of which would make sense in this context.

Choice (C) also corrects the false reference, but it introduces a redundancy: *immediately* means "without delay."

Choice (D) corrects the false reference, but its structure is very awkward. The direct object of a verb should be as close to the verb as possible. In this case, the verb *notify* is separated from its direct object *customers* by the clause *that the government is contemplating a forced recall of any of the manufacturer's products that*.

Choice (E) is correct because the singular pronoun *its* has the singular noun *a manufacturer* as its antecedent.

3. The answer is (D).

Choice (A) is incorrect. Since *United States* is denoting the collective country, it is singular and therefore cannot be correctly referred to by the plural pronoun *they*.

Choice (B) is not technically incorrect, but it lacks precision since it does not state who enacted the Marshall Plan. Further, it uses a passive construction: *was enacted*.

Choice (C) states who enacted the Marshall Plan, but it retains the passive construction *was enacted*.

Choice (E) does not violate the rules of grammar (though some strict grammarians do object to its use in this context). It is the second-best answer-choice. The phrase "*in order*" is unnecessary. In this context, the phase "*in order to*" has the same meaning as just the word "*to*." Choice (D) is the same as Choice (E), except for the redundant words "in order," so it is a better answer.

Choice (D) corrects the false reference by replacing *they* with *the United States*. Further, it uses the active verb *enacted* instead of the passive verb *was enacted*.

4. The sentence is correct as written. The answer is (A).

Choice (B) creates a run-on sentence by replacing the semicolon with a comma. Without a connecting word (*and, or, but*, etc.) two independent clauses must be joined by a semicolon or written as two separate sentences. Also, deleting *as desirable* changes the meaning of the sentence.
Choice (C) uses a very awkward construction: *are desirable of it*.

Choice (D) contains an error in tense. The sentence progresses from the past to the present, so the verb in the second clause should be *accept*, not *accepted*.

Choice (E) writes the two clauses as separate sentences, which is allowable, but it also changes the tense of the second clause to the future: *will accept*.

5. The answer is (B).

Choice (A) is incorrect since the relative pronoun *that* is redundant: the pronoun *one*, which refers to the newly discovered fault, is sufficient.

Although choice (C) reads more smoothly, it still contains the double pronouns.

Choice (D) is incorrect. Generally, relative pronouns such as *that* refer to whole ideas in previous clauses or sentences. Since the second sentence is about the fault and not its discovery, the pronoun *that* is appropriate.

Choice (E) is very tempting. It actually reads better than choice (A), but it contains a subtle flaw. *One* is the direct object of the verb *believes* and therefore cannot be the subject of the verb *acts*. Since *they* clearly is not the subject, the verb *acts* is without a subject.

Choice (B) has both the correct pronoun and the correct verb form.

6. The answer is (D).

Choice (A) is incorrect because the plural verb *have* does not agree with its singular subject *the rising cost*.

Both (B) and (C) are incorrect because they turn the sentence into a fragment.

Choice (E) is incorrect because *rising cost* is still singular.

Choice (D) is the correct answer since now the plural verb *have* agrees with its plural subject *the rising costs*.

7. The answer is (C).

Choice (A) is incorrect. Recall that intervening phrases have no effect on subject-verb agreement. In this sentence, the subject *ownership* is singular, but the verb *are* is plural.

Choice (B) is incorrect. Neither adding *each of* nor interchanging *shared* and *equally* addresses the issue of subject-verb agreement.

Choice (D) contains a faulty pronoun reference. The antecedent of the plural pronoun *their* would be the singular noun *material*.

Choice (E) is incorrect since it still contains the plural verb *are*.

8. The answer is (B).

Choice (A) has two flaws. First, the subject of the sentence *the rise* is singular, and therefore the verb *indicate* should not be plural. Second, the comma indicates that the sentence is made up of two independent clauses, but the relative pronoun *that* immediately following *therefore* forms a subordinate clause.

Choice (C) corrects the number of the verb, but retains the subordinating relative pronoun *that*.

Choice (D) corrects the number of the verb and eliminates the subordinating relative pronoun *that*. However, the verb *being* is less descriptive than the verb *becoming*: As negative attitudes toward foreigners increase, the country becomes correspondingly less tolerant. *Being* does not capture this notion of change.

Choice (E) corrects the verb's number, and by dropping the comma, makes the subordination allowable. However, it introduces the preposition *of* which does not have an object: less tolerant of what?

Choice (B) both corrects the verb's number and removes the subordinating relative pronoun *that*.

9. The answer is (D).

Choice (A) is incorrect since the singular subject *the harvest* requires a singular verb, not the plural verb *were*.

Choice (B) is illogical since it states that the harvest began to decrease in 1990 and then it states that it was the third straight year of decrease.

In choice (C) the plural verb *were* still does not agree with its singular subject *the harvest*.

Choice (E) contains the same flaw as choice (B).

Choice (D) has the singular verb *was* agreeing with its singular subject *the harvest*. Further, it places the phrase *in 1990* more naturally.

10. The answer is (D).

Choice (A) is incorrect since the compound subject *developing the ability to work with others and developing leadership skills* requires a plural verb, not the singular verb *is*.

Choice (B) uses the correct plural verb *are* but deletes the word *developing*, making the meaning of the sentence less clear.

Choice (C) uses a the natural order of subject then verb, but it is incorrect since the compound subject *developing the ability to work with others and developing leadership skills* requires a plural verb, not the singular verb *is*.

Choice (D) has the plural verb *are* agreeing with its compound subject *developing the ability to work with others and developing leadership skills*.

Choice (E) is incorrect since the compound subject *the development of the ability to work with others and the development leadership skills* requires a plural verb, not the singular verb *has*.

11. The answer is (B).

Choice (A) is incorrect since the plural subject *a number* requires a plural verb, not the singular verb *is*.

Choice (B) is the answer because it correctly uses the plural verb *are* with the plural subject *a number*.

Choice (C) is incorrect since the plural subject *a number* requires a plural verb, not the singular verb *was*. Further, the shift in verb tense from *was* to *have not been* is awkward.

Choice (D) is incorrect because the shift in verb tense from *were* to *have not been* is awkward.

Choice (E) is incorrect because it is awkward and changes the meaning of the sentence.

12. The answer is (E).

Choice (A) is incorrect since it implies that *the other causes of crime* are doing the focusing.

Choice (B) has the same flaw as Choice (A).

Choice (C) is incorrect. The phrase *by focusing on poverty* must modify the subject of the sentence, but *there* cannot be the subject since the construction *there are* is used to introduce a subject.

Choice (D) implies that *crimes* are focusing on poverty.

Choice (E) correctly puts the subject of the sentence *sociologists* immediately next to its modifying phrase *by focusing on poverty*.

13. The answer is (D).

Choice (A) is incorrect because the phrase *using the Hubble telescope* does not have a noun to modify.

Choice (B) is incorrect because the phrase *using the Hubble telescope* still does not have a noun to modify.

Choice (C) offers a noun, *astronomers*, but it is too far from the phrase *using the Hubble telescope*.

Choice (D) offers a noun, *astronomers*, and correctly places it immediately after the modifying phrase *using the Hubble telescope*.

In choice (E), the phrase *with the aid of the Hubble telescope* does not have a noun to modify.

14. The answer is (C).

Choice (A) is incorrect. As worded, the sentence implies that the cold should be well-insulated.

Choice (B) is awkward; besides, it still implies that the cold should be well-insulated.

Choice (C) is the answer since it correctly implies that the stranded motorists should be well-insulated with protective clothing.

Choice (D) does not indicate what should be insulated.

Choice (E), like choices (A) and (B), implies that the cold should be well-insulated.

15. The answer is (E).

Choice (A) has two flaws. First, the introductory phrase is too long. Second, the subject Ansel Adams should immediately follow the introductory phrase since it was Ansel Adams—not the year 1945—who was traveling and shooting the Southwest.

Choice (B) is incorrect because the phrase *traveling across . . . Southwest* is too far from its subject Ansel Adams. As written, the sentence seems to imply that the photographic career was traveling across and shooting the Southwest.

Choice (C) is inconsistent in verb tense. Further, it implies that Adams began his photographic career after he traveled across the Southwest.

Choice (D) is awkward.

Choice (E) is the best answer.

16. The answer is (B).

Choice (A) is incorrect because it implies that the Harmony virus should be inoculated when it's the computer system that needs to be protected.

Choice (B) is the answer since it correctly implies that the computer system should be inoculated, not the virus.

Choice (C) sounds better, but it is not clear what the pronoun *it* is referring to, the virus or the computer. Hence, it is not clear whether it's the virus or the computer that needs to be inoculated.

Choice (D) is awkward, and it implies that the Harmony virus should be inoculated when it's the computer system that needs to be protected.

Choice (E) is awkward, and it implies that the Harmony virus should be inoculated when it's the computer system that needs to be protected.

17. The answer is (E).

Choice (A) is incorrect because it implies that *we* are the head of the division instead of the actual head of the division *you*.

Although Choice (B) makes clear who is the head of the division (*you* not *we*), the structure *Seeing as you...* is too lose and informal.

Choice (C) makes the same mistake as the original sentence: It implies that *we* are the head of the division instead of the actual head of the division *you*.

Choice (D) is incorrect because it merely adds unnecessary words *are inclined to* which does not correct the flaw in the original sentence: It still implies that *we* are the head of the division instead of the actual head of the division *you*.

Choice (E) is the answer because the clause *that as head of the division* correctly modifies the head of the division *you*.

18. The answer is (D).

Choice (A) is incorrect because the phrase *during childhood* modifies *parent* illogically implying that the parent died during childhood.

Choice (B) is incorrect because the phrase *when a child* modifies *parent* illogically implying that the parent died during childhood.

Choice (C) is incorrect because the phrase *occurring when a child* modifies *parent* illogically implying that the parent died during childhood.

Choice (D) is the answer. Now, the phrase *during childhood* correctly modifies *people*.

Choice (E) is very awkward. The long clause *That people who . . . as adults* is the subject of the sentence. Although perhaps not ungrammatical, Choice (E) is very hard to read.

19. The answer is (C).

Choice (A) is incorrect because the phrase *Based on yarns of storytellers* modifies *linguistic archeologists* illogically implying that the archeologists are based on the yarns of storytellers.

Choice (B) is incorrect because the phrase *Basing on the yarns of storytellers* modifies *linguistic archeologists* illogically implying that the archeologists are based on the yarns of storytellers. Further, the phrase *Basing on the yarns of storytellers* is very awkward.

Choice (C) is the answer. The clause *Using the yarns of storytellers* correctly modifies *linguistic archeologists*, showing how they are using the yarns. The clause can also be placed after the subject it modifies: Linguistic archeologists using the yarns of storytellers . . ..

Choice (D) is incorrect because the phrase *coming to the realization* is wordy. Further, the phrase *Based on the yarns of storytellers* modifies *linguistic archeologists* illogically implying that the archeologists are based on the yarns of storytellers.

Choice (E) is incorrect because it is awkward and vague: What is *it* referring to?

20. The answer is (D).

Choice (A) is incorrect since *eating properly* (verb-adverb) is not parallel to *sensible exercise* (adjective-noun).

Choice (B) offers two parallel nouns, *exercise* and *diet*. However, a general truth should be expressed in the present tense, not in the past tense.

Choice (C) is not parallel since it pairs the noun *exercise* with the gerund (a verb acting as a noun) *dieting*.

Choice (E) makes the same mistake as choice (A).

Choice (D) offers two parallel nouns—*exercise* and *diet*—and two parallel verbs—*tells* and *results*.

21. The answer is (D).

Choice (A) is incorrect. Although the first two phrases, *war brewing in Europe* and *the industrial revolution well-established*, have different structures, the thoughts are parallel. However, the third phrase, *and a nascent communication age*, is not parallel to the first two.

Choice (B) does not make the third phrase parallel to the first two.

Choice (C) changes the meaning of the sentence: the new formulation states that war already existed in Europe while the original sentence states that war was only developing.

Choice (E) is not parallel. The first two phrases in the series are noun phrases, but the final phrase *saw the birth of the communication age* is a verb phrase.

Choice (D) offers three phrases in parallel form.

22. The answer is (E).

Choice (A) is incorrect since the verb *repairing* is not parallel to the verb *junk*.

In choice (B), the construction *have it junked* is awkward. Further, it changes the original construction from active to passive.

Choice (C) offers a parallel construction (*repairing/junking*), but it is awkward.

Choice (D) also offers a parallel construction (*repair/junk*), but the construction *try and* is not proper diction.

Choice (E) offers a parallel construction (*repair/junk*), and the formal structure — *try to*.

23. The answer is (B).

Choice (A) is incorrect since the verb *written* is not parallel to the construction *which was ... printed*. Choice (B) is the correct answer since the sentence is concise and the verb *written* is parallel to the verb *printed*. Choice (C) does offer a parallel structure (*which was written/which was printed*); however, choice (B) is more concise. Choice (D) rambles. The introduction *Written by ... 1988* is too long. Choice (E) also offers a parallel structure (*which was written/which was printed*); however, choice (B) is more concise.

24. The answer is (E).

Choice (A) is incorrect. We cannot leave the sentence as it is because the elements of the sentence need to be parallel in structure. Choice (B) is incorrect. The subject of the sentence is *Getaway Lodge*. The correct pronoun is *its* not *their*. Choice (C) is incorrect because it makes an unnecessary change. *Hospitality* functions better than *hospitable living*, so why change it? Choice (D) is incorrect for the same reason as Choice (C). *Comfort* is much more effective here than *comfortable living*. Choice (E) is the correct answer. As it is, *living in luxury* is not parallel to *hospitality* and *comfort*. We need to change it to *luxurious living*.

25. The answer is (C).

Choice (A) is incorrect. The passage thus far has focused on the guests rather than the subject of the room. Choice (B) is incorrect for the same reason as Choice (A). Choice (D) is incorrect because it implies that guests were simply *shown* their gift baskets. The passage clearly implies that the gift baskets are given to the guests. Choice (E) is not correct. It is a poorly constructed sentence, and it does not provide an effective transition from the subject of gift baskets to mountain views. Choice (C) is correct. Just as guests were *treated* to gift baskets, the mountain views serve as a treat as well. It works well to tie the sentences together. Additionally, the guests are the focus in this sentence just as in sentence three.

26. The answer is (C).

Choice (A) is incorrect. All element of the sentence need to be parallel; they are not parallel, so we cannot leave it as it is. Choice (B) is incorrect. Not only does the solution not address the problem of parallel structure in the sentence, but it takes away some of the interest of the sentence by replacing the word *enjoy* with *take*. Choice (D) is incorrect. It changes the wording of a part of the sentence that is not parallel, but the rewrite does not change the structure of the sentence. Choice (E) is incorrect because the solution does not correct the problem of balancing the parallelism of the sentence. Moreover, changing the order of the sentence takes away much of the interest of the sentence. Choice (C) is the correct answer. In this sentence, we needed to make *stroll through the garden* and *sitting by the fireplace* parallel. We could have corrected this by addressing *stroll* or *sitting*. This answer-choice offers a solution by changing *stroll* to *strolling*.

27. The answer is (C).

Choice (A) is incorrect because it uses the past perfect *had chosen*, which describes an event that has been completed before another event. But the sentence implies that teachers have and are continuing to return to the private sector. Hence, the present perfect tense should be used. Choice (B) is incorrect because it uses the present progressive tense *having chosen*, which describes an ongoing event. Although this is the case, it does not capture the fact that the event began in the past. Choice (C) is incorrect because it uses the simple past *chose*, which describes a past event. But again, the sentence implies that the teachers are continuing to opt for the private sector. Choice (D) is the correct answer because it uses the present perfect *have chosen* to describe an event that occurred in the past and is continuing into the present. Choice (E) is incorrect because it leaves the thought in the sentence uncompleted.

28. The answer is (C).

Choice (A) is incorrect because the simple past *were* does not express the fact that the homes had been built before the fire destroyed them. Choice (B) merely rearranges the wording while retaining the simple past *were*. Choice (C) is the correct answer because it uses the past perfect *had been* to indicate that the homes were completely built before they were destroyed by the fire. Choice (D) is incorrect because it uses the present perfect *have been*, which implies that the homes were destroyed before being built. Choice (E) is incorrect. Although removing *that were* makes the sentence more concise, the past progressive *were being* implies that the homes were destroyed while being built.

29. The answer is (A).

The sentence is grammatical as written, so the answer is (A). The present perfect verb *have ... signed* correctly indicates that they have not signed a peace treaty and are not on the verge of signing one. Further, the present perfect verb *have been* correctly indicates that in the past both countries have been reluctant to develop closer relations and are still reluctant. In choice (B), the simple past *did* does not capture the fact that they did not sign a peace treaty immediately after the war and still have not signed one. Choice (C) is very awkward, and the present progressive *being* does not capture the fact that the countries have been reluctant to thaw relations since after the war up through the present. In choice (D), the present tense *are* leaves open the possibility that in the past the countries may have desired closer relations but now no longer do. In choice (E), the present progressive tense *are ... signing*, as in choice (D), leaves open the possibility that in the past the countries may have desired closer relations but now no longer do.

30. The answer is (C).

Choice (A) is incorrect because the simple past *obtained* does not express the fact that the information was obtained before another past action—the sabotage. Choice (B) is incorrect because *used* is not parallel to *of resorting*. Choice (C) is correct because the phrase *of using* is parallel to the phrase *of resorting*. Further, the past perfect *had obtained* correctly expresses that a past action—the spying—was completed before another past action—the sabotage. Choice (D) is incorrect because *using* is not parallel to *of resorting* and the past perfect is not used. Choice (E) is incorrect because *to have used* is not parallel to *of resorting* and the past perfect is not used.

31. The answer is (D).

Choice (A) is incorrect. In this context, *graduate* requires the word *from*: "you will not *graduate from* medical school." The use of the passive voice in choices (B) and (C) weakens the sentence. Choice (D) is the answer since it uses the correct diction *graduate from*. Choice (E) changes the meaning of the sentence and does not correct the faulty diction.

32. The answer is (C).

Choice (A) is incorrect. *Retrospective* means looking back on the past. Hence, in the phrase *refers back*, the word *back* is redundant. Choice (B) is incorrect because *harkens back* is also redundant. Choice (C) is correct. Dropping the word *back* eliminates the redundancy. Choice (D) is incorrect because the preposition *from* is non-idiomatic. Choice (E) is incorrect because *looks back* is also redundant.

33. The answer is (D).

Choice (A) is incorrect. Although many educated writers and speakers begin sentences with *due to*, it is almost always incorrect. Choice (B) is incorrect: it is both redundant and awkward. Choice (C) is incorrect. The past perfect *had been delayed* implies the delay no longer exists. Hence, the meaning of the sentence has been changed. Choice (D) is correct. In general, *due to* should not be used as a substitute for *because of, by reason of*, etc. Choice (E) is incorrect. The future progressive *will be delaying* is unnecessary and ponderous. Had choice (E) used the simple future *will delay*, it would have been better that choice (D) because then it would be more direct and active.

34. The answer is (B).

Choice (A) is incorrect. Sentence four ends with *a focus that some feel is unhealthy*. Sentence five says that *a focus on self-improvement is very important in helping people grow in character*. The content of sentence five is in contrast to the content of sentence four, so we need a transition that shows contrast. *Moreover* is a transitional word used to show agreement. Choice (C) is incorrect for the same reason as Choice (A). Choice D is incorrect because *consequently* is a transitional word that precedes a result in a cause-effect relationship. Choice (E) is incorrect for the same reason as Choice (A) and (C). Choice (B) is correct because *on the contrary* shows the contrast between what is said in sentence four and what is said in sentence five.

35. The answer is (E).

Choice (A) is incorrect. We need to make sure that sentence 12 is parallel in structure to sentence 11 which says *impatience can be turned...* As it is now, sentence 12 is not parallel to sentence 11, so we cannot leave it as it is. Choice (B) is incorrect because the resulting new sentence would be *Strong will is turned into perseverance*. Again, this is not parallel to sentence 11, so this is not our solution. Choice (C) is not correct either. Let's look at the proposed new construction of the sentence: *Strong will shall turn into perseverance*. This again is not parallel. Choice (D) is incorrect. *Strong will becomes perseverance* is not parallel in structure. Choice (E) is the correct answer. Let's check the new sentence: *Strong will can be turned into perseverance*. This is parallel to *...impatience can be turned into determination...*

Rhetoric

Now that you know when to use a semicolon instead of a comma, and now that you know how to repair faulty grammar within a sentence, the final section the English test will test you on is rhetoric.

Rhetoric is literally the art of effective or persuasive writing, and it can be broken down into a few primary areas: style, structure, and strategy.

Style

The way a writer uses words and phrases to add personality to his writing is called *style*. A writer is to style as a figure skater is to skating. A writer can learn all the rules to make his writing correct, just as a figure skater can learn how to accomplish her jumps and footwork. But just learning the rules of grammar is not enough to create a well-written piece; learning just the rules of skating is not enough to earn a gold medal. The writer must bring his own methods and personality to his writing, just as a skater must invest her own personality and flair to her performance.

Many elements combine to form the writer's style; and, although style can be identified and examined, true style will only develop through practice. Let's look at some specific elements of style.

➢ **Transitions**—Transitional phrases are an important element of formal writing because they create coherence. They guide the reader from point A to point B. Look at the lists below for some examples of transitional words and phrases that help achieve cohesiveness.

> **Agreement:** *also, plus, in addition, further, furthermore, moreover, additionally, to add to that, next, in accordance with, accordingly, in agreement, finally, for instance, for example, in exemplification, exemplifying that, in fact, factually speaking, in terms of, and so forth, in coordination with, along those lines, collectively speaking, generally speaking, indeed, undoubtedly, obviously, to be sure, equally*

> **Contrast:** *however, in contrast, on the contrary, on the other hand, from a different angle, nonetheless, nevertheless, but, yet, a catch to this is, sadly enough, as a hindrance, oddly enough, instead, in direct opposition, still, rather*

> **Result:** *as a result, as a consequence, consequently, thus, therefore, hence, thereby, resulting in, ultimately, in the end, finally, in the overall analysis, in hindsight, in retrospect, retrospectively, vicariously, the long term effect, as a short term result, significantly, as a major effect, effectively, heretofore, hereafter, thereafter, in short, generally, over all, concluding*

✓ Check your work

Transitional words and phrases are helpful not only in linking ideas between sentences, but also in providing cohesiveness from paragraph to paragraph. Without this clarity, an essay will likely be choppy and difficult to read and understand. A word of caution, though: Be careful not to overuse transitional words and phrases. Overuse can make you sound like a pedantic writer rather than an intelligent one.

➤ **Varying Sentences**—No matter how well an essay flows, the reader will easily get bored if it consists only of sentences that contain the same words and follow the same structure.

> **Example:**
> Dogs help blind people. Dogs also help epileptic people. Dogs can sense when an epileptic person is about to have a seizure. Dogs are also used in rescue work. They help rescue skiers. They also help in catastrophic events. They rescue people after earthquakes.

There are several things wrong with this paragraph:
- Almost every sentence is the same length.
- The structure in each sentence is almost identical: Subject + Verb + Direct Object.
- The same words are used over and over: *dogs, they, rescue, help, people*.
- No description is used to further illustrate the writer's points.

✔ Check your work
To add more interest, try varying sentence length and structure. Try different sentence styles, employ a variety of words and use these words to paint a vivid picture of the subject. For example, you could begin your sentence with a subject and a predicate and then build on them using various words and phrases.

> **Cumulative sentence:**
> The energetic children played hard, chasing each other in all directions, occasionally falling and then scrambling to their feet, giggling at each other's antics and never stopping for even a moment to catch their breath.

> **Periodic sentence:**
> With flour in her hair, dough in between her fingers and sauce all over her face, she attempted to make a gourmet pizza.

Both of the above sentences not only add variety, but also bring rhythm and cadence to writing. This rhythm creates interest and is pleasant to read. Additionally, descriptive words paint a clear picture for the reader.

➤ **Figurative Language**—Another excellent way to paint a vivid picture is to use figures of speech. Figures of speech—like similes, metaphors, analogies, personification, hyperbole, irony, and allusion—when used correctly, add extra flair to writing. They add an extra element that takes writing from ordinary to extraordinary.

- *Similes* show a marked comparison between two things by using the phrases *like, as,* or, *as if:*

  The cat stood poised and *still as a statue*, waiting for the opportune moment to pounce.

- *Metaphors* show absolute comparison by omitting *like, as,* or, *as if:*

  She is Mother Theresa when it comes to her generosity and compassion.

Here the comparison is absolute because the writer states that this person *is* Mother Theresa, even though she is not actually Mother Theresa.

- *Analogies* compare the similar features of two dissimilar things, and they often bring clarity to writing by showing the reader another way of seeing something. Analogies are not limited to a sentence; sometimes an analogy streams its way through an entire piece of writing.

Example:
Office cooperation is like a soccer game. Each employee has a position on the playing field, and each position dictates an employee's function. Working together, the office completes passes by communicating well within each department. Shots on goal are taken when employees meet with prospective clients to pitch ideas, and the whole office triumphs when a goal is scored and a prospect becomes a client.

Although an office and a soccer team are two very unrelated things, the writer sees similarities between the two and uses these similarities to clearly show how an office works.

- *Personification* gives human characteristics to animals, inanimate objects and ideas in order to make them more real and understandable:

  The rusty car groaned, coughed, then gave one last sputter and died.

The car in this sentence comes to life even as it "dies" because of the human characteristics it is given.

- *Hyperbole* uses deliberate exaggeration or overstatement to show special emphasis or create humor.

  Example:
  Fat-free foods have become so popular that soon all vendors will want to sell them. Before you know it, Kentucky Fried Chicken will have fat-free fried chicken. Big Macs will contain 0 grams of fat. And the amount of fat in a Pizza Hut cheese pizza? You guessed it—none!

In order to show how excessive people's obsession with fat-free foods has become, this description purposefully exaggerates a world where the most unlikely things are fat-free.

- *Irony* uses language to make a suggestion that directly contrasts with the literal word or idea. It can offer humor to writing, or a bitter tone when it is used in sarcasm.

  Example:
  Scientists have worked hard to develop ways to decrease infant mortality rates and increase longevity. As a result, more people are living longer and scientists will soon have to develop some methods with which to control overpopulation.

This sentence uses irony by predicting that, because scientists have now discovered ways to increase a person's life span, they will soon have to deal with another problem—overpopulation.

- *Allusion* makes indirect reference to known cultural works, people or events. The familiarity allusions bring to writing helps the writer make connections with the reader:

  I have so much to do today, I feel like David must have felt as he approached Goliath.

David must have felt a bit intimidated when facing the giant, Goliath—a feeling this writer alludes to when thinking about everything that needs to be done.

✓ Check your work
Your goal as a writer is to create interest and coherence through your unique writing style. Using figures of speech and maintaining consistent use of tone, diction, and person are effective ways to create interest; and using transitional words help to create coherence. Remember, though, that part of creating coherence is being concise. Use only the details that are necessary to support your topic and avoid tedious descriptions. This isn't to say that you should avoid vivid imagery, but only that you should take care to ensure that the above methods add to your writing rather than detract from it.

The most important aspect to remember is that style can only develop through practice. Practice your writing and proofread, proofread, proofread. If you do all of these things, you'll be well on your way to becoming an effective, skillful writer.

Structure

Although style usually takes the front seat when it comes to rhetoric, structure is just as important.

In his book, *The Elements of Style,* William Strunk wrote that, "The more clearly the writer perceives the shape (of an essay), the better are the chances of success." No truer words have ever been spoken in regard to composition. Sure, it can be a pain to create a full outline. Sure, some writer's write better by the seat of their pants. But, for the most part, planning must be a deliberate prelude to writing. And since nearly half of the questions in the English section test rhetoric—writing style, structure, and strategy—it's important to understand the structure of an essay.

The two most important elements of structure are the introduction and the conclusion.

➤ **Introduction**—The introduction serves two structural purposes: It restates the topic so that the reader need not review the given question, and it offers a clear thesis—the main idea—so that the reader can discover the purpose of the essay.

> **Example:**
> Does the adoption of covenants in housing communities result in rising property values?
> In a letter to the residents of Rivermill Subdivision, a small group of homeowners stated that property values in nearby Providence were double the property values in Rivermill because of such a covenant.

Not only did the above example restate the topic, but it also sparked interest in the issue.

It may seem like a tall order to have to examine a passage and determine if it restates the topic, creates a thesis, AND makes the content captivating; but, if the writer uses one of the following techniques to start their essay, then it's a good bet that the rest of the essay will follow in good form.

- Begin the introduction with a question. Naturally, when a question is posed to the reader, he or she will want to keep reading to find out the answer.
- Begin the introduction with a quote.
- Begin with an anecdote. An anecdote is entertaining and will thus draw in the reader.
- Begin with an illustration or a hypothetical example based on the topic.
- Begin with a true-to-life example.
- Begin with vivid description of something pertaining to the topic.

➤ **Conclusion**—The conclusion of an essay is just as important as the introduction. It should wrap up the writer's thoughts and leave the reader satisfied that a convincing discussion has just taken place. The conclusion should include a restatement of the thesis and end with a general statement, perhaps a warning or a call to action.

✔ Check your work

It's important to understand the function of the introduction and conclusion of an essay. The ACT will often ask you to move a sentence to an area where it makes more sense, or it might ask you what the overall goal of an essay was and if the writer accomplished that goal.

Example:

(1) Stonehenge, one of the many magnificent wonders of the ancient world, has long been shrouded in mystery. (2) Its creation and purpose have generated numerous theories down the years. (3) One thing is for certain: it took many hours of manpower to develop this amazing site.

(4) Hundreds of men would have had to have helped with the construction because there were three phases of it. (5) In Phase 1, a circular ditch and bank were dug out of the ground, probably with the use of crude tools made from animal bones. (6) Phase 2 involved transporting approximately 80 stones, each weighing about 4 tons, from 240 miles away. (7) These stones were to be arranged in a circle, and, although such construction began, it was never finished. (8) Many speculate that a majority of the 4 ton stones that were hauled in were eventually removed and replaced by the larger stones used in Phase 3. (9) Approximately 30 stones were used in Phase 3, each weighing at least 25 tons and each originating 20 miles away from the Stonehenge site. (10) These stones were arranged in an outer circle and then capped with additional stones.

(11) How workers hoisted such heavy stones to their upright positions without modern-day cranes is one of the mysteries surrounding Stonehenge. (12) Without its enigma, however, it would not be the tourist attraction it is today.

1. What is the best version of sentence 4 (reproduced below)?

Hundreds of men would have had to have helped with the construction because there were three phases of it.

(A) Hundreds of men would have had to have helped with the construction because there were three phases of it.
(B) Hundreds of men must have helped with the construction because there were three phases of it.
(C) Hundreds of men must have helped with the construction because there were three phases of construction.
(D) Because there were three phases of construction, hundreds of men must have helped.
(E) Hundreds of men must have helped with the three phases of construction.

2. Which sentence would function best as a concluding sentence after sentence 12 (reproduced below)?

Without its enigma, however, it would not be the tourist attraction it is today.

(A) The purpose of Stonehenge is still an enigma too, although most believe that it was used as a sacred burial ground for prominent people.
(B) Thousands visit the site in Southern England each year, and work is in progress to better preserve Stonehenge so generations can enjoy the wonder.
(C) Tourists can stay in one of the many hotels that have been built within kilometers of Stonehenge.
(D) Many other tourist attractions are nearby as well.
(E) The sheer magnitude of the attraction is amazing.

3. Which transitional word or phrase would best work to improve the flow between sentences 7 and 8 (reproduced below)?

These stones were to be arranged in a circle, and, although such construction began, it was never finished. Many speculate that a majority of the 4 ton stones that were hauled in were eventually removed and replaced by the larger stones used in Phase 3.

(A) However, many speculate...
(B) Nevertheless, many speculate...
(C) Consequently, many speculate...
(D) Therefore, many speculate...
(E) In fact, many speculate...

Even though most questions on the English test will deal with punctuation and grammar, it will not be uncommon for you to come across strategy — or content — questions like the ones above. But we'll go more into detail on these during the Reading Test, which is next.

Reading Test

- **INTRODUCTION**

- **READING METHODS**
  Why Speed Reading Doesn't Work
  Why Previewing Questions Doesn't Work
  Why Pre-reading Topic Sentences Works

- **THE SIX QUESTIONS**
  Main Idea Questions
  Description Questions
  Writing Technique Questions
  Extension Questions
  Application Questions
  Tone Questions

- **PIVOTAL WORDS**

- **THE THREE-STEP METHOD**
  Preview Topic Sentences
  Circle the Pivotal Words and Annotate
  Understand the Six Questions

- **PRACTICE READING TEST**

Introduction

As mentioned earlier, it's too late to fake amnesia. Everyone knows that you know how to read. So the only thing to do now is prepare for the ACT's 35 minutes of reading fun.

Format of the Reading Test

The Reading Test is 35-minutes long and consists of 40 multiple-choice questions. The questions are separated into four sections, and each section tests a different subject. The test contains one passage in each of the following areas:

- **Humanities:** This passage can be about music, dance, theater, art, architecture, language, ethics, literary criticism, and even philosophy.
- **Social Studies:** The social studies passage can include sociology, anthropology, history, geography, psychology, political science, and economics.
- **Natural Sciences:** The natural science passage can cover chemistry, biology, physics, and other physical sciences.
- **Prose Fiction:** The fiction passage can be taken from a novel or a short story; however, don't expect to have seen the passage before.

So, if my math's correct, you'll have 35-minutes to read four passages and answer 10 multiple-choice questions on each passage, which brings us to a grand total of 40 questions.

➤ **Pivotal Words -** *Pivotal words* mark natural places for questions to be drawn. At a pivotal word, the author changes direction. The ACT writers form questions at these junctures to test whether you turned with the author or if you continued to go straight. Rarely do the ACT writers let a pivotal word pass without drawing a question from its sentence.

> **Common Pivotal Words:**
> - But
> - However
> - Despite
> - Nonetheless
> - In contrast
> - Although
> - Yet
> - Nevertheless
> - Except
> - Even though

As mentioned earlier, you will have 35 minutes to read four passages and answer ten questions concerning each passage. That leaves you with about 8 1/2 minutes to spend on each passage and their following questions. It's essential, therefore, to identify the places from which questions will most likely be drawn and concentrate your attention there.

Read the pages that follow carefully. The better you understand how the reading test is written, the better are your chances of success.

Reading Methods

Reading styles are subjective: there is no best method for approaching the written word. A reading technique that works for one person can be awkward and unnatural for another. However, it's really hard to believe that so many books advocate methods that don't work and often cause more confusion than necessary.

Speed Reading

Some books recommend speed-reading the passages on timed tests. This is a mistake. Speed-reading is designed for ordinary, nontechnical material, not for the fluff-less material you'll encounter on the ACT.

The passages on the ACT are often quoted articles that have been condensed to about one-third of their original length. Which means that all the fluff in the original article gets cut, making more room for essential material. This is why speed-reading will not work: the passages on the ACT just contain too much information.

Previewing Questions

Many books also recommend that the questions be read before the passage. Not only does this method seem like a cruel joke, but it also seems like it's advocated merely to give the reader the feeling that he or she is getting the inside stuff on how to ace the test. But there are two big problems with this method. First, some of the questions are almost a paragraph long; reading a paragraph-long question twice will use up precious time. Second, there are up to ten questions per passage, and psychologists have shown that we can hold in our minds a maximum of about three thoughts at any one time (some of us have trouble simply remembering a single phone number). After reading all ten questions, the student will turn to a passage with his mind clouded by half-remembered thoughts. This is, at best, a waste of time. Rather than helping the student better comprehend the passage, it will more likely turn the passage into a disjointed mass of information.

Pre-Reading Topic Sentences

However, one technique that you may find helpful is to preview the passage by reading the first sentence of each paragraph. Generally, the topic of a paragraph is contained in the first sentence. The topic sentence acts, in essence, as a summary of the following text. Furthermore, since each passage is only four to eight paragraphs long, previewing the topic sentences will not use up an inordinate amount of time.

The Six Questions

The key to performing well on the reading test is not the particular reading technique you use (so long as it's neither speed reading nor pre-reading). Rather, the key is to become familiar with the question types on the test, so that you can anticipate the questions that *might* be asked and answer those that *are* asked more quickly and efficiently.

Although you may encounter many different types of questions on the ACT, the following passage will illustrate six of the most common offenders. Read the passage slowly to get a good understanding of the issues.

There are two major systems of criminal procedure in the modern world—the adversarial and the inquisitorial. The former is associated with common law tradition and the latter with civil law tradition. Both systems were historically preceded by the system of private vengeance in which the victim of a crime fashioned his own remedy and administered it privately, either personally or through an agent. The vengeance system was a system of self-help, the essence of which was captured in the slogan "an eye for an eye, a tooth for a tooth." The modern adversarial system is only one historical step removed from the private vengeance system and still retains some of its characteristic features. Thus, for example, even though the right to institute criminal action has now been extended to all members of society and even though the police department has taken over the pretrial investigative functions on behalf of the prosecution, the adversarial system still leaves the defendant to conduct his own pretrial investigation. The trial is still viewed as a duel between two adversaries, refereed by a judge who, at the beginning of the trial, has no knowledge of the investigative background of the case. In the final analysis the adversarial system of criminal procedure symbolizes and regularizes the punitive combat.

By contrast, the inquisitorial system begins historically where the adversarial system stopped its development. It is two historical steps removed from the system of private vengeance. Therefore, from the standpoint of legal anthropology, it is historically superior to the adversarial system. Under the inquisitorial system the public investigator has the duty to investigate not just on behalf of the prosecutor but also on behalf of the defendant. Additionally, the public prosecutor has the duty to present to the court not only evidence that may lead to the conviction of the defendant but also evidence that may lead to his exoneration. This system mandates that both parties permit full pretrial discovery of the evidence in their possession. Finally, in an effort to make the trial less like a duel between two adversaries, the inquisitorial system mandates that the judge take an active part in the conduct of the trial, with a role that is both directive and protective.

Fact-finding is at the heart of the inquisitorial system. This system operates on the philosophical premise that in a criminal case the crucial factor is not the legal rule but the facts of the case and that the goal of the entire procedure is to experimentally recreate for the court the commission of the alleged crime.

➤ **Main Idea Questions** - The process of writing is the process of communicating; all authors have a point that they want to make in their writing. *Main idea questions* test your ability to identify and understand an author's intent. Main idea questions are usually the first questions asked after you read the passage.

> **Common Main Idea Questions:**
> Which one of the following best expresses the main idea of the passage?
> The primary purpose of the passage is to . . .
> In the passage, the author's primary concern is to discuss . . .

Main idea questions are rarely difficult, especially if the author is a clear communicator. If, however, after reading the passage, you don't have a feel for the main idea, review the first and last sentence of each paragraph; these should provide you with a main idea quick fix.

✔ Check your work

Because main idea questions are relatively easy, the ACT writers try to obscure the correct answer by surrounding it with semi-correct choices (detractors) that either overstate or understate the author's main point. Choices that stress specifics tend to understate the main idea; choices that go beyond the scope of the passage tend to overstate the main idea. To answer main idea questions correctly, remember that the answer will summarize the author's argument, yet it won't be too specific or broad.

> **Example:** (Refer to the original passage.)
> The primary purpose of the passage is to
> (A) explain why the inquisitorial system is the best system of criminal justice
> (B) explain how the adversarial and the inquisitorial systems of criminal justice both evolved from the system of private vengeance
> (C) show how the adversarial and inquisitorial systems of criminal justice are being combined into a new and better system
> (D) analyze two systems of criminal justice and deduce which one is better

Choice (A) is incorrect because it overstates the scope of the passage with its use of the extreme word *best*. Choice (B) is incorrect because it understates the scope of the passage by neglecting to mention that the author is trying to prove which system is better. And Choice (C) can be quickly dismissed since it's not mentioned in the passage.

The passage does two things: it presents two systems of criminal justice and shows why one is better than the other. So choice (D) is the correct answer.

➤ **Description Questions** - Description questions, as with main idea questions, refer to a point made by the author. However, description questions refer to a minor point or to incidental information, not to the author's main point.

> **Common Description Questions:**
> • According to the passage . . .
> • In line 37, the author mentions . . . for the purpose of . . .
> • The passage suggests that which one of the following would . . .

The answer to a description question must refer <u>directly</u> to a statement in the passage, not to something implied by it. However, the correct answer will paraphrase a statement in the passage, not give an exact quote. In fact, exact quotes ("Same language" traps) are often used to bait wrong answers.

Caution: When answering a description question, you must find the point in the passage from which the question is drawn. Don't rely on memory—too many obfuscating tactics are used with these questions.

Not only must the correct answer refer directly to a statement in the passage, it must refer to the relevant statement. The correct answer will be surrounded by wrong choices which refer directly to the passage but don't address the question. These choices can be tempting because they tend to be quite close to the actual answer.

Once you spot the sentence to which the question refers, you still must read a few sentences before and after it, to put the question in context. If a question refers to line 20, the information needed to answer it can occur anywhere from line 15 to 25. Even if you have spotted the answer in line 20, you should still read a couple more lines to make certain you have the proper perspective.

> **Example:** (Refer to the original passage.)
> According to the passage, the inquisitorial system differs from the adversarial system in that
> (F)   it does not make the defendant solely responsible for gathering evidence for his case
> (G)   it does not require the police department to work on behalf of the prosecution
> (H)   it does not allow the victim the satisfaction of private vengeance
> (J)   it requires the prosecution to drop a weak case

This is a description question, so the information needed to answer it must be stated in the passage—though not in the same language as in the answer. The needed information is contained at the end of second paragraph, which states that the public prosecutor has to investigate on behalf of both society and the defendant. Thus, the defendant is not solely responsible for investigating his case. Furthermore, the paragraph's opening implies that this feature is not found in the adversarial system. This illustrates why you must determine the context of the situation before you can safely answer the question. The answer is (F).

The other choices can be easily dismissed. (G) is the second best answer. The passage states that in the adversarial system the police assume the work of the prosecution, and the passage states that the inquisitorial system begins where the adversarial system stopped; this implies that in both systems the police work for the prosecution. (H) uses a false claim ploy. The passage states that both systems are removed from the system of private vengeance. (J) is probably true, but it is neither stated nor directly implied by the passage.

Often you will be asked to define a word or phrase based on its context. For this type of question, again you must look at a few lines before and after the word. <u>Don't</u> assume that because the word is familiar you know the definition requested. Words often have more than one meaning, and the ACT often asks for a peculiar or technical meaning of a common word. For example, as a noun *champion* means "the winner," but as a verb *champion* means "to be an advocate for someone." You must consider the word's context to get its correct meaning.

On the ACT, the definition of a word will not use as simple a structure as was used above to define *champion*. One common way the ACT introduces a defining word or phrase is to place it in <u>apposition</u> to the word being defined.

Don't confuse "apposition" with "opposition": they have antithetical [exactly opposite] meanings. Words or phrases in <u>apposition</u> are placed next to each other, and the second word or phrase defines, clarifies, or gives evidence for the first word or phrase. The second word or phrase will be set off from the first by a comma, semicolon, hyphen, or parentheses. (Note: If a comma is not followed by a linking word—such as *and, for, yet*—then the following phrase is probably appositional.)

Example:

The discussions were acrimonious, frequently degenerating into name-calling contests.

After the comma in this sentence, there is no linking word (such as *and, but, because, although*, etc.). Hence the phrase following the comma is in apposition to *acrimonious*—it defines or further clarifies the word. Now acrimonious means bitter, mean-spirited talk, which would aptly describe a name-calling contest.

➤ **Writing Technique Questions** - All coherent writing has a superstructure or blueprint. When writing, we don't just randomly jot down our thoughts; we organize our ideas and present them in a logical manner. For example, we may present evidence that builds up to a conclusion but intentionally leaves the conclusion unstated; or we may present a position and then contrast it with an opposing position; or we may even draw an extended analogy.

There are an endless number of writing techniques that authors use to present their ideas, so we cannot classify them all. However, some techniques are common enough on the ACT to acknowledge.

Compare & Contrast Technique - This technique has a number of variations, but the most common occurrence is when two ideas are developed and then contrasted.

Example: (Refer to the original passage.)

Which one of the following best describes the organization of the passage?

(A) Two systems of criminal justice are compared and contrasted, and one is deemed to be better than the other.
(B) One system of criminal justice is presented as better than another. Then evidence is offered to support that claim.
(C) Two systems of criminal justice are analyzed, and one specific example is examined in detail.
(D) A set of examples is furnished. Then a conclusion is drawn from them.

Clearly the author is comparing and contrasting two criminal justice systems; the opening makes this clear. The author opens the passage by developing (comparing) both systems and then shifts to developing just the adversarial system. He then opens the second paragraph by contrasting the two criminal justice systems and then further develops just the inquisitorial system. Finally, he closes by again contrasting the two systems and implying that the inquisitorial system is superior.

Only choices (A) and (B), have any real merit. They essentially say the same thing—though in different order.

In the passage, the author does not indicate which system is better until the end of paragraph one, and he does not make that certain until paragraph two. This contradicts the order given by choice (B). The answer is (A). (Note: In (A) the order is not specified and therefore is harder to attack, whereas in (B) the order is definite and therefore is easier to attack. Remember that a measured response is harder to attack and therefore is more likely to be the answer.)

Cause & Effect - In this technique, the author typically shows how a particular cause leads to a certain result or set of results. It's not uncommon for this method to introduce a sequence of causes and effects. A causes B, which causes C, which causes D, and so on. Hence B is both the effect of A and the cause of C. The variations on this rhetorical technique can be illustrated by the following schematics:

$$C \longrightarrow E \qquad C \begin{cases} \longrightarrow E \\ \longrightarrow E \\ \longrightarrow E \end{cases} \qquad C \longrightarrow C/E \longrightarrow C/E \longrightarrow E$$

Example *(Short Passage)*:

Thirdly, I worry about the private automobile. It is a dirty, noisy, wasteful, and lonely means of travel. It pollutes the air, ruins the safety and sociability of the street, and exercises upon the individual a discipline which takes away far more freedom than it gives him. It causes an enormous amount of land to be unnecessarily abstracted from nature and from plant life and to become devoid of any natural function. It explodes cities, grievously impairs the whole institution of neighborliness, and fragmentizes and destroys communities. It has already spelled the end of our cities as real cultural and social communities, and has made impossible the construction of any others in their place. Together with the airplane, it has crowded out other, more civilized and more convenient means of transport, leaving older people, infirm people, poor people and children in a worse situation than they were a hundred years ago. It continues to lend a terrible element of fragility to our civilization, placing us in a situation where our life would break down completely if anything ever interfered with the oil supply.

George F. Kennan

Which of the following best describes the organization of the passage?

(F) A problem is presented and then a possible solution is discussed.
(G) The benefits and demerits of the automobile are compared and contrasted.
(H) A topic is presented and a number of its effects are discussed.
(J) A set of examples is furnished to support a conclusion.

This passage is laden with effects. Kennan introduces the cause, the automobile, in the opening sentence and from there on presents a series of effects—the automobile pollutes, enslaves, and so on. Hence the answer is (H). Choice (J) is the second-best choice, but it is disqualified by two flaws: First, in this context, the word *examples* is not as precise as *effects*. Second, the order is wrong: the conclusion, "I worry about the private automobile" is presented first and then the examples: it pollutes, it enslaves, etc.

Position & Evidence - This technique is common with opinionated passages. Equally common is the reverse order. That is, the supporting evidence is presented and then the position or conclusion is stated. Sometimes an author will even present evidence that builds up an unstated position. If this is done skillfully the reader's conclusion will more than likely be the author's conclusion, even though it is unstated.

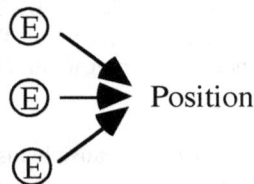

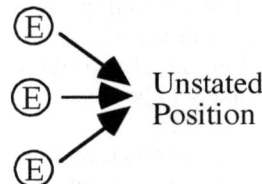

➤ **Extension Questions** - *Extension questions* are the most common question type on the reading test. They require you to go beyond what is stated in the passage, asking you to draw an inference from the passage, to make a conclusion based on the passage, or to identify one of the author's tacit assumptions.

Common Extension Questions:
• It can be inferred from the passage that . . .
• The passage suggests that . . .

✓ Check your work

Since extension questions require you to go beyond the passage, the correct answer must say *more* than what is said in the passage. Beware of language traps when answering these questions. The correct answer will often both paraphrase and extend a statement in the passage, but it will not directly quote it. The answer should not require a quantum leap in thought, but it will add significantly to the ideas presented in the passage.

Example: (Refer to the original passage.)
The author views the prosecution's role in the inquisitorial system as being
(A) an advocate for both society and the defendant
(B) solely responsible for starting a trial
(C) an investigator only
(D) an aggressive but fair investigator

The author states that the prosecutor is bound to present any evidence that may prove the defendant innocent and that he must disclose all pretrial evidence (i.e., have no tricks up his sleeve). This is the essence of fair play. So the answer is probably (D).

Choice (A) overstates the case. Although the prosecutor must disclose any evidence that might show the defendant innocent, the prosecutor is still advocating society's case against the defendant, not for the defendant. As for choice (B): although it is implied that in both systems the right to initiate a case is extended to all people through the prosecutor, it is not stated or implied that this is the only way to start a case. Finally, choice (C) is not mentioned or implied in the passage. The answer, therefore, is (D).

Application: *(Short passage)*
Often, the central problem in any business is that money is needed to make money. The following discusses the sale of equity, which is one response to this problem.

Sale of Capital Stock: a way to obtain capital through the sale of stock to individual investors beyond the scope of one's immediate acquaintances. Periods of high interest rates turn entrepreneurs to this equity market. This involves, of necessity, a dilution of ownership, and many owners are reluctant to take this step for that reason. Whether the owner is wise in declining to use outside equity financing depends upon the firm's long-range prospects. If there is an opportunity for substantial expansion on a continuing basis and if other sources are inadequate, the owner may decide logically to bring in other owners. Owning part of a larger business may be more profitable than owning all of a smaller business.

Small-Business Management, 6th Ed., © 1983 by South-Western Publishing Co.
The passage implies that an owner who chooses not to sell capital stock despite the prospect of continued expansion is
(A) subject to increased regulation
(B) more conservative than is wise under the circumstances
(C) likely to have her ownership of the business diluted
(D) sacrificing security for rapid growth

(A): No. This is not mentioned in the passage. **(B): Yes.** The passage states that *"the owner may decide logically to bring in other owners"*; in other words, the owner would be wise to sell stock in this situation. (C): No. By NOT selling stock, the owner retains full ownership. (D) No. Just the opposite: the owner would be sacrificing a measure of security for growth if she did sell stock.

➤ **Application Questions** - *Application questions* differ from extension questions only in degree. Extension questions ask you to apply what you have learned from the passage to derive new information about the same subject, whereas application questions go one step further, asking you to apply what you have learned from the passage to a different or hypothetical situation.

Common Application Questions:
* Which one of the following is the most likely source of the passage?
* Which one of the following actions would be most likely to have the same effect as the author's actions?

Or

* The author would most likely agree with which one of the following statements?
* Which one of the following sentences would the author be most likely to use to complete the last paragraph of the passage?

✓ Check your work
To answer an application question, take the author's perspective and ask yourself, "What am I arguing for?" Or, "What might make my argument stronger? What might make it weaker?"

Because these questions go well beyond the passage, they tend to be the most difficult. And because application and extension questions require a deeper understanding of the passage, skimming (or worse yet, speed-reading) the passage is ineffective. Skimming may give you the main idea and structure of the passage, but it is unlikely to give you the subtleties of the author's attitude.

> **Example:** (Refer to the original passage.)
> Based on the information in the passage, it can be inferred that which one of the following would most logically begin a paragraph immediately following the passage?
> (F)   Because of the inquisitorial system's thoroughness in conducting its pretrial investigation, it can be concluded that a defendant who is innocent would prefer to be tried under the inquisitorial system, whereas a defendant who is guilty would prefer to be tried under the adversarial system.
> (G)   As the preceding analysis shows, the legal system is in a constant state of flux. For now the inquisitorial system is ascendant, but it will probably be soon replaced by another system.
> (H)   The accusatorial system begins where the inquisitorial system ends. So it is three steps removed from the system of private vengeance, and therefore historically superior to it.
> (J)   Because in the inquisitorial system the judge must take an active role in the conduct of the trial, his competency and expertise have become critical.

The example passage compares and contrasts two systems of criminal justice, implying that the inquisitorial system is superior. We expect the concluding paragraph to sum up this position. The system of justice under which an innocent person would choose to be judged is a logical place for the author to conclude. The answer is (A).

➤ **Tone Questions** - *Tone questions* ask you to identify the writer's attitude or perspective. Is the writer's feeling toward the subject positive, negative, or neutral? Does the writer give his own opinion, or does he objectively present the opinions of others? However, if you're having a hard time feeling out the writer's tone for the subject, check the adjectives that he wrote.

Adjectives and, to a lesser extent, adverbs express our feelings toward a subject. For instance, if we agree with a person who holds strong feelings about a subject, we may describe his opinions as impassioned. On the other hand, if we disagree with him, we may describe his opinions as excitable, which has the same meaning as impassioned but carries a negative connotation.

> **Example:** (Refer to the original passage.)
> The author's attitude toward the adversarial system can best be described as
> (A)   encouraged that it is far removed from the system of private vengeance
> (B)   concerned that it does not allow all members of society to instigate legal action
> (C)   hopeful that it will be replaced by the inquisitorial system
> (D)   doubtful that it is the best vehicle for justice

The author does not reveal his feelings toward the adversarial system until the end of paragraph one. The clause *the adversarial system of criminal procedure symbolizes and regularizes the punitive combat* indicates that he has a negative attitude toward the system. This is confirmed in the second paragraph when he states that the inquisitorial system is historically superior to the adversarial system. So he feels that the adversarial system is deficient.

Only choices (C) and (D) have any real merit. Both are good answers, but which one is better? To decide between two choices attack each: the one that survives is the answer.

A tone question should be answered from what is directly stated in the passage, not from what it implies. Although the author has reservations toward the adversarial system, at no point does he say that he hopes the inquisitorial system will replace it, he may prefer a third system over both. This eliminates (C), so the answer is (D).

The remaining choices are not supported by the passage. Choice (A), using the same language as in the passage, overstates the author's feeling. Remember: **Be wary of extreme words**. Choice (A) would be a better choice if *far* were dropped. And choice (B) and (C) make false claims.

✔ Check your work

Beware of answers that contain extreme emotions. Remember that the passages are taken from academic journals; strong emotions are considered inappropriate. The writers want to display opinions that are considered and reasonable, not spontaneous and off-the-wall. So if an author's tone is negative, it may be disapproving, not snide. Or if his tone is positive, it may be approving, not ecstatic.

Answers must also be indisputable. If answers were subjective, then the writers of the ACT would be deluged with letters from angry test takers, complaining that their test-scores are unfair. To avoid such a difficult position, the writers of the ACT never allow the correct answer to be either controversial or grammatically questionable.

Let's use these theories to answer the following questions.

Example:

Which one of the following most accurately characterizes the author's attitude with respect to Phillis Wheatley's literary accomplishments?

(A)   enthusiastic advocacy
(B)   qualified admiration
(C)   dispassionate impartiality
(D)   detached ambivalence

Even without reference to the passage, this is not a difficult question to answer.

Scholars may advocate each other's work, but they are unlikely to be enthusiastic advocates. Furthermore, the context stretches the meaning of advocacy—to defend someone else's cause or plight. So (A) is unlikely to be the answer.

(B) is the measured response and therefore is probably the answer.

"Dispassionate impartiality" is a rather odd construction; additionally, it is redundant. It could never be the answer to an ACT question. This eliminates (C).

"Detached ambivalence" is not as odd as "dispassionate impartiality," but it is unusual. So (D) is unlikely to be the answer.

Hence, even without the passage we can still find the answer, (B).

Example:

Which one of the following best describes the author's attitude toward scientific techniques?

(A)   critical
(B)   hostile
(C)   idealistic
(D)   neutral

(A) is one of two measured responses offered. Now a scholar may be critical of a particular scientific technique, but only a crackpot would be critical of *all* scientific techniques—eliminate (A).

"Hostile" is far too negative. Scholars consider such emotions juvenile—eliminate (B).

"Idealistic," on the other hand, is too positive; it sounds pollyannaish—eliminate (C).

(D) is the other measured response, and by elimination it is the answer.

Points to Remember

1. The order of questions roughly corresponds to the order of the passage.

2. The six question types are:
    Main Idea
    Description
    Writing Technique
    Extension
    Application
    Tone

3. The main idea of a passage is usually stated in the last, sometimes the first, sentence of the first paragraph. If it's not there, it will probably be the last sentence of the entire passage.

4. If after the first reading you don't have a feel for the main idea, review the first and last sentence of each paragraph.

5. The answer to a description question must refer directly to a statement in the passage, not to something implied by it. However, the correct answer will paraphrase a passage statement, not quote it exactly. In fact, exact quotes are used with these questions to bait wrong answers.

6. When answering a description question, you must find the point in the passage from which the question is drawn.

7. If a description question refers to line 20, the information needed to answer it can occur anywhere from line 15 to 25.

8. Some writing techniques commonly used in the ACT passages are
    A. Compare & Contrast
    B. Cause & Effect
    C. Position & Evidence

9. For extension questions, any answer that refers explicitly to or repeats a statement in the passage is probably be wrong.

10. Application questions differ from extension questions only in degree. Extension questions ask you to apply what you have learned from the passage to derive new information about the same subject, whereas application questions go one step further, asking you to apply what you have learned from the passage to a different or hypothetical situation.

11. To answer an application question, take the perspective of the author and ask yourself, "What am I arguing for? What might make my argument stronger?" And, "What might make it weaker?"

12. Because application questions go well beyond the passage, they tend to be the most difficult.

13. For tone questions, decide whether the writer's tone is positive, negative, or neutral before you look at the answers.

14. If you do not have a feel for the writer's attitude after the first reading, check the adjectives that he chooses.

15. Beware of answers that contain extreme emotion. If an author's tone is negative, it may be disapproving, not snide. If his tone is positive, it may be approving, not ecstatic.

16. Answers must be indisputable. A correct answer will never be controversial or grammatically questionable.

Mentored Exercise

From Romania to Germany, from Tallinn to Belgrade, a major historical process—the death of communism—is taking place. The German Democratic Republic no longer exists as a separate state. And the former German Democratic Republic will serve as the first measure of the price a post-Communist society has to pay for entering the normal European orbit. In Yugoslavia we will see whether the federation can survive without communism.

One thing seems common to all these countries: dictatorship has been defeated and freedom has won, yet the victory of freedom has not yet meant the triumph of democracy. Democracy is something more than freedom. Democracy is freedom institutionalized, freedom submitted to the limits of the law, freedom functioning as an object of compromise between the major political forces on the scene.

We have freedom, but we still have not achieved the democratic order. That is why this freedom is so fragile. In the years of democratic opposition to communism, we supposed that the easiest thing would be to introduce changes in the economy. In fact, we thought that the march from a planned economy to a market economy would take place within the framework of the bureaucratic system and that the market within the Communist state would explode the totalitarian structures. Only then would the time come to build the institutions of a civil society; and only at the end, with the completion of the market economy and the civil society, would the time of great political transformations finally arrive.

The opposite happened. First came the big political change, the great shock, which either broke the monopoly and the principle of Communist Party rule or simply pushed the Communists out of power. Then came the creation of civil society, whose institutions were created in great pain, and which had trouble negotiating the empty space of freedom. Only then, as the third moment of change, the final task was undertaken: that of transforming the totalitarian economy into a normal economy where different forms of ownership and different economic actors will live one next to the other.

Today we are in a typical moment of transition. No one can say where we are headed. The people of the democratic opposition have the feeling that we won. We taste the sweetness of our victory the same way the Communists, only yesterday our prison guards, taste the bitterness of their defeat. Yet, even as we are conscious of our victory, we feel that we are, in a strange way, losing. In Bulgaria the Communists have won the parliamentary elections and will govern the country, without losing their social legitimacy. In Romania the National Salvation Front, largely dominated by people from the old Communist bureaucracy, has won. In other countries democratic institutions seem shaky, and the political horizon is cloudy.

The masquerade goes on: dozens of groups and parties are created, each announces similar slogans, each accuses its adversaries of all possible sins, and each declares itself representative of the national interest. Personal disputes are more important than disputes over values. Arguments over values are fiercer than arguments over ideas.

1. The author originally thought that the order of events in the transformation of communist society would be represented by which one of the following?
   (A) A great political shock would break the totalitarian monopoly, leaving in its wake a civil society whose task would be to change the state-controlled market into a free economy.
   (B) The transformation of the economy would destroy totalitarianism, after which a new and different social and political structure would be born.
   (C) First the people would freely elect political representatives who would transform the economy, which would then undermine the totalitarian structure.
   (D) The change to a democratic state would necessarily undermine totalitarianism, after which a new economic order would be created.

The answer is (B).

This is a description question, so you should locate the point in the passage from which it was drawn. In the third paragraph, the author recalls his expectation that, by introducing the market system, the communist system would topple from within.

Watch out for choice (A). It chronicles how the events actually occurred, not how they were anticipated to occur. It's also baited with the words like *great shock, monopoly,* and *civil society.* Remember: In a description question, the correct answer will paraphrase a passage statement, not quote it exactly. Quoted answer-choices are used as bait for wrong answers.

2. Beginning in the second paragraph, the author describes the complicated relationship between freedom and democracy. In the author's view, which one of the following statements best reflects that relationship?
   (F) A country can have freedom without having democracy.
   (G) If a country has freedom, it necessarily has democracy.
   (H) A country can have democracy without having freedom.
   (J) A country can never have democracy if it has freedom.

The answer is (F).

This is an extension question, so the answer must say more than what is said in the passage, without requiring a quantum leap in thought. The needed reference is *Democracy is something more than freedom* (middle of second paragraph). Since freedom can exist without democracy, freedom alone does not insure democracy.

3. From the passage, a reader could conclude that which one of the following best describes the author's attitude toward the events that have taken place in communist society?
   (A) Relieved that at last the democratic order has surfaced.
   (B) Clearly wants to return to the old order.
   (C) Disappointed with the nature of the democracy that has emerged.
   (D) Surprised that communism was toppled through political rather than economic means.

The answer is (C).

This is a tone question. The key to answering this question is found in the closing comments. There the author states that *The masquerade goes on,* referring to nascent democracies. So he has reservations about the newly emerging democracies.

Watch out for answer-choices like choice (D). Although it is supported by the passage and is a right-enough-sounding answer, its placement in the passage is key. (D) is pulled from a supporting paragraph. The ideas in a concluding paragraph take precedence over those in a supporting paragraph.

Remember: Multiple answer-choices can be slightly correct. You must, however, choose the BEST answer.

4. A cynic who has observed political systems in various countries would likely interpret the author's description of the situation at the end of the passage as
    (F) a distorted description of the new political system.
    (G) a necessary political reality that is a prelude to democracy.
    (H) a fair description of many democratic political systems.
    (J) evidence of the baseness of people.

The answer is (H).

This is an application question. These are like extension questions, but they go well beyond what is stated in the passage. In this case we are asked to interpret the author's comments from a cynic's perspective. Because application questions go well beyond the passage, they are often difficult, as is this one.

A cynic looks at reality from a negative perspective, usually with a sense of dark irony and hopelessness.

Don't make the mistake of choosing (J). Although a cynic is likely to make such a statement, it does not address the subject of the passage—political and economic systems. The passage is not about human nature, at least not directly.

5. Which one of the following does the author imply may have contributed to the difficulties involved in creating a new democratic order in eastern Europe?
    I. The people who existed under the totalitarian structure have not had the experience of negotiating the empty space of freedom.
    II. Mistaking the order in which political, economic, and social restructuring would occur.
    III. Excessive self-interest among the new political activists.
    (A) I only
    (B) II only
    (C) II and III only
    (D) I, II, and III

The answer is (D).

This is an extension question. Statement I is true. In the fourth paragraph, the author implies that the institutions of the new-born, free society were created with great pain because the people lacked experience. Statement II is true. Expectations that the market mechanisms would explode totalitarianism and usher in a new society were dashed, and having to read just one's expectations certainly makes a situation more difficult. Finally, statement III is true. It summarizes the thrust of the passage's closing lines.

6. By stating *even as we are conscious of our victory, we feel that we are, in a strange way, losing* (fifth paragraph) the author means that
    (A) some of the old governments are still unwilling to grant freedom at the individual level.
    (B) some of the new governments are not strong enough to exist as a single federation.
    (C) some of the new democratic governments are electing to retain the old political parties.
    (D) no new parties have been created to fill the vacuum created by the victory of freedom.

The answer is (C).

This is a hybrid extension and description question. Because it refers to a specific point in the passage, you must read a few sentences before and after it. The answer can be found in the fifth paragraph.

Solo Exercise

In the United States the per capita costs of schooling have risen almost as fast as the cost of medical treatment. But increased treatment by both doctors and teachers has shown steadily declining results. Medical expenses concentrated on those above forty-five have doubled several times over a period of forty years with a resulting 3 percent increase in the life expectancy of men. The increase in educational expenditures has produced even stranger results; otherwise President Nixon could not have been moved this spring to promise that every child shall soon have the "Right to Read" before leaving school.

In the United States it would take eighty billion dollars per year to provide what educators regard as equal treatment for all in grammar and high school. This is well over twice the $36 billion now being spent. Independent cost projections prepared at HEW and at the University of Florida indicate that by 1974 the comparable figures will be $107 billion as against the $45 billion now projected, and these figures wholly omit the enormous costs of what is called "higher education," for which demand is growing even faster. The United States, which spent nearly eighty billion dollars in 1969 for "defense," including its deployment in Vietnam, is obviously too poor to provide equal schooling. The President's committee for the study of school finance should ask not how to support or how to trim such increasing costs, but how they can be avoided.

Equal obligatory schooling must be recognized as at least economically unfeasible. In Latin America the amount of public money spent on each graduate student is between 350 and 1,500 times the amount spent on the median citizen (that is, the citizen who holds the middle ground between the poorest and the richest). In the United States the discrepancy is smaller, but the discrimination is keener. The richest parents, some 10 percent, can afford private education for their children and help them to benefit from foundation grants. But in addition they obtain ten times the per capita amount of public funds if this is compared with the per capita expenditure made on the children of the 10 percent who are poorest. The principal reasons for this are that rich children stay longer in school, that a year in a university is disproportionately more expensive than a year in high school, and that most private universities depend—at least indirectly—on tax-derived finances.

Obligatory schooling inevitably polarizes a society; it also grades the nations of the world according to an international caste system. Countries are rated like castes whose educational dignity is determined by the average years of schooling of its citizens, a rating which is closely related to per capita gross national product, and much more painful.

1. Which one of the following best expresses the main idea of the passage?
    (A) The educational shortcomings of the United States, in contrast to those of Latin America, are merely the result of poor allocation of available resources.
    (B) Defense spending is sapping funds which would be better spent in education.
    (C) Obligatory schooling must be scrapped if the goal of educational equality is to be realized.
    (D) Obligatory education does not and cannot provide equal education.

2. The author most likely would agree with which one of the following solutions to the problems presented by obligatory education?
    (F) Education should not be obligatory at all.
    (G) Education should not be obligatory for those who cannot afford it.
    (H) More money should be diverted to education for the poorest.
    (J) Future spending should be capped.

3. According to the passage, education is like health care in all of the following ways EXCEPT:
    (A) It has reached a point of diminishing returns, increased spending no longer results in significant improvement.
    (B) It is unfairly distributed between rich and poor.
    (C) The amount of money being spent on older students is increasing.
    (D) Its cost has increased nearly as fast.

4. Why does the author consider the results from increased educational expenditures to be "even stranger" than those from increased medical expenditures?
    (F) The aging of the population should have had an impact only on medical care, not on education.
    (G) The "Right to Read" should be a bare minimum, not a Presidential ideal.
    (H) Educational spending has shown even poorer results than spending on health care, despite greater increases.
    (J) It inevitably polarizes society.

5. Which one of the following most accurately characterizes the author's attitude with respect to obligatory schooling?
    (A) critical
    (B) neutral
    (C) ambivalent
    (D) resentful

Answers and Solutions to Solo Exercise

1. The answer to a main idea question will summarize the passage, without going beyond it, so the answer is (D).

(A) makes a false claim. The beginning of the third paragraph implies that the discrepancy in allocation of funds is greater in Latin America than the United States.

(B) is implied in the passage but never fully developed.

(C) is the second-best answer-choice. The answer to a main idea question, however, should sum up the passage, not make a conjecture about it. Clearly the author has serious reservations about obligatory schooling, but at no point does he state or imply that it should be scrapped.

(D) aptly summarizes the passage, without going beyond it. The key to seeing this is the opening to paragraph three: *Equal obligatory schooling must be recognized as at least economically unfeasible.* In other words, regardless of any other failings, it cannot succeed economically and therefore cannot provide equal education.

2. This is an application question. These questions tend to be rather difficult, though this one is not. To answer an application question, put yourself in the author's place. If you were arguing his case, which of the solutions would you advocate? The answer is (F).

(F) The author does not merely imply that obligatory education has some shortcomings; he suggests that it is fundamentally flawed. Again this is made clear by the opening to paragraph three, *Equal obligatory schooling must be recognized as at least economically unfeasible.*

(G) is incorrect because nothing in the passage suggests that the author would advocate a solution that would polarize society even more.

(H) is incorrect because it contradicts the author. Paragraph two is dedicated to showing that the United States is too poor to provide equal schooling. You can't divert money you don't have.

(J) is the second-best answer-choice. Although the author probably believes that future spending should be restrained or capped, this understates the thrust of his argument.

3. This is a description question, so we must find the place from which it is drawn. Through the process of elimination, the answer is (B).

(A) is eliminated by the first paragraph.

(B) is correct. In paragraph three, the author does state that there is a keen discrepancy in the funding of education between rich and poor, but a survey of the passage shows that at no point does he mention that this is also the case with health care.

(C) is eliminated by the first paragraph.

(D) is eliminated by the opening.

4. This is an extension question. We are asked to interpret a statement by the author. The needed reference is the closing sentence to paragraph one. Remember: extension questions require you to go beyond the passage, so the answer won't be explicitly stated in the reference—we will have to interpret it.

The implication of President Nixon's promise is that despite increased educational funding many children cannot even read when they graduate from school. The answer is (G).

Don't make the mistake of choosing (H). The opening line to the passage states that educational costs have risen "almost as fast" as medical costs, not faster. (F) is incorrect because the passage never mentions the aging of the population.

Many students who cannot solve this question choose (J)—don't. It uses bait language from the passage, *"inevitably polarizes a society."* The correct answer to an extension question will often both paraphrase and extend a passage statement but will not quote it directly, as in (J).

5. Like most tone questions this one is rather easy. The author clearly does not admire the obligatory school system. This eliminates (B) and (C). Although the author strongly opposes obligatory schooling, the word *resentful* in (D) is too strong and too personal. A scholar would never directly express resentment or envy, even if that is his true feeling. Hence, the answer is (A).

Pivotal Words

As mentioned earlier, you will have 35 minutes to read four passages and answer ten questions concerning each passage. That leaves you with about 8 1/2 minutes to spend on each passage and their following questions. It's essential, therefore, to identify the places from which questions will most likely be drawn and concentrate your attention there.

Pivotal words can help in this regard. Following are the most common pivotal words.

PIVOTAL WORDS

But	Although
However	Yet
Despite	Nevertheless
Nonetheless	Except
In contrast	Even though

As you may have noticed, these words indicate contrast. Pivotal words warn that the author is about to either make a U-turn or introduce a counter-premise (concession to a minor point that weakens the argument).

Example: (Counter-premise)

I submit that the strikers should accept the management's offer. Admittedly, it is less than what was demanded. But it does resolve the main grievance—inadequate health care. Furthermore, an independent study shows that a wage increase greater than 5% would leave the company unable to compete against Japan and Germany, forcing it into bankruptcy.

The conclusion, "the strikers should accept the management's offer," is stated in the first sentence. Then "Admittedly" introduces a concession (counter-premise); namely, that the offer was less than what was demanded. This weakens the speaker's case, but it addresses a potential criticism of his position before it can be made. The last two sentences of the argument present more compelling reasons to accept the offer and form the gist of the argument.

Pivotal words mark natural places for questions to be drawn. At a pivotal word, the author changes direction. The ACT writers form questions at these junctures to test whether you turned with the author or you continued to go straight. Rarely do the ACT writers let a pivotal word pass without drawing a question from its sentence.

Strategy: As you read a passage, circle the pivotal words and refer to them when answering the questions.

Let's apply this theory to the passage on criminal justice. For easy reference, the passage is reprinted here with explanations. The pivotal words are marked in bold.

****

There are two major systems of criminal procedure in the modern world—the adversarial and the inquisitorial. The former is associated with common law tradition and the latter with civil law tradition. Both systems were historically preceded by the system of private vengeance in which the victim of a crime fashioned his own remedy and administered it privately, either personally or through an agent. The vengeance system was a system of self-help, the essence of which was captured in the slogan "an eye for an eye, a tooth for a tooth." The modern adversarial system is only one historical step removed from the private vengeance system and still retains some of its characteristic features. Thus, for example, **even though** the right to institute criminal action has now been extended to all members of society and **even though** the police department has taken over the pretrial investigative functions on behalf of the prosecution, the adversarial system still leaves the defendant to conduct his own pretrial investigation. The trial is still viewed as a duel between two adversaries, refereed by a judge who, at the beginning of the trial has no knowledge of the investigative background of the case. In the final analysis the adversarial system of criminal procedure symbolizes and regularizes the punitive combat.

By contrast, the inquisitorial system begins historically where the adversarial system stopped its development. It is two historical steps removed from the system of private vengeance. Therefore, from the standpoint of legal anthropology, it is historically superior to the adversarial system. Under the inquisitorial system the public investigator has the duty to investigate not just on behalf of the prosecutor **but also** on behalf of the defendant. Additionally, the public prosecutor has the duty to present to the court not only evidence that may lead to the conviction of the defendant **but also** evidence that may lead to his exoneration. This system mandates that both parties permit full pretrial discovery of the evidence in their possession. Finally, in an effort to make the trial less like a duel between two adversaries, the inquisitorial system mandates that the judge take an active part in the conduct of the trial, with a role that is both directive and protective.

Fact-finding is at the heart of the inquisitorial system. This system operates on the philosophical premise that in a criminal case the crucial factor is not the legal rule but the facts of the case and that the goal of the entire procedure is to experimentally recreate for the court the commission of the alleged crime.

****

Even though—Here "even though" is introducing a concession. In the previous sentence, the author stated that the adversarial system is only one step removed from the private vengeance system. The author uses the two concessions as a hedge against potential criticism that he did not consider that the adversarial system has extended the right to institute criminal action to all members of society and that police departments now perform the pretrial investigation. But the author then states that the adversarial system still leaves the defendant to conduct his own pretrial investigation. This marks a good place from which to draw a question. Many people will misinterpret the two concessions as evidence that the adversarial system is two steps removed from the private vengeance system.

By contrast—In this case the pivotal word is not introducing a concession. Instead it indicates a change in thought: now the author is going to discuss the other criminal justice system. This is a natural place to test whether the student has made the transition and whether he will attribute the properties soon to be introduced to the inquisitorial system, not the adversarial system.

But also—In both places, "but also" indicates neither concession nor change in thought. Instead it is part of the coordinating conjunction "not only . . . but also . . . ." Rather than indicating contrast, it emphasizes the second element of the pair.

Let's see how these pivotal words can help answer the questions in the last section. The first is from the Description Section:

Example:
According to the passage, the inquisitorial system differs from the adversarial system in that
(A)   it does not make the defendant solely responsible for gathering evidence for his case
(B)   it does not require the police department to work on behalf of the prosecution
(C)   it does not allow the victim the satisfaction of private vengeance
(D)   it requires the prosecution to drop a weak case

The pivotal phrase "by contrast" flags the second paragraph as the place to begin looking. The pivotal phrase "but also" introduces the answer—namely that the prosecutor must also investigate "on behalf of the defendant." The answer is (A).

The next question is from the Writing Techniques Section:

Example:
Which one of the following best describes the organization of the passage?
(A)   Two systems of criminal justice are compared and contrasted, and one is deemed to be better than the other.
(B)   One system of criminal justice is presented as better than another. Then evidence is presented to support that claim.
(C)   Two systems of criminal justice are analyzed, and one specific example is examined in detail.
(D)   A set of examples is presented. Then a conclusion is drawn from them.

The pivotal phrase "by contrast" gives this question away. The author is comparing and contrasting two criminal justice systems, which the opening pivotal word introduces. Hence the answer is (A).

For our final example, consider the question from the Extension Section:

Example:
The author views the prosecution's role in the inquisitorial system as being
(A)   an advocate for both society and the defendant
(B)   solely responsible for starting a trial
(C)   an investigator only
(D)   an aggressive but fair investigator

The information needed to answer this question is introduced by the pivotal phrase, "but also." There it is stated that the prosecutor must present evidence that may exonerate the defendant; that is, he must act fairly. The answer is (D).

Points to Remember

1.   Pivotal words indicate that the author is about to make a U-turn in thought or introduce a counter-premise (concession to a minor point that weakens the argument).

2.   The following are the most common pivotal words:

But	**Although**	**Except**
However	**Yet**	**Even though**
Despite	**Nevertheless**	**In contrast**
Nonetheless		

3.   Pivotal words mark natural places for questions to be drawn. At a pivotal word, the author changes direction. The ACT writers form questions at these junctures to test whether you made the turn with the author or whether you continued to go straight. Rarely do the ACT writers pass a pivotal word without drawing a question from its sentence.

4.   As you read each passage, circle the pivotal words.

Mentored Exercise

Directions: This passage is followed by a group of questions to be answered based on what is stated or implied in the passage. Choose the best answer; the one that most accurately and completely answers the question. Hints, insights, and answers are given.

The premise with which the multiculturalists begin is unexceptional: that it is important to recognize and to celebrate the wide range of cultures that exist in the United States. In what sounds like a reflection of traditional American pluralism, the multiculturalists argue that we must recognize difference, that difference is legitimate; in its kindlier versions, multiculturalism represents the discovery on the part of minority groups that they can play a part in molding the larger culture even as they are molded by it. And on the campus multiculturalism, defined more locally as the need to recognize cultural variations among students, has tried with some success to talk about how a racially and ethnically diverse student body can enrich everyone's education.

Phillip Green, a political scientist at Smith and a thoughtful proponent of multiculturalism, notes that for a significant portion of the students the politics of identity is all-consuming. Students he says "are unhappy with the thin gruel of rationalism. They require a therapeutic curriculum to overcome not straightforward racism but ignorant stereotyping."

(1) But multiculturalism's hard-liners, who seem to make up the majority of the movement, damn as racism any attempt to draw the myriad of American groups into a common American culture. For these multiculturalists, differences are absolute, irreducible, intractable—occasions not for understanding but for separation. The multiculturalist, it turns out, is not especially interested in the great American hyphen, in the syncretistic (and therefore naturally tolerant) identities that allow Americans to belong to more than a single culture, to be both particularists and universalists.

The time-honored American mixture of assimilation and traditional allegiance is denounced as a danger to racial and gender authenticity. This is an extraordinary reversal of the traditional liberal commitment to a "truth" that transcends parochialisms. In the new race/class/gender formation, universality is replaced by, among other things, feminist science Nubian numerals (as part of an Afro-centric science), and what Marilyn Frankenstein of the University of Massachusetts-Boston describes as "ethno-mathematics," in which the cultural basis of counting comes to the fore.

The multiculturalists insist on seeing all perspectives as tainted by the perceiver's particular point of view. Impartial knowledge, they argue, is not possible, because ideas are simply the expression of individual identity, or of the unspoken but inescapable assumptions that are inscribed in a culture or a language. The problem, **(2) however,** with this warmed-over Nietzscheanism is that it threatens to leave no ground for anybody to stand on. So the multi-culturalists make a leap, necessary for their own intellectual survival, and proceed to argue that there are some categories, such as race and gender, that do in fact embody an unmistakable knowledge of oppression. Victims are at least epistemologically lucky. Objectivity is a mask for oppression. And so an appalled former 1960s radical complained to me that self-proclaimed witches were teaching classes on witchcraft. "They're not teaching students how to think," she said, "they're telling them what to believe."

****

There are two critical pivotal words in this passage—(1) **But**, and (2) **however**.

(1) **But**. Until this point, the author did not reveal his feeling toward multiculturalism. He presented an objective, if not positive, view of the movement. However, "**But**" introduced an abrupt change in direction (a U-turn). Before he talked about the "kindlier" multiculturalism—to which he appears to be sympathetic. Now he talks about "hard-line" multiculturalism, which he implies is intolerant and divisive.

The pivotal word "**but**" doesn't just change the direction of the passage, it introduces the main idea: that multiculturalism has become an extreme and self-contradictory movement.

(2) **however**. This is the second critical pivotal word. The author opened this paragraph by presenting the multiculturalist's view; now he will criticize their positions.

1. Which one of the following ideas would a multiculturalist NOT believe?
   (A) That we should recognize and celebrate the differences among the many cultures in the United States.
   (B) That we can never know the "truth" because "truth" is always shaped by one's culture.
   (C) That "difference" is more important than "sameness."
   (D) That different cultures should work to assimilate themselves into the mainstream culture so that eventually there will be no excuse for racism.

The sentence introduced by the pivotal word "**But**" gives away the answer to this question.

The answer is (D).

2. According to a hard-line multiculturalist, which one of the following groups is most likely to know the "truth" about political reality?
   (A) Educated people who have learned how to see reality from many different perspectives.
   (B) A minority group that has suffered oppression at the hands of the majority.
   (C) High government officials who have privileged access to secret information.
   (D) Minorities who through their education have risen above the socioeconomic position occupied by most members of their ethnic group.

This is a rather hard extension question.

Hint: A subjugated minority group has at least the "unmistakable knowledge of oppression" (last paragraph)

Don't make the mistake of choosing (D). Upper class minorities have simply exchanged one tainted point of view for another—and probably a more tainted one since the adopted position does not allow for knowledge of "oppression."

The answer is (B).

3. The author states that in a "kindlier version" of multiculturalism, minorities discover "that they can play a part in molding the larger culture even as they are molded by it." If no new ethnic groups were incorporated into the American culture for many centuries to come, which one of the following would be the most probable outcome of this "kindlier version"?

   (A) At some point in the future, there would be only one culture with no observable ethnic differences.
   (B) Eventually the dominant culture would overwhelm the minority cultures, who would then lose their ethnic identities.
   (C) The multiplicity of ethnic groups would remain but the characteristics of the different ethnic groups would change.
   (D) The smaller ethnic groups would remain, and they would retain their ethnic heritage.

This application question clearly goes well beyond the passage.

If no new ethnic groups were incorporated into the American culture, then the interplay between the larger and smaller groups would continue, with both groups changing, until there would be only one common (and different from any original) group.

The answer is (A).

4. The author speaks about the "politics of identity" that Phillip Green, a political scientist at Smith, notes is all-consuming for many of the students. Considering the subject of the passage, which one of the following best describes what the author means by "the politics of identity"?

    (A) The attempt to discover individual identities through political action
    (B) The political agenda that aspires to create a new pride of identity for Americans
    (C) The current obsession for therapy groups that help individuals discover their inner selves
    (D) The trend among minority students to discover their identities in their ethnic groups rather than in their individuality

    This is an extension question. You may find the classification of the these problems as "application" or "extension" to be somewhat arbitrary or even disagree with a particular classification. As mentioned before, application and extension questions differ only in degree. Question 3 is clearly an application question; by asking you to make a conjecture about the future, it goes well beyond the passage. How to classify Question 4, however, is not so clear. We classified it as an extension question because it seems to be asking merely for the author's true meaning of the phrase "the politics of identity." That is, it stays within the context of the passage.

    Trap: Don't be led astray by (B); it uses the word "political" to tempt you. Although it is perhaps a good description, it is not within the context of the passage, which focuses on ethnic politics, not national identities through "roots."

    The answer is (D).

5. Which one of the following best describes the attitude of the writer toward the multicultural movement?

    (A) Tolerant. It may have some faults, but it is well-meaning overall.
    (B) Critical. A formerly admirable movement has been taken over by radical intellectuals.
    (C) Disinterested. He seems to be presenting an objective report.
    (D) Enthusiastic. The author embraces the multiculturalist movement and is trying to present it in a favorable light.

    Like most tone questions this one is rather easy.

    To get a feel for the author's attitude, check the adjectives he chooses. The author starts by introducing the "kindlier" version of multiculturalism and describes a proponent of multiculturalism, Phillip Green, as "thoughtful." Then he introduces the "hard liners" who "damn" any attempt at cultural assimilation. He feels that the movement has changed; that it has gone bad.

    The answer is (B).

6. "Multiculturalist relativism" is the notion that there is no such thing as impartial or objective knowledge. The author seems to be grounding his criticism of this notion on

    (A) the clear evidence that science has indeed discovered "truths" that have been independent of both language and culture.
    (B) the conclusion that relativism leaves one with no clear notions of any one thing that is true.
    (C) the absurdity of claiming that knowledge of oppression is more valid than knowledge of scientific facts.
    (D) the agreement among peoples of all cultures as to certain undeniable truths—e.g., when the sky is clear, day is warmer than night.

    This is an another extension question.

    Hint: The answer can be derived from the pivotal sentence containing "however" (2).

    The answer is (B).

Solo Exercise

Directions: This passage is followed by a group of questions to be answered based on what is *stated* or *implied* in the passage. Choose the *best* answer - the one that most accurately and completely answers the question.

According to usage and conventions which are at last being questioned but have by no means been overcome, the social presence of a woman is different in kind from that of a man. A man's presence is dependent upon the promise of power which he embodies. If the promise is large and credible his presence is striking. If it is small or incredible, he is found to have little presence. The promised power may be moral, physical, temperamental, economic, social, sexual—but its object is always exterior to the man. A man's presence suggests what he is capable of doing to you or for you. His presence may be fabricated, in the sense that he pretends to be capable of what he is not. But the pretense is always toward a power which he exercises on others.

By contrast, a woman's presence expresses her own attitude to herself, and defines what can and cannot be done to her. Her presence is manifest in her gestures, voices, opinions, expressions, clothes, chosen surroundings, taste—indeed there is nothing she can do which does not contribute to her presence. Presence for a woman is so intrinsic to her person that men tend to think of it as an almost physical emanation, a kind of heat or smell or aura.

To be born a woman has been to be born, within an allotted and confined space, into the keeping of men. The social presence of women has developed as a result of their ingenuity in living under such tutelage within such a limited space. But this has been at the cost of a woman's self being split into two. A woman must continually watch herself. Whilst she is walking across a room or whilst she is weeping at the death of her father, she can scarcely avoid envisaging herself walking or weeping. From earliest childhood she has been taught and persuaded to survey herself continually.

And so she comes to consider the *surveyor* and the *surveyed* within her as the two constituent yet always distinct elements of her identity as a woman.

She has to survey everything she is and everything she does because how she appears to others, and ultimately how she appears to men, is of crucial importance for what is normally thought of as the success of her life. Her own sense of being in herself is supplanted by a sense of being appreciated as herself by another. Men survey women before treating them. Consequently how a woman appears to a man can determine how she will be treated. To acquire some control over this process, women must contain it and internalize it. That part of a woman's self which is the surveyor treats the part which is the surveyed so as to demonstrate to others how her whole self would like to be treated. And this exemplary treatment of herself by herself constitutes her presence. Every woman's presence regulates what is and is not "permissible" within her presence. Every one of her actions—whatever its direct purpose or motivation—is also read as an indication of how she would like to be treated. If a woman throws a glass on the floor, this is an example of how she treats her own emotion of anger and so of how she would wish to be treated by others. If a man does the same, his action is only read as an expression of his anger. If a woman makes a good joke this is an example of how she treats the joker in herself and accordingly of how she as joker-woman would like to be treated by others. Only a man can make a good joke for its own sake.

1. According to "usage and conventions," appearance is NECESSARILY a part of reality for

   (A) men
   (B) women
   (C) both men and women
   (D) neither men nor women

2. In analyzing a woman's customary "social presence," the author hopes to

   (A) justify and reinforce it.
   (B) understand and explain it.
   (C) expose and discredit it.
   (D) demonstrate and criticize it.

3. It can be inferred from the passage that a woman with a Ph.D. in psychology who gives a lecture to a group of students is probably MOST concerned with

   (A) whether her students learn the material.
   (B) what the males in the audience think of her.
   (C) how she comes off as a speaker in psychology.
   (D) finding a husband.

4. The passage portrays women as

   (A) victims
   (B) liars
   (C) actresses
   (D) politicians

5. Which one of the following is NOT implied by the passage?

   (A) Women have split personalities.
   (B) Men are not image-conscious.
   (C) Good looks are more important to women than to men.
   (D) A man is defined by what he does, whereas a woman is defined by how she appears.

6. The primary purpose of the passage is to

   (A) compare and contrast woman's presence and place in society with that of man's.
   (B) discuss a woman's presence and place in society and to contrast it with a man's presence and place.
   (C) illustrate how a woman is oppressed by society.
   (D) explain why men are better than women at telling jokes.

Answers and Solutions to Exercise

This passage is filled with pivotal words, some of which are crucial to following the author's train of thought. We will discuss only the critical pivotal words. The first pivotal word, "but" (middle of the first paragraph), introduces a distinction between a man's presence and a woman's: a man's is external, a woman's internal. The second pivotal word, "by contrast," introduces the main idea of the passage. The author opened the passage by defining a man's presence; now she will define a woman's presence. The last pivotal word, "but" (middle of the third paragraph), also introduces a change in thought. Now the author discusses how a woman's presence has split her identity into two parts—the *surveyor* and the *surveyed*. By closing with, *"Only a man can make a good joke for its own sake,"* the author is saying a man can concentrate on the punch line, whereas a woman must concentrate on its delivery.

1. This is a description question. The needed reference is contained in the second paragraph: *"there is nothing [a woman] can do which does not contribute to her presence. Presence for a woman is intrinsic to her person . . ."* If something is intrinsic to you, then it necessarily is part of your reality. Hence the answer is (B).

Note the question refers to "usage and conventions" discussed in the passage, not to any other way of viewing the world—such as your own!

2. Although the author opens the passage with a hint that she doesn't like the customary sex roles (*"conventions which are at last being questioned"*), the rest of the passage is explanatory and analytical. So (C) and (D) are too strong. The answer is (B).

3. This is an application question; we are asked to apply what we have learned from the passage to a hypothetical situation.

The best way to analyze this question is to compare the speaker to a joke-teller. The passage paints a portrait of a woman as most concerned with the image she presents to the world. She is not concerned with the speech or joke, *per se*, rather with how she delivers it. *"Only a man can make a good joke for its own sake."* The answer is (C).

Don't make the mistake of choosing (B). Although men have, in the main, molded her self-image, she has gone beyond that; she now measures herself in the abstract: "how will I come off to the ultimately critical audience?" and not "how will actual audience members see me?"

4. This description question is a bit tricky because the second-best choice is rather good. Women are concerned with the image they present, so they cannot be themselves—they must act their part. Hence, the answer is (C).

You may have been tempted by (A). According to the passage, women are thrown into the role of an actress, "into the keeping of men." So, like victims, they are not responsible for their social position. However, nothing in the passage directly suggests that it is wrong for women to be in this position or that women attempt to refuse this role. According to the passage, therefore, women are not, strictly speaking, victims. (*Victim* means "someone not in control of something injurious happening to him or her.")

5. This is an extension question. The passage discusses the fact that a man may fabricate his image (first paragraph). This suggests that men *are* conscious of their images, but the passage also states that image is not intrinsic to their personalities, as it is for women. The answer is (B).

6. This is a rather hard main idea question because the second-best choice, (A), is quite good.

The passage does open with a discussion of a man's presence. But in paragraph two the pivotal phrase "by contrast" introduces a woman's presence; from there the discussion of a man's presence is only in regard to how it affects a woman's. So a woman's presence is the main idea; contrasting it with a man's presence is secondary. (B) gives the proper emphasis to these two purposes.

The Three-Step Method

If speed-reading doesn't work — ever — and guessing just isn't your style, then what does work? If we combine three of the pivotal points we discussed earlier — previewing topic sentences, circling pivotal words, and understanding the six most common question types — then we can create a reading method that works. Otherwise known as the Three-Step Method.

The Three-Step Method:
1. (Optional) Preview the first sentence of each paragraph.
2. Read the passage at a slightly faster pace, and annotate the passage or circle any pivotal words. Use your marks as reference points when answering the following questions. Following are some guidance marks for your annotation pleasure.
   A = Author's Attitude
   C = Complex point
   ? = Question? I don't understand this part (you can bet that this area will be important to at least one question)
   SP = Significant point
   ! = Exclamation! Strong opinion
   W = Weak, questionable or unsupported argument or premise
3. Stay alert to places from which any of the six questions might be drawn:
   d. Main Idea
   e. Description
   f. Writing Technique
   g. Extension
   h. Application
   i. Tone

The *three-step method* should be viewed as a dynamic — not a static — process. Steps will often overlap each other and will not always be performed in the same order. Analyzing a passage to understand how it is constructed can be compared to dismantling an engine to understand how it was built. Some may dismantle the entire engine and then label the parts, while others may label the parts as they take them off the engine. Likewise, with writing, each person's process will be different.

Let's apply the three-step method to the following passage. Begin by previewing the first sentence of each paragraph:

Passage:

That placebos can cure everything from dandruff to leprosy is well known. They have a long history of use by witch doctors, faith healers, and even modern physicians, all of whom refuse to admit their efficacy. Modern distribution techniques can bring this most potent of medicines to the aid of everyone, not just those lucky enough to receive placebos in a medical testing program.

Every drug tested would prove effective if special steps were not taken to neutralize the placebo effect. This is why drug tests give half the patients the new medication and half a harmless substitute. These tests prove the value of placebos because approximately five percent of the patients taking them are cured even though the placebos are made from substances that have been carefully selected to be useless.

Most people feel that the lucky patients in a drug test get the experimental drug because the real drug provides them a chance to be cured. **(1) Yet** analysis shows that patients getting the placebo may be the lucky ones because they may be cured without risking any adverse effects the new drug may have. Furthermore, the drug may well be found worthless and to have severe side effects. No harmful side effects result from placebos.

Placebos regularly cure more than five percent of the patients and would cure considerably more if the doubts associated with the tests were eliminated. Cures are principally due to the patient's faith, **(2) yet** the patient must have doubts knowing that he may or may not be given the new drug, which itself may or may not prove to be an effective drug. Since he knows the probability of being given the true drug is about fifty percent, the placebo cure rate would be more than doubled by removing these doubts if cures are directly related to faith.

The actual curing power of placebos probably stems from the faith of the patient in the treatment. This suggests that cure rates in the ten percent range could be expected if patients are given placebos under the guise of a proven cure, even when patients know their problems are incurable.

It may take a while to reach the ten percent level of cure because any newly established program will not have cultivated the word-of-mouth advertising needed to insure its success. One person saying "I was told that my problem was beyond medical help, but they cured me," can direct countless people to the treatment with the required degree of faith. Furthermore, when only terminal illnesses are treated, those not cured tell no one of the failure.

Unfortunately, placebo treatment centers cannot operate as nonprofit businesses. The nonprofit idea was ruled out upon learning that the first rule of public medicine is never to give free medicine. Public health services know that medicine not paid for by patients is often not taken or not effective because the recipient feels the medicine is worth just what it cost him. **(3) Even though** the patients would not know they were taking sugar pills, the placebos cost so little that the patients would have no faith in the treatment. Therefore, though it is against higher principles, treatment centers must charge high fees for placebo treatments. This sacrifice of principles, however, is a small price to pay for the greater good of the patients.

Topic Sentence Previews:

j.   The sentence *"That placebos can cure everything from dandruff to leprosy is well known "*implies that the passage is about placebos and that they are perhaps cure-alls.

k.   The sentence *"Every drug tested would prove effective if special steps were not taken to neutralize the placebo effect"* gives the first bit of evidence supporting the topic sentence.

l.   The sentence *"Most people feel that the lucky patients in a drug test get the experimental drug because the real drug provides them a chance to be cured"* might be introducing a counter-premise or pivotal point. We won't know until we read the passage.

m.   The sentence *"Placebos regularly cure more than five percent of the patients and would cure considerably more if the doubts associated with the tests were eliminated"* provides more support for the topic sentence.

n.   The sentence *"The actual curing power of placebos probably stems from the faith of the patient in the treatment"* explains why the topic sentence is true.

o.   The sentence *"It may take a while to reach the ten percent level of cure because any newly established program will not have cultivated the word-of-mouth advertising needed to insure its success"* is hard to interpret, and doesn't really help with getting a glimpse of the passage.

p.   The sentence *"Unfortunately, placebo treatment centers cannot operate as nonprofit businesses"* seems to be off the subject. Again, this does not help us.

In summary, although the last two sentences were not useful, we now have a good idea of what the passage is about: *how* and *why* placebos are effective.

The next step in the Three-Step Method is to fully read the passage, all the while keeping an eye out for places where the writer's of the ACT might have drawn questions.

Go back to the passage. As you read it, circle pivotal words and annotate any key points that you think are relevant. I've already marked some pivotal word for you, so all you need to do is watch out for key points.

Done? Good. Remember: Don't be afraid to mark up the passages on the ACT. Not only will doing so help you understand the material you've just read, but it will also make the text easier to navigate the second time around, when answering questions.

Let's apply your knowledge of the passage on to some questions. Answers will immediately follow the questions.

1.   Which one of the following best expresses the main idea of the passage?
    (A) Placebo treatment is a proven tool of modern medicine and its expanded use would benefit society's health.
    (B) Because modern technology allows for distribution of drugs on a massive scale, the proven efficacy of the placebo is no longer limited to a privileged few.
    (C) The curative power of the placebo is so strong that it should replace proven drugs because the patients receiving the placebo will then be cured without risking any adverse side effects.
    (D) The price of placebo treatment must be kept artificially high because patients have little faith in inexpensive treatments.

This is a main idea question.

As we found by previewing the topic sentences, the passage is about the efficiency of placebo treatment. Careful reading shows that the passage also promotes expanded use of placebos. Hence, the answer is (A). The other choices can be quickly dismissed.

The other choices can be quickly dismissed. (B) is the second-best choice: the author *does* mention that modern distribution techniques can bring the curative power of placebos to everyone, but he does <u>not</u> fully develop that idea. This answer-choice is tempting because it is contained in the topic paragraph. As to (C), it overstates the author's claim. Although in the third paragraph, the author states that those who receive the placebos may be the lucky ones, this is referring to new, unproven drugs, not to established drugs. As to (D), it, like (B), is mentioned in the passage but is not fully developed. It's tempting because it appears in the last paragraph — a natural place for the conclusion. Finally, (E) is neither mentioned nor implied by the passage

2. Which one of the following is most analogous to the idea presented in the last paragraph?
    (F) Buying a television at a discount house
    (G) Making an additional pledge to charity
    (H) Choosing the most expensive dishwasher in a manufacturer's line
    (J) Waiting until a book comes out in paperback

This is an application question.

The information needed to answer this question is heralded by the pivotal phrase *Even though* (middle of last paragraph). The implication of that sentence is you get what you pay for. This would motivate one to buy the most expensive item in a manufacturer's line. The answer is (H).

3. According to the passage, when testing a new drug medical researchers give half of the subjects the test drug and half a placebo because
    (A) proper statistical controls should be observed.
    (B) this method reduces the risk of maiming too many subjects if the drug should prove to be harmful.
    (C) all drugs which are tested would prove to be effective otherwise.
    (D) most drugs would test positively otherwise.

This is a description question.

Since this is a description question, you must refer to the passage to answer it. The opening sentence to paragraph two contains the needed information. That sentence states *Every drug would prove effective if special steps were not taken to neutralize the placebo effect*. So the answer is (C).

Choice (D) illustrates why you must refer directly to the passage to answer a description question: unless you have a remarkable memory, you would be unsure whether the statement was that **all** or **most** drugs would prove effective.

4. It can be inferred from the passage that the author might
    (F) believe that the benefits of a placebo treatment program which leads patients to believe they were getting a real drug would outweigh the moral issue of lying.
    (G) support legislation outlawing the use of placebos.
    (H) open up a medical clinic that would treat patients exclusively through placebo methods.
    (J) believe that factors other than faith are responsible for the curative power of the placebo.

This is an extension question.

The answer is (F). One of the first clues to the author's view on this issue is contained in the pivotal clause *yet the patient . . . effective drug* (fourth paragraph). Later, in paragraph six, the author nearly advocates that the patient should not be told that he or she might be receiving a placebo. Finally, the closing line of the passage cinches it. There, the author implies that certain principles *can be* sacrificed for the greater good of the patients.

5. Which one of the following best describes the organization of the material presented in the passage?
    (A) A general proposition is stated; then evidence for its support is given.
    (B) Two types of drug treatment — placebo and non-placebo — are compared and contrasted.
    (C) A result is stated, its cause is explained, and an application is suggested.
    (D) A series of examples is presented; then a conclusion is drawn from them.

This is a writing technique question.

In the first paragraph the author claims that placebos can cure everything from dandruff to leprosy—this is a result. Then in paragraphs two, three, four, and five, he explains the causes of the result. Finally, he alludes to an application—the placebo treatment centers. The answer is (C).

6.   Which one of the following most accurately characterizes the author's attitude toward placebo treatment?
     (F)   reserved advocacy
     (G)   feigned objectivity
     (H)   summary dismissal
     (J)   perplexed by its effectiveness

This is a tone question.

This question is a little tricky. Only choices (F) and (G) have any real merit. Although the passage has a detached, third-person style, the author *does* present his opinions—namely that placebos work and that their use should be expanded. However, that advocacy is reserved, so the answer is (F).

The other choices can be quickly eliminated:
   (H)   *Summary dismissal* is not supported by the passage. Besides, a scholar would never summarily dismiss something; he would consider it carefully—or at least give the impression that he has— before rejecting it. This eliminates (H).
   (J)   Given the human ego, we are unlikely to admit that we don't understand the subject we are writing about. This eliminates (J).

Points to Remember

THE THREE-STEP METHOD
   1.   (Optional) Preview the first sentence of each paragraph.

   2.   Read the passage at a faster than usual pace (but not to the point that comprehension suffers), being alert to places from which any of the six questions might be drawn:
        a.   Main Idea
        b.   Description
        c.   Writing Technique
        d.   Extension
        e.   Application
        f.   Tone

   3.   Annotate the passage and circle any pivotal words. Then use these as reference points for answering the questions. Following are some common annotation marks (you may want to add to this list):
        A = **A**uthor's Attitude
        C = **C**omplex point
        ? = **Question?** I don't understand this part (you can bet that this area will be important to *at least* one question)
        SP = **S**ignificant **p**oint
        ! = **Exclamation!** Strong opinion
        W = **W**eak, questionable or unsupported argument or premise

One final word: Try to enjoy the passages. Although it may seem like a chore, some of the reading material on the ACT is very interesting. If you go into a passage with a positive outlook rather than a negative one, you might be surprised how much easier the material will be to read.

Mentored Exercise

<u>Directions:</u> This passage is followed by a group of questions to be answered based on what is <u>stated</u> or <u>implied</u> in the passage. Choose the <u>best</u> answer; the one that most accurately and completely answers the question.

Following the Three-Step Method, we preview the first sentence of each paragraph in the passage: (The body of the passage will be presented later.)

The enigmatic opening sentence *"Many readers, I suspect, will take the title of this article [Women, Fire, and Dangerous Things] as suggesting that women, fire, and dangerous things have something in common—say, that women are fiery and dangerous"* does not give us much of a clue to what the passage is about.

The sentence *"The classical view that categories are based on shared properties is not entirely wrong"* is more helpful. It tells us the passage is about categorization and that there are at least two theories about it: the classical view, which has merit, and the modern view, which is apparently superior.

The sentence *"Categorization is not a matter to be taken lightly"* merely confirms the subject of the passage.

Although only one sentence was helpful, previewing did reveal a lot about the passage's subject matter— categorization. Now we read the passage, circling pivotal words, annotating, and noting likely places from which any of the six questions might be drawn. After each paragraph, we will stop to analyze and interpret what the author has presented:

> Many readers, I suspect, will take the title of this article [*Women, Fire, and Dangerous Things*] as suggesting that women, fire, and dangerous things have something in common—say, that women are fiery and dangerous. Most feminists I've mentioned it to have loved the title for that reason, though some have hated it for the same reason. But the chain of inference—from conjunction to categorization to commonality—is the norm. The inference is based on the common idea of what it means to be in the same category: things are categorized together on the basis of what they have in common. The idea that categories are defined by common properties is not only our everyday folk theory of what a category is, it is also the principle technical theory—one that has been with us for more than two thousand years.

In this paragraph, the author introduces the subject matter of the passage—categorization. And the pivotal sentence, introduced by "but," explains the classical theory of categorization, albeit rather obtusely. Namely, like things are placed in the same category.

> Now we consider the second paragraph:

> The classical view that categories are based on shared properties is not entirely wrong. We often do categorize things on that basis. But that is only a small part of the story. In recent years it has become clear that categorization is far more complex than that. A new theory of categorization, called *prototype theory*, has emerged. It shows that human categorization is based on principles that extend far beyond those envisioned in the classical theory. One of our goals is to survey the complexities of the way people really categorize. For example, the title of this book was inspired by the Australian aboriginal language Dyirbal, which has a category, *balan*, that actually includes women, fire, and dangerous things. It also includes birds that are *not* dangerous, as well as exceptional animals, such as the platypus, bandicoot, and echidna. This is not simply a matter of categorization by common properties.

In this paragraph, the second pivotal word—but—is crucial. It introduces the main idea of the passage— the prototype theory of categorization. Now everything that is introduced should be attributed to the prototype theory, <u>not</u> to the classical theory. Wrong answer-choices are likely to be baited with just the opposite.

The author states that the prototype theory goes "far beyond" the classical theory. Although he does not tell us what the prototype theory *is*, he does tell us that it *is not* merely categorization by common properties.

Now we turn to the third paragraph:

> Categorization is not a matter to be taken lightly. There is nothing more basic than categorization to our thought, perception, action and speech. Every time we see something as a *kind* of thing, for example, a tree, we are categorizing. Whenever we reason about *kinds* of things—chairs, nations, illnesses, emotions, any kind of thing at all—we are employing categories. Whenever we intentionally perform any *kind* of action, say something as mundane as writing with a pencil, hammering with a hammer, or ironing clothes, we are using categories. The particular action we perform on that occasion is a *kind* of motor activity, that is, it is in a particular category of motor actions. They are never done in exactly the same way, yet despite the differences in particular movements, they are all movements of a kind, and we know how to make movements of that kind. And any time we either produce or understand any utterance of any reasonable length, we are employing dozens if not hundreds of categories: categories of speech sounds, of words, of phrases and clauses, as well as conceptual categories. Without the ability to categorize, we could not function at all, either in the physical world or in our social and intellectual lives.

Though the author does not explicitly state it, this paragraph defines the theory of prototypes. Notice the author likes to use an indirect, even cryptic, method of introducing or switching topics, which makes this a classic ACT type passage. The ACT writers have many opportunities here to test whether you are following the author's train of thought.

Now we attack the questions.

1. The author probably chose *Women, Fire, and Dangerous Things* as the title of the article because
   I.   he thought that since the Dyirbal placed all three items in the same category, women, fire, and dangerous things necessarily had something in common.
   II. he was hoping to draw attention to the fact that because items have been placed in the same category doesn't mean that they necessarily have anything in common.
   III. he wanted to use the Dyirbal classification system as an example of how primitive classifications are not as functional as contemporary Western classification systems.
   (A) I only
   (B) II only
   (C) III only
   (D) II and III only

This is an extension question. The second paragraph contains the information needed to answer it. There the author states that women, fire, and dangerous things belong to a category called *balan* in an Australian aboriginal language, which is <u>not</u> simply based on common properties. This eliminates Statement I and confirms Statement II.

The answer is (B).

2. According to the author,
   I.   categorizing is a fundamental activity of people.
   II. whenever a word refers to a kind of thing, it signifies a category.
   III. one has to be able to categorize in order to function in our culture.
   (A) I only
   (B) II only
   (C) I and II only
   (D) I, II, and III

This is a description question, so we must find the points in the passage from which the statements were drawn.

Remember, the answer to a description question will not directly quote a statement from the passage, but it will be closely related to one—often a paraphrase.

The needed references for Statements I, II, and III are all contained in the closing paragraph.

The answer is (D).

3. Which one of the following facts would most weaken the significance of the author's title?
   (A) The discovery that all the birds and animals classified as *balan* in Dyirbal are female
   (B) The discovery that the male Dyirbal culture considers females to be both fiery and dangerous
   (C) The discovery that all items in the *balan* category are considered female
   (D) The discovery that neither fire nor women are considered dangerous

To weaken an argument, attack one or more of its premises. Now the implication of the title is that *women, fire,* and *dangerous things* do not have anything in common. To weaken this implication, the answer should state that all things in the *balan* category have something in common.

The answer is (C).

3. To weaken an argument, attack one or more of its premises. Now the implication of the title is that *women, fire,* and *dangerous things* do not have anything in common. To weaken this implication, the answer should state that all things in the *balan* category have something in common.

The answer is (C).

4. If linguistic experts cannot perceive how women, fire, and dangerous things in the category *balan* have at least one thing in common, it follows that

   (A) there probably is something other than shared properties that led to all items in *balan* being placed in that category.
   (B) the anthropologists simply weren't able to perceive what the items had in common.
   (C) the anthropologists might not have been able to see what the items had in common.
   (D) the items do not have anything in common.

This is an extension question; we are asked to draw a conclusion based on the passage.

Hint: The thrust of the passage is that commonality is not the only way to categorize things.

The answer is (A).

5. Which one of the following sentences would best complete the last paragraph of the passage?

   (A) An understanding of how we categorize is central to any understanding of how we think and how we function, and therefore central to an understanding of what makes us human.
   (B) The prototype theory is only the latest in a series of new and improved theories of categorization; undoubtedly even better theories will replace it.
   (C) The prototype theory of categories has not only unified a major branch of linguistics, but it has applications to mathematics and physics as well.
   (D) An understanding of how the prototype theory of categorization evolved from the classical theory is essential to any understanding of how we think and how we function in society.

This is an application question; we are asked to complete a thought for the author.

Most of the third paragraph is introducing the prototype theory of categorization. But in the last sentence the author changes direction somewhat—without any notice, as is typical of his style. Now he is discussing the importance of the ability to categorize. The clause *"Without the ability to categorize, we could not function at all"* indicates that this ability is fundamental to our very being.

Be careful not to choose (D). Although it is probably true, it is too specific: in the final sentence the author is discussing categorization in general.

The answer is (A).

Solo Exercise

Directions: This passage is followed by a group of questions to be answered based on what is stated or implied in the passage. Choose the best answer; the one that most accurately and completely answers the question.

Global strategies to control infectious disease have historically included the erection of barriers to international travel and immigration. Keeping people with infectious diseases outside national borders has reemerged as an important public health policy in the human immunodeficiency virus (HIV) epidemic. Between 29 and 50 countries are reported to have introduced border restrictions on HIV-positive foreigners, usually those planning an extended stay in the country, such as students, workers, or seamen.

Travel restrictions have been established primarily by countries in the western Pacific and Mediterranean regions, where HIV seroprevalence is relatively low. However, the country with the broadest policy of testing and excluding foreigners is the United States. From December 1, 1987, when HIV infection was first classified in the United States as a contagious disease, through September 30, 1989, more than 3 million people seeking permanent residence in this country were tested for HIV antibodies. The U.S. policy has been sharply criticized by national and international organizations as being contrary to public health goals and human-rights principles. Many of these organizations are boycotting international meetings in the United States that are vital for the study of prevention, education, and treatment of HIV infection.

The Immigration and Nationality Act requires the Public Health Service to list "dangerous contagious diseases" for which aliens can be excluded from the United States. By 1987 there were seven designated diseases—five of them sexually transmitted (chancroid, gonorrhea, granuloma inguinale, lymphog-ranuloma venereum, and infectious syphilis) and two non-venereal (active tuberculosis and infectious leprosy). On June 8, 1987, in response to a Congressional direction in the Helms Amendment, the Public Health Service added HIV infection to the list of dangerous contagious diseases.

A just and efficacious travel and immigration policy would not exclude people because of their serologic status unless they posed a danger to the community through casual transmission. U.S. regulations should list only active tuberculosis as a contagious infectious disease. We support well-funded programs to protect the health of travelers infected with HIV through appropriate immunizations and prophylactic treatment and to reduce behaviors that may transmit infection.

We recognize that treating patients infected with HIV who immigrate to the United States will incur costs for the public sector. It is inequitable, however, to use cost as a reason to exclude people infected with HIV, for there are no similar exclusionary policies for those with other costly chronic diseases, such as heart disease or cancer.

Rather than arbitrarily restrict the movement of a subgroup of infected people, we must dedicate ourselves to the principles of justice, scientific cooperation, and a global response to the HIV pandemic.

1. According to the passage, countries in the western Pacific have

   (A) a very high frequency of HIV-positive immigrants and have a greater reason to be concerned over this issue than other countries.
   (B) opposed efforts on the part of Mediterranean states to establish travel restrictions on HIV-positive residents.
   (C) a low HIV seroprevalence and, in tandem with Mediterranean regions, have established travel restrictions on HIV-positive foreigners.
   (D) continued to obstruct efforts to unify policy concerning immigrant screening.

2. The authors of the passage conclude that

    (A)   it is unjust to exclude people based on their serological status without the knowledge that they pose a danger to the public.
    (B)   U.S. regulations should require more stringent testing to be implemented at all major border crossings.
    (C)   it is the responsibility of the public sector to absorb costs incurred by treatment of immigrants infected with HIV.
    (D)   the HIV pandemic is largely overstated and that, based on new epidemiological data, screening immigrants is not indicated.

3. It can be inferred from the passage that

    (A)   more than 3 million HIV-positive people have sought permanent residence in the United States.
    (B)   countries with a low seroprevalence of HIV have a disproportionate and unjustified concern over the spread of AIDS by immigration.
    (C)   the United States is more concerned with controlling the number of HIV-positive immigrants than with avoiding criticism from outside its borders.
    (D)   current law is meeting the demand for prudent handling of a potentially hazardous international issue.

4. Before the Helms Amendment in 1987, seven designated diseases were listed as being cause for denying immigration. We can conclude from the passage that

    (A)   the authors agree fully with this policy but disagree with adding HIV to the list.
    (B)   the authors believe that sexual diseases are appropriate reasons for denying immigration but not non-venereal diseases.
    (C)   the authors disagree with the amendment.
    (D)   the authors believe that non-venereal diseases are justifiable reasons for exclusion, but not sexually transmitted diseases.

5. In referring to the "costs" incurred by the public (opening of the fifth paragraph), the authors apparently mean

    (A)   financial costs.
    (B)   costs to the public health.
    (C)   costs in manpower.
    (D)   costs in international reputation.

Answers and Solutions to Exercise

Previewing the first sentence of each paragraph shows that the passage is about restricting travel of HIV-positive persons and that the authors feel there should be no restrictions. There are two pivotal words: "however" (second sentence of the second paragraph), and "Rather than" (opening of the last paragraph), which introduces the concluding paragraph.

1. This is a description question, so we must find the point in the passage from which the question is drawn. It is the opening sentence to paragraph two. There it is stated that countries in the western Pacific and Mediterranean regions have a low incidence of HIV infection and have introduced border restrictions. The answer, therefore, is (C).

2. This is another description question. The answer is (A). This is directly supported by the opening sentence of paragraph four. Note that (A) is a paraphrase of that sentence.

Be careful with (C). Although this is hinted at in paragraph five, it is never directly stated that the public sector is <u>responsible</u> for these costs, only that it would in fact pick up these costs. Remember: A description question must be answered from what is directly stated in the passage, not from what it implies.

3. This is an extension question. The second paragraph states *"U.S. policy has been sharply criticized by national and international organizations."* Given that this criticism has not caused the United States to change its policies, it must be more concerned with controlling the number of HIV-positive immigrants than with avoiding criticism. The answer, therefore, is (C).

Don't be tempted by (A); it's a same language trap. Every word in it is taken from the passage. However, the passage states that over 3 million people were tested for HIV antibodies (second paragraph), <u>not</u> that they were tested "positive" for HIV antibodies.

4. This is another extension question. At the end of the fourth paragraph, the authors state that only active tuberculosis should be listed as a dangerous contagious disease. We expect that they would oppose adding HIV to the list. The answer is (C).

5. Although governments have ostensibly restricted the immigration of HIV-positive persons out of fear that they may spread the disease, the authors apparently are referring to financial costs, not costs to public health. This is indicated by the end of the fifth paragraph, where they describe heart disease and cancer as non-contagious and costly, yet still admissible. The answer, therefore, is (A).

Practice Reading Test

On the actual ACT, you will read four full-length (around 750 words each) passages. Each passage will then be followed by ten questions. However, to help ease you into it all, this practice test will only ask you a few questions on each of the following passages. And, unlike the ACT, there is no time limit. So feel free to take your time. Remember: preview topic sentences, circle pivotal words, annotate the passage, and have fun!

Directions: Each passage in this group is followed by questions based on its content. After reading a passage, choose the best answer to each question. Answer all questions following a passage on the basis of what is stated or implied in that passage.

Passage 1:

Most students arrive at [college] using "discrete, concrete, and absolute categories to understand people, knowledge, and values." These students live with a *dualistic* view, seeing "the world in polar terms of we-right-good vs. other-wrong-bad." These students cannot acknowledge the existence of more than one point of view toward any issue. There is one "right" way. And because these absolutes are assumed by or imposed on the individual from external authority, they cannot be personally substantiated or authenticated by experience. These students are slaves to the generalizations of their authorities. An eye for eye! Capital punishment is apt justice for murder. The Bible says so.

Most students break through the dualistic stage to another equally frustrating stage—*multiplicity*. Within this stage, students see a variety of ways to deal with any given topic or problem. However, while these students accept multiple points of view, they are unable to evaluate or justify them. To have an opinion is everyone's right. While students in the dualistic stage are unable to produce evidence to support what they consider to be self-evident absolutes, students in the multiplistic stage are unable to connect instances into coherent generalizations. Every assertion, every point, is valid. In their democracy they are directionless. Capital punishment? What sense is there in answering one murder with another?

The third stage of development finds students living in a world of *relativism*. Knowledge is relative: right and wrong depend on the context. No longer recognizing the validity of each individual idea or action, relativists examine everything to find its place in an overall framework. While the multiplist views the world as unconnected, almost random, the relativist seeks always to place phenomena into coherent larger patterns. Students in this stage view the world analytically. They appreciate authority for its expertise, using it to defend their own generalizations. In addition, they accept or reject ostensible authority *after systematically* evaluating its validity. In this stage, however, students resist decision making. Suffering the ambivalence of finding several consistent and acceptable alternatives, they are almost overwhelmed by diversity and need means for managing it. Capital punishment is appropriate justice—in some instances.

In the final stage students manage diversity through individual *commitment*. Students do not deny relativism. Rather they assert an identity by forming commitments and assuming responsibility for them. They gather personal experience into a coherent framework, abstract principles to guide their actions, and use these principles to discipline and govern their thoughts and actions. The individual has chosen to join a particular community and agrees to live by its tenets. The accused has had the benefit of due process to guard his civil rights, a jury of peers has found him guilty, and the state has the right to end his life. This is a principle my community and I endorse.

1. It can be inferred from the passage that the author would consider which of the following to be good examples of dualistic thinking?
    I.   *People who think there is a right way and a wrong way to do things*
    II. *Teenagers who assume they know more about the real world than adults do*
    III. *People who back our country, right or wrong, when it goes to war*
    (A) I only
    (B) III only
    (C) I and II only
    (D) I and III only

2. Students who are dualistic thinkers may not be able to support their beliefs convincingly because
    (F) most of their beliefs *cannot* be supported by arguments.
    (G) they have accepted their truths simply because authorities have said these things are true.
    (H) they half-believe and half-disbelieve just about everything.
    (J) they are enslaved by their authorities.

3. Which one of the following assertions is supported by the passage?
    (A) *Committed* thinkers are not very sure of their positions.
    (B) *Relativistic* thinkers have learned how to make sense out of the world and have chosen their own positions in it.
    (C) *Multiplicity* thinkers have difficulty understanding the relationships between different points of view.
    (D) *Dualistic* thinkers have thought out the reasons for taking their positions.

4. In paragraph two, the author states that in their democracy students in the *multiplicity* stage are directionless. The writer describes *multiplicity* students as being in a democracy because
    (F) there are so many different kinds of people in a democracy.
    (G) in an ideal democracy, all people are considered equal; by extension, so are their opinions.
    (H) Democrats generally do not have a good sense of direction.
    (J) although democracies may grant freedom, they are generally acknowledged to be less efficient than more authoritarian forms of government.

5. Which one of the following kinds of thinking is NOT described in the passage?
    (A) People who assume that there is no right or wrong in any issue
    (B) People who believe that right or wrong depends on the situation
    (C) People who commit themselves to a particular point of view after having considered several alternative concepts
    (D) People who think that all behavior can be accounted for by cause and effect relationships

6. Which one of the following best describes the organization of the passage?
    (F) Four methods of thought are compared and contrasted.
    (G) Four methods of thought are presented, and each is shown to complement the other.
    (H) The evolution of thought from simplistic and provincial through considered and cosmopolitan is illustrated by four stages.
    (J) The evolution of thought through four stages is presented, and each stage is illustrated by how it views capital punishment.

Passage 2:
A growing taste for shark steaks and shark-fin soup has for the first time in 400 million years put the scourge of the sea at the wrong end of the food chain. Commercial landings of this toothsome fish have doubled every year since 1986, and shark populations are plunging. It is hardly a case of good riddance. Sharks do for gentler fish what lions do for the wildebeest: they check populations by feeding on the weak. Also, sharks apparently do not get cancer and may therefore harbor clues to the nature of that disease.

Finally, there is the issue of motherhood. Sharks are viviparous. That is, they bear their young alive and swimming (not sealed in eggs), after gestation periods lasting from nine months to two years. Shark mothers generally give birth to litters of from eight to twelve pups and bear only one litter every other year.

This is why sharks have one of the lowest fecundity rates in the ocean. The female cod, for example, spawns annually and lays a few million eggs at a time. If three quarters of the cod were to be fished this year, they could be back in full force in a few years. But if humans took that big of a bite out of the sharks, the population would not recover for 15 years.

So, late this summer, if all goes according to plan, the shark will join the bald eagle and the buffalo on the list of managed species. The federal government will cap the U.S. commercial catch at 5,800 metric tons, about half of the 1989 level, and limit sportsmen to two sharks per boat. Another provision discourages finning, the harvesting of shark fins alone, by limiting the weight of fins to 7 percent of that of all the carcasses.

Finning got under the skin of environmentalists, and the resulting anger helped to mobilize support for the new regulations. Finning itself is a fairly recent innovation. Shark fins contain noodle-like cartilaginous tissues that Chinese chefs have traditionally used to thicken and flavor soup. Over the past few years rising demand in Hong Kong has made the fins as valuable as the rest of the fish. Long strands are prized, so unusually large fins can be worth considerably more to the fisherman than the average price of about $10 a pound.

But can U.S. quotas save shark species that wander the whole Atlantic? The blue shark, for example, migrates into the waters of something

like 23 countries. John G. Casey, a biologist with the National Marine Fisheries Service Research Center in Narragansett, R.I., admits that international co-ordination will eventually be necessary. But he supports U.S. quotas as a first step in mobilizing other nations. Meanwhile the commercial fishermen are not waiting for the new rules to take effect. "There's a pre-quota rush on sharks," Casey says, "and it's going on as we speak."

7. According to the passage, shark populations are at greater risk than cod populations because
    (A) sharks are now being eaten more than cod.
    (B) the shark reproduction rate is lower than that of the cod.
    (C) sharks are quickly becoming fewer in number.
    (D) sharks are now as scarce as bald eagles and buffalo.

8. According to the passage, a decrease in shark populations
    I.   *might cause some fish populations to go unchecked.*
    II. *would hamper cancer research.*
    III. *to one-quarter the current level would take over a decade to recover from.*
    (A) II only
    (B) III only
    (C) I and III only
    (D) I and II only

9. If the species Homo logicus was determined to be viviparous and to have extremely low fecundity rates on land, we might expect that
    (A) *Homo logicus* could overpopulate its niche and should be controlled.
    (B) *Homo logicus* might be declared an endangered species.
    (C) *Homo logicus* would pose no danger to other species and would itself be in no danger.
    (D) None of these events would be expected with certainty.

10. Which one of the following best describes the author's attitude toward the efforts to protect shark populations?
    (A) strong advocate
    (B) impartial observer
    (C) opposed
    (D) resigned to their ineffectiveness

11. It can be inferred from the passage that
    I. *research efforts on cancer will be hindered if shark populations are threatened.*
    II. *U.S. quotas on shark fishing will have limited effectiveness in protecting certain species.*
    III. *some practices of Chinese chefs have angered environmentalists.*
    (F) I only
    (G) II only
    (H) I and II only
    (J) II and III only

12. An irony resulting from the announcement that sharks will be placed on the managed list is
    (A) we will now find out less about cancer, so by saving the sharks, we are hurting ourselves.
    (B) sharks are far more dangerous to other fish than we are to them.
    (C) more chefs are now using the cartilaginous tissues found in shark fins.
    (D) more sharks are being killed now than before the announcement.

Passage 3:

"A writer's job is to tell the truth," said Hemingway in 1942. No other writer of our time had so fiercely asserted, so pugnaciously defended or so consistently exemplified the writer's obligation to speak truly. His standard of truth-telling remained, moreover, so high and so rigorous that he was ordinarily unwilling to admit secondary evidence, whether literary evidence or evidence picked up from other sources than his own experience. "I only know what I have seen," was a statement which came often to his lips and pen. What he had personally done, or what he knew unforgettably by having gone through one version of it, was what he was interested in telling about. This is not to say that he refused to invent freely, but that he always made it a sacrosanct point to invent in terms of what he actually knew of.

The primary intent of his writing, from first to last, was to seize and project for the reader what he often called "the way it was." This is a characteristically simple phrase for a concept of extraordinary complexity, and Hemingway's conception of its meaning subtly changed several times in the course of his career—always in the direction of greater complexity. At the core of the concept, however, one can invariably discern the operation of three aesthetic instruments: the sense of place, the sense of fact, and the sense of scene.

The first of these, obviously a strong passion with Hemingway, is the sense of place. "Unless you have geography, background," he once told George Antheil, "you have nothing." You have, that is to say, a dramatic vacuum. Few writers have been more place-conscious. Few have so carefully charted out the geographical ground work of their novels while managing to keep background so conspicuously unobtrusive. Few, accordingly, have been able to record more economically and graphically the way it is when you walk through the streets of Paris in search of breakfast at a corner café . . . Or when, at around six o'clock of a Spanish dawn, you watch the bulls running from the corrals at the Puerta Rochapea through the streets of Pamplona towards the bullring.

"When I woke it was the sound of the rocket exploding that announced the release of the bulls from the corrals at the edge of town. Down below the narrow street was empty. All the balconies were crowded with people. Suddenly a crowd came down the street. They were all running, packed close together. They passed along and up the street toward the bullring and behind them came more men running faster, and then some stragglers who were really running. Behind them was a little bare space, and then the bulls, galloping, tossing their heads up and down. It all went out of sight around the corner. One man fell, rolled to the gutter, and lay quiet. But the bulls went right on and did not notice him. They were all running together."

This landscape is as morning-fresh as a design in India ink on clean white paper. First is the bare white street, seen from above, quiet and empty. Then one sees the first packed clot of runners. Behind these are the thinner ranks of those who move faster because they are closer to the bulls. Then the almost comic stragglers, who are "really running." Brilliantly behind these shines the "little bare space," a desperate margin for error. Then the clot of running bulls—closing the design, except of course for the man in the gutter making himself, like the designer's initials, as inconspicuous as possible.

13. From the author's comments and the example of the bulls (paragraph 4), what was the most likely reason that Hemingway took care to include details of place?
    (F) He felt that geography in some way illuminated other, more important events.
    (G) He thought readers generally did not have enough imagination to visualize the scenes for themselves.
    (H) He had no other recourse since he was avoiding the use of other literary sources.
    (J) He thought that landscapes were more important than characters to convey "the way it was."

14. One might infer from the passage that Hemingway preferred which one of the following sources for his novels and short stories?
    (A) Stories that he had heard from friends or chance acquaintances
    (B) Stories that he had read about in newspapers or other secondary sources
    (C) Stories that came to him in periods of meditation or in dreams
    (D) Stories that he had lived rather than read about

15. It has been suggested that part of Hemingway's genius lies in the way in which he removes himself from his stories in order to let readers experience the stories for themselves. Which of the following elements of the passage support this suggestion?
    I. *The comparison of the designer's initials to the man who fell and lay in the gutter (fourth* paragraph) *during the running of the bulls*
    II. *Hemingway's stated intent to project for the reader "the way it was" (*opening of the second paragraph)
    III. *Hemingway's ability to invent fascinating tales from his own experience*
    (F) I only
    (G) II only
    (H) I and II only
    (J) I and III only

16. From the passage, one can assume that which of the following statements would best describe Hemingway's attitude toward knowledge?
    (A) One can learn about life only by living it fully.
    (B) A wise person will read widely in order to learn about life.
    (C) Knowledge is a powerful tool that should be reserved only for those who know how to use it.
    (D) Experience is a poor teacher.

17. The author calls "the way it was" a characteristically simple phrase for a concept of extraordinary complexity (opening of the second paragraph) because
    (F) the phrase reflects Hemingway's talent for obscuring ordinary events.
    (G) the relationship between simplicity and complexity reflected the relationship between the style and content of Hemingway's writing.
    (H) Hemingway became increasingly confused about "the way it was" throughout the course of his career.
    (J) Hemingway's obsession for geographic details progressively overshadowed the dramatic element of his stories.

Passage 4:
Imagine that we stand on any ordinary seaside pier, and watch the waves rolling in and striking against the iron columns of the pier. Large waves pay very little attention to the columns—they divide right and left and re-unite after passing each column, much as a regiment of soldiers would if a tree stood in their way; it is almost as though the columns had not been there. But the short waves and ripples find the columns of the pier a much more formidable obstacle. When the short waves impinge on the columns, they are reflected back and spread as new ripples in all directions. To use the technical term, they are scattered. The obstacle provided by the iron columns hardly affects the long waves at all, but scatters the short ripples.

We have been watching a working model of the way in which sunlight struggles through the earth's atmosphere. Between us on earth and outer space the atmosphere interposes innumerable obstacles in the form of molecules of air, tiny droplets of water, and small particles of dust. They are represented by the columns of the pier.

The waves of the sea represent the sunlight. We know that sunlight is a blend of lights of many colors—as we can prove for ourselves by passing it through a prism, or even through a jug of water, or as Nature demonstrates to us when she passes it through the raindrops of a summer shower and produces a rainbow. We also know that light consists of waves, and that the different colors of light are produced by waves of different lengths, red light by long waves and blue light by short waves. The mixture of waves which constitutes sunlight has to struggle through the obstacles it meets in the atmosphere, just as the mixture of waves at the seaside has to struggle past the columns of the pier. And these obstacles treat the light waves much as the columns of the pier treat the sea-waves. The long waves which constitute red light are hardly affected, but the short waves which constitute blue light are scattered in all directions.

Thus, the different constituents of sunlight are treated in different ways as they struggle through the earth's atmosphere. A wave of blue light may be scattered by a dust particle, and turned out of its course. After a time a second dust particle again turns it out of its course, and so on, until finally it enters our eyes by a path as zigzag as that of a flash of lightning. Consequently, the blue waves of the sunlight enter our eyes from all directions. And that is why the sky looks blue.

18. We know from experience that if we look directly at the sun, we will see red light near the sun. This observation is supported by the passage for which one of the following reasons?

   (A) It seems reasonable to assume that red light would surround the sun because the sun is basically a large fireball.
   (B) It seems reasonable to assume that the other colors of light would either cancel each other or combine to produce red.
   (C) It seems reasonable to assume that red light would not be disturbed by the atmospheric particles and would consequently reach us by a relatively direct path from the sun to our eyes.
   (D) It is not supported by the passage. The author does not say what color of light should be near the sun, and he provides no reasons that would allow us to assume that the light would be red.

19. Scientists have observed that shorter wavelength light has more energy than longer wavelength light. From this we can conclude that

   (A) red light will exert more energy when it hits the surface of the earth than will blue light.
   (B) lightning is caused by the collision of blue light with particles in the air.
   (C) red light will travel faster than blue light.
   (D) blue light has more energy than red light.

20. A scientist makes new observations and learns that water waves of shorter wavelengths spread in all directions not only because they scatter off piers but also because they interact with previously scattered short water waves. Drawing upon the analogy between water waves and light waves, we might hypothesize which of the following?
    (A) Blue light waves act like ripples that other blue light waves meet and scatter from.
    (B) Red light waves will be scattered by blue light waves like incoming long water waves are scattered by outgoing ripples.
    (C) Red light waves can scatter blue light waves, but blue light waves cannot scatter red.
    (D) The analogy between water and light waves cannot be extended to include the way in which short water waves become ripples and scatter one another.

21. Which one of the following is a reason for assuming that sunlight is constituted of waves of many colors?
    (A) The mixture of waves that make up sunlight has to struggle through a variety of obstacles in the atmosphere.
    (B) When passing through water in the atmosphere, sunlight is sometimes broken down into an array of colors.
    (C) Many different wavelengths of light enter our eyes from all directions.
    (D) The mere fact that light waves can be scattered is a reason for assuming that sunlight is constituted of waves of different colors.

22. From the information presented in the passage, what can we conclude about the color of the sky on a day with a large quantity of dust in the air?
    (A) The sky would be even bluer
    (B) The sky would be redder
    (C) The sky would not change colors
    (D) We do not have enough information to determine a change in color

23. We all know that when there is a clear sky, the western sky appears red as the sun sets. From the information presented in the passage, this phenomenon would seem to be explained by which of the following?
    I.   Light meets more obstacles when passing parallel to the earth's surface than when traveling perpendicular. Consequently, even red light is diffused.
    II. The blue light may not make it through the denser pathway of the evening sky, leaving only the long light waves of red.
    III. The short red light waves have more energy and are the only waves that can make it through the thick atmosphere of the evening sky.
    (A) I only
    (B) II only
    (C) I and II only
    (D) II and III only

24. Which one of the following does the author seem to imply?
    (A) Waves of light and waves of water are identical.
    (B) Waves of light have the same physical shape as waves of water.
    (C) Waves of light and waves of water do not have very much in common.
    (D) Waves of water are only models of waves of light.

Answers and Solutions

1. D	7. B	13. F	19. D
2. G	8. C	14. D	20. D
3. C	9. D	15. H	21. B
4. G	10. B	16. A	22. D
5. D	11. G	17. G	23. C
6. J	12. D	18. C	24. D

1. This is an extension question. Statement I is true. This is the essential characteristic of dualistic (right/wrong) thinkers (opening lines of the first paragraph). This eliminates (B). Statement II is false. Dualistic thinkers grant authority (right thinking) to adults and adult figures. This is clear from the sentence, "These students are slaves to the generalizations of their authorities." This eliminates (C). Unfortunately, we have to check Statement III. It is true since Dualistic thinkers believe their group is right and the other group is wrong. (Again, see the opening lines of the first paragraph.) The answer, therefore is (D).

2. This is another extension question. Dualistic thinkers probably cannot give cogent arguments for their beliefs since they have adopted them unquestioningly from authority figures; dualistic thinkers do not know - or have never thought of - the reasons for which their beliefs are right or wrong. Hence the answer is (G).

3. This is a description question. Choice (A) is false. After carefully thinking through their reasons, committed thinkers are reasonably sure of their position. Choice (B) is also false. Relativistic thinkers make sense of the world, but they have not chosen their position. Choice (C) is true. Multiplicity thinkers see the world as randomly organized; they can't see the relationships that connect different positions. (See the first pivotal word, *however* [second paragraph].)

4. This is an extension question. Multiplicity students view all opinions as equally valid. They have yet to learn how to rank opinions (truths)—all votes (thoughts) count equally. The answer is (G). Note, (H) is offered to humor Republicans. The test-makers sometimes run out of tempting wrong choices. Don't dwell on such humorous nonsense.

5. This is another description question. Don't confuse (A) and (B). Multiplists acknowledge no right or wrong; whereas, Relativists acknowledge a morality, but one that is context dependent. The answer is (D).

6. This is a writing technique question. In each paragraph the author shows how a stage of thought evolved from a previous stage—except the dualistic stage, which starts the analysis. Furthermore, the thought process in each stage is illustrated by how it views capital punishment. So the answer is (J). Be careful not to choose (H). Although dualistic thinking certainly is simplistic and provincial, and committed thinking seems to be considered and cosmopolitan, neither of these judgments is stated nor implied by the passage.

7. This is a description question. Paragraph 3 contains the information needed to answer it. There it is stated that the cod population can replenish itself in a few years, but the shark population would take 15 years. Hence the answer is (B).

Don't make the mistake of choosing (C). Although it is certainly supported by the passage, it does not state how this relates to cod—they too may be decreasing in number. (C) uses the true-but-irrelevant ploy.

8. This is a description question. Statement I is true. It is supported by the analogy drawn between lions and sharks (first paragraph). This eliminates (A) and (B). Statement II is false. It is too strong an inference to draw from the information at the end of the first paragraph. If sharks were on the verge of extinction, this "could hamper" research. But given that the author does not claim or imply that sharks are near extinction, "would hamper" is too strong. Besides, the author does not state that sharks are being used in research, just that they may be useful in that regard. This eliminates (D). Hence, by process of elimination, we have learned the answer is (C).

9. This is an application question; we are asked to apply what we have learned in the passage to a hypothetical situation. A review of the passage shows that only (B) and (D) have any real merit. But sharks have survived for 400 million years with an extremely low fecundity rate. This eliminates (B). Hence the answer is (D).

10. This is a rather easy tone question. The passage has a matter-of-fact or journalistic tone to it, so the answer is (B).

11. This is an extension question. Statement I is incorrect: it overstates. Statement II is correct: we know that some species of sharks migrate into the waters of over 20 countries. U.S. quotas alone cannot protect these sharks, even if the quotas reduce the rate of killing in U.S. waters. Statement III is incorrect: the environmentalists are angry at the finning fishermen who are over-fishing the waters, but there is nothing in the passage to suggest that this anger is also directed towards the chefs. The answer is (G).

12. By announcing the impending classification, the federal government ironically encourages fishermen to kill as many sharks as they can before the regulations go into effect—stimulating the opposite of what was intended, i.e., the saving of sharks. The answer is (D).

13. This is an extension question. In the opening of the third paragraph, Hemingway effectively equates geography with background, and says that without them you have nothing. Later in third paragraph, the author refers to the geographical groundwork of Hemingway's novels. Both of these statements imply that details of place set the stage for other, more important events. Hence the answer is (F). Don't try to draw a distinction between geography, background, and landscape. The author uses them interchangeably when referring to details of place. Such latitude with labels is often mimicked by the Question-Writers.

14. Hemingway's primary intent was to project for the reader the way it was, as seen through his eyes. The answer is (D).

15. This is an extension question. Statement I is true: the last line of the passage states that the designer's initials (i.e., the writer's presence) are made as inconspicuous as possible. Statement II is also true: readers cannot see the way it was if they are looking through another medium (the author). Hemingway appears to say, in effect: *"I'm striving to report exactly what happened (and not my opinions about it). The readers must draw their own conclusions."* Statement III is false: in fact, a good case could be made that writing only from personal experience would tend to increase, not decrease, the presence of the writer in his writings. The answer is (H).

16. This is an application question; we are asked to put ourselves in Hemingway's mind. From Hemingway's statement "I only know what I have seen" and from the author's assertion that Hemingway refused to honor secondary sources, we can infer that he believed one can know only through experience. The answer is (A).

17. This is an extension question. The answer is (G). *Phrase* (in the passage) corresponds to *style* (in the answer-choice), and *concept* corresponds to *content*.

18. This is an extension question. According to the passage, red light would not be significantly deflected and consequently would pass through a relatively direct route from the sun to our eyes. Hence the answer is (C).

19. This is another extension question. Since the passage is a science selection, we should expect a lot of extension questions.
(A): No, if anything, blue light would exert more energy.
(B): No. We cannot infer this. The collision of blue light with particles in the air is the reason for a blue sky, not for lightning.
(C): No. Speed of light is not mentioned in the passage.
(D): Yes. Blue light has a shorter wavelength, consequently it has more energy than red light.

20. This is an application question since it introduces new information about water waves and asks us to conclude how the behavior of light waves might be similarly affected. Given this information, however, we can justify no conclusion about whether light waves imitate water waves in this new regard. The analogy might hold or it might break down. We don't yet know. (To find out we would have to do an experiment using light.) The answer is (D).

21. (A): No. We do not know anything about a "variety" of obstacles; even if we did, we would have no reason to assume that light is constituted of different colors.
(B): Yes. See the first part of the third paragraph. Rainbows occur because light is constituted of many colors.
(C): No. This is a distortion of the final lines of the passage, and it sounds illogical to boot.
(D): No. This gives no reason to assume that light is constituted of many colors.

22. (A): No. Although dust is mentioned as one of the three important obstacles (second paragraph), we simply do not have enough information to conclude how dust density would change sky color.
(B): No. While this idea may fit with the common lore that a lot of dust in the air creates great, red sunsets, the passage itself gives no basis to any conclusion regarding color change.
(C): No. Same reason as in (A) and (B).
(D): Yes. There is not enough information in the passage to determine a relationship between color change and dust density. The dust may give off a certain color of its own—we can't say for certain.

23. Statement I is true. There are obviously more particles on a horizontal than a vertical path. The glowing red sky is reasonable evidence for some diffusion. Note that Question 24 asks "what can we *conclude*" while this question asks what seems *plausible* (what "would seem to be explained"). So, while we are attempting to make very similar inferences in both questions, what we can do with the data depends, among other things, on the degree of certainty requested. Statement II is true. The path of evening light probably has a greater average density, since it spends more time passing through a zone of thicker atmosphere. It is reasonable to assume this significantly greater density, or the absolute number of particles, might present an obstacle to blue light. Statement III is false. There are two things wrong with this answer: (1) red light waves are not short, relative to blue; (2) we do not know that waves with more energy will more readily pass through obstacles. The passage, in fact, implies just the opposite. The answer is (C).

24. (A): No. Water waves offer only a model for light waves. As a model, they are identical in some ways but not in others.
(B): No. This is not implied by the passage. What they have in common is the way they act when they impinge on obstacles.
(C): No. Waves of water are used as a model because they have much in common with waves of light.
(D): Yes. See explanation for (A).

WRITING TEST

- **INTRODUCTION**

- **THE ESSAY**

  - **Re-Cap**
    Structure
    Style

  - **Presenting a Perspective on an Issue**
    Patterns of Development
    Writing Your Essay
    Sample Prompts & Essays
    Practice

- ➤ **SAMPLE ESSAYS**

Introduction

Format of the Writing Section

The Writing Test is 30 minutes long and consists of one prompt from which to write an essay. And, although the Writing Test is optional, three-quarters of colleges and universities require this section of the ACT. So it's probably a good idea to buckle down and take it. If you take it and your university *doesn't* require it, then you have nothing to lose. But if you don't take it and your university *does* require it, then you have everything to lose. Again, it's probably in your best interest to take the darn test.

How to Get a Top-Half Score

Since critical and creative skills will be tested and evaluated in a subjective manner, writing essays often raises anxieties in even the best test takers. This is known as performance anxiety. From having a difficult time understanding exactly what is being asked to having debilitating uncertainties about how to begin an answer, *Performance anxiety* can lead to a host of problems.

The best way to reduce such anxieties, and therefore increase your chance of obtaining a top-half score, is through *rehearsal*, which encompasses four activities that need to take place before taking the ACT:

1) understanding the writing tasks
2) knowing what the evaluators expect to find in top-half essays
3) anticipating an organizational scheme for the essay
4) practicing by writing an essay in response to at least one practice question in this book

After you can complete these four steps, you will be in an excellent position to approach the writing test with confidence and competency.

The Essay

Structure

Learning the rules that govern written English is one thing; putting your knowledge to use is another. We will discuss some specific tips that pertain to the type of essay you will be required to write, but for now, let's look at some general techniques to make your essay the best it can be.

➢ **Introduction** - The introduction should serve two structural purposes: It should restate the topic so that the reader need not review the given question, and it should offer a clear thesis so the reader knows what your purpose is. Simply defined, a *thesis* states the main idea of your essay.

In other words, your reader should be able to ascertain the issue or argument without reading the given topic. Suppose the ACT gives you this topic and assignment:

Prompt:
The new writing section was recently added to the ACT with the idea that such a section would encourage more teaching of writing. In turn, students would be more mature writers by graduation time.

Assignment:
Do you think that the added writing section will indeed improve writing skills? Plan and write an essay that depicts your point of view on this subject. Provide support on your position by pulling examples from your own experiences.

Your initial reaction to this assignment may be to begin your essay with a direct response such as *I agree with this assumption...* However, this introductory sentence does not provide adequate information because it does not specify *which* assumption and therefore it would leave the reader confused. Following is the beginning of an introduction that does give adequate information to the reader:

> "Does the new ACT really help improve the writing skills of high school graduates? The impetus behind the development of the new writing section is to prompt more in-depth teaching of writing. Added writing curriculum should turn out more mature writers. This is a valid assumption because..."

Not only should you restate the topic, but you should also do so in a way that will spark interest. It may seem like a tall order to restate your topic, create a thesis, AND make it captivating, but if you don't grab your reader's attention in the introduction, it doesn't matter how interesting the body of your essay is because readers won't feel compelled to read on. Think of your introduction as the worm on a fishhook, just dangling there enticing the fish to bite. There are several techniques you can employ to get your reader to bite and read on.

- Begin your introduction with a question. Naturally, when a question is posed to your reader, he or she will want to keep reading to find out the answer.
- Begin your introduction with a quote. Because you will not have time to research your topic for the ACT test, this may not be as feasible as, say, on a term paper for a college class; however, if you can remember a specific quote pertinent to your topic, use it.
- Begin with an anecdote. An anecdote is entertaining and will thus draw in the reader.

- Begin with an illustration or a hypothetical example based on the topic you are going to discuss.
- Begin with a true-to-life example.
- Begin with vivid description of something pertaining to your topic.

It is particularly important that, in the context of the ACT, you make a concerted effort to create a captivating introduction. Keep in mind that the scorers of your essays are the scorers of everyone else's essays. They read hundreds of responses to the same issues and arguments. You must make your essay stand out. What better way to make it stand out than to make it exceptional from the beginning?

➢ **Conclusion -** The conclusion of your essay is just as important as the introduction because it wraps up your thoughts and evidence. It should leave your reader satisfied that a convincing discussion has just taken place. Your conclusion should include a restatement of your thesis and then end with a more general statement, perhaps a warning or a call for action.

Tip: If time is running out and you get stuck trying to formulate a conclusion, try beginning with *In conclusion* or *In summary*. Then continue by restating your thesis.

Style

How does a writer make a piece of writing his own? And how does a writer add interest to his essays? The way a writer uses words and phrases to add personality to his writing is called *style*.

Although we talked about style earlier, let's briefly re-cap.

➢ **Transitions**—Transitional phrases are an important element of formal writing because they create coherence. They guide the reader from point A to point B. Look at the lists below for some examples of transitional words and phrases that help achieve cohesiveness.

Agreement: *also, plus, in addition, further, furthermore, moreover, additionally, to add to that, next, in accordance with, accordingly, in agreement, finally, for instance, for example, in exemplification, exemplifying that, in fact, factually speaking, in terms of, and so forth, in coordination with, along those lines, collectively speaking, generally speaking, indeed, undoubtedly, obviously, to be sure, equally*

Contrast: *however, in contrast, on the contrary, on the other hand, from a different angle, nonetheless, nevertheless, but, yet, a catch to this is, sadly enough, as a hindrance, oddly enough, instead, in direct opposition, still, rather*

Result: *as a result, as a consequence, consequently, thus, therefore, hence, thereby, resulting in, ultimately, in the end, finally, in the overall analysis, in hindsight, in retrospect, retrospectively, vicariously, the long term effect, as a short term result, significantly, as a major effect, effectively, heretofore, hereafter, thereafter, in short, generally, over all, concluding*

✔ Check your work
Transitional words and phrases are helpful not only in linking ideas between sentences, but also in providing cohesiveness from paragraph to paragraph. Without this clarity, an essay will likely be choppy and difficult to read and understand. A word of caution, though: Be careful not to overuse transitional words and phrases. Overuse can make you sound like a pedantic writer rather than an intelligent one.

➢ **Varying Sentences**—No matter how well an essay flows, the reader will easily get bored if it consists only of sentences that contain the same words and follow the same structure.

Example:
Dogs help blind people. Dogs also help epileptic people. Dogs can sense when an epileptic person is about to have a seizure. Dogs are also used in rescue work. They help rescue skiers. They also help in catastrophic events. They rescue people after earthquakes.

There are several things wrong with this paragraph:
- Almost every sentence is the same length.
- The structure in each sentence is almost identical: Subject + Verb + Direct Object.
- The same words are used over and over: *dogs, they, rescue, help, people.*
- No description is used to further illustrate the writer's points.

✔ Check your work
To add more interest, try varying sentence length and structure. Try different sentence styles, employ a variety of words and use these words to paint a vivid picture of the subject. For example, you could begin your sentence with a subject and a predicate and then build on them using various words and phrases.

Cumulative sentence:
The energetic children played hard, chasing each other in all directions, occasionally falling and then scrambling to their feet, giggling at each other's antics and never stopping for even a moment to catch their breath.

Periodic sentence:
With flour in her hair, dough in between her fingers and sauce all over her face, she attempted to make a gourmet pizza.

Both of the above sentences not only add variety, but also bring rhythm and cadence to the writing. This rhythm creates interest and is pleasant to read. Additionally, descriptive words paint a clear picture for the reader.

➢ **Figurative Language**—Another excellent way to paint a vivid picture is to use figures of speech. Figures of speech—like similes, metaphors, analogies, personification, hyperbole, irony, and allusion—when used correctly, add extra flair to writing. They add an extra element that takes writing from ordinary to extraordinary.

Similes show a marked comparison between two things by using the phrases *like, as,* or, *as if:*

The cat stood poised and *still as a statue*, waiting for the opportune moment to pounce.

Metaphors show absolute comparison by omitting *like, as,* or, *as if:*

She is Mother Theresa when it comes to her generosity and compassion.

Here the comparison is absolute because the writer states that this person *is* Mother Theresa, even though she is not actually Mother Theresa.

Analogies compare the similar features of two dissimilar things, and they often bring clarity to writing by showing the reader another way of seeing something. Analogies are not limited to a sentence; sometimes an analogy streams its way through an entire piece of writing.

Example:
Office cooperation is like a soccer game. Each employee has a position on the playing field, and each position dictates an employee's function. Working together, the office completes passes by communicating well within each department. Shots on goal are taken when employees meet with

prospective clients to pitch ideas, and the whole office triumphs when a goal is scored and a prospect becomes a client.

Although an office and a soccer team are two very unrelated things, the writer sees similarities between the two and uses these similarities to clearly show how an office works.

>   *Personification* gives human characteristics to animals, inanimate objects and ideas in order to make them more real and understandable:

>   The rusty car groaned, coughed, then gave one last sputter and died.

The car in this sentence comes to life even as it "dies" because of the human characteristics it is given.

>   *Hyperbole* uses deliberate exaggeration or overstatement to show special emphasis or create humor.

Example:
Fat-free foods have become so popular that soon all vendors will want to sell them. Before you know it, Kentucky Fried Chicken will have fat-free fried chicken. Big Macs will contain 0 grams of fat. And the amount of fat in a Pizza Hut cheese pizza? You guessed it—none!

In order to show how excessive people's obsession with fat-free foods has become, this description purposefully exaggerates a world where the most unlikely things are fat-free.

>   *Irony* uses language to make a suggestion that directly contrasts with the literal word or idea. It can offer humor to writing, or a bitter tone when it is used in sarcasm.

Example:
Scientists have worked hard to develop ways to decrease infant mortality rates and increase longevity. As a result, more people are living longer and scientists will soon have to develop some methods with which to control overpopulation.

This sentence uses irony by predicting that, because scientists have now discovered ways to increase a person's life span, they will soon have to deal with another problem—overpopulation.

>   *Allusion* makes indirect reference to known cultural works, people or events. The familiarity allusions bring to writing helps the writer make connections with the reader:

>   I have so much to do today, I feel like David must have felt as he approached Goliath.

David must have felt a bit intimidated when facing the giant, Goliath—a feeling this writer alludes to when thinking about everything that needs to be done.

➢   **Tone -** The words you choose will greatly affect the tone of your essay. Likewise, the tone you wish to achieve will depend on your audience. On the ACT, you know your audience will consist of men and women who will be quickly reading your essay and then assigning a score based on their impression and how well you handled the topic. Knowing this, you will want to use a professional, formal tone, the kind you will probably use in most of your college work. Using a formal tone means that you will want to keep some distance between you, the writer, and your audience, the scorer. Be courteous and polite but avoid being chummy or intimate in any way. Furthermore, you should avoid all colloquialisms and slang.

➢   **Diction -** While tone defines the overall language you use, diction deals with the specific kinds of words and phrases you choose for your essay. Since you have already determined your audience and thus ascertained that you need to portray a formal tone in your essay, you must be consistent with your diction, or word choice. Diction may be classified as technical (*homo sapien* rather than *human*), formal (*Please inform me when you are ready to depart.*), informal or colloquial (*Give me a buzz when you're ready to go.*), or slang (*She's a real couch potato and watches the tube from early morning 'til the cows come home.*) Knowing that your audience dictates a formal tone, you must also be consistent in maintaining formal diction. Look at the following example of inconsistent diction:

> Violence in schools has become an epidemic problem. School shootings occur regularly, and fights erupt daily in the nation's classrooms. Even with the addition of metal detectors at school entrances, violence will never be eradicated because the jocks are always ganging up on the geeks. If only we could just all get along.

This example begins with a formal tone and formal diction; however, it takes a quick turn when the writer uses slang words like *jocks* and *geeks*. The paragraph is concluded informally with *If only we could just all get along.*

As you write your essay, and later, when you proofread it, you should make sure that you preserve the formality your audience requires.

➤ **Person** - It is important to maintain consistency in person. For example, if you begin your essay in second person (*you*) do not shift to third person (*he*, *she*, *it*, *one*, or *they*). Let's look at a couple of examples illustrating a shift in person:

Example:
One can get excellent grades in school if you study hard.

The switch from *one* to *you* is confusing and awkward.

Example:
Off the coast of Puerto Rico, on the island of Vieques, is an old French mansion turned hotel. Here one can enjoy spacious guest rooms and a cozy library. One can lounge around the pool and indulge in the honorary pool bar. Because the hotel is not far from the ocean, you can also take a leisurely walk down to the white sandy beach where one can spend a lazy day basking in the sun.

The switch from *one* to *you* is confusing in this paragraph and detracts from the imagery. Decide from the beginning of your essay what person you wish to employ and make a conscious effort to stick to it.

✓ Check your work
Your goal as a writer is to create interest and coherence through your unique writing style. Using figures of speech and maintaining consistent use of tone, diction, and person are effective ways to create interest. Using transitional words help to create coherence. Remember, though, that part of creating coherence is being concise. Use only the details that are necessary to support your topic and avoid tedious descriptions. This isn't to say that you should avoid vivid imagery, but only that you should take care to ensure that the above methods add to your writing rather than detract from it.

The most important aspect to remember is that style can only develop through practice. Practice your writing and proofread, proofread, proofread. If you do all of these things, you'll be well on your way to becoming an effective, skillful writer.

Warm-Up Drills

Prompt:
It is more beneficial to complete independent study than to attend college.

Assignment:
Do you think that a student can benefit more from completing independent study than from attending college? Plan and develop an essay in which you provide detailed and persuasive support for your opinion.

1. This opinion is not valid and is clearly not based on any evidence that would prove its validity. One can't gain more knowledge by completing independent study instead of attending college. It is necessary to look at some evidence to prove this.

2. Some people think that there are too many distractions at college because there are so many other students who take up class time. Interaction with other students can provide valuable insight into topics you study in college. Other people's backgrounds and experience add differences in perspectives and, in some cases, valuable expertise. Professors add expertise as well since they are the experts in the areas they are teaching. When a student studies on his own, he is dependent only on what he knows. He is also dependent on what he can read about. He is also dependent on his own background and experiences. This is very limiting to the value he can obtain from his education.

3. Some people think that students can learn more discipline by studying independently at home instead of going to college. College students learn a lot of discipline. They are held accountable by their college professors. They are held accountable by fellow students too. They depend upon them to contribute to the class. Students who study on their own are only accountable to themselves. Many times, studies get set aside when life gets too busy. Studies get the boot when a student encounters a subject they're not too excited about.

4. Studying at home independently is not as beneficial as attending college because the degree you get, if you get a degree at all, will not carry as much weight with potential employers as will a college degree from an accredited college or university. Employers place more weight on someone whose expertise they can depend on. Employers feel they can depend more on the expertise of someone who has been trained at a college or university.

5. People should go to college. You can't depend on your own motivation to finish your studies at home. A student gains a lot more from the interaction they receive between other students and professors in college. Students who get a degree from a college may have a better chance of getting a good job after college.

Solutions to Warm-Up Drills

1. The opening sentence in this paragraph does not make an effective introduction. It does not restate the topic but rather makes a direct address to the topic question. A good introduction should not require the reader to read the topic. The second sentence of the paragraph gives a concise thesis statement but should be elaborated on a bit. Also, the contraction *can't* does not fit with the formal tone of the essay. The last sentence serves as a transition to the next paragraph, but it does not show much sophistication or subtlety.

    Better:
    Should a student give up a college education in order to complete an independent study at home? Although the financial savings of independent study may be substantial, one can gain more benefits by obtaining a college or university education. Studying at a college or university can give a student a broader education, can help him learn discipline through accountability, and can pay off in the long run.

    This introduction begins with a question, which is more effective than directly addressing the question/topic. The thesis statement concisely lists three reasons a formal education is better than independent study; this sentence gives the reader a clear idea of what the essay will be about.

2. The first sentence serves as a topic sentence for the paragraph; however, it should be reworded to act as a better transitional sentence, one that would tie in with the last sentence of the preceding paragraph. The second sentence would function better with a transitional phrase like *On the contrary* to introduce it. Also in this sentence, the use of second person *you* is inconsistent with the rest of the essay. The fourth sentence uses the same two words *add* and *expertise* that were used in the preceding sentence. These should be changed to add some variety. The next three sentences are repetitive and should be combined.

    Better:
    Some people think that distractions at college from other students who take up class time results in a narrow education. On the contrary, interaction with other students can provide valuable insight into the topics one studies in college. Other people's backgrounds and experience add different perspectives and, in some cases, valuable expertise. Professors offer much value as well since they are the experts in the areas they are teaching. When a student studies on his own, he is dependent only on what he knows or can read about and on his own background and experiences. This severely limits the value he can obtain from his education.

    The first sentence works as a transition because it uses the word *narrow*, which contrasts with the word *broader* from the thesis statement in the preceding paragraph.

3. The first sentence works well as a topic sentence, but it uses the same wording as the topic sentence for the preceding paragraph. In the fifth sentence, the use of *they* and *them* is confusing because it is unclear whether the pronoun reference is to the student or fellow students. The remaining sentences are all the same length and therefore choppy. The last sentence strays from the formal tone of the essay. In addition, the word *they* does not agree in person with *a student*.

    Better:
    One valuable lesson students can learn at college is discipline. College students learn a lot of discipline because they are held accountable by their professors. Moreover, they are often held accountable by fellow students who depend upon them to contribute to the class. Students who study on their own are accountable only to themselves. Many times, studies get set aside when life gets too busy or when a student encounters a subject for which he is not enthusiastic.

    The word *valuable* ties in well with the word *value* in the last sentence of the preceding paragraph. Thus, this sentence serves not only as a topic sentence but also as a transitional sentence.

4. Again, the first sentence provides a good topic sentence but not a good transition from the preceding paragraph. The second sentence unnecessarily repeats the word *weight* from the first sentence. In the third sentence, the text shifts to second person *you*. The last sentence repeats the word *depend* from the preceding sentence.

Better:

Studying at a college or university may not make every topic seem scintillating; however, when a student is held accountable, he is more driven. As he is driven to succeed, he will eventually earn a degree. Studying at home independently is not as beneficial as attending college because the degree a student gets, if he gets a degree at all, will not carry as much weight with potential employers as will a degree from an accredited college or university. Employers place more confidence in someone whose expertise they can rely on. Employers feel they can depend more on the expertise of someone who has been trained at a college or university.

The topic sentence in this paragraph provides transition because it refers to the preceding paragraph by relating *scintillating* courses to being *enthusiastic* about subjects.

5. The first sentence does not act as a thorough topic sentence, nor does it provide a good transition. The second sentence uses *you* and *your*, which is an inconsistent use of person. In addition, the contraction *can't* takes away from the formal tone of the essay. Overall, this last paragraph is not effective; it has short, choppy sentences and does not adequately conclude the subject by restating the topic and giving final remarks.

Better:

Whether one is trained at a university or opts to stay home to study independently, an education is extremely important; however, it is clear that a student can benefit more from a formal education than from independent study. Students should not depend on their own motivation to finish their studies, nor should they miss out on the opportunity to benefit from the interaction they will receive from other students and professors in college. Despite any financial savings a student may earn by studying independently, the rewards of a college education will pay off in the long run.

The transition here works well because the first sentence uses the word *trained*, which is used in the sentence before it. This final paragraph functions effectively as a conclusion because it restates the topic. It also brings the writing full circle by once again mentioning the monetary aspect of education, which, as you recall, was mentioned in the introductory paragraph.

Presenting a Perspective on an Issue

If you are the typical high school student, you are more than likely wriggling in you seat, waiting to ask the all important question: *How long does my essay have to be?* A good rule of thumb to follow is the five-paragraph essay. In a five-paragraph essay, your first paragraph introduces your topic, three body paragraphs support your topic, and the last paragraph acts as your concluding paragraph.

Writing five paragraphs on one topic may seem like a daunting task; however, there are tricks to developing your topic and organizing your thoughts into paragraphs.

Patterns of Development

Just as there is no universal answer to every question, there are many different strategies used to write an essay. These strategies, or methods, are called *patterns of development*. The type of pattern you choose to employ is dependent upon the question or prompt to which you are responding. Usually, an essay question will contain certain clues, which enable you to determine which pattern of development to use. Utilizing these patterns will help you to develop a clear, concise thesis, which, in turn, will affect the way you organize your essay.

> **Compare & Contrast -** When an essay prompt uses words that suggest similarity or difference, or if an essay prompt seeks to persuade you that one item is superior to another, chances are that the writers of the ACT are trying to tell you something. They're looking for a Compare & Contrast essay.

> **Example:**
> American cars are better than foreign cars.

Here, the author uses the word *than* to compare the two cars, and he seeks to persuade the reader that an American car is a wiser choice than a foreign one.

To write a compare and contrast essay, you will need to portray similarities and differences between two given items (here, cars) to prove which one is superior, either in agreement or disagreement with the prompt.

> **Cause & Effect -** If an essay prompt uses an "If...then" statement or lacks an effect, then the writer's of the ACT are again trying to tell you what type of essay they want to see. A Cause & Effect essay.

> **Example (if...then):**
> If college and university faculty spent time outside the academic world working in professions relevant to the courses they teach, then the overall quality of higher education would greatly increase.

The author is arguing that if faculty spent time outside the academic world, in professions relevant to their courses, a desirable effect is achieved. So, in your essay, you must prove that the prompt's cause actually does result in the overall quality of education increasing. Either that, or you must prove that the prompt is wrong by introducing a negative effect based on the original cause, which was teachers working in professions relevant to the courses they teach.

Example (lack of effect):
More restrictions should be set on teenage drivers.

In this call to action statement, the author offers no effects that will result if the action is taken. However, it is implied that, if the author feels the action should be taken, he assumes something positive will result.

To write an essay off a *lack of effect* prompt, you will need to support a position in agreement with the above statement or against it, thus proving or disproving the implied effect.

Definition - Sometimes an essay prompt will attempt to show that a particular idea or concept is of great value. When this happens, prompts can be quite difficult to decipher. While it's easy to recognize a great value prompt, it becomes harder when these prompts only show a limited definition of a particular idea or concept.

Example (limited definition):
A person's generosity can be determined by examining what he or she has given to charity.

In this example, the author seeks to provide a very limited definition of a generosity, when, in fact, generosity can be defined by much more than a person's wallet and the amount that they've given to charity. After reading this prompt, your job would then be to either support the author's definition with evidence or show that the definition is much broader, maybe even wrong.

Let's look at another example.

Example (great value):
Patriotism breaks down the walls of division.

The author believes that patriotism can do great things. Whether or not you agree or disagree, it would be your job to define patriotism and show that, because of its attributes and qualities, it has value or it lacks value.

Planning & Writing

Now that you're familiar with the different methods you can employ to write an essay, let's get down to the nitty gritty. Remember, you're aiming for a 6 essay, one that presents clear, concise evidence to support a view. Writing a 6 essay doesn't have to be a difficult task. All you have to do is follow seven simple steps.

(Although some of the following steps may include specific formulas, you won't need to enter complete, descriptive sentences into the formulas; simple notes and phrases should be enough.)

➢ **Step 1 – Understand the Issue -** In order to properly present your perspective on an issue, you must first understand the issue you are being asked to discuss. Understanding the issue allows you to fully develop your position, presenting your evidence in a way that is most effective and appropriate for the topic. There are two steps that will help you understand the issue.

First, take a couple of minutes to read the given question carefully. Second, ask yourself the following questions about the prompt:
- What does the statement mean?
- What is the issue at hand?
- What is implied by the statement?
- What is the writer's opinion of the issue?
- What, if any, evidence does the writer use to support his position?
- What, specifically, is the assignment?

➢ **Step 2 – Choose A Pattern of Development -** Keeping in mind our discussion about the three patterns of development, look for the necessary criteria in the prompt. If you think the question requires more than one method, choose the one you think works the best. Although, on a timed writing assignment, your essay will be fairly short and therefore you cannot adequately utilize two methods.

➢ **Step 3 – Develop Your Thesis -** The next and most important step is to develop your thesis. Your thesis states the purpose of your essay. Without a thesis statement, your reader does not know what you are setting out to prove. And without a thesis statement, it would be very difficult to organize your essay with clarity and coherence. Don't be intimidated by the task of formulating what is to be the crux of your essay. It can be quite simple.

> **THESIS FOR A COMPARE & CONTRAST ESSAY** *(formula 1-1)*:
> I believe that Item A, _____, is better than Item B, _____, because
> 1) _____, 2) _____, 3) _____.
>
> **THESIS FOR A CAUSE & EFFECT ESSAY** *(formula 1-2)*:
> If _____, then _____, because
> 1) _____, 2) _____, 3) _____.
>
> **THESIS FOR A DEFINITION ESSAY** *(formula 1-3)*:
> By definition, _____ possess(es) these qualities: 1) _____,
> 2) _____, 3) _____ which have a positive effect because
> A) _____, B) _____, C) _____.

➢ **Step 4 – Understand Counter Arguments -** Have you ever been in an argument and found that you're covering zero ground? This could be because you are failing to see things from the other person's point of view. Being able to see the other side of a coin can go a long way in proving your point and disarming your opponent's objections. By showing that you are aware, though perhaps not understanding, of the opposing side you are adding credibility to your argument because it is clear that you have viewed the issue from all angles. To write an effective essay, you must show that you have considered the other side of the argument.

COMPARISON & CONTRAST COUNTER CLAIM *(formula 2-1)*:

Others may think Item B is better than Item A because 1) _____,
2) _____, 3) _____.

(Note that these three points should contrast directly with the three points of your thesis.)(see *formula 1-1*)

CAUSE & EFFECT COUNTER CLAIM *(formula 2-2)*:

Some may feel that _____ would cause _____ based on _____.

(Note that this point should contrast directly with point #1 of your thesis.)
(see *formula 1-2*)

DEFINITION *(formula 2-3)*:

By definition some may feel that _____ exhibits or is defined by _____
which could be positive / negative.

(Note that this point should contrast directly with point #1 of your thesis.)
(see *formula 1-3*)

➤ **Step 5 – Organize Your Thoughts -** Each of the following formulas will prompt you to plug in your thesis and counter argument points. In addition, there are spaces in the formula for you to insert 1 or 2 pieces of supporting evidence. Don't be intimidated, though. The formulas are meant to be a skeleton for organizing your essay. If you practice writing essays using the sample prompts in this book, you'll soon get accustomed to using the outlines, and they will seem much less imposing.

COMPARISON & CONTRAST ESSAY OUTLINE *(formula 3-1)*:

I. Introduction – Paragraph 1
   A. Restate your topic
   B. Thesis statement *(formula 1-1)*
II. Support – Paragraph 2
   A. Counter Claim point #1 *(formula 2-1)*
   B. Thesis point #1 *(formula 1-1)*
      1. Support for thesis point #1
      2. Support for thesis point #1
III. Support – Paragraph 3
   A. Counter Claim point #2 *(formula 2-1)*
   B. Thesis point #2 *(formula 1-1)*
      1. Support for thesis point #2
      2. Support for thesis point #2
IV. Support – Paragraph 4
   A. Counter Claim point #3 *(formula 2-1)*
   B. Thesis point #3 *(formula 1-1)*
      1. Support for thesis point #3
      2. Support for thesis point #3
V. Conclusion – Paragraph 5
   A. Restate thesis
   B. Issue a warning or a call to action

CAUSE & EFFECT ESSAY OUTLINE *(formula 3-2)*:

I. Introduction – Paragraph 1
   A. Restate your topic
   B. Thesis statement *(formula 1-2)*
II. Support – Paragraph 2
   A. Counter Claim *(formula 2-2)*
   B. Thesis point #1 *(formula 1-2)*
      1. Support for thesis point #1
      2. Support for thesis point #1

III. Support – Paragraph 3 – Thesis point #2 *(formula 1-2)*
    A. Support for thesis point #2
    B. Support for thesis point #2
IV. Support – Paragraph 4 – Thesis point #3 *(formula 1-2)*
    A. Support for thesis point #3
    B. Support for thesis point #3
V. Conclusion – Paragraph 5
    A. Restate thesis
    B. Issue a warning or a call to action

DEFINITION ESSAY FORMULA *(formula 3-3)*:
I. Introduction – Paragraph 1
    A. Restate your topic
    B. Thesis statement *(formula 1-3)*
II. Support – Paragraph 2
    A. Counter Claim *(formula 2-3)*
    B. Thesis point #1 *(formula 1-3)*
        1. Support by using thesis point A *(formula 1-3)*
        2. Support by using thesis point A *(formula 1-3)*
III. Support – Paragraph 3 – Thesis point #2 *(formula 1-3)*
    A. Support by using point B *(formula 1-3)*
    B. Support by using point B *(formula 1-3)*
IV. Support – Paragraph 4 – Thesis point #3 *(formula 1-3)*
    A. Support by using point C *(formula 1-3)*
    B. Support by using point C *(formula 1-3)*
V. Conclusion – Paragraph 5
    A. Restate thesis
    B. Issue a warning or a call for action

➢ **Step 6 – Write Your Essay -** Now that you have organized your thought, it's time to write! The best strategy under the pressure of a time restraint is to just begin writing—as quickly as you can while still being careful. (You should allow yourself about 20 minutes for writing.) Organization should not be difficult with the help of your formulas and outlines, but don't forget to add transitional words, phrases and sentences to help give your essay coherence. As you write, remember the mechanical rules you learned earlier and keep in mind the techniques we discussed in the section *The Essay*. The key to successful, timed writing is to reserve a bit of time at the end so that you can go back and proofread. You'll need this time to add finishing touch that will better you essay and help your idea flow more smoothly.

➢ **Step 7 – Revise Your Essay -** Because you have written quickly, you must spend some time, about 5 minutes, at the end to review your essay, making necessary changes to enhance the clarity, coherence and grammatical accuracy of your writing. You must look for misspellings and mechanical errors while at the same time keeping in mind the following questions:
- Is my introduction captivating?
- Is my thesis statement concise?
- Do my body paragraphs clearly support my thesis?
- Have I used logical transitions that help the text flow smoothly between sentences and between paragraphs?
- Have I maintained a formal tone and proper diction throughout my essay?
- Have I maintained consistent use of person (i.e., first, second, third)?
- Is there a word, or are there words, which I have employed too often throughout the essay?
- Do my sentences vary in length and structure?

As you ask yourself these questions, make the necessary changes. If you still have time left after you have completed the initial revision, go back and read your essay again. A writer makes many, many revisions to his manuscript before it is ready to be published, so you can never proofread too many times!

Sample Prompts & Essays

Now let's apply the 7 steps to three examples.

> ## **Example 1: Comparison & Contrast Essay**

> **Prompt:**
> *A new custom home is a much better purchase than an older, run-down home.*

> **Assignment:**
> Is it more wise to purchase an older, run-down home than a new custom home? Based on your own experiences in your family, plan and write an essay in which you develop your opinion on the better choice between new and old homes. Provide effective support for your opinion.

> Step 1 – Understand the Issue

- What does the statement mean? *If you are in the market to buy a house, a new home would be a better value.*
- What is the issue at hand? *What kind of home is the best to buy?*
- What is implied by the statement? *That one who purchases an old home is not making a wise choice. Also implied is that an older home is run-down.*
- What is the writer's stand on the issue? *He believes a new home is superior to an old one.*
- What, if any, evidence does the writer use to support his position? *Old houses are run-down, new homes can be custom built.*
- What, specifically, is the assignment? *To give my opinion about which home I think would make a wiser choice—a new home or an old home. To give support to persuasively develop my opinion.*

> Step 2 – Choose A Pattern of Development

This prompt requires me to employ the Comparison & Contrast pattern of development because the statement uses the word *than*, a contrasting word. The author is also trying to convince me that it is better to buy a new home than an old one.

> Step 3 – Develop Your Thesis

THESIS FOR A COMPARISON & CONTRAST ESSAY *(formula 1-1)*:
I believe that Item A, an old home, is better than Item B, a new home, because 1) an old home exemplifies old-style motifs that are unique in today's market, 2) foundations are stronger in older homes, 3) can remodel an old home in any way.

> Step 4 – Understand Counter Arguments

COMPARISON & CONTRAST COUNTER CLAIM *(formula 2-1)*:
Others may think Item B is better than Item A because 1) you can "keep up with the Joneses" with your modern décor, 2) new homes may be built quickly for easy occupancy, 3) new homes can be custom-built. (Note that these three points should contrast directly with the three points of your thesis.) (see *formula 1-1*)

> Step 5 – Organize Your Thoughts

COMPARISON & CONTRAST ESSAY FORMULA *(formula 3-1)*:
I. Introduction – Paragraph 1
    A. Some people feel that the purchase of a new home is a smarter investment choice than the purchase of an older home.

   B. For anyone who puts stock in the aged and unique, the traditional home may be the choice of a lifetime with its old-fashioned motifs, its strong foundations, and its versatility to become the house its owner designs.

II. Support – Paragraph 2
   A. keeping up with the Joneses – modern décor
   B. bring back old-time motifs
      1. More choices – can choose from different time periods
      2. More unique versus "cookie cutter" homes of today

III. Support – Paragraph 3
   A. Homes can be built quicker
   B. As a result, foundations not as strong in new homes
      1. Mass production of homes – builder doesn't establish good foundation
      2. Older homes in better condition over long period of time because built more solidly

IV. Support – Paragraph 4
   A. Custom-built
   B. Can remodel any way owner wants
      1. No allowance restrictions placed on owner by builder

V. Conclusion – Paragraph 5
   A. Modern homes just don't offer the old-fashioned charm an older well-built, unique home can offer.
   B. When it comes to such an important decision as purchasing a home, the choice is clear: an older home has much more to offer and will last for many years to come.

➢ Step 6 – Write Your Essay

Modern-day housing developments are springing up everywhere, dotting hills and filling in every open space available. Characterized by "cookie cutter" homes, houses all cut from the same mold, the look of these communities lacks distinctiveness. For anyone who puts stock in the aged and unique rather than the new and ordinary, the traditional house may be the choice of a lifetime, with its old-fashioned motifs, its strong foundations, and its versatility to become the home of its owner's design.

Many homeowners do not feel the need to be the designer behind their home. Rather, they strive to "keep up with the Joneses" by filling their houses with the same modern décor that fills the homes of their neighbors. On the flip side, when seeking to invest in a traditional home, the buyer has a plethora of options because older homes offer so much uniqueness. This uniqueness can be seen in the motifs of style, which are almost non-existent in today's market of prefabricated homes but are powerful reminders of the past in older structures. These are the structures that offer a homeowner an admirable individuality.

Clearly, modern-day homes, which lack individuality, are built more quickly than homes of the past, a fact that seems to fit today's hurried society. But what does a homeowner have to show for this efficiency years down the road? There is much value added to a home constructed by a builder who takes time and pays attention to detail instead of putting up as many homes as possible in the shortest amount of time possible. For example, in the past when builders did take extra time and care, the foundations and overall structures were, and still are, much stronger. This is because many builders today, eager to make a quick buck, do not give homes ample time to settle on their foundation before continuing with the construction. Overall, older houses are in better condition, even over the course of time, because they were more solidly built.

Many prospective buyers today overlook the quality of a home's structure and are compelled to purchase by the alluring idea of custom building their house. These homebuyers enjoy the process of choosing paint colors, fixtures and floor coverings. Consider an older home, however. Here the possibilities are endless, and traditional buyers may even negotiate remodeling into the price of the house. What is more, there are no spending restrictions which contemporary builders often impose on their buyers.

Spending restrictions represent just one of many ways that freedom is limited when purchasing a new home instead of an older home. Whether one prefers an elegant, plantation-style mansion or a peaceful, rustic country getaway, the distinctive older home has much more to offer than the commonplace modern home set in communities of houses that all look the same. Simply put, it comes down to whether the prospective buyer is willing to trade quality and originality for expediency.

➢ Step 7 – Revise Your Essay

When critiquing other essays, you can often learn a lot about the strengths and weaknesses in your own writing. So here's an assignment: Complete the task required for each of the following questions.

- Is the introduction captivating? Why or why not? Do you recognize a certain method the author employed to make the introduction interesting?
- Is the thesis statement concise? Does it clearly show the purpose of the essay?

- Do the body paragraphs clearly support each point made in the thesis? If not, where does the essay lack necessary support?

- Are there logical transitions that make the text flow smoothly between sentences and between paragraphs? Underline each word, phrase or sentence that acts as a transition.

- Is the tone and diction consistent throughout the essay? If not, point out the places where consistency breaks down.

- Is the use of person consistent? If not, point out the places where consistency is not maintained.

- Is there a word, or are there words, which have been used too often in the essay? List these words. Also list the words that have been used to provide variety in the essay.

- Do the sentences vary in length and structure?

➢ **Example 2: Cause & Effect Essay**

Prompt:
Students should not be required to take courses outside their field of study.

Assignment:
Do you think that college students should be required to take a well-rounded selection of courses even if they do not pertain to their major? Plan and write a well-developed essay in which you discuss your opinion on this topic. Support your opinion with persuasive details.

➢ Step 1 – Understand the Issue

- What does the statement mean? *Colleges should not make students take courses, like General Education courses, if they do not pertain to their area of study.*
- What is the issue at hand? *Whether or not students benefit from taking college courses that don't pertain to their major.*
- What is implied by the statement? *That a student will be adequately prepared for the "real world" without taking a wide range of classes.*
- What is the writer's stand on the issue? *That students should not be required to take these classes.*
- What, if any, evidence does the writer use to support his position? *The writer does not give any evidence to support his view.*
- What, specifically, is the assignment? *To show my perspective on whether college students should have to take classes that do not have anything to do with their major. I need to give support that will persuade the reader that the college student will benefit based on my opinion.*

➢ Step 2 – Choose A Pattern of Development

This prompt is a call to action statement, and, although no effect is discussed, the writer implies that his recommended course of action would result in a positive effect.

➢ Step 3 – Develop Your Thesis

THESIS FOR CAUSE & EFFECT ESSAY *(formula 1-2)*:
If students are not required to take courses outside their field of study, then they will not be prepared, because 1) they will be ill-prepared if they fail to get a job in their field, 2) they will be lacking in important skills – communication or thinking/reasoning skills, 3) they will be close-minded and ignorant to things happening in the world around them.

➢ Step 4 – Understand Counter Arguments

CAUSE & EFFECT COUNTER CLAIM *(formula 2-2)*:
Some may feel that requiring students to take courses only in their field of study would cause students to be more knowledgeable in their field because they would have more thoroughly studied this area.
(Note that this point should contrast directly with point #1 of your thesis.)
(see *formula 1-2*)

➤ Step 5 – Organize Your Thoughts

CAUSE & EFFECT ESSAY FORMULA *(formula 3-2)*:

I. Introduction – Paragraph 1
  A. Some feel students should not be required to take courses outside their field of study.
  B. If students are not required to take courses outside their field of study, they will be ill-prepared should they fail to get a job in their field, they will lack important skills, and they will be close-minded and ignorant to things happening in the world around them.

II. Support – Paragraph 2
  A. Some may feel that requiring students to take courses only in their field of study would cause students to be more knowledgeable in their field because they would have more thoroughly studied this area.
  B. Many people are unable to get a job in their field after they graduate.
    1. Without some knowledge of other fields, these highly trained people will be stuck working menial jobs.

III. They will be lacking in important skills.
  A. Students studying the sciences will lack communication skills.
  B. Students studying the arts will lack critical thinking and reasoning skills.

IV. They will be close-minded and ignorant of things happening in the world around them.
  A. Lack of familiarity with certain fields promotes disinterest in these topics as they pertain to current events (politics, scientific research).
  B. This disinterest promotes apathy in participating in or supporting causes that result from these current events.

V. Conclusion – Paragraph 5
  A. Students must take a well-rounded schedule of classes in order to be prepared for work outside their field and so they will have adequate skills to use toward a common interest in society.
  B. Students should welcome an opportunity to learn about all areas of study.

➤ Step 6 – Write Your Essay

Colleges and universities require students, regardless of their majors, to complete General Education courses, basic courses that cover general subject areas. These classes include basic literature and writing courses, basic science and math courses, and basic arts classes like music and drama. Some feel students should not be required to take these General Education classes. However, if students are not required to take courses outside their major, they will be ill-prepared should they fail to get a job in their field, they will lack important skills, and they will be close-minded and ignorant of things happening in the world around them.

Many opponents of General Education classes are themselves unaware of the advantages of a well-rounded education. They focus only on the theory that students will be more fully prepared to enter their field as a result of more extensive study in their area. What they fail to see, however, is that many graduates are not able to find jobs in their field of expertise. So, without a broad range of knowledge, these highly trained graduates would be stuck in menial jobs.

Even if graduates do get jobs within their field, such a wide range of skills are required in the workplace in order to be successful that, without a diverse educational background, a graduate will not be fully competent in any job. For example, when a graduate begins looking for a job, she will discover that excellent communication skills are invaluable in the workplace, both in dealing with customers and with colleagues. Without some base of communication knowledge, such as a student would receive in a basic English class, the candidate will be overlooked for someone who does show strength in communication. Moreover, most jobs require strong problem-solving skills, skills that develop from learning how to think and reason critically. These skills are reinforced in math and science classes.

Lack of familiarity in certain educational arenas, like math and science, results in a provincial attitude. This lack of familiarity leads to disinterest in the areas where a student has not gained knowledge. Likewise, this disinterest leads to apathy in participating or supporting any causes that are linked to these fields of study.

For example, a student who has not studied science will be indifferent to scientific ideas, ideas which could become theories and could help all of mankind. A student who does not study politics and government will likely be apathetic toward participating in important political events such as elections.

It is important that a country's citizens take part in supporting causes and concepts that generate a common interest in society. Without a well-rounded schedule of classes in college, however, the citizen base will soon be filled with people who are unprepared and indifferent to anything that does not directly pertain to their area of interest. Instead of complaining about an opportunity to gain a broad range of knowledge, students should consider it a privilege and an asset.

➤ Step 7 – Revise Your Essay

Read over the essay above and then answer the following questions.

- Is the introduction captivating? Why or why not? Do you recognize a certain method the author employed to make the introduction interesting?

- Is the thesis statement concise? Does it clearly show the purpose of the essay?

- Do the body paragraphs clearly support each point made in the thesis? If not, where does the essay lack necessary support?

- Are there logical transitions that make the text flow smoothly between sentences and between paragraphs? Underline each word, phrase or sentence that acts as a transition.

- Is the tone and diction consistent throughout the essay? If not, point out the places where consistency breaks down.

- Is the use of person consistent? If not, point out the places where consistency is not maintained.

- Is there a word, or are there words, which have been used too often in the essay? List these words. Also list the words that have been used to provide variety in the essay.

- Do the sentences vary in length and structure?

➢ **Example 3: Definition Essay**

Prompt:
The positive effects of competition in a society far outweigh the negative effects.

Assignment:
Do you think that competition has a positive or negative effect on a community? Write an essay in which you develop your opinion. Support your perspective by drawing from personal experience and knowledge you have gained in your life. Make sure your support is specific and persuasive.

➢ Step 1 – Understand the Issue
- What does the statement mean? *Competition affects society in a good way, not a bad way.*
- What is the issue at hand? *Whether or not competition is good for society.*
- What is implied by the statement? *That a society benefits from competition amongst its members.*
- What is the writer's stand on the issue? *That competition is good and provides benefits.*
- What, if any, evidence does the writer use to support his position? *The writer does not give any evidence to support his view.*
- What, specifically, is the assignment? *To persuasively discuss with the reader my perspective on the effects of competition in society. I can use personal experience to make my points clear.*

➢ Step 2 – Choose A Pattern of Development
Although the comparison between a society driven by competition and one where competition plays little or no role seems to hint that the Compare & Contrast method should be used, the Definition pattern of development is a better fit because it is necessary to look at the qualities of competition that make it a positive influence rather than a negative one.

➢ Step 3 – Develop Your Thesis
THESIS FOR DEFINITION ESSAY *(formula 1-3)*:
By definition, competition possesses these qualities: 1) gives everyone the same chance at the beginning, 2) drives people to succeed, 3) provides a way to recognize people who advance which have a positive effect because A) no one can use the excuse that they didn't have the same opportunities; everyone has a chance to succeed, B) people want to be the best, and gives everyone their "place" in life, C) gives self-worth to those who are recognized for their accomplishments.

➢ Step 4 – Understand Counter Arguments
DEFINITION *(formula 2-3)*:
By definition, some may feel that competition helps only a few/pushing only a few to the top, leaving others feeling left out or insignificant which could be positive or **negative**.
(Note that this point should contrast directly with point #1 of your thesis.)
(see *formula 1-3*)

➢ Step 5 – Organize Your Thoughts
DEFINITION ESSAY FORMULA *(formula 3-3)*:
I. Introduction – Paragraph 1
  A. Competition benefits a society.
  B. Everyone is given a chance to succeed in a society where competition drives people to be the best and recognizes the accomplishments of the many who advance.
II. Support – Paragraph 2
  A. Some feel that competition helps only a few, leaving others feeling left out or insignificant. There is a push to eliminate salutatorian/valedictorian recognition speeches at graduation.
  B. Competition gives everyone the same chance at the beginning.
    1. Just like a marathon – everyone begins at the same starting line.
    2. No one has an excuse – it is up to each individual to decide how to run the race. Some want to work harder than others and therefore deserve recognition.
III. Competition drives people to be their best
  A. Everyone's "best" is different.
  B. Gives everyone their place in life – if no competition, we'd have a world full of custodians, no CEO's or vice versa.
IV. With competition comes the chance to recognize winners.

A. Gives self-worth to those recognized, causing them to set even greater goals.

B. Encourages those who were not recognized to try harder so that they too may be recognized.

V. Conclusion – Paragraph 5

    A. Competition is vital to a growing and thriving society.

    B. How will you run the race? Will you strive to be the best?

➢ Step 6 – Write Your Essay

On your mark! All the runners are at the starting line. *Get set!* The runners are poised, in position. *Go!* The runners take off. The spirit of competition is the driving force behind these runners' desire to win. And, as an integral part of society, competition brings many benefits. Everyone is given a chance to succeed in a society where competition drives people to be their best, and competition recognizes the accomplishments of those who advance.

Some feel that, although competition recognizes winners, there are so few winners that many are left feeling insignificant and alienated. This attitude has, for example, lead to a movement to eliminate salutatorian and valedictorian recognition and speeches at graduation ceremonies. Those in the movement claim that acknowledging salutatorian and valedictorian students for their scholastic achievements causes other students to feel slighted. This is a misguided assumption. Government gives everyone equal opportunity to attend school and to excel. Some students work harder than others and deserve special honors at graduation. Just like in a race, everyone begins at the same starting line and therefore has the same chance to succeed. Each person makes his own decision about how he will run the race. No one has an excuse, then, for not trying his best to succeed.

Competition drives people to achieve a goal. For most, this goal represents a person's best. Since everyone's concept of "best" is different, achievement differs for each person. Therefore, when an individual reaches his goal, this gives him a certain status. This status is different for each person, depending on the goal that was attained. This is extremely important because if competition did not place people at different positions in life, the resulting equality would be stultifying to society. For example, the work force would consist of only custodians and no CEO's or vice versa.

CEO's get to where they are only through competition. As an employee works hard and competes within a company, he is rewarded for his accomplishments with promotions. Not only does competition award people through tangible benefits like promotions, but competition also gives long-lasting psychological awards such as a feeling of self-worth or pride. This recognition encourages people who succeed to raise their personal goals even higher. Recognition also drives those who were not recognized to do better so that they too may be rewarded.

Because competition results in rewards, both tangible and emotional, it is essential for a growing and thriving society. Everyone begins at the same starting line and is given the same chance to succeed. When the starting gun fires, it is up to each runner to decide how he will run the race. This decision will ultimately determine who will become the winners. Driven by competition, these winners, along with the losers, comprise a successful society.

➢ Step 7 – Revise Your Essay

Read over the essay previous and then answer the following questions:

- Is the introduction captivating? Why or why not? Do you recognize a certain method the author employed to make the introduction interesting?
- Is the thesis statement concise? Does it clearly show the purpose of the essay?
- Do the body paragraphs clearly support each point made in the thesis? If not, where does the essay lack necessary support?
- Are there logical transitions that make the text flow smoothly between sentences and between paragraphs? Underline each word, phrase or sentence that acts as a transition.
- Is the tone and diction consistent throughout the essay? If not, point out the places where consistency breaks down.
- Is the use of person consistent? If not, point out the places where consistency is not maintained.
- Is there a word, or are there words, which have been used too often in the essay? List these words. Also list the words that have been used to provide variety in the essay.
- Do the sentences vary in length and structure?

Practice

Now it's your turn to practice some essays. Consider the five prompts and assignments below and write an essay, using the 7 steps that we've talked about in this section. Remember: the only way to become better at writing is through practice, practice, practice.

Prompt:
Museums should have the liberty to exhibit whatever displays they want without the interference of government censorship.

Assignment:
Do you think the government should impose censorship on controversial museum displays, or should museums be permitted to display whatever they choose? Plan and write an essay in which you discuss your perspective on this type of censorship. Support your opinion with clear and persuasive evidence.

Prompt:
When people work in teams, they are more productive than when they work individually.

Assignment:
Do you think that people work more effectively in teams or by themselves? Explain your opinion in a well-developed essay. Support your perspective by drawing from personal experience and knowledge you have gained.

Prompt:
If everyone would closely examine their past, they would realize that only a few individuals have played a role in shaping their behavior and their way of thinking.

Assignment:
Do you think your behavior and way of thinking was shaped by merely a few people, or were you impacted by many others? Thinking about your own personal experiences, plan and write an essay in which you discuss your perspective on the shaping of behavior.

Prompt:
Success is easily obtained but difficult to maintain.

Assignment:
In your opinion, is it easy or difficult to obtain success? Along the same lines, do you think that, once obtained, success is easy or difficult to maintain? Plan and write an essay in which you develop your opinion about success. Support your perspective by providing concise evidence.

Prompt:
Society is governed by two types of laws, just and unjust. People must obey just laws but are at liberty to defy those laws which they determine are frivolous or unjust.

Assignment:
Do you agree that some laws are just while others are unjust? Moreover, if you do agree with this statement, do you feel that people need only obey those laws which they deem just? Discuss your opinion about the justice of laws. Provide concrete and persuasive support for your opinion.

Sample Essays

There is little need for books today because one can learn just as much or more from television.

Assignment:
Do you think that television is a good replacement for books? Plan and write an essay in which you discuss your opinion on the relevance of books in today's world. Make sure you support your opinion by drawing on your experiences and knowledge.

When I was little, I would line up my stuffed animals and "read" to them. Although I was not old enough to know the letters formed words and the words formed sentences, I knew there was a story to tell, and I knew there was an audience who would be interested in hearing the story. Now I watch my two-year-old daughter do the same thing. In this media age, books often take a back seat to television, which is unfortunate because books offer so much more. Books are a better tool with which to build imagination. Moreover, readers can gain much more knowledge from the wide variety of books that are available.

Satellite dishes and improved cable offer hundreds of channels, a variety that some TV viewers argue is sufficient to replace reading. However, libraries and bookstores offer thousands, not hundreds, of titles from which to choose. Among these choices, a reader can find books on any theme he chooses, from topics of today to stories of every era in the past. Television, unfortunately, is controlled mostly by popular trends. Aside from a handful of specialty channels like *The History Channel*, there is little on TV about historical events. Furthermore, TV viewers' choices are limited since the television broadcasting companies choose what they will offer on each channel.

A limited choice of TV channels results in limited knowledge. The written word offers much more detail than television. Most TV shows are limited to two hours or less, and because of this time restriction, fewer details can be included in shows like movies and documentaries. For example, a TV documentary on orangutans would most likely be a one hour program which would offer some basic knowledge about orangutans, their habitat and their way of life. A book about orangutans, on the other hand, would educate the reader far beyond the basic knowledge he would gain from watching a television program.

In addition to offering more information on a greater number of subjects, the added description included in books helps readers improve vocabulary. In books, readers see unfamiliar words in context, enabling them to decipher the meaning. For TV viewers, unfamiliar words in conversation usually go unnoticed. In fact, many people watch TV simply to "veg," or, in other words, to sit and do nothing but be vaguely aware of the images flickering across the screen. Watching television requires little of the concentration that is required for reading books; consequently the viewer overlooks many details.

Because watching TV does not require active participation, the imagination suffers. Television programs take the viewer quickly from one scene to the next, prohibiting the viewer from taking notice of the details of the setting. Books inspire imagination, allowing the reader to picture for herself the setting and characters of the story. A book's character may be described as tall, dark complected, and wearing a bright purple robe; it is up to the reader to imagine exactly what the character looks like. Is the character Italian or perhaps Native American? Is the bright purple robe rather gaudy looking, or does it give the character an air of sophistication? Television makes those decisions for the viewer by placing in the program a specific actor in garb chosen by costume designers, thus leaving little room for imagination.

Imagination is the key to forward thinking, thinking that brings a person success in what he does. Without imagination, problems go unsolved and new and inventive ideas never make it to the drawing board. Imagination produces creativity, which inspires dreamers. I hope my daughter will continue to be a dreamer, allowing her imagination to blossom. And when the letters, then words, then sentences take form for her, she will have the added benefit of gaining boundless knowledge from books.

Prompt:
Many of today's technological conveniences were developed to save time. Ironically, these developments have created an even more hurried, fast-paced society, where people actually have less leisure time.

Assignment:
Do you think modern technological advances have resulted in a less relaxed society? Develop an essay in which you give your perspective on the effects of modern conveniences on today's society. Pull from your own experiences to persuasively support your opinion.

Ah, the good ol' days! When people sat on their front porch talking and watching the world go by instead of finishing up last-minute work on their laptops. When letters took a week to spread the latest news instead of a few seconds through e-mail. In a world of pagers, faxes, cell phones, and computers, a very hurried society is characterized by impatient workaholics whose nerves are on edge and whose lives are unknowingly empty.

Many of today's conveniences were developed to meet growing impatience with the speed it took to spread information. Through the development of such things as faxes, cell phones and e-mail, however, a new impatience was born. This new impatience is characterized by frustration with the sophistication and complexity of modern technology. Office workers grit their teeth in frustration when an e-mail takes too long to download. In annoyance, they may shut down their computer assuming there is something wrong with the machine. This wastes even more time while restarting the computer and finally retrieving the culprit e-mail. Overnight delivery services emerged to meet this all-consuming impatience as well. Oftentimes, however, even this speedy service is not expedient enough. Some find it necessary to rush a package to the airport so that it may arrive at its destination just a few hours earlier.

This annoyance with our more efficient world has thrown society into a frenzy where even the most technologically advanced equipment is unsatisfactorily slow. The resulting annoyance and impatience can turn into rage in the office and on the highway, with stressed out employees who "go postal," losing all rationale and even causing injury to colleagues. Preventable injuries occur on highways as road rage consumes drivers who are eager to get to their next destination.

In a world where people are eager to pass information ever more quickly and get to their next destination ever more quickly, this has truly become a society of workaholics. Because the transfer of information is so much more efficient with modern technologies, workers find they can accomplish much more in a given day. Driven by this fact, they work more hours. There is always time to make that last call or send a quick e-mail at the end of the day. And portable conveniences like laptops and palm pilots make it possible for people to work essentially anywhere; work is no longer confined to the office and is often completed at home.

Perhaps the most detrimental aspect of our more hurried society lies at home. Because many people spend more time working, and because work is transportable, many spouses discover that their partners spend more time with their computers and cell phones than with their family. Additionally, other conveniences like microwave meals encourage quick meals on-the-go. Rushed families rarely spend quality time together around the dinner table. Rather, they all go their separate ways to eat in front of the TV, at the computer, or at a desk reviewing reports.

At home, in the office and on the streets, a fast-paced society continues to become more hurried as technology continues to match a perpetually growing impatience. Is all of this annoyance, frustration, and rage worth the added convenience that technology has brought to our society? It hardly seems so. In fact, in looking back at the good 'ol days, it seems that in a world with far less vexation and anger, there was more happiness.

Prompt:
Character is created in a crisis.

Assignment:
Do you think character is created in a crisis or merely manifested? Plan and write an essay in which you define your opinion. Make sure you provide clear support for your answer.

In 1992, Hurricane Andrew slammed into Florida causing millions of dollars of damage. Many residents lost everything, including their homes. Those houses that had the strongest foundations withstood the storm most favorably. Additionally, the homes that had been adequately prepared to face the storm fared better than those whose windows were not boarded. Character is like a house. If your character has a strong foundation and displays traits of preparedness, you can weather a storm well. In this light, it is clear that character is not born from crisis, but rather, it merely emerges during difficult times.

It is not adversity but the small moments of life that create character. Poor decisions, regardless of how insignificant, break down your character. Anytime you are inconsistent in following your principles, no matter how small the compromise, cracks in your foundation undoubtedly weaken your character. On the positive side, though, you can learn a lot from your mistakes. In fact, lessons learned from failures are indispensable in building character. To discern the lesson to be learned, however, takes conscious effort. If you are unwilling to put effort into developing character, you will continue to repeat your mistakes, and your life will stagnate.

Part of building character and thus avoiding stagnation is building on your strengths. Taking what is good and making it exceptional is what character building is all about. Continued improvement in life makes you stronger. This too takes a conscious effort in using strengths to positively affect others around you. Channeling the positive to help others results in personal growth, which in turn builds character.

Only when you are willing to learn from your mistakes and make a conscious effort to grow can you face a crisis successfully. It is during this adversity that character comes to light. If you have learned from past failures, you will have the strength to face a crisis head on. You will have adequate problem-solving skills to overcome obstacles set before you. If you have made the conscious effort to build on your positive traits, you will have the means with which to get through the crisis positively with the will to move ahead.

The will and ability to move forward from crisis is the defining moment of your character. As you move forward, though, you should never stop working to improve, because the stronger your foundation is, the better it will weather any type of storm. What kind of storm can the foundation of your character withstand?

Practice Test

Time: 45 minutes for 73 questions.

Directions: Following are five passages with underlined portions. Alternate ways of stating the underlined portions come after the passages. Choose the best alternative; if the original is the best way of stating the underlined portion, choose NO CHANGE.

The test also has questions that refer to the passages or ask you to reorder the sentences within the passage. These questions are identified by a number in a box. Choose the best answer and shade in the corresponding oval on your answer sheet.

Passage 1:

Mind and Media: The Effects of Television, Video

Games, and Computers - Patricia Marks

Greenfield

[1]

If dynamic visual graphics, sound effects,
1
and, automatic scorekeeping are the features that
1
account for the popularity of video games (the

latter being addictive in nature), why are parents
2
so worried? All seem quite innocent. But another
3
source of concern is that the games available in

arcades have, almost without exception, themes

of physical aggression. There has long been the
4
belief that violent content may teach violent

behavior. And yet again our society finds a new

medium in which to present that content, and yet
5
again the demand is nearly insatiable could be
5   6
looked at as another instance where human

history has repeated it'self. And there is evidence
7
that violent video games breed violent behavior. 8

[2]

The effects of video violence are less

simple, however, than it at first appeared. The
9
same group of researchers who found negative

effects [from certain video games] has more
10
recently found that two-player aggressive video
10
games, whether cooperative or competitive,

reduce the level of aggression in children's

play, that is surprising.
11

[3]

It may be that the most harmful aspect of

the violent video games are that they are solitary
12
in nature. A two-person aggressive game (video

boxing, in this study) seems to provide a cathartic
13
or releasing effect for aggression, while a solitary
13
aggressive game (such as Space Invaders) may

stimulate further aggression. TV viewing typically
14
involves little social interaction. 15
14

394

1. A. NO CHANGE
   B. dynamic visual graphics, sound effects; and, automatic scorekeeping
   C. dynamic visual graphics, sound effects: and, automatic scorekeeping
   D. dynamic visual graphics, sound effects, and automatic scorekeeping

2. F. NO CHANGE
   G. last
   H. final
   J. latest

3. A. NO CHANGE
   B. All of these features seem quite innocent.
   C. All of those features seem quite innocent.
   D. All features seem quite innocent.

4. F. NO CHANGE
   G. There will long have been
   H. There could long have been
   J. There long is

5. A. NO CHANGE
   B. , and, yet again,
   C. and yet again
   D. , yet

6. F. NO CHANGE
   G. insatiable; could be
   H. insatiable, that could be
   J. insatiable, which could be

7. A. NO CHANGE
   B. itself
   C. it's self
   D. its self

8. Is it logical to omit the final sentence of paragraph one?
   F. Yes, because it restates information that has already been presented.
   G. Yes, because the conjunction *and* has been used to start too many sentence in the paragraph.
   H. No, because it sets up the topic for the next paragraph.
   J. No, because you should never delete anything from an essay, so that you never miss a point.

9. A. NO CHANGE
   B. he
   C. they
   D. them

10. F. NO CHANGE
    G. has, more recently found
    H. has been more recently finding
    J. have more recently found

11. A. NO CHANGE
    B. , which is surprising
    C. ; that is surprising
    D. . That is surprising.

12. F. NO CHANGE
    G. is
    H. will be
    J. OMIT UNDERLINED PORTION

13. A. NO CHANGE
    B. a cathartic, or releasing effect,
    C. a cathartic or releasing affect
    D. a cathartic, or releasing, effect

14. F. NO CHANGE
    G. TV viewing, typically, involves little social interaction.
    H. TV viewing involved little social interaction.
    J. OMIT UNDERLINED PORTION

15. According to the passage, which of the following would be likely to stimulate violent behavior in a child playing a video game?
    I. Watching the computer stage a battle between two opponents
    II. Controlling a character in battle against a computer
    III. Challenging another player to a battle in a non-cooperative two-person game
    A. II only
    B. III only
    C. I and II only
    D. II and III only

Passage 2:

The Technological Society - Jacques Ellul

[1]

The technical phenomenon, embracing all the separate techniques, forms a whole. Not only is it useless to look for differentiations (because they only exist secondarily)<u>, but it serves</u> almost
    ₁₆
no purpose. After the common features of the technical phenomenon are sharply drawn<u>, then</u> it
                                          ₁₇
is easy to discern that which is the technical phenomenon and that which is not. And the common features draw <u>themself.</u> [19]
                          ₁₈

[2]

To analyze these common features is tricky, but it is simple to grasp <u>them, just</u> as there
                                      ₂₀
are principles common to things as different as a wireless set and an internal-combustion engine, so to the organization of an office and the construction of an aircraft have certain identical features. <u>That is</u> the primary mark of that
        ₂₁
thoroughgoing <u>unity, it makes</u> the technical
              ₂₂
phenomenon a single essence despite the extreme diversity of its appearances. <u>The</u>
                                          ₂₃
<u>technical phenomenon is a single entity.</u>
          ₂₃

[3]

As a corollary, it is impossible to analyze this or that element out of <u>it--a</u> truth which is today
                                  ₂₄
particularly misunderstood. <u>The great tendency of</u>
                            ₂₅
<u>all persons who study techniques to make</u>
          ₂₅

<u>distinctions.</u> They distinguish between the
  ₂₅
different elements of <u>technique, maintaining some</u>
                        ₂₆
<u>and discarding others.</u> They distinguish <u>among</u>
  ₂₆   ₂₇
technique and the use to which it is put. These distinctions are completely invalid and show only that <u>he whose made them</u> understood nothing of
      ₂₈
the technical phenomenon. Its parts are ontologically tied together; <u>being that,</u> use is
                          ₂₉
inseparable from being. [30]

16. F. NO CHANGE
    G. , also it serves
    H. , but also it serves
    J. , but also looking serves

17. A. NO CHANGE
    B. ; it
    C. , it
    D. ; then,

18. F. NO CHANGE
    G. they
    H. themselves
    J. itself

19. The "technical phenomenon" referred to in the opening line can best be defined as
    A. all of the machinery in use today
    B. the abstract idea of the machine
    C. a way of thinking in modern society
    D. what all machines have in common

20. F. NO CHANGE
    G. them. Just
    H. them; just
    J. them just

21. A. NO CHANGE
    B. These distinctions are
    C. It is
    D. Which is

22. F. NO CHANGE
    G. unity that makes
    H. unity, which makes
    J. unity, so makes

23. A. NO CHANGE
    B. The technical phenomenon is not a single entity.
    C. The technical phenomenon is confusing.
    D. OMIT UNDERLINED PORTION

24. F. NO CHANGE
    G. it; a
    H. it, a truth
    J. it a truth

25. A. NO CHANGE
    B. The great tendency of all persons who study techniques is to make distinctions.
    C. The great tendency of all persons who study techniques are to make distinctions.
    D. OMIT UNDERLINED PORTION

26. F. NO CHANGE
    G. technique. Maintaining some and discarding others.
    H. technique...maintaining some and discarding others.
    J. technique; maintaining some and discarding others.

27. A. NO CHANGE
    B. over
    C. between
    D. against

28. F. NO CHANGE
    G. he who made those
    H. he whom had made them
    J. he who has made them

29. A. NO CHANGE
    B. in it,
    C. since,
    D. often,

30. The author wrote this essay for an assignment in which he had to describe a technical society. Did the author meet his assignment?
    F. Yes, because the technical phenomenon is about a technical society.
    G. Yes, because writing something with the word *technical* in it is better than writing nothing at all.
    H. No, because discussing the technical phenomenon does not describe the necessary elements of a technical society.
    J. No, because the essay makes no sense.

Passage 3:

A Shorter History of Science

- Sir William Cecil Dampier

[1]

As Xenophanes recognized as long ago as the sixth century before Christ, its certain that
<u>31</u>
man makes gods in his. <u>Being that the gods</u> of
<u>32</u>   <u>33</u>
Greek mythology first appear in the writings of Homer and Hesiod, and, from the character and actions of these picturesque and, for the most part, <u>if you think about it,</u> friendly beings, we get
<u>34</u>
some idea of the men who made them and brought them to Greece. <u>Homer is believed to</u>
<u>35</u>
<u>have been a writer and poet.</u>
<u>35</u>

[2]

But ritual is more fundamental than <u>mythology, the reason because Greek ritual</u>
<u>36</u>
during recent years has shown that, beneath the belief or skepticism with which the Olympians were regarded, <u>lie</u> an older magic, with traditional
<u>37</u>
rites for the promotion of fertility by the celebration of the annual cycle of life and death, and the propitiation of unfriendly <u>ghosts, gods or a demon</u>.
<u>38</u>
Some such survivals were doubtless widespread, and, prolonged into classical times, probably made the substance of Eleusinian and Orphic <u>mysteries, against</u> this dark and dangerous
<u>39</u>
background arose Olympic mythology on the one hand and early philosophy and science on the other.

[3]

In classical times the need of a creed higher than the Olympian was <u>felt; therefore,</u>
<u>40</u>
Aeschylus, Sophocles and Plato evolved from the pleasant but crude polytheism the idea of a single, supreme and righteous Zeus. <u>Having</u>
<u>41</u>
<u>changed,</u> the decay of Olympus led to a revival of
<u>41</u>
old and the invasion of new magic cults among the <u>people; while</u> some philosophers <u>were looking</u>
<u>42</u>   <u>43</u>
to a vision of the uniformity of nature under divine and universal law. <u>Greece had been changed by</u>
<u>44</u>
<u>the gods.</u> 45

31. A. NO CHANGE
    B. There is
    C. its'
    D. It is

32. F. NO CHANGE
    G. his own image
    H. their own image
    J. his own

33. A. NO CHANGE
    B. Since the gods
    C. The gods
    D. Because the gods

34. F. NO CHANGE
    G. if you thought about it,
    H. when you think about it,
    J. OMIT UNDERLINED PORTION

35. A. NO CHANGE
    B. Homer was believed to have been a writer
    and poet.
    C. Homer has been a writer and a poet.
    D. OMIT UNDERLINED PORTION

36. F. NO CHANGE
    G. mythology; the reason because Greek
    ritual
    H. mythology. Greek ritual
    J. mythology, the reason because, Greek
    ritual

37. A. NO CHANGE
    B. lay
    C. lies
    D. laid

38. F. NO CHANGE
    G. ghosts, gods, or a demon
    H. ghosts, a god or a demon
    J. ghosts, gods or demons

39. A. NO CHANGE
    B. mysteries: against
    C. mysteries. Against
    D. mysteries--against

40. F. NO CHANGE
    G. felt, therefore,
    H. felt. Therefore,
    J. OMIT UNDERLINED PORTION

41. A. NO CHANGE
    B. Being changed,
    C. To be changed,
    D. OMIT UNDERLINED PORTION

42. F. NO CHANGE
    G. people, while
    H. people: while
    J. people. While

43. A. NO CHANGE
    B. was looking
    C. are looking
    D. will be looking

44. F. NO CHANGE
    G. Greece will be changed by the gods.
    H. The gods changed Greece.
    J. The gods will be changed by Greece.

45. The main idea of the passage is that
    A. Olympic mythology evolved from ancient
    rituals and gave rise to early philosophy.
    B. early moves toward viewing nature as
    ordered by divine and universal law coincided
    with monotheistic impulses and the
    disintegration of classical mythology.
    C. early philosophy followed from classical
    mythology.
    D. the practice of science, i.e., empiricism,
    preceded scientific theory.

Passage 4:

Psychotherapy East and West - Alan W. Watts

[1]

The idea of stuff expresses no more than the experience of coming to a limit at which our senses or our instruments are not fine enough to make out the pattern. 46

[2]

Something of the same kind happens,
47
when, the scientist investigates any unit or pattern
47
so distinct to the naked eye that it has been considered a separate entity. At that time then he
48
finds that the more carefully he observes and describes it, the more he is *also* describing the environment in which it moves and other patterns to which it seems inseparably related. As Teilhard de Chardin has so well expressed it; the isolation
49
of individual, atomic patterns "is merely an
50
intellectual dodge. 51
50

[3]

Although the ancient cultures of Asia never attained the rigorously exact physical
52
knowledge of the modern West, they grasped in principle many things which are only now occurring to us. There way of life, Hinduism and
53
Buddhism, are impossible to classify as religion,
54
philosophy, science, or even mythology, or again as an amalgamation of all four, because departmentalization is foreign to them even in so basic a form as the separation of the spiritual and

the material, Buddhism is not a culture but a
55
critique of culture, an enduring nonviolent revolution, or "loyal opposition," to the culture with which it is involved. But this gives these ways of
56
liberation something, however, in common with
56
psychotherapy beyond the interest in changing states of consciousness. For the task of the psychotherapist is to bring about a reconciliation between individual feeling and social norms without sacrificing the integrity of the individual. He tries to help him to be himself and to go it
57
alone in the world (of social convention) but not of the world. And there lays the beauty of ancient
58
Asia. 59   60

46. Which sentence would make the topic idea of this paragraph clearer.
    F. NO CHANGE
    G. Stuff expresses the experience of coming to the limit at which our senses or instruments stop working.
    H. The limit at which our senses or instruments become less effective is because of the idea of stuff.
    J. The idea of stuff expresses the precipice at which our senses or instruments become inefficient at sensing a pattern.

47. A. NO CHANGE
    B. --when--
    C. . When,
    D. when

48. F. NO CHANGE
    G. At that time, then
    H. At that time; then
    J. OMIT UNDERLINED PORTION

49. A. NO CHANGE
    B. it, the
    C. it. The
    D. it, and the

50. F. NO CHANGE
    G. "'is merely an intellectual dodge.'"
    H. "is merely an intellectual dodge".
    J. 'is merely an intellectual dodge.'

51. For the sake of clarity, should the author provide a longer quote?
    A. Yes, because it is unclear whether the quote is about the isolation of an individual or atomic patterns.
    B. Yes, because only "is merely an intellectual dodge" is cutting the great Chardin short.
    C. No, because the quote is effective and concise as is.
    D. No, because long quotes are unnecessary.

52. F. NO CHANGE
    G. never attain
    H. never attains
    J. never attaining

53. A. NO CHANGE
    B. Their
    C. They're
    D. Theirs

54. F. NO CHANGE
    G. were
    H. to be
    J. is

55. A. NO CHANGE
    B. material; and Buddhism
    C. material. Buddhism
    D. material and Buddhism

56. F. NO CHANGE
    G. But this gives these ways of liberation something however
    H. But this gives these ways of liberation something
    J. But this however gives these ways of liberation something

57. A. NO CHANGE
    B. the individual
    C. her
    D. it

58. F. NO CHANGE
    G. have lain
    H. laid
    J. lies

59. For the sake of logic and coherence, where should the last sentence of the passage be placed?
    A. NO CHANGE
    B. paragraph 1, sentence 1
    C. paragraph 2, sentence 4
    D. paragraph 3, sentence 3

60. What does the passage suggest about the theme of the book from which it is excerpted?
    F. The book attempts to understand psychotherapy in the context of different and changing systems of thought.
    G. The book argues that psychotherapy unites elements of an exact science with elements of eastern philosophy.
    H. The book describes the origins of psychotherapy around the world.
    J. The book compares psychotherapy in the West and in the East.

Passage 5:

On Natural Death - Lewis Thomas

[1]

While an elm in our backyard caught the
                                    61
blight this summer and dropped stone dead,
                                    61
leafless, almost overnight. One weekend it was a
                    61
normal-looking elm, maybe a little bare in spots
                                                62
but nothing alarming, and the next weekend it
            62
was gone, passed over, departed, taken.

[2]

The dying of a field mouse, at the jaws of
an amiable household cat, is a spectacle I have
beheld many times. It used to make me wince. It
wasn't since I thought about it that I was lead or
          63   64
came to believe that Nature was an abomination.

[3]

Recently I've done some thinking about
that mouse, however, and I wonder if his dying is
                    65
necessarily all that different from the passing of
our elm. The main difference, if there is one,
would be in the matter of pain. Pain hurts. I do not
                                        66
believe that an elm tree has pain receptors, and
even so, the blight seems to me a relatively
painless way to go. But the mouse dangling tail-
down from the teeth of a gray cat is something
else again, with pain beyond bearing, you'd think,
all over his small body. There are now some
plausible reasons for thinking it is not like that at
all.

[4]

At the instant of being trapped and
penetrated by teeth, peptide hormones are
released by cells in the hypothalamus and the
pituitary gland; called endorphins, instantly these
                                            67
substances are attached to the surfaces of other
            67
cells responsible for pain perception; the

hormones has the pharmacologic properties of
            68
opium; there is no pain. Thus its that the mouse
                                    69
seems always to dangle so languidly from the
jaws, lies there so quietly when dropped, dies of
his injuries without a struggle. If a mouse could
shrug, he'd shrug....

[5]

Affectively, pain is useful for avoidance,
            70
for getting away when there's time to get away,
                                                71
when it is end game, and no way back, pain is
    71
likely to be turned off, and the mechanisms for
this are wonderfully precise and quick. If it were
up to Tom or I to design an ecosystem in which
            72
creatures had to live off each other and in which
dying was an indispensable part of living, I could
not think of a better way to manage. [73]

61. A. NO CHANGE
    B. Since an elm in our backyard caught the blight this summer and dropped stone dead, leafless, almost overnight.
    C. Until an elm in our backyard caught the blight this summer and dropped stone dead, leafless, almost overnight.
    D. An elm in our backyard caught the blight this summer and dropped stone dead, leafless, almost overnight.

62. F. NO CHANGE
    G. maybe a little bare in spots but nothing alarming.
    H. ; maybe a little bare in spots, but nothing alarming,
    J. OMIT UNDERLINED PORTION

63. A. NO CHANGE
    B. when
    C. until
    D. from

64. F. NO CHANGE
    G. led
    H. leads
    J. leading

65. A. NO CHANGE
    B. ; however,
    C. . However,
    D. however,

66. F. NO CHANGE
    G. Pain does not hurt.
    H. Pain hurts?
    J. OMIT UNDERLINED PORTION

67. A. NO CHANGE
    B. gland, called endorphins, instantly these substances are
    C. gland (called endorphins) instantly these substances are
    D. gland; instantly these substances, called endorphins, are

68. F. NO CHANGE
    G. hormones have
    H. hormone have
    J. hormones having

69. A. NO CHANGE
    B. its'
    C. it's
    D. OMIT UNDERLINED PORTION

70.   F. NO CHANGE
    G. Being that
    H. In effect
    J. In affect

71. A. NO CHANGE
    B. away. When
    C. away, and when
    D. away, but

72. F. NO CHANGE
    G. I or Tom
    H. Tom and I
    J. Tom or me

73. Which one of the following would best characterize the author's attitude toward the relationship between pain and death?
    A. Dismay at the inherent cruelty of nature
    B. Amusement at the irony of the relationship between pain and death
    C. Admiration for the ways in which animal life functions in the ecosystem
    D. A desire to conduct experiments

Answers and Solutions

1. D	16. J	31. D	46. J	61. D
2. G	17. C	32. G	47. D	62. F
3. B	18. H	33. C	48. J	63. C
4. F	19. C	34. J	49. B	64. G
5. A	20. G	35. D	50. F	65. A
6. J	21. B	36. H	51. C	66. J
7. B	22. H	37. B	52. F	67. D
8. H	23. D	38. J	53. B	68. G
9. C	24. F	39. C	54. J	69. C
10. J	25. B	40. F	55. C	70. H
11. B	26. F	41. D	56. H	71. B
12. G	27. C	42. G	57. B	72. J
13. A	28. J	43. A	58. J	73. C
14. J	29. B	44. H	59. D	
15. C	30. H	45. B	60. F	

1. When separating a series of words, phrases, or verbs, placing a comma before the conjunction (*and, or, nor*) is optional; however, a comma should never be used after the conjunction. Choice (B) and (C) change the comma before the conjunction to a semi-colon and a colon, even though this is incorrect, but they do not remove the comma after the conjunction. The answer is (D).

2. The word *latter*, even though it appears in the middle of a parenthetic phrase, is referring to the series of nouns underlined in sentence one. And since it is referring to the last word in a series of three words, *latter* is incorrect. *Latter* distinguishes between two things; *last* refers to the final thing in a series of three or more. The answer is (G).

3. Although this sentence is not quite a fragment, the pronoun *all* makes it very unclear. What seems quite innocent? There's no way to know for sure, unless you reword the sentence. The passage is written in the present tense, so choice (C)'s past *those features* is incorrect. Choice (D) makes it unclear which features the sentence is referring to, so the answer is (B).

4. As mentioned earlier, the passage is written in the present tense, so the present perfect tense *there has long been* is correct. The answer is (F).

5. *Yet again* is a transitional word phrase, so this question is really about combining two independent clauses with a comma and the conjunction *and*. Choice (B) could technically be correct, but since the author chooses not to set off *yet again* with commas the first time he uses it, the latter part of the compound sentence should be parallel with the former. Choice (C) removes the punctuation and creates a run-on sentence, and choice (D) removes part of the meaning of the sentence. The underlined portion is correct as is. The answer is (A).

6. Here we have a dependent clause being joined to an independent clause without punctuation. Choice (G) is wrong because a dependent clause cannot be joined to an independent clause with only a semicolon. Choice (H)'s use of a comma and *that* creates a subordinating clause but with the wrong subordinating conjunction. Choice (J) correctly joins the dependent clause to the sentence with a comma and the word *which,* creating a correct subordinating clause. The answer is (J).

7. The underlined portion joins *it is* with *self* by adding an apostrophe, which is incorrect. The correct pronoun, used to restate the noun *history,* is *itself*. The answer is (B).

8. This question is one of those tricky rhetoric, or strategy, questions we talked about earlier. Before answering a question like this, always ask yourself, "What is the BEST answer." Many choices will seem correct, but only one will be the *right* answer. The sentence in question is talking about *evidence* of violent

behavior; and, previously, the passage only spoke about the *belief* of violent behavior being connected with violent video games, so choice (F) is incorrect. While choice (G) is correct in a lot of ways, the sentence in question provides a smooth transition to the next paragraph. So a stylistic use of *and* at the beginning of a sentence should not be enough to cut the sentence entirely. Choice (J) is heresy, so the answer is (H).

9. Remember when we talked about pronouns? When we said that a pronoun must have the same number and gender of the noun or noun phrase it is replacing? The noun in this sentence is *effects,* and it is plural and neuter, so the pronoun must agree. *It* is singular, *he* is masculine, and *them* usually refers to the object of a clause instead of the subject (and we're talking about the subject here). *They* is plural and properly refers to the plural subject *effects.* The answer is (C).

10. It doesn't matter whether the verb follows directly after the subject, comes before the subject, or is separated from its subject by an intervening phrase, the subject and verb must always agree in number and person. The subject is *researchers*, and the verb is *has found*. If we put the two together, *researchers has found,* they sound odd, don't they? We need a plural verb for the plural subject, and the only answer-choice that addresses this is (J). The answer is (J).

11. The underlined portion joins two independent clauses with a comma, which is called a comma splice - and it is incorrect. Choice (C) changes the comma to a semicolon, but that is also incorrect. Choice (D) might be right if it wasn't at the end of the paragraph, but leaving a sentence like that at the end of a paragraph is distracting and weird. The best thing to do here is to drop the relative pronoun *that,* which is causing all the problems, and add *which,* creating a subordinating clause. The answer is (B).

12. This question is another subject-verb agreement fiasco. Being right next to *games, are* sounds correct, but it is not in agreement with its actual subject *aspect.* Since *aspect* is singular, it requires a singular verb. The answer is (G).

13. If everything looks right with an underlined portion and, more importantly, sounds right, more often than not it is right and should not be changed. The majority of people taking the ACT speak English natively and, as such, should use their ears and their gut. Not everything is a trick question. The underlined portion is correct as is and should not be changed. The answer is (A).

14. The underlined portion has absolutely nothing to do with violent video games or anything that the passage is talking about. Choice (G) and (H) reword and re-punctuate the needless sentence, but it should just be removed. The answer is (J).

15. Item I, True: Stimulation would occur. This choice is qualitatively the same as passively watching violence on television. Item II, True: Stimulation would also occur. This is another example of solitary aggression (implied by the second sentence of the last paragraph). Item III, False: No stimulation would occur. Two-player aggressive games are "cathartic" (again the needed reference is the second sentence of the last paragraph). The answer is (C).

16. Earlier in this sentence we saw the notorious correlative conjunction *not only*, so the underlined portion is testing your parallel *not only ... but also* knowledge. Choice (G) replaces *but* with *also*, but that is incorrect; choice (H) correctly uses *but also*, but the sentence still reads a bit funny. Remember, you will always be looking for the BEST answer. Choice (J) correctly uses *not only ... but also* but also clarifies the pronoun *it* by restating what *it* is replacing: *looking.* The answer is (J).

17. Many questions, like the previous one, will not only be testing the underlined portion, but also the sentence as a whole. Since the word *after* appears at the beginning of this sentence, *then* is redundant and should be removed. And since the only answer-choice that correctly joins a dependent clause with an independent clause without the word *then* is (C), the answer is (C).

18. This sentence is awkward, and normally I would say that it should be deleted, but we are not given the option to delete it. *Features* is the subject, and it is plural, so it needs a plural pronoun to restate it later in

the sentence. Choice (F) and (J) are singular, and choice (G) is in the subjunctive case and not the proper objective case. The answer is (H).

19. This question is pretty much a reading comprehension question, since the actual definition of the technical phenomenon is never stated in the passage. You must use all the information in the passage to choose the BEST answer. The answer is (C).

20. When reading certain underlined portions on the ACT, it is usually a good idea to read the sentence quietly out loud to yourself. Many readers are conditioned to ignore mistakes, even if they don't know it, and our brains like to subconsciously fix small mistakes without telling us. But what your eyes subconsciously skip over, your ears will almost always pick up. Remember, if it sounds wrong, it probably is. This question is a run-on sentence with a comma splice. Out of the answer-choices, choice (G) is the only one that correctly fixes the run-on by separating the two sentences with a period. The answer is (G).

21. Whenever you see the word *that* as the subject of a sentence, it should probably be replaced. Granted, sometimes sentences are so closely related that there is no doubt what *that* is referring to, but more often than not *that* is unclear. When sentences become unclear, complex, or just plain confusing, the best thing to do is to restate the subject. The answer is (B).

22. Here we have another run-on sentence. You can either separate the two independent clauses, or you can combine them. Choice (G) and (J) do not properly combine the two sentences, and since we are not given the option here to separate them, choice (H) is the only answer that properly combines both sentences with a comma and the subordinating conjunction *which*. The answer is (H).

23. In speech, many people restate a fact several times in succession, for fear that whoever is listening to them might have missed a point. In essay writing, however, this is taboo. The underlined portion is repeating, almost exactly, what was said in the previous sentence. This is redundant, and the sentence should be deleted. The answer is (D).

24. When faced with a question about a dash, it is often very difficult to know whether or not the mark was actually used correctly, because they are so commonly misused. In some writings, it would seem that the dash is the only mark of punctuation that the author knows, and in others, dashes are as alive and kicking as a T-rex. So all the dash confusion is understandable, but not on the ACT. In the context of this sentence, though, the dash is correct. And while a comma would have also been correct here, the use of a dash adds emphasis to the explanatory information that follows; thus, it is correct. The answer is (F).

25. Here is another example where reading quietly out loud could be helpful. While your eyes might fix the sentence fragment by adding the small verb it is missing, your ears would never let that happen, not without making you re-read the sentence. Choice (C) adds a verb, but it is plural when it should be singular. The answer is (B).

26. The underlined portion correctly separates the verbal phrase from the rest of the sentence. Choice (G) creates a sentence fragment, choice (H) misuses the ellipsis (although it has become, incorrectly, a one-size-fits-all mark of punctuation, judging from text messages and Facebook statuses), and choice (J) misuses the semi-colon. The answer is (F).

27. *Among* distinguishes between three or more things; *between* distinguishes between two. The answer is (C).

28. While you might think that this question is about the endless battle between *who* and *whom*, it is a trick question. *Whose* is simply being misused as *who's* or *who has*, so we need to replace it with the correct words. The answer is (J).

29. This question is a tough one. Anytime you see *being that* in a sentence, it is generally wrong. Choice (C) makes the following section a dependent clause, so it cannot be joined with a semi-colon. Choice (D) is not a proper transitional word, so it cannot be used as a conjunction. And since the underlined portion is

incorrect, that leaves choice (B), which is also a funky transition, yet it is the best answer, after checking the other options. The answer is (B).

30. Because of question 19, we know that the technical phenomenon is a way of thinking in a modern society. The authors assignment was to describe a technical society; instead, he described the way of thinking in said society and not the society itself. So both "yes" answers, choice (F) and (G), are incorrect, and choice (J) doesn't address the question at all, so the answer is (H).

31. When you come across *its* or *it's* in a question, always check and make sure that it is being properly used. Here, *its* is meant to mean *it is*, so the answer is (D).

32. This is not only a case of an unclear pronoun, but also, according to the answer-choices, the object of the sentence has been completely left out. Choice (J) still begs the question, "His own what?," and choice (H) uses a plural pronoun for the singular subject *man,* so that leaves choice (G). The answer is (G).

33. As mentioned earlier, anytime you see the phrase *being that* in a sentence, it is probably wrong. In fact, it doesn't even make sense for the beginning of this sentence to be a modifier at all. Choice (B) and (D) cut *being that* but still make the first clause a modifier of nothing. This independent clause should stand on its own. The answer is (C).

34. This is a common mistake for essay writers because people so often talk this way, which means that a lot of people will see nothing wrong with the underlined portion. This section is direct input from the author in a historical essay about the Greek gods. First of all, if we were to keep the underlined portion, it should either be parenthetical or between dashes. But since this phrase is wordy and provides no useful information, it should be omitted. The answer is (J).

35. While this sentence is grammatically correct, it gives no new information and acts as a poor transitional sentence into the next paragraph. It should be omitted. The answer is (D).

36. *The reason because* is redundant and wordy. Choices (G) and (J) change the punctuation but not *the reason because*. When it comes down to it, sometimes it is better to start a new sentence than to try to connect several sentences together with redundant transitional phrases. The answer is (H).

37. The verb *lie* is in the present tense, but the sentence is talking about something in the past. Even the author is referring to the Olympians in the past tense. The past tense of *lie* is *lay*. The answer is (B).

38. When items in a series, that are similar in content or function, are listed together, all of the parts must share the same grammatical form. In other words, they must be parallel. This question is not about comma usage, so choice (G) and (H) are incorrect. The only answer-choice that fixes the parallelism between *ghosts, gods,* and *demons* is (J). The answer is (J).

39. This is another run-on sentence with another comma splice. The second clause is not a list, and it is not redefining the first clause, so the use of the colon in choice (B) is incorrect. The same goes for choice (D). Again, sometimes the best thing to do with run-on sentences is to separate them. The answer is (C).

40. This is the correct usage of a semi-colon and the transitional word *therefore*; therefore, the answer is (F).

41. If you're left wondering, "What changed?" after reading an introductory phrase declaring, "Having changed," this is probably a good sign that you have a misplaced modifier on your hands. Choices (B) and (C) rephrase the modifier, but they don't change the fact that it is in the wrong place. And since we don't have the option of moving it, it is best to omit it. The answer is (D).

42. The latter part of the underlined portion is a dependent clause because of the word *while*, so it cannot be joined to an independent clause with only a semi-colon. It is also not a list, nor does it redefine the former part of the underlined portion, so the use of the colon in choice (H) is incorrect. And since we are talking

about a dependent clause, making it its own sentence, as in choice (J), is also incorrect. Remember, we connect dependent clauses to an independent clause with a comma. The answer is (G).

43. Just because a section is underlined on the ACT does not mean that it is incorrect. There are usually several NO CHANGE questions scattered throughout each passage. But beware of marking too many Fs or As. If your test is filled with those letters, chances are you've been tricked a few times into thinking something was correct when it was actually incorrect. This question, however, is correct as is. The answer is (A).

44. At first glance, there doesn't seem to be anything wrong with this underlined portion, but if you look at all the answer-choices, one by one, you should be able to notice a pattern. Although the wordings and meanings are all different, the underlined portion, choice (G), and choice (J) are all written in the passive voice. As we mentioned earlier - and as I'm sure your English teacher has mentioned a thousand times before as well - the passive voice should always be avoided. It's weak. Choice (H) is the only answer-choice that changes the construction of the sentence to the strong active voice. The answer is (H).

45. Most main idea questions are rather easy. This one is not—mainly, because the passage itself is not an easy read. To find the main idea of a passage, check the last sentence of the first paragraph; if it's not there, check the closing of the passage. Reviewing the last sentence of the first paragraph, we see that it hardly presents a statement, let alone the main idea. Turning to the line before the closing line of the passage, however, we find the key to this question. The passage describes a struggle for ascendancy amongst four opposing philosophies: magic and traditional rites vs. Olympic mythology vs. monotheism (Zeus) vs. early philosophy and science. The closing lines of the passage summarize this and add that Olympic mythology lost out to monotheism (Zeus), while magical cults enjoyed a revival and the germ of universal law was planted. The answer is (B).

46. It's not that the first paragraph is wrong, per se, only that the word choices, and the order of those words, makes the paragraph sound jumbled. Choices (G) and (H) do nothing to improve the clarity of the paragraph. Only choice (J) concisely and clearly explains the main idea of the paragraph. The answer is (J).

47. Since the word *when* is not an interjection or transitional word, it does not need to be set of by any punctuation marks. The answer is (D).

48. *At that time then* is redundant. A choice should be made between either *at that time* or *then*. But since we are not given the option to delete one or the other, it is best to omit the phrase all together. The answer is (J).

49. This is another case of joining a dependent clause to an independent clause with only a semi-colon. By this point in the test, we should know how to fix that. The answer is (B).

50. The underlined portion uses quotation marks correctly. All the other answer-choices misuse them. The answer is (F).

51. This might be a tricky question for you or it might not be, depending on the way you write essays. *Individual* and *atomic* are adjectives describing the noun *patterns*. And for a quote to be about an adjective is ridiculous; thus, choice (A) is incorrect. Also, the reader thinking that there isn't enough Chardin, which probably means that the reader is a big fan, should not affect whether or not the quote needs to be longer, so choice (B) is incorrect. Choice (C) is correct because choice (D) makes a nonsensical claim. The answer is (C).

52. *Never attained* is the correct verb tense. The answer is (F).

53. There, their, or they're. The *there* that is used here refers to a location and not people, so it is incorrect. Choice (C) means *there are,* and choice (D) is in the wrong tense. The answer is (B).

54. Subject-verb agreement should never be affected by intervening clauses like *Hinduism and Buddhism. Way of life* is the subject, and it is singular, so it needs a singular verb. The answer is (J).

55. This is a run-on sentence with a comma splice. We know how to fix those now, right? The best way to fix a run-on, especially if both sentences are long and have a lot of punctuation, is to separate them. The answer is (C).

56. *But* and *however* mean the same thing, so the underlined portion is redundant. We need to get rid of *but* or *however*, and the only answer-choice that does this is (H). The answer is (H).

57. This pronoun is very unclear. Is *he* trying to help *himself* be *himself*, or someone else be *himself*? *He* and *him* are more than likely replacing the subject and object from the previous sentence, *He* being the psychotherapist and *him* being *the individual*. The best answer-choice here is the one that restates the object from the previous sentence, for greater clarity. The answer is (B).

58. This is a question about the conjugation of *lay,* which is *lay, lie,* and *have lain. Laid* has no place here, so choice (H) is incorrect, and choice (F) and (G) are in the wrong tense. The answer is (J).

59. Where the sentence is placed now, it doesn't really make much sense. The best thing to do would be to look back over the passage and place the sentence where ancient Asia is being discussed. Since paragraph three is the only paragraph to talk about Asia, logic tells us that choice (D) is correct. The answer is (D).

60. (F): Yes, this is the most accurate inference from the passage. The passage discusses how the more carefully a scientist views and describes something the more he describes the environment in which it moves, and the passage traces similarities between psychotherapy and Eastern systems of (evolving) thought. (G): No, this is too narrow an interpretation of what the whole book would be doing. (H): No, too vague; the passage is too philosophical to be merely a history. (J): No, also too vague, meant to entrap those of you who relied on the title without thinking through the passage. The answer is (F).

61. Since the word *while* starts this sentence, making it a dependent clause, and since this dependent clause is not joined to an independent clause, this sentence is a fragment. Choices (B) and (C), with the words *since* and *until* starting them off, are also sentence fragments. Choice (D) fixes the problem by removing the subordinating conjunctions and prepositions. The answer is (D).

62. The underlined portion is a nonrestrictive phrase and is correctly set off with commas. The answer is (F).

63. *Since* is the wrong subordinating conjunction here and changes the meaning of the sentence. The only answer-choice that makes sense in the context of this sentence is (C). The answer is (C).

64. The *lead* being used here - pronounced LEED - is not the metal. It is the present tense of *led* and is commonly misused. *Lead* sounds right here only because many pronounce it like lead, the metal. The answer is (G).

65. *However* is a transitional word here, and it is correctly set off with commas. The answer is (A).

66. The realization, here, that pain hurts is something that everyone who is human knows very well. This small sentence serves as a distraction and ruins the flow of the essay. It should be omitted. The answer is (J).

67. *Called endorphins* is a nonrestrictive clause and not a transitional phrase or a conjunction, so as it follows directly after the semi-colon, it is a misplaced modifier. The only answer-choice that fixes the misplaced modifier's position is (D), so the answer is (D).

68. Here we have a plural subject and a singular verb. For subject-verb agreement, the verb must also be plural. Choice (H) makes the subject singular but the verb plural, and choice (J) creates a sentence fragment

by adding the beginning of a verbal phrase. Choice (G) has both a plural subject and a plural verb. The answer is (G).

69. The *its* that is used here is the possessive form; what is needed is the contraction *it's*, meaning *it is*. Choice (C) has this. The answer is (C).

70. *Affectively* is an adverb and not a transitional word, and it also means influenced by or resulting from emotions, which I'm sure is not what the author is trying to mean here. *Being that* is almost always incorrect, so choice (G) is incorrect. And the prepositional phrase *in affect* does not exist, so the answer is (H).

71. Here we have yet another run-on sentence, joined by a comma splice, and the best thing to do is separate the two independent clauses. The answer is (B).

72. Tom and I, me and you, you and I - the proper way to say a compound subject mixed with a pronoun can get confusing. But, when trying to decide whether to use *me* or *I*, the best thing to do is drop the other part of the compound subject and see which pronoun works. If we were to drop *Tom* here, *I* makes no sense, so the answer is (J).

73. The author's attitude toward the relationship between pain and death evolves through three stages. First, he expresses revulsion at the relationship. This is indicated in the second paragraph by the words *wince* and *abomination*. Then in the third paragraph, he adopts a more analytical attitude and questions his previous judgment. This is indicated by the clause, *I wonder if his dying is necessarily all that different from the passing of our elm*. And in closing the paragraph, he seems resigned to the fact that the relationship is not all that bad. This is indicated by the sentence, *If a mouse could shrug, he'd shrug*. Finally, in the last paragraph, he comes to express admiration for the relationship between pain and death. This is indicated by the phrase *wonderfully precise and quick*, and it is made definite by the closing line, *If I had to design an ecosystem . . . in which dying was an indispensable part of living, I could not think of a better way to manage*. Thus, the answer is (C).

Part Three
SCIENCE

ORIENTATION

PHYSICS

- Introduction
- Language of Motion
- Laws of Motion
- Gravitation
- Planes and Circles

BIOLOGY

- Introduction
- Biological Molecules
- Enzymes and Energy
- Cellular Metabolism
- DNA Structure and Function
- Viruses

CHEMISTRY

- Introduction
- Chemical Reactions
- Electronic Structure
- Organic Chemistry
- Alkanes

SCIENCE TESTS

- Test 1
- Test 2

ORIENTATION

Format of the Science Section

The science section typically includes 40 multiple-choice questions based on 7 passages and is 35 minutes long. The test measures analytical and problem solving skills associated with the basics of science.

You will not be tested on advanced concepts in science, but you will need to know the basic concepts and nomenclature of science. The test assumes that you are in the process of taking three or more years of science courses and have complete two years of study.

Section	Type	Time
Science	40 Multiple-choice Questions	35 minutes

Advanced mathematical skills are not needed for the science section, but you do need basics computational skills. So, you don't need any knowledge of Calculus, Trigonometry, or even much Algebra.

The science section is the fourth section of the test.

The science passages are typically taken from Biology, Chemistry, Physics, or closely related fields of science.

Scoring the ACT

The total score is reported on a scale from 1 to 36, with 36 being the highest score possible. The average total score is about 20. Do not become discouraged if you "blow" a few questions. The average ACT student misses about half of the questions on the science section.

In addition to the scaled score, you will be assigned a percentile ranking, which gives the percentage of students with scores below yours. For instance, if you score in the 80th percentile, then you will have scored better than 80 out of every 100 test takers.

Calculators

Although you may use a calculator on the math section of the test, oddly enough you cannot use it on the science section. So, when studying, avoid using a calculator when doing calculations. Otherwise, you may become dependent on it, and then struggle when you no longer have access to the calculator.

For the math section, you can use any standard scientific or graphing calculator. You cannot use advanced calculators, such as ones with built-in computer algebra systems (for example, TI-89). You also cannot use the calculator in a cell phone or any other electronic communication device.

Skipping and Guessing

Some questions on the ACT are rather hard, and it is a time-pressured test. So, you may not be able to finish the section.

Often students become obsessed with a particular problem and waste valuable time trying to solve it. To get a top score, learn to cut your losses and move on because all questions are worth the same number of points, regardless of difficulty level. So, often it is best to skip the hardest questions and concentrate on the easy and medium ones.

There is no guessing penalty on the ACT. So, if you skip a question or do not finish the section in time, be sure to mark an answer for every question. By the laws of probability, you should get about 1 out of every 4 guesses correct.

The Structure of this Section

Frist, a through review of the basics of Physics, Biology, and Chemistry is presented. Then 6 full-length Science Tests are presented so that you can test your skills and knowledge of science.

Physics Review 1
Introduction

A. Philosophy of the Physics Review Section

This review section is about the concepts of physics, with the goal to prepare you, the reader, to pass the science section of the ACT. This section of the ACT consist mainly of a series of passages, each with several questions or problems. Often the passages involve unfamiliar situations and, rather than numbers, explanations, relationships among various quantities, and extrapolations to new situations.

How do you prepare for such a thing?

The short answer is: by thinking and doing physics.

This review section actually has several goals. One is to give you a working knowledge of the basic concepts of physics. Although you will not need a battery of specialized equations, you should remember enough equations to understand the ideas.

Another goal is to teach you how to solve problems in science. But you cannot learn to solve problems by simply reading about physics. The way to learn is to solve problems. Then you can solve future problems, for example, on the ACT, by thinking in the same way as when you solved problems before. For this reason each chapter contains problems in the text with full explanations, as well as problems for you to solve at the end. The solutions tell you how to think about the problems, which clues to look for, and what methods to apply. The goal is for you to learn how to approach new problems.

In each chapter the initial problems are simple, in order to help you to practice your understanding of the concepts in that chapter. These problems may be easy questions or single problems involving some calculations. Although they are not a close approximation of ACT questions, you will have difficulty on the exam unless you learn to do these first. Gradually, the problems in a chapter become more difficult, and at the end of every chapter there are ACT-style passages.

B. Reading the Physics Review Section

Reading about physics is completely different from reading a novel. First of all, you should be at a desk and have paper and a pen or pencil. You should write down every equation, making sure you understand all the symbols. You should reproduce every diagram, working to understand, for example, why certain forces are there and no others, and so on. You may even try working the examples before reading the solutions and work the solutions out along side the text.

It is especially important that you keep an open mind and visualize what you read. In biology one can actually see organelles with an electron microscope. Understanding the operation of enzymes requires a little bit more imagination. In physics, you must rely on imagination even more, but it is not too different from imagining the working of enzymes. If you view physics as a mere collection of facts and equations to memorize, you will find it frustrating. Alternatively, if you approach physics looking for new concepts, themes and a new worldview, then your efforts will be better rewarded.

C. Units

A widely held belief is that unit analysis is the least interesting activity of the physical sciences. Indeed, carefully carrying units through a difficult formula is sometimes about as interesting as painting a barn. But there are several good reasons to pay attention to units.

You can lose valuable points if you drop units, substitute into a formula, and forget to convert cm to m or the like. One way to guard against this type of error is to automatically convert any number to MKS (meters, kilograms, and seconds) as you read the passage, or at least flag the units that are nonstandard (i.e., not meters, kilograms, and seconds). Another way is to keep track of the units any time the units in the problem are nonstandard.

Another reason to pay attention to units is that they can alert you if you have written an equation the wrong way. For example, you may remember that flow rate f is the volume (m^3) flowing past a point per unit time (s) and that it is related to the velocity v and cross-sectional area A of the pipe. But how do you relate $f\,[m^3/s]$, $v\,[m/s]$, and $A\,[m^2]$?

The only way to correctly obtain the units is to write something like

$$f = Av$$

that is

$$\left[\frac{m^3}{s}\right] = \left[m^2\right]\left[\frac{m}{s}\right]$$

where we may have left out a proportionality constant. In this case the formula is correct as written. Units may bring back to mind an equation you would have forgotten, counting for valuable points.

A third reason for keeping track of units is that they sometimes guide you to an answer without your having to use a formula or do much work, as the next example shows.

Example: How much volume does 0.4 kg of oxygen gas take up at $T = 27°$ C and $P = 12$ atm? (Use the gas constant $R = 0.0821$ L atm/K mol.)

Solution: Well, to the question, "How much oxygen?", we can answer either in kilograms or in liters. The problem gives kilograms and asks for liters, so this is a complicated units conversion problem. We will essentially construct the ideal gas equation using the units of the elements in the problem. We start with 0.4 kg.

$$\text{(amount of } O_2\text{)} = 0.4 \text{ kg } O_2$$

In order to apply the ideal gas equation we need to convert to moles. We can do this by including the factors:

$$\left(\frac{10^3 g O_2}{1 kg O_2}\right)\left(\frac{1 mole O_2}{32 g O_2}\right)$$

Both are equivalent to 1, but the units cancel, leaving us with moles.

$$\text{(amount of } O_2\text{)} = 0.4 \, kg O_2\left(\frac{10^3 g O_2}{1 kg O_2}\right)\left(\frac{1 mole O_2}{32 g O_2}\right)$$

Now we include a factor of R because it has liters in the numerator and moles in the denominator. We obtain

$$\left(\text{amount of } O_2\right) = 0.4\,\cancel{\text{kg}O_2}\left(\frac{10^3\,\cancel{g}O_2}{1\,\cancel{kg}O_2}\right)\left(\frac{1\,\text{mole}\,O_2}{32\,\cancel{g}O_2}\right)\left(\frac{0.0821\,\text{L atm}}{\text{K mol}}\right)$$

This leaves us with units of atm and K which we want to get rid of. In order to cancel them, we can just put them in. This may seem strange, but it works. (Recall $27°\,C = 300\,K$.) Thus we obtain

$$\left(\text{amount of } O_2\right) = 0.4\,\cancel{\text{kg}O_2}\left(\frac{10^3\,\cancel{g}O_2}{1\,\cancel{kg}O_2}\right)\left(\frac{1\,\text{mole}\,O_2}{32\,\cancel{g}O_2}\right)\left(\frac{0.0821\,\text{L}\,\cancel{atm}}{\cancel{K}\,\cancel{mol}}\right)300\,\cancel{K}\frac{1}{12\,\cancel{atm}}$$

$$= \frac{0.4 \cdot 1000 \cdot 0.0821 \cdot 300}{32 \cdot 12}\,L$$

For ACT problems, we generally work to one digit of accuracy, so we replace 0.0821 with 0.08, so that we have

$$\left(\text{amount of } O_2\right) = \frac{0.4 \cdot 1000 \cdot 0.0821 \cdot 300}{32 \cdot 12}$$

$$= \frac{4 \cdot 8 \cdot 300}{8 \cdot 5} = 24\,L$$

It is generally safe to round to one significant digit. If it happens that two choices are close, then you can always go back and gain more accuracy.

This example involved more arithmetic than most ACT problems, but its purpose was to point out that attention to units can speed up the solution to a problem. If this is the way you normally do such a problem, good. Most readers, however, would take longer working through this type of problem, using up valuable seconds on the ACT. Remember that seconds can add up to points.

D. Equations

Students generally have one of three attitudes toward equations:

1. sheer hatred (enough said),
2. cold pragmatism (plug in numbers and get an answer), and
3. warm fondness.

Try adopting the last attitude. Many students do not realize that equations are merely a way to contain useful information in a short form. They are sentences in the concise language of mathematics. You should not have to memorize most equations in the text, because by the time you learn each chapter, the equations should feel natural to you. They should feel like natural relationships among familiar quantities.

For example, consider one of the first equations you ever encountered, distance equals rate times time, that is

$$\Delta x = v\Delta t \tag{1}$$

It makes sense that, in a given time, we can go twice as far if we go twice as fast. Thus Δx is proportional to v. On the other hand, for a given speed, we can go twice as far if we travel twice as long a time. Thus Δx is proportional to Δt. We would never be tempted to write

$$v = \Delta x \Delta t$$

or

$$\Delta t = v \Delta x$$

because these equations give relationships among the quantities that we know to be wrong. Note also that the units work out correctly only in equation (1).

Another example is the second law of motion, which we will encounter in Section 3.B. If an object has a single force on it, then its acceleration is proportional to the magnitude of the force and inversely proportional to its mass. Instead of words, we simply write

$$a = F/m \qquad\qquad\qquad (2)$$

Now let's think about the equation. What would we do if we forgot it? If we stop to think about it, we could figure it out. First, we know that force, mass, and acceleration are connected somehow. If we have two objects of the same mass, and we apply three times as much force to the second object as to the first, then we have a picture like that in Figure 1-1. The greater force causes the greater acceleration, so we can guess that they are proportional. We write

$$a \sim F$$

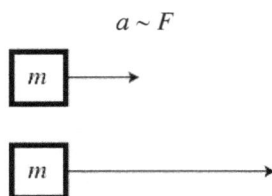

Figure 1-1

If we apply the same force to two objects of different masses, then we expect the smaller object to accelerate more (Figure 1-2). Thus we can guess that the acceleration is *inversely* proportional to the mass, so we write

$$a \sim 1/m$$

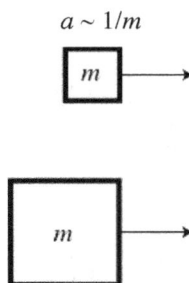

Figure 1-2

Combining these two proportions we get

$$a = F/m$$

as in equation (2).

When you take the ACT, you really should have the equation $F = ma$ in your head, but if you train yourself to think this way, it will be easier to keep the formulas in your head. This will make it possible to recover the formula if you forget it. And you will understand physics better. Most importantly, you will be better able to apply the concept behind the equation.

Some equations are a little more complicated. An example is Newton's law of gravity, which gives the force of gravity between two objects:

$$F_{\text{grav}} = \frac{Gm_1 m_2}{r^2} \qquad\qquad\qquad (3)$$

where G is a constant, m_1 and m_2 are masses of objects, and r is the distance between them. How would you ever remember this equation?

Well, start with the idea that objects with more mass have a greater force of gravity between them, so write

$$F_{grav} \sim m_1 m_2$$

Also, if objects are far apart, the force of gravity between them is less, so write

$$F_{grav} \sim \frac{m_1 m_2}{r}$$

There is a constant, so write

$$F_{grav} \sim \frac{Gm_1 m_2}{r}$$

The only part that needs to be memorized is the "square" in the denominator, so that we have

$$F_{grav} = \frac{Gm_1 m_2}{r^2}$$

That's why we call gravity an inverse-square force.

The ACT will not ask you to substitute into an equation like equation (3), but it may ask a question like, "What happens to the gravitational force between two objects if the distance between the objects is increased by a factor of four?"

We can tell from equation (3) that an increase in distance results in a decrease in force, because r is in the denominator. Because the r is squared, a factor of 4 in r will result in a factor of $4^2 = 16$ in F_{grav}. The answer is that the gravitational force decreases by a factor of 16.

If this last point seems opaque to you, try some numbers on a more familiar equation, such as that for the area of a circle

$$A = \pi r^2 \tag{4}$$

What happens to the area when the radius increases by a factor of 3? (Answer: It increases by a factor of 9.) Try it with $r_1 = 4$ m and $r_2 = 12$ m, or with some other numbers.

Another equation is that for the surface area of a sphere

$$A = 4\pi r^2 \tag{5}$$

What happens to the surface area of a sphere when the radius increases by a factor of 3? (Answer: It increases by a factor of 9. Surprised? What about the factor of 4? Try it with $r_1 = 4$ m and $r_2 = 12$ m.) The surface area of a sphere is an equation that you just have to memorize. It is difficult to get an intuitive grasp why the 4π should be there. On the other hand, the r^2 is natural in this equation. Why? (Think about units.)

Another example concerns the volume of a sphere

$$V = \frac{4\pi}{3} r^3 \tag{6}$$

What happens to the volume when the radius is doubled?

In this chapter we discussed the importance of units in solving problems. If a problem involves only simple proportionalities and there are no unitless proportionality constants, then we can obtain a quick solution simply by keeping track of units. The example in the text demonstrates all the techniques involved.

We also looked at equations as the language of physics. If you read equations as sentences containing information for you to understand, then the equations will seem less foreign than if you look at them as abstract collections of symbols. Each time you encounter a boxed equation in this section, you should spend some time thinking about what the equation means.

Physics Review 1 Problems

In any of the following problems you may want to use one of the constants

$$N_A = 6.02 \times 10^{23}$$
$$R = 0.0821 \text{ L atm/K mol}$$

1. In a certain assay, a number of microbes is measured by determining the mass of the sample. It is known that the average mass of a microbe (of this species) is 6.0×10^{-16} g. How many microbes are in a sample of mass 1.1×10^{-12} g?
   A. 1800
   B. 5500
   C. 6.6×10^4
   D. 6.6×10^{28}

2. A certain substance has a density $8.4 \, \mu\text{g/mL}$. What is the mass of 422.4 mL?
   A. 0.020 mg.
   B. 3.55 mg.
   C. 350.3 mg.
   D. 3550 mg.

3. What is the mass of a water molecule?
   A. 9.2×10^{-26} g.
   B. 1.7×10^{-24} g.
   C. 3.0×10^{-23} g.
   D. 0.018 g.

4. An electrical resistor is installed in a container of water to heat it. The resistor dissipates heat at a rate of 2.0 W, and the container holds 10 kg of water. How long would it take to raise the temperature of the water 5° C? (Note: The specific heat of water is 4.2×10^3 J/kg °C, and 1 W is 1 J/s.)

   A. 2.4×10^{-2} seconds.
   B. 4.2×10^3 seconds.
   C. 1.05×10^5 seconds.
   D. 4.2×10^5 seconds.

5. Two liters of argon gas are at 10 atm of pressure. If the sample is 16 g, what is the temperature?
   A. 16,000 K
   B. 610 K
   C. 6 K
   D. 4 K

Use the following information for questions 6–10:

For a circle we have the formula for the circumference

$$C = 2\pi r$$

and the area

$$A = \pi r^2$$

where r is the radius. For a sphere, the surface area is

$$A_{surf} = 4\pi r^2$$

and the volume is

$$V = 4/3 \, \pi r^3$$

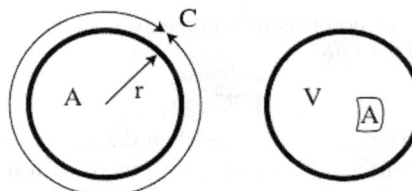

6. If the diameter of a circle is increased by a factor of 4, what happens to the circumference?
   A. It increases by a factor of 2.
   B. It increases by a factor of 4.
   C. It increases by a factor of 8.
   D. It increases by a factor of 16.

7. If the radius of a circle increases by a factor of 4, what happens to its area?
   A. It increases by a factor of 2.
   B. It increases by a factor of 4.
   C. It increases by a factor of 16.
   D. It increases by a factor of 64.

8. If the radius of a sphere increases by a factor of 4, what happens to its volume?
   A. It increases by a factor of 2.
   B. It increases by a factor of 4.
   C. It increases by a factor of 16.
   D. It increases by a factor of 64.

9. If the volume of a sphere decreases by a factor of 27, what happens to its diameter?
   A. It decreases by a factor of 9.
   B. It decreases by a factor of 3.
   C. It decreases by a factor of 4.5.
   D. It decreases by a factor of 1.5.

10. If the radius of a circle is increased by 30%, how does the area change?
    A. It increases by 30%.
    B. It increases by 60%.
    C. It increases by 69%.
    D. It increases by 75%.

Use the following information for questions 11–13:

A pendulum is a mass connected to a light string or rod which is connected to the ceiling. The period is the amount of time it takes the bob (as the mass is called) to swing from one side to the other and back. It is given by

$$T = 2\pi\sqrt{\frac{l}{g}}$$

where T is in s, l is the length of the string or rod (in m), and g is the acceleration due to gravity (m/s^2). (See Figure.)

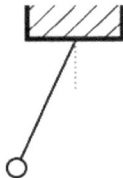

11. If the length of the string of a pendulum is increased by a factor of 4, how does the period change?
    A. It decreases by a factor of 16.
    B. It increases by a factor of 2.
    C. It increases by a factor of 4.
    D. It increases by a factor of 16.

12. The length of the rod of a certain pendulum is decreased, and the period then decreases by 20%. By how much was the rod length decreased?
    A. 20%
    B. 36%
    C. 40%
    D. 44%

13. If a pendulum is transported to the Moon, where the acceleration due to gravity is six times less than that here on Earth, how would the period of the pendulum change?
    A. It would decrease by a factor of 36.
    B. It would increase by a factor of 2.4.
    C. It would increase by a factor of 6.
    D. It would increase by a factor of 36.

Use the following information for questions 14–16:

A spring is characterized by a spring constant k (in N/m) which gives the stiffness of the spring, or how hard you have to pull to stretch it. If you connect a mass m on one end, and connect the other end to a fixed wall or ceiling, then the resulting system will vibrate. This vibration has period T given by

$$T = 2\pi\sqrt{\frac{m}{k}}$$

The frequency of the vibration is defined as

$$f = 1/T$$

14. If a mass of 60 g is connected to a certain spring, the frequency is 30 Hz. If a mass of 240 g is connected to the same spring, what is the frequency?
    A. 7.5 Hz
    B. 15 Hz
    C. 60 Hz
    D. 120 Hz

15. In two trials, two masses are attached to a spring and the periods recorded. Mass P resulted in a period 36 times larger than the period of mass Q. What can be concluded?
    A. Mass P is 1296 times larger than mass Q.
    B. Mass P is 6 times larger than mass Q.
    C. Mass P is 6 times smaller than mass Q.
    D. Mass P is 1296 times smaller than mass Q.

16. If the period increases by 50%, how does the frequency change?
    A. It decreases by 50%.
    B. It decreases by 40%.
    C. It decreases by 33%.
    D. It increases by 33%.

Passage 1

In a certain experiment, we are investigating the retarding force that a fluid exerts on an object moving through it. We guess that the size of the object is a factor, so we include A, the cross-sectional area, in an equation. The relative velocity between the object and the fluid is a factor v, as well as the density of the fluid ρ. So we guess

$$F = k\rho^m A^n v^p$$

where k is a proportionality constant with some appropriate units. Before we run the experiment, we do not know the values of the exponents m, n, and p.

The chart gives the data for a certain fluid.

Experiment	object	A (cm^2)	v (m/s)	F (N)
1	cork ball	1.5	7.0	0.020
2	cork ball	1.5	3.5	0.005
3	steel ball	1.5	3.5	0.005
4	steel ball	3.0	3.5	0.010
5	steel ball	4.5	3.5	0.015
6	steel ball	3.0	14.0	0.160

17. Which pair of experiments could be used to determine n?
    A. 2 and 3
    B. 3 and 4
    C. 4 and 6
    D. 5 and 6

18. What is the approximate value of p?
    A. −1
    B. 0
    C. 1
    D. 2

19. Which pair of experiments indicates that retarding force does not depend on the density of the object?
    A. 1 and 2
    B. 2 and 3
    C. 1 and 6
    D. 4 and 6

20. Let us say m and n are known. What combination of experiments would be considered a minimum set for determining p and k?
    A. 1 and 2
    B. 1, 2, and 3
    C. 3, 4, and 5
    D. 3 only

Passage 2

The amount of energy a car expends against air resistance is approximately given by

$$E = 0.2\rho_{air} ADv^2$$

where E is measured in Joules, ρ_{air} is the density of air (1.2 kg/m^3), A is the cross-sectional area of the car viewed from the front (in m^2), D is the distance traveled (in m), and v is the speed of the car (in m/s). Julie wants to drive from Tucson to Phoenix and get good gas mileage. For the following questions, assume that the energy loss is due solely to air resistance, and there is no wind.

21. If Julie increases her speed from 30 mph to 60 mph, how does the energy required to travel from Tucson to Phoenix change?
    A. It increases by a factor of 2.
    B. It increases by a factor of 4.
    C. It increases by a factor of 8.
    D. It increases by a factor of 16.

22. Julie usually drives at a certain speed. How much more energy will she use if she drives 20% faster?
    A. 20% more energy.
    B. 40% more energy.
    C. 44% more energy.
    D. 80% more energy.

23. Scott drives a very large 50s style car, and Laura drives a small 90s style car, so that every linear dimension of Scott's car is double that of Laura's car. *On the basis of energy loss due to air resistance alone*, how much more energy would you expect Scott's car to expend getting from Tucson to Phoenix than Laura's car?
    A. Twice as much energy.
    B. Four times as much energy.
    C. Eight times as much energy.
    D. Sixteen times as much energy.

24. How does Julie's energy usage change if she changes from driving 50 mph to 55 mph?
    A. It increases by 10%.
    B. It increases by 20%.
    C. It increases by 21%.
    D. It increases by 40%.

25. Julie modifies her car, so that the effective cross-sectional area is reduced by 20%. How much further can she drive and still use the same amount of energy?
    A. 10% further.
    B. 20% further.
    C. 25% further.
    D. 44% further.

Solutions

1. A.

We start with the information 1.1×10^{-12} g. Unit analysis takes us to the answer:

$$1.1 \times 10^{-12} g \left(\frac{1 \text{ microbe}}{6 \times 10^{-16} g} \right) = \frac{1.1}{6} \times 10^{-12+16} \text{ microbes}$$

$$\approx 0.2 \times 10^4 \text{ microbes}$$

$$\approx 2000 \text{ microbes}$$

Here we estimate (1.1)/6 to be about 0.2, which is close enough to give us an answer. Remember, all you need is an answer. You do not need to calculate a second digit.

2. B.

The question again is, "How much?" We have information in mL, and we want it in mg. Thus we write

$$422.4 \text{mL} \left(\frac{8.4 \mu g}{1 \text{mL}} \right) \left(\frac{1 \text{mg}}{10^3 \mu g} \right) \approx \frac{400 \cdot 8}{1000} \text{mg}$$

$$\approx \frac{3000}{1000} \text{mg}$$

$$= 3 \text{ mg}$$

Here we estimated 4 times 8 = 30. This is close enough to yield the answer B.

3. C.

Here we start with 1 molecule H_2O. Then we can convert to mol and g:

$$1 \text{ molec} \left(\frac{1 \text{ mol}}{6.02 \times 10^{23} \text{ molec}} \right) \left(\frac{18 \text{ g}}{1 \text{ mol}} \right) \approx \frac{18}{6} \times 10^{-23} g$$

$$\approx 3 \times 10^{-23} g$$

4. C.

We can guess that the amount of time required is proportional to the temperature change desired, so let's start with that. Next, we want to cancel the units °C, so we add a factor of $4.2 \times 10^3 \text{J/kg°C}$, giving

$$5°C \frac{4.2 \times 10^3 \text{J}}{\text{kg°C}}$$

We want to cancel kg, so we can just place a factor of 10 kg in the numerator, giving

$$5°C \frac{4.2 \times 10^3 \text{J}}{\text{kg°C}} \frac{10 \text{kg}}{1}$$

To cancel J, we can use the J from the power the resistor dissipates 2 W = 2 J/s. Thus

$$5°C \frac{4.2 \times 10^3 \text{J}}{\text{kg°C}} \frac{10 \text{kg}}{1} \frac{\text{s}}{2 \text{J}}$$

At this point we rejoice, because we have seconds in the numerator. Now we cut everything down to one digit and quickly multiply. This gives

$$\Delta t = \frac{5 \cdot 4 \cdot 10^3 \cdot 10}{2} \text{s} = \frac{20}{2} \cdot 10^4 \text{s} = 10^5 \text{s}$$

This is close to choice C.

Does this method always work? Clearly you cannot answer every conceivable question by looking at units. But it is surprising how many questions can be answered this way, specifically any question in which all the formulas involved are simple proportionalities without unitless proportionality constants.

5. B.

We know this involves the ideal gas equation, but how do we start a unit analysis? Since we know we want to end up with K in the numerator, we can just place it there at the outset:

$$\frac{\text{K mol}}{0.0821 \text{ L atm}}$$

Now we cancel L and atm, giving

$$\frac{\text{K mol}}{0.0821 \text{ L atm}} \frac{2 \text{ L}}{1} \frac{10 \text{ atm}}{1}$$

We can cancel mol if we think of a connection between mol and the 16 g Ar, so that we write

$$\frac{\text{K mol}}{0.0821 \text{ L atm}} \frac{2 \text{ L}}{1} \frac{10 \text{ atm}}{1} \frac{40 \text{ g}}{\text{mol}} \frac{1}{16 \text{ g Ar}}$$

$$\approx \frac{2 \cdot 10 \cdot 40}{0.08 \cdot 16} \text{K}$$

$$\approx \frac{100 \cdot 2 \cdot 10 \cdot 40}{8 \cdot 16} \text{K}$$

$$\approx \frac{10,000}{16} \text{K}$$

$$\approx 700 \text{K}$$

In the second step above, we multiplied numerator and denominator by 100. In the third step we calculated $2 \cdot 40/8 = 10$. Most calculations go pretty quickly if you look for these shortcuts. Our answer is close enough for us to realize the correct answer is B.

6. B.
If the diameter of a circle increases by a factor of 4, the radius increases by a factor of 4 also. (If you do not believe this, try it with a few numbers.) The circumference increases by a factor of 4 as well.

7. C.
Clearly the area increases, but since the radius is squared in the formula, the area increases by a factor of $4^2 = 16$. The π in the formula does not make any difference.

8. D.
This time there is an r^3 in the formula, so the volume increases by a factor of $4^3 = 64$.

9. B.
If the volume of a sphere decreases by a factor of 27, then its radius must decrease by a factor of 3, since $3^3 = 27$. If the radius decreases by a factor of 3, then the diameter decreases by a factor of 3 as well. Again, you should try this method with some numbers if it does not make sense to you.

10. C.
If the radius increases by 30%, that is the same as increasing by a factor of 1.3, since $(1 + 30/100) = 1.3$. If the radius increases by a factor of 1.3, then the area increases by a factor of $1.3^2 = 1.69$. An increase by such a factor is an increase by 69%, so the answer is C. Keep in mind that you need to know how to manipulate numbers like this quickly.

11. B.
Since l is in the numerator, T increases if l does. If l increases by a factor of 4, then T increases by a factor of

$$\sqrt{4} = 2$$

12. B
A problem like this is easier if we solve for l, giving

$$l = g(2\pi T)^2$$

$$l = 4\pi^2 g T^2$$

A decrease by 20% in the period is equivalent to multiplying the period by $(1 - 20/100) = 0.8$. If the period is multiplied by 0.8, then the length is multiplied by $0.8^2 = 0.64$. We can rewrite $0.64 = (1 - 36/100)$. Thus the length decreases by 36%.

13. B.
Since g is in the denominator, a decrease in g results in an increase in T. If g decreases by a factor of 6, then T increases by a factor of

$$\sqrt{6} = 2.4$$

Of course, you do not have to work out the square root. A glance at the answers indicates that B is correct.

14. B.
Since m is in the numerator, an increase in m will increase T. This results in a decrease in frequency f. Since m changes by a factor of 4, the period changes by a factor of

$$\sqrt{4} = 2$$

The frequency changes by a factor of 2, so the answer is B. This approach is the most straightforward way to do the problem. Any time spent calculating the value of k is wasted time.

15. A.
First, if the period is larger for mass P, then mass P must be larger. Next, for there to be a change of 36 in the period, there must be a change of 1296 inside the square root. Thus the answer is A.

16. C.
Since we have $(1 + 50/100) = 1.5$, the period is multiplied by 1.5. Thus the frequency is multiplied by $(1.5)^{-1} = 0.67$. We rewrite $0.67 = (1 - 33/100)$, so the frequency decreases by 33%.

Passage 1

17. B.
In order to determine n, we need two experiments where everything stays the same except for the area, so that we can investigate the results of a change in area. As for choice A, the object changes and the area does not, so that is out. In choice B, area changes from 1.5 to 3.0 cm^2, and nothing else changes, so B is correct. Choice C is incorrect because the velocity is the only thing that changes. In choice D, both A and v change, so we would not be able to tell how much change in F is due to A and how much is due to v.

18. D.
In the previous solution, we realized that experiments 4 and 6 have the property that all the input variables stay the same except for velocity v, which increases by a factor of 4. The force increases by a factor of 16, which means that p must be 2. That is, if p is 2, then an increase by a factor of 4 in v results in an increase by a factor of 4^2 in the force.

19. B.
In choice A, experiments 1 and 2 both use a cork ball. For choice C, many input variables are altered between experiments 1 and 6, so it is impossible to isolate the effect of object density. As for choice D, experiments 4 and 6 both use a steel ball. Choice B involves two experiments in which only the density of the object changes.

20. A.
As for choice A, experiments 1 and 2 could be used to determine p, since the velocity changes and nothing else does. Once p is determined, k can be determined by substituting in values from either experiment 1 or 2. Thus experiments 1 and 2 are sufficient. We can exclude choices B and C (not minimum sets). As for choice D, there is not enough information to obtain p or k.

Passage 2

21. B.
If v increases by a factor of 2, then the required energy increases by a factor of $2^2 = 4$.

22. C.
If Julie increases her speed by 20%, then she multiplies her speed by 1.2. Thus the required energy is multiplied by $(1.2)^2 = 1.44$, which is an increase of 44%.

23. B.
Comparing Scott's car to Laura's, all the linear dimensions are increased by a factor of 2 (see figure). The cross-sectional area A is width times height ($A = hw$), so if both h and w increase by a factor of 2, then A increases by a factor of 4. Thus the required energy increases by a factor of 4. The increase in length does not matter.

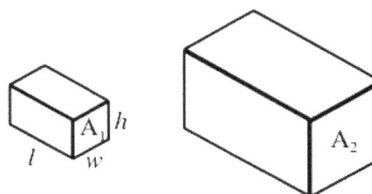

24. C.
Julie increases her speed by a factor of $55/50 = 1.1$, so the energy increases by a factor of $1.1^2 = 1.21$. This is an increase of 21%.

25. C
The easiest way to do this is to solve for D, giving

$$D = \frac{5E}{\rho_{air}Av^2}$$

If A is reduced by 20%, then A is multiplied by 0.8. According to the above equation, D is multiplied by $(0.8)^{-1} = 1.25$, representing an increase of 25%.

Physics Review 2
The Language of Motion

A. Introduction

Mechanics is about the motion of things. Before we can talk about motion in depth, we need to be able to describe motion and the things which affect it. Objects move, and we talk of how fast they go, that is, velocity. Their velocity changes, so we talk of acceleration. We can think of changes in acceleration, but it turns out (happily) that we rarely need to. Mechanics is concerned mainly with changes in velocity.

In this chapter we look at the fundamental elements of mechanics: force, mass, distance, velocity, and acceleration. Comparatively this chapter has a lot of equations (six that you should memorize) and the least interesting physics. It is an unpleasant way to begin, but it must be done.

B. Force

A *force* is a push or pull, and the units for force are [Newtons = N]. (Some countries continue to use an archaic unit called the "pound".) A Newton is approximately the amount of force that you would exert on an apple near the Earth's surface to keep it from falling.

Examples of forces include the force of a horse pulling a cart, the force of a spring pushing the chassis of a car, the force of gravity pulling you down, and the force on your head due to pressure when you are at the bottom of a pool.

C. Mass

We can think about mass in several ways. First, the *mass* of an object is a measure of the total amount of material (or stuff) in the object. The amount of stuff in an object is a fundamental property of the object. It doesn't change if you move the object to a new place, like a mountaintop or to Mars.

There is another way to think of mass. The mass of an object is a measure of how difficult it is to get it moving at a certain velocity if it starts from rest. For example, if John wants to set a car, initially at rest, to moving at 1 m/s, he has to push hard for a little while. We are assuming the car's motion has no friction. If John and the car were on the Moon, his task would be equally difficult. The fundamental concept here is the mass of the car, not the astronomical body the car is on. (See Figure 2-1.)

*A car has the same mass on the Moon as it has
on Earth. It takes just as much force and time to
get a car moving at a given velocity on the
Earth as on the Moon.*

Figure 2-1

Saying this another way, the mass of an object is a measure of how much it hurts if your stub you toe on it. Stubbing your toe on a bowling ball is a painful proposition, even on the Moon.

There is a *wrong* way to think about mass. Many people think the mass of an object is a measure of how difficult it is to pick it up. But that definition depends on where you are. It is easy to pick up a bowling ball on the Moon, but nearly impossible on the surface of Jupiter. The difficulty in picking up an object is a matter of weight, which is a force. And weight *does* depend on the astronomical body near by.

D. Vectors

In physics we often need to describe direction as well as size. For example, two forces F_1 and F_2 may both be 100 N and acting on a crocodile, but the crocodile's experience will be very different depending on whether the forces are both pointing north or one north and one south (Figure 2-2). In the former case he gets stretched, and in the latter case he goes flying. To describe forces we need to specify size and direction. That is, we need to use vectors. Force is a vector.

We denote vectors in diagrams by arrows, the length of the arrow showing the size of the vector and the direction of the arrow showing its direction.

We can add vectors by the tip-to-tail method. We leave the first vector fixed, and move the second vector so its tail is at the first vector's tip. If there are other vectors, then each vector gets added to the previous tip. The sum is the vector pointing from the first tail to the last tip.

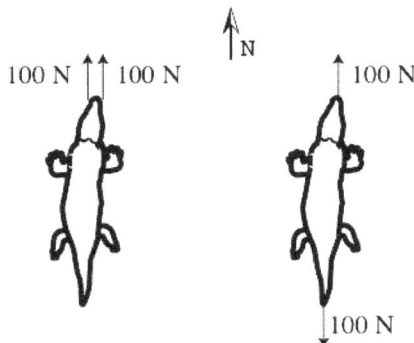

*Two forces on an object may add in
different ways, depending on the
relative directions of the forces.*

Figure 2-2

Example 1: For the crocodiles mentioned before, if the vectors (both 100 N) both point north, then the sum is a force of 200 N pointing north (Figure 2-3, where the sum is shown dashed).

If one vector points north and the other south, then the first tail coincides with the last tip and the sum is zero (Figure 2-3).

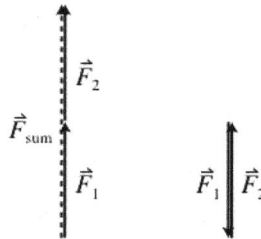

Forces are vectors and they add according to the tip-to-tail method.

Figure 2-3

Example 2: A crocodile has three forces acting on him: a 100-N force north, a 100-N force east, and a 100-N force southwest. What is the direction of the net force (that is, total force)?

Solution: We DRAW A DIAGRAM (Figure 2-4). The sum is a vector pointing northeast, about 40 N.

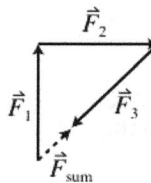

Figure 2-4

Note that, when you add vectors, the magnitude of the sum is equal to, at most, the sum of the individual magnitudes (and that only if they are pointing in the same direction). For instance, if three vectors of 100 N are acting on a crocodile, the sum can be anything from 0 N to 300 N, but no greater.

For ACT problems, vector addition need not get more sophisticated than this. It is useful to keep in mind the Pythagorean theorem and elementary trigonometry.

Example 3: A force of 4 N is acting to the north on a rock and a force of 3 N is acting to the east.

a. What is the magnitude of the total force?
b. What is $\cos\phi$, if ϕ is the deviation from north of the direction of the total force?

Solution: We DRAW A DIAGRAM (Figure 2-5). There is a right triangle, so we can write

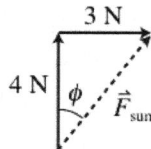

Figure 2-5

$$F^2_{sum} = (3N)^2 + (4N)^2 = 25N^2$$

$$F_{sum} = 5 \text{ N}$$

Also we write

$$\cos\phi = 4N/5N = 0.8$$

If your trigonometry is rusty, now is a good time to relearn the definitions of sine, cosine, and tangent.

A vector is denoted by a half-arrow on top of a letter, $\vec{F}$, for example.

E. Position, Displacement, and Time

To specify position, we must give three coordinates x, y, and z, generally measured in [meters = m]. The symbol s stands for the coordinates (x, y, z). If an object moves from one position to another, the vector giving the change in position is the *displacement vector*, $\Delta s = s_2 - s_1$. The magnitude of the displacement vector is called the *displacement*.

Time is a fundamental quantity in classical physics, denoted t, measured in [seconds = s]. Often we will speak of a *time interval* $\Delta t = t_2 - t_1$, that is, the time between a beginning time t_1 and ending time t_2. An *instant* is a single moment of time.

F. Velocity, Speed, and All That

We can think of the *velocity vector* in terms of a speedometer reading with units [meters/second = m/s] and a direction. The magnitude of the velocity vector (that is, just the speedometer reading) is called *speed*. The word "velocity" is sometimes used to refer to the vector and sometimes to the magnitude. When in doubt, you should assume it refers to the vector.

If an object is traveling such that its velocity vector is constant, we say it is in *uniform motion*. An example is a car going a constant 30 m/s (freeway speed) west. We can write the following equations for uniform motion in one dimension:

$$v = \frac{\Delta x}{\Delta t} \qquad (1a)$$

$$v = \frac{x_2 - x_1}{\Delta t} \qquad (1b)$$

When you see a formula in this text, instead of speeding by it, slow down and look at it. Ask yourself, "What is this equation telling me?" Equation (1a) is just another form of "distance equals rate times time" for an object in uniform motion. Since v is constant, this tells you, for instance, that a car will travel twice as far if it travels for twice the time. This makes sense.

Equation (1b) is like the first, only Δx is replaced by its definition $x_2 - x_1$. Do you see why it is this and not $x_1 - x_2$ or $x_2 + x_1$?

But in some problems the velocity does change, and we must pay attention to several velocities, that is,

$$v_1 \quad \text{initial velocity,}$$

$$v_2 \quad \text{final velocity,}$$

and

$$v_{avg} \quad \text{average velocity.}$$

The average velocity is defined as

$$v_{avg} = \frac{\Delta s}{\Delta t} \qquad (2)$$

This is different from equation (1). Equation (2) is the definition of an average velocity over a time interval when velocity is changing, whereas equation (1) defines a constant velocity and only holds for time intervals when the motion is uniform.

Example: A car goes west at 10 m/s for 6 s, then it goes north at 10 m/s for 5 s, and then it goes west again at 4 m/s for 15 s. What are v_1, v_2, and v_{avg}?

Solution: Well, we have $v_1 = 10$ m/s and $v_2 = 4$ m/s. For the average velocity we need to DRAW A DIAGRAM (Figure 2-6). The Pythagorean theorem gives us $\Delta s = 130$ m. Thus

$$v_{avg} = 130m/26s = 5 \text{ m/s}$$

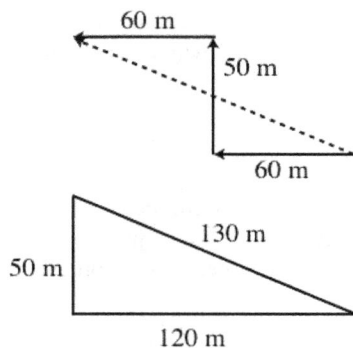

Figure 2-6

G. Acceleration

When an object's velocity vector is changing, the object is *accelerating*. Examples include a car speeding up ("accelerating" in common parlance), slowing down or braking ("decelerating", but physicists prefer to say "negatively accelerating"), and turning. In three dimensions, we define acceleration by

$$\vec{a} = \frac{\overrightarrow{\Delta v}}{\Delta t} \qquad (3a)$$

$$= \frac{\vec{v}_2 - \vec{v}_1}{\Delta t}. \qquad (3b)$$

The numerator for equation (3a) gives the change in the velocity vector, so there is an acceleration if either the magnitude or the direction of the velocity vector change. In one dimension the definition of acceleration is

$$a = \frac{\Delta v}{\Delta t} \qquad (4a)$$

$$= \frac{v_2 - v_1}{\Delta t} \qquad (4b)$$

The units for acceleration are $[(m/s)/s = m/s \cdot 1/s = m/s^2]$.

Example 1a: Take north to be positive. A car is traveling south and speeding up. What is the sign of the acceleration?

Solution: Since the velocity vector points south and the car is speeding up, the acceleration vector must point south. With this sign convention, acceleration is negative.

Example 1b: Take north to be positive. A car traveling south speeds up from 10 m/s to 15 m/s in 10 s. What is its acceleration?

Solution: We write

$$a = \frac{-15\frac{m}{s} - (-10)\frac{m}{s}}{10s} = -0.5\frac{m}{s^2}$$

This confirms our thinking in Example 1a.

Example 2a: Take north to be positive. A car is traveling north and slowing for a red light. What is the sign of the acceleration?

Solution: The velocity vector points north. Since this vector is shrinking, the acceleration vector must point south. Thus the acceleration is negative.

Example 2b: What is the acceleration for the car in Example 2a slowing from 10 m/s to 8 m/s in 1 s?
Solution: We write

$$a = \frac{8\frac{m}{s} - 10\frac{m}{s}}{1s} = -2\frac{m}{s^2}$$

Example 3: An Oldsmobile takes a certain amount of time to accelerate from 0 to 60 mph. A Porsche takes less time by a factor of 3 to accelerate from 0 to 60 mph. How does the Porsche acceleration compare with that of the Oldsmobile?

Solution: We look at equation (4)

$$a = \frac{\Delta v}{\Delta t}$$

Since Δv is constant, if Δt is smaller by a factor of 3, then a is larger by a factor of 3.

H. Graphs

Now we have three quantities, position, velocity, and acceleration, all related to each other algebraically. Often it is helpful to visualize these quantities graphically. The following principles apply

1. Given a graph of x versus t, the instantaneous slope at time t is the velocity v at time t.
2. Given a graph of v versus t, the instantaneous slope at time t is the acceleration a at time t.
3. Given a graph of a versus t, the area under the curve during interval Δt gives the change in velocity v during that interval.
4. Given a graph of v versus t, the area under the curve during interval Δt gives the change in position x during that interval.

Example 1: The graph of a versus t for a car which undergoes constant acceleration is shown in Figure 2-7. Sketch the graph of v versus t. Assume $v = 0$ m/s at $t = 0$ s.

Solution: The area under the curve between 0 and Δt is shown in a "forward-slash" hatch. This area is Δv, that is, the change in velocity during Δt. The reason for principle 3 above becomes clear if we recall the formula for the area of the rectangle representing the hatched region:

$$\text{area} = \text{height} \times \text{length}$$
$$\Delta v = a\Delta t$$

This is how we defined acceleration in equation (4). During the second interval Δt, the area is a Δt again. Thus the change in velocity is the same, as shown in Figure 2-8. For the next intervals of time, the quantity Δv is constant.

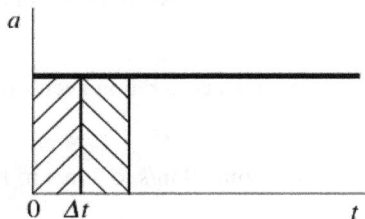

Figure 2-7

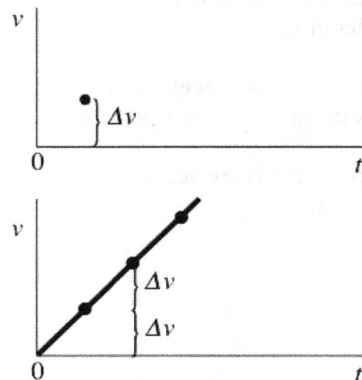

Figure 2-8

Note that Figures 2-7 and 2-8 give (almost) the same information in different forms. Figure 2-7 has the information that the acceleration is positive and constant, so the car is speeding up (if it is going forward). Figure 2-8 has the information that the velocity is increasing at a constant rate. This is the same thing.

Before you read the next example, consider an object thrown straight up. When it reaches the top of its path, what is the direction of its velocity? What is the direction of its acceleration?

Example 2: An apple is tossed straight up in the air. The graph of y versus t is shown in Figure 2-9. Sketch the graphs of v versus t and a versus t.

Solution: To obtain an instantaneous slope, we can use an imaginary electron microscope to look at a small portion of the graph. A small section of Figure 2-9 has been enlarged using such a microscope. This portion looks almost straight, so we could calculate its slope if we had some numbers. We can at least read that the slope is positive and very large, hence the first point in Figure 2-10.

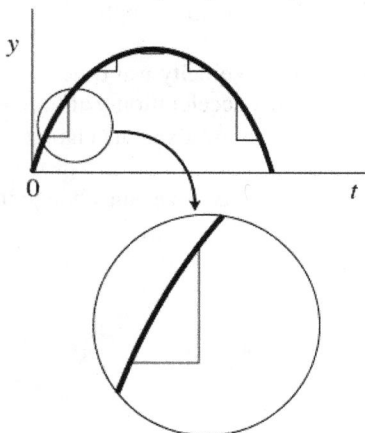

Figure 2-9

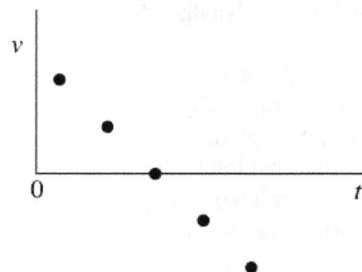

Figure 2-10

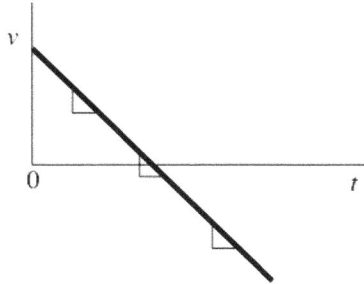

Figure 2-11

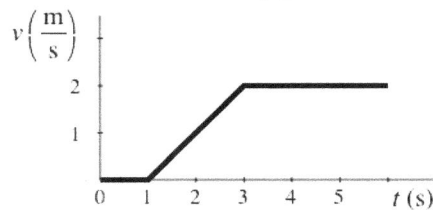

Figure 2-12

The second point on Figure 2-10 still has a positive slope, but smaller. The third point has a zero slope (see uppermost point in Figure 2-9). The fourth point has negative slope, and the fifth point has a slope more negative still.

It will not come as a surprise if we draw a straight line through these points, as in Figure 2-11. We take the slope at three points, but it is easy to see that the slope is constant and negative. We graph the acceleration in Figure 2-12.

Does this match your expectation? Particularly at the top of flight, did you know that the direction of the acceleration would be down?

Example 3: Figure 2-13 shows v versus t for a car. Sketch the graphs for x versus t and for a versus t. (Say $x = 0$ at $t = 0$.)

Solution: Let's graph x versus t first. From $t = 0$ to 1 s, there is no area under the curve, so x stays constant. From $t = 1$ to 2 s, the area under the curve is 0.5 m. (Recall the area of a triangle is $A = 1/2$ base x height.)

From $t = 2$ to 3 s the area under the curve is 1.5 m, so that the x value jumps to 2 m (see the first graph of Figure 2-14). Between $t = 3$ and 4 s, the area is 2 m and x jumps to 4 m, and so on. Figure 2-14 shows the result.

For the graph of a versus t, the slope of v versus t for any point between $t = 0$ and 1 s is zero. The slope jumps to 1 m/s^2 for the interval from 1 to 3 s and drops back down to zero for times after 3 s. (See Figure 2-15.)

Think about all three graphs for a while and note how they give the same information in different forms.

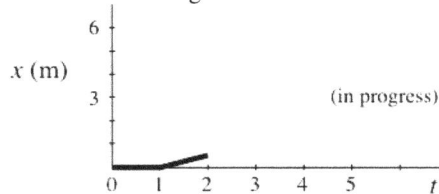

Figure 2-13

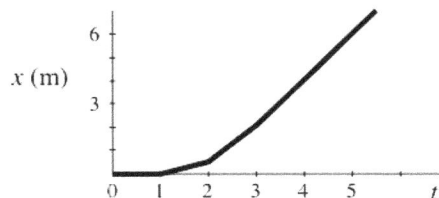

Figure 2-14

433

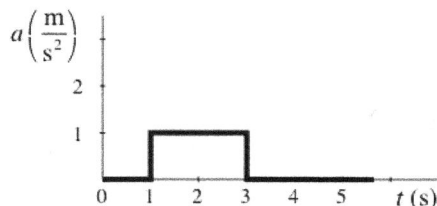

Figure 2-15

I. Uniform Acceleration

If an object has a constant acceleration vector, we say it undergoes *uniform acceleration*. Most ACT problems involving acceleration will involve uniform acceleration. For uniform acceleration, we have the following:

$$v_{avg} = \frac{1}{2}(v_1 + v_2) \qquad (5)$$

that is, the average velocity over a period of time is the average of the beginning and ending velocities. This may seem like a natural definition of average velocity, but the definition of v_{avg} is given by equation (2), and equation (5) holds only for uniform acceleration.

See Figures 2-7 and 2-8 for an example. The velocity v_1 is small, v_2 is large, and v_{avg} is exactly between them.

If we start with the definition of average velocity, we can write

$$\Delta x = v_{avg}\Delta t$$

$$\Delta x = \frac{1}{2}(v_1 + v_2)\Delta t$$

This is a useful equation if you do not have and do not need the acceleration (see equation [7] below). Furthermore, if we substitute $v_2 = v_1 + a\Delta t$ (from equation [4]), then we obtain

$$\Delta x = \frac{1}{2}(v_1 + (v_1 + a\Delta t))\Delta t$$

$$\boxed{\Delta x = v_1\Delta t + \frac{1}{2}a\Delta t^2 \qquad (6)}$$

This is the first equation which may seem a bit arcane. You should memorize it anyway. Working through the algebra will help you memorize it.

Example: A car is accelerating uniformly from rest. If it goes a distance d in the first second, how far will it go in the first four seconds?

Solution: We want an equation involving the quantities mentioned in the problem, a, $v_1 = 0$, Δx, and Δt, so equation (6) is it. With $v_1 = 0$, we obtain

$$\Delta x = \frac{1}{2}a\Delta t^2$$

If Δt increases by a factor of 4, the Δx increases, and it increases by a factor of $4^2 = 16$.

J. Kinematic Equations for Constant Acceleration

For uniform acceleration there are four equations you should know:

$$\Delta x = \frac{1}{2}\left(v_1 + v_2\right)\Delta t \qquad (7)$$

$$v_2 - v_1 = a\Delta t \qquad (8)$$

$$\Delta x = v_1\Delta t + \frac{1}{2}a\Delta t^2 \qquad (9)$$

$$v_2^2 = v_1^2 + 2a\Delta x \qquad (10)$$

The first equation we have seen before, the modified "distance equals rate times time" when velocity is changing. It should be easy to remember. The second equation is just the definition of acceleration. The third equation was in the last section. The last equation is the only one which is new, obtained by eliminating Δt from equations (7) and (8). It is useful for problems in which the time interval is neither specified nor desired.

Example 1: A cat drops from a ledge 2 m above the ground. If he accelerates 10 m/s² downward due to gravity, how much time does it take him to drop?

Solution: Let's choose "up" to be positive and DRAW A DIAGRAM (Figure 2-16). We write the quantities we know:

$$\Delta y = -2 \text{ m}$$

$$v_0 = 0 \text{ m/s}$$

$$a = -10 \text{ m/s2}$$

$$\Delta t = ?$$

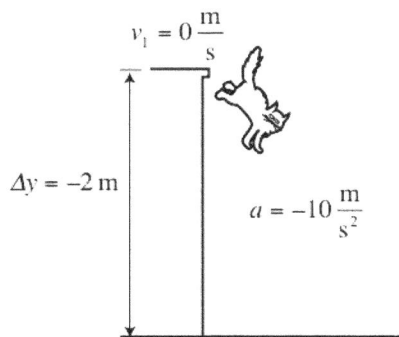

Figure 2-16

We look for an equation which involves these quantities and no others. Equation (9) fits, so that

$$-2\text{m} = 0\text{m} + \frac{1}{2}\left(-10\frac{m}{s^2}\right)\Delta t^2$$

$$\Delta t^2 = 0.4 \cdot \frac{s^2}{m}$$

$$\Delta t = 0.63\text{s}$$

Example 2: A man drops to his death from the sixth floor of a building (20 m). As he is falling, his acceleration is a constant 10 m/s² downward. What is his impact velocity? (He was a bad man, and if he had not died many other nice people would have.)

Solution: First we DRAW A DIAGRAM (Figure 2-17). The impact velocity is the man's velocity just before he hits the ground v_2. Thus our information summary is

$$v_1 = 0 \text{ m/s}$$

$$\Delta y = -20 \text{ m}$$

$$a = -10 \text{ m/s}^2$$

$$v_2 = ?$$

The formula which contains this information and nothing else is (10), so that

$$v_2^2 = v_1^2 + 2a\Delta y$$

$$v_2^2 = \left(0\frac{m}{s}\right)^2 + 2\left(-10\frac{m}{s^2}\right)(-20 \text{ m})$$

$$v_2^2 = 400\frac{m^2}{s^2}$$

$$v_2 = -20\frac{m}{s}$$

His impact velocity is 20 m/s.

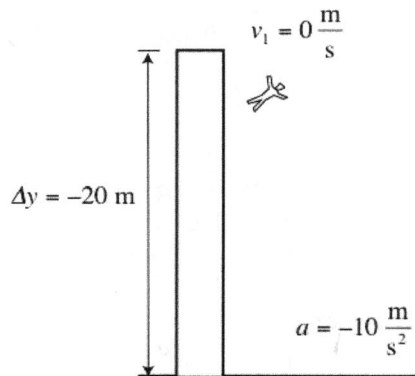

Figure 2-17

In this chapter we looked at the quantities which describe motion, that is, displacement, velocity, and acceleration, and the quantities which affect motion, that is, force and mass. Displacement is a change in location. Velocity is a measure of the change in location per unit time, while acceleration is a measure of the change in velocity per unit time. Displacement, velocity, acceleration, and force are all vectors, that is, they have direction as well as magnitude. Most of the mechanics problems on the ACT involve one dimension and uniform acceleration. In this case, we can derive four equations, shown in Section J.

In addition, you should know the equations for the definition of velocity for uniform motion and of average velocity.

Physics Review 2 Problems

1. The gravitational field of a planet or spherical astronomical body depends on its mass and on its radius. When the Moon is compared to Earth, its smaller mass makes for a smaller gravitational field, while its smaller radius favors a larger one. The net effect is that the gravitational field of the Moon at its surface is one sixth that of the Earth. A 10,000-kg mobile unit is transported to the Moon. What is its mass on the Moon?
    A. 1/36 (10,000) kg
    B. 1/6 (10,000) kg
    C. 10,000 kg
    D. 60,000 kg

Use the following information for questions 2 and 3:

A car is driving north at 2 m/s, and a fly in the car is flying west at 0.3 m/s (relative to the car).

2. Which of the following best shows the appropriate diagram for the fly's velocity relative to the ground (thick arrow)?

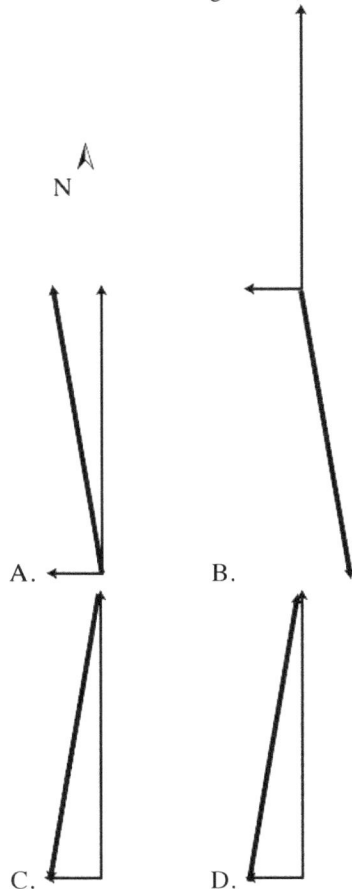

3. What is the speed of the fly?
    A. 1.7 m/s
    B. 2.02 m/s
    C. 2.3 m/s
    D. 4.09 m/s

4. The following diagram represents three vectors in a plane:

    What arrow best represents the direction of the sum?
    A. →
    B. ←
    C. ↑
    D. ↓

5. The following diagram represents three vectors in a plane:

    What arrow best represents the direction of the sum?
    A. ↓
    B. ↑
    C. The sum is zero.
    D. The diagram is invalid.

6. Two men pull on ropes connected to a large refrigerator with forces 3000 N and 4000 N. If there are no other (unbalanced) forces, which of the following is NOT a possibility for the magnitude of the net (total) force?
    A. 500 N
    B. 1000 N
    C. 3500 N
    D. 7000 N

7. If, in question 6, the two men are pulling at right angles to each other, what is the magnitude of the net force?
    A. 1000 N
    B. 5000 N
    C. 7000 N
    D. 8000 N

Use the following information for questions 8–11:

A woman is going to a friend's house to discuss opening a business. At 11:00 (exactly) she starts from rest and accelerates at a constant 2.5 m/s² for 9 s to get to her cruising speed. She then drives for 15 minutes at constant speed before she hits city traffic. She comes to a stop at her friend's house, which is 27 km away (straight-line distance), at 12:15 (exactly). Consider the interval from 11:00 to 12:15.

8. What is her initial velocity?
    A. 0 m/s
    B. 2.1 m/s
    C. 5.6 m/s
    D. 22.5 m/s

9. What is her final velocity?
    A. 0 m/s
    B. 2.1 m/s
    C. 5.6 m/s
    D. 22.5 m/s

10. What is her average velocity?
    A. 0 m/s
    B. 6 m/s
    C. 12 m/s
    D. 22.5 m/s

11. What is her velocity 9 s after 11:00?
    A. 0.28 m/s
    B. 6 m/s
    C. 11.25 m/s
    D. 22.5 m/s

Use the following information for questions 12–14:

A car accelerates uniformly in one dimension from 5 m/s to 30 m/s in 10 s.

12. What is the car's acceleration?
    A. 1.75 m/s²
    B. 2.5 m/s²
    C. 3.5 m/s²
    D. 15 m/s²

13. What is the car's average velocity for this time interval?
    A. 2.5 m/s
    B. 3.5 m/s
    C. 17.5 m/s
    D. This cannot be determined from the information given.

14. How far does the car travel during this time?
    A. 1.75 m
    B. 17.5 m
    C. 175 m
    D. This cannot be determined from the information given.

15. A car travels a certain distance at a constant velocity *v* for a time *t*. If the car were to travel three times as fast, covering the same distance, then the time of travel would be
    A. decreased by a factor of 9.
    B. decreased by a factor of 3.
    C. increased by a factor of 3.
    D. increased by a factor of 9.

16. A sparrow cruising at 1.5 m/s begins to accelerate at a constant 0.3 m/s² for 3 s. What is its change in velocity?
    A. 0.9 m/s
    B. 1.5 m/s
    C. 1.95 m/s
    D. 2.4 m/s

Use the following information for questions 17 and 18:

A dropped ball falls from a height of 10 m to the ground. Its acceleration is a constant 9.8 m/s² downward.

17. How long does it take to fall?
    A. 1.02 s
    B. 1.43 s
    C. 2.04 s
    D. This cannot be determined from the information given.

18. What is its velocity just before hitting the ground?
    A. 0.98 m/s
    B. 14 m/s
    C. 98 m/s
    D. This cannot be determined from the information given.

19. A car is going 20 m/s in traffic. When the traffic breaks, the driver steps on the accelerator pedal, accelerating at a constant 1.2 m/s^2 for 5 s. How far does he travel during these 5 s?
    A. 30 m
    B. 115 m
    C. 130 m
    D. 160 m

20. A car is going up a slight slope decelerating at 0.1 m/s^2. It comes to a stop after going for 5 s. What was its initial velocity?
    A. 0.02 m/s
    B. 0.25 m/s
    C. 0.5 m/s
    D. 1.0 s

Use the following information for questions 21 and 22:

A ball is initially rolling up a slight incline at 0.2 m/s. It decelerates uniformly at 0.05 m/s^2.

21. At what time does the ball come to a stop?
    A. 2 s
    B. 4 s
    C. 8 s
    D. 16 s

22. What is the ball's net displacement after 6 s?
    A. 0.3 m
    B. 0.4 m
    C. 0.5 m
    D. 1.7 m

Use the following information for questions 23 and 24:

A car is going backwards at 5 m/s. After 10 s of uniform acceleration, the car is going forward at 10 m/s.

23. What is the acceleration?
    A. 0.5 m/s^2
    B. 0.75 m/s^2
    C. 1.5 m/s^2
    D. 5 m/s^2

24. What is the net distance traveled?
    A. 25 m
    B. 41.7 m
    C. 45 m
    D. 50 m

25. A bicycle traveling at speed v covers a distance Δx during a time interval Δt. If a car travels at speed $3v$, how much time does it take the car to go the same distance?
    A. $\Delta t + 3$
    B. $3\Delta t$
    C. $\Delta t/3$
    D. $\Delta t - 3$

26. A car is traveling 25 m/s when it passes kilometer-marker 3000. The car accelerates at 0.02 m/s^2 for the next 500 s. What kilometer marker will the car pass at that time?
    A. 3015 km
    B. 3030 km
    C. 12000 km
    D. 18000 km

27. A squirrel is running along a wire with constant acceleration. If it has an initial velocity 0.4 m/s and final velocity 1.8 m/s after 4 s, how far does it run in that time?
    A. 1.6 m
    B. 4.4 m
    C. 5.6 m
    D. 8.8 m

28. If a bicycle starts accelerating uniformly from rest (at $t = 0$), it attains a certain velocity v after a time t. How fast would it be going after a time $3t$ (that is, a time $3t$ after the start $t = 0$)?
    A. $v + 9$
    B. $3v$
    C. $6v$
    D. $9v$

For questions 29 and 30, consider the following figure representing the velocity of a car along a street.

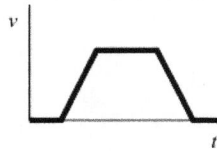

Consider also the following graphs:

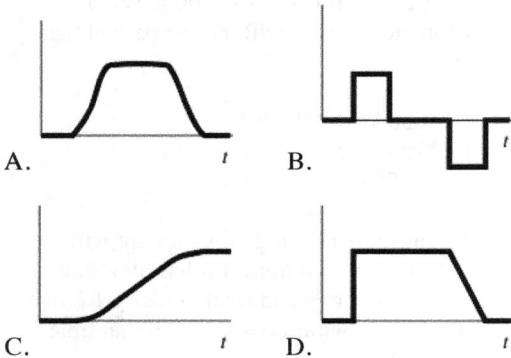

A.

B.

C.

D.

29. Which best represents the graph of displacement versus time?
   A. A
   B. B
   C. C
   D. D

30. Which best represents the graph of acceleration versus time?
   A. A
   B. B
   C. C
   D. D

For questions 31 and 32, consider the following figure representing the displacement of an object in one dimension.

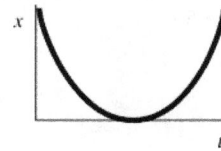

31. Which best represents the graph of acceleration versus time?

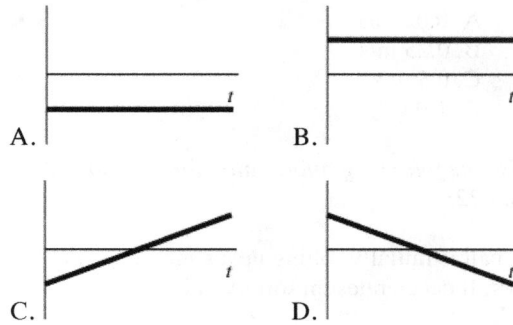

A.

B.

C.

D.

32. What can be concluded about the net displacement?
   A. It is zero.
   B. It is positive except for one point, where it is zero.
   C. It is negative, then zero, then positive.
   D. It is always positive?

Passage 1

A man is driving out of his driveway by backing up. He realizes he has forgotten his lunch, so he pulls back into the driveway. Car experts agree that the best way to do this is to press on the brake until the car comes to a complete stop, shift from reverse into first gear, then accelerate forward.

The driver, however, shifts into first gear while the car is rolling backward and pushes on the accelerator until he is going forward. This causes some wear on the transmission. The following chart shows some data about his progress. (Negative velocity = backwards.)

t (s)	x (m)	v (m/s)
0.0	1.35	−1.8
0.5	0.60	−1.2
1.0	0.15	−0.6
1.5	0.00	0.0
2.0	0.15	0.6
2.5	0.60	1.2
3.0	1.35	1.8

33. What is the value of his initial velocity?
    A. −1.8 m/s
    B. 0.0 m/s
    C. 1.2 m/s
    D. 1.8 m/s

34. What is the value of his average velocity?
    A. −1.8 m/s
    B. 0.0 m/s
    C. 1.2 m/s
    D. 1.8 m/s

35. Which of the following is evidence that the acceleration is uniform?
    A. The displacement x is always nonnegative.
    B. The velocity is always increasing.
    C. The velocity becomes zero at $t = 1.5$ s.
    D. Equal intervals of time correspond to equal intervals of velocity.

36. What is the magnitude of the acceleration from $t = 1.0$ s to 2.0 s?
    A. 0.0 m/s^2
    B. 0.6 m/s^2
    C. 1.0 m/s^2
    D. 1.2 m/s^2

37. What is the direction of the acceleration vector?
    A. forward
    B. backward
    C. up
    D. down

38. Which best represents the graph of acceleration versus time?

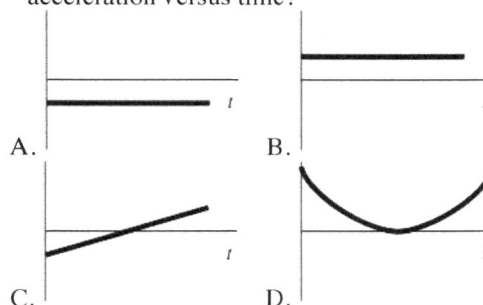

Passage 2

A physics student leans out of the fortieth story of the physics building and drops two balls of the same size at the same time. One is 0.8 kg and made of iron, and the other is 1.2 kg and made of lead. Not only do the two balls hit the ground at the same time, the heights of the two balls match all the way down.

This somewhat counterintuitive result is an example of a general principle: If air resistance is negligible, then an object in free fall at the surface of the Earth has a downward acceleration of $g = 9.8$ m/s^2. Free fall means that only the force of gravity is acting on an object.

In the following questions, consider a ball dropped from the fortieth story of a building, and consider "down" to be in the positive direction. Consider air resistance negligible unless noted otherwise.

39. How far does the object fall in the time interval from $t = 0$ to 4 s?
    A. 39.2 m
    B. 78.4 m
    C. 156.8 m
    D. 313.6 m

40. Which expression gives the change in velocity between $t_1 = 3$ s and $t_2 = 4$ s?
    A. $g(t_2 - t_1)/2$
    B. $g(t_2 - t_1)$
    C. $g(t_2 + t_1)/2$
    D. $g(t_2 + t_1)$

41. Which graph best represents velocity versus time?

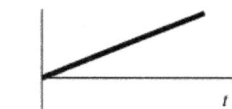

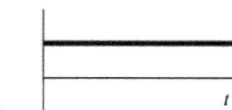

A.

B.

C.

D.

42. How does the change in velocity from $t = 1$ to 2 s compare with the change in velocity from $t = 3$ to 4 s?
    A. It is less.
    B. It is the same.
    C. It is greater.
    D. It depends on the object.

43. How does the change in height from $t = 1$ to 2 s compare with the change in height from $t = 3$ to 4 s?
    A. It is less.
    B. It is the same.
    C. It is greater.
    D. It depends on the object.

44. If an object falls a distance Δx during the first t seconds, how far does it fall during the first $3t$ seconds?
    A. $\Delta x + 3$
    B. $3\Delta x$
    C. $\Delta x + 9$
    D. $9\Delta x$

45. A Styrofoam ball of the same size as the lead ball takes a longer time to reach the ground. Which is a good explanation for this?
    A. The force of gravity does not act on the Styrofoam ball.
    B. The force of gravity on the Styrofoam ball is less than that on the lead ball.
    C. Air resistance is a significant force in this problem.
    D. There is a gravitational force between the ball and the building.

Solutions

1. C.

The mass of the mobile unit does not change just because we transport it to a different place.

2. A.

We add the fly's velocity to the car's velocity in order to obtain its total velocity relative to the ground. We move the fly velocity vector so that its tail coincides with the tip of the car velocity vector. The resulting total is just west of north (see diagram). In the choices, only choice A shows the correct total vector. The choice does not show the fly vector already moved. You must do that.

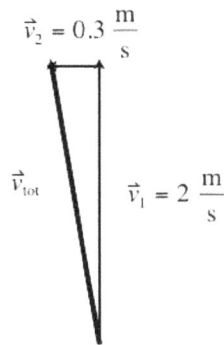

$$\vec{v}_2 = 0.3 \, \frac{\text{m}}{\text{s}}$$

$$\vec{v}_{\text{tot}} \qquad \vec{v}_1 = 2 \, \frac{\text{m}}{\text{s}}$$

3. B.

From the diagram of the previous solution, we can see that the answer must be slightly larger than 2 m/s and certainly not so large as 2.3 m/s, so B is correct. To do the numbers, we use the Pythagorean theorem:

$$\left(v_{\text{tot}}\right)^2 = \left(2\frac{\text{m}}{\text{s}}\right)^2 + \left(0.3\frac{\text{m}}{\text{s}}\right)^2$$

$$= 4.09\frac{\text{m}^2}{\text{s}^2}$$

$$v_{\text{tot}} = 2.02\frac{\text{m}}{\text{s}}$$

4. A.

First we move the horizontal vector, so its tail is on the tip of the top vector. Then we move the bottom vector, so its tail is on the tip of the horizontal vector. The resulting sum is the arrow from the first tail to the last tip (see diagram).

$$\vec{v}_{\text{tot}}$$

5. C.

Again we sequentially place the tail of one vector on the tip of the previous one. The resulting sum is zero (see diagram). We could see this in the diagram anyway, since the arrows seem to cancel out each other.

$$\vec{v}_{\text{tot}} = \vec{0}$$

6. A.

They exert the largest net force when they pull the same direction (see figure), giving the total 7000 N. They exert the smallest net force when they are directly opposed to each other, giving 1000 N. Therefore it is not possible for the net force to be 500 N. If this is unclear, try drawing a few vector diagrams to get a total of 500 N.

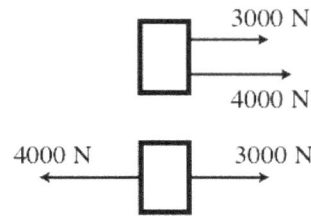

3000 N

4000 N

4000 N   3000 N

7. B.

If they pull at right angles, then we need to apply the Pythagorean theorem (see figure):

$$(F_{\text{tot}})^2 = (3000 \text{ N})^2 + (4000 \text{ N})^2$$

$$F_{\text{tot}} = 5000 \text{ N}$$

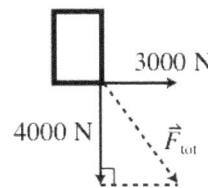

3000 N

4000 N $\vec{F}_{\text{tot}}$

8. A.

Since she starts from rest, her initial velocity is zero.

9. A.

Again, she ends at rest.

10. B.

The net displacement is $\Delta s = 27$ km $= 27,000$ m. The total time is $\Delta t = 75$ min $= 4500$ s. Thus the average velocity is $v_{\text{avg}} = \Delta s/\Delta t = 6$ m/s.

11. D.
During these 9 s, she was accelerating uniformly, so we can write the equation:

$$v_2 - v_1 = a\Delta t$$

$$v_2 = v_1 + a\Delta t$$

$$= 0 \text{ m/s} + (2.5 \text{ m/s}^2)(9\text{s})$$

$$= 22.5 \text{ m/s}$$

12. B.
Since the car is accelerating uniformly, we can write $a = \Delta v/\Delta t = (30 \text{ m/s} - 5 \text{ m/s})/10 \text{ s} = 2.5$ m/s^2.

13. C.
Since the car is accelerating uniformly, we can write $v_{avg} = 1/2 \, (v_1 + v_2) = 17.5$ m/s.

14. C.
We can write the equation

$$\Delta x = 1/2 \, (v_1 + v_2)\Delta t$$

$$= 1/2 \, (5 \text{ m/s} + 30 \text{ m/s})(10\text{s})$$

$$= 175 \text{ m}$$

15. B.
We want a formula which relates distance, velocity, and time, so we write

$$v = \frac{\Delta x}{\Delta t}$$

Now Δx is the same, while we want v to increase by a factor of 3. To do this we need Δt to decrease by a factor of 3. You could probably do this without writing down the formula. Other problems will not be so simple.

16. A.
We want to know change of velocity Δv, while we know acceleration $a = 0.3$ m/s^2, the time interval $\Delta t = 3$ s, and the initial velocity $v_1 = 1.5$ m/s. We need the definition of acceleration:

$$a = \Delta v/\Delta t$$

$$\Delta v = a\Delta t$$

$$= (0.3 \text{ m/s}^2)(3 \text{ s})$$

$$= 0.9 \text{ m/s}^2$$

So we did not need the value of v_1 at all. The key to many problems is making an inventory of what we know and what we want.

17. B.
We know $\Delta y = -10$ m, $a = -10$ m/s^2 (approximately), $v_1 = 0$ m/s (because it is dropped). We want Δt. Thus we have

$$\Delta x = v_1\Delta t + \frac{1}{2}a\Delta t^2$$

$$-10\text{m} = \frac{1}{2}\left(-10\frac{\text{m}}{\text{s}^2}\right)\Delta t^2$$

$$\Delta t = \sqrt{2}\,\text{s} = 1.4\text{s}$$

18. B.
If we want v_2, we use the equation:

$$v_2^2 = v_1^2 + 2a\Delta x$$

$$v_2^2 = \left(0\frac{\text{m}}{\text{s}}\right)^2 + 2\left(-10\frac{\text{m}}{\text{s}^2}\right)(-10\text{m})$$

$$v_2 = 10\sqrt{2}\frac{\text{m}}{\text{s}}$$

$$= 14\frac{\text{m}}{\text{s}}$$

19. B.
We know $v_1 = 20$ m/s, $a = 1.2$ m/s^2, and $\Delta t = 5$ s. Thus $\Delta x = v_1\Delta t + 1/2 \, a(\Delta t)^2 = 115$ m.

20. C.
We know $a = -0.1$ m/s^2, $v_2 = 0$ m/s (because it comes to a stop), and $\Delta t = 5$ s. We use the following equation:

$$v_2 - v_1 = a\Delta t$$

$$v_1 = v_2 - a\Delta t$$

$$v_1 = (0 \text{ m/s}) - (-0.1 \text{ m/s}^2)(5\text{s})$$

$$= 0.5 \text{ m/s}$$

21. B.
We know $v_1 = 0.2$ m/s and $a = -0.05$ m/s^2. If we want to know how long it takes to stop, we add the datum $v_2 = 0$ m/s. Thus we have

$$v_2 - v_1 = a\Delta t$$

$$0\frac{\text{m}}{\text{s}} - 0.2\frac{\text{m}}{\text{s}} = -0.05\frac{\text{m}}{\text{s}^2}\Delta t$$

$$\Delta t = \frac{-0.2\dfrac{\text{m}}{\text{s}}}{-0.05\dfrac{\text{m}}{\text{s}^2}}$$

$$= 4 \text{ s}$$

22. A.

We still use $v_1 = 0.2$ m/s and $a = -0.05$ m/s^2, but now we have $\Delta t = 6$ s. The net displacement is obtained from

$$\Delta s = v_1 \Delta t + 1/2 \, a\Delta t^2$$

$$= (0.2 \text{ m/s})(6 \text{ s}) + 1/2 \, (-0.05 \text{ m/s}^2)(6 \text{ s})^2$$

$$= 0.3 \text{ m}$$

It is important to pay attention to signs in this problem, translating "up" into positive and "decelerating" into negative. Also note that the ball travels further than 0.3 m, going 0.4 m up the slope before heading back. The net displacement is the difference between final position and initial position.

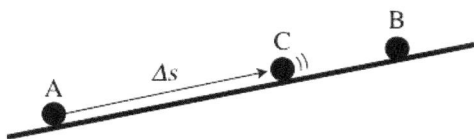

23. C.

Here we have $v_1 = -5$ m/s, $\Delta t = 10$ s, and $v_2 = 10$ m/s. We can obtain acceleration from its definition: $a = (v_2 - v_1)/\Delta t = 1.5$ m/s^2.

24. A.

We obtain the net displacement from $\Delta x = 1/2(v_1 + v_2)\Delta t = 25$ m.

25. C.

We want an equation which relates v, Δx, and Δt. This is $v = \Delta x/\Delta t$. If v increases by a factor of 3, then Δt must decrease by a factor of 3, so the answer is C.

26. A.

Here we know that $v_1 = 25$ m/s, $x_1 = 3000$ km, $a = 0.02$ m/s^2, and $\Delta t = 500$ s. We want x_2. We know that $\Delta x = x_2 - x_1$, so we can calculate

$$\Delta x = v_1 \Delta t + \frac{1}{2} a \Delta t^2$$

$$= (25 \frac{\text{m}}{\text{s}})(500\text{s}) + \frac{1}{2}\left(0.02 \frac{\text{m}}{\text{s}^2}\right)(500\text{s})^2$$

$$= 15000 \text{m}$$

$$= 15 \text{km}$$

Thus $x_2 = 3015$ km. Remember to be careful with the units.

27. B.

We calculate $\Delta x = 1/2 \, (v_1 + v_2)\Delta t = 4.4$ m.

28. B.

We want an equation involving velocity and time and possibly acceleration. Let's look at the equation

$$a = \frac{\Delta v}{\Delta t}$$

Here a is constant and Δt increases by a factor of 3. Thus Δv increases by a factor of 3 as well, giving B as an answer. Another way to see this is to rewrite the equation:

$$\Delta v = a\Delta t$$

so an increase in Δt yields an increase in v.

29. C.

The figure in the problem shows a car which starts from rest, speeds up to a cruising speed which it maintains, then slows to a stop. Let's keep this in mind.

The figure above shows v versus t, and we want to pick the best graph for x versus t. From point A to point B, there is no area under the graph, so the displacement is zero, and all the choices show this. From B to C, there is an increasing amount of area under the curve, eliminating choices B and D which show a jump in x versus t. From C to D, there is area under the curve, so Δx is positive for every interval Δt. This means x is increasing, which is shown only in choice C. After E, the velocity goes to zero, and Δx goes to zero. This means that no more increments get added to x. *But this does not mean* that x returns to the x-axis (as in choice A).

30. B.

Between A and B, the instantaneous slope is zero (see figure). Between points B and C, the instantaneous slope jumps to a constant value, eliminating A and C as choices. Between C and D, the instantaneous slope is zero, so the acceleration jumps back down to zero, so B is correct. Between points D and E, the acceleration is negative.

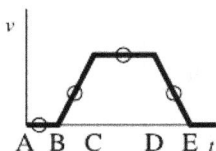

31. B.

The following figure is x versus t. We can obtain v versus t by looking at the instantaneous slope at various times. This gives the points shown in the second figure.

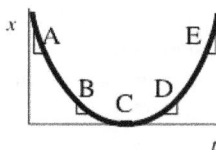

To obtain the acceleration, we need to take the instantaneous slope at various points in the second figure, but clearly the slope is always positive (and probably constant).

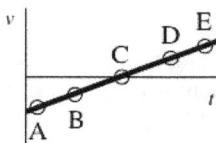

32. A.

The net displacement is $\Delta x = x_2 - x_1$, the difference between final and initial position. But in this case x_1 and x_2 are the same, so the net displacement is zero.

Passage 1

33. A.

The initial velocity is just that at the beginning of the experiment.

34. B.

The average velocity is $v_{avg} = \Delta x / \Delta t$. The net displacement is $\Delta x = 1.35$ m $- 1.35$ m $= 0$ m.

35. D.

This question consists entirely of words, but let us write an equation anyway. Uniform acceleration means a is constant, and $a = \Delta v / \Delta t$. Thus Δv and Δt are in a constant ratio. If one of the choices expresses this fact, then that would be the solution. (If not, we will have to think some more, perhaps find another equation.) D is the correct answer.

36. D.

We apply the definition of acceleration:

$$a = \frac{v_2 - v_1}{\Delta t}$$

$$= \frac{0.6 \frac{m}{s} - \left(-0.6 \frac{m}{s}\right)}{1s}$$

$$= 1.2 \frac{m}{s^2}$$

37. A.

Since acceleration is positive, the vector points in the forward direction (according to the sign convention of the passage).

38. B.

For any 0.5-s interval in the chart, the acceleration ($\Delta v / \Delta t$) is a constant 1.2 m/s^2, even for the intervals near $t = 1.5$ s, where the velocity is zero. Thus B is the best answer.

Passage 2

39. B.

We apply the formula $\Delta x = v_1 \Delta t + 1/2\, a(\Delta t)^2 = $ (0 m/s)(4 s) + 1/2 (10 m/s^2)(4 s)^2 = 80 m.

40. B.

The equation which involves change in velocity Δv and time is the definition of acceleration:

$$g = \Delta v / \Delta t$$

$$\Delta v = g \Delta t$$

$$\Delta v = g(t_2 - t_1)$$

41. C.

Since velocity starts at zero, we can eliminate D. The instantaneous slope for the graph of v versus t must be a constant $g = 9.8$ m/s^2. The graph to which this applies is C.

42. B.

Let's be clear about this by writing an equation. The equation involving Δv is the definition of acceleration (see solution to problem 45). Thus $\Delta v = g \Delta t$. The acceleration g is constant, and Δt is the same for the two situations (both have $\Delta t = 1$ s). Thus Δv is the same. The velocity increases at a constant rate throughout the fall.

43. A.

We can calculate the height at the four clock readings:

$$\Delta x\ (t = 1\text{s}) = v_1 \Delta t + 1/2\, a \Delta t^2$$

$$= (0 \text{ m/s})(1 \text{ s}) + 1/2\ (10 \text{ m/s}^2)(1 \text{ s})^2$$

$$= 5 \text{ m}$$

$$\Delta x\ (t = 2 \text{ s}) = 20 \text{ m}$$

$$\Delta x\ (t = 3 \text{ s}) = 45 \text{ m}$$

$$\Delta x\ (t = 4 \text{ s}) = 80 \text{ m}$$

Thus from 1 to 2 s, the object falls 15 m, while from 3 to 4 s, the object falls 35 m. This confirms our intuition that the distance fallen is greater for the later time interval. Notice the difference between this problem and the previous one.

44. D.

We use the equation involving Δx, Δt, and the acceleration (since we know its value):

$$\Delta x = v_1 \Delta t + 1/2\, g \Delta t^2$$

We have $v_1 = 0$ m/s, so we write

$$\Delta x = 1/2\, g \Delta t^2$$

If the time interval Δt increases by a factor of 3, what happens to Δx? Apparently it increases by a factor of 9.

45. C.

Choice A is nonsense. Choice B is a true statement, but it cannot be an adequate explanation for the fact, since the lead and iron balls fall at the same rate, and the force of gravity is presumably different on those two balls as well. Choice C is a good candidate, since the passage mentions air resistance as a caveat. Choice D is irrelevant.

Physics Review 3
Laws of Motion

A. First Law of Motion

The following is *not* a law of physics:

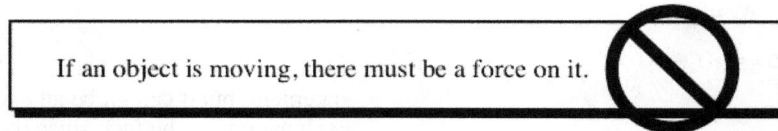

> If an object is moving, there must be a force on it. 🚫

Most people think the above statement is a law of nature. Some very intelligent thinkers thought it was a law of nature, including Aristotle (ancient Greek, no intellectual lightweight) and more recently Descartes (famous philosopher). Because it is common sense (right?) that if nothing pushes on an object, it eventually slows to a stop.

But sometimes closer scrutiny conflicts with common sense, and when that happens we have to change our thinking, to retune our intuition, so that what once seemed wrong now seems right. That can be difficult, but that's physics.

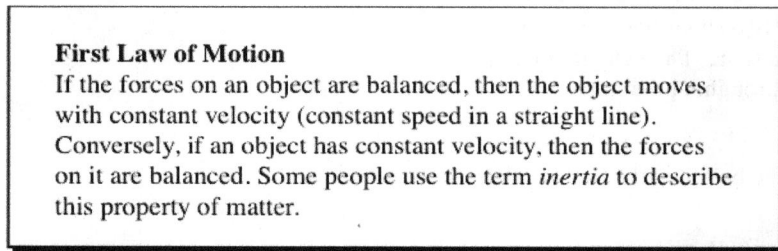

> **First Law of Motion**
> If the forces on an object are balanced, then the object moves with constant velocity (constant speed in a straight line). Conversely, if an object has constant velocity, then the forces on it are balanced. Some people use the term *inertia* to describe this property of matter.

Galileo discovered this law, although it's generally called Newton's first law of motion.

What does it mean for the forces to be balanced? Before we answer that question, let's look at a few cases. In the following figures (Figures 3-1a–f) we denote the motion of an object by "motion marks", so that ⊓ means the object is moving to the right.

Case a. There are no forces. In this case think of a rock in deep space moving along. The velocity vector is constant, meaning the rock continues traveling at constant speed to the right indefinitely.

Figure 3-1a

Case b. There are two opposed forces, equal in magnitude, perpendicular to the motion. In this case think of a marble rolling along a smooth level floor (no friction). Gravity pulls down, but the floor pushes up. The velocity vector is constant.

Figure 3-1b

Case c. This scenario is a nonexample, in which the right force is larger than the left force (hence unbalanced). The object will speed up.

Figure 3-1c

Case d. This scenario is also a nonexample with the left force larger than the right force. The object will slow down.

Figure 3-1d

Case e. Two opposed forces, left and right, are equal in magnitude. The case is between cases c and d. The object has constant velocity, that is, it will keep its speed indefinitely. Think about this one for a while. This stumps many people.

Figure 3-1e

Case f. The forces in all three directions are balanced. The object's velocity vector is constant.

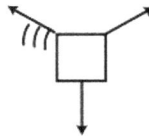

Figure 3-1f

The forces are balanced if the vector sum of all the forces on the object is zero. We define F_{net} by

$$F_{net} = F_1 + F_2 + ...$$

where F_1, F_2, ..., are all the forces acting on an object. The vector F_{net} is the total force on the object.

Example: A woman kicks a soccer ball, and it rolls for a while at constant speed, then another woman stops it. Draw a diagram showing all the forces on the ball at the three times: kicking, rolling, and stopping.

Solution: Part a: The ball is kicked (see Figure 3-2). The vector F_{grav} is the force of gravity, and F_{kick} is the force of the foot on the ball. The symbol N stands for "normal", a physics word meaning perpendicular to the ground. It is force the ground exerts on the ball.

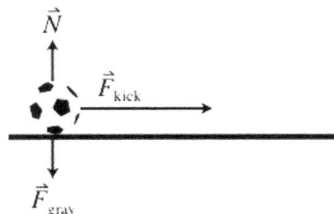

The woman kicks the ball.

Figure 3-2

Part b: The ball rolls along. It has only two forces acting on it (Figure 3-3). The ball does not remember (or care) what started it rolling. According to the first law, the balanced forces guarantee it will keep rolling indefinitely at constant speed.

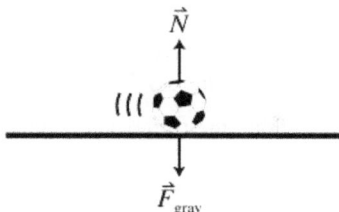

The ball rolls without friction.

Figure 3-3

Part c: The ball is stopped. Now there is a force of a foot on the ball as well (Figure 3-4).

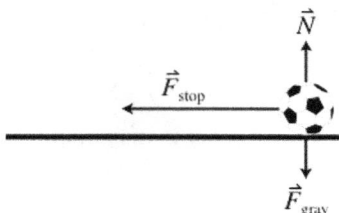

The woman stops the ball.

Figure 3-4

Over the next several chapters there will be many problems to test your intuition on the first law.

B. Second Law of Motion

So what happens if the forces on an object are not balanced? If the net force on an object is nonzero, then the velocity vector changes. There must be acceleration. In fact the larger the force, the larger the acceleration. (See Figure 3-5.) On the other hand, if we apply the same push to both a small car and a large car (Figure 3-6), the small car will have the larger acceleration.

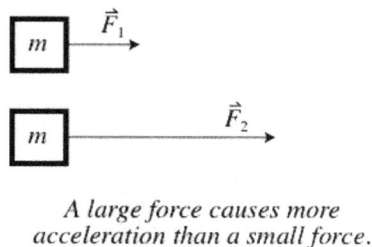

A large force causes more acceleration than a small force.

Figure 3-5

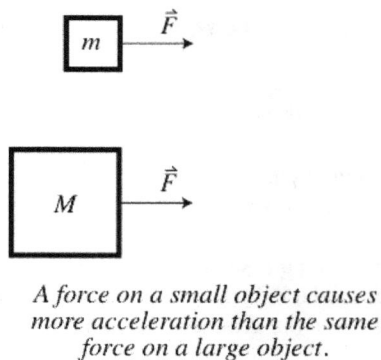

A force on a small object causes more acceleration than the same force on a large object.

Figure 3-6

We can write (in one dimension)

$$a = \frac{F_{net}}{m} \qquad (1)$$

We have not proven this equation, but the discussion in the previous paragraph should make it seem reasonable to you.

In three dimensions, we write what is often called Newton's second law:

Second Law of Motion

If an object has forces $\vec{F_1}, \vec{F_2}, \cdots$, acting on it, then the total force on the object is the vector sum

$$\vec{F}_{net} = \vec{F_1} + \vec{F_2} + \cdots,$$

and the acceleration $\vec{a}$ of the object is given by

$$\vec{F}_{net} = m\vec{a}. \tag{2}$$

Most often, however, we will break up equation (2) into components:

$$\left(F_{net}\right)_x = ma_x \tag{3a}$$
$$\left(F_{net}\right)_y = ma_y \tag{3b}$$

Equation (3a), for example, states that the sum of all the horizontal forces is mass times the horizontal acceleration. We will discuss breaking vectors into vertical and horizontal components in Section 4.D.

Finally, we are able to make the connection between the units for force [N] and for mass [kg], introduced in Chapter 1. The Newton is defined by

$$N = \frac{kgm}{s^2}$$

Example 1: Bruce pushes a car (500 kg) on level ground starting from rest with a force 100 N. How long does it take to get the car rolling 1 m/s? (Assume no friction.)

Solution: We have the information $m = 500$ kg, $v_1 = 0$ m/s, $F = 100$ N, and $v_2 = 1$ m/s, and we want Δt. We can find acceleration from equation (1), so we obtain

$$a = 100N/500kg$$

$$= 0.2 \text{ N/kg}$$

Then we can find Δt from

$$a = \frac{\left(v_2 - v_1\right)}{\Delta t}$$

$$\Delta t = 5 \text{ s}.$$

Example 2: A rocket provides a constant force to wagon A that rolls without friction. It starts from rest and after time t attains velocity v. A similar rocket providing the same force is attached to wagon B, which has five times the mass of A (Figure 3-7). How much time does it take wagon B to go from rest to velocity v? (Assume no friction.)

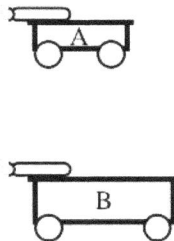

Figure 3-7

Solution: This one looks difficult, but if we write down the relevant equations, it is not so hard. We need to connect force and velocity, so we write,

$$F = ma$$

$$a = \frac{v_2 - v_1}{\Delta t} = \frac{v_2}{\Delta t}$$

We set v_1 to zero because the wagons start from rest. Substitution gives

$$F = m\frac{v_2}{\Delta t}$$

Since the problem asks about the change in time, we can solve for Δt to obtain

$$\Delta t = m\frac{v_2}{F}$$

Now, F and v_2 stay the same, but m is five times larger for wagon B, so Δt is five times larger. The answer is $5t$.

C. Third Law of Motion

The third law of motion is not so much a law about motion as it is a rule of thumb about pairs of forces. It is usually stated thus:

> To every action there is an equal and opposite reaction.

This is certainly poetic, but what does it mean? More clear (and less poetic) is the following:

> **The Third Law of Motion**
> If object 1 exerts a force $\vec{F}_{12}$ on object 2,
> then object 2 exerts a force $\vec{F}_{21}$ on object 1
> which is equal in magnitude, opposite in direction, and of the same type (gravity, friction, etc.):
> $\vec{F}_{12} = -\vec{F}_{21}$.

Example 1: The Sun and the Earth exert a force of gravity on each other. Draw a force diagram.

Solution: See Figure 3-8.

Figure 3-8

F_{ES} = gravitational force of the Earth on the Sun,

F_{SE} = gravitational force of the Sun on the Earth.

Example 2: Two spacecraft push off from each other. Draw a force diagram.

Solution: See Figure 3-9.

Figure 3-9

F_{12} = contact force of craft 1 on craft 2,

F_{21} = contact force of craft 2 on craft 1.

Example 3: A basketball player jumps up. While he is in the air, he pushes the basketball horizontally. Draw all the forces *while* he is pushing the ball. Ignore the tiny gravitational force between the player and the ball.

Solution: See Figure 3-10.

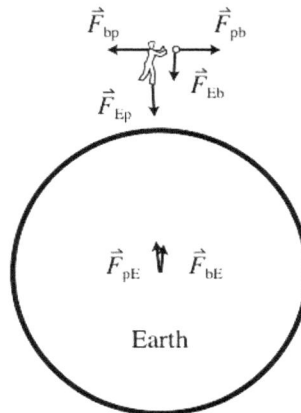

Figure 3-10

F_{pb} = contact force of player on ball,
F_{bp} = contact force of ball on player,
F_{Ep} = gravitational force of Earth on player,
F_{pE} = gravitational force of player on Earth,
F_{Eb} = gravitational force of Earth on ball,
F_{bE} = gravitational force of ball on Earth.

Notice that the magnitude of the force of the player on the ball is the same as that of the ball on the player. But the player moves hardly at all, while the ball springs toward another player. Why is the basketball affected more than the player? (Hint: Look at equation 1.)

D. Force Diagrams

Already in this chapter we have seen a number of force diagrams. In this section we discuss some rules for drawing force diagrams. There are two types of force diagrams:

  1. a diagram in which all the objects appear and the forces come in third-law pairs, and
  2. a diagram featuring one object and all its forces (or maybe several objects, but not all the objects in the situation).

In most problems we will want the second type, but it is important to know how to draw both, and knowing diagrams of the first type will help with the second type.

To draw the first type of diagram, we ask four questions:

1. What gravitational forces are important?
2. What things are touching? (These give contact forces.)
3. Does the problem mention any specific forces?
4. Do the net forces in the diagram conform to expectation?

For each force we draw an arrow whose tail lies on the object *on which the force acts*. This may seem unnatural at first, but it makes things easier in the end. For some examples, look at the diagrams we drew in Section C.

Example 1: A girl jumps horizontally from a boat in the water. Draw all the forces on the boat, the girl, and the Earth. Ignore the tiny gravitational force between the girl and the boat, and ignore the drag force of the water on the boat.

Solution: First we add the gravitational forces in pairs (Figure 3-11).

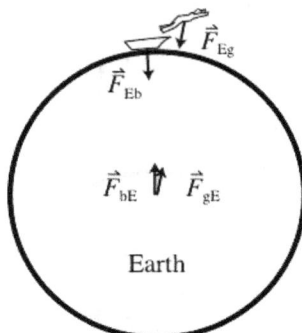

Figure 3-11

Then we add the forces due to the boat and girl touching (F_{bg} and F_{gb}) and the contact force between the Earth and the bat (N_{eb} and N_{bE}). See Figure 3-12.

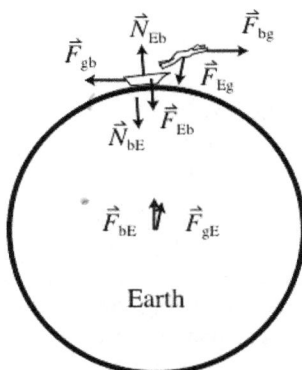

Figure 3-12

The net forces on the boat indicate that it accelerates backwards, which seems right. The net force on the girl indicates she would accelerate forward and down, which seems right. It is difficult to tell what is going on with the Earth.

Example 2: A vase sits on a table, which sits on the Earth. List all pairs of forces. Do this example on your own before you look at the solution.

Solution: See Figure 3-13.

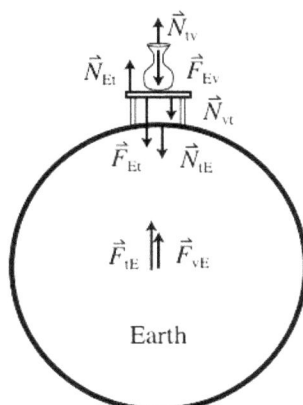

Figure 3-13

F_{Ev} = gravitational force of Earth on the vase,
F_{vE} = gravitational force of vase on the Earth,
F_{Et} = gravitational force of Earth on the table,
F_{tE} = gravitational force of table on the Earth,
N_{tv} = contact force of table on vase,
N_{vt} = contact force of vase on table,
N_{Et} = contact force of Earth on table,
N_{tE} = contact force of table on Earth.

Drawing a diagram of the second type is easier, but you have to be careful not to leave out any forces nor to add any ghost forces.

Example 3: A roller skate is rolling frictionlessly on level ground to the left. Draw all the forces on the roller skate. STOP! Try doing this problem before looking at the solution.

Solution: Gravity is pulling down (question 1). And the ground is touching the skate, pushing up (question 2). There is no friction, nor any other forces, so the force diagram is Figure 3-14.

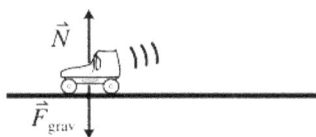

Figure 3-14

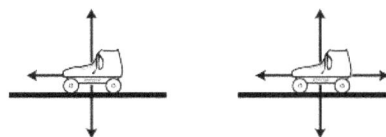

A   B

Figure 3-15

Did your diagram look like Figure 3-15 A or B? If so, you have not yet tuned your intuition about the first law of motion. Just because the skate is going to the left does not mean there is a force to the left. Only if the skate were speeding up to the left would we be forced to conclude that there was a force to the left.

In this chapter we studied Newton's laws of motion. In a sense, the first law of motion is the most subtle. If an object is moving at a constant velocity, then the forces on the object add to zero, and if the vector sum of the force vectors for an object is zero, then the object moves at constant velocity. Constant velocity means constant speed in a straight path. No force is required to keep an object moving.

The second law of motion concerns objects whose force vectors' sum is not zero: The acceleration of such an object is in the same direction as the total force, proportional to its magnitude and inversely proportional to the object's mass. That is $a = F_{net}/m$. Do you see why we use equations?

The third law states that forces come in pairs: If object 1 pushes object 2, then object 2 pushes object 1 in the opposite direction.

Pay especial attention to Section D on force diagrams. In solving problems, we are always interested in the forces on an object at a given instant in time. These include gravity, usually, and forces due to things touching the object at that moment. No other forces need to be included. In particular, do not include a force in a direction just because the object in moving in that direction.

Physics Review 3 Problems

Section A

1. Consider a paratrooper who has jumped from an airplane. After an initial accelerating plunge, he begins to fall at a constant speed in a straight vertical plunge (at *terminal velocity*). During the latter portion of his fall, are the forces on the paratrooper balanced?
   A. No, since a force balance exists only if an object is not moving.
   B. No, since gravity is not balanced by anything.
   C. No, since gravity is greater than the drag force.
   D. Yes, since he is moving at a constant velocity.

2. There is one force acting on an object. What can we definitely conclude from this?
   A. The object is speeding up or slowing down.
   B. The object is going at a constant speed, not necessarily in a straight line.
   C. The object is going at a constant speed in a straight line.
   D. None of the above may be definitely concluded.

3. A car's engine has died, and the car is slowing down as it coasts. What may we conclude about the forces acting on the car?
   A. There are no forces acting on the car.
   B. There are forces acting on the car, but the net force is zero.
   C. The net force acting on the car is not zero.
   D. None of the above may be definitely concluded.

4. An object is moving with uniform motion, that is, at constant speed in a straight line. There are two forces acting on the object. What can we definitely conclude from this?
   A. The net force is in the same direction that the object is moving.
   B. Both forces are in a direction perpendicular to the object's motion.
   C. The two forces have equal magnitudes but point in opposite directions.
   D. None of the above may be definitely concluded.

Section B

5. In the following diagram, the magnitude of force F_A is 400 N, and that of F_B is 300 N. What is the magnitude of the net force in the three cases?

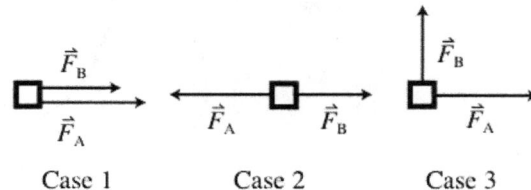

Case 1   Case 2   Case 3

   A. In case 1, the net force is 100 N; case 2, 700 N; and case 3, 500 N.
   B. In case 1, the net force is 700 N; case 2, 100 N; and case 3, 500 N.
   C. In case 1, the net force is 350 N; case 2, 50 N; and case 3, 450 N.
   D. In case 1, the net force is 350 N; case 2, 50 N; and case 3, 550 N.

Use the following information for questions 6 and 7:

A man is pulling his son in a toy wagon. The son and the wagon are 60 kg. For 3 s the man exerts a force which has the effect of uniformly accelerating the wagon from 1.5 m/s to 3.5 m/s.

6. What is the acceleration of the wagon with the son?
   A. 0.67 m/s^2
   B. 0.84 m/s^2
   C. 1.66 m/s^2
   D. 20 m/s^2

7. What is the net force on the wagon and son?
   A. 40 N
   B. 50 N
   C. 120 N
   D. 1200 N

Use the following information for questions 8–11:

A tiger (100 kg) sees a wildebeest and accelerates uniformly from rest to 20 m/s in 12 s.

8. What is the acceleration of the tiger?
    A. 0.60 m/s^2
    B. 0.83 m/s^2
    C. 1.67 m/s^2
    D. 240 m/s^2

9. How much distance does the tiger cover in those 12 s?
    A. 120 m
    B. 240 m
    C. 480 m
    D. 960 m

10. What is the magnitude of the net force on the tiger?
    A. 60 N
    B. 83 N
    C. 167 N
    D. 24000 N

11. What are all the forces acting on the tiger?
    A. Gravity, down.
    B. Gravity, down; and the normal force, up.
    C. Gravity, down; the normal force, up, and a horizontal force of the ground pushing the tiger.
    D. None of the above is correct.

12. Three men push on a station wagon with a net force F, producing an acceleration. (Assume there is no friction.) If they push with the same net force on a compact car (with half the mass), the acceleration of the compact car is
    A. four times the acceleration of the station wagon.
    B. twice the acceleration of the station wagon.
    C. half the acceleration of the station wagon.
    D. one quarter the acceleration of the station wagon.

13. Object A is acted upon by a net force F_A to produce an acceleration. If object B has three times the mass of A and is acted on by three times the force as A, the acceleration of B is
    A. 9 times that of A.
    B. 3 times that of A.
    C. the same as that of A.
    D. one third that of A.

14. At time $t = 0$ s, two dung beetles are pushing a small ball (0.5 g). One pushes east with a force 0.0015 N; the other pushes west with a force 0.0010 N. At $t = 0$ s, what is the acceleration of the ball?
    A. 1 m/s^2
    B. 2.5 m/s^2
    C. 3 m/s^2
    D. 5 m/s^2

15. A rocket ship (500 kg) is firing two jets at once. The two jets are at right angles, with one firing to yield a force of 5000 N and the other to yield a force of 12000 N. What is the magnitude of the acceleration of the rocket ship?
    A. 24 m/s^2
    B. 26 m/s^2
    C. 34 m/s^2
    D. 36 m/s^2

16. A girl shoves a 4-kg toy cart across the level floor with a speed of 15 m/s (so it is going 15 m/s when it leaves her hand). It slides to a rest in 5 s. Assuming a constant force slowing the cart, what is the magnitude of the force?
    A. 0.75 N
    B. 1.33 N
    C. 12 N
    D. 18.75 N

17. A piece of steel of mass 0.8 kg hangs from a string over the edge of a table. The string passes over a pulley and is connected in such a way as to maintain a tension force of 6 N (see figure).

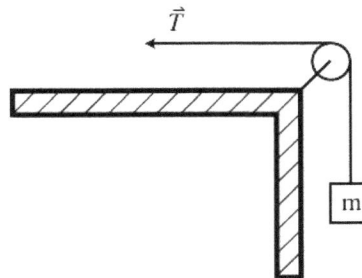

The force due to gravity on the steel is given by $F_{grav} = mg$, where $g = 10$ m/s^2 is the acceleration due to gravity. We allow the piece of steel to fall from rest for 5 s. What is the final acceleration of the piece of steel?
    A. 2 m/s^2
    B. 2.5 m/s^2
    C. 10 m/s^2
    D. 12.5 m/s^2

18. A woman is riding in an elevator which is going up at constant speed. The force of the floor against her feet
    A. is less than the force of gravity on her.
    B. is the same as the force of gravity on her.
    C. is greater than the force of gravity on her.
    D. has no relationship with the force of gravity on her that can be determined by the given information.

19. On September 12, 1966, astronauts conducted an experiment using the second law of motion. A Gemini spacecraft (measured to be 3400 kg) connected with an orbiting rocket case. The thrusters were fired to provide a force of 890 N for 7.0 s. The change in velocity of the spacecraft and rocket case was found to be 0.93 m/s. What was the mass of the rocket case?
    A. 120 kg
    B. 3300 kg
    C. 10,100 kg
    D. 15,400 kg

20. Car A starts from rest and accelerates uniformly for a period of time t to travel a distance d. Car B, which has four times the mass of car A, starts from rest and accelerates uniformly as well. If the magnitudes of the forces accelerating A and B are the same, how long does is take B to travel the same distance d?
    A. $16t$
    B. $4t$
    C. $2t$
    D. $t/4$

21. A car trailer is connected to a car, and both are traveling forward at velocity 3 m/s at time $t = 5$ s. The force the car exerts on the trailer is 105 N, the force of friction on the trailer is 30 N, and the force of air resistance on the trailer is 70 N. The force of gravity on the trailer is 8000 N, and the road exerts an upward force of 8000 N. What conclusion may be drawn about the trailer?
    A. It is speeding up.
    B. It is staying the same speed.
    C. It is slowing down.
    D. It is speeding up or staying the same speed.

Solutions

1. D.
From the first law of motion, a force balance on an object implies it has constant velocity. From this we conclude that the force of gravity and the drag force due to the air are *exactly balanced*.

2. D.
Since there is only one force, there must be a net force on the object; there is no way for forces to be balanced. From the first law of motion, we conclude that the object is not undergoing uniform motion, so it is speeding up, slowing down, or changing direction. But none of the choices can be definitely concluded.

3. C.
Since the car is not undergoing uniform motion (it is slowing), it has a net force on it. In fact, the net force points in the opposite direction the car is going.

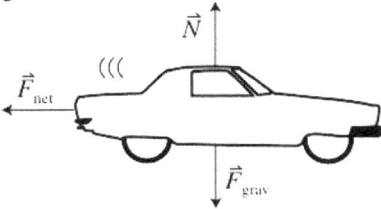

4. C.
Since the object is moving with uniform motion, the forces on the object must be balanced. Since there are exactly two forces, the only way for them to be balanced is that they be of equal magnitude in opposite directions, which is choice C. If you chose B, think of the example of the paratrooper falling in question 1, in which the downward force of gravity is balanced by the upward force of the air drag.

5. B.
In case 1, we move the tail of F_B to the tip of F_A (see figure). The sum, F_{net}, is drawn from the first tail to the last tip, giving a magnitude of 700 N. So choice B is correct. The same method for case 2 yields a magnitude 100 N. For case 3, we need to apply the Pythagorean theorem to obtain a magnitude 500 N.

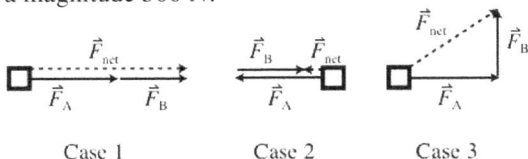

Case 1   Case 2   Case 3

6. A.
(This was a review problem.) We calculate a = (3.5 m/s – 1.5 m/s)/3 s = 0.67 m/s^2.

7. A.
We calculate F_{net} = ma = (60 kg) (0.67 m/s^2) = 40 N.

8. C.
We calculate a = (20 m/s – 0 m/s)/(12 s) = 1.67 m/s^2.

9. A.
We calculate (from Chapter 2) Δx = 1/2 (0 m/s + 20 m/s) (12 s) = 120 m.

10. C.
The magnitude of the net force is given by F_{net} = ma = 167 N.

11. C.
The vertical forces, which are balanced, are gravity (down) and the normal force of the ground (up). The one horizontal force accelerates the tiger, and it is due to the ground pushing forward. This may seem strange, but it is a result of the third law of motion. The tiger pushes the ground backward. There is then an equal force of the ground on the tiger pushing forward, even though there is no "active" agent creating the force. But it has to be the ground pushing the tiger forward, since that is the only thing touching him. Certainly he does not push himself forward (what would that even mean?).

12. B.
We want an equation which connects force, acceleration, and mass. This is $F = ma$. Since we are looking for the change in acceleration, we can write this equation $a = F/m$. If the mass decreases by a factor of 2, then the acceleration increases by a factor of 2.

13. C.
As in question 12, we write $a = F/m$. If F increases by a factor of 3 and m increases by a factor of 3, then a remains the same.

14. A.
We draw a diagram (see figure). We cannot calculate the acceleration using the methods of the previous chapter, but we can find a net force. In one dimension, we can call east positive, so F_{net} = 0.0015 N – 0.0010 N = 0.0005 N. Thus we can find acceleration $a = F_{net}/m$ = 0.0005 N/0.0005 kg = 1 m/s^2.

0.0010 N   0.0015 N

15. B.

We draw a diagram (see figure). We can obtain the net force by applying the Pythagorean theorem. The net force is 13000 N. From this we obtain the magnitude of the acceleration $a = F_{net}/m = 26$ m/s^2.

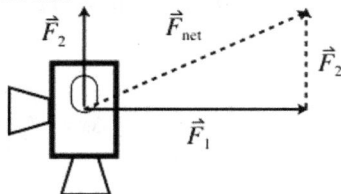

16. C.

We draw a diagram (see figure). We include the vertical forces of gravity and the normal force, which add to zero (that is, balance each other). There is nothing touching the truck except the ground (the girl has already let go), but there must be another force because the truck is changing velocity. This force is the drag force, pointing backward. (There is no forward force.) We want to know the magnitude of the drag force, since this is also the net force. We obtain the acceleration $a = (0$ m/s $- 15$ m/s$)/5$ s $= -3$ m/s^2. Thus, in magnitude, the net force is $F_{net} = ma = 12$ N.

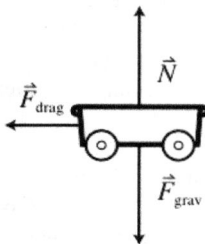

17. B.

We draw a diagram showing the forces on the mass (see figure). There is the force of gravity and the tension in the string, which pulls up. The net force (with down as positive) is $F_{net} = (0.8$ kg$) (10$ m/s$^2) - 6$ N $= 2$ N. The sign indicates the net force is down. Now we can calculate the acceleration $a = F_{net}/m = 2$ N/0.8 kg $= 2.5$ m/s^2.

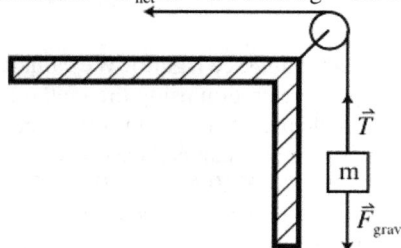

18. B.

We draw a diagram showing the forces on the woman. Since she is traveling at constant velocity, the net force on her is zero, and the forces are balanced. Thus the force of the floor against the woman's feet has the same magnitude as the force of gravity on her. This is just the first law of motion. If you chose C, then you need to study the first law of motion again.

19. B.

We can calculate an estimate of acceleration $a = \Delta v/\Delta t = (1$ m/s$)/(7$ s$) = 1/7$ m/s^2. Thus the total mass is given by $m = F_{net}/a = 900/(1/7)$ kg $= 6300$ kg. The mass of the rocket case is then $(6300 - 3300)$ kg $= 3000$ kg. This is close to B.

20. C.

We need an equation which connects time and mass (which differs from A to B). We also have information about F, v_1, and d. We can use $F = ma$ and $d = v_1\Delta t + 1/2\ a(\Delta t)^2$. Combining these, we obtain

$$d = v_1 + \frac{1}{2}a\Delta t^2$$

$$= \frac{1}{2}\left(\frac{F}{m}\right)\Delta t^2$$

$$\Delta t = \sqrt{\frac{2dm}{F}}$$

So if m increases by a factor of 4, then time increases by a factor of

$$\sqrt{4} = 2$$

21. A.

First we draw a diagram (see figure). The vertical forces balance. The net horizontal force is $F_{net} = 105$ N $- 30$ N $- 70$ N $= 5$ N. The net force is forward, so the car is speeding up.

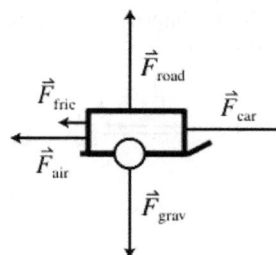

Physics Review 4
Gravitation

A. The Law of Gravitation

When a person does a great deal of work in a scientific field, it often happens that that person eventually receives credit for almost everything done by anybody (see Matthew 13:12 in the Christian Bible). For instance, Newton is given credit, at least in popular accounts, for almost every interesting thing that happened in science during the Renaissance. In fact, then as now, science is the activity of a community, with many people contributing to the revolution in thinking. For example, the essentials of Newton's first law of motion were discovered by Galileo, and Robert Hooke surmised the essential parts of the law of gravitation.

Newton's genius lay in his ability to see a simple underlying law for very different phenomena and to synthesize diverse branches of science. An example of this is his realization that both the motion of the Moon and the motion of a falling apple could be explained by the same force, the force of gravity. In this chapter we will study the physics of the gravitational force.

Newton's law of gravity states that any two objects exert an attractive force on each other given by

$$F_{grav} = \frac{Gm_1 m_2}{d^2} \qquad (1)$$

Here F_{grav} is the magnitude of the gravitational force between two objects, m_1 and m_2 are the masses of the objects, d is the distance between the centers of the objects, and G is a universal constant 6.67×10^{-11} m^3/kg s^2. Do not memorize G, but do remember the equation. We discussed it in Chapter 1.

Example 1: What is the force on a cow (200 kg) standing on the surface of the Earth? (Assume $M_{Earth} = 6.0 \times 10^{24}$ kg, $R_{Earth} = 6.4 \times 10^6$ m.)

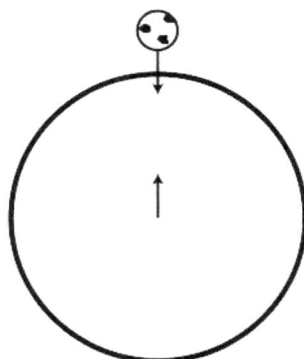

Figure 4-1

Solution: Let's assume we have a spherical cow (Figure 4-1). We calculate

$$F_{grav} = \frac{GM_{Earth}m_{cow}}{R_{Earth}^2}$$

$$= \frac{\left(6.67\times10^{-11}\frac{m^3}{kgs^2}\right)\left(6.0\times10^{24}\,kg\right)}{\left(6.4\times10^6\,m\right)^2}m_{cow}$$

$$= m_{cow}\left(9.8\frac{m}{s^2}\right)$$

$$= 1960\ N$$

Example 2: What is the motion of an apple (0.1 kg) which has let go of its tree?

Solution: First, we DRAW A DIAGRAM (Figure 4-2) showing all the forces on the apple while it is falling. There is only the force of gravity (nothing else is touching it), so we write

$$F_{grav} = \frac{GM_{Earth}m_{apple}}{R_{Earth}^2}$$

$$= \frac{\left(6.67\times10^{-11}\frac{m^3}{kgs^2}\right)\left(6.0\times10^{24}\,kg\right)\left(0.1kg\right)}{\left(6.4\times10^6\,m\right)^2}$$

$$= 0.98\ N$$

Figure 4-2

Since the total force is simply the gravitational force, we write

$$m_{apple}a = F_{net}$$

$$a = \frac{0.98\frac{kgm}{s^2}}{0.1kg} = 9.8\frac{m}{s^2}$$

So the apple accelerates downward at 9.8 m/s^2.

Equation (1) is easy to use in two types of problems:

1. obtaining the force between two planets (d is much larger than the radii of the planets), and
2. obtaining the force between a planet and a small object on its surface (d is essentially the radius of the planet).

The previous examples illustrated this second use.

B. Surface of the Earth

Most of us will spend most of our lives on or near the surface of the Earth. What is the force of gravity of the Earth on an object of mass m? The force is

$$F_{grav} = \frac{GM_{Earth}m}{R_{Earth}^2} = \left(9.8\frac{m}{s^2}\right)m$$

where we use a calculation from the previous section. This number 9.8 m/s^2 comes up so often in introductory physics that we have given it a name: The *acceleration due to gravity* is

$$g = 9.8\frac{m}{s^2} \qquad (2)$$

In working problems, however, we *always* approximate this as g = 10 m/s^2 (even if the problem says to use 9.8 m/s^2).

Please note: *Whenever* there is gravity and we are at the surface of the Earth, which is in most problems, we will use

$$F_{grav} = mg \qquad (3)$$

C. Free Fall

An object is said to be in *free fall* when nothing is touching it, so that the only force on it is gravity. Such an object is called a *projectile*. The simplest problem in free fall involves dropping objects near the surface of the Earth. We want to know which falls faster, a heavy object or a light one? Things become complicated if the object is too light, like a leaf fluttering to the ground, so at first we will consider two objects for which air resistance is only a small consideration. Let us start by doing a pair of examples.

Example 1: How long does it take a small rock (0.02 kg) to fall from rest 2 meters to the ground?

Solution: First, we DRAW A DIAGRAM (Figure 4-3). There is only one force since nothing touches the rock and we are neglecting air resistance. Second, we find the net force

$$F_{net} = F_{grav} = -mg$$
$$= -(0.02 \text{ kg})(10 \text{ m/s}^2)$$
$$= -0.2 \text{ N}$$

where the negative sign reminds us that gravity points down.

Figure 4-3

Third, we obtain acceleration by writing

$$F_{net} = ma$$
$$a = F_{net}/m = -0.2 \text{ N}/0.02 \text{ kg} = -10 \text{ m/s}^2$$

(This result should look familiar.)

We also have

$$v_1 = 0$$
$$\Delta y = -2 \text{ m}$$

so that

$$\Delta y = v_1 \Delta t + 1/2 \; a_y \Delta t^2$$
$$-2 \text{ m} = 1/2 \; (-10 \text{m/s}^2) \Delta t^2$$
$$\Delta t = 0.63 \text{ s}$$

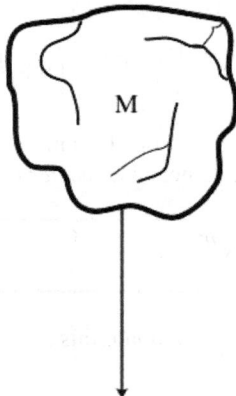

Figure 4-4

Example 2: How long does it take a medium-sized rock (0.2 kg) to fall 2 meters from rest?

Solution: The rock is larger, and so is the force of gravity (and the force arrow, see Figure 4-4). We write

$$F_{net} = F_{grav} = -Mg = -(0.2 \text{ kg})(10 \text{ m/s}^2) = -2 \text{ N}$$

The acceleration is

$$a = F_{net}/M = -2 \text{ N}/0.2 \text{ kg} = -10 \text{ m/s}^2$$

The rest of the problem is the same, so $\Delta t = 0.63$ s.

WHAT HAPPENED? The force of gravity was larger in Example 2, BUT the acceleration is inversely proportional to mass in the second law of motion. The net effect is that the acceleration is the same 9.8 m/s^2 for both rocks. Try this at home with a pen and a stapler or some such thing. It is difficult to gain an intuitive grasp of this situation, but think about it until you also understand *why* the two rocks have the same acceleration.

Let us revisit Example 2 in Section 2.H. There we saw an apple tossed straight up. It rose, came to a stop, and fell. We claimed that the acceleration was always negative (that is, down), even at the top point. We are now at a better position to understand why. Once the apple leaves the hand, there is only one force on the apple, the downward force of gravity. (See Figure 4-5.) The acceleration must be down as well. In fact, we now know the acceleration is a constant 9.8 m/s^2, down.

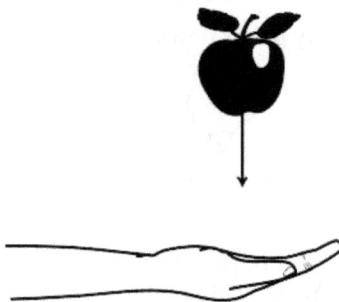

A tossed apple at the top of its flight
is accelerating down at $9.8 \dfrac{m}{s^2}$.

Figure 4-5

D. Horizontal and Vertical Motion

This section has no new equations but it does present one new idea, so prepare your imagination. A pencil and paper may prove handy.

Imagine you are sitting at the shore of a bay, and you see a boat traveling along at constant speed in a straight line. A sailor at the top of a vertical mast drops a grapefruit. (See Figure 4-6.) We will pretend air resistance plays no role (mostly true). Where will the grapefruit land?

    A. In front of the mast.
    B. At the foot of the mast.
    C. Behind the mast.

Choose your answer before you read any further.

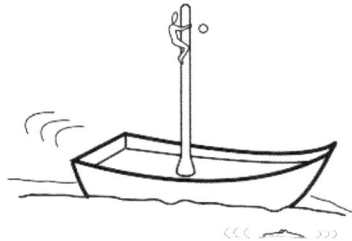

A boat moves with uniform motion.
A grapefruit falls from the mast.
Where does it land?
Figure 4-6

Few people choose A. Not many people choose B. If you are like most people, you chose C, thinking that somehow the boat moves out from under the grapefruit. If that was your answer, then you need to do some rethinking. Here is what really happens. Figure 4-7 shows two ships at four successive times, one ship at rest and the other in uniform motion. Sailors at the tops of the masts drop grapefruits at the same time. Both grapefruits drop to the foot of the corresponding mast.

The grapefruit on the moving ship retains its
horizontal motion regardless of vertical motion, and
it drops vertically regardless of its horizontal motion.
Figure 4-7

What is going on in the previous example? Just after the grapefruit is released from the hand on the second ship, it still has its horizontal motion. If air resistance does not affect it, then it maintains its same horizontal motion from start to finish. The vertical motion, on the other hand, proceeds on schedule regardless of the horizontal motion. At $t = 0.2$ s, both grapefruits have moved *vertically* 0.05 m (the second has moved horizontally as well). As time goes on, the second grapefruit keeps up with the ship, and both grapefruits hit the deck at the same time.

If you do not believe the figure, try the experiment yourself. While walking at a constant speed, release an apple above your head (and a little forward). It will fall in front of your face and land at your feet. (See Figure 4-8.)

Figure 4-8

The picture of a boat in the bay and the resulting principle are due to Galileo:

> Horizontal and vertical motion are independent. That is, motion in the *x*- and *y*-directions can be considered independently.

Now let's leave the bay and travel to the edge of a cliff with a large plain at the bottom. We have two cannonballs, and at the same time, we shoot one horizontally off the cliff and drop the other. Which will hit the plain first?

Again, most people will say the dropped ball hits first. As long as air resistance plays at most a small role, they will hit at the same time. (See Figure 4-9.) For the second ball, the vertical motion of falling is not affected at all by its horizontal motion. It may help your intuition to realize that the shot cannonball does have a larger total velocity all the way down. Notice that Figure 4-9 looks just like Figure 4-7 with the boats removed. It is the same physical principle.

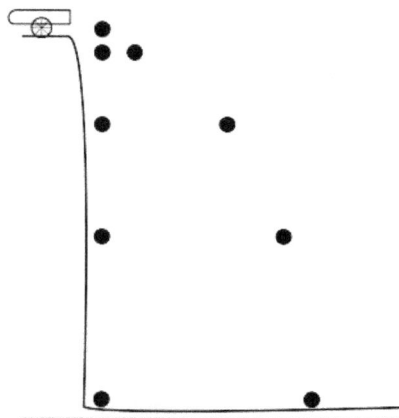

A dropped cannonball falls at the same rate as one shot horizontally.
Figure 4-9

Up until now we have been using v_1, v_2, and a to denote velocities and acceleration in one dimension. For these problems we will need to keep track of the vertical and horizontal pieces separately, so we need the symbols v_{1x}, v_{2x}, a_x, v_{1y}, v_{2y}, and a_y.

The following box shows how this principle gets translated into equations:

If the net vertical force is $(F_{net})_y$, then we can determine the vertical motion using

$$\left(F_{net}\right)_y = ma_y,$$

$$\Delta y = \frac{1}{2}\left(v_{1y} + v_{2y}\right)\Delta t,$$

$$v_{2y} = v_{1y} + a_y\Delta t,$$

$$\Delta y = v_{1y}\Delta t + \frac{1}{2}a_y\Delta t^2.$$

$$v_{2y}^2 = v_{1y}^2 + 2a_y\Delta y.$$

Similarly, we can determine the horizontal motion using similar equations with y replaced by x.

Objects in free fall experience only the force of gravity, so we can say more:

For an object in free fall at the surface of the Earth, we have

$$a_y = -9.8\,\frac{m}{s^2}. \tag{4a}$$

$$a_x = 0\,\frac{m}{s^2}. \tag{4b}$$

where "up" is positive and we use *the estimate* $10\,\frac{m}{s^2}$.

Example 1: A cliff stands 80 m above a flat plane. One cannonball is dropped, and another is fired horizontally at 120 m/s at the same time. How far from the first ball will the second ball land?

Solution: The first ball falls straight down, of course. Let's DRAW A DIAGRAM for the second ball while it is in flight (Figure 4-10). Note that the cannon exerts a force on the cannonball while it is in the cannon, but after the ball leaves the cannon, *the only force is gravity*.

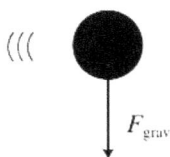

Figure 4-10

We record the information we have. We do not know the mass of the ball, but from Section B we know we do not need it. The acceleration vector is 10 m/s², down.

Vertical	horizontal
$v_{1y} = 0$	$v_{1x} = 120$ m/s
$\Delta y = -80$ m	$\Delta x = ?$
$a_y = -10$ m/s²	$a_x = 0$ m/s²
$\Delta y = v_{1y}\Delta t + 1/2\,a_y\Delta t^2$	
-80 m $= 1/2\,(-10$ m/s²$)\Delta t^2$	
$\Delta t = 4$ s	$\Delta t = 4$ s
	$\Delta x = v_{1x}\Delta t + 1/2\,a_x\Delta t^2$
	$\Delta x = (120$ m/s$)(4$ s$)$
	$\Delta x = 480$ m

We solved the vertical problem first because we had more vertical information than horizontal information. The time $\Delta t = 4$ s was the connection between the horizontal and vertical parts. You should work through this example yourself without looking at the book.

The following example involves a *projectile*.

Example 2: A cannon is fired on level ground, so that the ball's initial velocity is 300 m/s and directed 30° up from the horizontal. How far from the cannon will the ball fall? (See figure 4-11.)

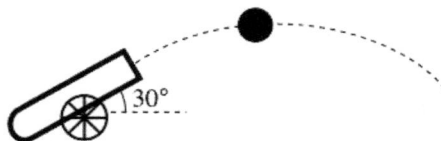

Figure 4-11

Interruption: We need to know the horizontal and vertical components of the initial velocity v_1. We need to find a horizontal vector v_{1x} and a vertical vector v_{1y} so that their sum is the original vector v_1 (see Figure 4-12). We can find the magnitudes of v_{1x} and v_{1y} using simple trigonometry. (You may need to review trigonometry at this point.)

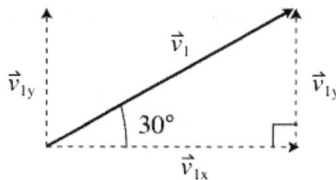

Figure 4-12

$$\frac{v_{1y}}{v_1} = \sin 30° \qquad\qquad \frac{v_{1x}}{v_1} = \cos 30°$$

$$v_{1y} = v_1 \sin 30° \qquad\qquad v_{1x} = v_1 \cos 30°$$

$$v_{1y} = 300 \left(\frac{1}{2}\right)\frac{m}{s} \qquad\qquad v_{1x} = 300\left(\frac{\sqrt{3}}{2}\right)\frac{m}{s}$$

$$v_{1y} = 150 \frac{m}{s} \qquad\qquad v_{1x} = 150\sqrt{3}\,\frac{m}{s}$$

Solution: The force diagram is the same as in Figure 4-10. The cannonball rises and then falls to the same height from which it started, so we have $\Delta y = 0$ m.

vertical	horizontal
$\Delta y = 0$ m	$\Delta x = ?$
$v_{1y} = 150$ m/s	$v_{1x} = 150\sqrt{3}\,\dfrac{m}{s}$
$a_y = -10$ m/s²	$a_x = 0$ m/s²
$\Delta y = v_{1y}\Delta t + 1/2\, a_y \Delta t^2$	
$0 = v_{1y}\Delta t + 1/2\, a_y \Delta t^2$	
$0 = v_{1y} + 1/2\, a_y \Delta t$	

In the last line, we have divided by a factor of Δt.

$$0 = (150 \text{ m/s}) + 1/2 \, (-10 \text{ m/s}^2) \, \Delta t$$
$$\Delta t = 30 \text{ s} \qquad\qquad\qquad \Delta t = 30 \text{ s}$$
$$\Delta x = v_{1x} \Delta t + 1/2 \, a_x \Delta t^2$$
$$\Delta x = \left(150\sqrt{3} \, \frac{\text{m}}{\text{s}}\right)(30\text{s})$$
$$\Delta x = 4500\sqrt{3} \text{m}$$
$$\Delta x = 7800 \text{ m}$$

We have been talking about grapefruits and cannonballs so far. Objects with a more complicated shape obey the same rules, as long as we use the center of mass to talk about the position of the object. Figure 4-13 shows a baseball bat fired from a cannon. The center of mass moves in a parabola, just like the cannonball in the previous example, even though the bat is rotating. In fact this is a definition of the center of mass. If an object is set to freely rotating, the center of mass is the point which refuses to rotate. The gravitational force acts as if it were exerted only at the center of mass.

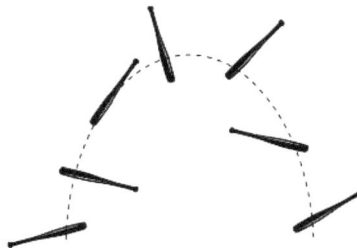

Figure 4-13

In this chapter we looked at the law of gravitation, whose grand form is

$$F_{\text{grav}} = Gm_1m_2/d^2$$

For most problems near the surface of the Earth we can use simply

$$F_{\text{grav}} = mg$$

where $g = GM_{\text{Earth}}/R_{\text{Earth}}^2 = 10\text{m/s}^2$

When any object near the Earth's surface has only gravity acting on it (freefall), it has a downward acceleration vector of magnitude 10 m/s^2. This curious result comes from the fact that the force of gravity is proportional to the mass, while the second law of motion states that the acceleration in inversely proportional to the mass.

We also explored the principle that horizontal and vertical motion are independent. This allows us to solve problems involving projectiles, that is, objects with only gravity acting on them. We will see more of this principle in the following chapter.

Physics Review 4 Problems

Sections A–C

Use the following information for questions 1–3:

In a binary star system, two stars revolve about their combined center of mass. They are held together by the force of gravity. For a certain system, the force of gravity between the stars (masses M_1 and M_2) is F_0.

1. If the mass of one of the stars could somehow be decreased by a factor of 2 at a given moment, how would this affect the force between them?
    A. It would decrease by a factor of 4.
    B. It would decrease by a factor of 2.
    C. It would stay the same.
    D. It would increase by a factor of 2.

2. If the distance between the stars were doubled, how would this affect the force between them?
    A. It would decrease by a factor of 4.
    B. It would decrease by a factor of 2.
    C. It would increase by a factor of 2.
    D. It would increase by a factor of 4.

3. In some binary systems, one star transfers material onto the other. If star 1 dumps half of its material onto star 2, which thus increases its mass by a factor of 5, how is the force affected if the distance between the stars' centers remains the same?
    A. The force increases by a factor of 5.
    B. The force increases by a factor of 2.5.
    C. The force remains the same.
    D. The force decreases by a factor of 2.5.

Use the following information for questions 4–6:

For a spherical planetary body, the gravitational field depends on its mass and radius. The strength of the gravitational field determines the acceleration due to gravity of freely falling objects at the planet's surface. At the surface of the Earth, for example, the acceleration due to gravity is $g_{Earth} = 9.8$ m/s^2. The Moon has a smaller mass and a smaller radius. The net result is that the acceleration due to gravity is $g_{Moon} = 1.6$ m/s^2. A metal block (12 kg on Earth) is taken to the Moon.

4. What is the mass of the block on the Moon?
    A. 2 kg
    B. 12 kg
    C. 24 kg
    D. 72 kg

5. The block is dropped from a height of 2 m to the surface of the Moon. How long does it take to drop to the surface?
    A. 1.6 s
    B. 2.4 s
    C. 6.3 s
    D. There is not enough information to answer this question.

6. What is the weight of the block on the Moon?
    A. 2 kg
    B. 12 kg
    C. 19 N
    D. 118 N

Use the following information for questions 7 and 8:

The colonization of Mars is a favorite topic among science fiction writers. It is a smaller planet than Earth and further from the Sun. Its radius is 0.5 times that of Earth, and its mass is 0.1 times that of Earth. It is 1.5 times further from the Sun than Earth. (Note: On Earth, the acceleration due to gravity is 10 m/s^2. Also, we have $G = 6.67 \times 10^{-11}$ N m^2/kg^2.)

7. If a person were standing on the surface of Mars and dropped a Martian rock, what is the approximate acceleration of the rock's fall?
    A. 0.3 m/s^2
    B. 1 m/s^2
    C. 2 m/s^2
    D. 4 m/s^2

8. How does the force of attraction between the Sun and Mars compare with that between the Sun and Earth?
    A. 0.04 times weaker.
    B. 0.07 times weaker.
    C. 0.10 times weaker.
    D. There is not enough information to answer this question.

Use the following information for questions 9 and 10:

The Earth and the Moon attract each other with the force of gravity. The Earth's radius is 3.67 times that of the Moon, and the Earth's mass is 81 times that of the Moon. The acceleration due to gravity on the surface of the Moon is one sixth the acceleration due to gravity on the Earth's surface.

9. How would the force of gravity between the Earth and the Moon be affected if the distance between the Earth and the Moon were decreased by a factor of 3?
   A. It would decrease by a factor of 9.
   B. It would decrease by a factor of 3.
   C. It would stay the same.
   D. It would increase by a factor of 9.

10. How does the Earth's gravitational pull on the Moon differ from the Moon's pull on the Earth?
    A. It is the same.
    B. It is 3.67 times larger.
    C. It is 6 times larger.
    D. It is 81 times larger.

Use the following information for questions 11 and 12:

A new planet is discovered whose mass is the same as that of Earth, although the acceleration of freely falling objects at the surface of this planet is three times larger than that corresponding to Earth. (That is, we have $g_{Earth} = 9.8$ m/s^2 and $g_{new} = 29.4$ m/s^2.)

11. What is the radius of this new planet?
    A. 9 times smaller than the radius of Earth.
    B. 3 times smaller than the radius of Earth.
    C. 1.7 times smaller than the radius of Earth.
    D. 3 times larger than the radius of Earth.

12. If an object were dropped from a height h on this planet, how much time would it take to reach the ground compared to the time it would take on Earth to drop the same distance h? (Assume no atmospheric resistance.)
    A. It would take the same amount of time.
    B. The time would be less by a factor of 1.7.
    C. The time would be less by a factor of 3.
    D. The time would be less by a factor of 9.

Use the following information for questions 13–15:

An astronaut is in a spaceship traveling at constant velocity toward the star Rigel and is far away from any other objects (planets and stars, etc.). There is racquet ball moving at 0.5 m/s on the spaceship. An astronaut blows air on the racquet ball, producing a small force of 0.08 N in the direction opposite the ball's velocity. The ball slows to a stop in 4 s.

13. What is the weight of the racquet ball?
    A. 0 N
    B. 0.016 N
    C. 0.4 N
    D. 6.4 N

14. What is the magnitude of the acceleration of the racquet ball?
    A. 0 m/s^2
    B. 0.125 m/s^2
    C. 0.2 m/s^2
    D. 0.4 m/s^2

15. What is the mass of the racquet ball?
    A. 0 kg
    B. 0.64 kg
    C. 1.6 kg
    D. 2.5 kg

Section D

Use the following information for questions 16–20:

In a certain sports event, called the appliance toss, men and women test their strength by hurling an electric can opener horizontally over a cliff. (See figure.) The cliff is very high, standing over a plain, and judges at the bottom determine where the openers land. When Barbara heaves her opener at $t = 0$ s, the opener has horizontal velocity 1.5 m/s when it leaves her hand. After 2 s, it is still in the air (point B in the diagram). (Use $g = 10$ m/s^2.)

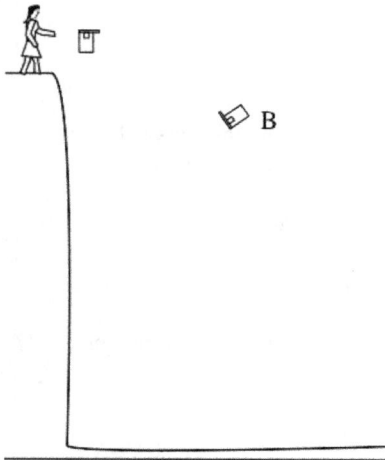

16. Which of the following best shows a force diagram for the can opener at point B?

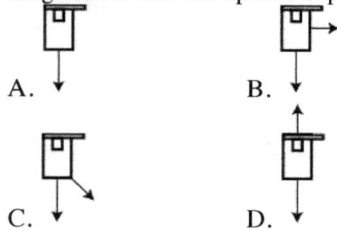

17. What vertical distance has the can opener fallen in the two seconds?
    A. 3 m
    B. 20 m
    C. 20.2 m
    D. 23 m

18. What horizontal distance has the can opener traversed in the two seconds?
    A. 3 m
    B. 20 m
    C. 20.2 m
    D. 23 m

19. At $t = 2$ s, what is the opener's vertical velocity?
    A. 0 m/s
    B. 1.5 m/s
    C. 20 m/s
    D. 21.5 m/s

20. At $t = 2$ s, what is the opener's horizontal velocity?
    A. 0 m/s
    B. 1.5 m/s
    C. 20 m/s
    D. 21.5 m/s

Use the following information for questions 21–27:

A ball (0.2 kg) rolls along a level table at 1.5 m/s and then rolls off the edge. The table is 1.25 m off the floor. Consider the time from the moment just after the ball leaves the table till the moment just before the ball touches the floor. See figure. (Use $g = 9.8$ m/s^2, and ignore any air resistance.)

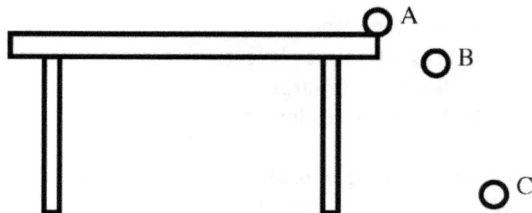

21. What is the ball's initial horizontal velocity?
    A. 0 m/s
    B. 1.5 m/s
    C. 5.0 m/s
    D. 5.2 m/s

22. What is the ball's initial vertical velocity?
    A. 0 m/s
    B. 1.5 m/s
    C. 5.0 m/s
    D. 5.2 m/s

23. When the ball is in midair (point B), what is the net force on the ball?
    A. 1.96 N
    B. 3.92 N
    C. 9.8 N
    D. 19.6 N

24. What is the vertical displacement of the ball during the fall?
    A. 0.76 m
    B. 1.47 m
    C. 1.25 m
    D. 2.25 m

25. How much time does the drop take?
    A. 0.26 s
    B. 0.51 s
    C. 0.83 s
    D. 1.01 s

26. What is the horizontal acceleration of the ball at point B?
    A. 0 m/s^2
    B. 0.2 m/s^2
    C. 1.96 m/s^2
    D. 9.8 m/s^2

27. What is the horizontal displacement of the ball during the fall?
    A. 0.76 m
    B. 1.47 m
    C. 1.25 m
    D. 2.25 m

Use the following information for questions 28–31:

Two girls are sitting on the edge of a building tossing coins over the edge. Alice is actually dropping her coins, each of which is 10 g. Barbara is tossing her coins horizontally at 0.3 m/s, and her coins are 40 g each. (See figure.) (Ignore air resistance.)

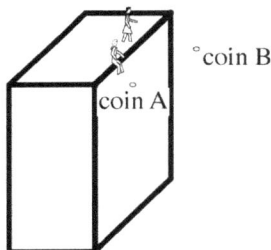

28. When the coins are in midair, how does the gravitational force on one of Alice's coins compare with the force on one of Barbara's?
    A. It is one fourth as large.
    B. It is the same.
    C. It is four times as large.
    D. It depends on the height at which the force is recorded.

29. When the coins are in midair, how does the acceleration of one of Alice's coins compare with the acceleration of one of Barbara's?
    A. It is one fourth as large.
    B. It is the same.
    C. It is four times as large.
    D. It depends on the height at which the acceleration is recorded.

30. How does the time to reach the ground for one of Alice's coins compare with the time of fall for Barbara's?
    A. The time for Alice's coins is less.
    B. The times are the same.
    C. The time for Alice's coins is greater.
    D. It depends on the height of the building.

31. Just before Alice's coin reaches the ground, it has speed s_A. Just before Barbara's coin reaches the ground, it has speed s_B. How does s_A compare with s_B?
    A. The speed s_A is less than s_B.
    B. The speed s_A is the same as s_B.
    C. The speed s_A is greater than s_B.
    D. It depends on the height of the building.

Use the following information for questions 32–33:

A woman (50 kg) is pulling a wagon behind her. In the wagon is her daughter by her first marriage; the daughter and the wagon are 60 kg. (See figure.) The woman pulls the handle with a tension 200 N, and the handle makes a 30° angle with the horizontal. There is a horizontal force of friction, and the wagon moves at a constant 2 m/s. (Use $g = 10$ m/s^2.)

32. What is the horizontal component of the force of the wagon handle on the wagon body?
    A. 0 N
    B. (200 N) (sin 30°)
    C. (200 N) (cos 30°)
    D. 200 N

33. What is the vertical component of the force of the wagon handle on the wagon body?
    A. 0 N
    B. (200 N) (sin 30°)
    C. (200 N) (cos 30°)
    D. 200 N

Solutions

1. B.
The fact that the stars revolve about their combined center of mass is irrelevant for calculating the force of gravity between them. That depends only on their masses and the distance between their centers. Since we have $F_{grav} = Gm_1m_2/d^2$, if one of the masses decreases by a factor of 2, then F_{grav} decreases by a factor of 2.

2. A.
The factor of d^2 in the denominator indicates that if d increases by a factor of 2, then F_{grav} decreases by a factor of $2^2 = 4$.

3. B.
If m_1 decreases by a factor of 2, and m_2 increases by a factor of 5, then F_{grav} changes by a factor of 5/2.

4. B.
I hope this one did not fool you. The mass of an object does not change just because you transport it somewhere.

5. A.
Objects in free fall on the Moon have a constant acceleration due to gravity 1.6 m/s² for the same reason that free-fall objects have $a = 9.8$ m/s² here on Earth. This comes from setting $F_{net} = ma$ equal to $F_{grav} = mg$, so that $a = g$. In this case, we have

$$a = -1.6 \text{ m/s}^2$$

$$v_1 = 0 \text{ m/s}$$

$$\Delta y = -2 \text{ m}$$

$$\Delta t = \text{?}$$

$$\Delta y = v_1\Delta t + 1/2\, a\Delta t^2$$

$$-2 \text{ m} = 1/2\,(-1.6 \text{ m/s}^2)\Delta t^2$$

$$\Delta t^2 = 2.5 \text{ s}^2$$

We only need to work as far as Δt^2 in order to eliminate choices B, C, and D.

6. C.
The weight of the block on the Moon is an exact analogy to its weight on Earth: $F_{grav} = mg_{Moon} = 20$ N.

7. D.
On Earth (or on any planetary body), we get the acceleration due to gravity on the surface by assuming that gravity is the only force acting on an object. So we set $F_{net} = ma$ equal to $F_{grav} = Gm_{planet}m/r^2$, where r is the radius of the planet:

$$ma = \frac{Gm_{planet}m}{r^2}$$

$$a = \frac{Gm_{planet}}{r^2}$$

See Example 2 in Section A. Now if the radius of the planet were multiplied by 0.5, then the acceleration due to gravity would be *divided* by $(0.5)^2$, giving us 40 m/s². (We expect an increase, since the acceleration increases if radius decreases.) But the mass of Mars is 0.1 of Earth's mass, so a factor of 0.1 in the numerator brings the acceleration down to 4 m/s².

8. A.
This time the relevant equation is

$$F_{grav} = \frac{Gm_{sun}m_{planet}}{d^2}$$

where d is the distance from the Sun to that planet. The mass of Mars is 0.1 times that of Earth, so that is a factor of 0.1. Another factor comes from the distance from the Sun to Mars, which is 1.5 times greater, so we *divide* by $(1.5)^2$, yielding about 0.04.

9. D.
The equation we need for this problem and the next is

$$F_{grav} = \frac{Gm_{Earth}m_{moon}}{d^2}$$

where d is the distance between the Earth and the Moon. If d decreases by a factor of 3, then F_{grav} increases by a factor of $3^2 = 9$.

10. A.
The Earth's gravitational pull on the Moon is the same as the Moon's on the Earth. That's the third law of motion. (Why does the Moon in its orbit move so much more than the Earth, then?)

11. C.
In problem 7, we worked out the surface acceleration due to gravity of a planet. Since we are looking for radius, we can solve for it, so we have

$$r = \sqrt{\frac{Gm_{\text{planet}}}{a}}$$

If the new planet has the same mass as Earth, but a larger acceleration due to gravity, then the radius must be smaller. And if a changes by a factor of 3, then r changes by a factor of $\sqrt{3}$, so the answer is B. (We don't need to know $\sqrt{3}$ to figure out which choice is right.)

12. B.
We want to relate acceleration and time, so we want an equation that involves these quantities. (We have seen enough of these problems to realize $v_1 = 0$.) We can use

$$h = v_1 \Delta t + 1/2\, g\Delta t^2$$
$$h = 1/2\, g\Delta t^2$$
$$\Delta t = \sqrt{\frac{2h}{g}}$$

If g increases by a factor of 3, then Δt decreases by a factor of $\sqrt{3}$.

13. A.
Since weight is the force of gravity on an object, and there are no massive planetary bodies around, the weight is zero.

14. B.
The acceleration is $a = (0\text{ m/s} - 0.5\text{ m/s})/(4\text{ s}) = -0.125\text{ m/s}^2$. (This was a review question.)

15. B.
Once we have the acceleration, we can calculate a mass $m = F/a = (0.08\text{ N})/(0.125\text{ m/s}^2) = 0.64$ kg.

16. A.
Certainly there is the force of gravity, down. There is nothing else touching the can opener, so gravity is the only force. Since there is no horizontal force, there is constant horizontal motion. But horizontal motion *does not* imply a horizontal force (see the first law of motion).

17. B.
Since we have a force diagram, we next need to inventory the information relevant to the vertical motion. We have $a_y = -10\text{ m/s}^2$ and $\Delta t = 2$ s. Because the opener is traveling *horizontally* when it leaves Barbara's hand, we have $v_{1y} = 0$ m/s. Since we want to know Δy, we use the equation $\Delta y = v_{1y}\Delta t + 1/2\, a_y(\Delta t)^2 = 20$ m.

18. A.
Since we are looking for Δx, we now inventory the horizontal information. We have $a_x = 0\text{ m/s}^2$ and $v_{1x} = 1.5$ m/s. Thus we have $\Delta x = v_{1x}\Delta t + 1/2 a_x(\Delta t)^2 = 3$ m.

19. C.
The problem asks for v_{2y}, so we write $v_{2y} = v_{1y} + a_y\Delta t = -20$ m/s. Since only positive choices are listed, we choose the magnitude 20 m/s.

20. B.
We can calculate $v_{2x} = v_{1x} + a_x\Delta t = 1.5$ m/s. Of course, we don't really have to do a calculation, since we know that the horizontal velocity is constant as long as there are no horizontal forces on the opener.

21. B.
As the ball just leaves the table, it is going 1.5 m/s horizontally, so $v_{1x} = 1.5$ m/s.

22. A.
Since the initial velocity is horizontal, we have $v_{1y} = 0$ m/s.

23. A.
We draw a diagram including all the forces (see figure). Since nothing is touching the ball, gravity is the only force. Thus $F_{\text{grav}} = mg = (0.2$ kg$)(10\text{ m/s}^2) = 2$ N.

24. C.
Since the ball simply drops the height of the table, we have $\Delta y = -1.25$ m (choosing "up" to be positive).

25. B.
For horizontal information, we have $a_x = 0$ m/s^2 and $v_{1x} = 1.5$ m/s, which is not enough to obtain Δt. For vertical information, we have

$$\Delta y = -1.25 \text{ m}$$
$$a_y = -10 \text{ m/s}^2$$
$$v_{1y} = 0 \text{ m/s}$$

We can calculate

$$\Delta y = v_{1y}\Delta t + 1/2 \, a_y\Delta t^2$$
$$\Delta t^2 = 2\Delta y/a_y$$
$$\Delta t^2 = 0.25 \text{ s}^2$$

We do not really need to take the square root to figure out the answer. If choice A is right, then $(\Delta t)^2 = (0.26 \text{ s})^2 \approx 0.12 \text{ s}^2$ (wrong). If choice B is right, then $(\Delta t)^2 = (0.5 \text{ s})^2 = 0.25 \text{ s}^2$. (Do not feel the need to work every arithmetic problem to its end.)

26. A.
There is no horizontal force on the ball.

27. A.
We want Δx. Since we now have Δt, we have enough information to calculate

$$\Delta x = v_{1x}\Delta t + 1/2 \, a_x\Delta t^2$$
$$\Delta x = 0.76 \text{ m}$$

28. A.
Since gravitational force is given by $F_{grav} = mg$, and since Barbara's coins have four times the mass of Alice's coins, the force on them is four times as large.

29. B.
The acceleration of Alice's coins is a constant 9.8 m/s^2 down, as is the acceleration of Barbara's.

30. B.
The vertical acceleration a_y is the same for both coins, and the initial vertical velocity v_{1y} is the same for both coins. The vertical displacement for the fall is certainly the same, so in the equation $\Delta y = v_{1y}\Delta t + 1/2 \, a_y(\Delta t)^2$, all the parameters are the same. This question combines the two ideas in this chapter, namely, for *freely falling bodies* near the surface of the Earth the vertical acceleration is 9.8 m/s^2 down, and for *all bodies* vertical motion is independent of horizontal motion.

31. A.
Both coins have the same vertical velocity. In addition, Barbara's coins retain their horizontal velocity.

32. C.
First, let's draw a diagram showing all the forces on the wagon body.

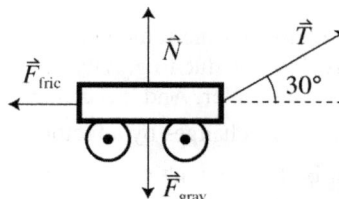

The handle and the ground are touching the wagon, so we include the tension force of the handle T and the upward force of the ground N. The problem mentions friction, so we include that as well. There are four forces on the wagon. We can redraw the force of the handle as the sum of two components, as shown in the second figure.

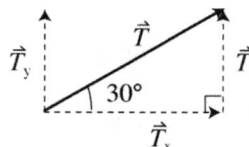

We calculate T_x as follows:

$$T_x/T = \cos 30°$$
$$T_x = T\cos 30°$$

33. B.
We calculate T_y as follows:

$$T_y/T = \sin 30°$$
$$T_y = T\sin 30°$$

Physics Review 5
Planes and Circles

A. Horizontal and Vertical Motion, Again

In the last chapter we solved problems with gravity as the only force. Well, gravity is a fine force indeed, but we need to understand problems in which other forces are present. That is the goal of this chapter.

In the last chapter we discussed the independence of vertical and horizontal motion for objects in freefall, but it turns out the principle works when other forces are acting as well:

Independence of Vertical and Horizontal Motion
An object has forces $\vec{F}_1, \vec{F}_2, \ldots,$ acting on it. If $F_{1y}, F_{2y}, \ldots,$ are the vertical components of the forces, then we have

$$F_{net.y} = F_{1y} + F_{2y} + \cdots, \qquad (1)$$

$$a_y = \frac{F_y}{m}. \qquad (2)$$

Similarly, if $F_{1x}, F_{2x}, \ldots,$ are the horizontal components of the forces, then we have

$$F_{net.x} = F_{1x} + F_{2x} + \cdots, \qquad (3)$$

$$a_x = \frac{F_x}{m}. \qquad (4)$$

This is a more useful form of $F_{net} = ma$, the equation that we discussed in Section 3.B. An example will help illustrate how the principle in the above box is used to solve problems.

In the following example, we find a toy wagon rolling on the ground. In general, when an object is on the ground or some other surface, that surface exerts one or two forces on it: always a normal force N pointing perpendicular to the surface and sometimes a frictional force F_{fric} pointing parallel to the surface.

Example: A boy pulls a red wagon (10 kg) with a constant force 20 N. The handle makes an angle $30°$ with the horizontal. Assume there is no friction.

   a. If the wagon starts from rest, how fast is it going after 3 seconds?
   b. What is the normal force acting on the wagon?

Solution: First we DRAW A DIAGRAM (Figure 5-1) showing all the forces on the wagon body. The handle and the ground are the only two things which touch it. So in addition to gravity, there are the tension due to the handle and the normal force. The tension T points along the handle, that is, $30°$ from the horizontal.

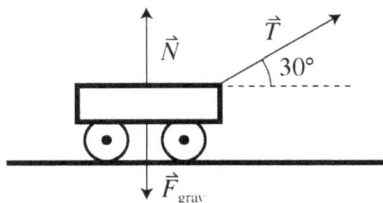

Figure 5-1

In Figure 5-2 we resolve the tension into components (recall trigonometry), so we have

$$\frac{T_y}{T} = \sin 30°$$

$$T_y = (20\text{N})\sin 30°$$

$$T_y = 10\text{N}$$

$$\frac{T_x}{T} = \cos 30°$$

$$T_x = (20\text{N})\cos 30°$$

$$T_x = 17\text{N}$$

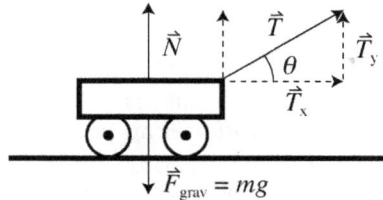

Figure 5-2

The normal force and gravity do not have horizontal components, so the only horizontal force is T_x. Thus we write

$(F_{net})_x = ma_x$,
$T_x = ma_x$,
$a_x, = T_x/m = 17\text{N}/10\text{kg} = 1.7 \text{ m/s}^2$

Using this and $v_{1x} = 0$ m/s and $\Delta t = 3$ s, we derive a horizontal velocity

$v_{2x} = v_{1x} + a_x\Delta t$
$= 0 \text{ m/s} + 1.7 \text{ m/s}^2(3\text{s}) = 4.1 \text{ m/s}$

which is the answer to part a.

If we consider the vertical components of force, then we can find $(F_{net})_y$ just by looking at the diagram, so we write

$$(F_{net})_y = N + T_y - F_{grav}$$

where we use the positive sign for forces which point up; negative for down. Now the second law of motion connects this with vertical acceleration, so that

$$(F_{net})_y = ma_y$$

But the cart is not moving vertically, so we know that v_y is constant (and zero) and thus a_y is zero. This means $(F_{net})_y$ is zero, so we have

$0 = N + T_y - F_{grav}$,
$N = F_{grav} - T_y$
$= mg - T_y$
$= (10\text{kg})(10\text{m/s}^2) - 10\text{N}$
$= 90 \text{ N}.$

Notice that the normal force is not the same as the gravitational force, a mistake often made by students. Why is the normal force not the same as gravity?

Note that in solving part a, we used information about forces to obtain the horizontal acceleration a_x and then the answer. In part b we reasoned the other way, using information about the vertical acceleration $a_y = 0$ to obtain information about the normal force. This strategy of reasoning in both directions will be useful in many problems.

B. Inclined Planes and Force Components

The following method generally works for force problems in two dimensions:

1. DRAW A DIAGRAM.
2. Draw all the forces on the object(s) in question (see Section 3.D).
3. Decide the orientation of the axes ("horizontal" and "vertical").
4. Divide the forces into components if necessary.
5. Solve $(F_{net})_y = ma_y$ and $(F_{net})_x = ma_x$.

For the last step, note that we often have $a_y = 0$, leading to $(F_{net})_y = 0$. Also, be on the lookout for the words "constant velocity" or the equivalent, since that implies $a_x = 0$ and $a_y = 0$, a force balance.

The principle of the independence of the components of the $F = ma$ equation is valid even when the axes are tilted, as the next example will show.

Example: A toy car of mass 40 grams is released at the top of an incline of plastic track, inclined 30° from the horizontal. The car starts from rest and travels 4 m to the floor. Assuming there is no friction, how much time does it take the car to reach the floor?

Solution: First we DRAW A DIAGRAM (Figure 5-3). In addition to gravity, the track touches the car and exerts a normal force. Since the track is inclined, the normal force points not up but perpendicular to the surface. There is no frictional force.

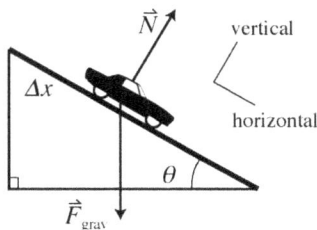

Figure 5-3

We will call "horizontal" the direction along the track and "vertical" the direction perpendicular to the track (Figure 5-3).

Next, we divide the gravitational force into components (Figure 5-4). Note that F_x and F_y are not new forces but pieces of F_{grav}. If we add F_x and F_y together like vectors (tip-to-tail), then we get F_{grav}. It may not be obvious that the two angles shown in Figure 5-4 should both be $\theta = 30°$. Note that both angles labeled θ are complementary to the angle between F_x and F_{grav}. On the other hand, in physics it is generally true that two small angles which look congruent are congruent(!).

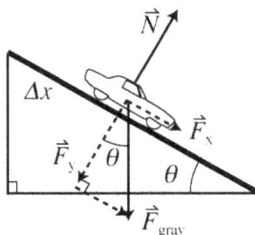

Figure 5-4

Now if we look at the triangle in Figure 5-4, we can write

$$\frac{F_x}{F_{grav}} = \sin\theta \qquad\qquad \frac{F_y}{F_{grav}} = \cos\theta$$

$$F_x = F_{grav}\sin\theta \qquad\qquad F_y = F_{grav}\cos\theta$$

$$F_x = mg\sin\theta \qquad\qquad F_y = mg\cos\theta$$

We care about the horizontal motion, so we write

$$(F_{net})_x = ma_x$$

The only horizontal force is F_x, so we write

$$F_x = ma_x$$

$$mg \sin \theta = ma_x$$

$$g \sin \theta = a_x$$

$$a_x = (10 \text{ m/s}^2)\sin 30° = 5 \text{ m/s}^2$$

We have $v_{1x} = 0$ m/s and $\Delta x = 4$ m, so we can find Δt by writing

$$\Delta x = v_{1x}\Delta t + \frac{1}{2}a_x\Delta t^2$$

$$\Delta t = \sqrt{\frac{2\Delta x}{a_x}}$$

$$= \sqrt{\frac{2(4\text{m})}{5\frac{\text{m}}{\text{s}^2}}}$$

$$= 1.3 \text{ s}$$

C. Circular Motion, Qualitative Description

Let's think a minute about a toy car moving along the floor and pretend the movement is frictionless. Figure 5-5 shows a top view, with the car moving to the right (see the motion marks behind the car). If we were to apply a rightward force F_A, by blowing the car with a portable hair dryer, for instance, this would clearly speed up the car. If we were to apply a leftward force F_B, this would slow it down. A force F_C applied (for just a moment) perpendicular to the motion would neither speed it up nor slow it down, but it would cause the car to veer from its straight path.

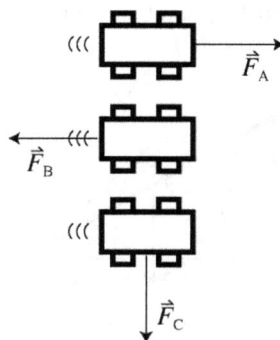

Figure 5-5

If we are using a hair dryer to exert F_C, then we can keep adjusting the direction of the force to keep it perpendicular to the motion of the car. The car will end up traveling in a circle (Figure 5-6). Given this discussion, the following box should seem reasonable.

480

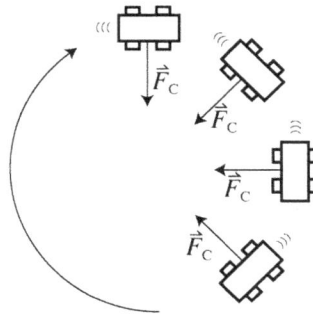

*An object moving in a circle with
constant speed has an acceleration
vector pointed towards the center
of the circle.*

Figure 5-6

> If an object is moving at constant speed in a circle, then the net
> force on the object points toward the center of the circle, and
> the acceleration vector points towards the center as well.

In normal English, we do not say that the car is accelerating when it is turning. But in physics language, an object that is moving at constant speed in a circle is "accelerating toward the center of the circle", because the *velocity vector* is changing. We call this *centripetal acceleration*, which is Latin for "toward the center". (Parenthetically, "centrifugal" means "away from the center".) The force which provides the centripetal acceleration is the *centripetal force*.

Example 1: The Earth moves around the Sun. What force provides the centripetal force?

Solution: The gravitational force provides the centripetal force (Figure 5-7).

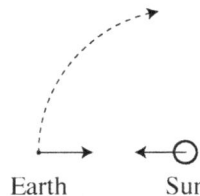

Earth   Sun
Figure 5-7

Example 2: A car goes around a curve to the left. What force provides the centripetal force?

Solution: This example is a bit more complicated. The driver turns her wheels to the left, so the wheels exert a force on the road to the right. By Newton's Third Law of Motion, the road exerts a force to the left on the wheels, turning the car left. In this case friction provides the centripetal force (Figure 5-8). (Think what would happen if there were no friction, for instance, if there were oil on the road.)

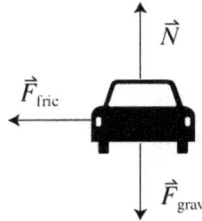

The car, seen from the rear, is turning left, and the frictional force provides the centripetal acceleration.

Figure 5-8

Example 3: A father is driving a car and turns to the left. There is a sack of groceries in the front passenger seat which crashes into the passenger door. The little brother Samson in the back seat asks the father why the groceries crashed into the door. The father says that was due to centrifugal force. The older sister Cadenza rolls her eyes at this, thinking about how much physics her brother will have to unlearn as he grows up. What is the correct explanation for the groceries' crashing into the door?

Solution: Figure 5-9 gives the real story. The groceries are going along a straight path, as we would expect according to the first law of motion. The car door is pulled into the path of the groceries. The father invents the word "centrifugal force" in order to hide his ignorance. Whenever you are tempted to explain something by centrifugal force, it is likely that you can explain it better with the ideas of first law of motion and a turning frame of reference (like the car).

The groceries in the passanger's seat crash into the car door because the door turns into their path (not because of "centrifugal force").

Figure 5-9

482

D. Circular Motion, Quantitative Description

An object moving in a circle has an acceleration which has, in general, two components: the centripetal acceleration and the tangential acceleration. The former is directed toward the center and is responsible for changing the direction of the object. The latter is responsible for changing the speed. The acceleration is given by

$$ \text{Tangential acceleration} \quad a_{\text{tang}} = \frac{\Delta \text{speed}}{\Delta t}. \qquad (5) $$

$$ \text{Centripetal acceleration} \quad a_{\text{cent}} = \frac{v^2}{r}. \qquad (6) $$

Example 1: A bombardier beetle sits on a blade of a windmill which is going counterclockwise and slowing down. The blade is at the top of its cycle. Sketch the acceleration vector.

Solution: In Figure 5-10, if the beetle is going left and slowing down, then the tangential acceleration must be to the right. The centripetal acceleration vector is down, and the total acceleration a is shown.

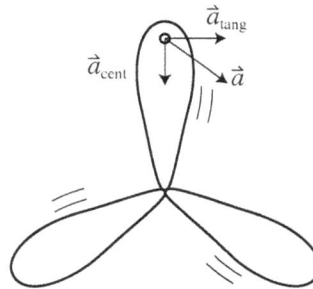

Figure 5-10

Example 2: Use the following information to find the mass of the sun:

$G = 6.67 \times 10^{-11}$ m^3/kg s^2
$R = 1.5 \times 10^{11}$ m (distance from the Sun to the Earth)

Solution: First, we DRAW A DIAGRAM showing all the forces (Figure 5-11). Some students are tempted to draw two forces on the Earth: a gravitational and a centripetal force. But the only force is gravity, and this provides the centripetal force in this problem. This last sentence provides the clue for solving the problem. We know expressions for gravitation and for centripetal acceleration, so that we have

$$ F_{\text{grav}} = F_{\text{cent}} $$
$$ \frac{GM_{\text{sun}}M_{\text{Earth}}}{R^2} = M_{Earth}\frac{v^2}{R} \qquad (7) $$

We use M_{Earth} on the right-hand side of the equation, because it is the Earth's acceleration we are concerned about. The Sun's acceleration is much smaller because its mass is larger. (Recall that the force the Earth exerts on the Sun is the same as that which the Sun exerts on the Earth.) Note that M_{Earth} cancels.

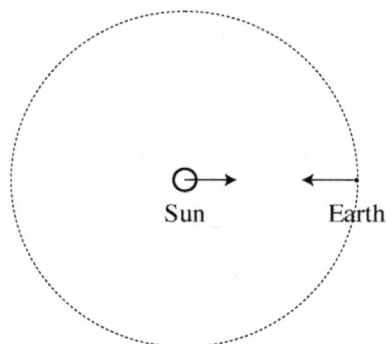

Figure 5-11

What expression shall we use for v? What is the velocity of the Earth? If the Earth travels a full circuit in a year, then velocity is simply distance per time, where the distance is the circumference of the circle. Thus we write

$$v = \frac{2\pi R}{T} \qquad (8)$$

where T is 1 year. Do not simply memorize this, but take a minute to think about why this equation is true, so it will come immediately to mind in any similar situations. Substituting this into equation (7) and doing some algebra gives

$$M_{sun} = \frac{4\pi^2 R^3}{GT^2}$$

into which we can substitute the values given in the problem, along with

$$T = 365\text{days}\left(\frac{24 \text{ hours}}{1 \text{ day}}\right)\left(\frac{3600 \text{ s}}{1 \text{ hour}}\right) = 3 \times 10^7 \text{ s}$$

to yield

$$M_{sun} = 2 \times 10^{30} \text{ kg}$$

The importance of this example does not lie in the arithmetic. The important parts are the method of setting two expressions for the same force equal to each other and the use of equation (8).

Example 3: A fan spins at a frequency of 50 cycles per second, and its plastic blades are 0.4 meters long. What is the centripetal acceleration of a piece of plastic at the tip of one of the blades?

Solution: You should try to work this out before you read the solution.

If the fan spins at 50 cycles per second, it must undergo one cycle in one fiftieth of a second, so $T = 1/50$ s $= 0.02$ s. The velocity is given by

$$v = \frac{2\pi r}{T} = \frac{2\pi(0.4\text{m})}{0.02\text{s}} = 126 \frac{\text{m}}{\text{s}}$$

so the acceleration is given by

$$a = \frac{v^2}{r} = \frac{\left(126\frac{\text{m}}{\text{s}}\right)^2}{0.4\text{m}} = 4 \times 10^4 \frac{\text{m}}{\text{s}^2}$$

Example 4: A space warrior must fly his spacecraft at constant speed around a spherical space station "Bad Star". Bad Star is large but not large enough to have an atmosphere or gravity worth considering. It is important for the warrior to stay close to the surface and maintain constant speed. A conventional rocket provides the thrust to maintain course, so the plume appears in the opposite direction of the desired thrust. In which direction (Figure 5-12) would we see the plume?

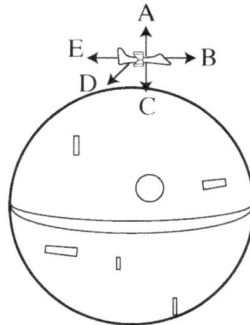

Figure 5-12

Stop! Think about his question and answer it before you look at the solution.

Solution: No one chooses B. Few people choose A. In fact, almost everyone chooses E, because they are thinking about a car driving on the surface of the Earth. But a car on the Earth's surface encounters the force of drag, both by friction and by air resistance, whereas the space warrior encounters neither. No force is required to maintain constant speed. If you chose E, it means you need to study the first law of motion again.

Okay, what is the correct way to think of this problem? The net force of the spacecraft is down, toward the center of Bad Star, because the craft is moving at constant speed in a circle. there is no gravity, no friction, no air drag, so the only force on the craft is due to the rockets. Therefore the rocket plume points in the direction of A.

Some students object that a rocket firing in the direction of A would push the craft into the Bad Star. This is the same as objecting that if the Earth pulls on the Moon, it ought to fall down. What holds up the Moon? The answer in both cases is that the centripetal force is large enough to keep the object (spacecraft or Moon) from moving away but not so large as to pull them into the ground. That is, in Figure 5-13, path 1 is the path the spacecraft takes if the warrior does not fire his rockets at all (no force). Path 2 is the path if he does not fire the rockets enough; and path 4, if he fires them too much. Path 3 is just right.

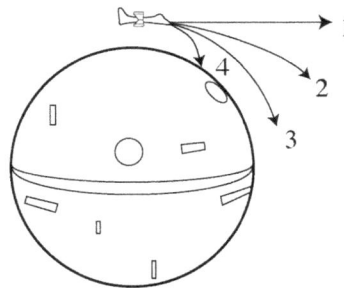

Figure 5-13

The most important concept in this chapter is the independence of horizontal and vertical motion. We saw this concept for the first time in Chapter 4. In this chapter we have used the concept to solve problems involving inclined planes and oblique forces, that is, forces which are neither horizontal nor vertical.

We also looked at circular motion. If an object is moving in a circle, its velocity vector is not constant, and the object must be accelerating. If the object is moving at constant speed, then the direction of the acceleration vector is toward the center, called centripetal acceleration, and its magnitude is $a_{\text{cent}} = v^2/r$.

Physics Review 5 Problems

Section A

Use the following information for questions 1–5:

A cannon shoots an orange (3 kg) straight up in the air with initial velocity 5 m/s (see figure). A horizontal wind exerts a force of 6 N on the orange while it is in the air. Use 10 m/s² for the acceleration due to gravity.

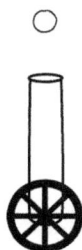

1. Which is the best force diagram while the orange is in the air?

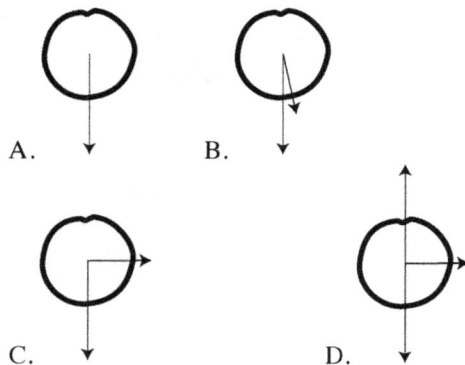

   A.
   B.
   C.
   D.

2. What is the vertical component of the net force on the orange while it is in the air?
   A. 0 N
   B. 2 N
   C. 30 N
   D. 32 N

3. How much time does it take the orange to reach the top of its path?
   A. 0.25 s
   B. 0.4 s
   C. 0.5 s
   D. 2.5 s

4. What is the horizontal component of the acceleration of the orange while it is in the air?
   A. 0 m/s²
   B. 2 m/s²
   C. 10 m/s²
   D. 18 m/s²

5. What is the horizontal velocity of the orange at the top of its path?
   A. 0 m/s
   B. 1 m/s
   C. 5 m/s
   D. 1.25 m/s

6. A shoe is being dragged to the right at constant velocity along a level floor by its string. The string is horizontal and bears a tension T in magnitude. The magnitude of the frictional force is F, the magnitude of the gravitational force is G, and the magnitude of the normal force is N. What can be definitely be concluded?
   A. $T < F$
   B. $T = F$
   C. $T > F$
   D. $T + F = G + N$

Use the following information for questions 7–11:

A winch pulls a crate of oranges (300 kg) up an incline (30° with the horizontal) by maintaining a tension on a rope over a pulley. The crate is moving at a constant speed 0.2 m/s. There is no friction. (Using $g = 10$ m/s².)

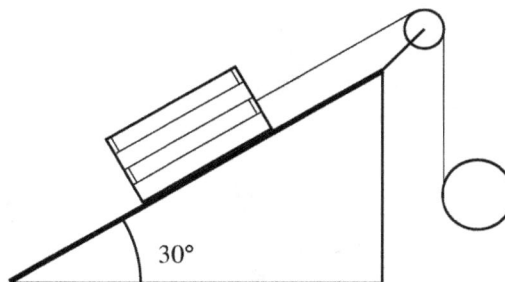

7. What is the component of the gravitational force perpendicular to the surface on which the crate sits?
   A. 0 N
   B. (3000 N) sin30°
   C. (3000 N) cos30°
   D. 3000 N

8. What is the component of the gravitational force parallel to the surface on which the crate sits?
   A. 0 N
   B. (3000 N) sin30°
   C. (3000 N) cos30°
   D. 3000 N

9. What is the normal force on the crate?
   A. 0 N
   B. (3000 N) sin30°
   C. (3000 N) cos30°
   D. 3000 N

10. What is the net force on the crate?
    A. 0 N
    B. (3000 N) sin30°
    C. (3000 N) cos30°
    D. 3000 N

11. What is the tension on the rope?
    A. 0 N
    B. (3000 N) sin30°
    C. (3000 N) cos30°
    D. 3000 N

Use the following information for questions 12–17:

A boy (60 kg) is pushing a sled (5 kg) with a stick, so that the stick makes a 30° angle with the vertical. He applies a force of 20 N, so that the force acts along the stick (i.e., there is no shear or friction force). There is negligible friction between the sled and the ground. At time $t = 0$ s, the sled is at rest.

12. Which of the following is the best force diagram for the sled after $t = 0$ s?

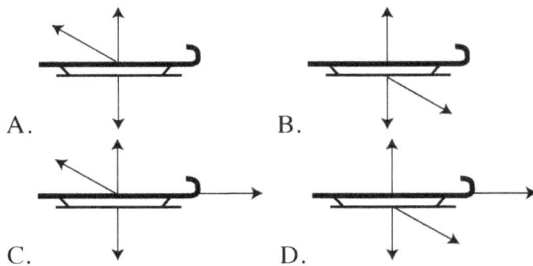

13. What is the horizontal component of the force due to the stick?
    A. 10 N
    B. 17 N
    C. 20 N
    D. 50 N

14. What is the vertical component of the force due to the stick?
    A. 10 N
    B. 17 N
    C. 20 N
    D. 50 N

15. What is the normal force of the ground on the sled?
    A. 17 N
    B. 33 N
    C. 50 N
    D. 67 N

16. What is the net force on the sled?
    A. 0 N
    B. 10 N
    C. 50 N
    D. 67 N

17. What is the acceleration of the sled?
    A. 0 m/s²
    B. 0.5 m/s²
    C. 2.0 m/s²
    D. 9.8 m/s²

Section B

18. A woman is driving a car along a road when she realizes, almost too late, that she needs to make a left hand turn. She quickly turns the wheel, and the books which were in the passenger seat go crashing against the passenger door. Consider the following statements:

    I. The books were pushed against the door by a centrifugal force.
    II. The books were pushed against the door by a centripetal force.
    III. The forces acting on the books while they are crashing against the door are gravity, the normal force, and a force toward the right.

    Which is (are) true?

    A. I and III are true.
    B. II and III are true.
    C. III only is true.
    D. None is true.

Use the following information for questions 19–23:

A stopper is swung on a string, one end of which is fixed at a point P. The diagram shows the stopper and string from the top, and the stopper is swinging counterclockwise at constant speed.

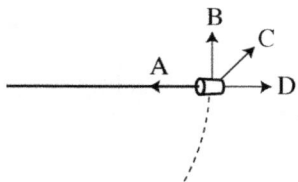

19. Which arrow best shows the direction of the velocity vector?
    A. A
    B. B
    C. C
    D. D

20. Which arrow best shows the direction of the acceleration vector?
    A. A
    B. B
    C. C
    D. D

21. Which arrow best shows the direction of the net force?
    A. A
    B. B
    C. C
    D. D

22. What provides the centripetal force?
    A. Gravity.
    B. Tension.
    C. Friction.
    D. Normal.

23. Which arrow best shows the direction the stopper would go if the string were to break at the moment shown in the diagram?
    A. A
    B. B
    C. C
    D. D

Use the following information for questions 24–27:

A '79 Buick Regal (1200 kg) is being driven at a constant speed 3 m/s and turning to the right on a curve of road which has effective radius 4 m.

24. Consider the car as viewed from the top. Ignore the gravitational and normal forces (which are vertical and add to zero anyway). Which is the best force diagram?

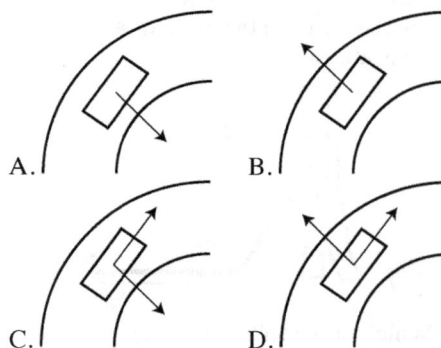

25. What is the acceleration of the Buick?
    A. 0 m/s^2
    B. 0.75 m/s^2
    C. 2.25 m/s^2
    D. 9.8 m/s^2

26. What is the net force on the Buick?
    A. 0 N
    B. 900 N
    C. 2700 N
    D. 11760 N

27. What force provides the centripetal force on the Buick?
    A. Gravity.
    B. Tension.
    C. Friction.
    D. Normal.

Use the following information for questions 28–29:

A bicycle wheel (mass 3 kg, radius 0.5 m) is spinning at a constant angular speed. It is situated horizontally, and a beetle (5 g) is sitting on the rim. The beetle is traveling at a speed 2 m/s. Use $g = 10$ m/s^2.

28. In the following diagrams, the wheel is viewed almost from the side, so that "down" is toward the bottom of the page. Which is the best force diagram?

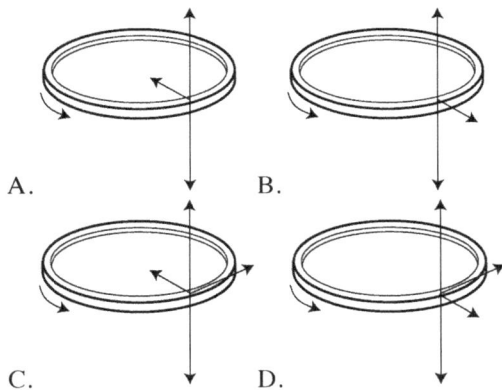

29. What is the acceleration of the beetle?
    A. 0 m/s^2
    B. 2 m/s^2
    C. 8 m/s^2
    D. 10 m/s^2

30. The figure shows a ball (from the top view) rolling on a table with a partial hoop. Which arrow best describes the path of the ball after it leaves the hoop?

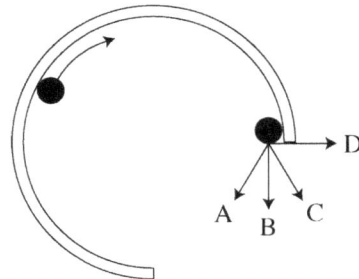

    A. A
    B. B
    C. C
    D. D

All Sections

Use the following information for questions 31 and 32:

A winch pulls a crate of apples (mass M) up an incline (making an angle α with the horizontal). (See figure.) The tension exerted by the winch is T. At the bottom of the incline the crate begins at rest at $t = 0$. Assume there is no friction.

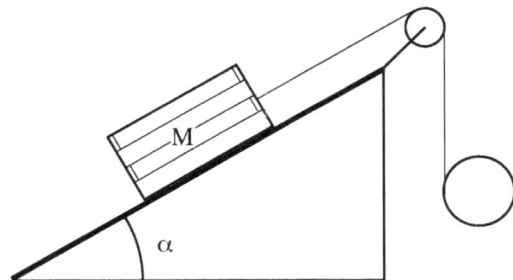

31. What is the normal force of the incline on the crate?
    A. Mg
    B. $Mg\cos\alpha$
    C. $Mg\sin\alpha$
    D. $Mg\sin\alpha - T$

32. What is the acceleration of the crate?
    A. 0
    B. g
    C. $N/M - g\cos\alpha$
    D. $T/M - g\sin\alpha$

Use the following information for questions 33 and 34:

A runner (50 kg) is running around a track (see figure). The curved portions of the track are arcs of a circle, and the dimensions of the track are shown. The runner is running a constant speed 8 m/s. Use 10 m/s^2 for the acceleration due to gravity.

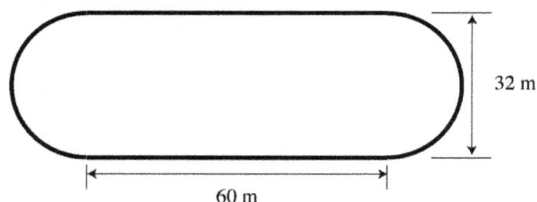

32 m

60 m

33. When the runner is on the curved portions of the track, what are the forces acting on her?
   A. Gravity, up; the normal force, down; and a force, inward.
   B. Gravity, up; the normal force, down; a force, inward; and a force, forward.
   C. Gravity, up; the normal force, down; and a force, outward.
   D. Gravity, up; the normal force, down; a force, outward; and a force, forward.

34. What is the net force on the runner on the curved portion of the track?
   A. 0 N
   B. 100 N
   C. 200 N
   D. 5000 N

Use the following information for questions 35–37:

A Ferris wheel (radius R) is turning in a counterclockwise direction at a given frequency (f).

35. How would the velocity of a chair on the Ferris wheel change if the frequency were doubled?
   A. It would stay the same.
   B. It would increase by a factor of 2.
   C. It would increase by a factor of 4.
   D. It would increase by a factor of 8.

36. How would the centripetal acceleration of a chair on the Ferris wheel change if the frequency were doubled?
   A. It would stay the same.
   B. It would increase by a factor of 2.
   C. It would increase by a factor of 4.
   D. It would increase by a factor of 8.

Solutions

1. C.

The force diagram should include gravity, pointing down. Nothing else is touching the orange, except the problem mentions that wind exerts a horizontal force, so we add that. The force diagram is shown.

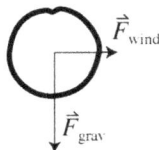

2. C.

The only vertical force is due to gravity, so $F_y = F_{grav} = mg = 30$ N.

3. C.

At the top of the orange's path we have $v_{2y} = 0$ m/s. Since this is vertical information, let's see what other vertical information we have. We have $a_y = -10$ m/s^2 and $v_{1y} = 5$ m/s. We want Δt, so we write $v_{2y} = v_{1y} + a_y\Delta t$ and obtain $\Delta t = 0.5$ s.

4. B.

We want a_x. The horizontal information we have is $v_{1x} = 0$ and $F_x = 6$ N. We don't have enough information for the equations of Chapter 2, but we can use $a_x = F_x/m = (6$ N$)/(3$ kg$) = 2$ m/s^2.

5. B.

Since we know a_x, v_{1x}, and Δt, we can find $v_{2x} = v_{1x} + a_x\Delta t = 0 + (2$ m/s$^2)(0.5$ s$) = 1$ m/s.

6. B.

First we draw a force diagram. This problem has those key words "at constant velocity", which means there is a force balance on the shoe. The horizontal forces are equal in magnitude so that their vector sum is zero, so B is correct. If you chose C, then go back and read the section on the first law of motion.

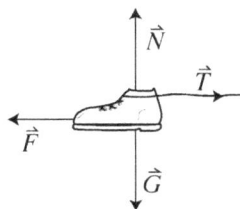

7. C.

First we draw a force diagram (see figure). In addition to gravity, we have two forces, normal and tension, due to two things touching the crate. There is no friction. The gravitational force vector can be separated into two components (see figure).

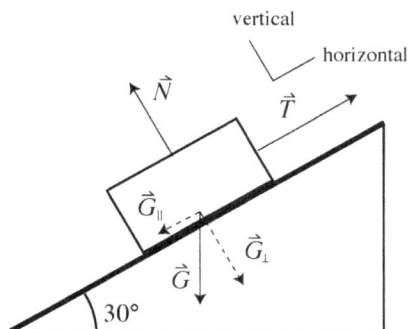

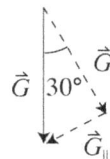

From trigonometry we know

$$\frac{G_\perp}{G} = \cos 30°$$

$$G_\perp = G\cos 30°$$

This gives us choice C.

8. B.

We get this from the same diagrams shown in the solution for 7.

9. C.

If we take the sum of all the perpendicular forces (in the text we called them "vertical"), we obtain $N - G_\perp = (F_{net})_y$. The negative sign denotes the "downward" direction of $G_\perp$. But the crate is moving at a constant velocity, which tells us that the acceleration is zero, and the net force is zero. Thus $N - G_\perp = 0$, giving choice C.

10. A.

As we noted, the net force is zero because of the information we have on the acceleration.

11. B.
This time we take the sum of parallel forces ("horizontal"), and we obtain $T - G_{\parallel} = (F_{net})_x = 0$. Again, we know the horizontal component of the net force is zero because the crate is moving at constant velocity. Thus the answer is B.

12. B.
There are two things touching the sled: the ground and the stick. So, in addition to gravity pointing down, we draw the normal force pointing up and the force due to the stick pointing down/right. There is no friction (which would act to the left). So B is the correct answer (see figure).

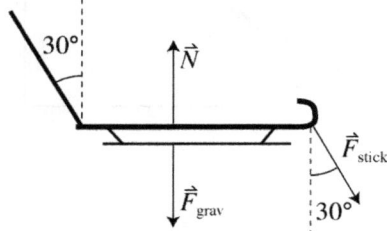

13. A.
We use the following diagram to obtain the vertical component of the stick's force.

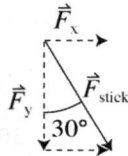

Using trigonometry, we obtain

$$\frac{F_x}{F_{stick}} = \sin 30°$$

$$F_x = F_{stick} \sin 30°$$

$$= (20N)\left(\frac{1}{2}\right)$$

$$= 10N$$

14. B.
Using the same diagram as in solution 13, we obtain $F_y/F_{stick} = \cos 30°$, and $F_y = 17$ N.

15. D.
In order to obtain the normal force, we need to consider all the vertical forces. We can obtain the vertical component of the net force by looking at the force diagram, so we write

$$(F_{net})_y = N - mg - F_y$$

Here we have used $F_{grav} = mg$ and have chosen "up" to be positive. But we know that the sled is

not moving up or down, so the vertical acceleration a_y is zero. And from second law of motion, we know that $(F_{net})_y = ma_y = 0$. The above equation becomes

$$0 = N - mg - F_y$$

$$N = mg + F_y$$

$$= (5 \text{ kg})(10 \text{ m/s}^2) + 17 \text{ N}$$

$$= 67 \text{ N}$$

16. B.
In the last problem, we talked about the vertical component of the net force being zero. We can tell from the force diagram that there is a net force, however, and this net force is the horizontal component F_x.

17. C.
The acceleration of the sled is given by $a_x = (F_{net})_x/m = 2.0 \text{ m/s}^2$

18. D.
The books are following a straight path. By turning the wheel, the driver pulls her car door into the path of the books, giving the impression that the books have a force on them.

19. B.
The direction of the velocity vector is always changing but not its magnitude. At the moment shown in the diagram, the velocity vector is pointing in the direction of the stopper's motion, that is, B.

20. A.
The tangential acceleration is zero, since the speed is constant. However, because the stopper is moving in a circle, the velocity vector is changing direction, and the acceleration vector points toward the center of the circle.

21. A.
Since the acceleration vector $\vec{a}$ points toward the center, we can conclude that the net force $\vec{F}_{net} = m\vec{a}$ points toward the center as well.

22. B.
The centripetal force is provided by the string, which is a force of tension.

23. B.
If the string were to break, then there would no longer be a force to affect the velocity vector. The velocity vector would be constant (first law of motion), so B is correct.

24. A.
Because the car moves in a circle, we know there is a centripetal acceleration and a centripetal force. This narrows the choices to A and C. There is no reason to assume there is a force acting forward on the car, especially since the tangential acceleration is zero (because of the car's constant speed). Hence A is correct. If you chose C, perhaps you were thinking that motion in the forward direction implies there must be a force in the forward direction. Not so.

25. C.
The acceleration is given by $a_{cent} = v^2/r = (3$ m/s$)^2/(4$ m$) = 2.25$ m/s^2.

26. C.
Once we know the acceleration of the car, we necessarily know the net force on the car: $F_{net} = ma = (1200$ kg$)(2.25$ m/s$^2) = 2700$ N.

27. C.
To see that the centripetal force is due to friction, consider what would happen if there were no friction between the tires and the road. The car would simply slide straight forward into the other lane.

28. A.
Gravity and the normal force add to zero. We know there is a net force toward the center of the wheel, because the beetle is moving in a circle, so this narrows our choices to A and C. Choice C includes a force in the forward direction, but since the wheel is rotating at constant speed, there is no tangential acceleration and no reason to assume there is a tangential force.

29. C.
The acceleration can be calculated $a = v^2/r = (2$ m/s$)^2/(0.5$ m$) = 8$ m/s^2.

30. B.
Once there is no longer a centripetal force, there is no longer a centripetal acceleration. According to the first law of motion, the velocity vector would be constant.

31. B.
We draw a diagram, including the three forces on the crate. We choose "horizontal" and "vertical" to be parallel and perpendicular to the surface, respectively, and we divide gravity into components (see figure).

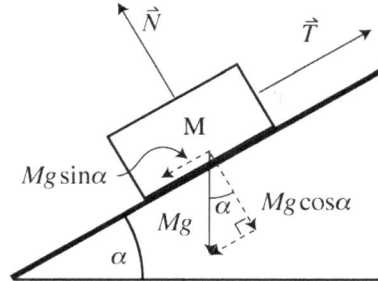

Since the normal force is "vertical", let us consider the vertical component of $F_{net} = a$. From the diagram we obtain

$$(F_{net})_y = N - Mg \cos\alpha$$

But we know that $a_y = 0$, because the crate is not moving up or down. This implies $(F_{net})_y = 0$, and we have

$$0 = N - Mg \cos\alpha$$

$$N = Mg \cos\alpha$$

32. D.
If we consider the "horizontal" component of $F_{net} = Ma$, then we can obtain from the diagram

$$(F_{net})_x = T - Mg \sin\alpha$$

where we have taken the positive direction to be up the incline. The acceleration is

$$a_x = \frac{(F_{net})_x}{M}$$

$$= \frac{T}{M} - g \sin\alpha$$

33. A.

The force inward is due to friction between the runner's shoes and the track. It may seem surprising that there is not a force forward, since the runner is actively running. There is a horizontal acceleration, and thus net force, only at the beginning of the race when the runner is accelerating. When she is going at a constant speed, she expends effort pushing down with the foot in contact with the track and moving it back fast enough.

34. C.

The net force is given by $F_{net} = ma$, and the only acceleration is centripetal, so we have $a = a_{cent} = v^2/r$.

35. B.

The frequency is the number of revolutions per unit of time. Each revolution represents a trip of length $2\pi R$. So the velocity is the total distance per time, that is, $v = 2\pi Rf$. If f is doubled, then v is doubled.

36. C.

On the other hand the centripetal acceleration is $a_{cent} = v^2/r$, so a_{cent} is increased by a factor of 4.

Biology Review 1
Introduction

A. Philosophy of the Biology Review Section

This review section is designed to help you understand major concepts in biology and to use this knowledge to solve problems. Each chapter contains ACT-style questions with answers and full explanations.

The ACT questions are written to test your knowledge of basic concepts in biology and problem solving abilities; they do not stress rote memorization of facts. The questions are based on short passages. Four to eight questions will be asked for each passage. These questions may require you to interpret data from graphs, tables or figures.

This introductory chapter will familiarize you with the concepts that form the foundations of biology. These key ideas are implicit in every topic of biology, and we recommend that you keep them in the back of your mind at all times.

B. Biology

We'll start with a simple definition of biology: *biology is the study of life*. This includes examination of the processes that govern how life is maintained and reproduced, and observation of how living things interact with each other and with the environment. Although this sounds rather simple, it involves studying many different and diverse areas, from the molecular level to the global scale.

There are two distinct perspectives from which one can study biological processes: *in vivo* or *in vitro*. *In vivo* means research is done in the body itself. *In vitro* means literally "in glass," as an experiment that is done in a test tube, or outside of the body. *In vivo* experiments, naturally, include all the factors that can influence a process; therefore, the reactions being studied represent a "real life" situation. However, all these factors and reactions can make for a very complex system that is not easily understood. *In vitro* studies, on the other hand, allow researchers to manipulate the system to study only one or two isolated factors. This helps to determine exactly what these factors do.

Although each approach has its merits and drawbacks, both perspectives are needed and work synergistically. For example, the study of AIDS has benefited from both *in vivo* and *in vitro* studies. The course of the illness, from infection with HIV to full blown AIDS, has been well characterized in humans through the use of *in vivo* studies. But the exact mechanism of how the virus invades a cell is known through *in vitro* studies. Drugs designed to fight the virus are first tested in vitro using HIV infected cells grown in the laboratory. Drugs that prove effective *in vitro* are then tested *in vivo*.

C. The Scientific Method

As with all sciences, biological research involves methodically searching for information. The procedure associated with this search is called the *scientific method*. It involves

1. asking questions, which are then followed by one or more *hypotheses* (educated guesses or hunches that answer or explain the question).
2. making predictions from the hypothesis, usually in the form of "if....then" statements (*if* the influenza virus causes the flu, *then* those exposed to it will become ill).

3. testing the predictions through experimentation, observation, model building, etc., including appropriate controls with which to compare the results.
4. repeating the investigations and devising new ways to further test the hypothesis (this may include modification of the hypothesis based on the results of the tests).
5. reporting the results and drawing conclusions from them.

A *theory* is similar to a hypothesis in that it is subjected to the scientific method, but a theory usually explains a broad range of related phenomena, not a single one. Theories are well supported hypotheses, shown to be valid under many different circumstances.

In science, there is no real beginning or end. All hypotheses are based on previous work, and all results and conclusions can be expanded in the future. Often experiments raise more questions than they answer.

D. Characteristics of Life

If biology is the study of life, then it is natural to ask: What is life? There is no one definition of life that can encompass all living things. However, there are certain characteristics that all living things share:

- *order and organization*: The basic unit of life is the cell. It is capable of performing all activities of life. For single-celled organisms, this is the limit of their organization. For multicellular organisms, cells may be arranged in tissues, tissues arranged in organs, and organs arranged in systems. Living things are further organized into populations, communities, ecosystems and, ultimately, the biosphere (the combined regions of the earth in which organisms can live). A corollary to this topic is the organization and structure of the genetic material: all living things have nucleic acids as the storage mechanism for genetic information.
- *growth and development*: All living things grow and develop during their life. This may be as simple as a bacterium that increases in size or as complex as a fertilized egg that develops into an elaborate, multicellular organism.
- *reproduction*: Organisms must reproduce in order for the species to survive. The exact mode of reproduction may be different (for example, *asexual* verses *sexual* reproduction), but the outcome is the same: an increase in the number of organisms.
- *energy metabolism*: All living things require energy to survive. Various processes are necessary in order to supply this energy. First of all, organisms must gain nutrition: those that can make their own food are called *autotrophs*, all others are called *heterotrophs*. The nutrients must be converted into energy, which includes the process of *respiration*. Finally, waste products must be eliminated.
- *stimuli response and homeostasis*: The ability to respond to the environment, whether it be the external or the internal environment, is a vital function in all living things. Organisms must regulate their life processes based on what is happening in the environment.
- *evolution*: The ability to change, to mutate, is an important characteristic of life. Were it not for this ability, the vast diversity of life would not exist on this planet. For that matter, no life would exist at all.

E. Structure and function

Another topic which underlies all aspects of biology is the correlation between structure and function. If the structure is known, often the function can be determined, and vice versa. For example, knowing the amino acid sequence of a protein (the structure) can help predict how that protein functions in a cell. Or, as another example, if an animal has the ability to see (the function), then it must have the structures necessary to support that function (eyes, optic nerves, a region of the brain to interpret nerve impulses, etc.).

F. Using this review section

Remember: the ACT stresses your problem solving skills and your knowledge of basic biological concepts. Therefore, you will be better prepared for the test by understanding these concepts rather than by just memorizing various facts and terms. These review sections will help you in this endeavor. Study to understand the topics, not just to memorize them.

Chapter 1 Problems

Passage

Karposi's sarcoma (KS) is a cancer marked by purple tumors on the skin. Although extremely rare in the population, it is found in approximately 25% of gay men infected with HIV, the virus that causes AIDS. It has been suggested that KS itself is caused by a virus, the human herpesvirus 8 (HHV8). To help confirm this hypothesis, the following observations were made:

Observation 1:

At regular intervals over a two-year period, samples of blood were taken from gay men who tested positive for HIV at the beginning of the study. In 38 of the subjects, no KS developed, although 18% had antibodies against HHV8 in their blood samples. However, in 40 subjects who developed KS, 80% had HHV8 antibodies. In 11 of these men, HHV8 antibodies were detected from the beginning of the study, but 21 of the men developed HHV8 antibodies during the study. In these subjects, the antibodies appeared several months before the onset of KS.

Observation 2:

Individuals not known to have been infected with HIV were tested for antibodies against HHV8. In 141 blood donors, only 1% were found to test positive for the antibodies. In addition, 300 hemophiliacs who had regular blood transfusions were also examined. Three percent had HHV8 antibodies.

Observation 3:

In 176 patients who had syphilis, a sexually transmitted disease, 36 (or 20%) had antibodies to HHV8.

1. What conclusion can be drawn from these observations?
    A. Although HHV8 is associated with KS, it has yet to be proven that it causes KS.
    B. In observation 1, the fact that some individuals tested positive for HHV8 but did not develop KS proves this virus does not cause the disease.
    C. Individuals with syphilis will also develop KS.
    D. Hemophiliacs are at no risk of developing KS.

2. Which is the best hypothesis for the mode of transmission of HHV8?
    A. blood transfusions
    B. casual contact
    C. sexual transmission
    D. airborne particles

3. In another study, it was found that KS is prevalent in transplant patients taking drugs which suppress their immune system to prevent rejection of the new organ. This, along with the above evidence, indicates:
    A. a virus other than HHV8 causes KS.
    B. a weakened immune system is probably necessary for KS to develop.
    C. both A and B
    D. neither A nor B

4. Many researchers argue that viruses are not alive. Which of the following supports this hypothesis?
    I. Some viruses carry their genetic information in the form of RNA, not DNA.
    II. Viruses cannot reproduce by themselves.
    III. Viruses do not evolve; that is, they do not mutate or change.
    A. I only
    B. II only
    C. I and II only
    D. II and III only

Solutions

1. A.

No direct evidence is presented to confirm that HHV8 causes KS, although it appears to be associated with the disease. Answer B is not the best choice as observation 1 was based on a 2-year study: those who tested positive for HHV8 may have developed KS at a later date. A statement about all syphilis patients developing KS is not valid, even if HHV8 is truly the cause of the disease: only a certain percentage would be predicted to develop the disease. And, conversely, it cannot be stated that all hemophiliacs are safe from the disease either.

2. C.

KS is prevalent in individuals with HIV and syphilis, two sexually transmitted diseases. Although HIV can also be contracted through blood transfusions, it appears HHV8 cannot due the hemophiliac data in observation 2. Casual contact and airborne transmission can also be ruled out as HHV8 antibodies are rarely found in HIV negative blood donors.

3. B.

No evidence is given that transplant patients had or didn't have HHV8, so the virus as a cause of KS cannot be ruled out based on this statement. However, since these transplant patients have a weakened immune system, as is found in AIDS, it appears KS thrives under this condition.

4. B.

Although some may argue that one characteristic of life is the storage of genetic information in the form of DNA, numerous viruses do contain DNA. Also, one outstanding feature of many viruses is their rapid mutation rate. However, all viruses need the cellular machinery to replicate: they cannot reproduce on their own.

Biology Review 2
Biological Molecules

A. Introduction

The study of *biochemistry* specifically explores the structure and function of important molecules found in living organisms. All important biomolecules are *organic*, that is, based on the carbon atom. Such molecules are often called *macromolecules*, because they are relatively large in comparison with the molecules studied by traditional, *inorganic* chemistry. Biological macromolecules are often *polymers* -- molecules formed by the stepwise addition of smaller subunits (*monomers*). Four major classes of biological molecules have been identified, each with unique structural properties and different roles.

B. Carbohydrates

Carbohydrates get their name from the fact that they are composed of only three types of atoms in particular combinations. The term literally means "carbon and water", belying their atomic composition: $[C(H_2O)]n$. This means that only carbon, hydrogen, and oxygen are present, and there is usually twice as much hydrogen as oxygen or carbon. In animals, the major function of carbohydrates is to provide energy for the organism. The fundamental carbohydrate subunit is the *monosaccharide* (see Figure 2.1). Monosaccharides can exist alone, or can be polymerized into larger *disaccharides* (see Figure 2.2) and *polysaccharides*.

- *Monosaccharides:* These are the simplest carbohydrate subunits found in nature. Along with disaccharides, they have a sweet taste and have thus been referred to historically and nutritionally as *sugars* or *simple carbohydrates*. Many nutritional monosaccharides are six-carbon compounds, such as *glucose* (the body's favorite fuel molecule), *fructose* ("fruit sugar"), and *galactose*. Other important monosaccharides are the five-carbon sugars *ribose* and *deoxyribose*, part of the nucleotides that compose DNA and RNA.
- *Disaccharides*: Composed of two monosaccharide units joined by a *glycosidic* bond, these are also recognized as sugars or simple carbohydrates nutritionally. *Sucrose*, or common table sugar, consists of one glucose and one fructose subunit. *Lactose* ("milk sugar") is made up of one glucose and one galactose subunit. *Maltose* ("malt sugar") is composed of two glucose subunits. All of these molecules must be broken down into their constituent monosaccharides before they can be utilized by the body.
- *Polysaccharides*: Polysaccharides are made up of many, often hundreds, of monosaccharide subunits. In nature, all of the important polysaccharides are glucose polymers, differing only in their physical arrangement and the type of bonds that join the subunits. Because they do not taste sweet, they are referred to nutritionally as complex carbohydrates, and include such compounds as starch and fiber. *Starch* is an energy storage molecule found in plants, and often makes up a large part of the human diet in the form of grains and vegetables. Because it is a polymer of glucose, starch is broken down into glucose subunits to be used as fuel in our bodies. Fiber, or *cellulose*, is a structural polysaccharide, composing the cell walls of plants. Due to the nature of the glycosidic bonds joining the glucose subunits, however, most animals (including humans) are unable to digest it. *Glycogen* is very similar to starch, and is sometimes referred to as "animal starch". Animals often store excess glucose in this form in their livers and muscles as an energy reserve.

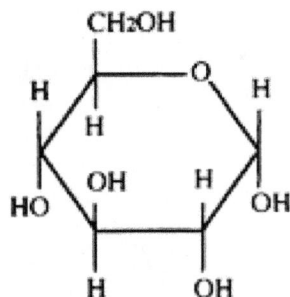

Figure 2.1: Glucose, a monosaccharide

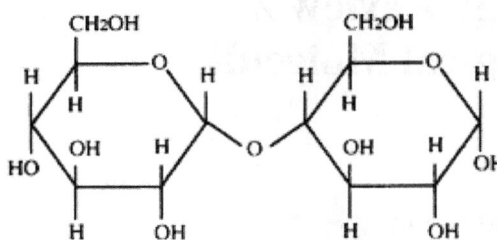

Figure 2.2: Maltose, a disaccharide

C. Lipids

Lipids are macromolecules grouped together for different reasons than are carbohydrates. They do not share any particularly constant chemical structure, but they do share an important physical property brought about by their basic chemical composition: lipids are biological molecules that do not dissolve appreciably in water. This is because they contain nonpolar covalent bonds, and are largely composed of hydrocarbon chains or rings. Since the body is a very watery place, lipids face a challenge, as they are not able to dissolve, and must be handled similarly with regard to their transportation and usage. Several types of lipids exist.

- *Triglycerides:* Triglycerides are composed of one molecule of the trialcohol *glycerol* covalently attached to three *fatty acid* molecules, hydrocarbon chains of varying lengths bonded through a terminal carboxylic acid group (see Figure 2.3). Traditionally called *fats* and *oils*, the major role of triglycerides in the body is long-term energy storage. Fats tend to be solid at room temperature because the fatty acid chains are *saturated*, which means they do not contain carbon-carbon double bonds. Chains containing double bonds are called *unsaturated*. The more unsaturated a fatty acid chain, the more liquid the triglyceride. Thus oils are often *polyunsaturated* triglycerides.

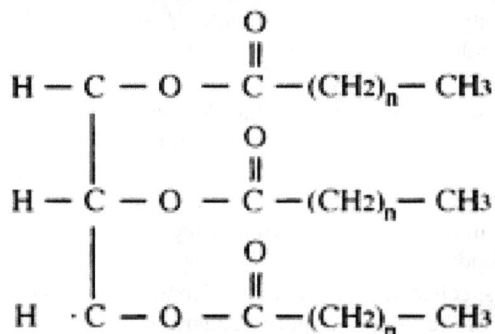

Figure 2.3: A saturated triglyceride

- *Phospholipids:* Phospholipids are a class of related compounds that structurally resemble triglycerides. In place of one of the fatty acids bonded to glycerol, however, is a hydrophilic molecule containing a phosphate group. This gives phospholipids a chemical "split personality". A portion of the molecule is *hydrophobic*, and unable to dissolve in water, while another portion is strongly charged and *hydrophilic*. This interesting combination of properties allows phospholipids to form the structures of plasma membranes and lipoproteins. They also act as emulsifying agents, allowing other lipids to dissolve more easily in the body.
- *Steroids:* Steroids are lipids that do not structurally resemble triglycerides, but are composed of a series of nonpolar rings (see Figure 2.4). *Cholesterol* is the most well known and prevalent steroid compound in the body. Cholesterol plays a role in the structure of cell membranes, as well as serving as the starting compound from which many others are synthesized. Other important steroids include the sex hormones and vitamin D.

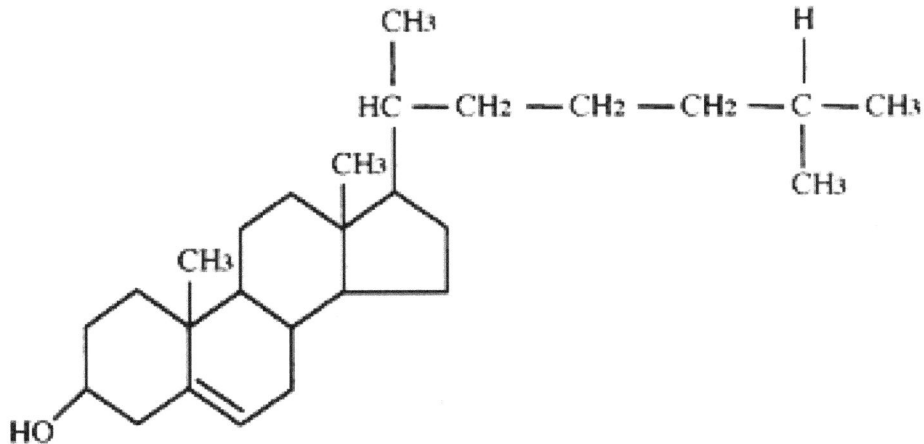

Figure 2.4: Cholesterol, a steroid lipid

D. Proteins

Proteins are polymeric macromolecules made up of subunits of *amino acids* (see Figure 2.5). As you might expect, amino acids all contain an amino group and a carboxylic acid group; what differentiates them is a variable portion referred to as the *R group*. In a sense, proteins are structurally simple, since every one consists of a number of amino acids linked by *peptide bonds*. There are twenty different amino acids, however, which can be linked together in any order, and a typical protein contains anywhere from 30 to 1,000 amino acids. Thus, a remarkably vast diversity of different proteins is possible, and this is exactly what we find. There are probably close to 100,000 different proteins in the human body, each with a different function. The remarkable diversity of protein function is made possible by the fact that once a chain of amino acids is linked together (also called a *polypeptide*), it undergoes additional folding so that the final protein molecule exists in a particular three-dimensional conformation. It is this shape that allows it to function in a unique way. We can identify four levels of protein structure (see Figure 2.6).

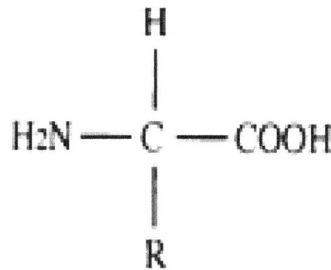

Figure 2.5: An amino acid

- *Primary structure:* A protein's primary structure simply refers to the linear order of amino acids it contains.
- *Secondary structure:* The secondary structure of a protein comes about due to local interactions, usually hydrogen bonds between atoms of adjacent amino and acid groups. Common secondary structures include the *alpha-helix* and the *beta-pleated sheet*.
- *Tertiary structure:* A protein's tertiary structure refers to its ultimate three-dimensional shape. It folds uniquely due to long range interactions between the R groups of the amino acids. Such interactions include hydrogen bonding, electrostatic interactions, and hydrophobic interactions. It is the tertiary structure that is responsible for the protein's function.
- *Quaternary structure:* Not all proteins have a quaternary structure; only those that consist of multiple polypeptide chains. Quaternary folding refers to the interactions between multiple chains of amino acids to achieve a protein that can only function in this complex state.

Proteins perform a vast array of functions, acting as enzymes, antibodies, structural components, hormones, and a wide variety of other functional entities. Well-known proteins include:

- *Hemoglobin*, which helps carry oxygen in the blood;
- *Collagen and Keratin*, major components of skin, hair, and connective tissues;
- *Insulin*, a hormone that regulates blood glucose levels;
- *Pepsin*, an enzyme that digests other proteins in the stomach;
- and others too numerous to list!

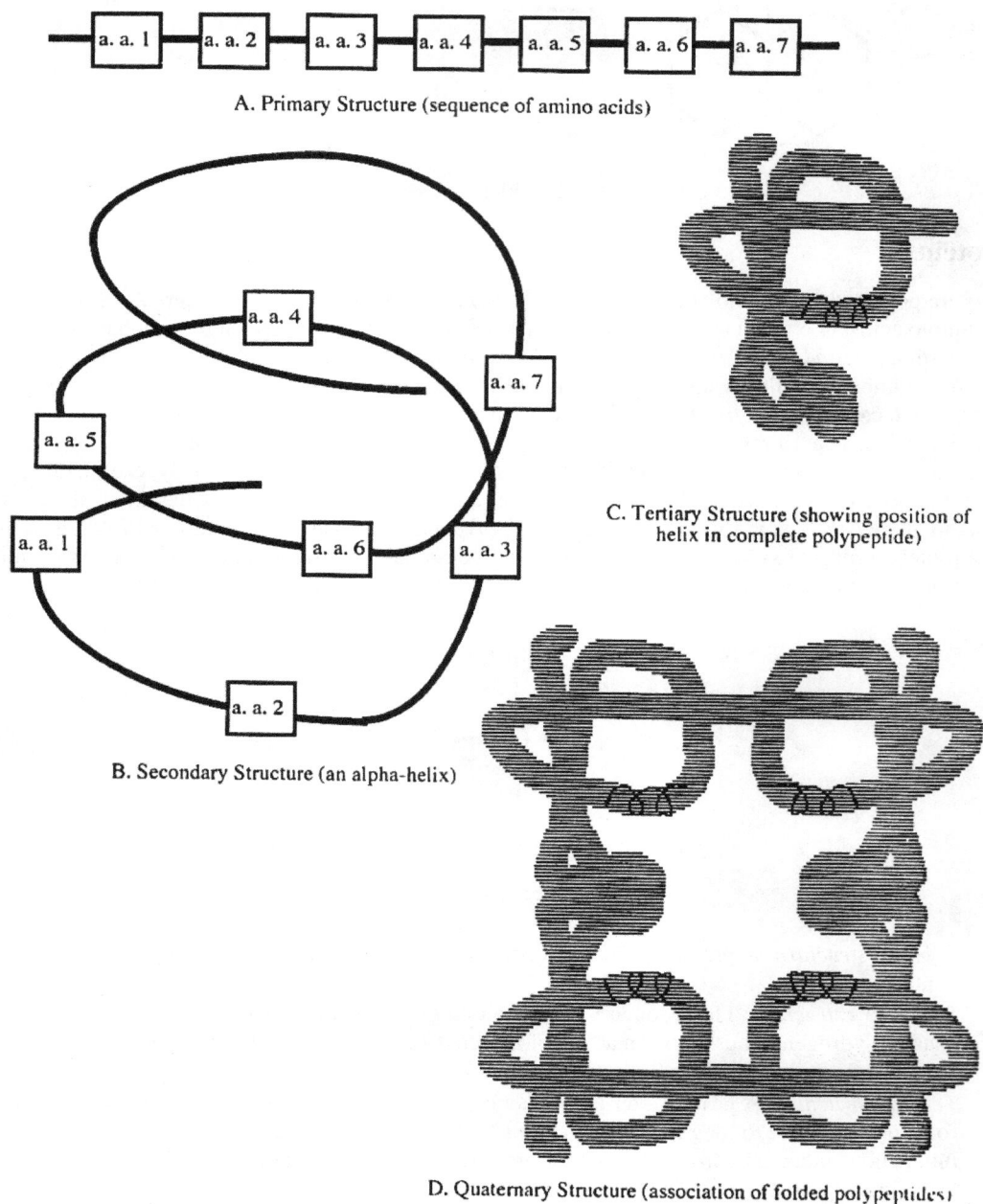

A. Primary Structure (sequence of amino acids)

B. Secondary Structure (an alpha-helix)

C. Tertiary Structure (showing position of helix in complete polypeptide)

D. Quaternary Structure (association of folded polypeptides)

Figure 2.6: Hierarchical folding of a hypothetical protein. aa: amino acid.

E. Nucleic Acids

Nucleic acids are also macromolecular polymers made up of a particular type of subunit, in this case, the *nucleotide* (see Figure 2.7). Nucleotides are more complex than the other subunits we have considered. Each one is made up of:

- a five-carbon sugar
- a nitrogenous base
- a phosphate group

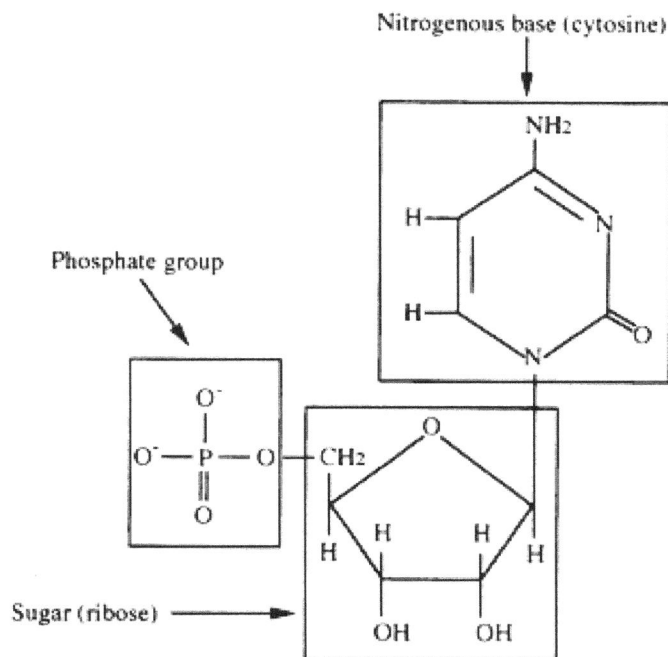

Figure 2.7: Cytidine monophosphate (CMP), a ribonucleotide

Two general types of nucleotides are recognized, depending upon which sugar they contain. Therefore, two major types of nucleic acids can be constructed, depending upon which kind of nucleotide is used.

- *DNA (deoxyribonucleic acid)* is made of nucleotides that contain the sugar *deoxyribose*.
- *RNA (ribonucleic acid)* is made of nucleotides that contain the sugar *ribose*.

Deoxyribonucleotides are of four types, depending upon which of four possible nitrogenous bases they contain. The four bases are:

- *Adenine*
- *Guanine*
- *Cytosine*
- *Thymine*

Ribonucleotides are of four types, depending upon which of four possible nitrogenous bases they contain. The four bases are

- *Adenine*
- *Guanine*
- *Cytosine*
- *Uracil*

As you can see, the bases are similar in DNA and RNA, with only one exception: the thymine of DNA is replaced by uracil in RNA. Due to their chemical structures, adenine and guanine are referred to as *purines*, while cytosine, thymine, and uracil are called *pyrimidines*.

Nucleotides are joined to one another by *phosphodiester bonds*, creating long chains. As with proteins, what makes one DNA molecule different from another is the sequence of bases that makes up the primary structure. This sequence carries encoded information, and is the basis for the "genetic code". In fact, the major functions of DNA and RNA all deal with the storage, transmission, and usage of genetic information.

It turns out that DNA normally exists in the form of a double helix in nature. Two antiparallel strands of nucleotides are held together by interactions between the bases to form a structure that resembles a twisted ladder. On the other hand, RNA is usually single-stranded.

Biology Review 2 Problems

1. Which of the following sugars does not need to undergo any enzymatic processing before it can be absorbed by the human digestive system?
   A. Lactose
   B. Maltose
   C. Galactose
   D. Sucrose

2. Which of the following is true of the differences between DNA and RNA?
   A. DNA contains a five-carbon sugar, while RNA contains a six-carbon sugar.
   B. DNA contains phosphate groups, while RNA does not.
   C. RNA contains the purine base adenine in place of the purine base guanine contained in DNA.
   D. RNA contains a different five-carbon sugar than DNA.

3. Which of the following statements is true regarding proteins?
   A. All proteins exhibit quaternary folding.
   B. The primary structure of a protein refers simply to the linear order of amino acids it contains.
   C. Not all proteins contain amino acids, only the ones that have extensive three-dimensional folding.
   D. All proteins are composed of one polypeptide chain.

4. Which of the following compounds would one expect to be liquid (with the lowest density) at room temperature?
   A. A saturated triglyceride
   B. A monounsaturated triglyceride
   C. A polyunsaturated triglyceride
   D. None of the above, as all would be solids at room temperature.

5. Which of the following carbohydrates is a polymer of the monosaccharide glucose?
   A. Cellulose
   B. Lactose
   C. Ribose
   D. None of the above

Solutions

1. C.
The human digestive system can only absorb sugars in the form of monosaccharides. Galactose is the only monosaccharide listed (glucose and fructose are the others). Lactose, maltose, and sucrose are all disaccharides, and must be enzymatically split before absorption.

2. D.
One of the major differences between DNA and RNA is that RNA contains the five-carbon sugar ribose, while DNA contains the five-carbon sugar deoxyribose. Both DNA and RNA contain phosphate groups, and both contain adenine and guanine. (RNA contains the pyrimidine base uracil instead of the pyrimidine base thymine.)

3. B.
Protein primary structure refers only to the linear order of amino acids. Secondary and tertiary folding are characteristics of all proteins, and involve interactions between various amino acids and ultimately cause specific three-dimensional folding. Both A and D are incorrect for related reasons; some proteins consist of more than one polypeptide chain, and it is only these proteins that exhibit quaternary folding (the association of multiple polypeptides). All proteins contain amino acids, by definition, so C cannot be correct.

4. C.
The major factor that determines whether or not a triglyceride will be solid or liquid at room temperature is the level of saturation of the fatty acids it contains. A completely saturated triglyceride is completely "filled" with hydrogen atoms, and is therefore linear in shape. This allows the molecules to pack closely and easily together, which results in a solid phase physical structure. We would call this type of molecule a "fat" or "saturated fat". A point of unsaturation occurs where a carbon-carbon double bond exists, and hydrogen atoms could potentially be added by hydrogenation. The more points of unsaturation, the more "kinks", or bends, the fatty acid will have. This makes packing together difficult, and we obtain a liquid, usually called an "oil".

5. A.
Cellulose is the only polysaccharide, or complex carbohydrate, listed. Lactose is a disaccharide, and ribose is a monosaccharide.

Biology Review 3
Enzymes and Energy

A. Introduction

The study of energy transformations, or *thermodynamics*, is covered in the chemistry. However, it is useful to remind ourselves that the laws of thermodynamics apply as much to living organisms and cells as they do to inanimate objects. Cells therefore had to evolve methods of obtaining and processing energy that are in accordance with the general principles of energy transformations. It is a general chemical principle that in order for a chemical reaction to proceed, a certain amount of energy, the *activation energy*, must be absorbed by the reactants to break the bonds already in place. One way of providing activation energy is simply to add heat to the reactants. This is what we do when we light a match to start a fire, which allows a combustion reaction to proceed. Living systems, however, cannot withstand the high temperatures necessary to overcome the activation energy barriers for biochemical reactions. Another method must exist to allow cells to facilitate and control chemical reactions. *Enzymes* are biological catalysts that facilitate reactions by lowering the necessary activation energy (see Figure 3.1).

B. Structure and Function of Enzymes

What types of molecules are enzymes and how do they work? Enzymes are almost always large protein molecules, folded into a particular three-dimensional configuration (see Chapter 2). Recently, some RNA molecules have been found to have enzymatic functions, but the vast majority of enzymes are proteins. The protein is folded so that a particular portion of the molecule, the *active site*, is accessible and forms a surface that attracts and aligns the reactant(s) in a favorable configuration. The reactant(s) are referred to as the enzyme's *substrate*, and when they associate with the enzyme, the intended reaction is able to proceed efficiently at the relatively low temperature of the cell. The amino acids that comprise the active site are close together in space, but may be far apart in the primary structure of the protein. Thus factors that disturb the overall folding of the protein may decrease or totally destroy the enzyme's ability to function.

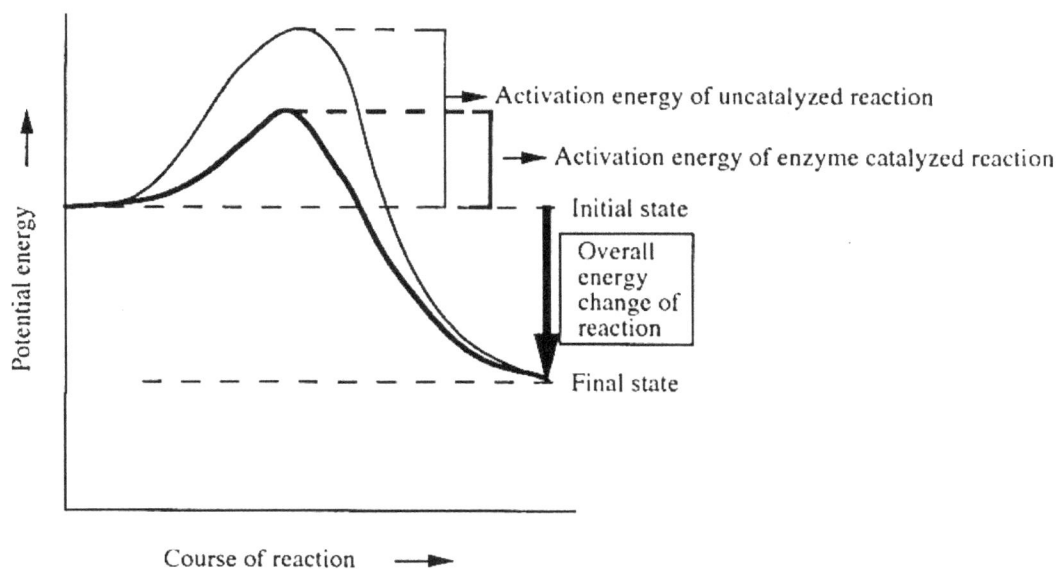

Figure 3.1: Activation energies of catalyzed and uncatalyzed reactions

The way the enzyme interacts with the substrate is only now becoming completely clear. Initially, the association was envisioned as a "lock and key" model, in which the shape of the active site matched the shape of the substrate exactly. This would account for their ability to come together easily. A more modern idea is the "induced fit" model, in which the active site and substrate have an affinity for each other, but the binding of the substrate may change the conformation of the active site, inducing a better fit and perhaps straining the bonds that will be broken in the substrate (see Figure 3.2).

Enzymes have great *specificity*, which means that one enzyme can catalyze only one reaction or a set of related reactions. This is of great benefit because it allows the cell to control different reactions independently, by regulating the activity or quantity of the enzyme involved. Furthermore, the enzyme is not permanently altered in any way by participating in the reaction, and so is "recyclable", being used over and over again. Therefore, enzymes typically do not need to be manufactured in large quantities.

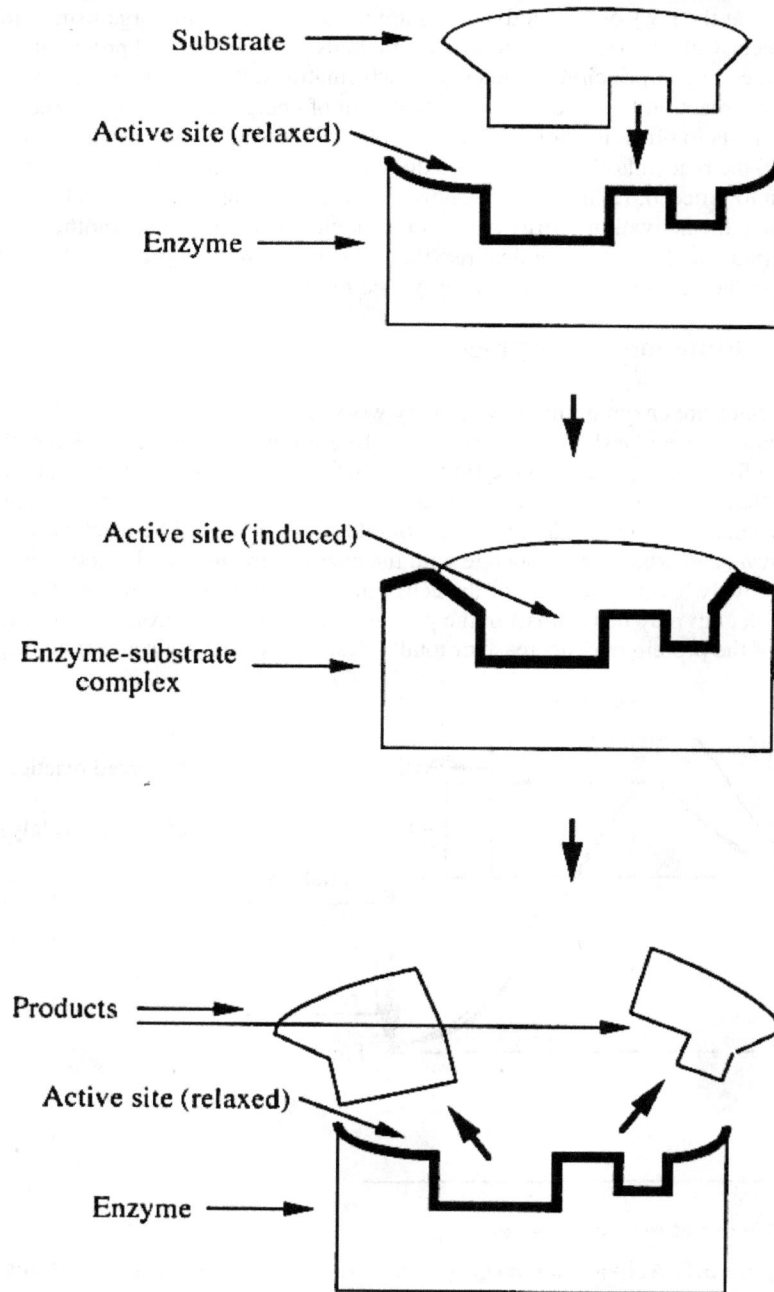

Figure 3.2: A model of enzyme action (induced fit)

C. Factors Affecting Enzyme Activity

Sometimes it takes more than just the presence of the substrate and the enzyme to allow a reaction to take place. Many enzymes require the presence of a *cofactor* to function. Simple cofactors are usually ionic minerals. For example, many enzymes require magnesium or zinc ions, for which they have binding sites, in order to act as catalysts. If the cofactor is not present, the enzyme will not work or will have reduced activity.

Sometimes the cofactor is a nonprotein organic molecule, called a *coenzyme*. The coenzyme plays a central role in the catalyzed reaction, often by accepting or providing electrons, and becoming *reduced* or *oxidized*, respectively, in the process. The vitamins of the B-complex group or their derivatives serve as coenzymes in the catabolic reactions that oxidize food molecules to release energy.

Environmental conditions also play a major role in determining an enzyme's effectiveness. In particular, temperature and pH influence enzyme activity enormously, and this is the major reason these parameters are so tightly controlled in humans. The temperature and pH of our bodies cannot vary considerably without dire consequences. Why are enzymes affected so profoundly by these environmental conditions?

Enzyme activity, in general, is reduced as the temperature drops and is increased as the temperature rises. If our body temperature becomes colder than normal, enzymes will function, but at slower and slower rates as the temperature falls. Ultimately, these rates will be too slow to sustain life. Raising the temperature will increase enzyme activity, to a certain point. If the temperature is too high, the interactions that maintain the shape of the enzyme will be disrupted, changing the overall shape of the protein and destroying, often irreversibly, the functionality of the active site. When an enzyme loses its activity due to disruption of its three-dimensional configuration, that enzyme has become *denatured*. Both low and high pH values can also denature enzymes by disrupting the interactions that hold them in their proper orientation, in this case by affecting the charges of various R groups and subsequently changing their affinities for each other. Every enzyme has an optimum pH and temperature at which it functions best; any deviation from these values will reduce its ability to catalyze reactions.

D. Control of Enzyme Activity

While ultimately the control of enzymes is accomplished genetically, several other processes affect when and how efficiently an enzyme works, so the cell carries out the desired reactions at the right times and rates. A classic example of an enzyme control mechanism is called *feedback inhibition*. Many enzymes, in addition to their active sites, contain binding sites for other molecules. These are referred to as *allosteric sites*, and enzymes that contain them are *allosteric enzymes*. If the allosteric site has an affinity for the product of the enzyme-catalyzed reaction, a feedback loop will automatically control how much of the product is produced. If product concentrations are low, the cell requires the reaction to proceed; little of the product exists to bind to the allosteric site, and the enzyme functions normally. As the reaction progresses, and enough of the product is made, it binds to the allosteric site. When this happens, the overall shape of the enzyme changes so that the active site is either hidden or disrupted, and the reaction will take place at a reduced rate or not at all. When product levels drop again, the product dissociates from the allosteric site, exposing the active site and allowing the reaction to resume. This process acts like a "thermostat", and is a common cellular strategy for regulating enzyme activity.

Sometimes molecules are present that act to inhibit an enzyme's function, and these are appropriately called *enzyme inhibitors*. *Competitive* inhibitors resemble the substrate, and thus compete with it for binding to the active site. *Non-competitive* inhibitors bind to an allosteric site, causing the enzyme's shape to change and affecting its function. Therefore, competitive inhibitors are less effective as the substrate concentration rises, while non-competitive inhibitors work regardless of the substrate concentration.

E. ATP as the Energy Currency of the Cell

Reactions that are *endergonic* require the input of energy. Cells must perform many endergonic reactions in order to remain alive; protein synthesis and DNA replication are just two examples. While enzymes are required to catalyze these reactions, they cannot provide the energy to drive them. Therefore, all endergonic reactions must be coupled to energy-releasing, or *exergonic*, reactions in order to proceed. While cells can ingest energy containing molecules in many forms (monosaccharides, fatty acids, amino acids, etc.), the energy contained in these molecules must be harvested and stored in a usable form by the cell. In almost all cases, this usable form of energy is the molecule *ATP (adenosine triphosphate),* the triphosphate form of the DNA nucleotide adenosine (see Figure 3.3). When the bond linking the terminal phosphate to the rest of the molecule is *hydrolyzed* (broken), *ADP (adenosine diphosphate)* and free phosphate are the products, and energy is released. Thus, this is an exergonic reaction. Many enzymes that catalyze endergonic reactions associate with ATP, and often contain *ATPase* (ATP hydrolyzing) activity in addition to their other catalytic capabilities. Thus, it is ATP that directly provides the energy required by enzymes to catalyze endergonic reactions. This intimate association of exergonic ATP hydrolysis with endergonic reactions is referred to as *coupling* of reactions. The next chapter addresses the process by which cells transform the chemical energy of food molecules into energy stored as ATP.

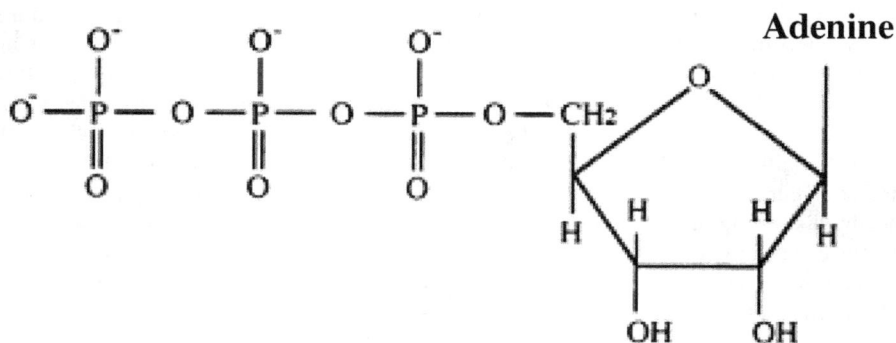

Figure 3.3: Adenosine triphosphate (ATP)

Biology Review 3 Problems

Passage

The reagent iodine potassium iodide (IKI) can be used to detect the presence of starch in a solution. IKI is normally light yellow in color; in the presence of starch it turns a deep blue. IKI can therefore be used to test for the presence and activity of the enzyme amylase, which breaks starch into maltose disaccharide units. (Maltose does not affect the color of IKI). Thus, if starch is initially present and mixed with IKI, the deep blue color created will begin to lighten and disappear if amylase is present as it begins to break down the starch to maltose. Using the same concentration of enzyme, the longer it takes for the blue color to disappear, the lower the amylase activity.

Amylase is usually present in vertebrates in two forms that work in different parts of the digestive tract. Salivary amylase, secreted in the saliva by the salivary glands, begins to break down starch in the mouth, which has a slightly acidic pH. Pancreatic amylase is manufactured by the pancreas and released into the small intestine, where it similarly breaks down remaining starch molecules to maltose.

The following tables show the results of an experiment designed to test the activities of one form of amylase at various pH's and temperatures.

pH	Time for blue color to disappear (in minutes)
3	10
6	1
9	5
12	30

Temperature (°C)	Time for blue color to disappear (minutes)
15	10
30	5
37	1
60	blue color never disappears

1. Which of the following is the enzyme being tested?
   A. Human salivary amylase
   B. Shark salivary amylase
   C. Human pancreatic amylase
   D. Shark pancreatic amylase

2. What is the most likely explanation for the observation that the blue color never disappears at 60° C?
   A. The chemical bonds in starch are stabilized by the heat so that it cannot break down even though the enzyme is highly active.
   B. Heat causes the IKI to become unable to stain the starch.
   C. The amylase has become denatured at this temperature.
   D. All of the above are reasonable explanations.

3. What is the optimal temperature and pH for the enzyme being tested?
   A. 15° C, pH 12
   B. 37° C, pH 6
   C. 37° C, pH 12
   D. 15° C, pH 6

4. The breakdown of starch is an exergonic reaction, which would occur spontaneously at temperatures of about 200° C. Amylase allows the reaction to proceed at physiological temperatures by:
   A. Increasing the activation energy for the reaction.
   B. Increasing the potential energy of the reactants.
   C. Changing the amount of energy released by the reaction.
   D. Lowering the activation energy of the reaction.

Solutions

1. A.
From the information given, we can tell that the optimal temperature and pH for the enzyme in question is 37 degrees C, pH 6 (the values at which the reaction proceeds to completion most quickly). As with the previous passage, the high temperature rules out any shark enzymes (choices B and D), and the mildly acidic pH could only exist in the mouth, not the small intestine (which is mildly alkaline).

2. C.
A human enzyme would likely become denatured at 60° C, as we saw in the last passage, and this would account for the lack of activity (the failure of the blue color to disappear implies that the starch remains present forever, since the enzyme cannot break it down). Choice A does not make sense, since heat will always tend to destabilize chemical bonds. Choice B could not be correct, because the IKI is still active; it is responsible for the blue color. Logically, this leaves out choice D, too.

3. B.
The explanation is the same as in question 1.

4. D.
This question is simply testing your general knowledge of how an enzyme functions in the context of this passage. Namely, an enzyme always functions by lowering the activation energy of a reaction (usually by providing a surface at the active site that puts the reactant(s) in a proper orientation and proximity). A is incorrect since it states the opposite of this idea. Choice B reflects what would happen if we were to facilitate a reaction by adding heat; the whole point of enzymes is to facilitate the reaction at a temperature that would not be harmful to life. With regard to choice C, an enzyme or any catalyst can never alter the change in free energy during a reaction, it can only affect the rate of that reaction! (This is a basic principle of thermodynamics and enzyme function).

Biology Review 4
Cellular Metabolism

A. Introduction

All living organisms, as we have already discussed, require energy in order to survive. Animals obtain this energy by ingesting compounds that contain potential chemical energy (carbohydrates, fats, and proteins), and metabolizing them so that energy is released and stored in the form of ATP (see Chapter 3). Energy is almost always used directly in the form of ATP. What processes occur at the cellular level to accomplish these energy transformations and create ATP? The net sum of all reactions that take place in a cell or organism is called *metabolism*, but often the term metabolism is used to refer to the *catabolic* (breaking down) reactions that make energy available to the cell. These are the reactions on which we will focus in this chapter.

B. Types of Metabolism

While in theory there are many pathways cells could utilize to metabolize their food, in nature, especially in animals, only a few pathways are used. While rather complex, these pathways vary little from organism to organism. Two major pathways are generally available to heterotrophic animal cells during metabolism: *aerobic respiration* and *fermentation*. Aerobic respiration is an oxygen requiring series of reactions, and is necessary in all vertebrates. Fermentation does not require oxygen, and while most vertebrates can perform fermentation reactions, it serves them mainly in emergencies when extra energy is needed. Only organisms such as yeast and some bacteria can live entirely by engaging in fermentation.

While many molecules may be metabolized (monosaccharides, amino acids, fatty acids, etc.), most cells prefer glucose as their source of fuel. It is therefore convenient to examine glucose metabolism as a model for the overall process, while keeping in mind that other molecules may also be used. Whichever pathways are ultimately utilized to harvest energy from glucose, they always involve the oxidation of glucose and always begin with a series of reactions called *glycolysis*. If the aerobic pathway is used, glycolysis is followed by two processes: the *Krebs cycle*, a cyclic series of reactions, and the *electron transport chain (ETC)*, where much ATP is synthesized. Let's look at each of these processes in more detail.

C. Understanding Glycolysis

Glycolysis, which literally means "splitting sugar", is a series of nine reactions that partially oxidize glucose and harvest two molecules of ATP. Figure 4.1 shows all nine of the reactions, but it is not necessary to attempt to memorize them all in this context. We are most interested in understanding the major events and the ultimate products of glycolysis.

Glycolysis occurs in the cytoplasm of animal cells, and it is important to remember three major aspects of the process:

- Glucose, a six-carbon compound, is ultimately broken down into 2 molecules of pyruvic acid, a three-carbon compound.
- Two molecules of ATP are produced when glycolysis is complete.
- Two molecules of the coenzyme *NAD⁺ (nicotinamide adenine dinucleotide)* are reduced to *NADH* when glycolysis is complete.

A few comments may be helpful at this point.

- Glycolysis is the first step in glucose metabolism in all vertebrates and almost all living cells.
- The ATP made during the process is generated by *substrate level phosphorylation*, which simply means a phosphate group attaches to ADP directly from one of the reactants in the pathway to make ATP.

• NAD$^+$ is a common coenzyme (see Chapter 3) that acts as an electron shuttle. It contains more potential energy when it is reduced to NADH than in its oxidized form, so the generation of NADH represents the temporary storage of energy.

D. The Anaerobic Option: Fermentation

Glycolysis occurs as the first step in glucose metabolism regardless of whether the cell is performing fermentation or aerobic respiration. It is important to note that glycolysis can never

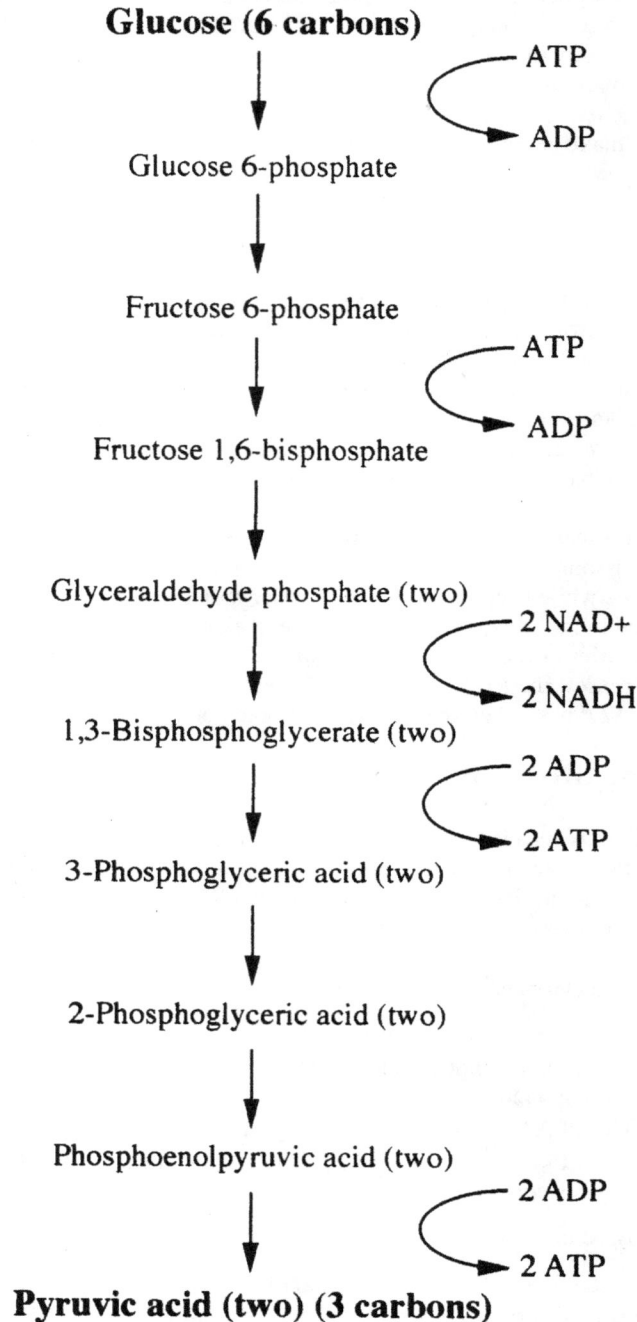

Glucose (6 carbons)

ATP → ADP

Glucose 6-phosphate

Fructose 6-phosphate

ATP → ADP

Fructose 1,6-bisphosphate

Glyceraldehyde phosphate (two)

2 NAD+ → 2 NADH

1,3-Bisphosphoglycerate (two)

2 ADP → 2 ATP

3-Phosphoglyceric acid (two)

2-Phosphoglyceric acid (two)

Phosphoenolpyruvic acid (two)

2 ADP → 2 ATP

Pyruvic acid (two) (3 carbons)

Figure 4.1: A summary of glycolysis

occur alone. It must be coupled to other reactions to be useful. Since fermentation is a comparatively simple process, we will examine it first. If a cell performs fermentation, no oxygen is required, but the pyruvic acid generated in glycolysis must be further processed. While countless variations exist, two major types of fermentation are common (see Figure 4.2):

- In *ethanol fermentation*, pyruvic acid is broken down into ethanol (a two-carbon compound) and carbon dioxide (CO_2). This type of fermentation is especially prevalent in yeast, and is utilized in many commercial processes, including the baking of bread and the making of alcoholic beverages.
- In *lactic acid* fermentation, the atoms of pyruvic acid are rearranged to form lactic acid (another three-carbon compound). This type of fermentation is carried out by vertebrates, usually in their muscle tissues. During heavy exertion, not enough oxygen may be available to supply ATP needs via the aerobic pathway.

A. Ethanol fermentation

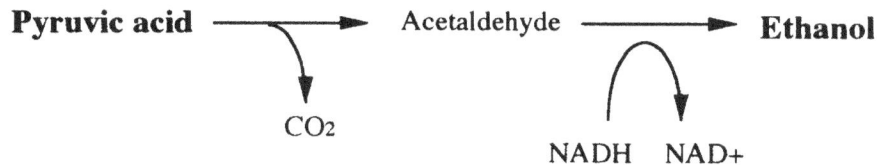

Pyruvic acid ⟶ Acetaldehyde ⟶ **Ethanol**

CO_2

NADH   NAD+

B. Lactic Acid fermentation

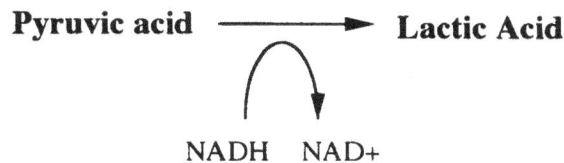

Pyruvic acid ⟶ **Lactic Acid**

NADH   NAD+

Figure 4.2: a summary of fermentation reactions

It is important to note in examining Figure 4.2 that no additional ATP is produced by either of the fermentation reactions. Why, therefore, must they occur? The answer is simple: the two molecules of NADH formed during glycolysis are oxidized back to NAD^+ during the fermentation reactions. If this did not occur, all of the NAD^+ in a cell would quickly be used up, and glycolysis could no longer continue. This explains why glycolysis can never "stand alone".

E. The Aerobic Option: Cellular Respiration

Vertebrates must perform *aerobic cellular respiration* in order to obtain enough ATP to live. This means that they need a constant supply of oxygen (a major participant in the reactions), and produce carbon dioxide as a waste. This explains the need for breathing, or *physiological* respiration. The reactions of aerobic respiration take place in the *mitochondria*, so, after glycolysis, the pyruvic acid to be processed must be transported to this organelle. We should note here that the mitochondrion (singular) is surrounded by two membranes; this creates an *intermembrane space*. In addition, the inner membrane is folded to increase its surface area, and the folds are referred to as *cristae*. The inner, liquid portion of the mitochondria is called the *matrix*.

F. The Krebs Cycle

Pyruvic acid must now enter a cyclic series of reaction, the *Krebs cycle*, also known as the *citric acid cycle* or the *TCA (tricarboxylic acid) cycle*. The reactions of the Krebs cycle take place in the mitochondrial matrix, and are summarized in Figure 4.3. Again, it is inadvisable to attempt to memorize all of these reactions. Before pyruvic acid can enter the cycle, it must undergo some initial preparatory steps:

- Pyruvic acid is oxidized, releasing one molecule of CO_2 and a two-carbon acetyl group.
- The acetyl group is attached to a molecule called *Coenzyme A*, to form *acetyl CoA*.
- In the process, a molecule of NAD^+ is reduced to NADH.

It is important to note that carbon atoms from pyruvic acid can enter the Krebs cycle only in the form of acetyl CoA.

Next, the acetyl group is donated to the four-carbon molecule *oxaloacetic acid* to form *citric acid*, a six-carbon compound. The citric acid is subsequently broken down, in a series of steps, back to oxaloacetic acid. As with glycolysis, there are three main points to keep in mind regarding the Krebs cycle. Specifically, for each turn of the cycle:

- Two carbons enter the cycle as an acetyl group, and two carbons are released as carbon dioxide.
- One molecule of ATP is harvested.
- Three molecules of NAD^+ are reduced to NADH, and one molecule of another coenzyme, *FAD*, is reduced to $FADH_2$.

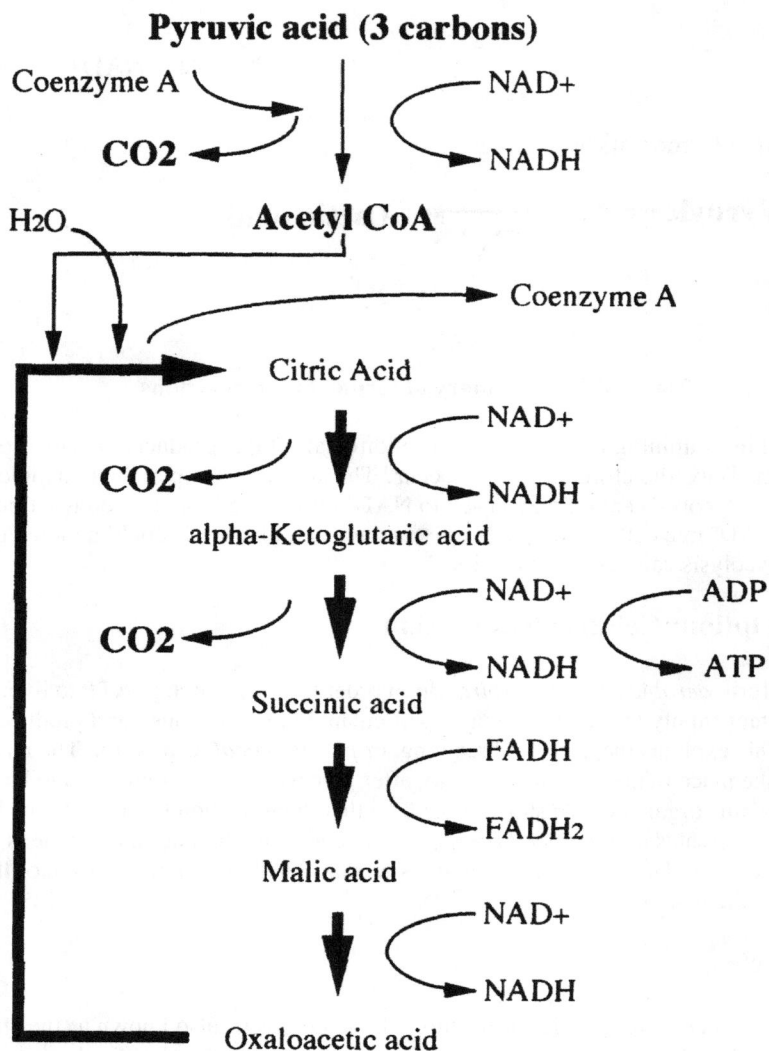

Figure 4.3: Highlights of the Krebs cycle

It is important to remember that for every glucose molecule we started with, two molecules of pyruvic acid were created. Since we have only been keeping track of one pyruvic acid molecule as it travels through the Krebs cycle, we must multiply our totals by two if wish to know the yield per molecule of glucose. If we consider the preparatory events with those of the Krebs cycle itself, we can summarize as follows:

- For each three-carbon molecule of pyruvic acid that enter the mitochondria, three molecules of carbon dioxide are released, for a total of six carbon dioxides. This is the source of the CO_2 we exhale.
- A total of two molecules of ATP are harvested.
- Overall, eight molecules of NAD^+ are reduced to NADH, and two FAD molecules are reduced to $FADH_2$.

G. The Electron Transport Chain: ATP Harvesting

After the Krebs cycle, the original glucose molecule has been completely oxidized, which means that its potential energy has been released. One glucose molecule theoretically contains enough potential energy to manufacture close to one hundred molecules of ATP. It is clear that we have not stored a significant amount of the released energy in this form yet. Where is the energy?

The energy is temporarily residing in the reduced coenzyme molecules NADH and $FADH_2$. During the final stages of respiration, *the electron transport chain*, these coenzymes will donate electrons to a series, or chain, of carriers, and will become oxidized in the process, back to NAD^+ and FAD (the coenzymes can then go back and participate in glycolysis and the Krebs cycle). The carriers are physically located in the inner mitochondrial membrane, and include *cytochrome* proteins, among other molecules. As electrons are passed down the chain, energy is released; the final electron acceptor is molecular oxygen (O2), which is reduced and converted to water as it accepts electrons (this is where the oxygen we inhale is actually used). The energy released is temporarily stored and ultimately used to make ATP by *oxidative phosphorylation*. The *chemiosmotic model* explains how ATP is produced this way (see Figure 4.4). The model highlights three major points:

- The reduced coenzymes NADH and $FADH_2$ ultimately react with oxygen by donating electrons through a series of intermediaries. This reaction causes oxidation of the coenzymes to NAD^+ and FAD, and reduction of oxygen to water. A large amount of energy is released in the process. If the intermediate carriers did not exist, all of the energy would be released at once, which would be difficult for the cell to control and manage.
- As energy is slowly released, it is used to pump *protons* (H^+ ions) from the matrix into the intermembrane space by active transport. This establishes an *electrochemical proton gradient* which stores the energy that has been released. This gradient can be used to do work.
- The enzyme *ATP synthase* is embedded in the inner membrane, and protons diffuse through a channel in this protein back into the matrix. As the protons "fall" through the enzyme, the energy they release is used to do work: the *phosphorylation* (addition of a phosphate group) of ADP to make ATP.

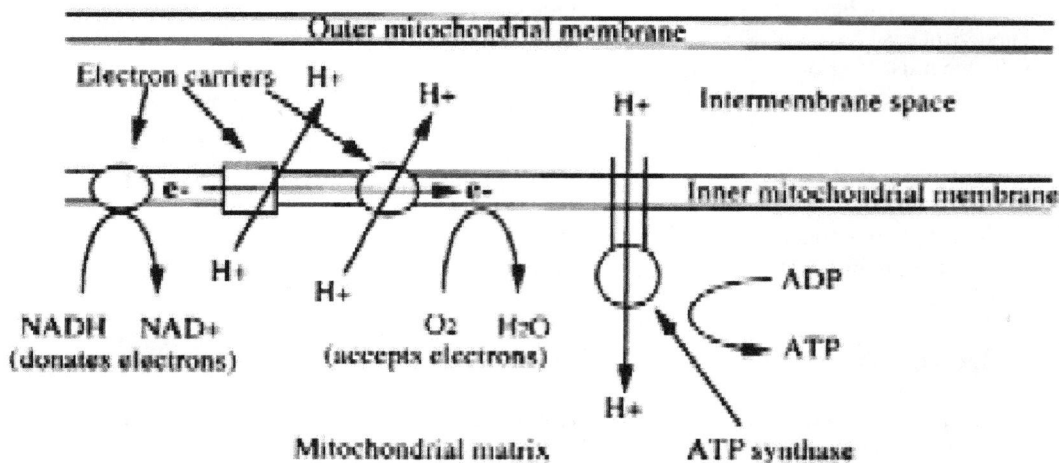

Figure 4.4: The electron transport chain and oxidative phosphorylation

When all is said and done, 32 ATP molecules are harvested by the electron transport chain from all of the reduced cofactors generated through glycolysis and the Krebs cycle. If we add this to the 2 ATP molecules obtained from glycolysis and the 2 produced in the Krebs cycle, we come up with a grand total of 38 molecules of ATP harvested. However, the net amount is 36 ATP molecules because some energy is used to transport pyruvic acid into the mitochondria.

H. Overall Energy Harvest

Given that glucose, if burned in a calorimeter, releases 686 kilocalories/mole, and ATP hydrolysis usually yields approximately 7 kilocalories/mole, we can calculate the efficiency of aerobic respiration. If we harvest 36 ATP molecules and multiply by 7 kilocalories/mole, we have obtained 252 kilocalories/mole of glucose burned. This represents an efficiency of 252/686, or approximately 37%. While far from perfect, it is certainly preferable to the efficiency of fermentation, which by the same logic is approximately 2%. Where does the rest of the energy go? The first law of thermodynamics tells us that energy can never be created or destroyed, so it must have been transformed into another type of energy. In fact, it was converted to heat, and is in effect "wasted" energy. Birds and mammals, however, have figured out another use for this energy so that it is not completely wasted: it is the major source of internal heat used to maintain a relatively high body temperatures.

I. Summary of Aerobic Respiration

After looking at all of the details of respiration, we can formulate a net equation that takes them all into account. That equation is:

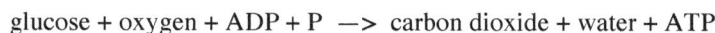

glucose + oxygen + ADP + P —> carbon dioxide + water + ATP

We can make this a proper, balanced chemical equation:

$$C_6H_{12}O_6 + 6O_2 + 36ADP + 36P \longrightarrow 6CO_2 + 6H_2O + 36 \text{ ATP}$$

Biology Review 4 Problems

Passage

Many chemicals that are poisons exert their toxic effects by interfering with some aspect of aerobic respiration, usually involving the electron transport chain of the mitochondria. Three such poisons are cyanide, 2,4-dinitrophenol, and the antibiotic oligomycin.

Cyanide is a potent and deadly human poison. It causes its effects by binding to one of the electron carriers and inhibiting the passage of electrons to oxygen, so that electron transport, proton-pumping, and ATP synthesis stop virtually instantaneously.

2,4-dinitrophenol is also a deadly poison to humans. It is an example of the general class of poisons known as "uncouplers", which allow protons to pass back from the intermembrane space to the matrix without passing through the ATP synthase enzyme. Electron transport and proton pumping continue, but ATP is not made. Such uncouplers are also called ionophores.

Oligomycin, an antibiotic, is not deadly to humans, but does interfere with respiration, which is how it kills bacteria, and accounts for its side effects in humans. It is representative of a group of poisons that directly inhibit ATP synthase by blocking the passageway for protons. As with the uncouplers, electron transport and proton pumping continue, but ATP is not made (although for a different reason).

Use the information above, the following observations, and your knowledge of respiration when answering the questions.

Observation 1

When a person breathes a particular deadly poison (compound A), the following effects are observed. Clinically, body temperature quickly increases, causing profuse sweating, and ultimate death. At the biochemical level it is noted that normal to greater than normal amounts of oxygen are used, and normal to greater amounts of carbon dioxide are produced. The pH of the mitochondrial intermembrane space does not change appreciably; if it does, it may increase slightly.

Observation 2

When a person ingests a particular toxin (compound B), the following effects are observed. At the biochemical level, it is noted that the Krebs cycle continues to function, producing NADH, and that the NADH is oxidized back to NAD+ as it donates electrons to the electron transport chain. Strikingly, the pH of the mitochondrial intermembrane space is noted to drop significantly.

1. The toxin ingested that is referred to as compound A in observation 1 is likely to be:
    A. Cyanide.
    B. 2,4-dinitrophenol.
    C. Oligomycin.
    D. The information presented does not allow differentiation of the three.

2. The toxin ingested that is referred to as compound B in observation 2 is likely to be:
    A. Cyanide.
    B. 2,4-dinitrophenol.
    C. Oligomycin.
    D. The information presented does not allow differentiation of the three.

3. During cyanide poisoning, which of the following molecules would increase its concentration dramatically?
    A. NAD+
    B. NADH
    C. Carbon dioxide
    D. FAD

4. In the 1950s, certain weak uncoupling agents were used to promote weight loss. They worked very well; in fact, they worked so well at "burning calories" that many people died from using them and they were pulled from the market. Which of the following statements explains how uncouplers could cause weight loss?

    A. Uncouplers allow ATP to be made but prevent its transport out of the mitochondria, thus uncoupling its manufacture from its use.

    B. Uncouplers increase the metabolic rate, and allow caloric energy temporarily stored in reduced coenzymes to remain "unharvested" as ATP; it is simply released as heat.

    C. Uncouplers prevent oxygen from accepting electrons, so that ATP is not made, and energy is not available to digest and absorb food.

    D. Uncouplers, due to their toxic effects, cause appetite suppression, and lower the overall metabolic rate.

Solutions

1. B.

The important information to remember when answering both questions 1 and 2 is the following: First, with cyanide poisoning, electron transport stops completely; this causes a buildup of NADH, and the ultimate shutdown of all previous processes, including the Krebs cycle and glycolysis, due to the unavailability of NAD+. Cyanide poisoning would therefore not allow any oxygen to be used up or carbon dioxide to be manufactured. In addition, no energy is released, as all processes are stopped. Since ATP synthase is still functioning, the proton gradient will eventually disappear, causing the pH in the intermembrane space to rise dramatically, as equilibrium with the matrix is reached. With 2,4-dinitrophenol, or any uncoupler, electron transport continues, and so do oxygen consumption and carbon dioxide evolution. Since the membrane is leaky to protons, they will flow back to the matrix without making ATP; the energy released will be dissipated as heat, which accounts for the increased body temperature. To the extent the proton gradient is relieved, the pH will rise in the intermembrane space. With an ATP synthase inhibitor like oligomycin, again, oxygen will continue to be used and carbon dioxide produced, as electron transport will continue. Since protons cannot re-enter the matrix, however, the gradient will be come steeper and steeper, and the pH in the intermembrane space will drop dramatically as it becomes very acidic.

So, the high body temperature of the person from observation 1, coupled with continued oxygen consumption and the relatively unchanged or alkaline pH of the intermembrane space, identifies the poisoning agent as an uncoupler.

2. C.

Refer to the information from question 1. The dropping pH in the intermembrane space alone allows identification of this toxin as an ATP synthase inhibitor.

3. B.

Again, refer to the information from question 1. NADH will build up as electron transport is discontinued, as it has no place to give up electrons. NAD+ and FAD, the oxidized forms of coenzymes, will eventually decrease in amount until there are none left. Carbon dioxide will ultimately stop being produced, so its concentration will not change very much.

4. B.

As we have seen from the solution to question 1, uncouplers function by allowing the inner mitochondrial membrane to become permeable to protons, and we know from question six that energy is released but not used (harvested as ATP); it is simply dissipated as heat. Choice A is incorrect because uncouplers decrease the formation of ATP; choice C is incorrect because it describes a cyanide-like poison that shuts down electron transport. Choice D makes little sense; if anything, an uncoupler would cause the metabolic rate to rise.

Biology Review 5
DNA Structure and Function

A. Introduction

Perhaps the most important molecule in all of biology is *DNA, deoxyribonucleic acid*.

All living things contain DNA as the storage unit of genetic information. The DNA molecule in every organism has the exact same structure and function. How it is copied by the cell (*replication*) and how it is interpreted (*transcription* and *translation*) may differ in some details; however, the basics are the same in every living entity. We will concentrate on eukaryotic cells in this chapter.

B. The Function of DNA

Earlier, in Chapter 1, we considered the relationship between structure and function. We will now see how the structure of DNA directly relates to its function. In brief, the functions of DNA are

- to carry the genetic information of the organism;
- to control the development of the cell and the organism;
- to direct the function of the cell, including its reproduction and metabolism.

Since DNA has the same structure in all organisms, and it dictates the function of the cell, it is natural to wonder what makes species different. It is not the basic structure of the DNA, but rather the exact arrangement of the components of DNA that determines this difference. In fact, this arrangement not only accounts for the difference among species, but also for the uniqueness of individuals in the same species.

C. The Chemical Structure of DNA

By the early 1950s, it was well known that DNA was a polymer made up of monomers called *nucleotides*. Each nucleotide consists of three chemical groups (see Figure 5.1, see also Chapter 2):

- a 5 carbon sugar, *deoxyribose*;
- a nitrogen rich *base* attached to the first carbon of the sugar;
- a *phosphate group* attached to the fifth carbon of the sugar.

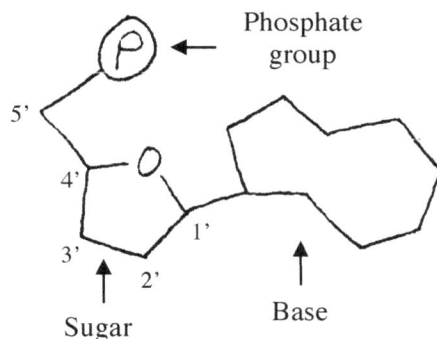

Figure 5.1: General structure of a nucleotide

Four types of nucleotides exist, and each differ only at the nitrogenous base:

- *adenine* (*A*),
- *cytosine* (*C*),
- *guanine* (*G*) and
- *thymine* (*T*).

In 1953, James Watson and Francis Crick proposed a model for the structure of DNA by considering a wide variety of data from other researchers. In particular, two observations became crucial to their model:

- Erwin Chargaff had discovered that, in every molecule of DNA, the amount of *A* was always equal to the amount of *T*, and the amount of *C* was always equal to the amount of *G*.
- Rosiland Franklin had obtained X ray diffraction data that showed DNA exists in a *double helix*, similar in structure to a winding staircase.

From this information, Watson and Crick were able to correctly determine the structure of the polymer (see Figure 5.2).

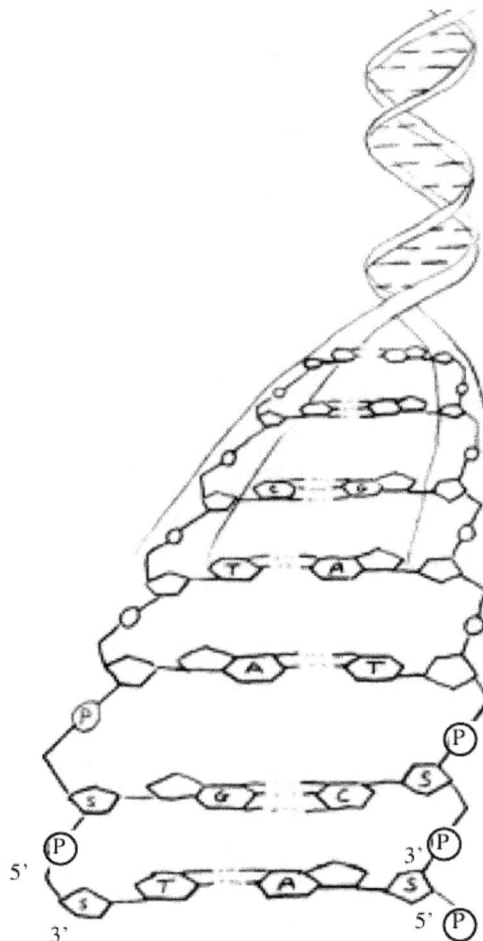

Figure 5.2: The structure of DNA. S: sugar; P: phosphate; A, C, G and T: nitrogenous bases

The monomers of DNA are linked together via the sugar and the phosphate groups in the nucleotides. This is often called the *sugar-phosphate backbone*, and the bond that forms between the monomeric nucleotides is called *a phosphodiester bond*. Remember how the phosphate group is attached to the fifth carbon on the deoxyribose? The phosphate from one nucleotide attaches to the sugar of another nucleotide at the third carbon. This actually gives DNA a direction, like north and south, except we call it 5' and 3' (pronounced "5 prime" and "3 prime," see Figure 5.2). We'll talk more about this attachment a little later.

One strand (polymer) of DNA is usually found attached to another strand of DNA, forming a double stranded molecule. The bases on each strand bond to form a pair. This pairing follows a strict rule: *A* always pairs with *T*, and *C* always pairs with *G* (this is what Chargaff saw). We call this *complementary base pairing*. When the strands of DNA come together to form a double strand, the structure twists around itself, creating a double helix (see Figure 5.2). By knowing the *sequence* (arrangements of nucleotides) of one strand, the sequence of the second strand can be determined. It is this sequence that determines the structure and function of the cell and the organism.

The base pairs are held together by *hydrogen bonds*, weak bonds that form between hydrogens and oxygens or hydrogens and nitrogens. The G-C base pairs form 3 hydrogen bonds while the A-T base pairs form only 2. This makes the G-C pairs inherently stronger and more stable.

Another interesting feature of the double helix is that, in order for the bases to pair correctly, the two strands of DNA must run in opposite directions, or in an antiparallel fashion. This means that the 5' end of one strand pairs with the 3' end of the other strand (see Figure 5.2).

D. Chromosome Structure

Before going any further, let's look at the structure of the DNA as it exists in a cell. If you could remove the DNA from one of your cells and stretch it out, it would be approximately one meter long. How can so much DNA fit into a microscopic cell? The answer is in the packaging. DNA is highly organized into a structure called a *chromosome*. The chromosome is made up of DNA and proteins. The DNA double helix is wrapped around proteins known as *histones*, and the histones form complexes called *nucleosomes* (see Figure 5.3). The nucleosomes are further packaged into *supercoiled loops* sometimes called *solinoids*. These are packaged into chromosomes.

Human cells contain 23 pairs of chromosomes (46 total). Certain genetic diseases can be diagnosed by examining the chromosome. This is what is done when a pregnant woman has an amniocentesis. The field of biology that studies chromosomes is called *cytogenetics*.

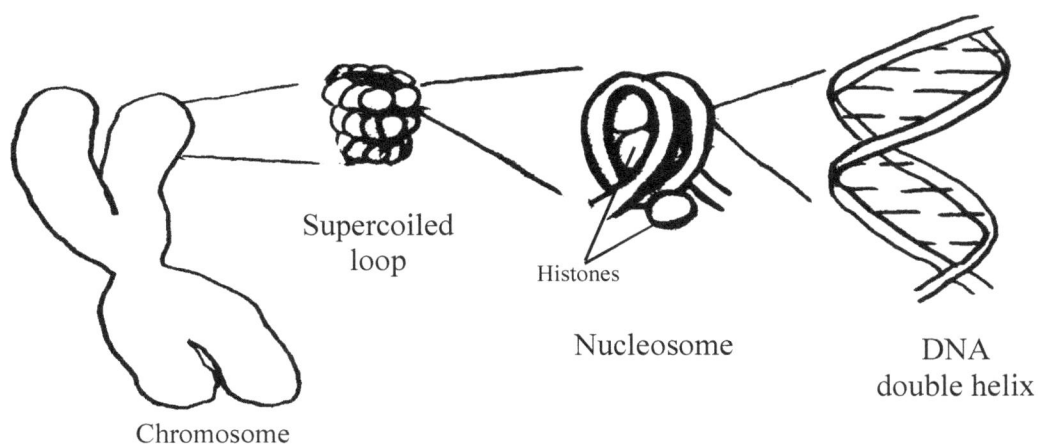

Figure 5.3: Levels of DNA packaging

E. RNA Structure

This is an opportune time to examine the structure of *RNA (ribonucleic acid),* a molecule closely related to DNA. RNA is also a polymer of nucleotides, but differs from DNA in three major respects:

- RNA is usually single stranded, meaning it is not usually found base paired with another RNA molecule;
- the sugar in an RNA nucleotide is *ribose*, not deoxyribose. The difference is found on the 2' carbon of the sugar: ribose has an OH group attached while deoxyribose has only an H;
- a nitrogenous base called *uracil* (*U*) substitutes for thymine (T) in RNA. Uracil is similar in structure to thymine, and will base pair with adenine (this will become important when we discuss transcription and translation).

F. Replication

When a cell divides, the new cell (or *daughter* cell) must receive the same genetic information as the original cell, or the daughter cell will not function correctly. Therefore, before a cell divides, the DNA must be copied, or *replicated*, faithfully. It must also be transferred to the new cell. This entire process is known as *mitosis*. The details of how DNA is replicated will be discussed here.

The beauty of the structure of DNA is that it simplifies its own replication. Due to the base pairing rules, each strand of the helix serves as a template to make a new strand. The copy is the complement of the template, and is identical to the strand originally bound to the template. This type of replication is referred to as *semiconservative*. Let's consider the details.

G. The Replication Machinery

One of the most important concepts to remember is that polymers of nucleotides can be built only in one direction, in the 5' to 3' direction. The phosphate from one nucleotide binds to the 3' carbon of the sugar in the preceding nucleotide (refer to Figure 5.2). The process can never occur in reverse.

Before the DNA can be replicated, the two strands must dissociate (this is sometimes referred to as unzipping, as the DNA double helix resembles a zipper). The physical point at which the DNA is unzipped is referred to as the *replication fork* (see Figure 5.4).

The main enzyme involved in replication is called *DNA polymerase*. It binds to each single stranded DNA chain and builds a complementary strand by reading the template strand. We will now examine some of the details of this process.

H. Leading and Lagging Strand Synthesis

Since DNA is synthesized from 5' to 3', the template DNA must be read from 3' to 5' (remember the antiparallel structure of the double helix). This causes a problem at the replication fork: one strand can be copied *continuously* as the fork extends, but the other strand must be copied *discontinuously*. This discontinuous replication occurs in the following manner (see Figure 5.4):

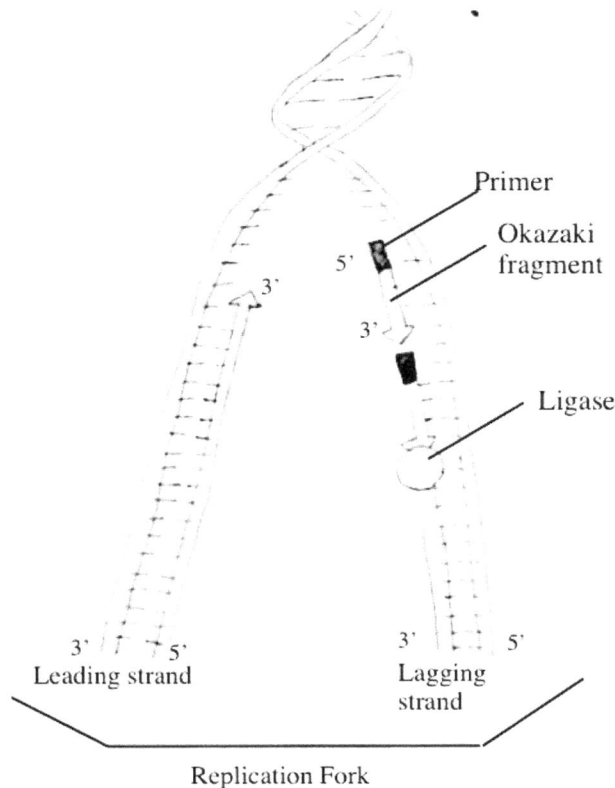

Figure 5.4: DNA replication

1. An RNA *primer* (a short stretch of nucleotides) attaches to one strand via complementary base pairing. The primer is synthesized by a *primase* enzyme.

2. The DNA polymerase begins synthesizing a new, complementary strand in the 5' to 3' direction. The strands made between RNA primers are known as *Okazaki fragments*.

3. The primers are degraded and the Okazaki fragments are linked together by the enzyme *DNA ligase*.

The strand that is synthesized continuously is called the *leading strand*. The other strand, synthesized discontinuously, is referred to as the *lagging strand*.

I. Proofreading and Repair

Everyone makes mistakes, and so does DNA polymerase. When this enzyme puts the wrong nucleotide into the growing chain, the result is a *mutation* which changes the genetic make up of an organism. Therefore, mistakes cannot be tolerated.

Fortunately, DNA polymerase has another ability besides synthesizing DNA strands: it also proofreads its work. If an error is detected, the enzyme cuts out the incorrect nucleotide and replaces it with the correct one.

In addition to random errors during replication, DNA can be mutated by other factors, such as UV light and cancer causing agents (*carcinogens*). If these mutations are not fixed, the function of the cell will be altered. This may cause the cell to die, or to grow in an unregulated fashion (cancer). Many repair mechanisms exist in the cell to detect and correct mutations, and more often than not they work just fine.

Biology Review 5 Problems

Passage (Questions 1-4)

The Watson and Crick model of the structure of DNA eloquently suggested the method of DNA replication. The double helical nature, and the complementary base pairing, implied that one strand of DNA provided the information for making the other strand. Once the strands of DNA separated, each would be used as a template to make a new, complementary strand. Therefore, the two resulting strands of DNA would contain both an old strand and a new strand. This is known as the *semiconservative* theory of replication. The *conservative* theory stated that one double helix would contain only the newly synthesized DNA while the other would contain only the original strands.

In 1958, Matthew Meselson and Franklin Stahl confirmed the semiconcervative model. They grew the bacterium *E. coli* for many generations in a heavy isotope of nitrogen, ^{15}N. The isotope was incorporated into the DNA.

The bacteria were then placed in medium that contained only the light isotope of nitrogen, ^{14}N. The bacteria were sampled over a period of time. Their DNA was extracted and subjected to centrifugation techniques, which would separate the DNA based on density.

DNA containing solely ^{15}N was "heavy" whereas DNA containing solely ^{14}N was "light". After one round of division in the medium containing ^{14}N, all the DNA was found to be intermediate in size, between the light and heavy types.

This "intermediate" DNA was further analyzed. The hydrogen bonds between the base pairs were broken so the DNA was single stranded. These strands were then centrifuged. Half of the single stranded DNA was in the heavy form, and half was in the light form.

1. If the replication theory suggested by Watson and Crick's model was correct, then the density of the double stranded DNA after 2 rounds of replication in ^{14}N medium would be:
    A. half heavy, half light
    B. half heavy, half intermediate
    C. half intermediate, half light
    D. all intermediate

2. ^{14}N and ^{15}N were good choices as isotopes because they would be incorporated into the DNA via:
    I. the deoxyribose sugar
    II. the phosphate group
    III. the bases
    A. I only
    B. II only
    C. III only
    D. I and III

3. If DNA replication was conservative, after 1 round of replication in ^{14}N, the density of the double stranded DNA would be:
    A. all intermediate
    B. all heavy
    C. half intermediate, half heavy
    D. half heavy, half light

4. In this experiment, the Okazaki fragments would contain:
    A. only ^{14}N
    B. only ^{15}N
    C. neither ^{14}N nor ^{15}N
    D. both ^{14}N and ^{15}N

Questions 5 - 7 are independent of any passage and independent of each other.

5. Heat is often used to separate or denature double stranded DNA into single stranded DNA by breaking the hydrogen bonds between base pairs. Which of the following statements is true?
    A. G-C base pairs would require higher temperatures to break than A-T base pairs.
    B. A-T base pairs would require higher temperatures to break than G-C base pairs.
    C. All long DNA chains should denature at the same temperature.
    D. DNA-DNA double strands would require higher temperatures to denature that DNA-RNA double strands containing the same sequence.

6. Part of the process of purifying DNA from isolated chromosomes must involve:
    A. adding DNase, an enzyme that breaks apart DNA.
    B. adding proteases, enzymes that break apart proteins.
    C. adding RNase, an enzyme that breaks apart RNA.
    D. adding detergents, chemicals that break apart lipids.

7. An RNA molecule was synthesized to complementary base pair with a DNA molecule. The sequence of the DNA was: 5' ATCCGCTAAG 3'. The RNA sequence should be:
    A. 5' CUUAGCGGAU 3'
    B. 5' UAGGCGAUUC 3'
    C. 5' CTTAGCGGAT 3'
    D. 5' TAGGCGATTC 3'

Solutions

1. C.
After one round of replication, all the DNA was found to be intermediate in density, with one strand containing the light isotope and one containing the heavy isotope. A second round of replication would mean that these intermediate DNA double strands would now serve as the template strands. The resulting copies would contain the light isotope. Therefore, from the template strand containing the heavy isotope, the resulting double strand would be intermediate, and from the template containing the light isotope, the double strand would contain only the light isotope. This would result in half the DNA being intermediate and half being light.

2. C.
Only the bases in a nucleotide contain nitrogen.

3. D.
Conservative replication implies that the template strands remain together and the copied strands form the new double stranded DNA molecule. If this were true, then the template strands would contain only ^{15}N, the heavy isotope, and the copy strands would contain only ^{14}N, the light isotope.

4. A.
Okazaki fragments are generated during replication of the lagging strand. Therefore, they would contain only ^{14}N.

5. A.
Since G-C base pairs contain three hydrogen bonds, whereas A-T base pairs contain only two, the G-C pairing would require more energy, and hence a higher temperature, to disrupt. Extending this idea, long chains of DNA require different temperatures to denature depending on how many G-C pairs they have relative to A-T base pairs. Since there is no difference in the number of hydrogen bonds between a DNA-DNA double strand and a DNA-RNA double strand with the same sequence (A-U base pairs only contain two, just like A-T), there would be no difference in the temperature necessary to denature them.

6. B.
Chromosomes contain DNA and proteins. It is necessary to keep the DNA intact during isolation for further experiments, so adding DNase would not be wise. Since chromosomes do not contain RNA or lipids, reagents used to degrade these components are not necessary. However, to purify the DNA, proteins must be removed. Proteases are often used to accomplish this.

7. A.
Since RNA contains *U* instead of *T*, the answers using *T* can be eliminated automatically. This question stresses the property of base pairing that requires the strands to be in the opposite orientation (antiparallel). Therefore, although the sequence UAGGCGAUUC (response B) matches the DNA sequence as written, the 5' and 3' ends are not in the correct orientation. If the sequence was reversed, as in answer A, the two strands would complementary base pair.

Biology Review 6
Viruses

A. Introduction

As we have already discussed, viruses are not considered to be alive. They cannot, on their own, perform many of the processes that are characteristic of life, including reproduction. Viruses absolutely require a host cell to propagate.

All viruses have the same basic structure. They are comprised of a protein coat surrounding the genetic material (which can be either DNA or RNA). In some viruses, an outer envelope is present, comprised of lipids and proteins derived from the cell membrane of their host.

Viruses come in a wide variety of shapes and sizes and have great capacity to mutate, especially in their protein coat and outer envelope. This often makes it difficult for the host organism to mount an immune response.

B. Life Cycle

Although viruses are not alive, they do have a "life cycle," a series of events that results in their reproduction. In general, viral replication involves four steps:

1. The virus attaches to a specific type of cell.
2. The genetic material enters the host cell.
3. The viral genetic material forces the host cell to produce copies of viral proteins and genetic material.
4. New viruses are released from the cell.

C. Bacteriophages

Bacteriophages (*phages* for short) are viruses that infect only bacteria. The most widely studied bacteriophages are *lambda* (λ) and the "T even" phages, *T2* and *T4*. The viruses contain DNA as their genetic material. The basic structure consists of the *head* and *tail* regions (see Figure 6.1). The head contains the protein coat (called a *capsid*) and the DNA. The tail is made up of a tube called a *sheath*, and, in the T even phages, several long *tail fibers* connected to the base of the sheath. The tail region attaches to a bacterial cell, and the DNA is injected into the cell through the sheath.

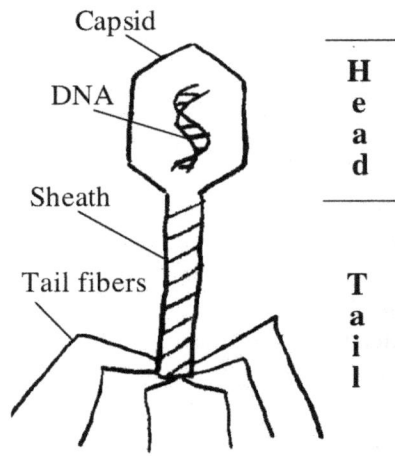

Figure 6.1: Structure of a bacteriophage

Once the DNA is inside the cell, two pathways are possible (λ can follow either pathway; the T even phages only follow the lytic cycle):

- *The lytic cycle*: The phage DNA instructs the cell to produce more viral particles. The cell *lyses*, or breaks, resulting in cell death. New bacteriophages are released and can infect other cells.

- *The lysogenic cycle*: Once infected, the virus enters a latent period, and the host cell is neither damaged nor destroyed. The phage DNA incorporates into the host cell chromosome and is replicated along with the host DNA. At this stage, the virus is technically called a *prophage*. The viral DNA, therefore, is passed on during cell division. Under appropriate conditions, the phage DNA will excise itself from the chromosome and enter the lytic cycle, thus destroying the host cell.

D. Animal Viruses

Animal viruses are very diverse in their size and structure, and the exact nature of their genetic material, which can be double or single stranded RNA or DNA. We will consider the *Human Immunodeficiency Virus (HIV)* as an example of an animal virus (see Figure 6.2).

The first stage of HIV infection involves attachment of the virus to the host cell. HIV has proteins on its outer membrane that recognize a specific protein (the *receptor*) on the host cell. After docking to the receptor, the virus enters the cell via endocytosis.

Some RNA viruses, such as HIV, must have their RNA copied into DNA for the cell to use it (these viruses are called *retroviruses*). This is accomplished by the viral enzyme *reverse transcriptase*. The DNA copy is made in the cytoplasm of the host cell and is then transported into the nucleus, where it can incorporate with the host DNA (the virus is now called a *provirus*, analogous to a prophage). Newly synthesized viral particles can be released via exocitosis. Therefore, the virus does not always kill the host cell.

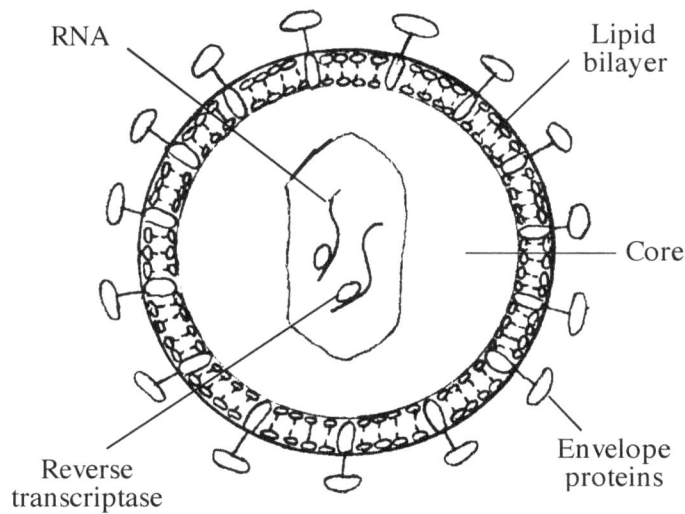

Figure 6.2: Structure of HIV

E. The Effect of HIV on Humans

HIV is such a deadly virus, and is so difficult to fight off, because it specifically targets cells in the immune system. The receptor for HIV is a protein called CD4, mostly found on helper T cells. In the progression of AIDS, the CD4 bearing cells are killed and the ability of the immune system to fight off other diseases and opportunistic infections is drastically reduced. Individuals do not die from AIDS, but rather from infections that can normally be fought off by a healthy immune system.

Chapter 6 Problems

Passage (Questions 1-4)

The activity of bacteriophages is easily assayed. Bacteria are spread on a solid nutrient agar plate. Under appropriate growth conditions, the bacteria will form a cloudy layer completely covering the dish. In microbiology, this is called a *lawn*, as opposed to isolated spots, or *colonies*, of bacteria. If bacteriophages are introduced to the lawn of bacteria, the phages will infect single cells. Once the phages have reproduced, they will lyse the cells and the progeny phage will infect the surrounding bacterial cells. In a relatively short period of time, the phages will have lysed all the bacteria within a radius of the initial infection, causing a clear, circular spot to form in the lawn of bacteria. This is called a *plaque*.

A researcher working with bacteriophages set up the following experiment:

Condition 1:
Bacteria were spread on agar plates and incubated at 37°C for 24 hours. A lawn was clearly visible and no plaques formed.

Condition 2:
The same strain of bacteria was mixed with a preparation of lambda bacteriophage. The mixture was spread on agar plates and incubated for 24 hours at 37°C. An average of twenty plaques formed on the bacterial lawn on each plate.

Condition 3:
The same strain of bacteria was spread on agar plates and then exposed to UV light. After incubation at 37°C for 24 hours, lawns grew and approximately fifty plaques formed on each plate.

1. After incubating the plates from condition 2 for an additional 5 days, the plates became totally clear. What is the most likely explanation for this result?
    A. Newly produced phages infected all bacteria on the dish, thus killing everything.
    B. The bacteria died off due to lack of nutrients.
    C. The bacteria protected themselves from the phages by slowing their growth.
    D. The phage forced all the bacteria to go into the lysogenic cycle and stop growing.

2. What happened in condition 3?
    A. Phage contaminated the dishes causing infection and lysis of the bacteria.
    B. The nutrients in the agar were insufficient to support bacterial growth.
    C. The bacteria were probably a lysogenic strain induced by UV light.
    D. The bacteria were not healthy and died off when exposed to UV light.

3. If a fourth experiment was done, where bacteria were mixed with lambda and exposed to UV light, what would you predict?
    A. The results would be similar to condition 2, with approximately 20 plaques per plate.
    B. The results would be similar to condition 3, with approximately 50 plaques per plate.
    C. There would be approximately 35 plaques per plate.
    D. There would be approximately 70 plaques per plate.

4. Before the phage life cycle was understood, researchers called the results from condition 3 *autolysis*. They thought an enzyme in the bacteria caused its own destruction and the destruction of surrounding cells. Which of the following would lend support to the viral theory and help to disprove autolysis?
    A. Within a week, all the bacterial cells in condition 3 die.
    B. Viral particles can be purified from the plates in condition 3.
    C. Exposure of bacteria to X rays also causes plaques to form.
    D. With or without exposure to UV light, no bacteria grow at 4°C.

Questions 5-6 are independent of any passage and independent of each other.

5. Strategies to fight the AIDS virus include drugs that mimic nucleotides, called *nucleotide analogs*. Reverse transcriptase incorporates these analogs into the newly formed viral DNA strand. The host cell cannot interpret the DNA correctly, so the virus does not propagate. Unfortunately, this therapy only works for a short time in infected individuals, probably because:
   A. the outer protein coat of the virus mutates so it is no longer recognized by the immune system.
   B. the patient's immune system starts to fight off the analog.
   C. the reverse transcriptase mutates to prevent incorporation of the analog.
   D. the viral DNA no longer incorporates into the host DNA.

6. Immunizations for viruses such as influenza and polio rely on the body's ability to recognize the virus and make antibodies against it. All of the following would allow for antibody production to prevent a virus from entering a cell <u>except</u>:
   A. injection of a small amount of "live" virus.
   B. injection of "heat killed" virus.
   C. injection of part of the outer coat of the virus.
   D. injection of viral reverse transcriptase.

Solutions

1. A.
All the bacteria were infected by the phage and lysed. The other conditions, whether true or not, deal with growth or death of bacteria and would not cause lysis of the bacteria. Therefore, the plate would remain cloudy. Only lysis causes the plates to appear clear.

2. C.
The control in this experiment (condition 1) rules out answers A and B. If UV light killed the bacteria, as suggested in D (and as can happen, depending on conditions), then all the bacteria would die. (Although it is possible that only a small percentage would die, it would be highly unlikely that this lethality would show a plaque pattern.) C is the only plausible answer, and we know that UV light can induce lysogenic strains to become lytic.

3. D.
Under both conditions, infection and induction, lysis would occur. Therefore, on average for these experimental conditions, infection would produce 20 plaques per plate and induction would produce 50 plaques per plate, for a total of 70 plaques per plate.

4. B.
Once induction occurs, viral particles are produced that can go on to infect other bacterial cells. Therefore, the isolation of bacteriophage from cultures would not support the theory of autolysis. Answer A is possible in the realm of either theory, C would not distinguish between the two, and D has nothing to do with either theory, as bacteria that grow well at 37°C will not grow at 4°C.

5. C.
The action of the analogs is at the level of reverse transcription. If the reverse transcriptase mutates to no longer allow incorporation of the analogs, then the virus can continue on its normal path. It is unlikely the body would mount an immune response to these analogs (choice B) as these analogs are so similar to normal nucleotides. Although the outer protein coat can and does mutate (choice A), this has nothing to do with the analogs. And the virus must incorporate into the host chromosome, so choice D is also incorrect.

6. D.
Antibody production against reverse transcriptase would not prevent the virus from entering the cell. All other conditions would allow the immune system to make antibodies against the intact virus, as it exists outside the cells where the immune system can detect it.

Chemistry Review 1
Introduction

The science portion of the ACT consists of questions that test the basic concepts in chemistry. The concepts are tested with respect to application, problem solving, and analytical thinking. These skills, which are measured by the test, are considered essential in the study of college level material. The questions asked are based on passages.

The ACT tests your ability to understand new concepts based on high school science courses. Sometimes the passages contain topics and data that you have not seen before. Nevertheless, you do not need advanced courses in chemistry to be successful in the ACT. All you need is to understand the basic concepts in chemistry. You should be familiar with the common equations and constants that are used in the high school level of studies. For example, simple formulas such as the density-mass equation or the gas equations. More importantly, you should know how to use the equations in both numerical and conceptual situations. Advanced equations will be provided to you in the passages, if necessary.

When studying this section, you should not focus just on facts. You should grasp the reasoning behind the facts and think conceptually about the various ideas in chemistry.

Matter

A. INTRODUCTION

A firm grasp of the basic ideas of division of matter is important for the understanding of physical sciences. These basic ideas presented here are not only used in chemistry and physics, but in many diverse fields such as medicine, engineering, astronomy, geology, and so on. In this chapter, we will discuss ideas about atoms and molecules, and related aspects such as moles, Avogadro number, percentage composition, atomic mass, atomic weight, and subatomic particles.

B. ATOMS

Atoms are the basic units of elements and compounds. In normal chemical reactions, atoms retain their identity. In this section, we will present a quick review of some of the basic terms and concepts such as elements, compounds, and mixtures.

Elements

An element is defined as matter that is made of only one type of atom. Elements are the basic building blocks of more complex matter. Some examples of elements include hydrogen (H), helium (He), potassium (K), carbon (C), and mercury (Hg).

Compounds

A compound is matter formed by the combination of two or more elements in fixed ratios. Let's consider an example. Hydrogen peroxide (H_2O_2) is a compound composed of two elements, hydrogen and oxygen, in a fixed ratio.

Mixtures

A combination of different elements, or a combination of elements and compounds, or a combination of different compounds is called a mixture. For example, an aqueous solution of potassium hydroxide (KOH + H_2O). In this example, the two components are potassium hydroxide and water.

Though these definitions illustrate basic ideas, you need to understand them fully; otherwise it will be almost impossible to decipher higher concepts that are based on these simple ideas. The ACT tests your understanding of basic concepts by incorporating simple ideas into passages. So in order to succeed on the test, you need to thoroughly understand the basics.

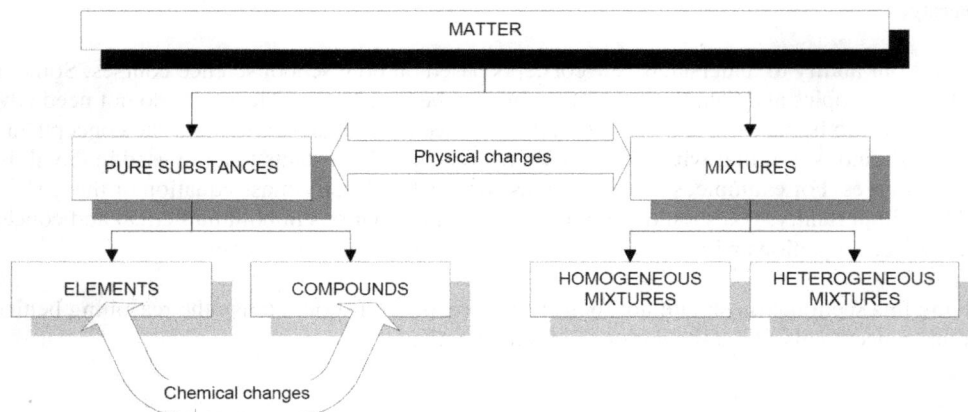

C. DALTON'S ATOMIC THEORY

In 1803, John Dalton proposed the atomic theory of matter. The main postulates of his atomic theory can be summarized as follows:

1) Matter is composed of indivisible particles - atoms.

2) An element is composed of only one kind of atom. These atoms in a particular element have the same properties such as mass, size, or even shape.

3) A compound is composed of two or more elements combined in fixed ratios or proportions.

4) In a chemical reaction, the atoms in the reactants recombine, resulting in products which represent the combination of atoms present in the reactants. In the process, atoms are neither created, nor destroyed. So a chemical reaction is essentially a rearrangement of atoms.

Ramifications of Dalton's Theory

The atomic theory put forward by Dalton is consistent with the law of conservation of mass. As the fourth postulate says, chemical reaction is just a rearrangement of atoms, and thus the total mass remains constant during a chemical reaction.

The postulates also account for the law of definite proportions. Compounds are made of elements in fixed or definite proportions. Since the atoms have fixed mass, compounds should have elements in a fixed ratio with respect to mass. Finally, these postulates predict what is known as the law of multiple proportions. According to this law, if two elements form two or more different compounds, the ratio of the mass of one element of these compounds to a fixed mass of the other element is a simple whole number.

D. THE GENERAL STRUCTURE OF THE ATOM

During the early twentieth century, scientists discovered that atoms can be divided into more basic particles. Their findings made it clear that atoms contain a central portion called the nucleus. The nucleus contains protons and neutrons. Protons are positively charged, and neutrons are neutral. Whirling about the nucleus are particles called electrons which are negatively charged. The electrons are relatively small in mass. Take a look at Table 1-1 for a size comparison.

Table 1-1

PARTICLE	ABSOLUTE CHARGE (Coulombs)	RELATIVE CHARGE	MASS (kg)
Neutron	0	0	1.675×10^{-27}
Proton	$+1.6 \times 10^{-19}$	$+1$	1.673×10^{-27}
Electron	-1.6×10^{-19}	-1	9.11×10^{-31}

E. ELECTRONS

As mentioned above, the late nineteenth century scientists conducted several experiments, and found that atoms are divisible. They conducted experiments with gas discharge tubes.

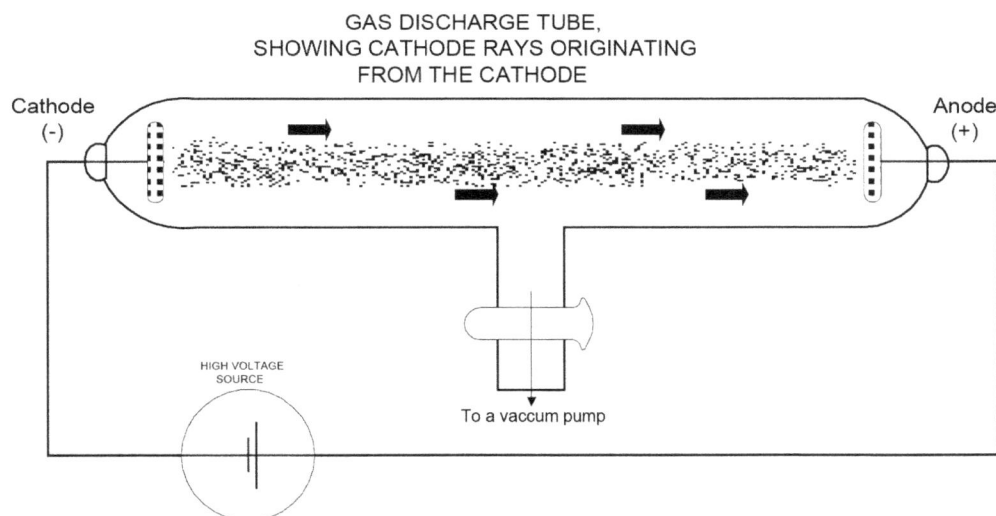

Figure 1-1 Gas discharge tube

A gas discharge tube is shown in Figure 1-1. The gas discharge tube is an evacuated glass tube and has two electrodes, a cathode (negative electrode) and an anode (positive electrode). The electrodes are connected to a high voltage source. Inside the tube, an electric discharge occurs between the electrodes. The discharge or 'rays' originate from the cathode and move toward the anode, and hence are called cathode rays. Using luminescent techniques, the cathode rays are made visible and it was found that these rays are deflected away from negatively charged plates. The scientist J. J. Thompson concluded that the cathode ray consists of negatively charged particles (electrons).

Charge of Electrons

R. A. Millikan conducted the famous oil drop experiments and came to several conclusions: The charge of an electron is -1.602×10^{-19} C. From the charge-to-mass ratio, the mass of an electron was also calculated.

$$\frac{\text{Charge}}{\text{Mass}} = -1.76 \times 10^{8} \text{ Coulombs / gram}$$

$$\text{mass} = \frac{-1.6 \times 10^{-19}}{-1.76 \times 10^{8}} = 9.11 \times 10^{-23} \text{ g} = 9.11 \times 10^{-31} \text{ kg}$$

F. PROTONS

Protons are positively charged nuclear particles. The charge of a proton is (positive electronic charge) $+1.6 \times 10^{-19}$ C. The net positive charge of the nucleus is due to the presence of the protons. A proton is about 1800 times more massive than an electron.

G. NEUTRONS

Neutrons have mass comparable to that of protons, but neutrons are devoid of any electric charge. We will talk more about neutrons and their whereabouts when we study radioactivity.

Now a natural question is whether electrons, protons, and neutrons are the most fundamental particles. The answer is no. These fundamental particles are made of more fundamental particles called quarks. But, we don't have to go that far for the ACT. Just be aware that such sub-fundamental particles exist, fundamental particles being electrons, protons, and neutrons.

H. ATOMIC NUMBER AND MASS NUMBER

The atomic number denotes the number of protons in an atom's nucleus. The mass number denotes the total number of protons and neutrons. Protons and neutrons are often called nucleons. By convention, the atomic number is usually written to the left of the elemental notation, and the mass number to the left above the elemental notation as represented by the example below. The element shown is aluminum.

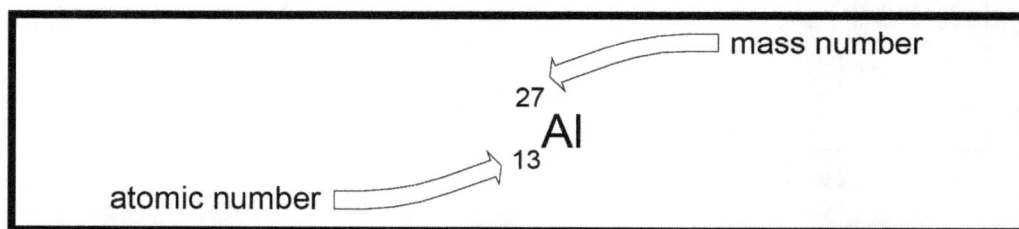

Some atoms have the same atomic number, but different mass numbers. This means different number of neutrons. Such atoms are called isotopes.

I. ATOMIC WEIGHT

The atomic weight of an element is the average weight of all the isotopic masses of the element, calculated on the basis of their relative abundance in nature. The atomic weights are set on a "carbon-12" scale. This is the standard weight scale that is used worldwide to express atomic weights. Exploring this further, we can say that 12 atomic mass units (amu) make up the mass of one atom of $_6^{12}C$ isotope. In other words, one amu is equal to 1/12 the mass of one carbon-12 atom. We can also say that the atomic weight of carbon-12 is 12 amu. Even though it is popular to use the term atomic weight, atomic mass is a more appropriate term since we are really talking about the mass rather than the weight.

J. MOLECULES

A molecule is a set or group of atoms which are chemically bonded. It can be represented by a molecular formula. A molecular formula represents the different kinds of atoms that are present in a molecule, along with the actual ratio of its atomic combination in forming that molecule.

A molecule of H_2O (water) contains two hydrogen atoms bonded to one atom of oxygen.

NaOH   Sodium Hydroxide

A molecule of sodium hydroxide contains one sodium atom, one oxygen atom, and one hydrogen atom. The point is that molecular formula represents the molecules and the actual ratio of the atoms present in them.

Molecular Weight

Molecular weight represents the sum of the atomic weights of all the atoms in that molecule. Molecular weight is also known as formula weight.

Example 1-1

Calculate the molecular weight of sulfuric acid (H_2SO_4).

2 hydrogens	2 x 1 = 2
1 sulfur	1 x 32 = 32
4 oxygens	4 x 16 = 64
	98 g/mol

Example 1- 2

Calculate the molecular weight of carbon dioxide (CO_2).

1 carbon	1 x 12 = 12
2 oxygens	2 x 16 = 32
	44 g/mol

Empirical Formula

Empirical formula of a molecule represents the simplest ratio of the atoms present in the molecule. For example, acetylene has the molecular formula C_2H_2. The empirical formula of acetylene is CH. In essence, empirical formula gives the simplest ratio of atoms in a molecule.

Problem 1-1

Write the empirical formula of the following molecules.

1. H_2O_2
2) C_2H_6
3) H_2O

Answers:

1) HO
2) CH_3
3) H_2O

Notice that sometimes the empirical formula is the same as the molecular formula as in the case of water (H_2O).

K. THE CONCEPT OF MOLE

The quantity of a given substance that contains as many units or molecules as the number of atoms in 12 grams of carbon-12 is called a **mole**. For example, one mole of glucose contains the same number of glucose molecules as in 12 grams of carbon-12. The mass of one mole of a substance is called its *molar mass*. The number of atoms in 12 grams of carbon-12 is represented by the *Avogadro number* (6.023 x 10^{23}). So one mole of any substance contains Avogadro number of units in them.

To understand this concept thoroughly, try different possible scenarios where the Avogadro number can be used. Here are some. One mole of hydrogen atoms contains Avogadro number of hydrogen atoms. One mole of hydrogen molecules contains Avogadro number of hydrogen molecules. A mole of water contains 6.023 x 10^{23} water molecules. These are all different ways of expressing the same concept.

The molar mass of a substance is equal to the molecular weight of that substance. The molecular weight (formula weight) of water is 18 amu. Since this is the molar mass, we can express it as 18 grams/mol.

Example 1-3

Calculate the mass of one molecule of sodium hydroxide (NaOH).

Answer: We know that the formula weight of sodium hydroxide is 40 g/mol.

Sodium	23
Oxygen	16
Hydrogen	1
	40 g/mol

We also know that one mole of NaOH contains Avogadro number of molecules. So the mass of the NaOH molecule can be found by the following method:
Mass of one molecule of sodium hydroxide

$$= \frac{40g}{6.02 \times 10^{23}} = 6.64 \times 10^{-23}g$$

Example 1-4

Calculate the number of moles in 109.5 grams of hydrogen chloride.

Answer: Just like the last example, we have to find the molar mass of the molecule. The molar mass is 35.5 + 1 = 36.5 g/mol.

$$\text{Number of moles} = 109.5 \text{ g HCI} \times \frac{1 \text{ mol HCI}}{36.5 \text{ g HCI}} = 3 \text{ moles HCI}$$

So, 109.5 grams of HCl correspond to 3 moles of HCl.

You should be able to do these types of conversions back and forth, from grams to moles and moles to grams.

Try the next problem to see whether you have mastered the idea.

Problem 1-2

Calculate the number of grams in 8 moles of sulfur dioxide.

Answer: If your answer is close to 512.8 g, you solved the problem correctly.

L. COMPOSITION BY PERCENTAGE

The ACT often contains percentage composition problems. Percentage composition is the percentage contribution (by weight) of each element to the total mass. Let's explore this idea by looking at some examples.

Example 1-5

Calcium carbonate ($CaCO_3$), commonly known as limestone is used in the preparation of a variety of compounds. Calculate the percentage composition of each element in calcium carbonate.

Solution:

# of atoms per molecule	molar weight of the atoms	total mass of the element per mol
1 Calcium	1 x 40.1 g	40.1 g
1 Carbon	1 x 12.0 g	12.0 g
3 Oxygen	3 x 16.0 g	48.0 g
		100.1 g

The percentage composition of each element can be found as follows:

$$\% \text{ of calcium} = \frac{40.1}{100.1} \times 100 = 40.1\% \text{ calcium}$$

$$\% \text{ of carbon} = \frac{12}{100.1} \times 100 = 12\% \text{ carbon}$$

$$\% \text{ of oxygen} = \frac{48}{100.1} \times 100 = 47.9\% \text{ oxygen}$$

Predicting Formulas from Percentage Compositions

You should be able to predict the formula of a compound on the basis of a given data of percentage compositions. Study the next example to understand how it is done.

Example 1-6

A carbon compound contains 27.27% carbon and 72.73% oxygen by mass. Predict the simplest ratio or formula of the compound.

Solution:

The best way to approach this problem is to consider that we have 100 grams of this compound. Logically it should contain 27.27 grams of carbon and 72.73 grams of oxygen. With that in mind, we can calculate the number of moles of each element or atom. After that we can obtain the simple ratio.

Step 1

# of moles of carbon atoms equals 27.27/12 = 2.275 moles of carbon atoms
# of moles of oxygen atoms equals 72.73/16 = 4.546 moles of oxygen atoms

Step 2

Divide every number of moles with the smallest number of moles that you got in Step 1. Here the smaller one is 2.2725. So divide the number of moles of carbon atoms and the number of moles of oxygen atoms by 2.2725. That will give you the simplest ratio between them.

$$Carbon: 2.2725/2.2725 = 1$$

$$Oxygen: 4.546/2.2725 \approx 2$$

Since the ratio of carbon to oxygen is 1:2, the compound is CO_2.

Example 1-7

Calculate the mass of sulfur in 150 grams of H_2SO_4.

Solution:

The easiest way to calculate this is to find the percentage composition of sulfur. Then, use that percentage to find the mass of sulfur in the given amount of substance.

Step 1

$$\% \text{ of sulfur} = 32.1/98 \times 100, \text{ roughly } 33\%$$

Step 2

The mass of sulfur present in 150 grams of sulfuric acid is

$$150 \times 33\%/100 = 49.5 \text{ g}$$

M. DENSITY

Density is defined as the mass per unit volume.

$$\boxed{\text{Density} = \frac{\text{mass}}{\text{volume}}}$$

This property can be used to identify a compound or an element, since the density of a pure substance is a constant. Since density relates mass and volume, it can be used to find the volume occupied by a given mass, or if the volume is known, we can find the mass.

Density of water is 1.0 g/ml.

Let's explore some calculations involving density. You'll see that these calculations have tremendous laboratory significance.

Example 1-8

The density of carbon tetrachloride is about 1.6 g/ml at 20°C. Calculate the volume occupied by 320 g of CCl_4.

Solution:

$$\text{Density} = \frac{\text{mass}}{\text{volume}}$$

$$\text{Volume} = \frac{\text{mass}}{\text{density}} = \frac{320 \text{ g}}{1.6 \text{g} / \text{ml}} = 200 \text{ ml}$$

So, 320 grams of carbon tetrachloride will occupy a volume of 200 ml.

Example 1-9

A 20 ml sample of mercury has a mass of 271 g. Calculate the density of mercury.
Solution:

$$\text{Density} = \frac{\text{mass}}{\text{volume}} = \frac{271 \text{ g}}{20 \text{ ml}} = 13.55 \text{ g} / \text{ml}$$

This question tests your knowledge of a basic equation. Though the equation is simple, you should be able to manipulate this equation so that you can connect this piece of information with other facts and formulas that are given in your test question or passage.

Chemistry Review 1 Problems

1. A student preparing a solution for an experiment measured the weight of the sample solute to be used. If she is supposed to use 2 moles of calcium hydroxide, she must use:
A. 57.1 grams.
B. 74.1 grams.
C. 114.2 grams.
D. 148.2 grams.

2. Which of the following best represents the total number of ions present in a sample of NaCl weighing 102 g?
A. 6.0×10^{23} ions
B. 10.5×10^{23} ions
C. 12.0×10^{23} ions
D. 21×10^{23} ions

3. Experiments conducted with gas discharge tubes during the late 19th century resulted in many important conclusions in atomic chemistry. Among those, one of the most important was the discovery of rays known as cathode rays. Cathode rays when passed near negative plates will most likely:
A. bend toward the negative plate.
B. bend away from the negative plate.
C. will not bend, because they are uncharged.
D. will not bend, because they are high energy radiations.

4. Which of the following is true regarding a typical atom?
A. Neutrons and electrons have the same mass.
B. The mass of neutrons is much less than that of electrons.
C. Neutrons and protons together make the nucleus electrically neutral.
D. Protons are more massive than electrons.

5. The empirical formula of butane is:
A. CH_3
B. C_2H_5
C. C_4H_{10}
D. CH_2

6. The mass of one mol of a substance is numerically equal to:
A. mass number.
B. Avogadro number.
C. molecular weight.
D. 22.4.

7. If m represents the number of moles of a substance, M represents the molar mass of the substance, and d represents the density of the substance, which of the following expressions equals to the volume of the sample substance?
A. mM/d
B. m/dM
C. d/mM
D. m/d

8. The mass of oxygen in 96 grams of sulfur dioxide is closest to:
A. 16 g.
B. 24 g.
C. 32 g.
D. 47 g.

9. Choose the best value that corresponds to the percentage composition of chlorine in carbon tetrachloride?
A. 92%
B. 90%
C. 86%
D. None of the above

10. A student researcher analyzing the identity of the by-product of a reaction found that the compound contained 63.6% nitrogen and 36.4% oxygen. What is the most likely formula of this compound?
A. NO
B. NO_2
C. N_2O
D. N_2O_3

Questions 11-14 are based on the following passage.

Passage

The following reactions were conducted in a lab for studies related to reaction kinetics. Consider the reactions shown:

Reaction 1

$$CH_4 + 2O_2 \rightarrow CO_2 + 2H_2O$$

$$2C_2H_6 + 7O_2 \rightarrow 4CO_2 + 6H_2O$$
Reaction 2

11. Reaction 2 is best described by which of the following?
A. A metathesis reaction
B. A combustion reaction
C. An endothermic reaction
D. A decomposition reaction

12. In Reaction 2, if 54 g of water was formed, how much ethane and oxygen must have reacted?
A. 30 g of ethane and 224 g of oxygen
B. 60 g of ethane and 224 g of oxygen
C. 30 g of ethane and 112 g of oxygen
D. 60 g of ethane and 112 g of oxygen

13. Which of the following is the actual formula of dextrose, if the empirical proportion is 1:2:1, where the proportion number 2 is that of hydrogen. Dextrose has a molecular weight of 180 g/mol? (Dextrose molecule is composed of carbon, hydrogen, and oxygen)
A. CHO
B. $C_6H_{12}O_6$
C. $C_{12}H_6O_3$
D. CH_2O

14. Which of the following equals the number of hydrogen atoms in 40 grams of methane?
A. 1.5×10^{24}
B. 2.4×10^{24}
C. 6.0×10^{24}
D. 6.023×10^{23}

Solutions

1. The answer is D. This question tests your understanding of the concept of mole. The student is preparing a solution using calcium hydroxide. The formula of calcium hydroxide is $Ca(OH)_2$. The formula weight of calcium hydroxide is 74.1 grams/mol. Here, the student added two moles of it. So the answer is 74.1 x 2 = 148.2 g.

2. The answer is D. The sample weighs 56 g. The formula weight of O_2 is 32 g/mol. So the number of moles of oxygen present is roughly 1.75. Remember that 1 mol contains Avogadro number of particles. Since 1.75 moles of oxygen is present, there are 1.75 x 6.0 x 10^{23} molecules of oxygen. Are we done at this point? No! The question asks for the total number of ions present in the sample. Since each oxygen molecule is composed of oxygen atoms, the total number of atoms in this sample equals 2 x 1.75 x 6.0 x 10^{23} = 21 x 10^{23}.

3. The answer is B. Gas discharge tubes are vacuum tubes with electrodes connected to very high voltages. Cathode rays are emitted from the cathode of the tube. A cathode ray consists of a beam of electrons. Since electrons are negatively charged, cathode rays will bend away from a negatively charged plate.

4. The answer is D. This question asks for a true statement from the choices. Let's look at each of those choices. Choice A is incorrect, because neutrons and electrons do not have the same mass. Choice B claims that the mass of a neutron is less than that of an electron. That is not true either. Protons are positive and neutrons are neutral. They cannot together make the nucleus neutral. In fact, the nucleus is positively charged, not electrically neutral. So Choice C is wrong. The last choice makes perfect sense. A proton is more massive than an electron.

5. The answer is B. The actual formula of butane is C_4H_{10}. But the question is not about butane's actual formula. The question asks for the empirical formula of butane. Empirical formula is the most simplified ratio of the actual formula. So the correct answer is C_2H_5.

6. The answer is C. Let's look at the question carefully. If you did not get the right answer, carefully think about it again. The question is simply testing your understanding of a definition. The mass of a substance in one mole of it is numerically equal to its molecular weight.

7. The answer is A. Density is equal to mass per volume. Further more, the mass is equal to the product of number moles and molar mass. Equating these two equations we can get the answer. Using the letter notations given in the question, the expression of volume is given by Choice A.

8. The answer is D. The formula of sulfur dioxide is SO_2. The formula weight of SO_2 is 64 g/mol. This sample of SO_2 contains 1.5 moles of it. If we calculate the percentage mass of the oxygen, we can see that the oxygen's mass contribution is 50% in SO_2. So regardless of the amount of SO_2 present, half of its mass is due to the presence of oxygen and the other half is due to the presence of sulfur. Here we have 96 g of SO_2. Now, one half of 96 g gives 48 g.

9. The answer is A. The formula of carbon tetrachloride is CCl_4. The formula weight of CCl_4 is 154 g/mol. The percentage composition of Cl can be calculated as follows:

$$\% \text{ of chlorine} = \frac{\text{mass of chlorine}}{\text{mass of } CCl_4} \times 100\% = \frac{142}{154} \times 100\% \approx 92\%$$

10. The answer is C. In the question, the percentage compositions of nitrogen and oxygen are given. With that information, we have to find the formula of that compound. Just as discussed in our review, assume that we have 100 grams of this compound. If there are 100 grams, logically it should contain 63.6 grams of nitrogen and 36.4 grams of oxygen.

Step 1

$$\text{\# of moles of nitrogen} = 63.6/14 \approx 4.5 \text{ moles of nitrogen}$$
$$\text{\# of moles of oxygen} = 36.4/16 \approx 2.275 \text{ moles of oxygen}$$

Step 2
Divide every number of moles with the smallest number of moles calculated in Step 1. Here the smaller one is 2.275. Divide both mole numbers by 2.275. This will give you the simplest ratio between them.

$$\text{Nitrogen} \quad 4.5/2.275 \approx 2 \qquad \text{Oxygen} \quad 2.275/2.275 \approx 1$$

Since the ratio of nitrogen to oxygen is 2:1, the compound is N_2O.

11. The answer is B. Reaction 2 is a typical example of a combustion reaction.

12. The answer is C.

$$2C_2H_6 \quad + \quad 7O_2 \quad \longrightarrow \quad 4CO_2 \quad + \quad 6H_2O$$

Reaction 2

According to Reaction 2, two moles of ethane will react with 7 moles of oxygen to form 4 moles of carbon dioxide and 6 moles of water. In the question, it is given that 54 g of water was formed. This corresponds to 3 moles of water. From the equation, we can say that 1 mol of ethane must have reacted to form 3 moles of water. We can also say that 3.5 moles of oxygen must have reacted in the formation of 3 moles of water. The last step is the conversion of moles to grams. The corresponding quantities in grams are 30 g of ethane and 112 g of oxygen.

13. The answer is B. From the question, we can say that the empirical formula of dextrose is CH_2O. The molecular weight of dextrose is also given. Let's first calculate the weight of the empirical formula. Maybe the empirical formula represents the actual formula. The weight of the empirical formula is 30 g/mol. But the question says it is 180 g/mol. In this case, the molecular formula is not the same as the empirical formula. By dividing the actual weight by the empirical weight, we will get the coefficient with which we have to multiply the empirical formula to get the actual formula. The coefficient is 180/30 = 6. So the molecular formula is $C_6H_{12}O_6$. Have you heard of glucose? Well, dextrose is the same thing. If you knew that, you could have picked the answer right away. But more importantly, it is the process that you have to learn from this question.

14. The answer is C. The formula of methane is CH_4. The molecular weight is 16 g/mol. We have 40 g of methane. That means we have 2.5 moles of methane. So the number of hydrogen atoms can be calculated.

$$6.0 \times 10^{23} \times 2.5 \text{ moles} \times 4 \text{ hydrogen atoms/mol} = 6.0 \times 10^{24} \text{ atoms}$$

Chemistry Review 2
Chemical Reactions

A. INTRODUCTION

Chemical reaction is a process at the molecular or ionic level by which one or more types of substances are transformed into one or more new types of substances by different modes of combination. In this chapter, we will explore the different types of chemical reactions including oxidation-reduction reactions. We will also learn how to balance equations.

B. CHEMICAL REACTIONS

A chemical reaction can be represented by a chemical equation. In a chemical equation representing an irreversible reaction, the substances that react (reactants) are written on the left side, while the resulting substances (products) are written on the right side of an arrow.

$$2 H_2 \quad + \quad O_2 \quad \longrightarrow \quad 2 H_2O$$

In the reaction shown above, two molecules of hydrogen react with one molecule of oxygen, forming two molecules of water. Balancing of equations will be covered a little later in this chapter.

C. TYPES OF CHEMICAL REACTIONS

There are five types of chemical reactions.

1) Combination reaction
2) Combustion reaction
3) Decomposition reaction
4) Displacement reaction or single-replacement reaction
5) Metathesis reaction or double-replacement reaction

Combination Reaction

A reaction involving the formation of a compound from two or more substances is called a combination reaction.

Some representative combination reactions

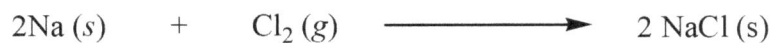

$$2Na\,(s) \quad + \quad Cl_2\,(g) \quad \longrightarrow \quad 2\,NaCl\,(s)$$

$$SO_2\,(g) \quad + \quad H_2O\,(l) \quad \longrightarrow \quad H_2SO_3\,(aq)$$

Combustion Reaction

A combustion reaction involves the reaction of substances with oxygen, and it is usually accompanied by the release of large amounts of heat. Combustion reactions are thus highly exothermic.

Some representative combustion reactions

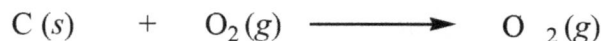

$$C\ (s)\ +\ O_2\ (g)\ \longrightarrow\ O\ _2\ (g)$$

$$2\ H_2S\ (g)\ +\ 3\ O_2\ (g)\ \longrightarrow\ 2\ SO_2\ (g)\ +\ 2\ H_2O\ (g)$$

Decomposition Reaction

A decomposition reaction is a process in which one compound decomposes or splits to form two or more simpler compounds and/or elements.

A representative decomposition reaction

$$CaCO_3\ (s)\ \longrightarrow\ CaO\ (s)\ +\ CO_2\ (g)$$

Displacement Reaction (single-replacement reaction)

In a *single-replacement reaction*, an element reacts with a compound, and results in the displacement of an element or group from the compound. An example of a single-replacement reaction is shown.

A single-replacement reaction

$$Zn\ (s)\ +\ CuCl_2\ (aq)\ \rightarrow\ ZnCl_2\ (aq)\ +\ Cu\ (s)$$

In this reaction, Zn substitutes for Cu.

Metathesis Reaction (double-replacement reaction)

A *metathesis (double-replacement) reaction* involves the exchange of two groups or two ions among the reactants. Remember that in a single-replacement reaction, there is only one group or ion being switched. A metathesis reaction can often result in an insoluble product from soluble reactants, and the insoluble compound formed is called a precipitate.

A metathesis reaction

$$AgNO_3\ (aq)\ +\ NaCl\ (aq)\ \longrightarrow\ AgCl\ (s)\ +\ NaNO_3\ (aq)$$

Note that this reaction involves the formation of a precipitate of AgCl.

With respect to the types of reactions, your objective should be to understand the basis behind the categorization.

D. BALANCING SIMPLE EQUATIONS

A chemical equation is said to be balanced if all the atoms present in the reactants appear in the same numbers among the products. Here is an example.

Example 2-1

Balance the following equation.

$$Fe + O_2 \longrightarrow Fe_2O_3$$

Solution:

Start by balancing the oxygen atoms. There are two oxygen atoms on the reactant side and three oxygen atoms on the product side. To balance this, put 3 as the coefficient of oxygen on the reactant side. When we write '3 O_2,' that means we have **6** oxygen atoms on the reactant side. To make the same number of oxygen atoms on the product side, let's put **2** as the coefficient of Fe_2O_3. Now the oxygen atoms seem to be balanced.

Let's take a look at Fe. Since the coefficient of Fe_2O_3 is **2**, we have 4 atoms of Fe on the product side. We can balance this by writing 4 as the coefficient of Fe on the reactant side. So the balanced equation is as follows:

$$4\,Fe + 3\,O_2 \longrightarrow 2\,Fe_2O_3$$

Problem 2-1

Balance the following equations:

(a)  $Cu + AgNO_3 \longrightarrow Ag + Cu(NO_3)_2$

(b) 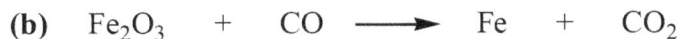 $Fe_2O_3 + CO \longrightarrow Fe + CO_2$

(c) 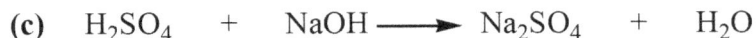 $H_2SO_4 + NaOH \longrightarrow Na_2SO_4 + H_2O$

(d) 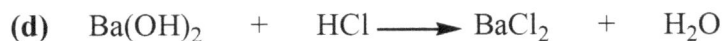 $Ba(OH)_2 + HCl \longrightarrow BaCl_2 + H_2O$

Answers:

(a)  $Cu + 2\,AgNO_3 \longrightarrow 2\,Ag + Cu(NO_3)_2$

(b)  $Fe_2O_3 + 3\,CO \longrightarrow 2\,Fe + 3\,CO_2$

(c) 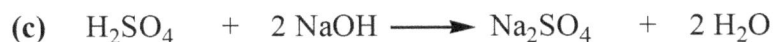 $H_2SO_4 + 2\,NaOH \longrightarrow Na_2SO_4 + 2\,H_2O$

(d)  $Ba(OH)_2 + 2\,HCl \longrightarrow BaCl_2 + 2\,H_2O$

E. OXIDATION NUMBER

Electrons are exchanged during oxidation-reduction reactions. The behavior of atoms or ions in terms of the number of electrons transferred is expressed as the oxidation state (oxidation number). We can define oxidation number as the charge of an atom or ion, based on a set of standard rules. If the given species is an ion containing a single atom, then its oxidation state is its charge itself. Let's analyze this by looking at a few examples.

In NaCl, the oxidation state of sodium is +1 and the oxidation state of chlorine is –1. Generally, the elements at the top right corner of the periodic table are assigned negative oxidation numbers. Some of the elements on the right side of the periodic table can have positive or negative oxidation numbers depending upon the atom to which the given element is bonded to. The elements in the middle and the left portions of the periodic table have almost exclusively positive oxidation numbers.

Table 1-1

General guidelines for assigning oxidation numbers

1. The elemental natural state oxidation number of any atom is zero. For example, the oxidation number of oxygen atom in O_2 is zero.
2. The sum of the oxidation numbers of the atoms in a compound should be zero.
3. The sum of the oxidation numbers of the atoms in an ionic species (a species with a net charge) should equal the net charge of the ionic species.
4. The oxidation number of a given ion containing a single atom is its charge itself.

Oxidation numbers of some common elements

1. The common oxidation number of Group IA metals is +1. E.g., lithium, sodium, potassium.
2. The common oxidation number of Group IIA metals is +2. E.g., beryllium, magnesium, calcium.
3. The common oxidation number of Group IIIA is +3. E.g., aluminum, boron.
4. The common oxidation number of Group IVA is +4. +2 is also seen in some compounds such as CO.
5. The common oxidation numbers of Group V A are +5 and –3.
6. The common oxidation number of Group VIA is –2.
7. The common oxidation number of Group VIIA is –1.
8. The common oxidation number of H is +1. In some metal hydrides, hydrogen shows an oxidation number of –1.

The above list of common oxidation numbers is not comprehensive. Nevertheless, it gives you a basic and essential picture about assigning oxidation numbers in common compounds and ionic species. Most elements can have multiple oxidation states, depending on the element or ionic species they are bonded to. You have to always follow the general guidelines in Table 1-1, and check whether the items listed are satisfied.

Now that we have learned the theory of assigning oxidation numbers, let's do an example to see how it works.

Example 2-2

What is the oxidation number of sulfur in sulfuric acid?

Solution:

Sulfuric acid is H_2SO_4. The oxidation number of hydrogen is +1. But we have two hydrogens which add up to a charge of +2. Since the total charge of this molecule should be zero, we can say that the charge of sulfate ion is –2. We also know that the oxidation number of oxygen is –2. But there are four oxygens in a sulfate ion. So the charge adds to –8. Now let's solve this algebraically.

ON^{Sulfur} - Oxidation number of sulfur
ON^{Oxygen} - Oxidation number of oxygen
$ON^{Sulfur} + 4 (ON^{Oxygen}) = -2$
$ON^{Sulfur} + 4 (-2) = -2$
$ON^{Sulfur} = +6$

So the oxidation number of sulfur in sulfuric acid is +6.

Problem 2-2

Calculate the oxidation state of the element indicated in each of the following problems.

(a) What is the oxidation state of hydrogen in MgH_2?
(b) What is the oxidation state of chlorine in ClO_3^- ?
(c) What is the oxidation state of oxygen in Na_2O_2?
(d) What is the oxidation state of nitrogen in NH_3?
(e) What is the oxidation state of oxygen in O_2?
(f) What is the oxidation state of bromine in $HBrO_2$?
(g) What is the oxidation state of manganese in $KMnO_4$?

Answers:

(a) –1
(b) +5
(c) –1
(d) –3
(e) 0
(f) +3
(g) +7

F. OXIDATION-REDUCTION REACTIONS

Oxidation-reduction (redox) reactions involve the transfer of electrons from one compound or species to another. In this section, we will discuss oxidation-reduction reactions and learn how to balance them.

Oxidation is the process by which an atom or species loses its electrons. In *reduction*, an atom or species gains electrons. Let's first consider oxidation and reduction separately.

Consider the conversion of iron from its neutral elemental state to its ionic form.

$$Fe \longrightarrow Fe^{2+} + 2\,e^-$$

Notice that in the process iron lost electrons. The process is oxidation.

Consider another example. An example involving the conversion of bromine to its ionic form.

$$Br_2 + 2\,e^- \longrightarrow 2\,Br^-$$

Notice that in the process bromine gained electrons. The process is reduction.

Now let's go one step forward. Consider the next reaction.

$$2 \text{ Fe} \; + \; 3 \text{ Br}_2 \longrightarrow 2 \text{ FeBr}_3$$

This reaction is a typical example of an oxidation-reduction reaction. The oxidation number of iron on the reactant side is 0. The oxidation number of bromine on the reactant side is also 0. What are the oxidation numbers of iron and bromine in FeBr_3? Well, we know that bromine has an oxidation number of -1. So the oxidation number of iron in FeBr_3 is $+3$. Thus iron is oxidized and bromine is reduced. The species that gets oxidized is called the reducing agent. The species that gets reduced is called the *oxidizing agent*. In this reaction, evidently iron acts as the *reducing agent*, and bromine acts as the oxidizing agent.

Oxidation results in an increase in the oxidation number. In the process of oxidation, electrons are lost.

Reduction results in a decrease in the oxidation number. In the process, electrons are gained.

Balancing Oxidation-Reduction Reactions

Balancing of an oxidation-reduction reaction is a little more complex than balancing a simple reaction. The main rule that you have to follow when balancing oxidation-reduction reactions is that the absolute value of the increase in oxidation number of all the atoms that are oxidized should equal the absolute value of the decrease in oxidation number of all the atoms that are reduced. Balancing oxidation-reduction reaction is sometimes time-consuming and quite often frustrating. We will look at two methods of balancing oxidation-reduction reactions.

Method A

1. Write the unbalanced equation.
2. Find the oxidation numbers of the atoms that undergo change in oxidation states and write on top of each atom the corresponding oxidation number.
3. By this process, we will be able to see which atoms are getting oxidized and reduced.
4. Compare and indicate the change in oxidation numbers from the reactant side and the product side, and write down the change in the oxidation numbers.
5. Make the necessary changes by writing coefficients that will equalize the changes in the oxidation numbers. In other words, the net decrease in the oxidation numbers should equal the net increase in the oxidation numbers. Add water if necessary.
6. Do a final check on whether all the atoms and charges balance out.

Method B

1. Write the unbalanced equation.
2. Separate the two half-reactions, write them out, and balance any of the atoms. From this point onward, we balance the reactions separately. Do the obvious or the simple balancing by inspection if possible.
3. Balance the oxygen atoms by adding water on the appropriate side of the half-reaction.
4. Balance the hydrogen atoms by adding H^+ on the appropriate side of the half-reaction.
5. Add sufficient number of electrons so that the charges are balanced.
6. Once the half-reactions are balanced, combine the half-reactions and cancel out any common terms that appear on both sides of the equation to get the refined and balanced oxidation-reduction equation.

Example 2-3

Balance the following oxidation-reduction reaction.

$$\text{Zn} \; + \; \text{NO}_3^- \longrightarrow \text{Zn}^{2+} \; + \; \text{N}_2\text{O}$$

Method A

1. Zn + NO_3^- $\longrightarrow$ Zn^{2+} + N_2O

2. $\overset{0}{Zn}$ + $\overset{+5}{NO_3^-}$ $\longrightarrow$ $\overset{+2}{Zn^{2+}}$ + $\overset{+1}{N_2O}$

3. $\overset{0}{Zn}$ + $\overset{+5}{2\,NO_3^-}$ $\longrightarrow$ $\overset{+2}{Zn^{2+}}$ + $\overset{+1}{N_2O}$

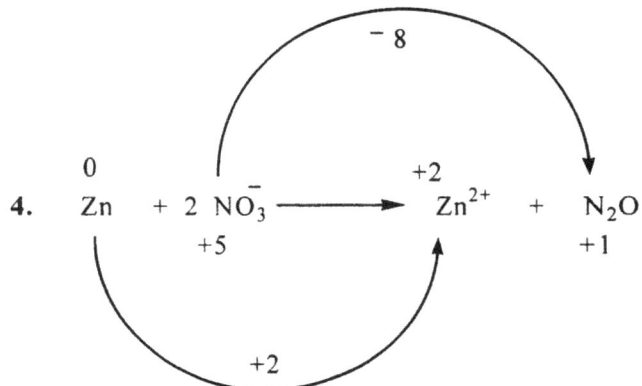

4. $\overset{0}{Zn}$ + $\underset{+5}{2\,NO_3^-}$ $\longrightarrow$ $\overset{+2}{Zn^{2+}}$ + $\overset{+1}{N_2O}$

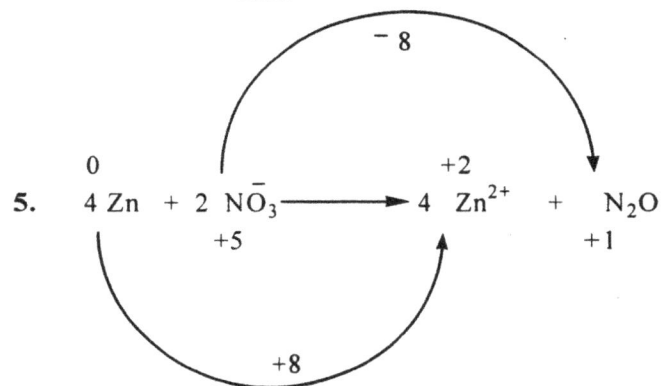

5. $\overset{0}{4\,Zn}$ + $\underset{+5}{2\,NO_3^-}$ $\longrightarrow$ $4\,\overset{+2}{Zn^{2+}}$ + $\overset{+1}{N_2O}$

6. $$10\,H^+ + 4\,Zn + 2\,NO_3^- \longrightarrow 4\,Zn^{2+} + N_2O + 5\,H_2O$$

Method B

$$Zn \ + \ NO_3^- \longrightarrow Zn^{2+} \ + \ N_2O$$

Half-reaction I

1. $Zn \longrightarrow Zn^{2+}$

2. $Zn \longrightarrow Zn^{2+} + 2e^-$

Half-reaction II

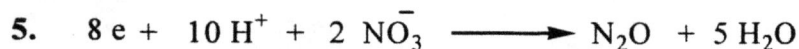

1. $NO_3^- \longrightarrow N_2O$

2. $2 NO_3^- \longrightarrow N_2O$

3. $2 NO_3^- \longrightarrow N_2O + 5 H_2O$

4. $10 H^+ + 2 NO_3^- \longrightarrow N_2O + 5 H_2O$

5. $8e + 10 H^+ + 2 NO_3^- \longrightarrow N_2O + 5 H_2O$

Before we combine the equations, the electrons need to be balanced out. So multiplying the balanced half-reaction # (I) by 4, we get

$$4 Zn \longrightarrow 4 Zn^{2+} + 8e^-$$

Combining the two half reactions

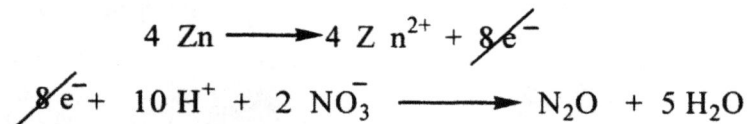

$$4 Zn \longrightarrow 4 Zn^{2+} + \cancel{8e^-}$$
$$\cancel{8e^-} + 10 H^+ + 2 NO_3^- \longrightarrow N_2O + 5 H_2O$$

$$10 H^+ + 4 Zn + 2 NO_3^- \longrightarrow 4 Zn^{2+} + N_2O + 5 H_2O$$

G. CALCULATIONS INVOLVING CHEMICAL REACTIONS

In this section, we will look at some chemical equations and find what we can do with the information represented in a chemical equation. The equation shown below represents the reaction of methane and oxygen to form carbon dioxide and water.

$$CH_4 \quad + \quad 2\,O_2 \quad \longrightarrow \quad CO_2 \quad + \quad 2\,H_2O$$

From this balanced equation we can infer many things. Let's consider a few.

1) One molecule of methane reacts with 2 molecules of oxygen to form 1 molecule of carbon dioxide and 2 molecules of water.

2) We can also say that 1 mole of methane reacts with 2 moles of oxygen to form 1 mole of carbon dioxide and 2 moles of water.

3) Since one mole contains Avogadro number of molecules, we can say that 6.023×10^{23} molecules of methane reacts with 1.2046×10^{24} ($= 2 \times 6.023 \times 10^{23}$) molecules of oxygen to form 6.023×10^{23} molecules of carbon dioxide and 1.2046×10^{24} molecules of water.

4) We can confidently say that 16 g of methane reacts with 64 g of oxygen to form 44 g of carbon dioxide and 36 g of water.

Example 2-4

Calculate the number of moles of water produced when 5.25 moles of methane undergo the reaction depicted below. (Assume there is plenty of oxygen for the reaction)

$$CH_4 \quad + \quad 2\,O_2 \quad \longrightarrow \quad CO_2 \quad + \quad 2\,H_2O$$

Solution:

From the equation, it is clear that for every mole of methane, 2 moles of water are formed. So without any elaborate calculations, you should be able to come up with the correct answer. It is very much like a ratio problem. Since there are 5.25 moles of methane, 10.5 moles of water will be formed.

Number of moles of water formed = 5.25 x 2 = 10.5 moles.

Example 2-5

110 g of CO_2 were formed as a result of the reaction shown below. How many grams of oxygen must have reacted to form that much carbon dioxide?

$$CH_4 \quad + \quad 2\,O_2 \quad \longrightarrow \quad CO_2 \quad + \quad 2\,H_2O$$

Solution:

According to the equation, 2 moles of oxygen result in 1 mole of carbon dioxide. For example, if 2 moles of carbon dioxide were formed, 4 moles of oxygen must have reacted. Here, the amount of carbon dioxide formed is given in terms of grams. So the first step is to convert the grams to moles.

$$\text{Moles of carbon dioxide} = \frac{110\text{ g}}{44\text{ g}/\text{mol}} = 2.5 \text{ moles}$$

Hence, <u>5 moles of oxygen</u> must have reacted to form 2.5 moles of carbon dioxide. But the question asks for this quantity in grams. So the final step is to convert moles to grams.

$$\text{The amount of required oxygen} = 5 \text{ moles} \times \frac{32 \text{ g}}{1 \text{ mol}} = 160 \text{ g}$$

H. THE CONCEPT OF LIMITING REAGENT

So far we have been considering reactions in which all the reactants exist in adequate quantities. In this section, we will consider what happens when the amount of one of the reactants available is less than the amount required to complete the reaction. When such a condition exists, we call that reactant or reagent the limiting reagent.

We will further explore this scenario through the following examples.

Example 2-6

A reaction mixture contains 60.75 g magnesium and 146 g hydrogen chloride. Predict the limiting reagent if the reaction occurs as shown.

$$Mg \quad + \quad 2\,HCl \quad \longrightarrow \quad H_2 \quad + \quad MgCl_2$$

Solution:

First, we have to convert the grams of the substances to moles. Then make the comparison to see which one is the limiting reagent. By now, you should be comfortable with the conversion of moles to grams and vice versa. The number of moles of magnesium present is 2.5 moles. According to the equation, 1 mole of magnesium reacts with 2 moles of hydrogen chloride. For magnesium to completely react, there should be at least 5 moles of hydrogen chloride present. If you calculate the number of moles of hydrogen chloride present, you will get 4 moles. This amount of hydrogen chloride is not enough to completely react with the amount of magnesium present. So the limiting reagent is hydrogen chloride.

I. PERCENT YIELD

If we know the chemical equation and the amounts of reactants, we can calculate the theoretical yield of that reaction. But in reality, the yield depends on many other factors also. Most of the time in synthesis reactions, even in your own lab experiments, you probably noticed that the actual yield is lower than the theoretical yield. The percent yield denotes the amount of actual yield in terms of the theoretical yield. The formula to find the percent yield is given below:

$$\text{Percent yield} = \frac{\text{actual yield of the product}}{\text{theoretical yield of the product}} \times 100\%$$

Example 2-7

$$NaNO_2 \ + \ HCl \ \longrightarrow \ HNO_2 \ + \ NaCl$$

A student conducted the above reaction in a lab as a part of her research assignment. She used 138 g of sodium nitrite, with excess of hydrogen chloride. What is the percent yield of HNO_2, if the actual yield of HNO_2 was 61.1 g?

Solution:

First, you should find the number of moles of $NaNO_2$. Since she used 138 g, the number of moles of $NaNO_2$ is 2 (Mol.wt of $NaNO_2$ is 69 g/mol). Since the ratio of formation of HNO_2 is 1:1 with respect to $NaNO_2$, theoretically 2 moles of HNO_2 should be formed. Two moles of HNO_2 correspond to 94 g. But actually, only 61.1 g of HNO_2 was formed. Now it is just a matter of plug and chug in the percent yield formula.

$$\text{The percentage yield of } HNO_2 = \frac{61.1 \text{ grams}}{94 \text{ grams}} \times 100\% = 65\%$$

In this experiment, the actual yield was not high (i.e., only 65% of the theoretically predicted yield) as expected.

Example 2-8

Match the following reactions with the appropriate type of reaction

1. $2KClO_3 \longrightarrow 2KCl + 3O_2$ **A.** Combination reaction

2. $2KCl + Cl_2 \longrightarrow 2KCl$ **B.** Double-replacement reaction

3. $HNO_3 + NaOH \longrightarrow NaNO_3 + H_2O$ **C.** Decomposition reaction

Solution:

$2KClO_3 \longrightarrow 2KCl + 3O_2$ **C.** Decomposition reaction

$2KCl + Cl_2 \longrightarrow 2KCl$ **A.** Combination reaction

$HNO_3 + NaOH \longrightarrow NaNO_3 + H_2O$ **B.** Double-replacement reaction

Chemistry Review 2 Problems

1. The reaction shown here can be best classified as a:

$$2HI + PbCl_2 \rightarrow PbI_2 + 2HCl$$

A. combustion reaction.
B. combination reaction.
C. single-replacement reaction.
D. double-replacement reaction.

2. All the following reactant-combinations are neutralization reactions, except:

A. $HNO_2 + NaOH$
B. $KOH + HCl$
C. $Al^+ + 3OH$
D. $H_3PO_4 + NaOH$

3. An unbalanced equation is shown. What is the coefficient of aluminum hydroxide in the final balanced equation?

$$H_2SO_4 + Al(OH)_3 \rightarrow H_2O + Al_2(SO_4)_3$$

A. 1
B. 2
C. 3
D. 7

4. How many grams of sodium chloride are required to synthesize 73 grams of hydrogen chloride, if the reaction involves sodium chloride and sulfuric acid?

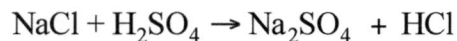

$$NaCl + H_2SO_4 \rightarrow Na_2SO_4 + HCl$$

A. 58.5 grams
B. 117 grams
C. 175.5 grams
D. 234 grams

5. In some reactions, you will often encounter ions in aqueous solutions which are not actually involved in the reaction. Such ions are best termed:

A. cations.
B. anions.
C. salt-bridge ions.
D. spectator ions.

6. Some substances can act as a base or an acid. Such substances are called:

A. aliphatic substances.
B. amphibasic substances.
C. lyophilic substances.
D. amphoteric substances.

7. Predict the coefficient of iron in the balanced equation for a reaction in which iron reacts with oxygen to form Fe_2O_3.

A. 1
B. 2
C. 3
D. 4

8. The number of molecules are the same in which of the following pairs?

A. 32 grams of O_2 and 32 grams of SO_2
B. 49 grams of NO_2 and 40 grams of NaOH
C. 20 grams of HF and 36 grams of H_2O
D. 60 grams of C_2H_6 and 156 grams of C_6H_6

Questions 9-15 are based on the following passage.

Passage 1

Information regarding the amounts of substances that actually react to form the products are of extreme help. Analyzing reactions and having the balanced equations help chemists to determine the correct and optimum proportions of reactants to be used. There are various other factors besides the amount of reactants, which determine the efficiency of reactions.

Experiment 1

$$2\,Al + Fe_2O_3 \rightarrow 2\,Fe + Al_2O_3$$

Student 1 used 40.5 g of aluminum and 80 g of Fe_2O_3 for Reaction I. A second student conducted the same reaction with a different amount for one of the reactants. The second student used 40.5 g of aluminum, and 90 grams of Fe_2O_3. A third student also conducted the same reaction with 54 g of aluminum and the same amount of Fe_2O_3 used by the first student.

Experiment 2

Reaction II involved the production of Al_2O_3 from aluminum hydroxide This was done by heating aluminum hydroxide.

$$2\,Al(OH)_3(s) \rightarrow Al_2O_3(s) + \text{product x}$$

Experiment 3

$$Fe_2O_3(s) + 3\,CO(g) \xrightarrow[\text{heat}]{} 2\,Fe(s) + 3\,CO_2(g)$$

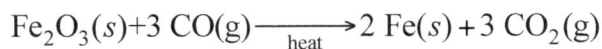

9. What is the most likely identity of product x?

A. aluminum
B. water
C. hydrogen
D. oxygen

10. In Experiment 3, which of the following is the limiting reagent?

A. Fe_2O_3 because there is only 1 mole of it
B. CO because of its gas phase
C. Fe because of its insufficiency
D. Cannot be determined without more data

11. Based on the given information, which of the following are true regarding Experiment 1?

I. The second student had the highest yield for aluminum oxide.
II. The third student had a higher yield for aluminum oxide than the first student.
III. The first and the third students had the same yield for aluminum oxide.

A. I only
B. I and II only
C. I and III only
D. II and III only

12. Which of the following changes will further increase the overall yield for the reactions conducted in the Experiment 1?

A. Increasing the amount of aluminum used by Student 1
B. Increasing the amount of aluminum used by Student 2
C. Increasing the amount of Fe_2O_3 used by Student 2
D. None of the above

13. Roughly 80 g of Fe_2O_3 was present in Experiment 3, and upon completion of the reaction, it was measured that 22 g of CO_2 was formed. If this is true, how much CO must have reacted before reaching completion of the reaction?

A. 14 grams
B. 28 grams
C. 56 grams
D. 84 grams

14. In the previous question, which of the reactants acts as the limiting reagent?

A. Fe_2O_3
B. CO
C. CO_2
D. Cannot be determined

15. If 0.1 mol of CO was reacted with excess of Fe_2O_3, how many molecules of carbon dioxide will be produced?

A. 6.0×10^{23} molecules
B. 6.0×10^{22} molecules
C. 3.0×10^{23} molecules
D. 18.0×10^{23} molecules

Solutions

1. The answer is D. This question tests your understanding of the general classification of reactions. The reaction is clearly not a combustion reaction. Combustion reactions occur in the presence of oxygen and involve release of heat. There is no indication of that in the given reaction. You might be tempted to select Choice C since the given reaction is a replacement reaction, but double-replacement reaction best describes the given reaction. In the reaction, the iodine is replaced with the chlorine, and the chlorine is replaced with the iodine.

2. The answer is C. Choices A, B, and D are all acid-base reactions, which are neutralization reactions. Choice C is actually the formation of a base ($AlOH_3$), and it is not a neutralization reaction.

3. The answer is B. Let's start balancing the equation from the sulfate point of view. You have 3 sulfate groups in aluminum sulfate. It has to come from the sulfuric acid. So the coefficient is 3 for the sulfuric acid. Since there are 2 aluminums in aluminum sulfate, we can assign a coefficient of 2 to the aluminum hydroxide. The rest of the hydrogens and oxygens can be balanced with water.

The balanced equation should look like this:

$$3\ H_2SO_4 + 2\ Al(OH)_3 \longrightarrow 6\ H_2O + Al_2(SO_4)_3$$

4. The answer is B. First, we have to check whether the given reaction is balanced. Without the balanced equation, the calculations will be incorrect. As a matter of fact, the given reaction is not balanced. The balanced equation is this:

$$2\ NaCl + H_2SO_4 \longrightarrow Na_2SO_4 + 2\ HCl$$

Now we can work out our magic calculations. The question specifies the grams of HCl synthesized. The 73 grams converted to moles should give 2 moles. According to the equation, 2 moles of NaCl are required to synthesize two moles of HCl. All you have to do now is to convert moles to grams. The correct value is 117 grams of NaCl.

5. The answer is D. This is a straightforward definition-type question. The ions that are present in the solution sometimes do not actually participate in the reaction. By writing the complete ionic equation of such a reaction, we can see that the spectator ions on both sides of the equation are in the same state or form. We can cancel them out and get the net equation of the reaction. Spectator ions are not usually depicted in the net ionic equation.

6. The answer is D. This is also a definition-type question. Amphoteric substances can exhibit both acidic and basic properties depending on the environment that they are subjected to.

7. The answer is D. The reaction mentioned in this question is the rusting of iron. The balanced reaction should look like this:

$$4\ Fe + 3\ O_2 \longrightarrow 2\ Fe_2O_3$$

8. The answer is D. The question tests your understanding of the concept of mole. In Choice A, we have 32 g of O_2 which corresponds to 1 mol of oxygen, and 32 g of SO_2 which corresponds to half a mol. Choice A is not correct. In Choice B, we have 49 g of NO_2 which corresponds to a little more than 1 mol, and 40 g of NaOH which corresponds to 1 mol. So this may be our answer. Choice C is not correct, because we have 20 g of HF which is 1 mol, and 36 g of water which is 2 moles. So Choice C is incorrect. Choice D has 60 g of C_2H_6 which is 2 moles, and 156 g of C_6H_6 is also 2 moles. So D is a better choice than B.

9. The answer is B. To answer this question, you have to use your intuition. The reaction occurs by means of the heat supplied to the aluminum hydroxide, and it is a dehydration reaction. So the most plausible answer is water.

10. The answer is D. The reactant coefficients in a balanced equation cannot be used to determine the identity of the limiting reagent. Without comparing the amounts of reactants that are actually present, we cannot determine the identity of the limiting reagent. CO being a gas has nothing to do with being the limiting reagent for the given reaction. Choice C is not logical, because it is a product. The best answer is that we cannot determine the identity of the limiting reagent, if any, without any data regarding the amount of reactants used.

11. The answer is C. Look at the items one by one. Item I says that the second student had the highest yield of products. In Experiment 1, the first student used 40.5 g of Al and 80 g of Fe_2O_3. This translates to 1.5 moles of Al and roughly 0.5 moles of Fe_2O_3. Here Fe_2O_3 is the limiting reagent. What was the second student doing? Well, the second student increased the amount of Fe_2O_3 used, keeping the same amount of Al. Since Fe_2O_3 is the limiting reagent, an increase of Fe_2O_3 will increase the product yield. So the second student must have had more yield than the first student. The first and the third students have the same yield for aluminum oxide, because the amount of limiting reagent present is the same in both cases. So items I and II are true.

12. The answer is C. By increasing the amount of aluminum used by the first student, there will not be an increase in the yield because Fe_2O_3 is the limiting reagent. Hence, Choice A is not correct. The same reasoning rules out Choice B. Increasing the amount of Fe_2O_3 by the second student will increase the yield further, because we actually have unreacted Al left according to the amounts used in the experiment. Hence, if we further increase the amount of Fe_2O_3 used, it will increase the yield until the Al runs out. Choice D is wrong.

13. The answer is A. In the question, we are given that 80 g of Fe_2O_3 is used in the reaction mixture. How much of this actually reacted is another story. That is to be found out from the yield data. The amount of CO_2 produced is 22 g. Based on the balanced equation, we can infer that for every 3 moles of CO reacted, 3 moles of CO_2 are produced. So CO and CO_2 have a 1:1 ratio. If 22 g or 0.5 moles of CO_2 is produced, 0.5 moles of CO must have reacted.

14. The answer is B. Based on the question, we can say that about 0.5 mol of Fe_2O_3 and 0.5 mol CO was present in the reacting mixture. Since the Fe_2O_3 to CO reacting ratio is 1:3, CO will completely react, and there will be some leftover unreacted Fe_2O_3 after the reaction is complete. So the limiting reagent is CO.

15. The answer is B. This question tests your understanding of the mole concept. Since we have excess amounts of Fe_2O_3, we do not have to worry about it. But, what you should consider is that the amount of CO present dictates the reaction. One mol of CO_2 contains Avogadro number (6.02×10^{23}) of molecules. The reaction results in 0.1 mol of CO_2. So 0.1 mol of CO_2 contains 6.02×10^{22} molecules.

Chemistry Review 3
Electronic Structure

A. INTRODUCTION

In this chapter, we will discuss the electronic arrangement of atoms. We will also talk about quantum numbers, orbitals, various rules pertaining to electron-filling, and electronic configuration.

B. ATOMIC STRUCTURE

The first ideas about electronic arrangement in atoms were primarily figured out from atomic emission spectra. In various experiments, atoms were made to be thermally or electrically excited, and this resulted in different kinds of bands or lines on photographic plates. Our understanding of atomic structure is based on these types of experiments. All elements have their characteristic line spectra with which they can be analyzed and identified.

Electromagnetic Waves

Before we discuss the atomic structure, we will touch on the topic of electromagnetic radiation to have a better analytical understanding of the key ideas. All electromagnetic radiations travel with a constant speed of 3×10^8 m/s. The electromagnetic spectrum ranges from radio waves to gamma rays.

The Wave Nature

Light has wave nature. It has electric and magnetic fields which are perpendicular to each other, and can travel through space. No medium is required. Because of its wave character, we can define light in terms of frequency and wave length. The distance between two adjacent crests or troughs, or any two adjacent identical points on a wave is called *wave length* (λ). *Frequency* (f) is the number of wavelengths passing through a point in unit time. Wavelength and frequency are related by the relation given below. Frequency is usually expressed in 1/second (s^{-1}), which is otherwise known as *hertz* (Hz).

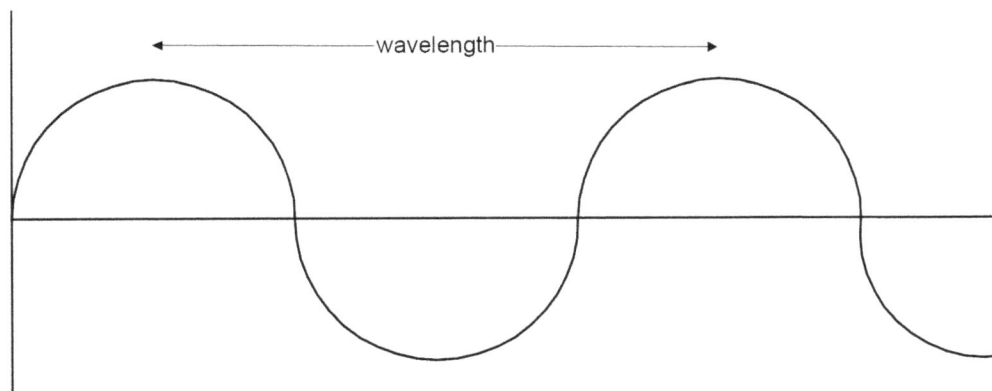

$$\text{Velocity} = \text{frequency} \times \text{wavelength}$$

$$c = f \, \lambda$$

The Particle Nature and Quantum Theory

Light has particle nature. These particles or forms (packages) of energy are called quanta. A more modern term for such as particle of light is photon. The energy of a photon can be expressed in terms of the following formula.

Energy = h f,

where h is the Planck's constant, and f is the frequency.

Planck's constant = 6.63×10^{-34} J.s

According to *Heisenberg's Uncertainty Principle*, we cannot determine both the momentum and the position of subatomic particles simultaneously. This is because we are using other particles (electromagnetic particles-like photons) of comparable energy to detect these subatomic particles, and by the time these other particles find the subatomic particles (say electrons), they are also disturbing the pathway of these electrons. In essence, the study of something extremely small and fast (about the magnitude of electrons) cannot be done without interference of its natural course or position.

Photoelectric Effect

The Photoelectric Effect can be defined as the ejection of electrons from a metal surface when light rays strike on it. The ejected electrons are often called "photoelectrons." The ejection of electrons occurs only if the incident light has a certain minimum or *threshold frequency*. The required threshold frequency is a characteristic specific to each metal. Experimentally, it has been found that the photoelectrons emitted with maximum energy do not have the full energy equivalent supplied by the incident photon. This is because energy is required to break loose the electrons from the surface of the metal. The energy required for this is called "work function," which is characteristic of each metal. The photoelectrons can be accelerated to a positively charged plate, creating a flow of charges along a wire-photocurrent. The current can be measured by an ammeter connected to the wire.

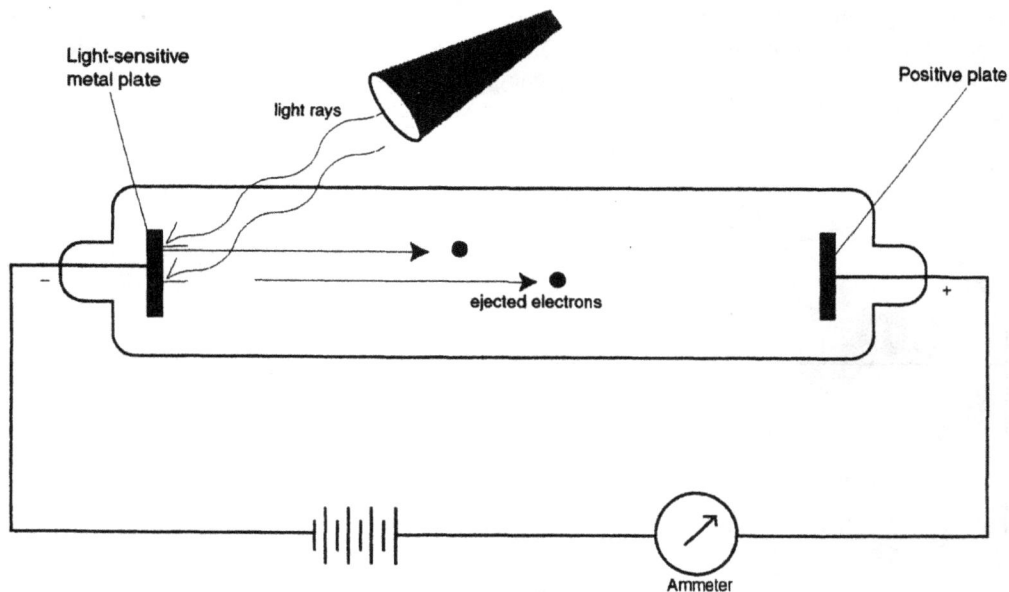

The maximum kinetic energy (K_{max}) of a photoelectron is given by the following equation:

$$K_{max} = 1/2\ mv_{max}{}^2 = hf - \varphi$$

In this equation, m is the mass of an electron, v_{max} is the maximum velocity of the electrons, h is the Planck's constant, f is the frequency of the incident light, φ (pronounced *phi*) is the "work function" of the metal. The entity hf represents the energy of the incident photon.

Key Observations on Photoelectric Effect

1) The photoelectric effect exemplifies the particle nature of light.

2) Based on conservation of energy, no photoelectron can have energy more than that of an incident photon.

3) The energy of the photoelectrons is always less than that of the incident photons, because some energy (work function) is required to break the electrons loose.

4) The maximum energy of the photoelectrons is independent of the intensity of the incident light.

5) Electrons are not ejected no matter how high the intensity of the incident light is, unless the incident light has the energy corresponding to the threshold frequency characteristic of a particular metal.

Atomic Emission Spectra

When we pass white light through a prism, dispersion of the light occurs resulting in *continuous spectrum* of wavelengths. Another type of spectrum results when heated gas emits light. This results in a *line spectrum*. Line spectrum contains only certain specific wavelengths of light. The wavelengths in the visible spectrum of hydrogen is given by the following formula:

$$\frac{1}{\lambda} = \frac{R}{hc}\left(\frac{1}{4} - \frac{1}{n^2}\right)$$

where λ is the wavelength of the light, R (Rydberg constant) = 2.18×10^{-18} J, h (Planck's constant) = 6.63×10^{-34} J.s, c (speed of light) = 3.0×10^8 m/s, and n is some whole number that is greater than 2 which corresponds to the orbit-number from which the electron is making the transition. For example, if the transition of an electron is from orbit number 4 to 2, the n value is 4.

Bohr's Model of Hydrogen Atom

Niel Bohr's explanation of the hydrogen spectrum was a major breakthrough toward the understanding of atomic structure. The following are the postulates:

1) In each hydrogen atom, the electron revolves around the nucleus in one of the several stable orbits.

2) Each orbit has a definite radius and thus has a definite energy associated with it.

3) An electron in an orbit closest to the nucleus has the lowest energy, and if the electron is in the lowest orbit the atom is said to be in its *ground state*.

4) The electron in an atom may absorb discrete amounts of energy and move to another orbit with higher energy, and this state is called the *excited state*.

5) An electron in an excited atom can go back to a lower energy level and this process will result in the release of excess energy as light.

6) The amount of energy released or absorbed is equal to the difference between the energies of the initial and final orbits.

Based on Bohr's theory, light energy is emitted when an electron in a higher energy level ($E_{initial}$) jumps to a lower energy level (E_{final}). Based on the law of conservation of energy, the sum of energies of the emitted photon (hf) and the electron's final energy (E_{final}) should be equal to the electron's initial energy ($E_{initial}$). This can be represented mathematically as follows:

$$hf + E_{final} = E_{initial}$$

Transitions of the electron in the hydrogen atom result in different spectral lines.

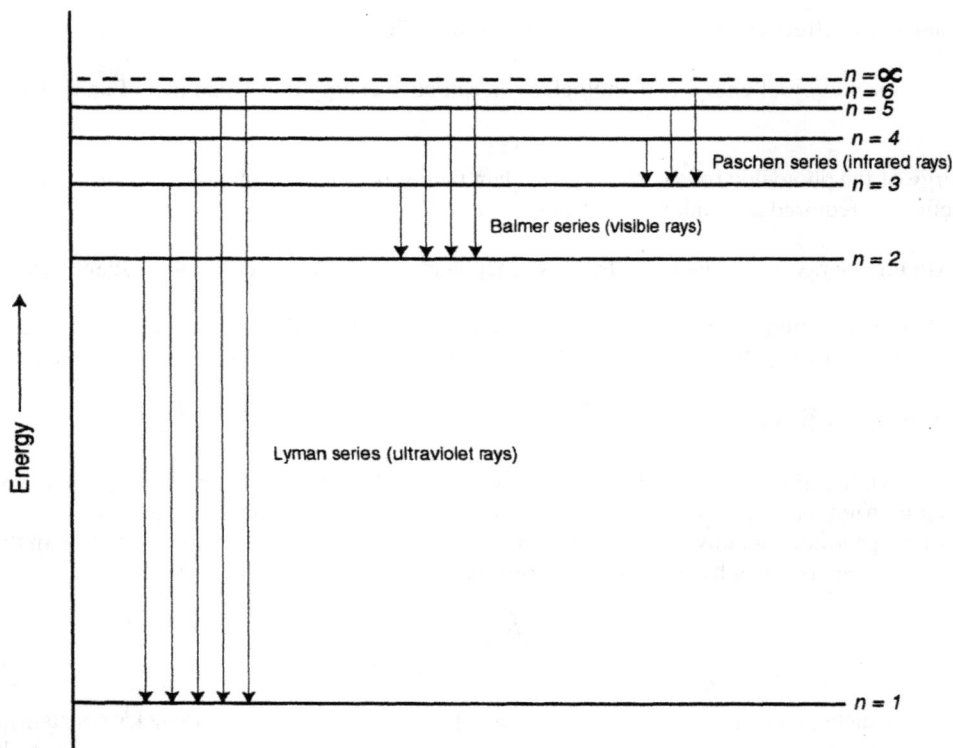

The energy of the emitted photon

$$hf = R\left(\frac{1}{n_{final}^2} - \frac{1}{n_{initial}^2}\right)$$

where n_{final} and $n_{initial}$ are the principal quantum numbers of final and initial energy levels, and R is the Rydberg constant (2.18×10^{-18} J). The figure given above shows the transitions that can result in the Lyman (ultraviolet region), Balmer (visible region), and Paschen series (infrared region) for n_{final} values 1, 2, and 3, respectively.

A photon is emitted when an electron in an atom jumps from a higher to a lower energy level. The energy of the emitted photon is equal to the difference in energy between the two energy levels.

C. QUANTUM NUMBERS

All electrons present in an atom have specific addresses or attributes by which each electron can be referred to. The four quantum numbers are the ones with which we can describe each and every electron that is present in an atom. One of the quantum numbers describes the shape or the most probable area around the nucleus where we can find the particular electrons of interest. This wave function of an electron is called an *orbital*.

Principal quantum number (*n*). The principal quantum number denotes the energy level of electrons. The larger the principal quantum number is, the larger the energy. The smaller the principal quantum number is, the lower the energy. The shells are often named K, L, M, N, . . ., which correspond to the principal quantum numbers 1, 2, 3, 4, . . ., respectively.

Letter	K	L	M	N . . .
n	1	2	3	4 . . .

Angular momentum quantum number (*l*). Angular momentum quantum number (azimuthal quantum number) denotes the shape of the orbital. The values range from 0 to n − 1, where n stands for the principal quantum number. If an electron has a principal quantum number of 4, the values of angular momentum quantum numbers are 0, 1, 2, and 3. The angular momentum quantum numbers correspond to different subshells. An angular momentum quantum number 0 corresponds to *s* subshell, 1 to *p* subshell, 2 to *d* subshell, 3 to *f* subshell, and so on. For instance, 3*d* denotes a subshell with quantum numbers *n* = 3 and *l* = 2

Orbital	s	p	d	f . . .
l	0	1	2	3 . . .

s orbital

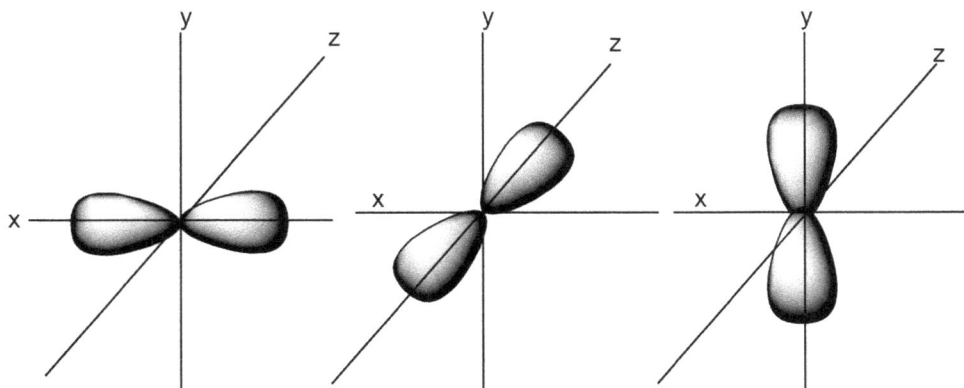

2 *p*$_x$ orbital   2 *p*$_y$ orbital   2 *p*$_z$ orbital

Magnetic quantum number (m_l). Magnetic quantum numbers define the different spatial orientations of the orbitals. The values from $-l$ to $+l$. For example, let's say the value of l is 1. So the magnetic quantum numbers will be $-1, 0$, and $+1$. The l value corresponds to p sublevel and the three magnetic quantum numbers correspond to the three atomic orbitals in the p subshell.

Spin quantum number (m_s). Spin quantum number has to do with the spin orientations of an electron. The two possible spins are denoted by the spin quantum numbers $+1/2$ and $-1/2$.

Spatial orientation of d orbitals

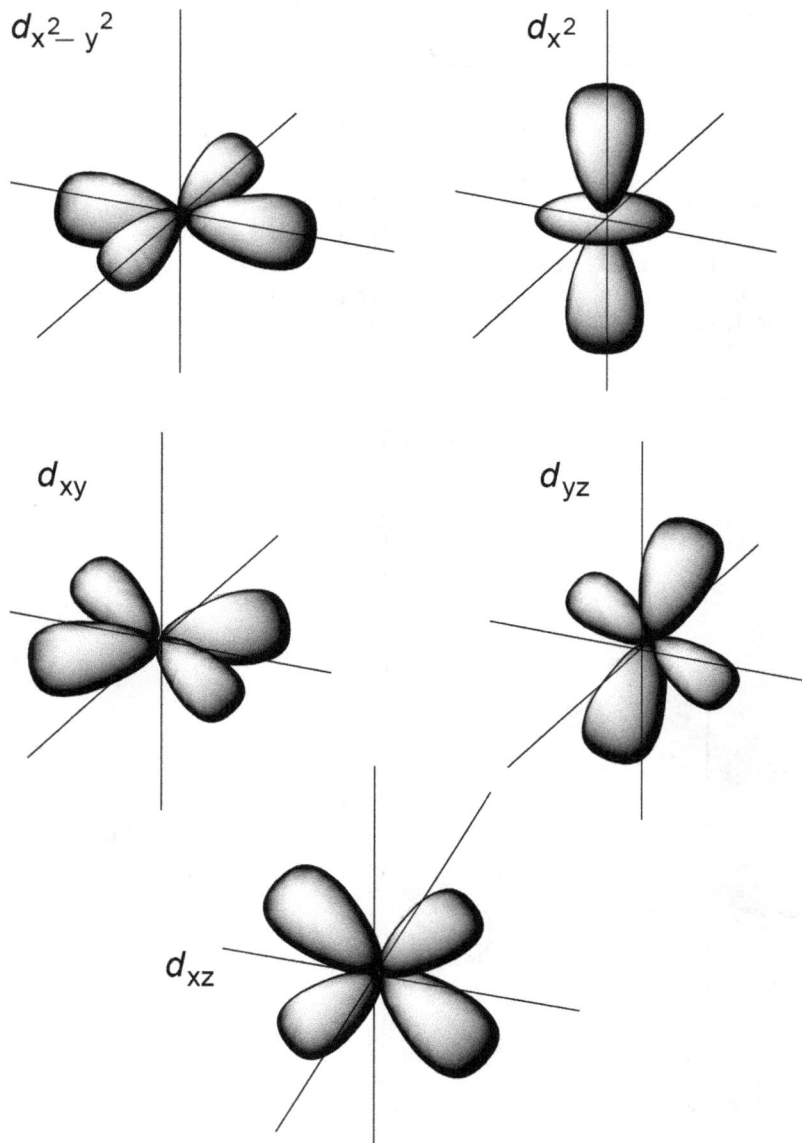

$d_{x^2-y^2}$

d_{x^2}

d_{xy}

d_{yz}

d_{xz}

D. ELECTRONIC CONFIGURATION

We talked about quantum numbers and atomic orbitals. In this section, we will focus our attention mainly on writing the electronic configuration of atoms and the rules associated with it. First, let's talk about the ground state electronic configuration. The ground state configuration means the electronic configuration at the lowest energy state.

There are certain rules that should be applied to the filling of orbitals. In order to do that properly, we need to know the Aufbau principle. According to the Aufbau principle, the filling order of electrons obeys a general pattern in which the electrons try to occupy the orbitals in such a way as to minimize the total energy; that is, they occupy the lowest energy orbitals first and then step-by-step go to the next available higher energy levels successively. Of course, there are some exceptions to these generalizations. Some students find it hard to remember the order of filling. The diagram given below may help you. So take a close look. Filling order can be depicted as follows:

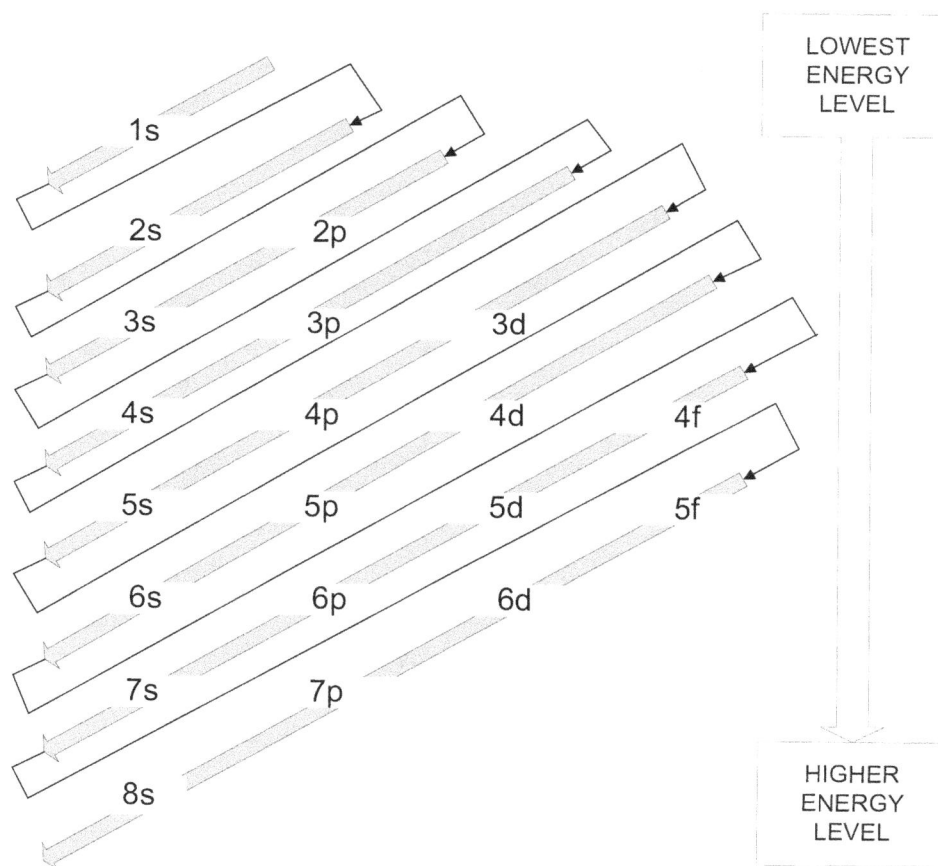

This is an easy way to remember the general order of electron-filling in the subshells. The order of filling is $1s, 2s, 2p, 3s, 3p, 4s, 4p, 5s, \ldots$, and so on.

An *s* orbital is spherical in shape. All *p* orbitals have dumbbell shape with two lobes aligned along an axis. All *d* orbitals have slightly complex shapes and are beyond the scope of our discussion. Each orbital can accommodate a maximum of two electrons. Hence, an *s* subshell, (only one orbital) can accommodate a maximum of two electrons. Similarly, *p* (three orbitals), *d* (five orbitals), and *f* (seven orbitals) subshells can have maximum of six, ten, and fourteen electrons, respectively.

Table 3-1 Some possible combinations of quantum numbers for atomic orbitals

Principal quantum number (*n*)	Angular momentum quantum number (*l*)	Magnetic quantum number (*m$_l$*)	Subshells	Number of orbitals	Maximum number of electrons
1	0	0	1*s*	1	2
2	0	0	2*s*	1	2
2	1	-1,0,+1	2*p*	3	6
3	0	0	3*s*	1	2
3	1	-1,0,+1	3*p*	3	6
3	2	-2,-1,0,+1,+2	3*d*	5	10
4	0	0	4*s*	1	2
4	1	-1,0,+1	4*p*	3	6
4	2	-2,-1,0,+1,+2	4*d*	5	10
4	3	-3,-2,-1,0,+1,+2,+3	4*f*	7	14

Example 3-1

Write the electronic configuration of lithium.

Solution: From the periodic table, we can get the atomic number of lithium. The lithium atom has 3 electrons. As we know, 1*s* subshell is the first one to be filled. The *s* orbital can hold a maximum of 2 electrons. We have one electron remaining. It will occupy the 2*s* subshell which is the next energy level. So the third electron will occupy the 2*s* subshell. Hence, the configuration of lithium is $1s^2 2s^1$.

Example 3-2

Write the electronic configuration of oxygen in its ground state form.

Solution: The oxygen atom contains 8 electrons. The first 2 electrons will go to the 1*s* level. The next 2 electrons will occupy the 2*s* level. We have 4 electrons remaining. What is the next subshell according to the filling order? It is 2*p*. The *p* subshell can hold a maximum of 6 electrons in its orbitals. So the remaining 4 electrons will occupy the 2*p* level. Hence, the configuration of oxygen is $1s^2\, 2s^2\, 2p^4$.

Hund's Rule

We have learned the order of filling the subshells. Now let's take a closer look at the filling of electrons in an orbital level. Each orbital can be occupied by a maximum of 2 electrons, and these electrons will have opposite spins as dictated by the spin quantum number. Hund's rule describes the way the electrons fill up the orbitals. According to the Hund's rule, each electron starts filling up each orbital of a given subshell. After all the orbitals in a given subshell have been filled singly (half-filled), then the electrons start pairing. Let's look at some examples.

Example 3-3

Write the electronic configuration of sulfur and also show the filling of electrons with orbital notation.

Solution: Sulfur atom has 16 electrons. The electronic configuration is written as $1s^2 \, 2s^2 \, 2p^6 \, 3s^2 \, 3p^4$. To see the significance of the Hund's rule, look at the $3p$ subshell. In the $3p$ subshell, we have 3 orbitals.

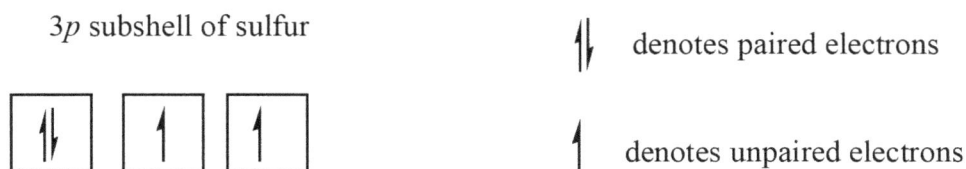

3p subshell of sulfur

↿⇂ denotes paired electrons

↿ denotes unpaired electrons

Note that the electrons first occupy singly in the orbitals. Altogether there are 4 electrons in the $3p$ subshell. Instead of filling the orbitals in pairs, the first 3 electrons start filling the three orbitals singly, and then the remaining electron occupies the orbital with the other electron as paired electrons. (See the orbital notation of $3p$ subshell shown above.) If this were not the case, you would have seen two electron-paired orbitals followed by an empty orbital.

Another idea we want to touch on concerns paramagnetic and diamagnetic substances. Substances that have unpaired electrons are called paramagnetic. Substances that have only paired electrons are called diamagnetic.

Chemistry Review 3 Problems

1. Which of the following shows the correct order of filling of subshells?

A. $3s, 3p, 4s, 3d, 4p$
B. $3s, 3p, 3d, 4s, 4p$
C. $3s, 3d, 3p, 4s, 4p$
D. $3s, 3d, 3p, 4p, 4s$

2. Which of the following represents the outer most shell configuration of an inert gas?

A. $4s^2 4p^2$
B. $4s^2 4p^3$
C. $4s^1 4p^6$
D. $4s^2 4p^6$

3. The electronic configuration shown is that of the element:

$$[Kr] 5s^2 4d^{10} 5p^2$$

A. Sb.
B. Rb.
C. In.
D. Sn.

4. The maximum number of electrons that can occupy the energy levels is calculated using a formula, where n represents the number corresponding to the energy level. The formula is:

A. n^2
B. $2n^2$
C. $2n + 1$
D. $4n + 2$

5. Consider this statement: No two electrons of an atom can have the same sets of four quantum numbers. This is known as the:

A. Heisenberg's Uncertainty Principle.
B. Hund's Rule.
C. Pauli Exclusion Principle.
D. Aufbau Principle.

6. Which of the following is true with respect to subshells?

A. The $4p$ subshell has higher energy than the $5s$ subshell.
B. The $3p$ subshell can have a maximum of 3 electrons.
C. The $5d$ subshell has higher energy than the $6s$ subshell.
D. The $4f$ subshell has higher energy than the $5d$ subshell.

7. Which of the following is NOT isoelectronic with any of the noble gases?

A. Ca^{2+}
B. Br^-
C. S^{2-}
D. Mg^+

8. Which of the following is not a possible set of quantum number values for the nitrogen atom, in the order of principal quantum number, azimuthal quantum number, magnetic quantum number, and spin quantum number?

A. $1, 0, 0, -1/2$
B. $2, 1, +1, +1/2$
C. $2, 0, 0, -1/2$
D. $2, 1, +2, +1/2$

9. The electronic configuration $[Ar] 3d^{10} 4s^2 4p^2$ is that of:

A. Ge.
B. Zn.
C. Se.
D. Ar.

10. The electronic configuration of a given element has a $4d$ subshell. This cannot be the electronic configuration of:

A. Os.
B. Cu.
C. Ag.
D. Ra.

Solutions

1. The answer is A. The correct order of filling from $3s$ onward is $3s$, $3p$, $4s$, $3d$, and $4p$.

2. The answer is D. Inert gases (noble gases) have the completed outermost s and p subshells. Helium is an exception to this.

3. The answer is D. The atomic number of Kr (krypton) is 36. After the representation of Kr, how many electrons do we have? There are 14 more electrons. That adds up to an atomic number of 50. The atomic number 50 corresponds to the element Sn.

4. The correct answer is B. This is a straightforward question. The maximum number of electrons that can occupy the principal energy level is calculated using the formula $2n^2$.

5. The answer is C. The statement "no two electrons of an atom can have the same set of four quantum numbers" is Pauli exclusion principle.

6. The answer is C. The only correct statement in the set of choices is "the $5d$ subshell has higher energy than the $6s$ subshell." All other choices are wrong.

7. The answer is D. The question asks us to pick the species that is not isoelectronic (same number of electrons) with the noble gases. In order to solve this problem, you have to find the number of electrons present in them, and if it matches with the number of electrons in any of the noble gases, you can eliminate that choice. All the ions match with one or other noble gas in terms of the number of electrons, except Mg^+.

8. The answer is D. The nitrogen atom has a total of 7 electrons. The principal quantum number could be 1 or 2. With that alone, we cannot rule out any of the choices. The next quantum number given is the azimuthal quantum number, also known as the angular momentum quantum number. The angular momentum quantum number can have values from 0 to $n-1$, where n represents the principal quantum number. Since 2 denotes the maximum n value, we cannot rule out any of the choices yet. Look at the next quantum number, which is the magnetic quantum number. The magnetic quantum number can have values from $-l$ to $+l$, where l represents angular momentum quantum number. So the magnetic quantum number cannot be +2 for nitrogen.

9. The answer is A. This question tests your ability to recognize a given electronic configuration. The fastest way to approach this type of question is to look at the root element given. The atomic number of argon is 18. We can count 14 more electrons in the given configuration to get a total of 32 electrons. The atomic number 32 is that of germanium (Ge).

10. The answer is B. Osmium, silver, and radium can have the $4d$ subshell. Copper belongs to the 4th period and therefore cannot have a $4d$ subshell. All the other elements listed belong to the periods 5, 6 and 7.

PERIODIC TABLE OF ELEMENTS

IA	IIA	IIIB	IVB	VB	VIB	VIIB	VIII	VIII	VIII	IB	IIB	IIIA	IVA	VA	VIA	VIIA	O
1 H 1.0																	2 He 4.0
3 Li 6.9	4 Be 9.0											5 B 10.8	6 C 12.0	7 N 14.0	8 O 16.0	9 F 19.0	10 Ne 20.2
11 Na 23.0	12 Mg 24.3											13 Al 27.0	14 Si 28.1	15 P 31.0	16 S 32.1	17 Cl 35.5	18 Ar 39.9
19 K 39.1	20 Ca 40.1	21 Sc 45.0	22 Ti 47.9	23 V 50.9	24 Cr 52.0	25 Mn 54.9	26 Fe 55.8	27 Co 58.9	28 Ni 58.7	29 Cu 63.5	30 Zn 65.4	31 Ga 69.7	32 Ge 72.6	33 As 74.9	34 Se 79.0	35 Br 79.9	36 Kr 83.8
37 Rb 85.5	38 Sr 87.6	39 Y 88.9	40 Zr 91.2	41 Nb 92.9	42 Mo 95.9	43 Tc (98)	44 Ru 101.1	45 Rh 102.9	46 Pd 106.4	47 Ag 107.9	48 Cd 112.4	49 In 114.8	50 Sn 118.7	51 Sb 121.8	52 Te 127.6	53 I 126.9	54 Xe 131.3
55 Cs 132.9	56 Ba 137.3	57 La* 138.9	72 Hf 178.5	73 Ta 180.9	74 W 183.9	75 Re 186.2	76 Os 190.2	77 Ir 192.2	78 Pt 195.1	79 Au 197.0	80 Hg 200.6	81 Tl 204.4	82 Pb 207.2	83 Bi 209.0	84 Po (209)	85 At (210)	86 Rn (222)
87 Fr (223)	88 Ra 226.0	89 Ac** 227.0	104 Unq (261)	105 Unp (262)	106 Unh (263)	107 Uns (262)	108 Uno (265)	109 Une (267)									

s BLOCK · d BLOCK · p BLOCK

f BLOCK

*

58 Ce 140.1	59 Pr 140.9	60 Nd 144.2	61 Pm (145)	62 Sm 150.4	63 Eu 152.0	64 Gd 157.3	65 Tb 158.9	66 Dy 162.5	67 Ho 164.9	68 Er 167.3	69 Tm 168.9	70 Yb 173.0	71 Lu 175.0

**

90 Th 232.0	91 Pa (231)	92 U 238.0	93 Np (237)	94 Pu (244)	95 Am (243)	96 Cm (247)	97 Bk (247)	98 Cf (251)	99 Es (252)	100 Fm (257)	101 Md (258)	102 No (259)	103 Lr (260)

Chemistry Review 4
Organic Chemistry

A. INTRODUCTION

Organic Chemistry is the study of carbon compounds. Carbon can form a wide array of compounds, because of its size and ability to form covalent bonds with other carbon atoms. In addition, carbon can form bonds with many other elements. This property of carbon increases the facility of forming multitudes of different compounds. The particular electronegativity of carbon also plays a key role in its versatility. In this chapter, we will review some of the fundamental aspects of carbon atom and the main types of hybridizations involving carbon compounds.

B. THE CARBON ATOM

Electrons are found in regions around the nucleus in an atom, and those regions are called *orbitals*. The orbitals can be defined and differentiated by size, shape, and orientation. *Valence electrons* are electrons that are found in the outermost shell. The carbon atom has four valence electrons. These valence electrons are involved in chemical reactions and bonding.

The electronic configuration:

Carbon	Atomic number — 6
	Electronic configuration — $1s^2 2s^2 2p^2$

C. BONDING

Ionic bond – Ionic bond is formed between an electropositive and electronegative atom (ion), or generally we can define it as an attractive force between a positive and a negative ion (e.g., KCl).

Covalent bond – Covalent bond is formed by the sharing of a pair of electrons between two atoms. Carbon compounds generally contain covalent bonds.

D. HYBRIDIZATION OF ORBITALS

The six electrons of a carbon atom are distributed in the orbitals as follows:

Electronic configuration — $1s^2 2s^2 2p^2$

Ground state carbon atom

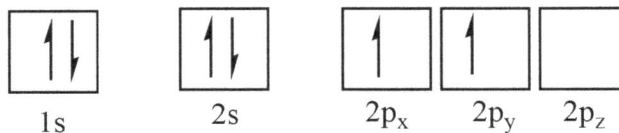

577

*sp*³ **Hybridization**

The carbon atoms of alkanes (e.g., methane, ethane) are sp^3 hybridized. In order to form the four bonds in methane, a carbon atom needs four half-filled orbitals. In order to have more free half-filled orbitals, the carbon atoms undergo hybridization.

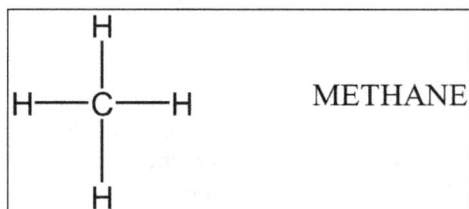

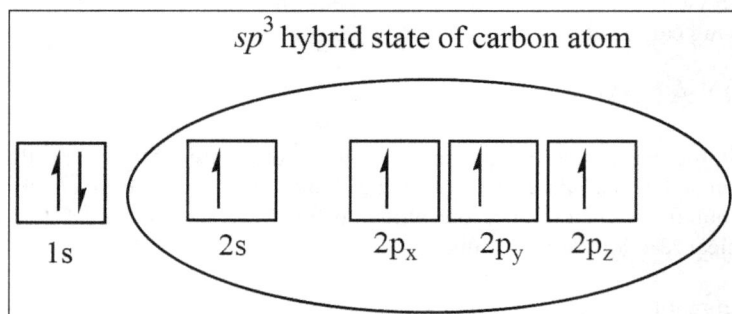

```
        H
        |
H ————— C ————— H        METHANE
        |
        H
```

sp^3 hybrid state of carbon atom

```
  ↑↓      ↑       ↑     ↑     ↑
  1s      2s     2pₓ   2p_y  2p_z
```

The hybridization results in one half-filled **2s** orbital, and three half-filled **2p** orbitals (a total of four half-filled orbitals). These unpaired electrons form the sp^3 hybridized carbon, which can form the four covalent bonds in the methane molecule. The four sp^3 hybrids are directed to the corners of a tetrahedron with bond angles of 109.5^0.

*sp*² **Hybridization**

In carbon-carbon double bonds, the carbons undergo another type of hybridization called the sp^2 hybridization. In this hybridization, only one **2s**, and two **2p** orbitals are involved. The C=C contains a sigma (σ) bond and a pi (π) bond. The pi bond is formed by the unhybridized **2p** orbital overlap. The three equal hybrids lie in an xy-plane with bond angles of 120^0.

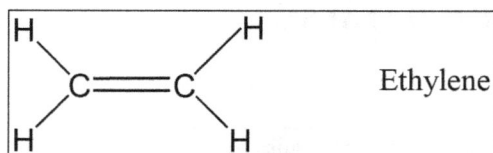

```
H               H
  \            /
    C ======= C          Ethylene
  /            \
H               H
```

sp^2 hybrid state of carbon atom

One 2s and two 2p orbitals

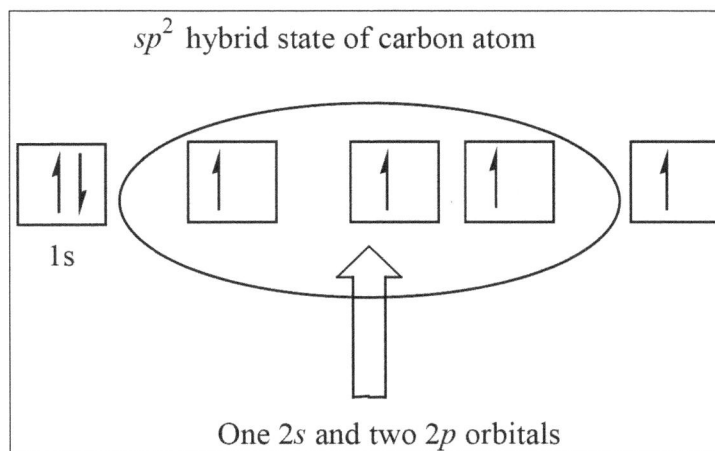

sp Hybridization

Yet another hybridization called the *sp* hybridization exists in carbon-carbon triple bonds. An *sp* hybridized carbon atom is bonded only to two other atoms. In this type of hybridization, one 2s orbital and one 2p orbital are involved. A carbon-carbon triple bond contains one sigma bond and two pi bonds.

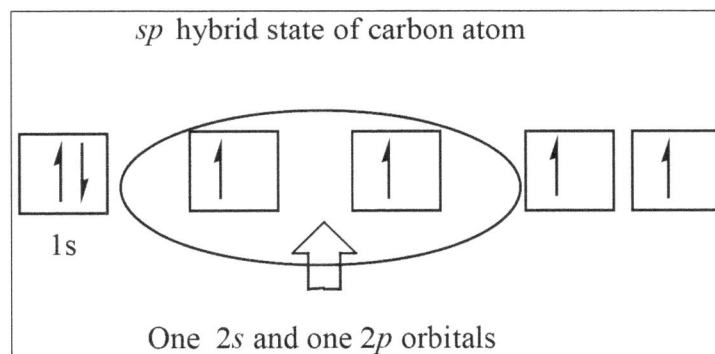

HC ≡ CH   Acetylene

sp hybrid state of carbon atom

One 2s and one 2p orbitals

E. RESONANCE

Resonance is an important aspect in Organic chemistry. Though we represent definite Lewis structures of molecules, in reality the electrons are not localized. They are shared and delocalized by the atoms in a molecule to have the most stable electron distribution. This is called *resonance*. Resonance promotes stability.

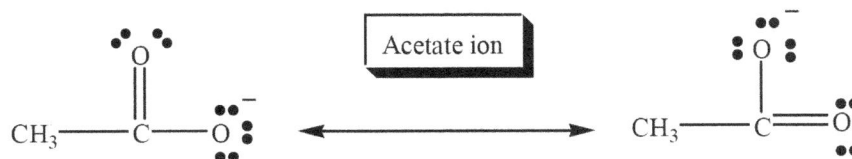

Acetate ion

F. FUNCTIONAL GROUPS

IMPORTANT FUNCTIONAL GROUPS

$R-\overset{\overset{\displaystyle O}{\|\|}}{C}-X$ Acid halide	$R-\overset{\overset{\displaystyle O}{\|\|}}{C}-O-\overset{\overset{\displaystyle O}{\|\|}}{C}-R$ Acid anhydride	R-OH Alcohol
$R-\overset{\overset{\displaystyle O}{\|\|}}{C}-H$ Aldehyde	R-H Alkane	$R_2C{=}CR_2$ Alkene
$R_2C{\equiv}CR_2$ Alkyne	R X Alkyl/aryl halide	$R-\overset{\overset{\displaystyle O}{\|\|}}{C}-NR_2$ Amide
$R-NH_2$ Amine (1^0)	R_2-NH Amine (2^0)	R_3-N Amine (3^0)
$R-\overset{\overset{\displaystyle O}{\|\|}}{C}OH$ Carboxylic cid	$R-\overset{\overset{\displaystyle O}{\|\|}}{C}-OR$ Ester	ROR Ether
$R-\overset{\overset{\displaystyle O}{\|\|}}{C}-R$ Ketone	R-SH Thiol	

Chemistry Review 4 Problems

1. The carbon indicated by the arrow has which of the following hybridizations?

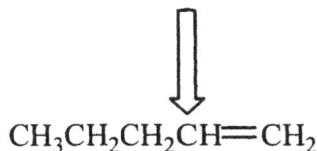

$$CH_3CH_2CH_2CH{=}CH_2$$

A. *sp* hybridization
B. sp^2 hybridization
C. sp^3 hybridization
D. sp^3d^2 hybridization

2. In acetylene, how many sigma bonds are present between the two carbons?

A. One
B. Two
C. Three
D. Four

3. The triple bond of 2-propyne contains:
A. one sigma bond and one pi bond.
B. one sigma bond and two pi bonds.
C. two sigma bonds and one pi bond.
D. three sigma bonds.

4. Which of the following represents the arrangement of the sp^3 hybrid orbitals in methane?

A. Planar
B. Tetragonal planar
C. Tetrahedral
D. Bipyramidal

5. How many electrons are actually involved in the carbon-carbon bond of acetylene?

A. 2
B. 3
C. 4
D. 6

6. Which of the following best represents the hydrogen-carbon-hydrogen bond angles in methane?

A. $90°$
B. $109.5°$
C. $120°$
D. $180°$

7. Which of the following bonds indicated by the arrows has the shortest bond length?

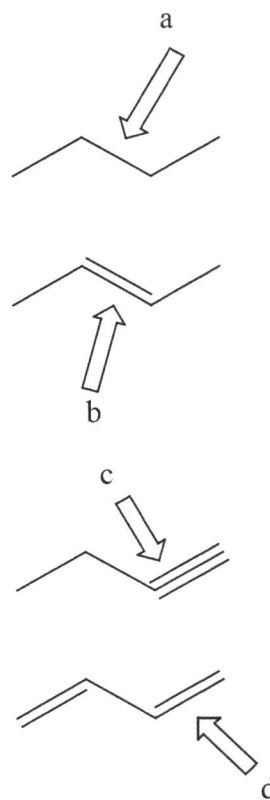

Figure for Q-7

A. a
B. b
C. c
D. d

8. The carbon-hydrogen bond in propane can be best described as:

A. an ionic bond.
B. a covalent bond.
C. a hydrogen bond.
D. a dipole-dipole bond.

Solutions

1. The answer is B. The carbon indicated by the arrow is an sp^2 hybridized carbon atom. Notice that the indicated carbon has a double bond and two single bonds. The double bond connects this carbon to the end-carbon. A hydrogen atom and the 3rd carbon are attached to this carbon via single bonds.

2. The answer is A. Acetylene is the first member of the alkyne group. The carbon-carbon bond is a triple bond which contains only one sigma bond.

3. The answer is B. The triple bond of 2-propyne (an alkyne) contains one sigma bond and two pi bonds.

4. The answer is C. The sp^3 hybrid orbitals such as those seen in alkanes have a tetrahedral orientation.

5. The answer is D. This question also tests your basic knowledge of hybridization in carbon compounds. A triple bond means three bonds. Since there are three bonds, six electrons are involved in the bond.

6. The answer is B. Methane has a tetrahedral geometry. So the hydrogen-carbon-hydrogen bond angle is closest to 109.5°.

7. The answer is C. The triple bond is the shortest among the bonds indicated by the arrows. The only triple bond-bearing compound given is Choice C.

8. The answer is B. The carbon-hydrogen bond is a single covalent bond.

Chemistry Review 5
Alkanes

A. INTRODUCTION

Hydrocarbons are compounds containing only carbon and hydrogen. They are classified into *aliphatic* and *aromatic hydrocarbons*. Aliphatic hydrocarbons can be divided into three major groups – *alkanes*, *alkenes*, and *alkynes*. Alkanes come under saturated hydrocarbons, because they have carbon-carbon single bonds. Alkenes and alkynes are unsaturated hydrocarbons, since they have carbon-carbon double and triple bonds, respectively.

B. ALKANES

Alkanes have the general molecular formula C_nH_{2n+2}. Hence, if we know the number of carbons present in an alkane, we can calculate the number of hydrogens in it or vice versa. Methane is the first member of the alkane family. It has a molecular formula of CH_4. Natural gases which are found in petroleum deposits contain gases such as methane, ethane, and propane. They are the first three members of the alkane family.

ALKANES WITH 1-12 CARBON ATOMS

Methane	CH_4	Heptane	C_7H_{16}
Ethane	C_2H_6	Octane	C_8H_{18}
Propane	C_3H_8	Nonane	C_9H_{20}
Butane	C_4H_{10}	Decane	$C_{10}H_{22}$
Pentane	C_5H_{12}	Undecane	$C_{11}H_{24}$
Hexane	C_6H_{14}	Dodecane	$C_{12}H_{26}$

Methane is a colorless, odorless gas. Ethane, propane, and butane are also gases, with butane having the highest boiling point among these. What kind of trend can we see from these observations? As the number of carbons and hydrogens increases, the boiling point increases. Each carbon in an alkane is sp^3 hybridized.

C. PROPERTIES OF ALKANES

At room temperature, the first four members of the alkane family are gases. The straight chain alkanes from pentane and up are liquids, and octadecane (18 carbons) and up in the alkane family are solids. As the number of carbons increases, the boiling point increases. Branched alkanes have lesser boiling points than their unbranched or less branched isomeric counterparts. The reason for this is that the unbranched molecules have more intermolecular interactions than the branched ones.

D. STRAIGHT CHAIN AND BRANCHED ALKANES

Butane (C_4H_{10}) and the other alkanes above it can exhibit *constitutional isomerism*. If the alkane is unbranched and has a straight chain, it is called *n*-alkane. For example, the straight chain pentane is called *n*-Pentane.

n-Pentane $CH_3CH_2CH_2CH_2CH_3$

n-Butane $CH_3CH_2CH_2CH_3$

> *Constitutional (structural) isomers are isomers with the same molecular formula, but are different in terms of the order in which the atoms are connected.*

Butane has two possible isomers: *n*-Butane and Isobutane

n-Butane　　　　　　　**Isobutane**

$CH_3CH_2CH_2CH_3$

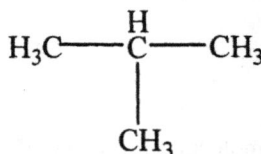

Pentane has three isomers: *n*-Pentane, Isopentane, and neopentane

$CH_3CH_2CH_2CH_2CH_3$ 　　 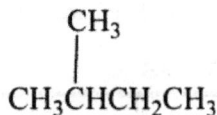 　　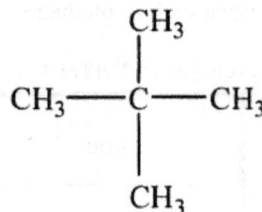

n-Pentane　　　　　　**Isopentane**　　　　　　**Neopentane**

The only way to find the number of possible isomers is by drawing out the structures sequentially and systematically, starting from the straight chain compound. There is no simple general formula to calculate the number of possible isomers of an alkane.

E. ALKYL GROUPS

Alkyl groups are groups which lack one hydrogen atom compared to its parent alkane. For example, methyl group is CH_3—, which lacks one hydrogen atom with respect to its parent alkane, methane (CH_4). Similarly, ethyl group (C_2H_5—) lacks one hydrogen atom compared to ethane (C_2H_6).

Some common alkyl groups

$CH_3CH_2CH_2$——　　　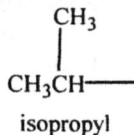　　　$CH_3CH_2CH_2CH_2$——　　　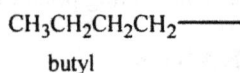

propyl (*n*-propyl)　　　isopropyl　　　butyl　　　isobutyl

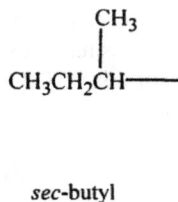　　　　　　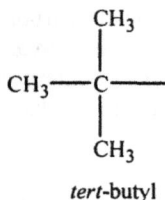

sec-butyl　　　　　　*tert*-butyl

F. THE IUPAC NAMING OF ALKANES

Main rules and strategies for the IUPAC naming of alkanes

1. Write out the expanded structural formula, if it is not given in the expanded form.
2. Find the longest carbon chain.
3. Then identify the alkyl or other substituents that are connected to this long chain.
4. The numbering of carbons should start from the specific end of the long chain, so that the numbers assigned for the substituents are the lowest.

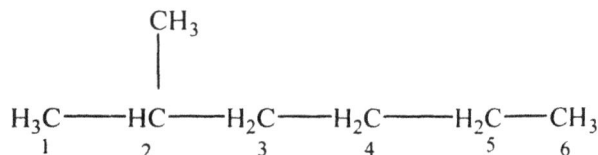

2-methyl hexane

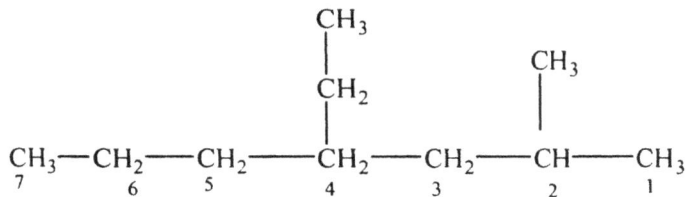

4-ethyl-2-methyl heptane

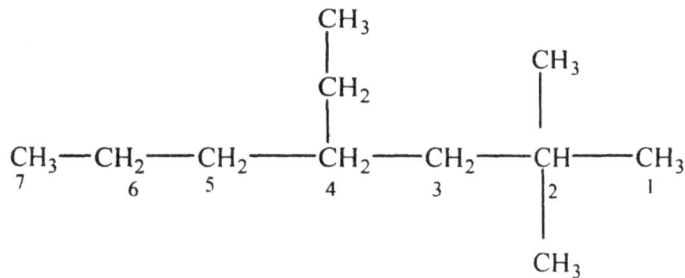

2,2-dimethyl-4-ethyl heptane

G. CYCLOALKANES

Cycloalkanes are cyclic compounds with ring structures. The general molecular formula of a cycloalkane is C_nH_{2n}.

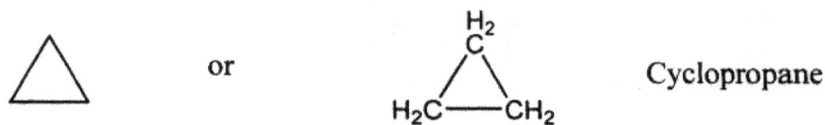

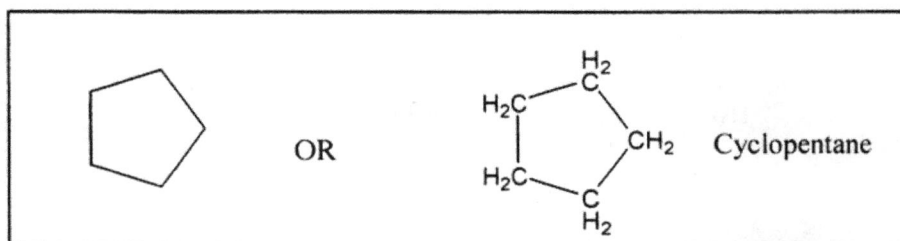

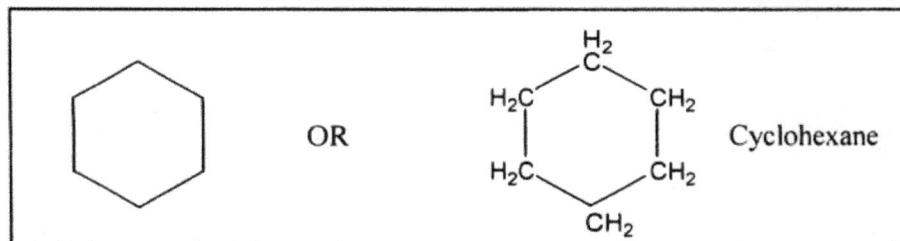

Cyclopropane

Cyclopentane

Cyclohexane

H. REACTIONS OF ALKANES

Combustion

Hydrocarbons undergo combustion reactions in the presence of oxygen to form carbon dioxide and water as products. Combustion reactions are very exothermic giving out energy, as they burn in the presence of oxygen.

Sample reaction 15-1

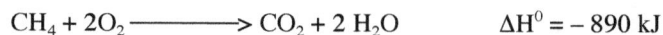

$$CH_4 + 2O_2 \longrightarrow CO_2 + 2H_2O \qquad \Delta H^0 = -890 \text{ kJ}$$

Halogenation

The *halogenation reaction* can be generalized as follows:

$$RH \ + \ X_2 \longrightarrow RX \ + \ HX$$

In this substitution reaction, the halogen (fluorine, chlorine, bromine, iodine) substitutes one hydrogen atom in the alkane, forming hydrogen halide and alkyl halide as the products. The reactivity of halogens in the halogenation reactions is as follows:

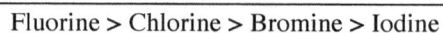

Fluorine > Chlorine > Bromine > Iodine

Fluorine is the most reactive among halogens in halogenation reactions, and iodine is the least reactive.

I. MECHANISM OF FREE RADICAL SUBSTITUTION OF ALKANES

Halogenation reactions occur via a mechanism called *free radical substitution*. There are three main steps in the free radical mechanism. They are:

(1) initiation
(2) propagation
(3) termination.

The overall reaction of chlorination of methane.

$$CH_4 + Cl_2 \longrightarrow CH_3Cl + HCl$$

(1) Initiation

This step involves the dissociation of the halogen molecule (e.g., chlorine molecule) into two chlorine atoms. Even though the total reaction is exothermic, initially energy should be supplied for the reaction to proceed.

:Cl : Cl: ⟶ 2 (•Cl:)

Chlorine molecule — 2 Chlorine atoms

(2) Propagation steps

During the propagation step, the hydrogen atom is abstracted from methane by a chlorine atom. This is followed by the reaction between the methyl radical and the chlorine molecule.

:Cl• + CH₃:H ⟶ H:Cl: + •CH₃

Chlorine atom   Methane — 2 Chlorine atoms   Methyl radical

:Cl:Cl: + CH₃• ⟶ •Cl: + CH₃:Cl:

Chlorine molecule   Methyl radical — Chlorine atom   Methyl chloride

(3) Termination

The termination steps involve the combination of the radicals.

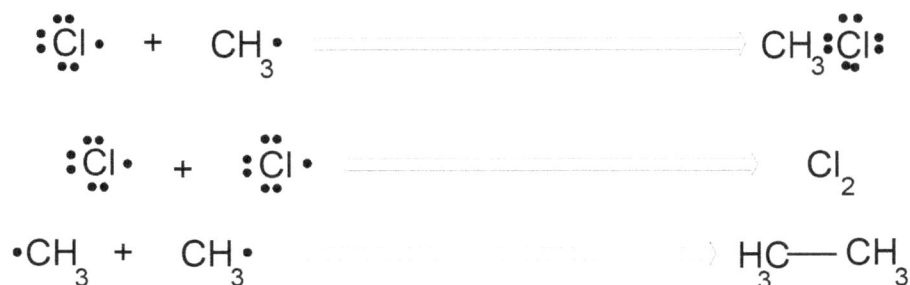

:Cl• + CH₃• ⟶ CH₃:Cl:

:Cl• + :Cl• ⟶ Cl₂

•CH₃ + CH₃• ⟶ H₃C—CH₃

J. REACTIVITY OF ALKANES

Primary, Secondary, and Tertiary Carbons

A carbon which is attached directly to only one other carbon is called a primary (1^0) carbon. If it is attached directly to two other carbons, it is a secondary (2^0) carbon. A carbon is called a tertiary (3^0) carbon, if it is directly attached to three other carbons.

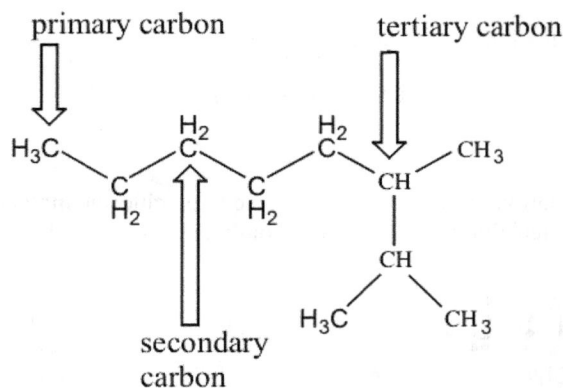

Though alkanes are not so reactive, they can undergo some reactions by forming intermediates. These intermediates can be alkyl radicals, carbocations, or carbanions. Alkyl radicals are intermediates of free radical reactions. Carbocations (carbonium ions) are species with a positive charge on one of the carbon atoms. A carbanion has a negative charge on one of its carbon atoms. Some major trends are given below:

Carbocation/Alkyl radical stability
$3^0 > 2^0 > 1^0 >$ methyl

Carbocation/Akyl radical reactivity
$3^0 < 2^0 < 1^0 <$ methyl

Carbanion stability
$3^0 < 2^0 < 1^0 <$ methyl

Carbanion reactivity
$3^0 > 2^0 > 1^0 >$ methyl

K. CONFORMATION AND STABILITY OF ALKANES

Conformations

Alkanes can have different conformations. By analyzing the structure of ethane, we can define certain aspects regarding its conformations. *Conformations* are different arrangements of the atoms in a molecule, as a result of rotation around a single bond.

Figure 15-1

STAGGERED CONFORMATION

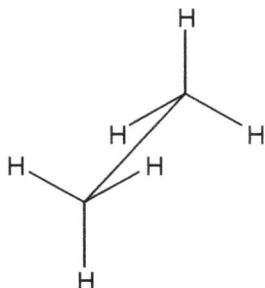

SAWHORSE REPRESENTATION   NEWMAN PROJECTION

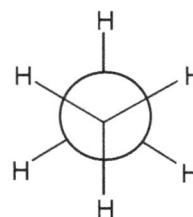

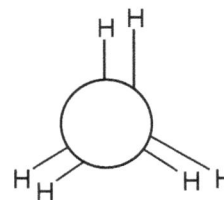

In *staggered conformation*, the torsional angle is 60^0. In *eclipsed conformation*, each carbon-hydrogen bond is aligned with the carbon-hydrogen bond of the next carbon.

Figure 15-2

ECLIPSED CONFORMATION

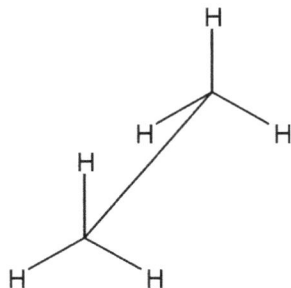

SAWHORSE REPRESENTATION   NEWMAN PROJECTION

In eclipsed conformations, the torsional angle is $0°$. In staggered conformations, the torsional angles can either be $60°$ (*gauche*) or $180°$ (*anti*). The anti conformation is more stable than the gauche conformation. We should also consider the fact that in this analysis of staggered conformation, the ethane molecule looks the same in the Newman projections, whether it is gauche or anti. Reason: There are no substituents other than just hydrogens. To denote the positional significance, the hydrogens are indicated in bold in the diagrams shown in Figure 15-4.

Eclipsed

0^0

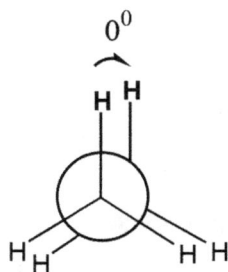

ANGLE OF TORSION
IS 0^0
Figure 15-3

Gauche

60^0

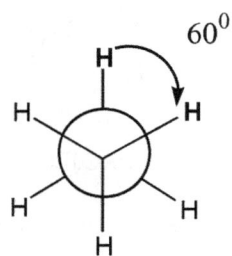

ANGLE OF TORSION
IS 60^0

Anti

180^0

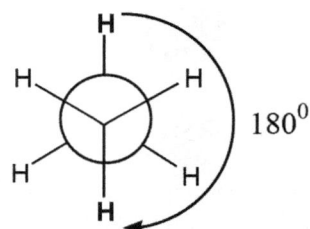

ANGLE OF TORSION
IS 180^0

Figure 15-4

Chemistry Review 5 Problems

1. A student is assigned to identify an unknown compound in an organic chemistry class. She is sure that the compound contains only carbon and hydrogen atoms. In addition, the unknown compound is a saturated hydrocarbon. If there are fourteen hydrogens in a molecule of this unknown compound, and it does not have a ring structure, what is the most likely number of carbons in this compound?

A. 3
B. 6
C. 7
D. 14

2. Which of the following represents the general formula of an alkane?

A. C_nH_{2n+2}
B. C_nH_{2n}
C. C_nH_{2n-2}
D. C_nH_n

3. n-Butane and isobutane are best described as:

A. stereoisomers.
B. anomers.
C. diastereomers.
D. constitutional isomers.

4. Choose the correct name of the following compound from the choices given below.

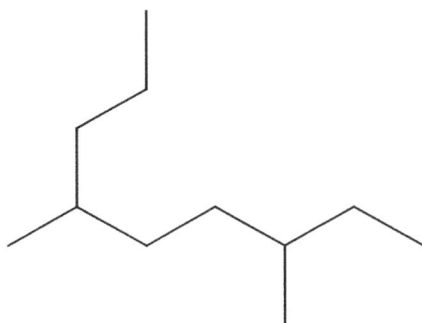

A. 2-propyl-5-methyl heptane
B. 3-methyl-6-propyl heptane
C. 3,6-dimethyl nonane
D. 4,7-dimethyl nonane

5. In the combustion reaction of butane, how many moles of carbon dioxide are formed, if one mole of butane undergoes complete combustion in a controlled environment in the presence of excess oxygen?

A. one
B. two
C. four
D. eight

6. Which of the following represents secondary carbons?

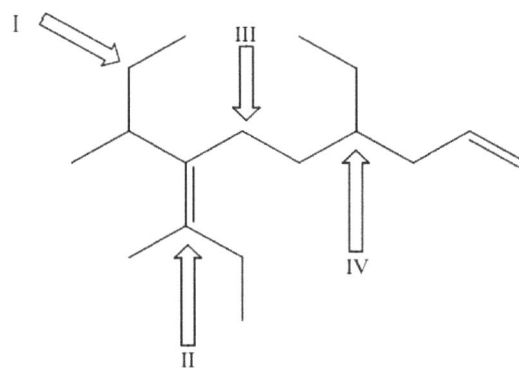

A. I & II only
B. I & III only
C. II & IV only
D. I, II, III & IV

7. Carbonium ions have:

A. a positive charge.
B. a negative charge.
C. no charge.
D. either a positive or a negative charge.

8. The gauche conformation is a form of:

A. eclipsed conformation.
B. anti-conformation.
C. staggered conformation.
D. none of the above conformations.

9. In cycloalkanes which of the following bond angles will have the least angle strain?

A. 90°
B. 110°
C. 125°
D. 180°

10. Which of the following alkanes has the highest boiling point?

I

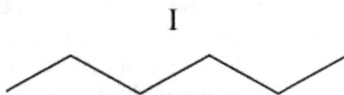

II

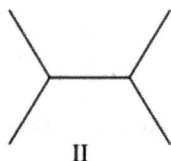

III

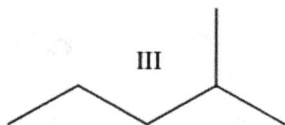

IV

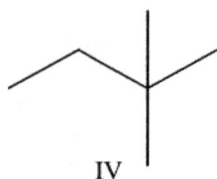

A. I
B. II
C. III
D. IV

Questions 11-14 are based on the following passage.

Passage

Hydrocarbons are compounds composed of carbon and hydrogen atoms. Alkanes are hydrocarbons. As the number of carbons increases in straight-chain alkanes, there is a steady gradation of properties which can be easily compared and predicted. The properties of branched alkanes vary considerably and are hard to predict because of other intervening forces that come into play. The boiling points of a few alkanes are given below:

methane	−161.6° C
propane	−88.6° C
pentane	36.1° C
hexane	68.7° C
octane	125.6° C
3-methylpentane	63.3° C

11. Which of the following intermolecular forces are important with respect to alkanes?

A. Hydrogen bonding
B. Dipole-dipole electrostatic forces
C. Ionic forces
D. Van der Waals forces

12. The melting point of butane is close to:

A. 37.5° C.
B. 55.1° C.
C. 24° C.
D. −138° C.

13. Alkenes can undergo free radical substitution reactions with halogens. Which of the following best represents a chain propagation step during the free radical chlorination of methane?

A. $Cl_2 \longrightarrow 2$:$\overset{..}{\underset{..}{Cl}}$•

B. •CH_3 + :$\overset{..}{\underset{..}{Cl}}$• $\longrightarrow CH_3Cl$

C. •CH_3 + $Cl_2 \longrightarrow CH_3Cl$ + :$\overset{..}{\underset{..}{Cl}}$•

D. •CH_3 + •$CH_3 \longrightarrow CH_3CH_3$

14. What is the most likely boiling point of 2,3-dimethylbutane?

A. 58° C
B. 63.3° C
C. 68.7° C
D. 75.8° C

Solutions

1. The answer is B.

To answer this question, we can use the following clues from the question:

> i) The compound is composed of only carbon and hydrogen atoms.
> ii) It is a saturated hydrocarbon.
> iii) It does not have a ring structure.

So the compound is an alkane. Alkanes have the general formula C_nH_{2n+2}. Now this becomes a simple algebra problem. Since there are 14 hydrogens, $2n + 2 = 14$.

So,

$$n = (14 - 2)/2 = 6$$

2. The answer is A.

3. The answer is D. Constitution isomers are compounds with the same molecular formula, but differ in the order with which the atoms are bonded. This definition matches the relationship between n-butane and isobutane.

4. The answer is C. First, we have to number the carbon chain to get the longest possible chain in the structure. The numbering should be done in such a way that the branches will have the smallest substituent number. The numbering is done as follows:

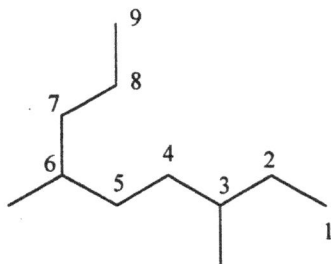

There are 9 carbons in the parent chain. So the parent chain is clear and the complete name ends with "nonane." This rules out Choices A and B. There are 2 methyl groups on carbons 3 and 6. So the compound is 3,6-dimethyl nonane.

5. The answer is C. Butane contains 4 carbon atoms and if one mole of butane is completely combusted, at least 4 moles of carbon dioxide will be formed provided that there is enough oxygen.

6. The answer is B. A secondary carbon atom should be attached to two other carbon atoms. The carbon atoms indicated by arrows I and III are secondary carbon atoms.

7. The answer is A. A carbonium ion is the same as a carbocation. A carbocation is a positively charged species.

8. The answer is C. Gauche conformation is a form of staggered conformation. The conformation is Gauche if the relative separation of two substituents on adjacent atoms is 60°. The Newman representation of a Gauche conformation is shown:

Gauche

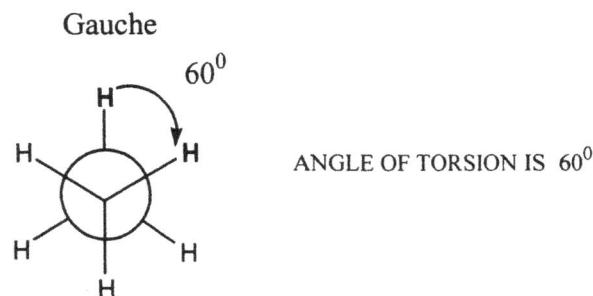

ANGLE OF TORSION IS 60^0

9. The answer is B. The angle closest to 109.5° is 110°. That is the most likely bond angle, having the least angle strain.

10. The answer is A. All the given choices are alkanes. Item I is an unbranched alkane. Items II, III, IV have increasing degrees of branching. Branching decreases the area of contact and thereby decreases the intermolecular interactions. So the unbranched alkane has the highest boiling point. Keep in mind that without actually measuring the properties, we can only compare compounds of comparable weights and number of carbons with reasonable accuracy.

11. The answer is D. The question asks for the type of force that is important with respect to alkanes. Alkanes cannot undergo hydrogen bonding. So Choice A is out. Choice B is generally not important in alkanes. Since there are no ionic bonds in an alkane, Choice C is wrong. The correct choice is Van der Waals forces.

12. The answer is D. To answer this question you have to do some intuitive thinking based on the information given in the passage. Butane is a four-carbon alkane with the formula C_4H_{10}. It is a bigger molecule than propane, but a smaller molecule than pentane. So the boiling point of butane should be between propane and pentane. We are talking in terms of the relative boiling points. But the question asks for the melting point. So let's translate this idea in terms of melting point. Obviously, the melting point of a substance should be below its boiling point. So the answer cannot be either 37.5°C or 55.1°C. This rules out Choices A and B. Choice C is not a sensible answer because butane is a gas at 25°C.

13. The answer is C. Choice A is an initiation step. Choice B is a chain termination step. Choice D is also a chain termination step. The only choice that represents a chain propagation step is Choice C.

14. The answer is A. This question tests your knowledge of intermolecular forces and other interactions that give rise to some of the chemical and physical properties of compounds. Let's take a look at the compound 2,3-dimethylbutane. We do not have a clue about the precise properties of the compound asked in this question. But what we do know is the boiling point of one of its relatives. In the table given in the passage, we are told that the boiling point of 3-methylpentane is 63.3° C. If we compare these two compounds, we see that they have the same number of carbons and hydrogens – both are six-carbon alkanes. If the boiling point of 3-methylpentane is 63.3° C, then 2,3-dimethylbutane will have a boiling point lower than that. The only choice with a lower value is Choice A.

SCIENCE TESTS

Test 1

(35 Minutes—40 Questions)

Passage 1

Often, bacteria are grown on a medium that contains all of the components they need to survive. This includes an energy source, a carbon source, and sources of all the mineral salts the bacteria require to carry out their metabolic reactions. Sometimes, a mutant bacterium is isolated that needs more than the usual minimum requirements, because it cannot carry out the reactions necessary to produce a needed substance. These mutants are referred to as *auxotrophs*; if they are to grow, they must be supplemented with the substance they need but cannot manufacture.

Experiment 1

Bacteria were grown on media containing different radioactively labeled atoms to determine which types of biological molecules would be radioactively labeled. Molecules become labeled as they are synthesized by the bacteria using the raw materials provided by the medium. The bacteria were grown for a period of time that was sufficient to label all molecules that could be labeled, and the major types of biomolecules were isolated and tested for the presence of radioactivity. The following table shows the various strains of bacteria and the radioactive element present in the media in which they were grown.

Bacterial strain	Radioactive element
strain 1	carbon
strain 2	phosphorous
strain 3	nitrogen
strain 4	oxygen

Experiment 2

Auxotrophic bacteria were grown on media supplemented with the substance that they need but cannot manufacture. If they were not supplemented in this way, no growth would be observed. The following table shows two auxotrophic strains and the substance with which they were supplemented.

Auxotrophic strain	Supplement
strain A	arginine, an amino acid
strain B	decanoic acid, a fatty acid

Experiment 3

Auxotrophic strain A (from Experiment 2) was grown on a medium that contained supplemental arginine *and* radioactive phosphorus, and the major types of biomolecules were again isolated and tested for radioactivity.

1. Which of the following biomolecules isolated from Strain 2 would we expect to be radioactively labeled according to the table from experiment 1?
   A. RNA
   B. Proteins
   C. Glucose
   D. Amino acids

2. Which of the following biomolecules isolated from Strain 3 would we expect to be radioactively labeled according to the table from experiment 1?
   A. DNA, but not RNA
   B. DNA and RNA, but not proteins
   C. RNA and proteins
   D. DNA and fatty acids

3. Which of the following biomolecules isolated from Strain 1 would we expect to be radioactively labeled according to the table from experiment 1?
   A. Cholesterol
   B. Phospholipids
   C. Both A and B
   D. Neither A nor B

4. In experiment 2, the arginine requiring auxotrophic strain A was supplemented with arginine to allow growth. If the cells were not supplemented with arginine, the cells could not grow because arginine is directly required for the synthesis of:
   A. DNA.
   B. Proteins.
   C. Fatty acids.
   D. RNA.

5. In experiment 3, which of the following biomolecules would we expect to become labeled?
   A. All proteins, DNA, and RNA
   B. Only proteins containing arginine, but not DNA or RNA
   C. DNA, RNA, and only those proteins that contain arginine
   D. RNA and phospholipids

Passage 2

In a parallel-plate capacitor, two parallel metal plates are connected to a voltage source which maintains a potential V across the plates. Positive charges collect on one side of the capacitor and negative charges on the other side, thus creating an electric field E between the plates. The magnitude of the electric field is related to the potential and the separation between the plates according to

$$V = Ed$$

where V is measured in volts, E in J/m, and d in m. A charged particle placed between the plates will experience a force given in magnitude by

$$F = qE$$

where q is the charge of the particle in Coulombs, and F is the force in N.

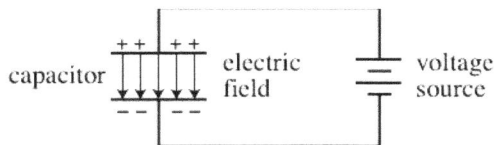

6. If a new battery is installed, so that the voltage between the plates is increased by a factor of 9, how is the electric field affected?
   A. It decreases by a factor of 9.
   B. It increases by a factor of 3.
   C. It increases by a factor of 9.
   D. It increases by a factor of 81.

7. If the voltage in a given experiment is held constant, but the distance between the plates is increased by a factor of 3, how is the electric field affected?
   A. It decreases by a factor of 9.
   B. It decreases by a factor of 3.
   C. It stays the same.
   D. It increases by a factor of 3.

8. In a given experiment, both a proton and a bare helium nucleus are between the plates. How does the force on the helium nucleus compare to the force on the proton?
   A. It is the same.
   B. It is twice as great.
   C. It is four times as great.
   D. There is no force on the helium.

9. In a given experiment, all other things being held constant, what happens to the force on a proton between the plates if the separation of the plates is increased by a factor of 2?
   A. It decreases by a factor of 4.
   B. It decreases by a factor of 2.
   C. It stays the same.
   D. It increases by a factor of 2.

10. Which graph best show the relationship between the potential V and the electric field E?

Passage 3

The behavior of gases can be predicted to a large extent on the basis of various laws. Gases are expressed mainly in terms of pressure, volume, and temperature. Many gases obey the ideal gas laws and those gases are called ideal gases. If we are not doing precision experiments, we can normally ignore the slight deviations that occur under normal conditions. Nevertheless, we cannot completely ignore the deviation factors.

According to Boyle's law, the pressure is inversely proportional to the volume at a constant temperature. Charles' law states that the volume is directly proportional to the temperature at a constant pressure. Combining these laws and Avogadro's law gives the combined gas law.

$$PV = nRT$$
(The ideal gas law)

Not all gases behave ideally. There are often deviations from the ideal behavior. At low temperatures, gases often behave differently apart from what is described by kinetic-molecular theory of gases. Considering these correction factors, the modified gas equation is:

$$\left(P + \frac{n^2 a}{V^2}\right)(V - nb) = nRT$$

The correction constants or Vander Waal constants, a and b, of gases are experimentally found. The Van der Waal constants of some gases are given in Table 1.

Table 1

Gas	a (L².atm/mol²)	b (L/mol)
Carbon monoxide	1.470	0.039
Hydrogen	0.245	0.026
Chlorine	6.340	0.054
Fluorine	1.170	0.029
Hydrogen sulfide	4.540	0.043
Nitrogen	1.380	0.039
Carbon dioxide	3.660	0.043
Argon	1.360	0.032
Propane	9.390	0.091

11. Under which of the following conditions will gases behave most ideally?
    A. Low temperature and high pressure
    B. High temperature and low pressure
    C. Low temperature and low pressure
    D. Gas behavior does not depend on temperature and pressure if the gas is an ideal gas, and such a gas will behave ideally regardless of the conditions

12. If the Vander Waal constant a is found to be zero for gas A, what are true regarding this gas?

    I. Gas A does not behave ideally.
    II. Gas A behaves ideally.
    III. Gas A is Xenon.

    A. I only
    B. II only
    C. II & III only
    D. III only

13. Equal volumes of gases will contain the same number of molecules at the same temperature and pressure. This prediction is directly based on:
    A. Charles law.
    B. Boyle's law.
    C. kinetic-molecular theory.
    D. Avogadro's law.

14. Based on kinetic-molecular theory, which of the following are true?

    I. At a given temperature, all gases have the same average kinetic energy.
    II. At a given temperature, different gases have different average velocities.
    III. The average kinetic energy is proportional to the absolute temperature.

    A. I only
    B. II only
    C. I & III only
    D. I, II & III

Passage 4

We perform an experiment which involves two masses m and M connected by a string which we will consider to be massless. Mass m hangs over the edge of a table. The string passes over a pulley at the edge of the table and mass M sits on the table, such that it moves along the table without friction. (See figure.) The tension in the string is the force that the string exerts where it is connected to another object or to more string. It is generally true that the tension anywhere along the string is the same as the tension anywhere else in the string.

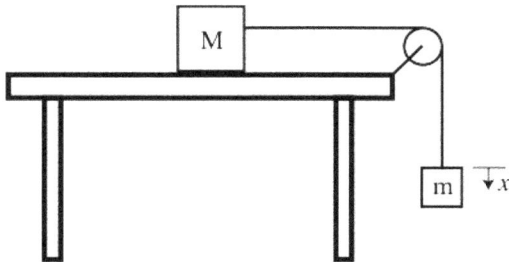

In this experiment the mass m is initially at rest and allowed to drop. Its position x is measured downward from its initial position. At various times, the position x and velocity v of mass m are measured and the results are recorded in the table which follows:

t (s)	x (m)	v (m/s)
0.0	0.00	0.0
0.2	0.01	0.1
0.4	0.04	0.2
0.6	0.09	0.3

15. Which of the following is evidence that the acceleration is uniform?
    A. The entries for x are nonnegative and increasing.
    B. The entries for v are nonnegative and increasing.
    C. The entries for v are always greater than x.
    D. Any interval Δv is proportional to the interval Δt.

16. What are the forces on the mass m?
    A. The force of gravity.
    B. The force of gravity and the tension of the string.
    C. The force of gravity and the force due to mass M.
    D. The force of gravity, the tension of the string, and the force due to M.

17. What are the forces on the mass M?
    A. The force of gravity and the upward force of the table.
    B. The force of gravity, the upward force of the table, and the tension in the string.
    C. The force of gravity, the upward force of the table, and the force due to m.
    D. The force of gravity, the upward force of the table, the force due to m, and the tension in the string.

18. What is the average velocity v_{avg} for the interval of time shown in the table?
    A. 0.0 m/s
    B. 0.1 m/s
    C. 0.15 m/s
    D. 0.3 m/s

19. After the experiment has run a while, the mass m hits the floor and the string goes slack. But mass M continues going forward until it hits the pulley. After the string goes slack but before M hits the pulley, what are the forces on mass M?
    A. There are no forces on M.
    B. The force of gravity.
    C. The force of gravity, and the upward force of the table.
    D. The force of gravity, the upward force of the table, and a forward force.

Passage 5

In general, enzymes are protein molecules which must be folded in a specific three-dimensional shape in order to function properly. Certain environmental parameters can affect enzyme activity, including pH and temperature. If an enzyme's shape changes significantly and it can no longer function, the enzyme is said to have become denatured.

The enzyme pancreatic amylase is manufactured and secreted by the pancreas into the duodenum (the large, beginning portion of the small intestine). Pancreatic amylase breaks down starch into maltose, a disaccharide. Pepsin is an enzyme that is released by the epithelium of the stomach, and functions in the stomach to break down proteins into smaller polypeptide units.

The following graphs show the activities of various enzymes under various environmental conditions.

Graph 1:

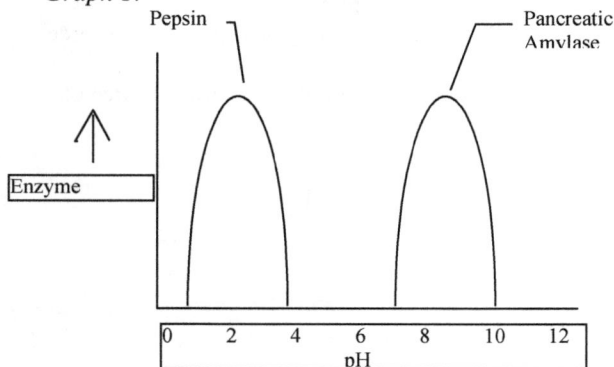

Graph 2:

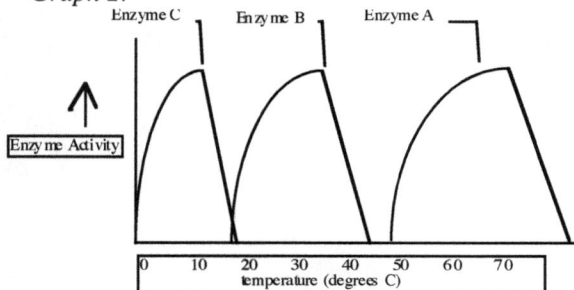

20. Which of the following statements is true with respect to graph 1?
    A. Pepsin and pancreatic amylase could never function together in the same part of the body at the same time.
    B. Pancreatic amylase could function in the stomach, but its activity would be low.
    C. The optimal pH for the functioning of pepsin is approximately 8.5.
    D. Normally, the small intestine must be slightly acidic.

21. Trypsin is a protein digesting enzyme that functions in the small intestine. Which of the following statements should be true about trypsin?
    A. The optimum pH for the functioning of trypsin is approximately 2.
    B. Both trypsin and pepsin would be expected to be found working together in the same part of the body.
    C. The optimum pH for the functioning of trypsin is approximately 8.5.
    D. Trypsin could function well in a solution containing 1 molar hydrochloric acid.

22. Graph 2 depicts the activities of three enzymes. Which curve illustrates the functioning of human DNA polymerase, which functions in the nucleus of cells?
    A. Enzyme A
    B. Enzyme B
    C. Enzyme C
    D. None of the above could represent the activity of human DNA polymerase.

23. Which curve illustrates the functioning of DNA polymerase from a shark?
    A. Enzyme A
    B. Enzyme B
    C. Enzyme C
    D. None of the above, since sharks, like all fish, do not contain DNA polymerase.

24. At what temperature would enzyme B be completely denatured?
    A. 37° C
    B. 15° C
    C. 5° C
    D. 50° C

Passage 6

A phase diagram illustrates the physical state of a substance with respect to the temperature and the pressure of the surroundings. The points plotted to draw the phase diagram are derived experimentally, and are usually plotted with temperature on the x-axis and pressure on the y-axis. A typical phase diagram is shown in Figure-1.

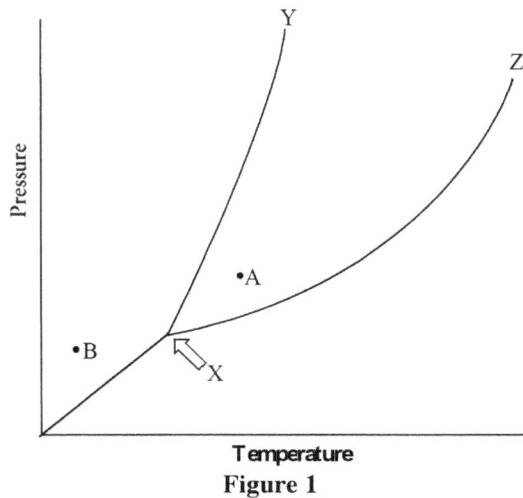

Figure 1

25. Which of the following represents the correct phase diagram of water?

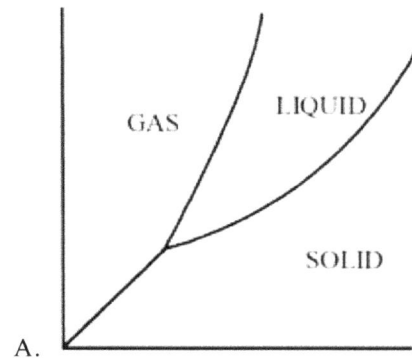

A.

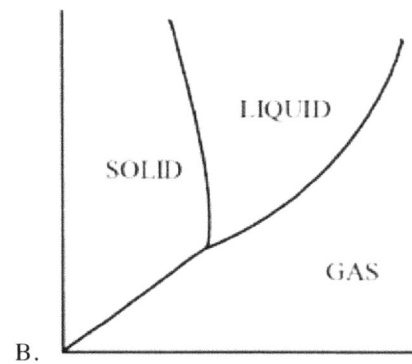

B.

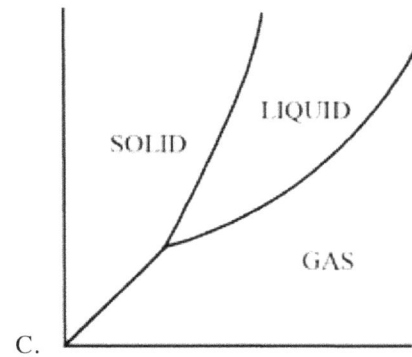

C.

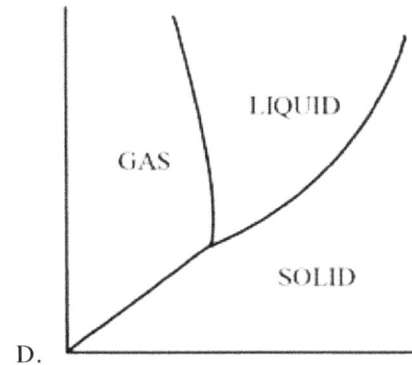

D.

26. The phase diagram given in the passage cannot be that of:
   A. CO_2
   B. H_2O
   C. CO
   D. O_2

27. From the phase diagram given in the passage, predict the likely phase change if the following changes happen. Consider point A as the current phase of substance M. What is the most likely effect on substance M, if the pressure was decreased without changing the temperature of the system?
   A. Gas to liquid
   B. Liquid to gas
   C. Liquid to solid
   D. Solid to liquid

28. The point marked 'X' in the phase diagram given in the passage is called:
   A. the critical point.
   B. the maximum point.
   C. the triple point.
   D. the critical pressure point.

29. The critical temperature of a substance is best defined as:
   A. the temperature below which a gas cannot be liquefied.
   B. the temperature above which a liquid cannot be vaporized.
   C. the temperature above which a substance exists only as gas.
   D. the temperature which is essential for a substance to obey ideal gas laws.

30. The segment XZ in the phase diagram given in the passage represents the equilibrium between:
   A. gas and liquid.
   B. liquid and solid.
   C. solid and gas.
   D. gas and plasma.

Passage 7

A sport at a nearby educational institute involves running along the roof of an apartment building, jumping off the edge, and falling into the pool below. This dangerous sport involves a combination of strength of spirit, braggadocio, and inebriation.

Let's say a student (50 kg) accelerates uniformly from rest at one side of the building to the jumping edge, a distance of 5 m. Just after his feet leave the building, he is traveling horizontally at a speed 5 m/s. The building is 7.2 m high, and the pool is 4.5 m from the edge of the building. Use $g = 10$ m/s^2.

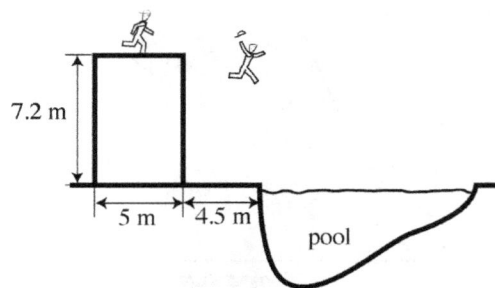

31. How much time does it take the student to accelerate as he is running along the roof?
   A. 1.00 s
   B. 1.20 s
   C. 1.44 s
   D. 2.00 s

32. Which diagram best represents the force diagram for the student while he is on the roof?

33. Which diagram best represents the force diagram for the student while he is in the air?

34. What is his horizontal velocity just before he lands?
 A. 0 m/s
 B. 5 m/s
 C. 12 m/s
 D. 13 m/s

Passage 8

Yeast are unicellular fungi that are considered to be facultatively anaerobic. This means that in the presence of oxygen they can and will undergo aerobic respiration, but at the same time they will likely be fermenting glucose. Furthermore, when no oxygen is present they can survive, potentially forever, by fermentation. Yeast use ethanol fermentation, and this produces carbon dioxide as one of its final products.

One way of quantifying the rate of fermentation in yeast is to measure the rate at which the volume of gas changes in a test tube connected to a solution of yeast being fed with glucose. Since carbon dioxide is the only gas involved in fermentation, the rate of gas production should mirror the rate of fermentation.

The following table shows the amount of gas evolved in such an experiment under different environmental conditions.

pH	Gas evolved (in ml)
5	5
6	10
7	20
8	30
9	25
10	10

35. At which pH is the most ethanol produced?
 A. 5
 B. 7
 C. 8
 D. 9

36. It is likely that oxygen is present in this system, so that aerobic respiration is going on at the same time as fermentation. Taking this into account, which of the following statements is true?
 A. Since oxygen will be used up, using the net change in overall gas production as an indicator of the fermentation rate will be inaccurate.
 B. It is irrelevant to our experiment whether or not aerobic respiration is taking place or not; using the net change in overall gas production as an indicator of the fermentation rate will be accurate.
 C. Under these conditions, no fermentation will occur, since according to the passage yeast only undergo fermentation when no oxygen is available.
 D. The experiment is further complicated by the fact that the yeast will use up some of the carbon dioxide during glycolysis, so using the net change in overall gas production as an indicator of the fermentation rate will be inaccurate.

Passage 9

Consider an object sitting on a scale at the surface of the Earth. The scale reading is the magnitude of the normal force which the scale exerts on the object. To a first approximation, there is force balance, and the magnitude of the scale's force is the magnitude of the gravitational force:

$$F_{grav} = \frac{GM_{Earth}m}{R_{Earth}^2} \qquad (1)$$

where G is Newton's constant, M_{Earth} is the mass of the Earth, and R_{Earth} is the radius of the Earth. The simple result is that the force of gravity, and the reading of the scale, is proportional to the mass:

$$F_{grav} = mg \qquad (2)$$

where g has the value $GM_{Earth}/R_{Earth}^2 = 9.8$ m/s^2. We have made several idealizations, however, and if we want to calculate the scale reading, we need to be more careful. For example, we have ignored the rotation of the Earth. Consider a man standing on a scale at the equator. Because he is moving in a circle, there is a centripetal acceleration. The result is that the scale will not give a reading equal to the force of gravity (equation [1]). We have also assumed that the Earth is a perfect sphere. Because it is rotating, the distance from the center of the Earth to the equator is greater than the distance from center to pole by about 0.1%. A third effect we have ignored is that the Earth has local irregularities which make it necessary to measure g in the local laboratory, if we need an exact value of the effective acceleration due to gravity.

37. For a man standing at the equator of a rotating Earth, which expression gives the best expression of his velocity? (Let T_{day} be the time of one rotation, 1 day.)
    A. R_{Earth}/T_{day}
    B. $2\pi R_{Earth}/T_{day}$
    C. gT_{day}
    D. $2\pi gT_{day}$

38. Which is the best force diagram for a man standing at the equator of a rotating Earth?

A. $|\vec{F}_{net}| = 0$

B. $\vec{F}_{net}$ points into the page.

C. $|\vec{F}_{grav}| < |\vec{F}_{scale}|$

D. $|\vec{F}_{grav}| > |\vec{F}_{scale}|$

39. If the man at the equator stood on a scale, how would the scale read compared to the scale reading for an identical man standing at the equator of a nonrotating Earth?
    A. It would read less than on a nonrotating Earth.
    B. It would read the same as on a nonrotating Earth.
    C. It would read greater than on a nonrotating Earth.
    D. It would depend on where the man is.

40. If two identical men stood on scales at the South Pole and at the equator of an Earth identical to this one but nonrotating, how would the reading of the polar scale compare to the equatorial one?
    A. It would be less.
    B. It would be the same.
    C. It would be greater.
    D. There is not enough information to answer this question.

Test 1 Solutions

Passage 1

1. A.
RNA, a nucleic acid, is the only molecule listed which contains phosphorus (in the phosphate group portion of the nucleotide). Thus radioactive phosphorus will not show up in proteins, glucose (a carbohydrate), or amino acids (protein subunits).

2. C.
Both RNA and proteins contain nitrogen, RNA in the nitrogenous base portion of the nucleotide, and proteins in the amino group of every amino acid. A and B are not correct because they exclude RNA or proteins. D is incorrect because fatty acids, constituents of triglycerides, do not contain nitrogen.

3. C.
Both cholesterol and phospholipids contain carbon, as do all of the major biomolecules we discussed, as they are organic. Therefore, radioactive carbon would show up in all the biomolecules we mentioned.

4. B.
We are told that arginine is an amino acid, and amino acids are the building blocks of proteins. DNA and RNA are made up of nucleotides, while fatty acids are long chain hydrocarbons that are not considered polymers, and certainly are not formed from amino acids.

5. D.
This question combines aspects of both of the preceding experiments in an attempt to cause confusion. Arginine simply allows the cells to grow, as they could not make proteins without it. However, since neither arginine nor any other amino acids contain phosphorus, no proteins, whether they contain arginine or not, should be labeled. The only remaining choice recognizes that both RNA and phospholipids contain phosphorus, in the phosphate group that each contains as part of its structure.

Passage 2

6. C.
The separation of the plates is unchanged, so the electric field increases by a factor of 9.

7. B.
According to the first equation, the electric field and the plate separation are inversely related, so an increase in d results in a decrease in E, so that B is the answer. If this is unclear, solve for E in the first equation.

8. B.
For this question we need to remember that a helium nucleus has two protons (its atomic number on the periodic table), so the bare helium nucleus has twice the charge of a proton. Thus the force on it is twice as great.

9. B.
If the separation of the plates increases by a factor of 2, then the electric field decreases by a factor of 2. And the force on the proton decreases by a factor of 2.

10. A.
The voltage V and electric field E are proportional, so A is correct. For C to be correct, the equation would need to be $V = Ed + V_0$.

Passage 3

11. B.
Gases best behave the most ideally under conditions such as high temperature and low pressure. Choice D is wrong. The passage makes the behavior of gases clear: They depend on the prevailing temperature and pressure.

12. A.
A value of zero alone will not ensure ideal behavior. So gas A does not behave ideally. Hence item I is correct. Item II contradicts what we just said. We cannot say whether gas A is xenon. So item III is not a valid statement.

13. D.

14. D.
According to the kinetic-molecular theory, all the items are true.

Passage 4

15. D.

Choices A and B are irrelevant, and comparisons, such as those in choice C, are meaningless if the units do not match. The correct choice is D. From the table we can see that equal jumps of time (for example, 0.2 s to 0.4 s) result in equal jumps of velocity (0.1 m/s to 0.2 m/s). This is consistent with the statement that $\Delta v/\Delta t$ is a constant, or that acceleration is constant.

16. B.

Gravity certainly acts on m. The only thing touching mass m is the string, so B is correct. (See figure.)

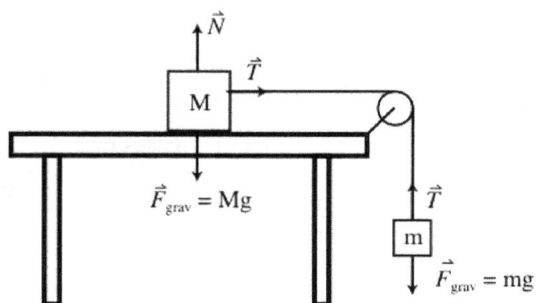

17. B.

The things touching mass M are the table and the string. It is true that the tension in the string is, in some sense, caused by mass m, but M does not know or care what the other end of the string is connected to. It only cares that there is a force due to a string which is directed to the right.

18. C.

By definition, we have $v_{avg} = \Delta x/\Delta t = (0.09\ m - 0.0\ m)/(0.06\ s - 0.0\ s) = 0.15$ m/s.

19. C.

Only the table and the string are touching mass M, but the string has no tension in it, so the answer is C.

Passage 5

20. A.

We can tell that this is true because the ranges of activity depicted by the graph do not overlap. Therefore, no pH value exists at which both enzymes will be even slightly active. It is assumed that the general pH values are known for the stomach and small intestine, approximately 2 and 8 respectively. Therefore, the graph confirms that pancreatic amylase will

have no activity at pH 2 (choice B), but that this is the optimum for pepsin (not 8.5, as is suggested in choice C.) The graph additionally shows that pancreatic amylase loses all activity at pH 7, so that it could not function in an acidic environment. Since the passage tells us that pancreatic amylase functions in the small intestine, choice D must be incorrect.

21. C.

The key here is to understand that trypsin, like pancreatic amylase, functions in the small intestine, and therefore must have a similar optimal pH as does pancreatic amylase. The graph shows that optimum as 8.5. For the same reasons stated above for pepsin and pancreatic amylase, pepsin and trypsin could never work under similar conditions (choice B). Additionally, both choices A and D must be incorrect because they demand that trypsin could function at pH 2 and 0 (the pH of 1M HCl, which you should at least know is acidic).

22. B.

Since humans are endotherms and maintain a constant body temperature of approximately 37^0 C (98.6^0 F), all human enzymes should share this optimal temperature. Curves A and C depict very different optimal temperatures.

23. C.

Since sharks are fish, they are ectothermic and will assume the temperature of their environment. While there is no way for you to know exactly what this value is, it is certainly colder than 37^0 C, and the optimal temperature of the enzyme shown in graph A, about 12^0 C (about 50^0 F), is reasonable for cool water, since you have to pick one choice. D cannot be true; everything that is alive must contain a DNA polymerase!

24. D.

Denaturation implies that the enzyme has lost all function because its shape has significantly changed. According to the graph, enzyme B has no activity below 17^0 C or above 43^0 C. Therefore, choice A is incorrect because this is the optimal temperature. Both choices B and C are out of the activity range, but cold temperatures do not cause denaturation, they simply cause a slowing of the reaction rate based on general kinetic principles until it is ultimately zero. Only high temperatures will cause denaturation, so choice D (50^0 C) must be correct.

Passage 6

25. B.
To answer this question, we need to recall some basic aspects regarding phase diagrams. Just by knowing those, we can eliminate some of the choices right away. In Choices A and D, the phases are wrongly labeled. The phases are correctly labeled only in Choices B and C. This rules out Choices A and D. Water has some anomalous properties. Such properties make water unique. In fact, the solid-liquid segment in the phase diagram of water has a negative slope.

26. B.
See the explanation for the previous question.

27. B.
The question describes a phase change scenario based on the diagram given in the passage. Substance M will be a liquid at point A. If the pressure is decreased, the most likely phase change will be from liquid (the phase before the change) to gas.

28. C.
This is a definition-type question. The point indicated by the X mark is called "triple point." At the triple point of a substance, the three phases coexist at equilibrium. Below this point, the solid to gas conversion or vice versa is direct without the intermediate liquid phase.

29. C.
The critical temperature is defined to be the temperature above which a gas cannot be changed into a liquid. The choice that best reflects this idea is C.

30. A.
In the phase diagram given in the passage, locate the segment XZ. This segment separates the liquid and the gas phases.

Passage 7

31. D.
For the student running along the roof, he starts from rest ($v_1 = 0$ m/s) and ends up running $v_2 = 5$ m/s. We have $\Delta x = 5$ m, and we want Δt. We use $\Delta x = 1/2 (v_1 + v_2)\Delta t$ to obtain $\Delta t = 2$ s.

32. B.
We know gravity pulls down and the roof pushes up, and these forces add to zero. In addition, there must be a force accelerating the student forward (to the right). Surprisingly, it is the roof which exerts the force forward. His feet push backwards on the roof, and the roof (by the third law of motion) pushes forward on him.

33. A.
We know gravity pulls down. Since nothing else touches the student, there is no other force.

34. B.
All during the fall the student has the same horizontal velocity 5 m/s.

Passage 8

35. C.
Ethanol fermentation produces two products from the pyruvic acid made during glycolysis: ethanol and carbon dioxide. Logically, then, the pH at which the most carbon dioxide is produced will be the same pH at which the most ethanol is produced.

36. B.
If aerobic respiration is occurring, it should not affect the net amount of gas present because for every molecule of oxygen that is used up, a molecule of carbon dioxide will be produced. Thus the net production of gas will accurately reflect the carbon dioxide produced by fermentation. The passage clearly states that fermentation and aerobic respiration can occur simultaneously, so choice C must be incorrect. Choice D must be wrong because carbon dioxide is never used up or created by glycolysis.

Passage 9

37. B.
Each day the man travels a distance given by the circumference of the Earth $C = 2\pi R_{Earth}$.

38. D.
Since the man is traveling in a circle at constant speed, his acceleration vector points toward the center of rotation, and so does the net force vector. For this to be so, the magnitude of the gravitational force must be greater than the magnitude of the force of the ground.

39. A.
The gravitational force for the two men is the same. Since the scale reading on a rotating Earth is less than the gravitational force, the correct answer is A.

40. C.
According to Newton's law of gravitation, if the distance in the denominator is less, then the gravitational force is greater.

Test 1 Conversion Chart

Scale Score Conversion Chart

Raw Score	Scale Score	Percentile Ranking
40	36	99
39	35	99
38	34	99
37	33	99
36	32	98
—	31	98
35	30	97
34	29	95
33	28	94
31–32	27	91
30	26	88
29	25	84
27–28	24	77
25–26	23	71
24	22	64
22–23	21	56
20–21	20	48
19	19	38
17–18	18	30
15–16	17	23
14	16	18
13	15	14
11–12	14	10
10	13	7
9	12	5
7–8	11	3
6	10	1
5	9	1
4	8	1
3	7	1
—	6	1
2	5	1
—	4	1
1	3	1
—	2	1
0	1	1

Test 2

(35 Minutes—40 Questions)

Passage 1

The Drum of Discomfort is an amusement park ride which consists of a large vertical hollow cylinder which turns on its axis. A person of mass M enters the drum (inside-radius R) while the drum is still and stands against the wall. The drum begins to turn, until it achieves uniform rotation with period T and the rider feels as if some force is pushing him against the wall (see figure). Then the floor drops down, so there is nothing touching the bottoms of the rider's shoes.

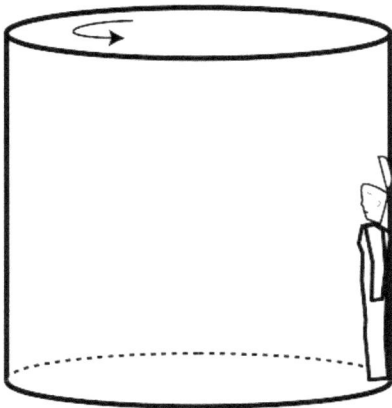

Assume the coefficient of friction between the rider's clothes and the surface of the drum is μ.

1. During uniform rotation, after the floor drops, what are the forces acting on a rider, besides gravity acting down and a force acting up?
   A. There is a force pointing inward.
   B. There is a force pointing inward and a force pointing in the same direction the rider is moving.
   C. There is a force pointing outward.
   D. There is a force pointing outward and a force pointing in the same direction the rider is moving.

2. After the floor drops, what force provides the centripetal force?
   A. The normal force.
   B. Friction.
   C. Gravitation.
   D. Tension.

3. After the floor drops, which direction does the acceleration vector point?
   A. Toward the center of rotation.
   B. Away from the center of rotation.
   C. In the direction of the rider is moving.
   D. The acceleration is zero.

4. Which gives an expression for the speed v the rider is going?
   A. $R/2\pi T$
   B. R/T
   C. $2\pi R/T$
   D. $2\pi T/R$

5. What is the magnitude of the upward force on the rider?
   A. Mg
   B. μMg
   C. Mv^2/r
   D. $\mu Mv^2/r$

Passage 2

Since only four types of nucleotides (adenine, guanine, cytosine and thymine) make up DNA, many scientists were skeptical that this was the hereditary molecule of life. Most believed proteins, with their building blocks of 20 amino acids, provided the complexity necessary to carry the genetic information.

In 1952, Alfred Hershey and Martha Chase designed an experiment to determine whether DNA or protein was the genetic material. They used a *bacteriophage* (a virus that infects bacteria) called T2. This bacteriophage was only composed of proteins and DNA. A short time after infecting a bacterial cell, the cell would *lyse* (break open) and release new T2 particles. T2 reprogrammed the cell to make more phage, but did it use DNA or proteins?

Hershey and Chase infected bacteria with T2 phage in growth medium containing radioactive sulfur (which labels proteins) and radioactive phosphate (which labels DNA). The resulting radioactive phages were then incubated with nonradioactive bacteria and allowed to infect these cells. After a short time, the mixture was placed in a blender to shake loose any phage particles remaining outside of or attached to the bacteria. The mixture was then centrifuged: bacterial cells would form a *pellet* at the bottom of the tube while any phage outside the cell would remain in the liquid portion (the *supernatant*). The radioactivity in each sample was measured.

6. Radioactive sulfur was found exclusively in the supernatant fraction, while the radioactive phosphate was found in the pellet fraction. This indicated:
   A. phage protein entered the cell, but the DNA did not.
   B. phage DNA entered the cell, but protein did not.
   C. both protein and DNA entered the cell.
   D. the phage did not infect the bacterial cell.

7. If the bacterial pellet were incubated in an appropriate growth medium, what would most likely occur?
   A. No phage would be produced as the protein coat was removed.
   B. Bacteria would survive as there is no proof they were infected with phage.
   C. Phage should be produced and kill the cells.
   D. The radioactive phosphate would kill the cells immediately.

8. A possible alternative to the blender technique used in this experiment would be:
   A. add a competitive inhibitor to the bacteria before adding phage.
   B. break apart the cell membranes with a strong detergent.
   C. incubate bacteria with a mutant phage that could not bind to the cells.
   D. shake the cell/phage mixture vigorously.

9. A modern experiment that confirms this experiment would be:
   A. injecting DNA into a cell which causes the cell to produce an enzyme it never had before.
   B. fertilizing an egg with a sperm in vitro.
   C. prescribing enzyme pills to help cystic fibrosis patients with digestion.
   D. consuming radioactive barium to view internal organs with X-rays.

Passage 3

The concentration of solutions are generally expressed in terms of molarity, molality, normality, and weight percent. The formation of the solutions itself has many ramifications. The solubility of solutes differ considerably from one other. Some of the factors that can influence the solubility include temperature and pressure. Solubility depends on other factors as well. Given below in Figure-1 is a graph which depicts solubility differences of some solutes.

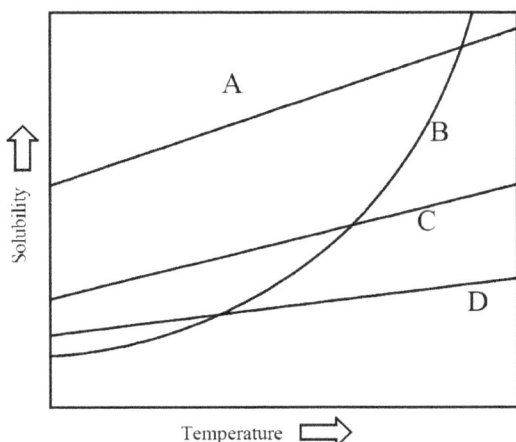

Figure-1

Quite often, the freezing and boiling point changes that are brought about by the dissolved solutes can be predicted reasonably. But this is not always the case.

The predictions and calculations are done for freezing point depression (ΔT_f) based on the following formula:

$$\Delta T_f = K_f\, m,$$

where m is the molality and K_f is the freezing point depression constant. ($K_f = 1.86\ ^\circ C/m$)

For boiling point elevation (ΔT_b), the calculations are based on the following formula:

$$\Delta T_b = K_b\, m,$$

where m is the molality and K_b is the boiling point elevation constant. ($K_b = 0.512\ ^\circ C/m$)

10. The graph in the passage shows the solubilities of some compounds (salts). Which of the following is most likely true regarding the Compounds A, B, C and D?
A. The solubility process of Compound B is exothermic, and those of Compounds A, C and D are endothermic.
B. The solubility process of Compound B is endothermic, and those of Compounds A, C and D are exothermic.
C. The solubility processes of Compounds A, B, C and D are exothermic.
D. The solubility processes of Compounds A, B, C and D are endothermic.

11. Two experiments were conducted for analyzing the solubility properties and their effects on colligative properties. In Experiment I, a 1.0 m solution of KBr was analyzed and in Experiment II, a 2.3 m solution of KBr was analyzed. The experimental values of freezing and boiling points were slightly different from the expected values based on the theoretical calculations discussed in the passage. Which of the following is most likely correct regarding the two experiments?
A. The experimental values of the solution in Experiment I was more different from the theoretical calculations than the solution in Experiment II.
B. The experimental values of the solution in Experiment II was more different from the theoretical calculations than the solution in Experiment I.
C. Both experiments have the same extent of differences from the theoretical predictions.
D. The discrepancy noted in the experiments is absolutely a result of instrumental error, because the differences in Experiments I & II cannot change colligative properties.

12. A solution was made by using 315 g of glucose in 750 g of water. The boiling point of this solution is 101.2°. If the amount of glucose used in this solution is doubled, while the amount of water stays the same, what must happen to the boiling point of the solution?
A. It will double.
B. It will quadruple.
C. It will decrease slightly.
D. It will increase slightly.

13. Which of the following statements is true regarding solutions?
    A. As the concentration of a solution increases, the vapor pressure increases.
    B. As the concentration of a solution decreases, the vapor pressure decreases.
    C. As the concentration of a solution increases, the vapor pressure decreases.
    D. None of the above

Passage 4

Engineers often make scale models of structures they plan to build in order to test function and stability. Sometimes, however, structures fail even when the models function, so engineers have developed extensive theory in order to determine how to build proper scale models and extrapolate reliable results from them.

At first we might assume that a model made of the same material as the intended final structure with each dimension scaled by a single factor will accurately reproduce the behavior of the final structure. That this is not so was known in antiquity by tragic observation, and it was first explained by Galileo around AD 1600. We will not present his detailed argument but will sketch some of the conclusions.

To summarize Galileo's conclusion on this point, when the linear dimensions of a structure are all increased by a factor, the load across any surface increases by the cube of that factor, whereas the strength, or the maximum force the structure can hold across any surface increases by the square of that factor. Therefore, as a structure gets larger, it tends to become unstable, more susceptible to failure.

To illustrate the point, let's consider a block of metal connected to a cylinder, which has much greater length than its diameter and is connected to the ceiling (part A in figure). The *stress* in the cylinder is the force per area across a cross section. Each material has a threshold stress, such that stress larger than the threshold causes the material to fail. If all the linear dimensions are increased by a factor (part B in figure), then the volume of the block increases by the cube of the factor, as well as the mass and weight of the block. The cross-sectional area of the cylinder increases by the square of the factor, so the stress increases as the factor itself.

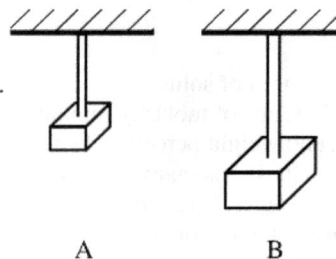

A   B

This is the simplest example of the subtlety involved in model building.

14. The figure below depicts a human biceps, which when flexed, has a cross-sectional area at its center of 5×10^{-3} m^2 and cross-sectional area at the forearm of 5×10^{-5} m^2. If the force exerted at the forearm is F_0, what is the force exerted at the shoulder?

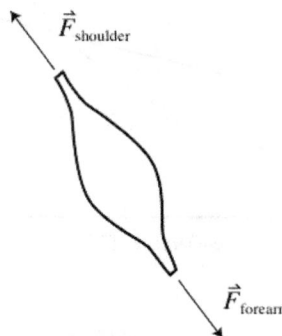

    A. $F_0/100$
    B. F_0
    C. $100F_0$
    D. $10^4 F_0$

15. Referring to the previous question, if the stress at the center of the biceps is 10^5 Pa, what is the stress at the forearm? Note: Stress, force, and area are related by the equation

$$Stress = F/A$$

    A. 10^3 Pa
    B. 10^5 Pa
    C. 10^7 Pa
    D. 10^9 Pa

16. The figure below shows two elephant statues which are the same shape, both made of plaster of paris. Statue B has twice the linear dimension of statue A. If statue A weighs 40 N, how much does statue B weigh? Note: $mass = \rho V$, where ρ is the density and V is the volume. And $weight = mg$, where m is the mass and g is gravity.

A   B

A. 48 N
B. 80 N
C. 160 N
D. 320 N

17. In the previous question, how does the pressure (stress) exerted by the right front foot of statue B compare with the pressure exerted by the corresponding foot of statue A?
A. It would be the same.
B. It would be twice as large.
C. It would be four times as large.
D. It would be eight times as large.

18. A lantern is hanging from a cable of negligible mass. The cable breaks when the weight of the lantern exceeds W_{max}. What would be the breaking weight for a similar cable (same material, same cross section) which was 10 times longer?
A. $W_{max}/100$
B. $W_{max}/10$
C. W_{max}
D. $10W_{max}$

Passage 5

The activity of bacteriophages is easily assayed. Bacteria are spread on a solid nutrient agar plate. Under appropriate growth conditions, the bacteria will form a cloudy layer completely covering the dish. In microbiology, this is called a *lawn*, as opposed to isolated spots, or *colonies*, of bacteria. If bacteriophages are introduced to the lawn of bacteria, the phages will infect single cells. Once the phages have reproduced, they will lyse the cells and the progeny phage will infect the surrounding bacterial cells. In a relatively short period of time, the phages will have lysed all the bacteria within a radius of the

initial infection, causing a clear, circular spot to form in the lawn of bacteria. This is called a *plaque*.

A researcher working with bacteriophages set up the following experiment:

Condition 1:
Bacteria were spread on agar plates and incubated at 37°C for 24 hours. A lawn was clearly visible and no plaques formed.

Condition 2:
The same strain of bacteria was mixed with a preparation of lambda bacteriophage. The mixture was spread on agar plates and incubated for 24 hours at 37°C. An average of twenty plaques formed on the bacterial lawn on each plate.

Condition 3:
The same strain of bacteria was spread on agar plates and then exposed to UV light. After incubation at 37°C for 24 hours, lawns grew and approximately fifty plaques formed on each plate.

19. After incubating the plates from condition 2 for an additional 5 days, the plates became totally clear. What is the most likely explanation for this result?
   A. Newly produced phages infected all bacteria on the dish, thus killing everything.
   B. The bacteria died off due to lack of nutrients.
   C. The bacteria protected themselves from the phages by slowing their growth.
   D. The phage forced all the bacteria to go into the lysogenic cycle and stop growing.

20. What happened in condition 3?
   A. Phage contaminated the dishes causing infection and lysis of the bacteria.
   B. The nutrients in the agar were insufficient to support bacterial growth.
   C. The bacteria were probably a lysogenic strain induced by UV light.
   D. The bacteria were not healthy and died off when exposed to UV light.

21. If a fourth experiment was done, where bacteria were mixed with lambda and exposed to UV light, what would you predict?
    A. The results would be similar to condition 2, with approximately 20 plaques per plate.
    B. The results would be similar to condition 3, with approximately 50 plaques per plate.
    C. There would be approximately 35 plaques per plate.
    D. There would be approximately 70 plaques per plate.

22. Before the phage life cycle was understood, researchers called the results from condition 3 *autolysis*. They thought an enzyme in the bacteria caused its own destruction and the destruction of surrounding cells. Which of the following would lend support to the viral theory and help to disprove autolysis?
    A. Within a week, all the bacterial cells in condition 3 die.
    B. Viral particles can be purified from the plates in condition 3.
    C. Exposure of bacteria to X rays also causes plaques to form.
    D. With or without exposure to UV light, no bacteria grow at 4°C.

Passage 6

In nuclear reactions, significant changes occur in the composition of the nuclei of the atoms involved. These reactions usually release tremendous amounts of energy. One of the reasons for the nuclear changes can be attributed to the stability of the nucleus.

The formation of nucleus from the subatomic particles - neutrons and protons, results in the release of energy. The mass of these individual particles in the nucleus is greater than that of the actual nucleus that is formed. This loss of mass is due to the change of mass into energy. The energy-mass relation can be represented in terms of the equation:

$$E = mc^2,$$

where m represents the mass, and c represents the speed of light (3×10^8 m/s).

If the nucleus of an atom is not stable, it can get transformed into another nucleus. A plot of the number of neutrons versus the number of protons

is often used to assess the stability trends of elements. If the number of protons and neutrons are equal, the nucleus is considered to be reasonably stable. As the atomic number increases, the trend changes.

Isotopes of elements having atomic numbers above ≈83 are unstable atoms. These unstable atoms can undergo disintegrations. The half-lives of some radioactive elements are shown in Table 1.

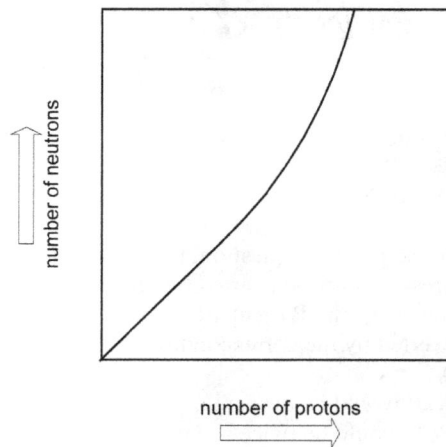

number of protons

TABLE 1

atom	half-life
Carbon 14	5.73×10^3 years
Uranium 238	4.47×10^9 years
Radon 222	3.82 days
Radium 226	1.6×10^3 years
Krypton 89	3.2 minutes

23. A sample of ^{226}Ra disintegrates to 3% of its original quantity. How many half-lives have this sample passed? Note: Half-life is the amount of time required for a radioactive substance to disintegrate to half its initial quantity.
    A. two
    B. three
    C. four
    D. five

24. Which of the following is true regarding radioactivity?
    A. As the atomic number increases, eventually the neutron-proton ratio values become ≤ 1.
    B. As the atomic number increases, eventually the neutron-proton ratio values become ≥ 1.
    C. As the atomic number increases, eventually the proton-neutron ratio values become ≥ 1.
    D. None of the above

25. When a helium nucleus is formed, there is always some degree of loss of mass. If the loss of mass equals 3.1×10^{-5} kg during the formation of one mol of it, what is the binding energy? Note: Mass loss can be calculated using the equation $E = mc^2$.
    A. 3.1×10^{-5} J
    B. 1.8×10^{19} J
    C. 9.3×10^3 J
    D. 2.8×10^{12} J

Passage 7

A rocket engine operates on the principle that hot gas is expelled backwards through a nozzle in order to produce a thrust on the ship in the opposite direction. Since momentum is conserved in this operation, we can derive the result that the effective force on the ship is

$$F_{\text{effective}} = Mu$$

where M is the mass expulsion rate, and u is the exhaust velocity relative to the ship. Thus it is important for both M and u to be high. The exhaust velocity varies as the square root of the ratio of the temperature of the combustion chamber and the molecular mass of the exhaust.

In conventional rocket engine design, large fuel tanks carry liquid hydrogen and oxygen, and these react by chemical combustion to yield water vapor. The water vapor, due to its high temperature, shoots out of the nozzle, and the ship is thrust forward.

In an experimental engine design, nuclear fission of uranium is used to heat a supply of hydrogen to high temperatures (around 2200 K). The hydrogen is then expelled through a nozzle at 1.0×10^4 m/s, about twice the exhaust velocity as that for conventional rockets. One major engineering problem involves the heat exchange between the hydrogen gas and the site where the nuclear reaction takes place. Engineers are improving the design so that the hydrogen is heated at a faster rate than it is in current designs.

26. When a rocket ship expels gas in order to produce a thrust, this is an example of
    A. the first law of motion: If the forces on an object are balanced, then the object moves with constant velocity.
    B. the second law of motion: The force acting on an object is equal to the mass of that object times its acceleration ($F = ma$).
    C. the third law of motion: To every action there is an equal and opposite reaction.
    D. the law of universal gravitation: Any two bodies attract each other with a force that is directly proportional to the product of their masses and inversely proportional to the square of the distance between them ($F = Gm_1m_2/r^2$).

27. Could heavier neon gas work instead of hydrogen in the design of the nuclear engine?
    A. No, since neon is not a product of uranium fission.
    B. No, since neon is an inert gas.
    C. Yes, but the engine would not be as efficient because of exhaust velocity.
    D. Yes, it would work approximately as well.

28. What, according to the passage, is a disadvantage of nuclear engines compared to conventional engines?
    A. The molecular mass of the exhaust is too low.
    B. The molecular mass of the exhaust is too high.
    C. Some of the energy is lost as heat.
    D. The mass expulsion rate is too low.

29. A rocket ship is going forward at 2000 m/s and fires its engines in order to speed up but not turn. If the absolute velocity of the exhaust gases is 3000 m/s going backwards, what is the exhaust velocity u relative to the ship?
    A. 1000 m/s
    B. 2000 m/s
    C. 3000 m/s
    D. 5000 m/s

30. We can model a rocket and its exhaust with two carts sitting on a level, frictionless one-dimensional track. The large cart (rocket) has a mass 10 kg, and the small cart (exhaust gas), 0.1 kg. There is a small explosive between them. At a certain time the explosive goes off and the two carts go flying apart. The less massive cart recoils with velocity 20 m/s. The explosion is over in about 0.2 s. What is the final velocity of the larger mass? Note: Use the principle of conservation of momentum: $P_{before} = P_{after}$.
   A. 0.2 m/s
   B. 1.0 m/s
   C. 20 m/s
   D. 2000 m/s

Passage 8

Interestingly, many, if not most, bacterial cells can communicate with other cells in the same species. The bacteria secrete proteins, and, once enough bacteria are present, the concentration of the proteins increases. A high concentration often triggers the bacteria to turn on other proteins so the colony can perform a function. For example, individuals who have impaired immune systems or who have the genetic disease *cystic fibrosis* (*CF*) are often infected by the respiratory bacterium, *Pseudomonas aeruginosa*. Only when enough bacteria have accumulated, *P. aeruginosa* will produce an enzyme that degrades lung tissue, which allows the bacteria to invade the blood stream.

Although many examples of this intraspecies communication exist, scientists wondered if different species can communicate with each other. To answer this question, researchers examined the relationship between *P. aeruginosa* and *Burkholderia cepacia*. *B. cepacia* causes fatal lung infections in CF patients, but only after these individuals have also been infected by *P. aeruginosa*.

Experiment 1:
P. aeruginosa were grown in an appropriate liquid medium in the laboratory. The culture was centrifuged to remove the bacterial cells. A culture of *B. cepacia* was then grown in the medium. These bacteria increased production of molecules necessary for survival.

Experiment 2:
Mutant *P. aeruginosa* were grown in the laboratory in liquid medium. After

centrifugation, the medium was used to incubate cultures of *B. cepacia*. Very few "survival molecules" were produced in the *B. cepacia*.

31. The experiments indicate:
   A. the two bacterial strains can communicate with each other.
   B. the *P. aeruginosa* bacteria help turn on production of survival molecules in *B. cepacia*.
   C. *B. cepacia* bacteria help turn on production of survival molecules in *P. aeruginosa*.
   D. no communication exists between the two bacterial strains.

32. The key to communication between these two bacteria is probably due to:
   A. a soluble protein secreted by *P. aeruginosa*.
   B. direct interaction between the two bacteria, possibly via cells of each species binding to each other.
   C. a soluble protein secreted by *B. cepacia*.
   D. unable to determine based on the available data.

33. A similar communication system exists between:
   I. nerve cells
   II. hormones and receptors
   III. photoreceptors in the eye
   A. I only
   B. II only
   C. I and II only
   D. III only

34. One important control that should be included in this experiment is:
   A. grow *P. aeruginosa* in medium used to grow *B. cepacia* first.
   B. infect mice with both species of bacteria.
   C. grow *B. cepacia* in medium that had not been used to grow *P. aeruginosa*
   D. no other control is necessary for this experiment.

35. The mutant *P. aeruginosa* used in Experiment 2 were most likely deficient in:
   A. replication
   B. transcription
   C. translation
   D. secretion

36. If the doubling time of a strain of bacteria is 30 minutes, approximately how many cells would there be after 5 hours if the original culture had 1×10^5 cells?
    A. 5×10^5
    B. 3.2×10^6
    C. 1×10^8
    D. 1×10^{25}

Passage 9

In a certain experiment, a piston chamber is used as part of a primitive engine. The apparatus consists of a pipe closed at one end with a piston at the other end. A valve in the cylinder allows fuel gases to be introduced or waste gases to be expelled.

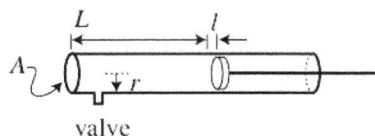

valve

In the operation of this engine, hydrogen and oxygen are introduced in a 2:1 ratio (in order to ensure complete combustion) at ambient temperature T_{amb} and atmospheric pressure P_{atm}. The following reaction is ignited

$$2H_{2(g)} + O_{2(g)} \rightarrow 2H_2O_{(g)}$$

with a heat of reaction

$$\Delta H_{rea} = -4.8 \times 10^5 \text{ J/mol}$$

The pressure rises to P_{burn}.

Next the piston slowly moves back a distance l, from which the engine derives useful work. The distance l is short enough that the pressure and temperature inside the chamber remain roughly constant.

The waste gases are then expelled, and the piston is restored to its original position.

The radius of the cylinder is r, and the cross-sectional area is A. The length of the cylinder before the piston moves back is L, which is much larger than l. The number of moles of oxygen introduced is n.

37. After the combustion occurs, why does the pressure go up?
    A. There are more gas particles on the left side of the reaction.
    B. The temperature rises considerably.
    C. The reaction is spontaneous.
    D. The heat of reaction is negative.

38. What would happen if the ratio in the second paragraph were not 2:1?
    A. The heat of reaction would be less than 4.8×10^5 J/mol.
    B. The combustion would not ignite.
    C. Some of the waste gas would be intermediate products of incomplete combustion.
    D. Some of the waste gas would be oxygen or hydrogen.

39. If the reaction shown were performed in a closed chamber isothermally at $500°C$, what would happen to the pressure?
    A. The pressure would decrease.
    B. The pressure would stay the same.
    C. The pressure would increase.
    D. There is not enough information to solve this problem.

40. What would be the consequence of making l larger? During the piston movement,
    A. pressure in the chamber would decrease, and temperature would decrease.
    B. pressure in the chamber would decrease, and temperature would increase.
    C. pressure in the chamber would increase, and temperature would decrease.
    D. pressure in the chamber would increase, and temperature would increase.

Test 2 Solutions

Passage 1

1. A.
We draw a force diagram including the force of gravity.

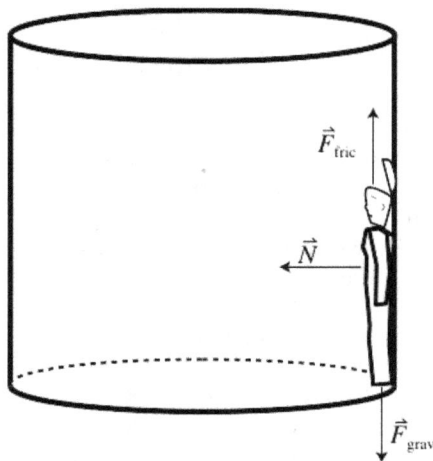

The only thing touching the rider once the floor drops is the side of the drum, which exerts a normal force that ends up being toward the axis of rotation. It also exerts a frictional force, which is up (balancing gravity). For uniform circular motion, we know the net force must be toward the center of rotation, so we can see that this force diagram is complete.

2. A.
From the diagram we can see that the normal force provides the centripetal force.

3. A.
Because the motion is uniform circular rotation, the acceleration vector points toward the center of rotation.

4. C.
The rider traverses the circumference of the circle ($2\pi R$) during each period of time T. Thus his speed is $2\pi R/T$.

5. A.
The upward force must balance the gravitational force, so the magnitude of the upward force must be Mg as well.

Passage 2

6. B.
Detection of radioactive phosphate in the pellet indicates the bacteria now contain the DNA of the bacteriophage. Radioactive sulfur in the supernatant suggests the protein of the phage did not enter the cell. Since the bacteria took up something from the phage, answer D is unlikely, as it does appear the phage infected the cell.

7. C.
The experiment verified that the DNA of the phage entered the cell. Therefore, the bacteria were indeed infected. It is not likely the protein coats are necessary for further functioning of the phage as they never entered the cell. It is also unlikely the radioactive phosphate would immediately kill the cells (after all, phage were propagated in bacteria grown in medium containing the isotope). The most likely answer is that the phage would reproduce as normal.

8. D.
Answer D is the only choice that makes any sense. All the other answers defeat the purpose of the experiment: a competitive inhibitor would prevent the phage from entering the cells at all; breaking apart the cell membrane would cause the contents of the cell to be released, where they would be found in the supernatant, along with the components of the phage that did not infect the cell; a mutant phage that could not bind to the cell would probably not infect the cell.

9. A.
Bacteriophages work by making the target cell do something it could not do before. Fertilization results in a new type of cell and is the beginning of a developmental cycle, not the best analogy to the phage experiment. Consuming enzymes would not fundamentally change an organism. Although the T2 experiment used radioactivity, not all experiments involving radioactive isotopes examine the same phenomenon.

Passage 3

10. D.
All the solubilities shown in the graph are endothermic. In fact most compounds (solids) dissolve endothermically. The graph shows that as the temperature increases, the solubility of the salts increases. In other words, as the temperature increases, more and more of the salt present is dissociated into ions. This is exactly how an endothermic process works.

11. B.
The observed changes in colligative properties are less than what was theoretically predicted. This is because the ionization of salts in water is not as complete as we expect. Some of the oppositely charged ions stick together and function as a unit. So the number of particles (units) is lower than what we expect. As the concentration increases, the possibility of the oppositely charged ions sticking together is greater than that in dilute solutions.

12. D.
This question is a bit tricky. You may have selected Choice A. But you have to understand what exactly is asked in the question. The question is not asking about the change in boiling point (ΔT). Instead, it asks what happens to the boiling point. It will not double; it will only increase slightly.

13. C.
Choice C is the only true statement given. Looking closely at Choices A and B, you should realize that they represent the same relationship. Since you cannot have two correct answers, this rules out Choices A and B. Thus, such logical elimination-techniques can be used to solve many problems on the test and save valuable time.

Passage 4

14. B.
Don't let the information in the problem distract you from the fact that there must be a force balance on the muscle, since the muscle is not accelerating. Thus the magnitudes of $F_{forearm}$ and $F_{shoulder}$ are the same.

15. C.
The force exerted at the center of the biceps is the same as the force exerted at the forearm (force balance, see previous question), and the area is 100 times smaller. Thus the stress at the forearm is 100 times larger. (You may have done this problem by an intermediate step by calculating that force to be 500 N.)

16. D.
Statue B has 8 times the volume of statue A. Since *mass* = ρV, statue B has 8 times the mass. Since *weight* = *mg*, statue B has 8 times the weight as well.

17. B.
Stress is force/area. The force (weight) increases by a factor of 8, and the area increases by a factor of 4, so the stress increases by a factor of 8/4 = 2. Also, see the last sentence of the fourth paragraph of the passage.

18. C.
The passage indicates that the breaking point is related to the threshold stress for the material in the cable. Stress is force per area. Increasing the length does not change the force of the load (the lantern weight) or the cross-sectional area, so the breaking weight would be the same.

Passage 5

19. A.
All the bacteria were infected by the phage and lysed. The other conditions, whether true or not, deal with growth or death of bacteria and would not cause lysis of the bacteria. Therefore, the plate would remain cloudy. Only lysis causes the plates to appear clear.

20. C.
The control in this experiment (condition 1) rules out answers A and B. If UV light killed the bacteria, as suggested in D (and as can happen, depending on conditions), then all the bacteria would die. (Although it is possible that only a small percentage would die, it would be highly unlikely that this lethality would show a plaque pattern.) C is the only plausible answer, and we know that UV light can induce lysogenic strains to become lytic.

21. D.
Under both conditions, infection and induction, lysis would occur. Therefore, on average for these experimental conditions, infection would produce 20 plaques per plate and induction would produce 50 plaques per plate, for a total of 70 plaques per plate.

22. B.
Once induction occurs, viral particles are produced that can go on to infect other bacterial cells. Therefore, the isolation of bacteriophage from cultures would not support the theory of autolysis. Answer A is possible in the realm of either theory, C would not distinguish between the two, and D has nothing to do with either theory, as bacteria that grow well at 37°C will not grow at 4°C.

Passage 6

23. D.
The sample described in the question has disintegrated to 3% of its original quantity. The disintegration can be analyzed as follows:

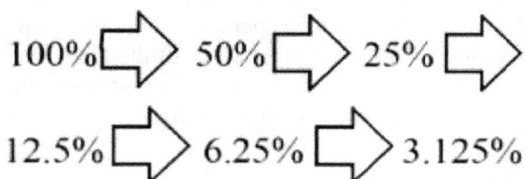

This means, at least 5 half-lives must have elapsed.

24. B.
According to the figure given in the passage, as the number of protons increases the neutron-proton ratio increases and becomes greater than or equal to one. (Clue: Look at the slope)

25. D.
The mass loss can be equated with the binding energy. In essence, mass loss can be calculated using the equation $E = mc^2$.

$$\text{Energy} = (3.1 \times 10^{-5}\ \text{kg})(3 \times 10^8\ \text{m/s})^2 = 2.8 \times 10^{12}\ \text{kg} \cdot \text{m/s}^2 = 2.8 \times 10^{12}\ \text{J}.$$

Passage 7

26. C.
Both the first and second laws of motion concern unbalanced forces. But the third law of motion states that, if the ship exerts a force on the gas, then the gas exerts an equal and oppositely directed force on the ship, so C is correct.

27. C.
Choice A is a true statement: Neon is not a product of uranium fission, but neither is hydrogen. The passage says that hydrogen is heated and then expelled. This is different from conventional rockets in which the products of the reaction themselves are expelled. Choice B is a true statement but also irrelevant, because the hydrogen does not react chemically in this process either. Concerning choice C, let's think of exhaust velocity. It is related to temperature and molecular mass of the exhaust gas. Since neon is more massive, the exhaust velocity will be less, and the thrust will be less. Choice C is correct.

28. D.
According to the passage, the hydrogen cannot be heated fast enough. This would result in a low mass expulsion rate.

29. D.
It helps to visualize this problem if we draw a diagram (see figure).

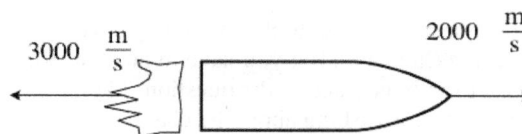

From the figure we can see that, relative to the ship, the gases are going 5000 m/s.

30. A.
Let's draw a diagram of the system.

before:

after:

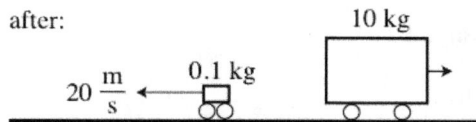

We can do this by momentum conservation:

$$P_{\text{before}} = P_{\text{after}}$$

$$0 = (0.1\ \text{kg})(-20\ \text{m/s}) + (10\ \text{kg})v_t$$

$$v_t = 0.2\ \text{m/s}$$

Passage 8

31. B.
The experiment shows that a soluble factor released by *P. aeruginosa* is probably present in the supernatant (the medium which was then used to grow *B. cepacia*). This factor induced the production of survival molecules in *B. cepacia*. Therefore, we know that *P. aeruginosa* can communicate with *B. cepacia*. We are given no experimental evidence to indicate if *B. cepacia* is able to communicate with *P. aeruginosa* .

32. A.
Since *B. cepacia* were grown in the liquid medium after the *P. aeruginosa* had been removed by centrifugation, a soluble factor, probably a protein, must have been present. No direct cell-to-cell contact could have taken place. In addition, we have no direct evidence that *B. cepacia* secreted any proteins.

33. C.
Nerve cells communicate chemically by releasing factors into the synapse between each other. Hormones are released from one gland and travel to a target tissue or organ where they are detected by receptors. Both systems use communication systems similar to the release of protein from one bacterial cell and detection by another.

34. C.
It is important to control this experiment. This can be accomplished by incubating *B. cepacia* in medium that had not been used to grow another strain of bacteria. In this manner, we could directly see the effects of *P. aeruginosa* on *B. cepacia*.

35. D.
The most likely answer to this question is that the *P. aeruginosa* were defective in secretion. If they had mutations in any other system, they would be unlikely to survive and reproduce.

36. C.
After five hours, there would be ten doublings since the doubling time is 30 minutes. Initially, there are 10^5 cells. So, after 30 minutes, there are 2×10^5 cells. After 1 hour, there are $2 \times 2 \times 10^5$ cells. After 10 iterations, we get

$$2 \times 2 \times \cdots \times 2 \times 10^5 = 2^{10} \times 10^5 = 1024 \times 10^5 \approx 10^3 \times 10^5 = 10^8$$

Passage 9

37. B.
It is true that there are more particles on the left side of the reaction, but that would tend to make the pressure go down, not up, so A is false. The pressure goes up because the temperature goes up, so B seems a good choice. Spontaneous reactions can have either an increase or a decrease in pressure, so C is incorrect. D is incorrect for the same reason.

38. D.
One of the reactants would be in excess. The heat of reaction is unchanged, so A is false. The combustion would still ignite, so B is out. The answer is C or D. If any of the intermediates in the reaction were stable compounds, then some of those compounds could end up in the waste gas. But the reaction of hydrogen with water is clean, and the waste gas would contain only leftover hydrogen or oxygen.

39. A.
If the reaction were performed isothermally, then the number of gas particles would be less after the reaction than before the reaction. Since pressure at a given volume and temperature is proportional to the number of gas particles by the ideal gas law, the pressure would decrease.

40. A.
We have assumed that the piston movement is small and the pressure stays about the same. If the piston movement were larger, the increase in volume would decrease the pressure. The gas in the chamber is doing work against the piston, so the internal energy of the gas must decrease. The temperature must decrease as well.

Test 2 Conversion Chart

Scale Score Conversion Chart

Raw Score	Scale Score	Percentile Ranking
40	36	99
39	35	99
38	34	99
37	33	99
36	32	98
—	31	98
35	30	97
34	29	95
33	28	94
31–32	27	91
30	26	88
29	25	84
27–28	24	77
25–26	23	71
24	22	64
22–23	21	56
20–21	20	48
19	19	38
17–18	18	30
15–16	17	23
14	16	18
13	15	14
11–12	14	10
10	13	7
9	12	5
7–8	11	3
6	10	1
5	9	1
4	8	1
3	7	1
—	6	1
2	5	1
—	4	1
1	3	1
—	2	1
0	1	1

www.ingramcontent.com/pod-product-compliance
Lightning Source LLC
Chambersburg PA
CBHW080407270326

41929CB00018B/2932